920 non ah.

STREETER

from Frank

Christmas 1947

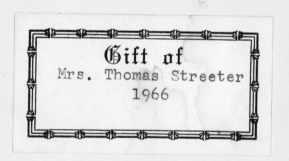
W9-CJJ-041

Also a Borzoi Book

THE AMERICAN NOVELS AND STORIES OF
Henry James

Edited, with an Introduction, by F·O·Matthiessen

Published in New York by Alfred·A·Knopf

The James Family

*Henry James and William James,
in England, about 1901*

The James Family

INCLUDING SELECTIONS FROM

THE WRITINGS OF

HENRY JAMES, SENIOR,

WILLIAM, HENRY,

& ALICE JAMES

By F. O. MATTHIESSEN

NEW YORK

ALFRED · A · KNOPF

1947

Principles of Psychology, copyright 1890 by Henry Holt and Company; copyright 1918 by Alice H. James

Picture and Text, copyright 1893 by Harper & Brothers; copyright 1920 by Mrs. Henry James

Essays in London and Elsewhere, copyright 1893 by Harper & Brothers; copyright 1920 by Mrs. Henry James

Talks to Teachers on Psychology, copyright 1899 by William James; copyright 1926 by Henry James

Varieties of Religious Experience, copyright 1902 by William James; copyright 1929 by Henry James

Pragmatism, copyright 1907 by William James; copyright 1934 by Henry James

The American Scene, copyright 1907 by Harper & Brothers; copyright 1935 by Henry James

Memories and Studies, copyright 1911 by Henry James Jr.; copyright 1938 by Henry James

A Small Boy and Others, copyright 1913 by Charles Scribner's Sons; copyright 1941 by Henry James

Notes on Novelists, copyright 1914 by Charles Scribner's Sons; copyright 1942 by Henry James

Notes of a Son and Brother, copyright 1914 by Charles Scribner's Sons; copyright 1942 by Henry James

The Middle Years, copyright 1917 by Charles Scribner's Sons; copyright 1945 by Charles Scribner's Sons

The Letters of Henry James, copyright 1920 by Charles Scribner's Sons

The Letters of William James, 1920 by Henry James

Alice James: Her Brothers—Her Journal, copyright 1934 by Dodd, Mead & Company

The Thought and Character of William James, copyright 1935 by Henry James

FIRST EDITION

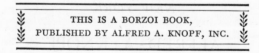

THIS IS A BORZOI BOOK,
PUBLISHED BY ALFRED A. KNOPF, INC.

PREFACE

I HAVE TRIED to present here a particular kind of biography, the biography not of an individual but of a family, and of a family of minds. The James family—that is to say, Henry James, Senior, his wife Mary Walsh, and their five children, notably William, Henry Junior, and Alice—constitute one of the most vivid and varied groups that our American nineteenth century produced. Henry Senior, true to his time and place, possessed radical ideas on most subjects, including education. He was in a position to put his educational theory into practice, to embrace the opportunities of Europe as well as of America; and his two oldest sons especially are fascinating examples of how any educational theory, depending upon the temperaments it has to deal with, can yield extraordinarily opposite results. Active and passive, participating and detached, scientific and æsthetic, William James and Henry James, Junior, as our narrative will disclose, divided and ranged in so many contrasting directions that, between them, they touched upon nearly all the major cultural interests of their age. Indeed, after surveying their father's ideas and his children's reactions to them, after listening to the family's discussions of religion and philosophy and literature and politics and society, we may feel that we have gained a fairly full index to American intellectual history from the time of Emerson to that of the first World War.

At least we shall have shared intimately in what one remarkably sensitive and alert family group thought and talked and argued about. The fact that no less than four members of this group developed unusual gifts of expression has determined the principle of organization for my volume. Henry Senior believed, with Emerson, that "words and deeds" are both "modes of the divine energy," that "words are also actions, and actions are a kind of words." Since the James family's essential biography is internal rather than external, a biography of minds in action, it can be presented best in their own language. Too many biographies of writers merely skirt or take for granted what gives their subjects their chief claim upon our interest, but by far the most revelatory material for understanding the James family consists of

v

eopy 1

letters and journals and essays, some hitherto unprinted, the bulk widely scattered in several dozen different volumes, most of which are out of print and hard to come by. These writers were overwhelmingly prolific, and since they were often on opposite sides of the Atlantic and in frequent correspondence, the record—if presented with the living concrete fullness that both the psychologist and novelist brothers demanded —could be encompassed only with amplitude, only by including some characteristic instances of every facet of their thought. Their biography, as I have conceived it, becomes also a comprehensive anthology.[1]

My own role has been something like that of the director of a play. I have tried to see to it that the actors were assembled in a series of significant and representative scenes, that the various scripts—in many cases the two halves of a hitherto separated correspondence—were dovetailed together, that any necessary cuts and foreshortenings should be made, and that the cues should fall pat. Then I have sat back and enjoyed the performance, without the usual nervousness as to how my extraordinary cast would acquit itself.

The drama, I repeat, finds its center in what happened in that family circle. It would have been impossible, within the confines of any one volume, to attempt further definitive accounts of William James' psychology and philosophy and of Henry Junior's fiction. My more elementary aim has been to uncover the sources of their seminal ideas in the matrix that formed them, and then to discover whatever I could of the implications of these ideas, not in isolation, but through whatever juxtapositions, comparisons, and contrasts I could contrive to bring them into. By this means the various members of the family have served in turn as one another's most searching critics. They have scrutinized and "placed" one another, just as they feasted upon and scrutinized and "placed" every book and character and event that came their way. In this role no one has been more helpful or winning than the relatively little-known Alice. She, along with the self-effacing mother, serves most to emphasize that though the family debated their differences with trenchancy and vigor, they were always held together by humor and by affection. For that reason, the story of their minds, far flung as it is through the vast range of their works, possesses the kind of natural center of composition upon which Henry Junior insisted. This gives their story the coherence to illuminate their times; and since they wrote so well, their words still possess for our time the enkindling energy that Emerson knew to inhere in thought and art.

---

[1] In order to let the flow of the narrative be as uninterrupted as possible, the same typography has been used for the writings of the Jameses and for my connecting commentary. Whenever this arrangement might lead to any possible confusion, breaks between my text and one of theirs have been indicated by five asterisks to mark the beginning of a citation and three asterisks to mark the end.

ACKNOWLEDGMENTS

THIS RECORD of the Jameses was made possible by my having access to the wealth of family manuscripts now in the Houghton Library at Harvard. The sections of my volume dealing with William James could hardly have been undertaken without the source material provided by Ralph Barton Perry's monumental work, *The Thought and Character of William James* (1935), upon which I have continually drawn. For other aspects of the family history I am also indebted in particular to the work done by Harold Larrabee, by Austin Warren on Henry James, Senior, and by Hartley Grattan, who also recognized the three most famous members of my group as constituting "a family of minds."

I have received unfailing co-operation from the staff of the Houghton Library; Stanley and Eileen Geist and Patricia Stange have given exacting scrutiny to my text; and I am grateful for inestimable courtesies to the present Henry, William, and Alice James.

I wish also to acknowledge the following permissions for copyrighted material:

To Henry Holt & Company for *The Principles of Psychology* and *Talks to Teachers on Psychology* by William James.

To Charles Scribner's Sons for *The Letters of Henry James, A Small Boy and Others, Notes of a Son and Brother, The Middle Years, Notes on Novelists* by Henry James; and *Winds of Doctrine* by George Santayana.

To Harper & Brothers for *Picture and Text, Essays in London,* and *The American Scene* by Henry James.

To Longmans, Green & Company for *The Will to Believe* by William James.

To Ralph Barton Perry for *The Thought and Character of William James.*

To Henry James for *The Letters of William James, The Varieties of*
vii

Religious Experience, Pragmatism, The Meaning of Truth, Essays in Radical Empiricism, Memories and Studies, Collected Essays and Reviews by William James.

To Dodd, Mead & Company for *Alice James: Her Brothers—Her Journal.*

To D. Appleton-Century Company for *A Backward Glance* by Edith Wharton.

To Houghton Mifflin Company for *The Early Years of the Saturday Club* by E. W. Emerson.

To Mildred Howells for *The Life in Letters of William Dean Howells.*

To the Essex Institute for *Proceedings in Commemoration of the One Hundredth Anniversary of Hawthorne's Birth.*

F. O. M.

Kittery, Maine

CONTENTS

BOOK FIVE

BOOK SIX

BOOK SEVEN

EPILOGUE

NOTE ON THE ILLUSTRATIONS

THERE ARE MANY excellent likenesses of the James family, ranging in painting from Duveneck to Sargent, and in photography from Brady to Alice Boughton. In several cases the Jameses also contributed their own comments on the likenesses, as in Henry Junior's accounts of the experience of sitting for Brady and Sargent, and in the passage from Alice James' *Journal* describing the heretofore unpublished photograph that was taken the year before her death. Of the various other descriptions, the following may supplement the pictures and text:

Howells, on Henry James, Senior: "As I write of him I see him before me: his white bearded face, with a kindly intensity which at first seemed fierce, the mouth humorously shaping the mustache, the eyes vague behind the glasses; his sensitive hand gripping the stick on which he rested his weight to ease it from the artificial limb he wore."

Henry James, the eldest son of William James, on his father: "He was of medium height (about five feet eight and one-half inches), and though he was muscular and compact, his frame was slight and he appeared to be slender in youth, spare in his last years. His carriage was erect and his tread was firm to the end. Until he was over fifty he used to take the stairs of his own house two, or even three, steps at a bound. He moved rapidly, not to say impatiently, but with an assurance that invested his figure with an informal sort of dignity . . .

"In talking he gesticulated very little, but his face and voice were unusually expressive. His eyes were of that not very dark shade whose depth and color changes with alterations of mood. Mrs. Henry Whitman, who knew him well and painted his portrait, called them 'irascible blue eyes.' He talked in a voice that was low-pitched rather than deep —an unforgettably agreeable voice, that was admirable for conversation or a small lecture-room, although in a very large hall it vibrated and lacked resonance. His speech was full of earnest, humorous and tender cadences . . . The story of the solemn-minded student who stemmed

the full tide of a lecture one day by exclaiming, 'But, Doctor, Doctor
—to be serious for a moment—,' is already well known."

*Theodora Bosanquet, who became Henry James' secretary in 1907,
on the impression he made*: "He was much more massive than I had expected, much broader and stouter and stronger. I remembered that
someone had told me he used to be taken for a sea-captain when he wore
a beard, but it was clear that now, with the beard shaved away, he would
hardly have passed for, say, an admiral, in spite of the keen grey eyes
set in a face burned to a colourable sea-faring brown by the Italian sun.
No successful naval officer could have afforded to keep that sensitive
mobile mouth . . . He had reacted with so much success against both
the American accent and the English manner that he seemed only doubtfully Anglo-Saxon. He might perhaps have been some species of disguised cardinal, or even a Roman nobleman amusing himself by playing
the part of a Sussex squire. The observer could at least have guessed
that any part he chose to assume would be finely conceived and generously played, for his features were all cast in the classical mould of
greatness."

This last fits in with Edmund Gosse's remark: "I remember once
seeing a Canon preaching in the Cathedral of Toulouse who was the
picture of Henry James in his unction, his gravity, and his vehemence."

Illustrations

From *A Small Boy and Others*: "I shall have strained the last drop of
romance from this vision of our towny summers with the quite sharp
reminiscence of my first sitting for my daguerreotype. I repaired
with my father on an August day to the great Broadway establishment
of Mr. Brady, supreme in that then beautiful art . . . Sharp again is
my sense of not being so adequately dressed as I should have taken
thought for had I foreseen my exposure; though the resources of my
wardrobe as then constituted could surely have left me but few alternatives. The main resource of a small New York boy in this line
at that time was the little sheath-like jacket, tight to the body, closed
at the neck and adorned in front with a single row of brass buttons—a
garment of scant grace assuredly and comprised to my consciousness,
above all, by a strange ironic light from an unforgotten source. It was
but a short time before those days that the great Mr. Thackeray had
come to America to lecture on The English Humourists, and still

present to me is the voice proceeding from my father's library, in which some glimpse of me hovering at an opening of the door, in passage or on staircase, prompted him to the formidable words: 'Come here, little boy, and show me your extraordinary jacket!' My sense of my jacket became from that hour a heavy one—further enriched as my vision is by my shyness of posture before the seated, the celebrated visitor, who struck me, in the sunny light of the animated room, as enormously big and who, though he laid on my shoulder the hand of benevolence, bent on my native costume the spectacles of wonder. I was to know later on why he had been so amused and why, after asking me if this were the common uniform of my age and class, he remarked that in England, were I to go there, I should be addressed as 'Buttons.' It had been revealed to me thus in a flash that we were somehow *queer*, and though never exactly crushed by it I became aware that I at least felt so as I stood with my head in Mr. Brady's vise. Beautiful most decidedly the lost art of the daguerreotype; I remember the 'exposure' as on this occasion interminably long, yet with the result of a facial anguish far less harshly reproduced than my suffered snapshots of a later age."

On June 18, 1913, HJ wrote to his nephew William Junior about how interesting he had found, "during the last three weeks, my regular sittings for my portrait to Sargent; which have numbered now some seven or eight, I forget which, and with but a couple more to come. So the thing is, I make out, very nearly finished, and the head apparently (as I much hope) to have almost nothing more done to it. It is, I infer, a very great success; a number of the competent and intelligent have seen it, and so pronounce it in the strongest terms . . . In short it seems likely to be one of S's very fine things. One is almost full-face, with one's left arm over the corner of one's chair-back and the hand brought round so that the thumb is caught in the arm-hole of one's waistcoat, and said hand therefore, with the fingers a bit folded, entirely visible and 'treated.' Of course I'm sitting a little askance in the chair. The canvas comes down to just where my watch-chain (such as it is, poor thing!) is hung across the waistcoat: which latter, in itself, is found to be splendidly (poor thing though it also be) and most interestingly treated. Sargent *can* make such things so in-teresting—such things as my coat-lappet and shoulder and sleeve too! But what is most interesting, every one is agreed, is the mouth—than which even he has never painted a more living and, as I am told, 'ex-pressive'! In fact I can quite see that myself; and really, I seem to feel, the thing will be all that can at the best (the best with such a subject!) have been expected of it. I only wish that you and Alice [William Junior's wife] had assisted at some of the sittings—as Sargent likes animated, sympathetic, beautiful, talkative friends to do, in order to correct by their presence too lugubrious expressions."

He added, a week later, to Rhoda Broughton: "It is now finished, *parachevé* (I sat for the last time a couple of days ago;) and it is nothing less evidently, than a very fine thing indeed, Sargent at his very best and poor H.J. not at his worst; in short a living breathing likeness and a masterpiece of painting. I am really quite ashamed to admire it so much and so loudly—it's so much as if I were calling at-tention to my own fine points. I don't, alas, exhibit a 'point' in it, but am all large and luscious rotundity—by which you may see how true a thing it is. And I am sorry to have ceased to sit, in spite of the re-peated big holes it made in my precious mornings: J.S.S. being so genial and delightful a *nature de grand maître* to have to do with, and his beautiful high cool studio, opening upon a balcony that overhangs a charming Chelsea green garden, adding a charm to everything. He liked always a friend or two to be in to break the spell of a settled gloom in my countenance by their prattle; though you will doubtless think this effect but little achieved when I tell you that, having my-self found the thing, as it grew, more and more like Sir Joshua's Dr. Johnson, and said so, a perceptive friend reinforced me a couple of sittings later by breaking out irrepressibly with the same judgment."

WILLIAM JAMES, BY ALICE BOUGHTON, 1907   588

Alice Boughton in *Photographing the Famous*, gave this account of her experience with William James: "After taking Mr. Henry James' picture, I was asked so many times if I had not done Professor Wil-liam James, that I finally wrote a note to Mrs. Herbert Lord, when I found Professor James was staying at her house. Knowing that he had liked the picture I had done of his brother, I asked him to give me a sitting—if he had the time and if he felt like it. He had been lecturing at Columbia, had hosts of friends demanding his time, and I knew that he was far from well and had but a limited amount of strength. No reply for several days and I forgot all about it. Then one morning when I was all packed to go out and do an artist for Scribner's there came a knock at the door, and there stood Mr. James. I had never seen him, but knew at once that it must be he, when stepping into the room, he said in a quiet voice, 'I am Mr. James. You wrote a note to my friend Mrs. Lord, and being susceptible to flattery, I am here." The artist and Scribner's were forgotten and I got to work at once, and had, it is needless to say, one of the pleasantest mornings I had ever spent. He stayed perhaps two hours, at times talking delightfully, and giving me the impression of having any amount of leisure to listen. He had the gift of seeming to be interested in another's point of view, whether you were the photographer or the scrub woman. Kindly and genial . . . putting one at ease without one's being conscious that this was so. As he was leaving I asked him whether he would allow his picture to be published, and whether I had permission to let his friends have them. He said, 'Yes certainly, if anyone cares to have them.' I had said goodbye and he had gone when a few moments later he knocked at the door, this time to say, 'You won't let the yellow press have it, will you?' "

HENRY JAMES, BY ALICE BOUGHTON, 1906   654

Miss Boughton's description of Henry James was even more detailed: "Henry James was, I may truthfully say, the only sitter who ever terrified me. I was to do him for publication, and though the time was set for early afternoon, he did not come until nearly four o'clock. It was April, and a warm day, ending in a thunder shower, the sky getting blacker by the minute and the light going. Finally he came, dignified and impressive, with manners almost courtly, and wearing a top hat several sizes too big. I saw that he took in everything in the room, and his keen, keen eye followed me about as I moved around, trying for the best spot, and to squeeze out as much light as possible from the leaden sky. When I could no longer endure the eye, I went to the book-shelves and took down *The Amazing Marriage* and asked him to read while I got ready. He took the book but continued to watch me over the top, then I said, 'Please pay no attention to me but read—really read, and I will tell you when I am ready.' And so he did, and became so absorbed, that when I wanted him to look into the camera I failed to get his attention. For the third time I said, very loudly, 'Mr. James, look into the camera!' He came to quickly, turned his head and uttered a sharp 'Eh?' And there you are! At the time, my latest acquisition was a small painting of a mother and child by Arthur Davies. This was hanging near the door, and on his way out Mr. James stopped before it and looked at it a long time, bending forward, in his top hat, his stick behind him. 'Just one more, please—

I must do this, for you look like a Daumier!' He seemed really amused, but remained in the same position until I photographed him again. Then we shook hands and he departed. My assistant, who had none too much reverence in her makeup, looking out of the window after he had gone, said, 'He's trying to find the subway and he does look like the Mad Hatter.' Not more than five or ten minutes after he had gone, Mr. Davies came in, and I told him about Mr. James standing in his top hat, hands behind him, examining the painting and how he looked so like a Daumier picture. To which Mr. Davies replied, 'Very tactful of you to tell him that!' 'Why tactful?' 'Because Mr. James has always been a great admirer of Daumier and years ago wrote an article about him for Harper's.' It was luck, not tact, on my part."

BOOK ONE

BOOK ONE

HENRY JAMES, SENIOR

ALMOST A CENTURY ago, in 1849, Henry James, Senior, wrote from New York a now famous letter to Emerson. The father of five small children, and necessarily concerned with education, he projected the scheme of taking his family to Europe for a few years, thereby "allowing them to absorb French and German and get a better sensuous education than they are likely to get here." Such an interest in the training of the senses was unique in America at that time. It was the strongest single influence in assuring that his children's minds would not be dry and abstract, but freshly and alertly perceptive.

William and Henry James, Junior, were contemporaries and friends of Wendell Holmes and Henry Adams, but they were not products of puritan New England. Indeed, as Henry was to remark in retrospect, being a New Englander had been "a danger after all escaped." Holmes' career drew upon the heritage that constituted the norm for the New England renaissance. His father had applied the term "Brahmin-caste" to those who, like Emerson, Lowell, and himself, were descended from a line of ministers. The progression from Abiel Holmes, a rigorous follower of Jonathan Edwards, to Oliver Wendell Holmes, the free-thinking Unitarian wit and man of science, to Wendell Holmes, the liberal jurist, was the familiar pattern. The Adams family went through a less easily explicable evolution when, after several generations of solid but undistinguished farmers at Quincy, John Adams suddenly emerged as a legal mind of great energy. But thereafter the continuity of intellectual distinction ran uninterrupted for four generations, though perhaps finally with some of the degradation of energy that Henry Adams brooded upon.

At the time when Abiel Holmes was about to become a Congregational clergyman in Cambridge, and young John Quincy Adams had already assisted his father in negotiating the treaty of peace with Great Britain, the founder of the James family in America, William James

(1771–1832), was just arriving as an immigrant of eighteen from County Cavan, Ireland. This son of another William James and of Susan McCartney brought along with him, according to the family legend, "a very small sum of money, a Latin grammar in which he had already made some progress at home, and a desire to visit the field of one of the revolutionary battles." He soon settled in Albany and advanced with an era of expansion. From clerk to master of a tobacco shop to operator of an express business between Albany and Utica, he rapidly went on to acquire great holdings in real estate and public utilities. A strong backer of the prosperous Erie Canal, he was finally second in the community only to Stephen Van Rensselaer, the last of the old patroons. "When old Billy James came to Syracuse," a citizen recalled, "things went as *he* wished."

This robust and dynamic character married three times and begat thirteen children. A stern Presbyterian, he also exhibited a serious interest in education, and became a benefactor and trustee of Union College. He died in the same year as a younger Albany businessman, Allan Melville. But whereas Herman Melville's father left his eight children bankrupt, William James bequeathed to his heirs three million dollars, the largest fortune in the state save for John Jacob Astor's.

His surviving portraits present him, in the words of one of his great-grandsons, as "of medium height, rather portly, clean-shaven, hearty, friendly, confident, and distinctly Irish." He was a man of astute practical intelligence, capable of being the orator of the day at the opening of the Canal, and of delivering a speech filled with sound sense rather than with oratory. But if we are trying to trace the James family mind to its roots, there is nothing to suggest that "William of Albany" was to be the father of a religious philosopher and speculative social theorist. If we turn to his third wife, Catharine Barber, the fourth of whose ten children was Henry James, Senior (1811–82), we find in that son's description that she was "a good wife and mother, nothing else—save, to be sure, a kindly friend and neighbor. . . . She was the most democratic person by temperament I ever knew." That such a description is meant for adoring praise we can tell only if we know how much value he habitually attached to such fundamental relationships and qualities. But we must look farther to account for his own unexpected bent as a Swedenborgian and Fourierist. Perhaps we need no more from his heredity to explain him than the fertile interplay between Presbyterian earnestness and Scotch-Irish effervescence. His son the novelist, writing late in life his *Notes of a Son and Brother*, dwelt fondly on the fact that through the Barbers some English blood had flowed into their stock. But he was quite wrong. Catharine's grandfather, Patrick Barber, had come from County Longford, Ireland, and her mother was the daughter of Matthew Rhea. When Henry James,

Senior, in turn, married Mary Robertson Walsh (1810–82), he prolonged the pure Scotch-Irish strain another generation.

But the environmental factors that contributed to the formation of
Henry James, Senior, were as marked as the somewhat different ones
that he induced upon his sons. The inheritance of enough money to
make him financially independent could by itself have caused a deflec-
tion from his father's sphere. As Henry Junior put it: "The rupture
with my grandfather's tradition and attitude was complete; we were
never in a single case, I think, for two generations, guilty of a stroke of
business; the most that could be said ·of us was that, though about
equally wanting, all round, in any faculty of acquisition, we happened
to pay for the amiable weakness less in some connections than in others." The connections in which many of the descent did pay for it were
suggested by another passage in these memoirs dwelling on "the numerous dawnings on which in many cases the deepening and final dark-
nesses were so soon to follow," and on how "our father's family was to
offer such a chronicle of early deaths, arrested careers, broken promises, orphaned children." Of the eleven of William James' sons and
daughters who reached maturity, seven were dead by forty. Variously
genial, charming, dissipated, or unstable, these Jameses, and the Temples
and Emmets with whom they intermarried are suggested further
through the glimpse, in *The Wings of the Dove*, of Milly Theale's
New York forebears: an "extravagant unregulated cluster, with free-
living ancestors, handsome dead cousins, lurid uncles, beautiful vanished aunts, persons all busts and curls."

The only other member of his generation who manifested anything
of Henry Senior's particular interests was an older half brother, the
Reverend William James, who, having been ordained as a Presbyterian
minister in 1820, gradually drifted away from orthodoxy and devoted
his later years to philosophical research. There was nothing gradual
about the revolt of Henry Senior. It is beyond conjecture to say how
much of his inwardness was determined by his disqualification for
active life through his loss of a leg at thirteen as the result of stamping
out a fire caused by a boy's balloon. He had shown a high-strung sensibility even before this accident,[1] and a letter from his maturity describes his temperament as it no doubt would have been inclined in any
event. "The bent of my nature," he wrote, "is towards affection and
thought rather than action. I love the fireside rather than the forum.
I can give ecstatic hours to worship or meditation but moments spent
in original deed, such as putting a button upon my coat or cleansing
my garden-walk of weeds, weigh very heavily upon my shoulders."

---

[1] See the account of his earliest years in his fragment of an autobiography, pp.
17–38 below.

Coming of age intellectually at the dawn of the transcendental era, it was almost inevitable that he should feel impelled to join in the moral argument against Calvinism. But what separates him from many of the thin-blooded clergymen who surrounded Emerson is a vivid love of life. While he was a student at Union, in the class of 1830, there were reports of a fondness for oysters and segars and stylish clothes, which wanton extravagance brought from one of his father's friends a letter saying: "Some consider you already as lost, irretrievably lost." He just failed of election to Phi Beta Kappa, but was among the very first American undergraduates to sport a fraternity pin. He opposed his father's desire that he study law, and he brooked his father's wrath by his deviations from unquestioning faith. However, three years after his father's death he was still sufficiently orthodox to decide to enter the Princeton Theological School, which was strongly Presbyterian. He withdrew in dissatisfaction after a couple of years, which had been punctuated by a summer's trip to Europe that included a return to his father's birthplace in County Cavan.

There followed a period of considerable uncertainty as to his future. In 1840 he married the sister of one of his Princeton classmates, and the fullness of his love for her is suggested by his remark to Emerson: "The flesh said, It is for me, and the spirit said, It is for me." But though the pair settled down happily to raising a family, the pressures under which James' mind was seething are evident from the questions he began to hurl at Emerson from the moment he first heard him lecture, in the month of his oldest son's birth.[1] Two years later, when he and his wife were in England with their two infant sons, James underwent a nervous and spiritual collapse which left him with the conviction of "the nothingness of selfhood." The dramatic crisis of his fear and the steps by which, through the help of the writings of Swedenborg, he found his way back to faith in life are recorded in his book *Society the Redeemed Form of Man.*[2] By the time of his return to this country in 1845 he had at last found his vocation, and he devoted the rest of his long career to the production of a series of lectures, pamphlets, essays, and books.[3]

---

[1] See below, p. 39.

[2] Pp. 161ff. below.

[3] These have been so nearly forgotten that the enumeration of his chief titles may serve to remind us of the volume of his work:

What Constitutes the State (1846);

Tracts for the New Times. No. 1. Letter to a Swedenborgian (1847);

Moralism and Christianity; or, Man's Experience and Destiny (1850);

Lectures and Miscellanies (1852);

The Church of Christ not an Ecclesiasticism: A Letter of Remonstrance to a member of the soi-disant *New Church* (1854);

The Nature of Evil (1855);

The Social Significance of our Institutions (1861);

Substance and Shadow; or Morality and Religion in Their Relation to Life: An Essay on the Physics of Creation (1866);

The Secret of Swedenborg: Being an

Henry James, Senior, is ordinarily thought of as the father of two far more notable sons, but he was a magnificent personality in his own right. When Bernard Shaw indulged his love of trying to shock by declaring to Henry Junior that the most interesting member of his family was neither himself nor his brother but their father, he found that no praise could have been more welcome. Put beside either son, the father displays, in his maturity, a unique spaciousness and serenity. We may discriminate his particular quality by pondering the coincidence that he was born eight years after Emerson, and eight years before Melville. He combines many of the traits of both. Although he was immensely stimulated by Emerson, he gradually found himself disappointed by that seer's lack of intellectual coherence and his airy dismissal of evil. There seems to be no evidence that James ever knew the author of *Moby Dick*, and the fact that Melville began by writing narratives of Pacific adventure doomed him to be ignored by other serious readers of the time, who, like James, were predominantly readers of philosophy rather than of fiction. There is hardly a more unfortunate occurrence in the long annals of the isolation of the artist in nineteenth-century America, since of all men in Albany and New York, James and Melville ought to have had most to say to each other. Both wrestled with the problem of evil, but both had an immense gusto for humanity. And both possessed the classic breadth of nature that marks them as men of our heroic age.

Since William James undertook a full exposition of his father's religious and philosophical system, as an introduction to his *Literary Remains*,[1] there is no need to repeat that in detail here. The grounds of Henry Senior's reaction against his father's Presbyterianism can be seen in his account of his boyhood, where he evokes the tortured sufferings of a child before a God of fear. When he grew up, he denounced such a God as one of "essential malignity," and declared that his sense of salvation was of salvation from Calvinism. Yet he stood strikingly apart from the religious drift of his age in maintaining that there was, nevertheless, more truth in the old orthodoxy than in the new uplifting liberalism. Unlike the optimistic humanitarians and perfectionists, he insisted on the reality of evil. He held to the tragic essence of Christianity, to death as the way to life. He believed that religion must begin with despair, that before a man can hope to know grace, he must first view himself "as so much mere rubbish." He took his stand, therefore, against all versions of genteel respectability. He

---

Elucidation of his Doctrine of the Divine Natural Humanity (1869);

Society the Redeemed Form of Man, and the Earnest of God's Omnipotence in Human Nature (1879);

The Literary Remains of Henry James, edited with an Introduction by William James (1884).

[1] Pp. 139-87 below.

repudiated self-righteous moralism in an effort to recapture a humbler piety.

All these aspects of his thought bring him closer to a generation that has rediscovered religious truth through Kierkegaard and existential philosophy. But James remained a child of his expansive age in working out a highly individual solution. If he knew evil, he also knew good; and his final tone is distinguished by an exuberance quite foreign to the existential strain. He had learned, in his terrible crisis, that "the curse of mankind is its sense of selfhood." From that perception he developed his own version of the Fall. That event was symbolized for him in "the gradual access of self-love, and the consequent cessation of love to God and the neighbor," in "the pride of moralism" and the conceit of one's own endowments, "which make a man feel that he has an absolute or independent selfhood, and lead him therefore to make much of the differences between himself and other men. This is original sin, the great parental fount of all the evils that desolate humanity."

By emphasizing the sympathetic bonds that link us with our fellow men, by singling out egotistic pride as the source of evil, James made the kind of opposition between heart and head that is also recurrent in Melville, from *Redburn* through *Billy Budd*. James put this opposition explicitly in a tribute to Mill's essay *On Liberty*, which he felt so "full of manly sympathy for the wants of the time": "His intellect appears to me thoroughly penetrated and vivified by his heart. . . . In all Mr. Mill's books one feels the man very much more than the author; feels the upright human heart throbbing to such purpose, that he is certain the somewhat narrow systematic head will one day or other encounter the necessary enlargement."

James found his own enlargement in the doctrine of "our glorified natural humanity," the three terms of which blended for him into an organic whole. Here his thought was interpenetrated with Swedenborg's, particularly in his conception of the relation of humanity to divinity. Humanity must remain natural, since God, in all his infiniteness, is not an external being, but can be realized only through "the inmost and inseparable life of every man." But natural humanity can be glorified only through transforming love. James found nothing to revere in the cold figure of the traditional Jehovah: "That style of deity exerts no attraction either upon my heart or understanding. Any mother who suckles her babe upon her own breast, any bitch in fact who litters her periodical brood of pups, presents to my imagination a vastly nearer and sweeter Divine charm."

In his affirmation of the beauty of passional energies, in his belief that "true worship is always spontaneous, the offspring of delight not duty," James was closely akin to Blake, whose *Songs of Innocence and Experience* he greatly admired. Why he felt humanity to be capable of regeneration and thus latently divine is made manifest in a remarkable passage on "the universality of the human form" in *Christianity the Logic of Creation,* a passage more like Blake in its tone of poetic celebration than it is like their common source in Swedenborg:

"One animal preys upon another; one half of the animal kingdom lives by destroying the other half. Now man, so far as his natural form is concerned, resumes all these distinctive differences of the lower natures, and fuses them in the bosom of his own unity. He is not only devouring as the fire, and unstable as the water: he is fixed as the rock, hard as the iron, sensitive as the flower, graceful and flowing as the vine, majestic as the oak, lowly as the shrub. But especially does he reproduce in himself all the animal characteristics. He is indolent as the sloth, he is busy as the bee, he is stupid as the ox, he is provident as the beaver, he is blind as the bat, he is far-sighted as the eagle, he grovels like the mole, he soars like the lark, he is bold as the lion, timid as the fawn, cunning as the fox, artless as the sheep, venomous as the serpent, harmless as the dove: in short, all the irreconcilable antagonisms of animate nature meet and kiss one another in the unity of the human form. It perfectly melts and fuses the most obdurate contrarieties in the lap of its own universality. It is this universality of the human form which endows it with the supremacy of nature, and fits it to embosom the Divine infinitude. Because it adequately resumes in its own unity the universe of life; because it sops up, so to speak, and reproduces in its own individuality all mineral, all vegetable, and all animal forms, it claims the rightful lordship of nature, or coerces nature under its own subjection. Thus the marriage I speak of [i.e., 'between a common nature and a specific subject'] is perfectly ratified only in the human form, because in that form alone does the feminine or individual element bear any just ratio to the masculine and universal one. In short, man is the sole measure of the universe, because he alone combines in the form of his natural individuality every conceivable characteristic of universal life."

In these terms of gnomic and proverbial wisdom James recaptured the ancient doctrine of the microcosm and the macrocosm, the doctrine of the harmonious correspondence between the inner and the outer worlds. Through the majesty of such a conception, James, like the great poets and thinkers of the sixteenth-century renaissance, reaffirmed the potentially heroic stature of man. James' elation over transfigured humanity sprang from a faith that was not troubled like Melville's. "A sceptical state," he once declared, "I have never known for a moment"; whereas Melville was racked with a skepticism often akin to Hamlet's.

This should not imply that James, even when his crisis was years behind him, ever degenerated into complacence. The keenness of his sensibilities prevented that, and his love, particularly his devotion to his children, was often intense to the point of agony. "Henry James said to me," Emerson noted, that "he wished sometimes the lightning would strike his wife and children out of existence, and he should suffer no more from loving them." James regarded all such selfish anxiety as a sin, which he did his fallible best to struggle against. "Thanks for your cheering letter," he wrote to his friend Julia Kellogg in 1869. "It is right good to hear of your growth in grace and knowledge of the Lord, and I am encouraged by your example to persevere in the hope of overcoming my own worse infirmities. My besetting sin is anxiety; and no sooner does any occasion for it arise, *ab extra,* than the whole 'clanging rookery' of hell comes darkening the air, and settling down in my devoted bosom as if it were their undisputed nest. But they find themselves mistaken, *laus deo!* They are obliged to take back a little of the unrest they give, I flatter myself. For I am not in the least disposed to mistake their influx for the fruit of the soil. I do not in the least mistake their dusky visages and croaking voices for my own. I loathe and hate them with such undissembled emotions that none of David's rages against his enemies in the Psalms appears more than a faint type of the execration I owe them and cordially bestow upon them, for that matter. I hate tyranny, and spiritual tyranny above all other forms of it, i.e. the tyranny that prevails against you by availing itself of your ignorance or prejudice in respect to truth, and so putting you in hopeless conflict with yourself; and pray to God to stifle it."

To this same correspondent, who published after his death the first intelligent account of his philosophy, he also phrased a vivid account of the precarious but triumphant means by which he managed to maintain his spiritual poise:

"The other day I had a *living* experience of the truth. . . . The conditions were simple, but the spiritual result has nothing to do with great or small. . . . I was obliged to go out some two miles into the New York harbour, to see a prisoner confined there on one of the islands. The steamboat which goes early in the morning had left to my regret, and I was obliged to take a small row-boat, rowed by an old man. The day was stormy, the wind blew a piercing blast, the waves ran high, and I said to myself as my nerves began to quiver, it looks as if we should never get safe across. The thought of wife and child and friend no more to be seen on earth, gave me a shudder of disgust, and very soon my bosom was a scene of most uncomfortable disorder and perturbation. I made a desperate inward effort to save myself from childishness by seizing vigorously upon the truth, when a soft voice—angelically sweet and potent though inaudible—reduced my rising chaos to instant order and peace, by telling me that all this appearance of things, this conflict of good and evil, of safety and danger, and so forth, was a *mere* appearance Divinely permitted in the interest of our eventual spiritual freedom, while the sole reality or truth was God, in whom all was infinite serenity success and safety for all his creatures, without the slightest justification consequently, even for a moment, of any of our perturbations or anxieties. O how delicious a calm thereupon came over the uplifted waves of my breast! My poor old oarsman, who seemed a moment before an inauspicious Charon ferrying me over to death and its shades, grew into a laughing vigorous youth sporting forever on summer seas, and we chatted lovingly and freely as if our bark were bearing us away from turmoil and insanity to enchanted isles of innocence and bliss. I could only adore the Divine greatness in silence, and lament that I could hope to keep up the savour of His presence only so feebly after I should come back to Broadway and falsity."

That last phrase can serve to contrast James with Whitman, who, always more at his ease, found his divine humanity in the midst of the city and felt no need for transfiguration. William James may very well have taken his father for the model of some of the attributes of saintliness that he enumerated in *The Varieties of Religious Experience*, particularly the "immense elation of freedom, as the outlines of the confining selfhood melt down," and the "affinity between joyousness and tenderness." But in ranking his father explicitly among the "band of saints and mystics," he also added that Henry Senior was "as drastic and unsentimental as old Epictetus or even Diogenes himself." [1] Yet, to an even greater degree than this son, Henry Senior "believed in believing," and the "one great truth" in his ontology was God's alienation for the sake of an ultimate free and blissful reunion. He dwelt, mainly, not on the fall, but on the promise of the rise of the common man.

When writing about his father, in the 1880's, William James described his philosophy almost exclusively in religious terms. Fourierism was long since dead, and the only political attitude that a liberal Harvard professor apparently found tenable during the long reign of Republicanism was that of a Mugwump. Henry Senior's politics, particularly in the period before the Civil War, had been far more positive and thoroughgoing. A second-generation American whose wealth enabled him to recross the sea at will and to be an international cosmopolitan, he grew ever stauncher in his preference for America as the land of the future. He made no separation between his religion and his politics. In one of his earliest pamphlets he denounced the American church, in all its sects, because "it wholly ignores all questions of political and social reform, or if it does recognize them at all, it is only to stigmatize their gathering urgency with the name of 'infidelity.'" In "Democracy and Its Issues" (1850) he pledged allegiance to our institu-

---

[1] P. 167 below.

tions, not on the ground that they had already brought to fulfillment "the democratic idea," but that, however imperfect, they had at least exploded "the old conceptions of government, as having an authority derived from some other source than the people." He was an uncompromising equalitarian, but on the basis that "the democratic idea . . . everywhere proclaims the superiority of man to institutions, allowing the latter no respect, however consecrated by past worth, save insofar as they also reflect the present interests of humanity."

Fourierism helped him to a vocabulary wherewith to articulate his conception of true popular sovereignty. He found no inconsistency in fusing it with his Swedenborgianism.[1] Just as he offset the living spiritual against the dead moral, so he opposed the social to the selfish. He held that "our entire system of trade, as based upon what is called 'unlimited competition,' is a system of rapacity and robbery." In another lecture in the winter of 1850, on "Property as a Symbol," he made his socialism explicit: "A true society would guarantee to every man woman and child, for the whole term of his natural life, food, clothing, shelter, and the opportunities of an education adapted to his tastes; leaving all the *distinction* he might achieve to himself, to his own genius freely influencing the homage of his fellow men." If that sounds very innocent in its knowledge of human nature, it should be remembered that James was always talking about potentiality rather than actuality. He took exception to the ethical assumptions of Fourier and Comte for their naturalistic optimism. The good society, in his view, was not the natural but "the redeemed form of man." Although he followed Fourier in counterbalancing dynamic "socialism" against outworn "civilization,"[2] he was not really concerned with forms of government, but with social relationships. He believed the Fourierists to be wrong whenever they substituted external organization for inner regeneration.

James was staunchly opposed to the atomic individualism of so many of the other thinkers of his age, and criticized Emerson on those grounds. His pages are filled with such sentences as: "Life is simply the passage of idea into action," and, "The measure of a man's goodness is his use to society." In a country that tended to put an excessive emphasis on personal liberty to the neglect of fraternity, he kept reaffirming the need for social solidarity, which he described as "the great unitary life of God in our nature," or as "the unity or personality of the human race itself." Yet, despite all these emphases upon society, James' own career

[1] He was not out of step with his times. In 1849 a book appeared in New York called *The True Organization of the New Church as indicated by Emanuel Swedenborg and scientifically demonstrated by Charles Fourier.* Many writers for Brook Farm's magazine, the *Harbinger,* were also concerned with this reconciliation, just as many writers of our day have been engaged with reconciling Marx and Freud.

[2] See pp. 49–58 below.

operated almost entirely in a void. What brought about such a paradox? What caused his failure to command almost any audience at all?

The intransigent reformer Stephen Pearl Andrews, who had engaged with James in a debate on free love, believed that he had the answer. He praised James as "an astute and terribly searching and merciless, though not altogether a sound and reliable critic of the old." But for the purposes of new social organization, Andrews, who was among the supporters of the community Modern Times, on Long Island, dismissed James as one who "tends powerfully toward metaphysical subtleties and spiritual entities, until he is completely lifted off the solid earth, and loses all knowledge of practical things." What he needed was some contact with "a workshop or a counting-house or the scramble of political life, anything which would have related him to the actual world around him." The natural distrust of the poor man for the well-to-do led Andrews to picture James as one "of the class of purely ideal reformers, men who will lounge at their ease upon damask sofas and dream of a harmonic and beautiful world to be created hereafter." That was particularly unfair, since probably James' best-known remark is that, "to a right-minded man," a crowded horse-car is "the nearest approach to heaven upon earth." His satisfaction with the ordinary people against whom he jostled was due to the fact that they had not been vitiated by the pretensions and affectations of the rich and the respectable. They were still close to the solid earth. "They talk so heartily of household expenses and weather and raising chickens that it is sweet to be near them."

James' failure to attract many readers may have justified Andrews' final reproach that he belonged to "the school of seers and prophets . . . a mere *jet d'eau* of aspiration, reaching a higher elevation at some points than almost any other man, but breaking into spray and impalpable mist, glittering in the sun, and descending to earth with no weight or mechanical force to effect any great end." Yet, in retrospect, Andrews' philosophical anarchism, as expressed in his *Science of Society*, seems quite as utopian as anything in James. The aspirations of both were tinged with the millennial dreams of the 1840's and '50's. But so, for that matter, were those of most of the generous minds of that time, Emerson and Whitman among them. James' lifelong preoccupation with theology in a period that was basing its thought increasingly in other terms undoubtedly contributed to his isolation. But the lack of an immediate audience for originality was hardly unusual when Whitman had to give away most of the first issue of *Leaves of Grass*, and *Moby Dick* quickly sank out of sight. The question is whether James' books also contained some energy that his age overlooked.

In none of them can be found the nut-like concentration that has

salvaged *Walden* from its initial neglect. To read through any of his
longer works is to be reminded of Howells' comment on *The Secret of
Swedenborg,* that James "kept it." His problem of communication was
bound up with one of the tendencies that Tocqueville noted in the
literature of our democracy, the tendency, in a society without traditions or barriers, to go at one leap from the individual to the universal.
In his eagerness to transcend the merely private and to open his embrace to what could be shared with all, James sometimes lost touch with
the image of any concrete man. His ballooning mind was filled with a
heady cosmic gas that defied condensation.

Yet no less exacting a critic than E. L. Godkin, the founder of the
Nation, though baffled as to the precise nature of James' philosophy,
declared: "He was a writer of extraordinary vigor and picturesqueness,
and I suppose there was not in his day a more formidable master of
English style." In the midst of many abstract and seemingly diffuse
wastes, you suddenly come upon passages that richly justify that praise.
These passages derive their power from some concrete core. They bear
out the theory of language that he shared with Emerson, that words
derive all their "substance or body from things, or the contents of our
sensible experience." James was a master of the spirited and witty character sketch, as his reminiscences of Emerson and Carlyle and the Boston Saturday Club demonstrate.[1] He was often loose in his handling of
philosophic terms, but when he was depicting traits of mind or personality, his style became "vascular," as William James said, racily colloquial, satiric, stinging, and tender, in robust and ardent sequence. He
resolved near the outset of his career to "make all my work sabbatical,
and expressive only of irrepressive inward health and impulsion." His
best pages seem to rise from the kind of fertile relaxation that Melville
urged upon "the harpooners of this world": to throw their darts "from
out of idleness, and not from out of toil."

James also possessed command over a startling rhetoric, which
stemmed back to the bolder days of the seventeenth century. He handled invective with exuberance, as when he wrote to the editor of the
New York Observer about "the stagnant slipslop which your weekly
ladle deals out"; or when he dismissed some current writing as the
"stale and mercenary circus tricks" of "our ordinary literary posture-
mongers"; or when he embarked on one of his many flights against the
God of orthodoxy: "Against this lurid power—half-pedagogue, half-
policeman, but wholly imbecile in both aspects—I . . . raise my glee-
ful fist, I lift my scornful foot." In such moods James believed that the
only way to enliven correct and torpid theological discussions was "to
burst asunder in the midst."

---

[1] Pp. 434–8, 460–78, 479–80 below.

The more constrained Emerson entertained some doubts about his friend's "elegant Billingsgate," but James wanted to go just as far in expressing scorn as his age would let him. He wrote once to the editor of the *New York Evening Post,* to whom he had submitted a communication: "Please run your eye, or rather your nose, along my Ms. till it comes to the word 'stink' and substitute for it the less honest and pictorial word 'scourge.' . . . It is a good Anglo-Saxon word much disliked by those to whom the thing signified by it is dear; but I presume it is better to conciliate the weaklings when nothing is to be got by affronting them."

But James' prevailing temper is affectionate rather than satirical. It is suggested in a letter to a friend, of whom he says that all his "thoughts and dispositions are as genial and caressing as bread to butter, or strawberries to cream, or mutton to turnips." Howells remembered that quality when reviewing William's *Principles of Psychology*: "Those who know the rich and cordial properties of Henry James the elder, will find a kindred heartiness in the speculations of his son, and will be directly at home with him."

The problem in repossessing the elder James is, therefore, akin to one to which he himself gave recurrent attention, the problem of waste and its conversion into something of substantial value. Henry noted how often his father dwelt on that theme when discussing the apparent false turns and dead ends to which their many educational experiments generally came. Nothing was lost, his father insisted, so long as it had enriched their human experience. In a kindred sense, much may now be salvaged from his father's long-buried writings. The description he gave of Swedenborg's books may prepare us for his own: "You need never go to them for any *direct* help upon existing social and scientific problems. You might as well go to a waving wheat-field to demand a loaf of bread." But James developed his metaphor in order to stress how such a wheat-field may "really nourish and quicken" the mind by compelling it to function for itself: "of no use to any one who does not enter in to gather and bind his own golden sheaves, and then proceed to thresh and grind his grain, to bolt his flour, to mix his bread, to build it up and bake it in such shapely and succulent loaves as his own intellectual bread-pan alone determines."

Three of James' contemporaries, who were impressed by his striking personality, may combine to give us an even better clue to what to expect from him. Emerson pronounced him "true comfort—wise, gentle, polished, with heroic manners, and a serenity like the sun." Ellery Channing, struck by the fact that his manners were not of Concord but of New York, described him in a letter to Thoreau as "a little fat, rosy Swedenborgian amateur, with the look of a broker, and the brains and heart of a Pascal." The "glowing fire" of his "animal spirits," which he rejoiced in as a boy, never deserted him. We may find his concentrated essence in a single witty phrase by Annie Fields, that he was "aninted with the Isle of Patmos." Concord and Boston were familiar enough with apocalyptic, if somewhat thin-blooded Yankees. But Henry James, Senior, was unique in that circle in being not only apocalyptic, but also full-bloodedly Hibernian.

*Henry James, Senior, about 1880, from
the portrait by Frank Duveneck*

HENRY JAMES, SENIOR

Autobiography

In publishing his father's fragment of an autobiography, William James said that it had been started many years before his father's death: "He had often been urged by members of his family to express his religious philosophy under the form of a personal evolution of opinion. But egotistic analysis was less to his taste than enunciation of objective results; so that, although he sat down to the autobiographic task a good many times, it was at long intervals. . . . The Stephen Dewhurst, whose confessions it is supposed to be, is an entirely fictitious personage. The few items of personal and geographic fact he gives have been rectified in foot-notes, so as to be true of Mr. James rather than of his imaginary mouthpiece. . . . Probably no one will read what is here printed without a deep regret that the work should not have extended over later years of the author's life." To make up for that loss, William James wove into his introduction [1] most of the other autobiographical passages to be found in his father's works.

* * * * * *

I. MY EARLIEST RECOLLECTIONS

I will not attempt to state the year in which I was born,[2] because it is not a fact embraced in my own knowledge, but content myself with saying instead, that the earliest event of my biographic consciousness is that of my having been carried out into the streets one night, in the arms of my negro nurse, to witness a grand illumination in honor of the treaty of peace then just signed with Great Britain. From this circumstance I infer of course that I was born before the year 1815, but it gives me no warrant to say just how long before. The net fact is that

---

[1] See pp. 139–87 below.   [2] June 2, 1811.

my historic consciousness, or my earliest self-recognition, dates from this municipal illumination in honor of peace. So, far, however,. as my share in that spectacle is concerned, I am free to say it was a failure. That is, the only impression left by the illumination upon my imagination was the contrast of the awful dark of the sky with the feeble glitter of the streets; as if the animus of the display had been, not to eclipse the darkness, but to make it visible. You, of course, may put what interpretation you choose upon the incident, but it seems to me rather emblematic of the intellect, that its earliest sensible foundations should thus be laid in "a horror of great darkness."

My father [1] was a successful merchant, who early in life had forsaken his native Somerset County,[2] with its watery horizons, to settle in Baltimore; [3] where on the strength of a good primary education, in which I was glad to observe some knowledge of Latin had mingled, he got employment as a clerk in a considerable mercantile house, and by his general intelligence and business sagacity erelong laid the foundations of a prosperous career. When I was very young I do not remember to have had much intellectual contact with my father save at family prayers and at meals, for he was always occupied during the day with business; and even in the frank domestic intercourse of the evening, when he was fond of hearing his children read to him, and would frequently exercise them in their studies, I cannot recollect that he ever questioned me about my out-of-door occupations, or about my companions, or showed any extreme solicitude about my standing in school. He was certainly a very easy parent, and I might have been left to regard him perhaps as a rather indifferent one, if it had not been for a severe illness which befell me from a gun-shot wound in my arm, and which confined me for a long time to the house, when his tenderness to me showed itself so assiduous and indeed extreme as to give me an exalted sense of his affection.[4] My wound had been very severe, being followed by a morbid process in the bone which ever and anon called for some sharp surgery; and on these occasions I remember—for the use of anæsthetics was still wholly undreamt of—his sympathy with my sufferings was so excessive that my mother had the greatest possible difficulty in imposing due prudence upon his expression of it.

My mother [5] was a good wife and mother, nothing else,—save, to be sure, a kindly friend and neighbor. The tradition of the house, indeed, was a very charitable one. I remember that my father was in the habit of having a great quantity of beef and pork and potatoes laid by in the

---

[1] William James.

[2] County Cavan, Ireland.

[3] Albany, N. Y.

[4] At the age of thirteen, Mr. James had his right leg so severely burned while playing the then not usual game of fire-ball that he was confined to his bed for two years, and two thigh amputations had to be performed.

[5] Catharine Barber.

beginning of winter for the needy poor, the distribution of which my mother regulated; and no sooner was the original stock exhausted than the supply was renewed with ungrudging hand. My mother, I repeat, was maternity itself in form; and I remember, as a touching evidence of this, that I have frequently seen her during my protracted illness, when I had been greatly reduced and required the most watchful nursing, come to my bedside fast asleep with her candle in her hand, and go through the forms of covering my shoulders, adjusting my pillows, and so forth, just as carefully as if she were awake. The only other thing I have to remark about her is, that she was the most democratic person by temperament I ever knew. Her father,[1] who spent the evening of his days in our family, was a farmer of great respectability and considerable substance. He had borne arms in the Revolutionary War, was very fond of historic reading, had a tenacious memory, and used to exercise it upon his grandchildren at times to their sufficient *ennui*. I never felt any affectionate leaning to him. Two of his brothers had served throughout the war in the army,—one of them, Colonel F. B.,[2] having been a distinguished and very efficient officer in various engagements, and a trusted friend of Washington; the other, Major W. B.,[3] who, if my memory serve me, was an aid of General Lafayette. These of course are never ungratifying facts to the carnal mind; and when accordingly we children used to ask our mother for tales about her uncles, she gave us to be sure what she had to give with good-will, but I could very well see that for some reason or other she never was able to put herself in our precise point of view in reference to them. She seemed someway ashamed, as well as I could gather, of having had distinguished relations. And then I remember I used to feel surprised to see how much satisfaction she could take in chatting with her respectable sewing-women, and how she gravitated as a general thing into relations of the frankest sympathy with every one conventionally beneath her. I should say, indeed, looking back, that she felt a tacit quarrel with the fortunes of her life in that they had sought to make her a flower or a shrub, when she herself would so willingly have remained mere lowly grass.

But I must say one word of my mother's mother, whose memory I cherish much more than that of my grandfather. She came to us at times in winter, and as long as she lived we spent a month of every summer with her in the country, where I delighted to drive the empty ox-cart far afield to bring in a load of fragrant hay, or gather apples for the cider-press, refreshing myself the while with a well-selected apricot or two. She was of a grave, thoughtful aspect, but she had a most vivacious love of children, and a very exceptional gift of interest-

---

[1] John Barber, of (then) Montgomery, Orange Co., N. Y. (near Newburgh).

[2] Francis Barber.

[3] William Barber.

ing them in conversation, which greatly endeared her society to me. It was not till I had grown up, and she herself was among the blessed, that I discovered she had undergone a great deal of mental suffering, and dimly associated this fact somehow with the great conscience she had always made of us children. She had been from youth a very religious person, without a shadow of scepticism or indifference in her mental temperament; but as life matured and her heart became mellowed under its discipline, she fell to doubting whether the dogmatic traditions in which she had been bred effectively represented Divine truth. And the conflict grew so active erelong between this quickened allegiance of her heart to God, and the merely habitual deference her intellect was under to men's opinions, as to allow her afterwards no fixed rest this side of the grave. In her most depressed condition, however, she maintained an equable front before the world, fulfilled all her duties to her family and her neighborhood, and yielded at last to death, as I afterwards learned, in smiling confidence of a speedy resolution of all her doubts. I never failed to contrast the soft flexibility and sweetness of her demeanor with the stoicism of my grandfather's character, and early noted the signal difference between the rich spontaneous favor we children enjoyed at her hands, and the purely voluntary or polite attentions we received from him. Nor could I doubt when in after years my own hour of tribulation sounded, and I too felt my first immortal longing "to bathe myself in innocency," that this dear old lady had found in the ignorance and innocence of the grandchildren whom she loved to hug to her bosom a truer gospel balm, a far more soothing and satisfactory echo of Divine knowledge, than she had ever caught from the logic of John Calvin.

I have nothing to say of my brothers and sisters, who were seven [1] in number, except that our relations proved always cordially affectionate; so much so, indeed, that I cannot now recall any instance of serious envy or jealousy between us. The law of the house, within the limits of religious decency, was freedom itself, and the parental will or wisdom had very seldom to be appealed to to settle our trivial discords. I should think indeed that our domestic intercourse had been on the whole most innocent as well as happy, were it not for a certain lack of oxygen which is indeed incidental to the family atmosphere, and which I may characterize as the lack of any ideal of action but that of self-preservation. It is the curse of the worldly mind, as of the civic or political state of man to which it affords a material basis; it is the curse of the religious mind, as of the ecclesiastical forms to which it furnishes

---

[1] My grandfather married three times, and had in all eleven children. The seven of whom my father speaks were his *own* brothers and sisters, born of the third marriage. [WJ must refer to the eleven children who reached maturity.]

a spiritual base,—that they both alike constitute their own ideal, or practically ignore any ulterior Divine end. I say it is their curse, because they thus conflict with the principles of universal justice, or God's providential order in the earth, which rigidly enjoins that *each particular thing exist for all, and that all things in general exist for each*. Our family at all events perfectly illustrated this common vice of contented isolation. Like all the other families of the land it gave no sign of a *spontaneous* religious culture, or of affections touched to the dimensions of universal man. In fact, religious truth at that day, as it seems to me, was at the very lowest ebb of formal remorseless dogmatism it has ever reached, and offered nothing whatever to conciliate the enmity of unwilling hearts. When I remember the clergy who used to frequent my father's house, which offered the freest hospitality to any number of the cloth, and recall the tone of the religious world generally with which I was familiar, I find my memory is charged with absolutely no incident either of manners or conversation which would ever lead me to suppose that religion was anything more in its votaries than a higher prudence, or that there was anything whatever in the Divine character as revealed in the gospel of Christ to inflame in common minds an enthusiasm of devotion, or beget anything like a passionate ardor of self-abasement.

Thus the entire strain of the Orthodox faith of the period was at fault, and restricted the motions of the divine life in us to the working out at most of a conventionally virtuous and pious repute. It was eminently respectable to belong to the church, and there were few insatiate worldings, I suspect, who did not count upon giving in a prudent adhesion to it at the last. We children of the church had been traditionally taught to contemplate God as a strictly *super*natural being, bigger personally than all the world; and not only therefore out of all sympathy with our pigmy infirmities, but exceedingly jealous of the hypocritical homage we paid to his contemptuous forbearance. This dramatic homage, however, being of an altogether negative complexion, was exceedingly trying to us. Notoriously our Orthodox Protestant faith, however denominated, is not intellectually a cheerful one, though it is not so inwardly demoralizing doubtless as the Catholic teaching; but it makes absolutely no ecclesiastical provision in the way of spectacle for engaging the affections of childhood. The innocent carnal delights of children are ignored by the church save at Christmas; and as Christmas comes but once a year, we poor little ones were practically shut up for all our spiritual limbering, or training in the divine life, to the influence of our ordinary paralytic Sunday routine. That is, we were taught not to play, not to dance nor to sing, not to read story-books, not to con over our school-lessons for Monday even; not to whistle, not to ride the pony, nor to take a walk in the country, nor a swim in the river; nor, in short, to do anything which nature specially craved. How my particular heels ached for exercise, and all my senses pined to be free, it is not worth while to recount; suffice it to say, that although I know my parents were not so Sabbatarian as many, I cannot flatter myself that our household sanctity ever presented a pleasant aspect to the angels. Nothing is so hard for a child as *not-to-do;* that is, to keep his hands and feet and tongue in enforced inactivity. It is a cruel wrong to put such an obligation upon him, while his reflective faculties are still undeveloped, and his senses urge him to unrestricted action. I am persuaded, for my part at all events, that the number of things I was conventionally bound *not-to-do* at that tender age, has made Sunday to my imagination ever since the most oppressive or least gracious and hallowed day of the week; and I should not wonder if the repression it riveted upon my youthful freedom had had much to do with the habitual unamiableness and irritability I discover in myself.

My boyish Sundays however had one slight alleviation. The church to which I was born occupied one extremity of a block, and sided upon a public street. Our family pew was a large square one, and embraced in part a window which gave upon the street, and whose movable blinds with their cords and tassels gave much quiet entertainment to my restless fingers. It was my delight to get to church early, in order to secure a certain corner of the pew which commanded the sidewalk on both sides of the street, and so furnished me many pregnant topics of speculation. Two huge chains indeed extended across the street at either extremity of the church, debarring vehicles from passing. But pedestrians enjoyed their liberty unimpeded, and took on a certain halo to my imagination from the independent air with which they used it. Sometimes a person would saunter past in modish costume, puffing a cigar, and gayly switching ever and anon the legs of his resonant well-starched trousers; and though I secretly envied him his power to convert the sacred day into a festivity, I could not but indulge some doubts as to where that comfortable state of mind tended. Most of my *dramatis personæ* in fact wore an air of careless ease or idleness, as if they had risen from a good night's sleep to a late breakfast, and were now disposing themselves for a genuine holiday of delights. I was doubtless not untouched inwardly by the gospel flavor and relish of the spectacle, but of course it presented to my legal or carnal apprehension of spiritual things a far more perilous method of sanctifying the day, than that offered by men's voluntary denial of all their spontaneous instincts, of all their æsthetic culture.

I may say, however, that one vision was pretty constant, and left no pharisaic pang behind it. Opposite the sacred edifice stood the dwelling-house and office of Mr. O—r, a Justice of the Peace; and every Sunday morning, just as the sermon was getting well under way, Mr. O—r's housemaid would appear upon the threshold with her crumb-cloth in hand, and proceed very leisurely to shake it over the side of the steps, glancing the while, as well as I could observe, with critical appreciation at the well-dressed people who passed by. She would do her work as I have said in a very leisurely way, leaving the cloth, for example, hanging upon the balustrade of the steps while she would go into the house, and then returning again and again to shake it, as if she loved the task, and could not help lingering over it. Perhaps her mistress might have estimated the performance differently, but fortunately she was in church; and I at all events was unfeignedly obliged to the shapely maid for giving my senses so much innocent occupation when their need was sorest. Her pleasant image has always remained a fixture of my memory; and if I shall ever be able to identify her in the populous world to which we are hastening, be assured I will not let the opportunity slip of telling her how much I owe her for the fresh, breezy, natural life she used to impart to those otherwise lifeless, stagnant, most unnatural Sunday mornings.

II. CONFLICT BETWEEN MY MORAL AND MY SPIRITUAL LIFE

THE AIM of all formal religious worship, as it stood impressed upon my youthful imagination, was to save the soul of the worshipper from a certain liability to Divine wrath which he had incurred as the inheritor of a fallen nature, and from which he could only get relief through the merits of Christ imputed to him, and apprehended by faith. I had been traditionally taught, and I traditionally took for granted, that all souls had originally forfeited the creative good-will in the person of Adam, their attorney or representative, even if they should never have aggravated that catastrophe subsequently in their own persons; so that practically every man of woman born comes into the world charged with a weight of Divine obstruction or limitation utterly hopeless and crushing, unless relieved by actual faith in the atoning blood of Christ. I ought not to say that I actually believed this puerile and disgusting caricature of the gospel, for one believes only with the heart, and my heart at all events inmostly loathed this dogmatic fouling of the creative name, even while it passively endured its authoritative imposition. I accepted it in short only as an Orthodox tradition,—just as all the world does,—commended to my unquestioning faith by the previous acceptance of those I loved and honored. And so accepting it, its inevitable effect was, I may say, perpetually to inflame a self-love and love of the world in me which needed everything but inflaming.

My boyish animal spirits, or my excessive enjoyment of life, allowed me no doubt very little time for reflection; yet it was very seldom that

I lay down at night without a present thought of God, and some little effort of recoil upon myself. My days bowled themselves out one after another, like waves upon the shore, and as a general thing deafened me by their clamor to any inward voice; but the dark silent night usually led in the spectral eye of God, and set me to wondering and pondering evermore how I should effectually baffle its gaze. Now I cannot conceive any less wholesome or innocent occupation for the childish mind than to keep a debtor and creditor account with God; for the effect of such discipline is either to make the child insufferably conceited, or else to harden him in indifference to the Divine name. The parent, or whoso occupies the parent's place, should be the only authorized medium of the Divine communion with the child; and if the parent repugn this function, he is by so much disqualified as parent. Men have their instructed reason and their experience to guide them in Divine things, and guard them from false teaching; but nothing can be so fatal to the tender awe and reverence which should always sanctify the Divine name to the youthful mind and heart, as to put the child in a bargaining or huckstering attitude towards God, as was done by the current religious teaching of my early days. I was habitually led by my teachers to conceive that at best a chronic apathy existed on God's part towards me, superinduced by Christ's work upon the active enmity he had formerly felt towards us; and the only reason why this teaching did not leave my mind in a similarly apathetic condition towards him was, as I have since become persuaded, that it always met in my soul, and was practically paralyzed by, a profounder Divine instinct which affirmed his stainless and ineffable love. I should never indeed have felt my intellectual tranquillity so much as jostled by the insane superstition in question, if it had not been that my headlong eagerness in the pursuit of pleasure plunged me incessantly into perturbations and disturbances of conscience, which had the effect often to convert God's chronic apathy or indifference into a sentiment of acute personal hostility. Whenever this experience occurred, I was down in the dust of self-abasement, and then tried every way I possibly could to *transact* with God—on the basis of course of his revealed clemency in Christ— by the most profuse acknowledgments of indebtedness, and the most profuse promises of future payment. Obviously I could not be expected at that early age to entertain problems which my elders themselves were unable to solve. Thus I never stopped to ask myself how a being whose clemency to the sinner wears so flatly commercial an aspect,— being the fruit of an actual purchase, of a most literal and cogent *quid pro quo* duly in hand paid,—could ever hope to awaken any spiritual love or confidence in the human breast, or ever pretend consequently to challenge permanent Divine honor. In short, I was incapable as a child of accepting any theologic dogma as *true*, and received it simply on the authority of the Church; and whenever accordingly I had pungently violated conscience in any manner, I was only too happy to betake myself to the feet of Christ, to plead his healing and gracious words, and pray that *my* offences also might be blotted out in his atoning blood.

But I must guard against giving you a false impression in respect to these devotional exercises of my childhood. I have always in looking back been struck with the fact, and used at first to be somewhat disconcerted by it, that my conscience, even in my earliest years, never charged itself with merely literal or ritual defilement; that is to say, with offences which did not contain an element of active or spiritual malignity to somebody else. For example, there was a shoemaker's shop in our neighborhood, at which the family were supplied with shoes. The business was conducted by two brothers who had recently inherited it of their father, and who were themselves uncommonly bright, intelligent, and personable young men. From the circumstance that all the principal families of the neighborhood were customers of the shop, the boys of these families in going there to be fitted, or to give orders, frequently encountered each other, and at last got to making it an habitual rendezvous. There were two apartments belonging to the shop,—one small, giving upon the street, which contained all the stock of the concern, and where customers were received; the other, in which the young men worked at their trade and where we boys were wont to congregate, much larger, in the rear, and descending towards a garden. I was in the habit of taking with me a pocket full of apples or other fruit from home, on my visits to the shop, for the delectation of its occupants, several of the other lads doing the same; and I frequently carried them books, especially novels, which they were fond of reading, and their judgments of which seemed to me very intelligent. The truth is, that we chits were rather proud to crony with these young men, who were so much older than ourselves, and had so much more knowledge of the world; and if their influence over us had been really educative, almost any beneficial results might have been anticipated. I do not know exactly how it came about, but one step probably led to another, until at last we found ourselves providing them an actual feast, some of us supplying edibles and other potables from our own larders and cellars. I used, I recollect, to take eggs in any number from the ample, uncounted, and unguarded stores at home, cakes, fruits, and whatever else it was handy to carry; and I do not know to what lengths our mutual emulation in these hospitable offices might not have pushed us, when it was brought to a sudden stop. Among the urchins engaged in these foraging exploits were two sons of the governor of the State, who was a widower, and whose household affairs were consequently not so well looked after as they might have been. By the connivance of their father's butler, these young gentlemen were in the habit of storing certain dainties in their own room at the top of the house, whence they could be conveniently transported to the shop at their leisure without attracting observation. But the governor unfortunately saw fit to re-marry soon after our drama opened, and his new wife took such good order in the house, that my young friends were forced thereafter to accomplish their ends by profounder strategy. And so it happened that their step-mother, sitting one warm summer evening at her open but unilluminated chamber-window to enjoy the breeze, suddenly became aware of a dark object defining itself upon the void between her face and the stars, but in much too close proximity to the former to be agreeable, and naturally put forth her hand to determine the law of its projection. It proved to be a bottle of Madeira, whose age was duly authenticated by cobwebs and weather-stains; and from the apparatus of stout twine connected with it there seemed to be no reasonable doubt that some able engineering was at the bottom of the phenomenon. Search was made, and the engineers discovered. And to make a long story short, this discovery did not fail of course to propagate a salutary rumor of itself, and eke a tremor, to the wonted scene of our festivities, begetting on the part of the *habitués* of the place a much more discreet conduct for the future.

But this is not by any means the only or the chief immorality that distinguished my boyish days. My father, for example, habitually kept a quantity of loose silver in a drawer of his dressing-table, with a view I suppose to his own and my mother's convenience in paying house-bills. It more than covered the bottom of the drawer, and though I never essayed to count it, I should judge it usually amounted to a sum of eight or ten dollars, perhaps double that sum, in Spanish sixpences, shillings, and quarters. The drawer was seldom locked, and even when locked usually had the key remaining in the lock, so that it offered no practical obstacle to the curiosity of servants and children. Our servants I suppose were very honest, as I do not recollect to have ever heard any of them suspected of interfering with the glittering treasure, nor indeed do I know that they were at all aware of its exposed existence. From my earliest days I remember that I myself cherished the greatest practical reverence for the sacred deposit, and seldom went near it except at the bidding of my mother occasionally, to replenish her purse against the frequent domestic demands made upon it, or the exaction of my own weekly stipend. My youthful imagination, to be sure, was often impressed on these occasions with the apparently inexhaustible resources provided by this small drawer against human want, but my necessities at that early day were not so pronounced as to suggest any thought of actual cupidity. But as I grew in years, and approached the very mundane age of seven or eight, the nascent pleasures of the palate began to alternate to my consciousness with those of my muscular activity,—such as marbles, kite-flying, and ball-playing; and I was gradually led in concert with my companions to frequent a very tempting confectioner's-shop in my neighborhood, kept by a colored woman, with whom my credit was very good, and to whom accordingly, whenever my slender store of pocket money was exhausted, I did not hesitate to run in debt to the amount of five, ten, or twenty cents. This trivial debt it was, however, which, growing at length somewhat embarrassing in amount, furnished the beginning of my moral, self-conscious, or distinctively human experience.

It did this all simply in making me for the first time think with an immense, though still timorous sigh of relief, of my father's magical drawer. Thus my country's proverbial taste for confectionery furnished my particular introduction to "the tree of knowledge of good and evil." This tragical tree, which man is forbidden to eat of under pain of finding his pleasant paradisiacal existence shadowed by death, symbolizes his dawning spiritual life, which always to his own perception begins in literal or subjective darkness and evil. For what after all is spiritual life in sum? It is the heartfelt discovery by man that God his creator is alone good, and that he himself, the creature, is by necessary contrast evil. But this life in man, being divine and immortal, is bound to avouch its proper grandeur, by thoroughly subjugating evil or death to itself; that is, absorbing it in its own infinitude. Hence it is that man, constitutionally requiring the most intimate handling of evil, or the intensest spiritual familiarity with it, actually finds *himself provisionally identified* with that principle, and so far furthered consequently on his way to immortal life.

The sentiment of relief which I felt at the remembrance of this wellstocked drawer, remained a sentiment for a considerable time however before it precipitated itself in actual form. I enjoyed in thought the possibility of relief a long time before I dared to convert it into an actuality. The temptation to do this was absolutely my first experience of spiritual daybreak, my first glimpse of its distinctively moral or death-giving principle. Until then, spiritual existence had been unknown to me save by the hearing of the ear. That is to say, it was mere intellectual gibberish to me. Our experience of the spiritual world dates in truth only from our first unaffected shiver at guilt. Our youthful innocence, like every other divine-natural endowment of humanity, dwells in us in altogether latent or unconscious form, and we never truly recognize it until we have forever forfeited it to the exigencies of a more spiritual and living innocence. It is sure, for example, never to come to direct consciousness in us until we are seriously tempted to do some conventionally opprobrious thing, and have incontinently yielded to the temptation; after that, looking back at our-

selves to see what change has befallen us, we become aware of our
loss, and immediately, like the inapprehensive spiritual noodles we are,
we bend all our energies to recover this fugacious innocence, and become henceforth its *conscious* guardians!—as if man were ever capable
by *consciousness* of embracing anything good! As if the human *conscience* were *ever* open to anything else but evil in some of its myriad-
fold modulations!

I doubtless relieved myself of debt, then, by two or three times
borrowing freely from my father's drawer, without any thought of
ever making restitution. But it is idle to pretend that my action in
any of these cases was spiritually criminal. It was clandestine of course,
as it could hardly help being if it were destined ever to take place at all,
and was indeed every way reprehensible when judged from the established family routine or order. I had no idea at the time, of course,
that the act was not sinful, for no one existed within my knowledge
capable of giving me that idea. But though I should have felt excessively ashamed of myself, doubtless, if my parents had ever discovered
or even suspected my clandestine operations, yet when my religious
conscience became quickened and I had learned to charge myself with
sin against God, I practically never found that acts of this sort very
heavily burdened my penitential memory. I did not fail, I presume, to
ventilate them occasionally in my daily litany, but I am sure they never
any of them gave me a sense of spiritual defilement, nor ever cost me
consequently a pang of godly sorrow. The reason why they did not
spiritually degrade me in my own esteem was, I suppose, that they were
at worst offences committed against my parents; and no child as it
seems to me with the heart of a child, or who has not been utterly
moralized out of his natural innocency and turned into a precocious
prig, can help secretly feeling a property in his parents so absolute or
unconditional as to make him *a priori* sure, do what he will, of preserving their affection. It would not have seemed so in ancient days, I
grant. The parental bond was then predominantly paternal, whereas of
late years it is becoming predominantly maternal. At that period it was
very nearly altogether authoritative and even tyrannous with respect
to the child; while in our own day it is fast growing to be one of the
utmost relaxation, indulgence, and even servility. My father was
weakly, nay painfully, sensitive to his children's claims upon his sympathy; and I myself, when I became a father in my turn, felt that I
could freely sacrifice property and life to save my children from unhappiness. In fact, the family sentiment has become within the last
hundred years so refined of its original gross literality, so shorn of its
absolute consequence, by being practically considered as a rudiment to
the larger social sentiment, that no intelligent conscientious parent now
thinks of himself as primary in that relation, but cheerfully subordi-

nates himself to the welfare of his children. What sensible parent now thinks it a good thing to repress the natural instincts of childhood, and not rather diligently to utilize them as so many divinely endowed educational forces? No doubt much honest misgiving is felt and much honest alarm expressed as to the effect of these new ideas upon the future of our existing civilization. But these alarms and misgivings beset those only who are intellectually indifferent to the truth of man's social destiny. For my own part, I delight to witness this outward demoralization of the parental bond, because I see in it the pregnant evidence of a growing spiritualization of human life, or an expanding *social* consciousness among men, which will erelong exalt them out of the mire and slime of their frivolous and obscene private personality, into a chaste and dignified natural manhood. This social conscience of manhood is becoming so pronounced and irresistible that almost no one who deserves the name of parent but feels the tie that binds him to his child outgrowing its old moral or obligatory limitations, and putting on free, spiritual, or spontaneous lineaments. Indeed, the multitude of devout minds in either sex is perpetually enlarging who sincerely feel themselves unfit to bear, to rear, and above all to educate and discipline, children without the enlightened aid and furtherance of all mankind. And it is only the silliest, most selfish and arrogant of men that can afford to make light of this very significant fact.

But to resume. What I want particularly to impress upon your understanding is that my religious conscience in its early beginnings practically disowned a moral or outward genesis, and took on a free, inward, or spiritual evolution. Not any literal thing I did, so much as the temper of mind with which it was done, had power to humble me before God or degrade me in my own conceit. What filled my breast with acute contrition, amounting at times to anguish, was never any technical offence which I had committed against established decorum, but always some wanton ungenerous word or deed by which I had wounded the vital self-respect of another, or imposed upon him gratuitous personal suffering. Things of this sort arrayed me to my own consciousness in flagrant hostility to God, and I never could contemplate them without feeling the deepest sense of sin. I sometimes wantonly mocked the sister who was nearest me in age, and now and then violently repelled the overtures of a younger brother who aspired to associate himself with me in my sports and pastimes. But when I remembered these things upon my bed, the terrors of hell encompassed me, and I was fairly heartbroken with a dread of being estranged from God and all good men. Even now I cannot recur to these instances of youthful depravity in me without a pungent feeling of self-abasement, without a meltingly tender recognition of the Divine magnanimity. I was very susceptible of gratitude, moreover, and this furnished another

spur to my religious conscience. For although I abounded in youthful
cupidity of every sort, I never got the satisfaction of my wishes without a sensible religious thankfulness. Especially rife was this sentiment
whenever I had had a marked escape from fatal calamity. For I was
an ardent angler and gunner from my earliest remembrance, and in my
eagerness for sport used to expose myself to accidents so grave as to
keep my parents in perpetual dread of my being brought home some
day disabled or dead. I distinctly remember how frequently on these
occasions, feeling what a narrow escape I had had from rock or river,
I was wont to be visited by the most remorseful sense of my own headlong folly, and the most adoring grateful sentiment of the Divine long-
suffering.

To sum up all in a word: my religious conscience, as well as I can
recall it, was from infancy an intensely *living* one, acknowledging no
ritual bonds, and admitting only *quasi* spiritual, that is natural, satisfactions. There was of course a certain established order in the house
as to coming and going, as to sleeping and waking, as to meal-times and
morning prayers, as to study hours and play hours, and so forth. I
certainly never exhibited any wilful disrespect for this order, but
doubtless I felt no absolute respect for it, and even violated it egre-
giously whenever my occasions demanded. But at the same time nothing could be more painful to me than to find that I had wounded my
father's or mother's feelings, or disappointed any specific confidence
they had reposed in me. And I acutely bemoaned my evil lot whenever
I came into chance personal collision with my brothers or sisters. In
short, I am satisfied that if there had been the least spiritual Divine
leaven discernible within the compass of the family bond; if there had
been the least recognizable subordination in it to any objective or
public and universal ends,—I should have been very sensitive to the
fact, and responsive to the influences it exerted. But there was nothing
of the sort. Our family righteousness had as little felt relation to the
public life of the world, as little connection with the common hopes
and fears of mankind, as the number and form of the rooms we inhabited; and we contentedly lived the same life of stagnant isolation
fram the race which the great mass of our modern families live, its
surface never dimpled by anything but the duties and courtesies we
owed to our private friends and acquaintances.

The truth is, that the family tie,—the tie of reciprocal ownership
which binds together parent and child, brother and sister,—was when
it existed in its integrity a purely legal, formal, typical tie, intended
merely to *represent* or symbolize to men's imagination the universal
family, or household of faith, eventually to appear upon the earth. But
it never had the least suspicion of its own spiritual mission. It was
bound in fact in the interest of self-preservation to ignore this its vital

representative function, to regard itself as its own end, and coerce its children consequently into an allegiance often very detrimental to their future spiritual manhood. For any refining or humanizing influence accordingly which the family is to exert upon its members, we must look exclusively to the future of the institution, when it will be glorified for the first time into a natural or universal bond. It is a denial of order to demand of the subterranean germ what we expect of the full corn in the ear. If for example the family as it once existed had ever been conscious of its strictly *representative* virtue; if it had for a moment recognized that spiritual Divine end of blessing to *universal* man which alone inwardly consecrated it,—it would have incontinently shrivelled up in its own esteem, and ceased thereupon to propagate itself; so defeating its own end. For the only spiritual Divine end which has ever sanctified the family institution and shaped its issues, is the evolution of a free society or fellowship among men; inasmuch as the family is literally the seminary of the race, or constitutes the sole Divine seed out of which the social consciousness of man ultimately flowers. Thus the only true Divine life or order practicable within the family precinct, the only sentiment truly spiritual appropriate to the isolated family as such, would have been fatal to its existence, as it would have taken from it its proper pride of life; for it would have consisted in each of its members freely *disowning* all the rest in the faith of a strictly unitary *spiritual* paternity or being to all men, and a strictly universal *natural* maternity or existence.

We seem in fact only now becoming qualified to realize the spiritual worth of the family considered as a *representative* economy. For un-questionably we do *as a people* constitutionally reject—in the symbols of priest and king—the only two hitherto sacred pillars upon which the ark of man's salvation has rested, or which have based his public and private righteousness; and it is very clear that we could not have rejected the symbol unless the substance had first come empowering us so to do. That is to say, we as a people are without any proper political and religious life or consciousness which is not exclusively generated by the *social* spirit in humanity, or the truth of an approaching marriage between the public and private, the universal and the particular interests of the race; so that our future welfare, spiritual and material, stands frankly committed to the energies of that untried spirit. Happy they who in this twilight of ever-deepening spiritual unbelief within the compass of the old symbolic Church, and hence of ever-widening moral earthquake, confusion, and desolation within the compass of the old symbolic State, intelligently recognize the serene immaculate divinity of the social spirit, feel their souls stayed upon the sheer impregnable truth of human society, human fellowship, human equality, on earth and in heaven! For they cannot fail to discern in the gathering "clouds of heaven," or the thickening obscuration which to so many despairing eyes is befalling the once bright earth of human hope, the radiant chariot-wheels of the long-looked-for Son of Man, bringing freedom, peace, and unity to all the realm of God's dominion. But these persons will be the promptest to perceive, and the most eager to confess, that the family bond with us, as it has always been restricted to rigidly literal dimensions, and never been allowed the faintest spiritual significance, so it must henceforth depend for its consideration wholly and solely upon the measure in which it freely lends itself to reproduce and embody the distinctively social instincts and aspirations of the race.

III. SAME GENERAL SUBJECT

CONSIDERING the state of things I have been depicting as incident to my boyish experience of the family, the church, and the world, you will hardly be surprised to hear me express my conviction that the influences—domestic, ecclesiastical, and secular—to which I was subjected, exerted a most unhappy bearing upon my intellectual development. They could not fail to do so in stimulating in me as they did a morbid doctrinal conscience.

The great worth of one's childhood to his future manhood consists in its being a storehouse of innocent natural emotions and affections, based upon ignorance, which offer themselves as an admirable Divine mould or anchorage to the subsequent development of his spiritual life or freedom. Accordingly in so far as you inconsiderately shorten this period of infantile innocence and ignorance in the child, you weaken his chances of a future manly character. I am sure that my own experience proves this truth. I am sure that the early development of my moral sense was every way fatal to my natural innocence, the innocence essential to a free evolution of one's spiritual character, and put me in an attitude of incessant exaction—in fact, of the most unhandsome mendicancy and higgling—towards my creative source. The thought of God in every childish mind is one of the utmost awe and reverence, arising from the tradition or rumor of his incomparable perfection; and the only legitimate effect of the thought, accordingly, when it is left unsophisticate, is to lower his tone of self-sufficiency, and implant in his bosom the germs of a *social* consciousness,—that is, of a tender, equal regard for other people. But when the child has been assiduously taught, as I was, that an essential conflict of interests exists between man and his Maker, then his natural awe of the Divine name practically comes in only to aggravate his acquired sense of danger in that direction, and thus preternaturally inflame all his most selfish and sinister cupidities. Our native appreciation of ourselves or what belongs to us is sufficiently high at its lowest estate; but you have only to dispute or put in peril any recognized interest of man, and you instantly enhance his appreciation of it a hundred-fold.

Our selfhood, or *proprium*, is all we have got to dike out the inflowing tides of the spiritual world, or serve as a barricade against the otherwise overwhelming influence of heaven and hell. My body isolates me from the world, or separates between me and the outward or finite; but I should be literally stifled in my own inward genesis, actually suffocated in my creative substance, were it not for this sentiment of selfhood,—the sentiment of a life *within* so much nearer and dearer to me than that of the world, so much more intimately and exquisitely *my own* than the life of the world is, as spiritually to guarantee me even against God or the infinite. The world gives me sensible constitution or existence, and if consequently you put yourself between me and the world, you doubtless inflict a sensible but not necessarily a vital injury upon me. But my selfhood, or *proprium*, is all I know of spiritual life or inward immortal being, is all I am able consciously to realize of God himself, in short; and whenever therefore you impinge upon that,—as when you assail my vital self-respect, when you expose me to gratuitous contumely or contempt, when you in any manner suppress or coerce my personal freedom to your own profit,—you put yourself as it were between me and God, at all events between me and all I thus far spiritually or *livingly* know of God; you darken my life's sun at its very centre, and reduce me to the torpor of death. You fill my interiors in short with an unspeakable anguish, and a resentment that knows no bounds; that will stickle at absolutely nothing to give me relief from your intolerable invasion.

Now, I had been thoroughly disciplined as a child in the Christian doctrine. My juvenile faith as enforced upon me at home, at church, and at Sunday-school, amounted substantially to this: that a profound natural enmity existed from the beginning between man and God, which however Christ had finally allayed, and that I ought therefore gratefully to submit myself to the law of Christ. I never had a misgiving about my absolute duty in the premises, but practically the thing was impossible. For this law of Christ, as it was authoritatively interpreted to my imagination, revolted instead of conciliating my allegiance, inasmuch as it put me at internecine odds with my own nature, or obliged me to maintain an ascetic instead of a spontaneous relation to it. If there be any pretension more absurd philosophically than another, it is that any person or anything *can* act contrarily to their own nature. And if there be any pretension more immoral practically than another, it is that any person or thing *ought* to act in that manner. No higher obligation is incumbent upon any man in respect to the demands either of honesty or honor, than to act according to his nature; and if his action prove to be vicious or disorderly, we may be sure that his nature is still imperfectly developed, or is not allowed fair play. Of course I never actually framed the thought to myself that Christ's law as interpreted by the church was essentially burdensome, nor should I have dared to confess it, if my intellect had been ripe enough to suggest such a thing; but I instinctively felt it to be so, simply because it represented Christ as sequestrating to himself henceforth that personal allegiance on our part which is the due exclusively of our nature. For this according to the church is precisely what Christ does. All men have forfeited their natural title to God's favor; Christ pays the forfeit in his proper person, and so confiscates to himself ever after the debt which men once owed exclusively to their nature.

This doubtless was the reason—at least I can imagine none other so potent—why I began very early to discover disorderly tendencies, or prove rebellious to religious restraints. I cannot imagine anything more damaging to the infant mind than to desecrate its natural delights, or impose upon it an ascetic regimen. For nature is eternal in all her subjects, and when the child's natural instincts are violently suppressed or driven inwards by some overpowering outward authority, a moral feverishness is sure to result, which would finally exhaust or consume every possibility of his future manhood, if nature did not incontinently put him to seeking a clandestine satisfaction of her will. I felt this impulse very strongly; I doubt whether ever any one more so. I had always had the keenest savor and relish of whatsoever came to me by nature's frank inspiration or free gift. The common ore of existence perpetually converted itself into the gold of life in the glowing fire of my animal spirits. I lived in every fibre of my body. The dawn always found me on my feet; and I can still vividly recall the divine rapture which filled my blood as I pursued under the magical light of morning the sports of the river, the wood, or the field. And here was a law which frowned—nay, scowled—upon that jocund unconscious existence; which drew a pall over the lovely outlying world of sense, and gave me to feel that I pursued its pleasures only at the imminent risk of immortal loss. Just conceive the horror of leading the tender mind of childhood to believe that the Divine being could under any circumstance grudge it its natural delights; could care, for example, for the holiness of any stupid day of the seven in comparison with the holiness of its innocent mind and body! Herod's politic slaughter of the innocents were mercy itself beside this wanton outrage to nature.

This, accordingly, is the offence I charge upon my early religious training,—that it prematurely *forced* my manhood, or gave it a hot-bed development, by imposing upon my credulous mind the fiction of a natural estrangement between me and God. My sense of individuality, my feeling of myself as a power endowed with the mastery of my own actions, was prematurely vitalized by my being taught to conceive myself capable of a direct—that is, of a personal or moral—commerce with the most High. I do not mean of course that my individuality was perfectly hatched, so to say, while I was thus subject to parental authority; but only that it was altogether unduly stimulated or quickened, by my having been led at that very tender age to deem myself capable of maintaining good and evil relations with God. It is amazing to me how little sensitive people are to the blasphemy of this pretension, whether in the child or the man. That the stream should reproduce in its own sinuous self the life of the fountain, and rejoice in it the while as its own life,—nothing can be better or more orderly. But that the stream should pretend actually to revert to the creative source whence all its life and motion are instantly derived, and affect to deplore the tortuous career which alone gives it phenomenal identity, as an absolute defect of nature or wrong done to the parent fount,— can anything be imagined more flagrantly audacious and impudent, if it were not first of all so supremely stupid?

But be this abstractly as you please, my own experience profoundly avouches its concrete truth. The thought of God as a power foreign to my nature, and with interests therefore hostile to my own, would have wilted my manhood in its cradle, would have made a thoughtful, anxious, and weary little slave of me before I had entered upon my teens, if it had not been for Nature's indomitable uprightness. It aroused a reflective self-consciousness in me when I ought by natural right to have been wholly immersed in my senses, and known nothing but the innocent pleasures and salutary pains they impart. I doubt whether any lad had ever just so thorough and pervading a belief in God's existence as an outside and contrarious force to humanity, as I had. The conviction of his supernatural being and attributes was burnt into me as with a red-hot iron, and I am sure no childish sinews were ever more strained than mine were in wrestling with the subtle terror of his name. This insane terror pervaded my consciousness more or less. It turned every hour of unallowed pleasure I enjoyed into an actual boon wrung from his forbearance; made me loath at night to lose myself in sleep, lest his dread hand should clip my thread of life without time for a parting sob of penitence, and grovel at morning dawn with an abject slavish gratitude that the sweet sights and sounds of Nature and of man were still around me. The terror was all but overpowering; yet not quite that, because it called out a juvenile strategy in me which gave me as it were a new *proprium*, or at all events enabled me *bel et bien* to hold my own. That is to say, Nature itself came to my aid when all outward resources proved treacherous, and enabled me to find in conventionally illicit relations with my kind a gospel succor and refreshment which my lawful ties were all too poor to allow.

There was nothing very dreadful to be sure in these relations, and I only bring myself to allude to them by way of illustrating the gradual fading out or loss of *stamina* which the isolated family tie is undergoing in this country, and indeed everywhere, in obedience to the growing access of the social sentiment. Man is destined to experience the broadest conceivable unity with his kind,—a unity regulated by the principle of spontaneous taste or attraction exclusively; and it is only our puerile civic *régime*, with its divisions of rich and poor, high and low, wise and ignorant, free and bond, which keeps him from freely realizing this destiny: or rather let us say that it is the debasing influence which this civic *régime* exerts upon the heart and mind of men, that keeps them as yet strangers even in thought to their divine destiny. Now, the isolated family bond is the nucleus or citadel of this provisional civic economy; and practically, therefore, the interest of the isolated family is the chief obstacle still presented to the full evolution of human nature. Accordingly, even in infancy the family subject feels an instinct of opposition to domestic rule. Even as a child he feels the family bond irksome, and finds his most precious enjoyments and friendships outside the home precinct. I do not say that the family in this country *consciously* antagonizes the social spirit in humanity, or is at all aware, indeed, of that deeper instinct of race-unity which is beginning to assert itself. For the family with us is not an institution, as it is and always has been in Europe, but only a transmitted prejudice, having no public *prestige* in any case but what it derives from the private worth of its members. Still, it is a very rancorous and deep-rooted prejudice, and speculatively operates every sort of vexatious hindrance to the spread of the social sp   The "rich" family looks down upon the "poor" family, the "cultivated" family upon the "uncultivated" one,—the consequence being that this old convention which we have inherited from our European ancestry still profoundly colors our practical ethics, and blights every effort and aspiration towards race-harmony.

I have no desire, either, to intimate that I myself suffered from any particularly stringent administration of the family bond. My intercourse with my parents was almost wholly destitute of a moral or voluntary hue. Whether it was that the children of the family were exceptionally void in their personal relations of malignity or not, I do not know; but, strive as I may, I cannot remember anything but a most infrequent exhibition of authority towards us on my father's part. And as to my mother, who was all anxiety and painstaking over our material interests, she made her own personal welfare or dignity of so little account in her habitual dealings with us as to constitute herself for the most part a law only to our affections. I presume, however, that our childish intercourse with one another was unusually affectionate, since it incessantly gave birth to relations of the most frankly humoristic quality, which would have been repugnant to any tie of a mere dutiful regard.

Nevertheless, I was never so happy at home as away from it. And even within the walls of home my happiest moments were those spent in the stable talking horse-talk with Asher Foot, the family coachman; in the wood-house talking pigeons, chickens, and rabbits with Francis Piles, the out-door servant; in the kitchen, in the evenings, hearing Dinah Foot the cook, and Peter Woods the waiter, discourse of rheumatism, methodism, and miracle, with a picturesque good faith, superstition, and suavity that made the parlor converse seem insipid; or, finally, in the bedrooms teasing the good-natured chambermaids till their rage died out in convulsions of impotent laughter, and they threatened the next time they caught me to kiss me till my cheeks burnt crimson. These were my purest household delights, because they were free or imprescriptible; that is, did not appeal to my living heart through the medium of my prudential understanding. But sweet as these "stolen waters" were, they were not near so refreshing as those I enjoyed outside the house. For obviously my relation to the household servants, however democratic my youthful tendencies might be, could not be one of true fellowship, because the inequality of our positions prevented its ever being perfectly spontaneous.

I was indebted for my earliest practical initiation into a freer sentiment to the friendly intimacy I chanced to contract with my neighbors the shoe-makers, whom I have described in a former chapter. Unfortunately, these plausible young men had really no more moral elevation than if they openly cultivated some form of dubious industry; and they were willing, I think, to take advantage of our boyish frankness and generosity to an extent which, on the whole, rendered their acquaintance very harmful to us. I cannot in the least justify them, but on the contrary hand their memory over to the unfaltering Nemesis which waits upon wronged innocence. But at the same time I must say that their friendship for awhile most beneficially housed my expanding consciousness, or served to give it an outward and objective direction. They had, to begin with, such an immense force of animal spirits as magnetized one out of all self-distrust or timidity, barely to be with them. And then they were so utterly void of all religious sensibility or perturbation that my mental sinews relaxed at once into comparative ease and freedom, so that the force of nature within me then felt, I may say, its first authentication. They gave me, for example, my earliest relish of living art and art criticism. There was no theatre at that time in the city, but its place was held by an amateur Thespian company, whose exhibition they assiduously attended; and the delight they manifested in the drama, and the impassioned criticism they indulged in

upon its acting, made me long for the day when I too should enter
upon the romance of life. They were also great admirers of the triumphs of eloquence, and I used to bring collections of speeches from
our own library to read to them by the hour. It was a huge pleasure
to be able to compel their rapt attention to some eloquent defence
of liberty or appeal to patriotism which I had become familiar with in
my school or home reading. There was an old workman in the shop,
an uncle of the principals, who sacrificed occasionally to Bacchus, and
whose eyes used to drip very freely when I read Robert Emmet's
famous speech, or the plea of the prisoner's counsel at the trial scene
in "The Heart of Midlothian." He even went so far in his enthusiasm
as to predict for the reader a distinguished career at the bar; but apparently prophecy was not my friend's strong point.

NOTE.—*The Autobiography was interrupted by Mr. James at this
point, and never finished.—W. J.*

* * *

HENRY JAMES, SENIOR

Letters to Emerson

On March 3, 1842 Emerson lectured in New York on "The Times," and drew forth this response:

*   *   *   *   *

March 3, 1842
New York City

My dear Sir:

I listened to your address this evening, and as my bosom glowed with many a true word that fell from your lips I felt erelong fully assured that before me I beheld a man who in very truth was seeking the realities of things. I said to myself, I will try when I go home how far this man follows reality—how far he loves truth and goodness. For I will write to him that I, too, in my small degree am coveting to understand the truth which surrounds me and embraces me, am seeking worthily to apprehend, or to be more worthily apprehended of, the love which underlies and vivifies all the seeming barrenness of our most unloving world; but that yet for every step I have taken I find myself severed from friends and kindred, so that at last, and just when I am become more consciously worthy of love than I ever was, in so far as being more consciously and universally loving may argue me so, I find my free manifestations compressed into the sphere of my own fireside. I will further tell him that to talk familiarly with one who earnestly follows truth through whatever frowning ways she beckons him on, and loves her with so true a love as never to have been baffled from her pursuit by all the wearisome forms of error he may have encountered in the way, has never been my lot for one half-hour even; and that he, therefore, if he be now the generous lover of truth and of her friends which he seems to be, may give me this untasted pleasure, and let me once feel the cordial grasp of a fellow pilgrim, and remember for long days the cheering Godspeed and the ringing laugh with which he bounded on from my sight at parting. I will not insult his reverence for truth equally with my own by saying that I desire his guidance in any way, but I will tell him that when once my voice is known, I may now and then call him back to interpret some of the hieroglyphics which here and there line our way, and which my own skill in tongues may be unequal to,—which slight services he cannot well deny. I will tell him that I do not value his substantive discoveries, whatever they may be, perhaps half so highly as he values them, but that I chiefly value that erect attitude of mind about him which in God's universe undauntedly seeks the worthiest tidings of God, and calmly defies every mumbling phantom which would herein challenge its freedom. And finally, not to try his patience also, I will tell him that should his zeal for realities and his contempt of vulgar shows abide the ordeal I had thus contrived for them, I should gladly await his visit to me whenever he should be pleased to appoint it.

This in substance is what I said to myself. Now that I have told it to you also, you have become a sort of confidant between me and myself, and so in a manner bound to promote harmony there. If you shrink from the confidence thus thrust upon you, *I* shall certainly be blamed by *myself*, for making so indiscreet a communication to you; but if you abide it, *I* shall with equal certainty be highly felicitated by *myself* for achieving a result so undeniably auspicious to both. In every event, I remain, your true well-wisher,

H. James

P.S. My residence is at No. 5, Washington Place. This Place runs from Broadway to Washington Square, and forms, or is formed by, the row of buildings between the University building and Broadway. My occupations are all indoor, so that I am generally at home—always in the evenings.

* * *

According to the family legend, as reported in Henry Junior's autobiography, Emerson, on his very first visit, was "proudly and pressingly 'taken upstairs' to admire and give his blessing to the lately-born babe who was to become the second American William James. The blessing was to be renewed, I may mention, in the sense that among the impressions of the next early years I easily distinguish that of the great and urbane Emerson's occasional presence in Fourteenth Street, a centre of many images, where the parental tent was . . . to pitch itself and rest awhile."

The ensuing letters show the mixture of fascination and disappointment that James was to experience in his intercourse with Emerson. It soon became apparent that Emerson's mind was far less intense in its demands than James' was, that having retired from the Unitarian

clergy a decade before, Emerson no longer felt pressed by theological
questions, but was content with passively contemplating the moments
of inspiration.

*   *   *   *   *

New York City, 1842

To the Invisible Emerson, the Emerson that thinks and feels and
lives, this letter is addressed; and not to the Emerson that talks and
bewitches one out of his serious thought when one talks to him, by the
beautiful serenity of his behaviour. This latter Emerson I shall begin
to hate soon for keeping my stupid eyes so continually away from the
profounder Emerson who alone can do one any good. But I will now
have the true man's ear alone. I came home tonight from my lecture a
little disposed to think from the smart reduction of my audience that
I had about as well not prepared my lectures, especially that I get no
tidings of having interested one of the sort (the religious) for whom
they were wholly designed. And now I say to myself "the first step
in your outgoing to the world having thus failed you, no second
step of course offers itself, but you must come back to your perch,
and look round the horizon for some other flight." No sooner said than
done—my eyes are already open to look, and shall continue patiently
open always. When I next see you I want a half-hour's help from you
in this matter. And the purpose of this letter is to secure it. Whenever
I am with you I get no help from you—that is, of the sort which you
can give me, I feel sure—and this letter is to let you know what it is
I want before I come next. Usually the temper you shew, of perfect
repose, of perfect candour, so perfectly free from all sickening partizan-
ship, so full of magnanimous tenderness towards all creatures, makes me
forget my wants in your lavish plenty. But I know you have the same
wants as I have, deep down in your bosom hidden from my sight, and
it is by these I want somewhat to know you. Henceforth I commit the
visible man to my wife for her reproof—and mine in leisure hours.

I am led, quite without any conscious wilfulness either, to seek the
laws of these appearances that swim round us in God's great museum—
to get hold of some central *facts* which may make all other facts
properly circumferential, and *orderly* so—and you continually dis-
hearten me by your apparent indifference to such law and central
facts: by the dishonour you seem to cast upon our intelligence, as if
it stood much in our way. Now my conviction at present is that my
intelligence is the necessary digestive apparatus for my life. . . . Is it
not so in truth with you? Is not your life continually fed by knowledge, and could you have any life but brute life without it? Do you
not feel the necessity of reaching after these laws all the while,—some
inner fact which shall link together mighty masses of now conflicting
facts; and suddenly by getting hold of such fact, are you not sensibly

lifted up to far vaster freedom of life? . . . But I cannot say what I want to say—what aches to say itself in me—and so I'll hold up till I see you, and try once more to get some better furtherance by my own effort.

Here am I thirty-one years in life, ignorant in all outward science, but having patient habits of meditation which never know disgust or weariness, and feeling a force of impulsive love toward all humanity which will not let me rest wholly mute—a force which grows against all resistance that I can muster against it. What shall I do? Shall I get me a little nook in the country and communicate with my *living* kind, not my talking kind—by life only—a word, may be, of *that* communication, a fit word, once a year? Or shall I follow some commoner method, learn science and bring myself first into men's respect, that thus I may the better speak to them? I confess this last theory seems rank with earthliness—to belong to days forever past. Can the invisible Emerson then put up from his depths some heart-secret-law which shall find itself reproduced in mine and so further me, or at least *stay* me? Let him try, and above all let him forgive *more suo* all my botherings.

                                                                    H. James

                                                        New York, May 11, 1843

My dear Emerson:

Your letter was well-come, I assure you, every way, even in that of flesh and blood, as it bade begone a spell of the blues which two days prevalence of east winds and dyspepsia had conjured over me. . . . Something or other disturbs the deep serene of my rejoicing in you. . . . All that I can at present say is that, being better satisfied with you than any man I ever met, I am worst satisfied: which being interpreted means, that while your *life* is of that sort which, so far as I can detect it, lays hold of my profoundest love, ever and anon some provokingly perverse way of speech breaks forth which does not seem to me to come from the life, and incontinently knocks me into downright *pi* again. It all comes of some lurking narrowness in me, which shall be discovered if so it be—but which nevertheless shall be legitimately discovered, that is, through the experience of growing life. . . . So by and bye, when I come into greener and freer pastures, I will wonder at the straitness of my present paddock, which I am so blindly bent on deeming ample for your accommodation. Till then bear with me. . . .

I am cheered by the coming of Carlyle's new book,[1] which Greeley announces, and shall hasten off, as soon as I have leisure, for it. The title is provokingly enigmatical. Thought enough will be there, no doubt, whatever it may be named. Thought heaped up to topheaviness

---

[1] *Past and Present.*

and inevitable lopsidedness, but more interesting thought to me than comes from any other quarter of Europe. Interesting for the man's sake whom it shews. According to my notion Carlyle is the very best interpreter of spiritual philosophy which could be devised *for this age*, the age of transition and conflict. And what renders him so is his natural birth- and education-place. Just to think of a *Scotchman* with a heart widened to German spiritualities! To have overcome his educational bigotries far enough to listen to the new ideas, this was wonderful. But then to give all his native shrewdness and humour to the service of making them *tell* to the minds of his people—what more fortunate thing for the time could there be than this? You don't look upon Calvinism as a fact at all, wherein you are to my mind philosophically infirm, and impaired as to your universality. I can see in Carlyle's writing the advantage his familiarity with this fact gives him over you with a general audience. What is highest in Carlyle is built upon that lowest. At least so I read. I believe Jonathan Edwards *redivivus* in true blue would, after an honest study of the philosophy that has grown up since his day, make the best possible reconciler and critic of philosophy—far better than Schelling *redivivus*. . . .

* * *

Exasperated at not being able to pin Emerson down, James once apostrophized him: "Oh you man without a handle!" Emerson's side of the intermittent correspondence was far less intimate and outspoken. But he soon introduced his New York friend to Thoreau, whose first reaction was that James "makes humanity seem more erect." On further acquaintance, however, they did not really take to each other. After James' later appearance at one of Alcott's "conversations," Thoreau reported that he "is a hearty man enough, with whom you can differ very satisfactorily, on account of both his doctrines and his good temper. He utters *quasi* philanthropic dogmas in a metaphysic dress; but they are for all practical purposes very crude. He charges society with all the crime committed, and praises the criminal for committing it. But I think that all the remedies he suggests out of his head—for he goes no farther, hearty as he is—would leave us about where we are now." On his side, James was finally repelled by Thoreau's extreme individualism, and declared that he "was literally the most childlike, unconscious and unblushing egotist it has ever been my fortune to encounter in the ranks of manhood; so that, if he happened to visit you on a Sunday morning, when possibly you were in a devout frame of mind, as like as not you would soon find yourself intoning subaudible praises to the meticulous skill which had at last succeeded in visibly marrying such sheer and mountainous inward self-esteem with such harmless and beautiful force of outward demeanor."

James' irreverent opposition to Alcott's far more towering self-esteem soon exploded the "conversation." A report of another meeting between these two in New York stated that "Mr. Alcott could not condone the attempt to translate his sayings into common sense, and said abruptly to Mr. James, 'You'll continue a sinner to all eternity; you are damaged goods.' He claimed that he himself was one with Pythagoras and Jesus. The three had never sinned, and had all that advantage over other men. Mr. James pushed his point: 'You say you and Jesus are one. Have you ever said 'I am the resurrection and the life?' 'Yes, often,' was the reply. 'Has any one ever believed you?' The conversation here ended abruptly, Mr. Alcott saying, 'I won't talk any more with you.' " But whatever their differences, James, who loved such a fight, maintained that his personal relations with Alcott were ever "most frank, cordial and friendly." James was even said to have "beamed with delight" when he was shaken by Emerson's Aunt Mary Moody for having attacked "Morality."

In the summer of 1849 Emerson's invitation for James to lecture at the Town and Country Club in Boston brought this reply:

* * * * *

I am horrified at the prospect of speaking before so urbane an assemblage as I am likely to meet, and nothing but the protection of your magnanimous countenance reconciles me. There is nothing I dread so much as literary men, especially *our* literary men. Catch them out of the range of mere personal gossip about authors and books, and ask them for honest sympathy with your sentiment or an honest repugnancy of it, and you will find the company of stage-drivers sweeter and more comforting to your soul. In truth the questions which are beginning to fill the best books and will fill the best for a long time to come, are not related to what men have called literature, and are as well—I think better—judged by those whom books have at all events not belittled. It seems to me the authorial vocation will not be so reputable in the future as in the past. If, as we are promised by all signs, the life which has hitherto glistened only in the intellect of men shall come down to their senses and put on every palpable form, I suspect the library will fall into disuse, and men will begin to believe that the only way for each to help the other is to live one's own life.

Your own books suggest this conviction incessantly. I never read you as an author at all. Your books are not literature but life, and criticism always strikes me, therefore, as infinitely laughable when applied to you. The opposite of this in literary men is what makes me hate them. You come to them with some grand secret that opens heaven to the lowest and most excluded hut, that lifts your own life out of bottomless and stifling mud, where living is abject toil, and expect some involuntary token of human sympathy, even of natural curiosity,—but no, a supercilious smile decks every visage, and the only notice taken of you is a muttered invocation of this, that and the other accepted name. These men do not live, and if books turn men into this parrot existence, I hope the Astor Library will meet the same fate as the Alexandrian. When a man lives he can scarcely write. He cannot read, I apprehend, at all. All his writing will be algebraized—put in the form of sonnets and proverbs, and the community will feel itself insulted to be offered a great book, as though it were stupid and wanted tedious drilling like a child.

But I have lost sight of what I wanted to say. I am totally unfit to appear before your people except upon the subjects which usually engage my most earnest thought. I should greatly like to consider socialism from the highest point of view, but the name is a stench in the nostrils of all the devout and honourable, and I would not willingly outrage your kindness in introducing me by *obtruding* the topic upon my audience. Do you then think that any chance exists for my getting heard without long offense upon that subject? I cannot conceal my whole thought about it, if I speak at all, and therefore I await your dictum before I set to work. In case you think I had better leave this topic, I should like to read a paper on sin. It seems to me that a very beautiful philosophy underlies all our experiences in that line, and I should greatly like to say all I feel upon the subject. But on second thoughts, this would be very shocking, too, to prejudiced people, and besides would involve a practical social bearing; so it is perhaps rather worse than the other. The fact is, I am in a very bad way I am afraid, for I cannot heartily engage in any topic in which I shall appear to advantage. However, I will do what I can, and take on with me certificates of good citizenship from my wife and family and neighbours, in case the worst comes to the worst.

My wife and I are obliged—so numerous has waxed our family—to enlarge our house in town, and get a country house for the summer. These things look expensive and temporary to us, besides being an additional care; and so, looking upon our four stout boys, who have no play-room within doors, and import shocking bad manners from the street, with much pity, we gravely ponder whether it would not be better to go abroad for a few years with them, allowing them to absorb French and German and get a better sensuous education than they are likely to get here. To be sure, this is but a glimpse of our ground of proceeding—but perhaps you know some decisive word which shall dispense us from any further consideration of the subject. When my paper to the Town and Country Club shall be read I shall be functionless, and may study as well, and, better perhaps, abroad as here. Anyhow, and everywhere, I am, yours faithfully,

H. James

* * *

Confronted with the heady alternative of a discussion of socialism or of sin, Emerson inclined to the former: "Socialism is as good a topic as a brave man who likes it can choose. We all have a leaning towards it from the 'anxious benches,' an expectation of being convicted and converted, on account of a certain geometry that is in it, notwithstanding that we are born hermits." So James delivered his paper on "Socialism and Civilization in Relation to the Development of the Individual Life." The expedition to Europe was postponed indefinitely, and he continued to lecture, during the next few years, on such subjects as "Democracy and Its Issues," "Property as a Symbol," "The Principle of Universality in Art," and "The Old and the New Theology." His son Henry preserved the memory of his father's having had,

* * * * *

before our migration of 1855, a considerable lecturing activity. A confused, yet perfectly recoverable recollection, on my own part, of these years, connects itself with our knowledge that our father engaged in that practice and that he went forth for the purpose, with my mother always in earnest and confident even though slightly fluttered attendance, at about the hour of our upward procession to bed; which fact lent to the proceeding—that is to *his*—a strange air of unnatural riot, quite as of torch-lighted and wind-blown dissipation. We went to plays and ballets, and they had comparatively speaking no mystery; but at no lecture had we ever been present, and these put on for my fancy at least a richer light and shade, very much as if we ourselves had been on the performing side of the curtain, or the wonder of admiring (in our mother's person) and of being admired (in our father's) had been rolled for us into a single glory. This glory moreover was not menaced, but only made more of a thrill by the prime admirer's anxiety, always displayed at the last, as to whether they were not starting without the feature of features, the *corpus delicti* or manuscript itself; which it was legendary with us that the admired had been known to drive back for in an abashed flurry at the moment we were launched in dreams of him as in full, though mysterious, operation. I can see him now, from the parlour window, at the door of the carriage and under the gusty street-lamp, produce it from a coat-tail pocket and shake it, for her ideal comfort, in the face of his companion. The following, to Emerson, I surmise, is of some early date in the autumn of '52:

"Your note finds me on the eve of starting for Albany, whence I leave for Boston next Tuesday, meaning to lecture there Wednesday evening (Nov. 5) at the Masonic Temple. . . . I should be greatly— appalled in some respects, but still—charmed to have you for an auditor, seeing thus an hundred empty seats obliterated; but I beg of you don't let any engagement suffer by such kindness to me.

"Looking over the lectures again they horrify me with their loud-mouthed imbecility. But I hope they may fall upon less hardened ears in some cases. I am sure that the thought which is in them, or rather seems to me to struggle to be in them, is worthy of all men's rapturous homage, and I will trust that a glimpse of it may somehow befall my patient auditory. The fact is that a vital truth can never be transferred from one mind to another, because life alone appreciates it. The most one can do for another is to plant some rude formula of such truth in his memory, leaving his own spiritual chemistry to set free the germ whenever the demands of his life exact it. The reason why the Gods seem so powerless to the sensuous understanding, and suffer themselves to be so long defamed by our crazy theologies, is that they are life, and can consequently be revealed only to life. But life is simply the passage of idea into action. And our crazy theologies forbid ideas to come into action any further than our existing institutions warrant. . . . However I shall try to convert *myself*, at least, into an army of Goths and Huns, to overrun and destroy our existing sanctities, that the supernal splendours may at length become credible and even visible. . . . Good-bye till we meet in Boston, then, and cultivate your good nature according to my extensive needs. Yours ever faithfully. . . ."

* * *

James' recurrent disheartenment and perennial hopefulness over his lectures remained with him to the end. His wife wrote, more than twenty years later, to their son Henry, then in Europe: "Father came back comfortably from his Providence spree, but rather discouraged, I think, as he always is, after giving a lecture. All that he has to say seems so good and glorious, and easily understood to him, but it falls so dead upon the dull or skeptical ears who come to hear him, that I do not wonder he feels so."

In his reminiscences of the earlier years, Henry described the anomalous position in which he and his brothers found themselves through their father's not being in business in a country which, to their young eyes, seemed to divide itself into only three classes: "the busy, the tipsy, and Daniel Webster."

"I remember well how when we were all young together we had, under pressure of the American ideal in that matter, then so rigid, felt it tasteless and even humiliating that the head of our little family was *not* in business, and that even among our relatives on each side we couldn't so much as name proudly anyone who was—with the sole exception of our maternal uncle Robertson Walsh, who looked, ever so benevolently, after our father's 'affairs,' happily for us. Such had never been the case with the father of any body of our acquaintance; the business in which the boy's father gloriously *was* stood forth inveterately as the very first note of our comrade's impressiveness. *We* had no note of that sort to produce, and I perfectly recover the effect

of my own repeated appeal to our parent for some presentable account
of him that would prove us respectable. Business alone was respectable
—if one meant by it, that is, the calling of a lawyer, a doctor or a
minister (we never spoke of clergymen) as well; I think that if we had
had the Pope among us we should have supposed the Pope in business,
just as I remember my friend Simpson's telling me crushingly, at one
of our New York schools, on my hanging back with the fatal truth
about our credentials, that the author of *his* being (we spoke no more
of 'governors' than we did of 'parsons') was in the business of a steve-
dore. That struck me as a great card to play—the word was fine and
mysterious; so that 'What shall we tell them that you *are*, don't you
see?' could but become on our lips at home a more constant appeal. It
seemed wantonly to be prompted for our father, and indeed greatly
to amuse him, that he should put us off with strange unheard-of attri-
butions, such as would have made us ridiculous in our special circles;
his 'Say I'm a philosopher, say I'm a seeker for truth, say I'm a lover
of my kind, say I'm an author of books if you like; or, best of all, just
say I'm a Student,' saw us so very little further. Abject it certainly
appeared to be reduced to the 'student' plea; and I must have lacked even
the confidence of my brother Bob, who, challenged, in my hearing and
the usual way, was ready not only with the fact that our parent 'wrote,'
but with the further fact that he had written *Lectures and Miscellanies
James*."

"Father's Ideas" came to be their shorthand indication of the mysterious realm that took their parent away from the family circle. A representative sampling of those ideas, in James' early prime, is afforded by
the lecture on "Socialism and Civilization," and by the 4th of July oration on "The Social Significance of Our Institutions," which he delivered a decade later, after their return from Europe to Newport. The
nature of his more formal religious writing may be judged by the
copious quotations in William's essay.[1]

---

[1] Pp. 139–87 below.

HENRY JAMES, SENIOR

Socialism and Civilization

* * * * *

GENTLEMEN:

I propose to discuss the relative bearing of Socialism and Civilization on human destiny, or the development of the individual life.

By Socialism, I mean not any special system of social organization, like that of Fourier, Owen, or St. Simon, but what is common to all these systems, namely, the idea of a perfect fellowship or society among men. And by Civilization, of course, I mean the present political constitution of the nations. Between the fundamental idea of Socialism, which affirms the possibility of a perfect life on earth, or the insubjection of man both to nature and his fellow-man, and the fundamental idea of Civilization, which affirms the perpetual imperfection of human life, or the permanent subjection of man to nature and society, a great discrepancy exists; and I hope to interest my audience in a brief examination of its features. I am sure you cannot bestow your spontaneous attention upon the subject without the greatest advantage.

The differences of detail which characterize the systems of St. Simon, Owen, Fourier, and other societary reformers, are of very little present account to us. What is of great present account is the signal agreement of these men in point of principle. They agree in holding our present social condition to be not only vicious, which every one will admit, but also stupid, which is not so universally obvious. They declare that it is entirely competent to us at any time to organize relations of profound and enduring harmony among men, and thus to banish crime, vice, and suffering from the earth; and that nothing but an ignorance of the true principles of human nature stands between us and this most desirable consummation. Crime, vice and suffering, they allege, are not essential to human society, but are merely incidental to its infancy or

49

nonage, and are sure to disappear before the advancing wisdom of its majority. Thus the socialist maintains the inherent righteousness of humanity, and resolves all its disorders into imperfect science.

Here, then, we have the fundamental difference between Socialism and Civilization. The socialist affirms the inherent righteousness of humanity, affirms,that man is sufficient unto himself, and needs no outward ordinances for his guidance, save during his minority. The conservative, on the other hand, or the advocate of the present, affirms the inherent depravity of man, affirms that he is insufficient unto himself, and requires the dominion of tutors and governors all his appointed days upon the earth. This accordingly is the quarrel which has first to be settled—the quarrel between Socialism and Civilization, before men will care in any considerable numbers to balance the claims of rival socialists. Let it first of all be made plain to us that Socialism is true in idea, is true as against Civilization; then we shall willingly enough discuss the relative superiority of St. Simon to Owen, or of Fourier to both.

How then shall this grand preliminary quarrel be settled? Of course, historically or actually, it will be settled only by the march of events. But how shall it be settled meanwhile, intellectually, or to your and my individual satisfaction? Each of us, doubtless, will judge it in the light of his own ideas and aspirations. If, for example, Socialism appear to promise better things than Civilization to the highest life of man, we cannot fail, of course, to bid it God-speed, and predict its speedy triumph. If the reverse judgment should ensue, we shall, equally of course, execrate it, and leave it to the contempt of mankind. . . .

I have no hesitation in affirming, that society, as at present, or rather as heretofore, constituted, arrays the lower interest in conflict with the higher, and debases man into subject slavery to itself. Society affords no succor to the divine life in man. Any culture we can give to that life, is owing not to society, but to our fortunate independence of it. For the incessant action of society is to shut up all my time and thought to the interests of my mere visible existence, to the necessity of providing subsistence, education, and social respect for myself and my children. To these narrow limits society confines all my passion, all my intellect, all my activity; and so far denies me self-development. My true or divine selfhood is completely swamped in transient frivolous cares. Indeed so rigorous is our social tyranny, so complete a servitude does society impose upon the individual, that we have almost lost the tradition of our essential freedom, and scarcely one in a million believes that he has any individuality or sacredness apart from his natural and social ties. He who constitutes our private and distinctive individuality, He who ceaselessly pants to become avouched and appropriated to every man as his nearest and most inseparable self, is for the most part

banished from the glowing heart of humanity, into frigid and extra-
mundane isolation, so that we actually seem to have no life above the
natural and social spheres.

But this appearance is fallacious. It is a correspondence of that fallacy
of the senses which makes the earth central, and the heavens circumferential. I will not deny that the most genial relations bind God and
my body, bind God and my neighbor; but I will deny *totis viribus*
that either my body or my neighbor forms the true point of contact
between God and me. He is infinitely nearer to me than my own body;
infinitely nearer to me also than my neighbor. In short He is with me
not only finitely but infinitely, not only by the medium of the physical
and moral life, but also in my spontaneous attractions and tendencies.
Here pre-eminently do I find God. Here alone do I behold the infinite
Beauty. Here alone do I perfectly lose myself and perfectly find myself.
Here alone, in short, do I feel empowered to say, what every true
creature of God is bound to say: I and my father are one.

I repeat that the whole strain of society is adverse to this spontaneous
and divine life in man. It relegates his whole energy to the service of
his physical and moral interest, that is to its own direct advantage, and
beyond this point takes no cognizance of him. It utterly ignores his
proper, God-given, and æsthetic life, the life whose supreme law is the
good pleasure of the subject; or recognises it only to profane and corrupt it. It is melancholy to see the crawling thing which society
christens Art, and feeds into fawning sycophancy. It has no other conception of Art than as polished labor, labor stripped of its jacket and
apron, and put into parlor costume. The Artist is merely the aboriginal
ditcher refined into the painter, poet, or sculptor. Art is not the gush
of God's life into every form of spontaneous speech and act; it is the
talent of successfully imitating nature—the trick of a good eye, a good
ear, or a good hand. It is not a really infinite life, consubstantiate with
the subject and lifting him into ever new and unpremeditated powers
and achievements; it is an accomplishment, a grace to be learned, and to
be put off and on at one's convenience.

Accordingly society establishes academies of Art, gives out rules for
its prosecution, and issues diplomas to the Artist, by which he may be
visibly discriminated from ordinary people. But always on this condition, that he hallow, by every work of his hands, its existing prejudices
and traditions; that he devote his perfectly docile genius to the consecration of its morality. If he would be truly its child, let him confine
himself to the safe paths of portraiture and bust making, to the reproduction of the reigning sanctities in church and state, their exemplary
consorts and interesting families. By this door many of our aspiring
"artists" have entered the best society. But if the disciple be skittish,
and insist on "sowing the wild oats" of his genius, let him, at most,

boldly allegorize the Calvinistic divinity or the Unitarian morality into Voyages of Life and similar contrivances, or dash off ineffectual brigands and Magdalens that should find no forgiveness in this world or the next. But these things are trivial. If society did no greater harm to God's life in man than to misconceive the nature and misapply the name of Art, it would be foolish to complain. But the evil it does is positive and profound, and justifies a perfectly remorseless criticism.

For the true complaint against society is not the little it does actually to promote the divine life in man, but the much it does actually to hinder that life by giving him a conscience of sin against God, and so falsifying the true relation between them. If I fail in my allegiance to society, if I violate any of its enactments, in forcibly taking, for example, the property of my neighbor, society is not thereupon content to visit me with the penalty provided for the case: it has the hardihood also to proclaim me a sinner against God, and threaten me with His wrath. Society has the presumption to identify its own will with the will of God. It assumes that whatsoever it declares to be property, or to belong to A., B. and C., is also viewed as such property, or as so belonging, on the part of God; and that hence in violating this property I offend God no less than itself. Certainly it is contrary to the divine will that any man should violate his neighbor's property. We may say that such a thing is *absolutely* contrary to the divine will, and cannot therefore be done. It would be an aspersion of the divine power to say that He gave me a property which any other man had power to take away from me. Or it would be an aspersion of His goodness to suppose Him giving me a certain property, and at the same time giving another power to deprive me of it. The whole conception of a man really sinning against God is intolerably puerile.

The error of society herein lies in its giving man what Swedenborg calls a *false proprium*, that is a property which God does not give him. Society does all it can to finite man, to include or shut up his proprium, his selfhood, within itself, and so render him its abject vassal or dependent. The more external property it gives him, the more houses, lands, flocks, and perishable goods of all sorts, the more it finites him and renders him dependent on itself. For society alone confers and guarantees this property. Abstract the protection of society, and no man could keep it a day. God, on the contrary, seeks incessantly to aggrandize His child, and render him *in-finite*. He strives to insinuate a proprium, which shall lift him above all outward limitation. He makes Himself over to him in an inward and invisible way, and so endows him with a property both incorruptible and inviolable, which no moth can corrupt, and no thief break through and steal. . . .

If the evils I have described be real, if civilization be fraught with these and all other forms of hindrance to the divine life, then clearly civilization stands condemned by its fruits, and has no title to prejudice the promise of Socialism. Socialism claims to be nothing more than a remedy for the physical and moral ills which inhere in civilization, which result from its very genius. The whole promise of Socialism may be thus summed up.—It promises to lift man out of the harassing bondage which he is under to nature and society, out of that crushing responsibility which he is under to his own body and his fellow-man, and so leave him subject forever to God's unimpeded inspiration, leave him, in fact, the very play-thing of God, a mere pipe for the finger of Deity to play what stops it pleases. It proceeds upon a double postulate, namely, that every creature of God, by virtue of his creation, is entitled, 1, to an ample physical subsistence, that is, to the satisfaction of all his natural appetites; 2, to an ample social subsistence, that is, to the respect and affection of every other creature of God. Whatever institution violates these principles by nonconformity, it pronounces tyrannous and void.

Thus Socialism condemns, after a certain stage of human progress, the institution of limited property. It demands for man an infinite property, that is to say a property in universal nature and in all the affections and thoughts of humanity. It is silly to charge it with a tendency to destroy property. It aims indeed to destroy all merely limited and conventional property, all such property as is held not by any inward fitness of the subject, but merely by external police or convention; but it aims to destroy even this property only in the pacific way of superseding it, that is, by giving the subject possession of the whole earth, or a property commensurate with his inward and essential infinitude.

This, I confess, is what attracts me in the programme of Socialism, the unconscious service it renders to the divine life in me, the complete inauguration and fulfilment it affords to the Christian hope of individual perfection. Christianity is a virtual denial of all mystery to Deity, and an affirmation of His essential intelligibility. It denies to Deity any mere passive or inoperative perfection, and affirms His existence exclusively within human conditions. It reveals a perfect harmony between God in His infinitude and man in his lowest natural and social debasement, even when devoid of all physical grace and comeliness, and when despised, cast out, and rejected of the best virtue of his time. In short it affirms the unity of God and Man. Two things hinder the consciousness of this unity on the part of man—nature and society, the one by limiting his power, the other by limiting his sympathies; the one by finiting his body, the other by finiting his soul. Accordingly, the Christ, or representative Divine Man, is seen warring with and subjugating both nature and society, making time and space so fluent and plastic to his desires as to avouch his actual bodily infinitude, and ex-

erting so wholly genial an influence upon the opposite extremes of
society—saint and sinner, Jew and Gentile,—as to avouch his equal
spiritual infinitude.

Now what is here typically reported of the Christ is to be actually
fulfilled in universal humanity, in every man, according to the promise,
"What things ye see me do, ye shall do also, and greater things than
these." Nature and society are to be glorified into the footstool of
Almighty God, enshrined in every human bosom. I have no idea that
man will ever be able literally to change water into wine, or to feed
his body upon inadequate food, or to pass through stone walls at
pleasure, or to satisfy the tax-gatherer out of the mouth of fishes. But
I believe that the various internal reality of these symbols will be
fully accomplished in us, that nature and society will become in the
progress of science so vivid with divine meaning, that the infinite desire
of man will receive a complete *present* satisfaction, and that instead of
our relegating the vision of God, as now, to an exclusively *post-mortem*
experience, He will become revealed to the natural senses with such an
emphasis as to make the most frolicsome sports of childhood more
worshipful than all piety.

Now Socialism alone supplies the science of this great consummation.
It reveals the incessant operation of laws by which man's physical and
social relations will be brought into the complete subjection of his inward or divine personality. It is the demonstration of a plenary unity
between man and nature and man and man. It convinces me of infinitely
more extended relations to nature than those which now define me,
and of infinitely sweeter ties with man than those which bind me to the
Tom, Dick and Harry of my present chance acquaintanceship.

Let this unity then become visible, become organized, and I shall
instantly realize the divine freedom, realize my true and infinite selfhood. For then I shall become released from this finite and false
proprium which now enslaves me and keeps me grovelling in the dust.
If I am one with nature and my fellow-man, if there be a sovereign
unity and not enmity pervading all our reciprocal relations, then clearly
every appetite and affection both of my physical and moral nature become instantly legitimated, and I stand henceforth absolved from all
defilement, a new creature of God triumphant over death and hell, nay
more, taking death and hell into friendly subjection, and suffusing
their hitherto dusk and dejected visages with the roseate flush of
omnipresent and omnipotent Life.

I repeat that the curse of our present ties, that which eliminates all
their poetry, is our limited property in men and things, is the finite
selfhood imposed on us by the present evil world. My internal property
or selfhood, that which God gives me, is nothing short of infinite, is
Himself in truth. To match this divine internal, nature gives me my

feeble body, society gives me a petty score of relatives and friends. Whilst I accept this niggardly service from nature and society, whilst I strive to compel my internal aspirations within these outward bounds, I suffer torments which are appeased only to be renewed. This body is incompetent to the subjugation of nature which my spirit demands. I may battle stoutly for a while, but I accomplish after all only a grave. But suppose the battle to have been never so successful in a material point of view, suppose me to have realized any amount of superfluous potatoes, yet after all how mere a potato-cask do I remain, destitute of inward pith and riches! The battle with nature, the battle for animal subsistence, leaves us merely animal, leaves us actually unvivified of God, leaves us only the dimmest and most fluctuating hope of God in realms beyond the grave.

But society imposes the most torturing disability. Affiliating me to one man, and that man incapable seven times out of eight of supplying my bare necessities; restricting me to the fraternity of two or three persons whom probably the penury of our joint resources converts into mutual rivals and foes; committing my profoundest passional interests to the keeping of one frail will; turning the most sacred depths of passion within me into an arena of public traffic, into material of habitual and vulgar gossip; society does its utmost to ensure me a daily profanation, and turn God's otherwise joyful force in me into the force of a giant despair, into the force of an eventual deadly retribution.

Let any one consider for a moment the best endowment he gets from present society, or the extent of limitation it imposes upon him, and then reply whether it can be long tolerable to God.

In the first place, we have the tie of the insulated family, which enjoins a superior affection to all involved in it than to any others. Let my father's interests clash with his neighbors; let my mother and the mother of any body else, come into rivalry; let my brother or sister conceive a quarrel with any unrelated person: you know that in all these cases I am a natural partisan, and that if I should practically disown the obligation, that blissful home which furnishes the theme of so much sincere as well as dishonest sentimentality, would become on the instant a very hell incapable of pacification. Conduct so unnatural on my part, no matter how just it might be in the abstract, would convert these natural brethren into my envenomed foes, and even disqualify me for any very cordial welcome from their original antagonist, the person for whose cause I had forsaken theirs. Take the tie of township or country, that which generates the old-fashioned virtue called patriotism, and you see it to be full of the same iniquitous bondage.

In fact there exists no tie either natural or social, as society is now constituted, which does not tend to slavery, which does not cheat man's soul of its fair proportions. I love my father and mother, my brother and sister, but I deny their unconditional property in me. Society having been incompetent hitherto to fulfil its duties to me, has deputed the care and sustenance of my tender years to them. I acknowledge gratefully the kindness I have received at their hands. But if they ask any other reward for this kindness than the satisfaction of seeing me a man, if they expect me to continue their humble satellite and partisan, instead of God's conscript and votary solely, I am bound to disappoint them. I will be the property of no person, and I will accept property in no person. I will be the son of my father, and the husband of my wife, and the parent of my child, but I will be all these things in a thoroughly divine way, or only as they involve no obloquy to my inward righteousness, only as they impose no injustice on me toward others.

You all remember those grand mystic sayings of the Christ, "whoso will lose his life in this world shall keep it unto life eternal," and "whoso will leave father or mother, or brother or sister, or wife or child, for my sake, shall find all these relations multiplied a hundredfold." Now what is the great spiritual burden of these divine words, for you know every divine word is so mainly from within. Is it not that our primary dignity is divine, and flows from God within us instead of from our outward relations? Is it not that each of us is under paramount allegiance to his own spontaneous life, and that if we insist first on the fulfilment of this allegiance, all these secondary or derivative relations will fall of themselves into harmony?

But you know this truth experimentally also. You know that you never find perfect peace or contentment in your outward and finite *proprium.* You know by experience that you cannot set your life's happiness upon any outward possession, be it wife or child, or riches, without an incessant and shuddering dread of betrayal. The infinite faculty within you steadfastly refuses these limited satisfactions. But when you rejoice first of all in that infinite faculty, when you seek above all things to give it development by the medium of appropriate action, by the medium of Art, then the house of your peace is built upon a rock, against which the windows of heaven are opened in vain. Let a man then renounce all enforced property in persons and things, accepting only such things and persons as actually gravitate to him; let him renounce all tale-bearing and recourse to the police, and come into universal candor, into complete whiteness of soul towards all men and things, how instantly would every heart expand to him as to God's melting sunshine, and the earth swarm with fragrant kisses for his feet!

To become possible, however, in any great degree for the individual man, this quality of manhood must first become universal, and to make it universal is the function of Socialism, is the aim of social science. Socialism lifts us out of these frivolous and pottering responsibilities we are under to man, and leaves us under responsibility to God alone, or our inmost life. The way it does this, is by revealing the existence and operation of laws, which shall provide every man, woman, and child, the orderly and ample satisfaction of their natural appetites and affections, the unlimited expansion of their intellect, and the complete education of their faculty of action, however infinitely various that faculty may be. In short it reveals the method of man's perpetual re-creation, a re-creation so complete that every day shall come clad to him with all the freshness of God's dewy hand, stifling both memory and hope in the amplitude of a present bliss. Suppose Socialism then to have attained its end, suppose the Divine Life to have become by its means universalized, what a temple of enchantment this lacerated earth would become! For when all things and persons become free, become self-pronounced, then a universal reverence and truth spring up, every manifestation of character claiming and enjoying the homage we now pay only to unmanifested Deity.

Besides we degrade and disesteem whatsoever we absolutely own. We degrade by owning and just in the degree of our owning. It is a proverb, that no man values the good he has in hand, but only that which is to come. This is signally true in respect to persons. We degrade and disesteem every person we own absolutely, every person bound to us by any other tenure than his own spontaneous affection. Of course one values one's brothers and sisters in the present state of things, if from nothing else, then from self-love; for society is so unfriendly and torpid to us that the domestic hearth gathers a warmth not wholly its own. But who is ever found idealizing a brother or sister? Our instinct of Friendship is profaned where a brother is the claimant, and Love expires of sheer self-loathing in the presence of a sister.

It is the indispensable condition of a perfect respect, that a person be inwardly individualized, that is, possess the complete supremacy of his own actions. Then all his relations are of an inevitable dignity. When the wife of Quisquis declined his merely dutiful or voluntary allegiance, when she insisted upon erasing the marriage-bond as a stain upon his truth, and giving to their relation the sole sanction of spontaneity, her husband found that relation instantly glorified, or purged of its abundant meanness. His home became henceforth a livelier sanctuary than the church, and his wife a diviner page than all the prophets. So also one's child, how tiresome he grows when he does nothing morning, noon or night, but reflect the paternal dullness, when he is sedulous to do all the father prescribes and avoid all the mother condemns! Yet how beautiful he becomes, when he ever and anon flashes forth some spontaneous grace, some self-prompted courtesy!

Why is it esteemed disgraceful for the mature man to consult his natural father and mother in every enterprise, and be led by their advice? The cause of this judgment is spiritual, and lies in the truth that man is destined by the fact of his divine genesis to self-sufficiency, to self-government, that he is destined to find all guidance within him and none whatever without him, and that he cannot persist accordingly in the infantile habit of seeking help beyond himself without flagrant detriment to his manhood, to his destiny. All our natural and social phenomena, in fact, are symbolic, and have no worth apart from the spiritual verities they embalm and typify.

To conclude, Socialism promises to make God's great life in man possible, promises to make all our relations so just, so beautiful and helpful, that we shall be no longer conscious of finiteness, of imperfection, but only of life and power utterly infinite. I am not able to satisfy any one's reasonable curiosity on this subject. Every one who trusts in a living and therefore active God, in that God who is quite as active and original in our day as He was six thousand years ago, in short every one whose hope for humanity is alert, behooves to acquaint himself forthwith with the marvellous literature of Socialism, above all with the writings of CHARLES FOURIER. You will doubtless find in Fourier things of an apostolic hardness to the understanding; you will find many things to startle, many things perhaps to disgust you; but you will find vastly more both in the way of criticism and of constructive science to satisfy and invigorate your understanding, while such glimpses will open on every hand of God's ravishing harmonies yet to ensue on earth, that your imagination will fairly ache with contentment, and plead to be let off.

These are what you will find in Fourier, provided you have no secret interest dogging your candor and watching to betray it. Let me also tell you what you will *not* find there. You will find no such defaming thought of God as makes His glory to depend upon the antagonism of His creature's shame. You will find no allegation of an essential and eternal contrariety between man and his creative source. Whatever be Fourier's errors and faults, this crowning and bottomless infamy by no means attaches to him. On the contrary, if the highest homage paid to Deity be that of the understanding, then Fourier's piety may safely claim pre-eminence. For it was not a traditional piety, that piety of habit which keeps our churches open—and cheerless; nor was it a selfish piety, the piety which springs from jail-bird conceptions of Deity, and paints him as a colossal spider bestriding the web of destiny and victimizing with fell alacrity every heedless human fly that gets entangled in it; but a piety as broad as human science, co-extensive in fact with the sphere of his senses, for its prayers were the passions or wants of the universal human heart, its praises the laws or methods of the human understanding, and its deeds the innumerable forms of spontaneous human action.

* * *

HENRY JAMES, SENIOR

The Social Significance of Our Institutions

THE IMPASSIONED tone of this address, "delivered by request of the citizens at Newport, R. I." on July 4, 1861, was naturally heightened by the fact that it was a product of the first summer of the Civil War, when the North's indignation against England's encouragement of the South was mounting. James characteristically discovered the cardinal significance of the Declaration of Independence to lie, not in any doctrine of individualistic freedom, but in its religious affirmation that all men are "*created* equal," and in its social implication that they find therefore their human fulfillment through "fellowship" and "fraternity."

* * * * *

A friend observed to me a few days since, as I accepted the invitation with which your Committee of Arrangements has honored me, to officiate as your orator on this occasion, that I could hardly expect, under the circumstances, to regale my auditors with the usual amount of spread-eagleism. I replied, that that depended upon what he meant by spread-eagleism. If he meant what was commonly meant by it, namely, so clearly defined a Providential destiny for our Union, that, do what we please, we shall never fall short of it, I could never, under any circumstances, the most opposed even to existing ones, consent to flatter my hearers with that unscrupulous rubbish. No doubt many men, whose consciences have been drugged by our past political prosperity, do fancy some such inevitable destiny as this before us,—do fancy that we may become so besotted with the lust of gain as to permit the greatest rapacity on the part of our public servants, the most undisguised and persistent corruption on the part of our municipal and private agents, without forfeiting the Providential favor. From that

sort of spread-eagleism I told my friend that I hoped we were now undergoing a timely and permanent deliverance. But if he meant by that
uncouth word an undiminished, yea, a heightened confidence in our
political sanity and vigor, and in the fresh and glowing manhood which
is to be in yet larger measure than ever the legitimate fruit of our institutions, I could assure him that my soul was full of it, and it would be
wholly my fault if my auditors did not feelingly respond to it.

I never felt proud of my country for what many seem to consider
her prime distinction, namely, her ability to foster the rapid accumulation of private wealth. It does not seem to me a particularly creditable
thing, that a greater number of people annually grow richer under our
institutions than they do anywhere else. It is a fact, no doubt, and like
all facts has its proper amiable signification when exposed to the recti-
fying light of Truth. But it is not the fact which in a foreign land, for
example, has made my heart to throb and my cheeks to glow when I
remembered the great and happy people beyond the ʹsea, when I
thought of the vast and fertile land that lay blossoming and beckoning
to all mankind beyond the setting sun. For there in Europe one sees
this same private wealth, in less diffused form, it is true, concentrated
in greatly fewer hands, but at the same time associated in many cases
with things that go every way to dignify it or give it a lustre not its
own,—associated with traditional family refinement, with inoffensive
unostentatious manners, with the practice of art and science and literature, and sometimes with the pursuit of toilsome and honorable personal adventure. Every one knows, on the other hand, how little *we*
exact from our rich men; how meagre and mean and creeping a race
we permit our rich men to be, if their meanness is only flavored with
profusion. I have not been favored with a great many rich acquaintance,
but still I have known a not inconsiderable number, and I have never
found them the persons to whom one would spontaneously resort in
his least personal moments, or communicate with the most naturally in
his hours of the purest intellectual elation or despondency. Of course I
have known exceptions to this rule, men whose money only serves to
illustrate their superior human sweetness, men of whose friendship
everybody is proud. But as a general thing, nevertheless, one likes best
to introduce one's foreign acquaintance, not to our commercial nabobs,
who aggravate the price of house-rent and butcher's meat so awfully to
us poor Newporters; not to our fast financiers and bank cashiers, who
on a salary of three thousand a year contrive to support in luxury, beside their proper wife and offspring, a dozen domestic servants and as
many horses; but to our, in the main, upright, self-respecting, and, if
you please, untutored, but at the same time unsophisticated, children of
toil, who are the real fathers and mothers of our future distinctive manhood.

No; what makes one's pulse to bound when he remembers his own home under foreign skies, is never the rich man, nor the learned man, nor the distinguished man of any sort who illustrates its history, for in all these petty products almost every country may favorably, at all events tediously, compete with our own; but it is all simply the abstract manhood itself of the country, man himself unqualified by convention, the man to whom all these conventional men have been simply introductory, the man who—let me say it—for the first time in human history finding himself in his own right erect under God's sky, and feeling himself in his own right the peer of every other man, spontaneously aspires and attains to a far freer and profounder culture of his nature than has ever yet illustrated humanity.

Shallow people call this pretension of ours the offspring of national vanity, and stigmatize it as implying the greatest immodesty in every one who asserts it. Is it not the same as saying, they ask, that ignorance is as good as experience, weakness as good as skill, nature as good as culture, the crude ore as good as the polished metal which is extracted from it? . . .

No American, who is not immersed in abject spread-eagleism,—that is to say, no American who has had the least glimpse of the rich social promise of our institutions, or of the free play they accord to the spiritual activities of our nature,—values the mere political prestige of his nation, or the repute it enjoys with other nations, as the true ground of its glory. . . .

As Americans, we love our country, it is true, but not because it is *ours* simply; on the contrary, we are proud to belong to it, because it is the country of all mankind, because she opens her teeming lap to the exile of every land, and bares her hospitable breast to whatsoever wears the human form. This is where the ordinary European mind inevitably fails to do us any justice. The purblind piddling mercenaries of literature, like Dickens, and the ominous scribes and Pharisees of the Saturday Review, have just enough of cheap wit to see and caricature the cordial complacency we feel in our virgin and beautiful mother; but it takes an acumen bred of no London police-courts, and an education of the heart which all the studies of Oxford will never yield, to see the rich human soul that vivifies that complacency, that burns away all its dross, and makes it laughable only to literary louts and flunkies who live by pandering to the prejudices of the average human understanding.

The American misses in European countries and institutions this exquisite human savor, this exquisite honor which is due to man alone, and this exquisite indifference which is due to persons. In European institutions,—I do not say in existing European *sentiment*, for that, no doubt, is greatly in advance of the institutions,—but in European institutions persons are everything and man comparatively nothing. It is always the skilled man, or the learned man, or the mighty man, or the noble man, in short the propertied or qualified man of some sort, that is had in reverence; never our common humanity itself, which, on the contrary, is starved in garrets in order that the man of quality may live in plenty, is ground to powder by toil in order to keep up his iniquitous state, is butchered in crowds to maintain his peace, and rots in prisons to avouch his purity. Abroad every American sees, of course and accordingly, any amount of merely political energy and efficiency, sees governments flourishing by the permanent demoralization of their people. He sees every appliance of luxurious art, all manner of imposing edifices, of elaborate gardens and pleasure-places, the deadliest arsenals of war, armies innumerable, and navies disciplined with infernal force, all consecrated to the sole purpose of keeping up the purely *political* status of the country, or aggrandizing its own selfish aims and repute to the eyes of other nations and its own people. And he cries aloud to his own heart, May America perish out of all remembrance, before what men blasphemously call public order finds itself promoted there by this costly human degradation! Disguise it as you will in your own weak, wilful way, in no country in Europe has the citizen as yet consciously risen into the man. In no country of Europe does the government consciously represent, or even so much as affect to represent, the unqualified manhood of the country, its lustrous human worth, the honest unadulterate blood of its myriad beautiful and loving bosoms, its fathers and mothers, its brothers and sisters, its sons and daughters, its husbands and wives, its lovers and friends, every throb of whose life is sacred with God's sole inspiration; but only the adulterate streams which course through the veins of some insignificant conventional aristocracy. Take England itself for an example of the perfect truth of my allegations. We may easily do injustice to England just now; may easily forget the shining and proud pre-eminence which belongs to her political development among all the polities of the earth. Another nation so great, so vowed in its political form to freedom, so renowned for arms, for art, for industry, for the intelligence of its scholars, for its public and private morality, does not illustrate human annals; and yet, because she now thinks of herself before she thinks of us, because she listens to the prayer of her starving operatives before she listens to the demands of our betrayed nationality, we are ready to forget her glorious past, and pronounce her a miracle of selfishness. But no truly human virtue is compatible with an empty stomach; and England, like everybody else, must .be allowed first of all to secure her own subsistence before she bestows a thought upon other people. I will not blame England, then, for her present timidity. I will never forget the inappreciable services she has rendered to the cause of political progress. But just as little can I be blind to the immense limitations she exhibits when measured by American humanitary ideas. She claims to be the freest of European nations; and so she is, as I have already admitted, so far as her public or political life is concerned. But viewed internally, viewed as to her *social* condition, you observe such a destitution of personal freedom and ease and courtesy among her children as distinguishes no other people, and absolutely shocks an American. Conventional routine, a wholly artificial morality, has so bitten itself into the life of the people, into the national manners and countenance even, that the kindly human heart within is never allowed to come to the surface, and what accordingly is meant among them for civility to each other is so coldly and grudgingly rendered as to strike the stranger like insult. The intensely artificial structure of society in England renders it inevitable in fact, that her people should be simply the worst-mannered people in Christendom. Indeed, I venture to say that no average American resides a year in England without getting a sense so acute and stifling of its hideous class-distinctions, and of the consequent awkwardness and *brusquerie* of its upper classes, and the consequent abject snobbery or inbred and ineradicable servility of its lower classes, as makes the manners of Choctaws and Potawatamies sweet and christian, and gives to a log-cabin in Oregon the charm of comparative dignity and peace.

For, after all, what do we prize in men? Is it their selfish or social worth? Is it their personal or their human significance? Unquestionably, only the latter. All the refinement, all the accomplishment, all the power, all the genius under heaven, is only a nuisance to us if it minister to individual vanity, or be associated with a sentiment of aloofness to the common life, to the great race which bears us upon her spotless bosom and nourishes us with the milk of her own immortality. What is the joy we feel when we see the gifted man, the man of genius, the man of high conventional place of whatever sort, come down to the recognition of the lowliest social obligations,—what is it but a testimony that the purest personal worth is then more pure when it denies itself, when it leaps over the privileged interval which separates it from the common life, and comes down to identify itself with the commonest? This sentiment of human unity, of the sole original sacredness of man and the purely derivative sanctity of persons, no matter who they are, *is what we are born to*, and what we must not fail to assert with an emphasis and good-will which may, if need be, make the world resound. For it is our very life, the absolute breath of our nostrils, which alone qualifies us to exist. I lived, recently, nearly a year in St. John's Wood in London, and was daily in the habit of riding down to the city in the omnibus along with my immediate neighbors, men of business and professional men, who resided in that healthy suburb, and fared forth from it every morning to lay up honest, toilsome bread for the buxom domestic angels who sanctified their homes, and the fair-haired cherubs who sweetened them. Very nice men, to use their own lingo, they were, for the most part; tidy, unpretending, irreproachable in dress and deportment; men in whose truth and honesty you would confide at a glance; and yet, after eight months' assiduous bosom solicitation of their hardened stolid visages, I never was favored with the slightest overture to human intercourse from one of them. I never once caught the eye of one of them. If ever I came nigh doing so, an instant film would surge up from their more vital parts, if such parts there were, just as a Newport fog suddenly surges up from the cold remorseless sea, and wrap the organ in the dullest, fishiest, most disheartening of stares. They took such extreme pains never to look at one another, that I knew they must be living men, devoutly intent each on disowning the other's life; otherwise I could well have believed them so many sad well-seasoned immortals, revisiting their old London haunts by way of a nudge to their present less carnal satisfactions. I had myself many cherished observations to make upon the weather, upon the lingering green of the autumn fields, upon the pretty suburban cottages we caught a passing glimpse of, upon the endless growth of London, and other equally conservative topics; but I got no chance to ventilate them, and the poor things died at last of hope deferred. The honest truth is what Dr. Johnson told Boswell, that the nation is deficient in human sentiment. "Dr. Johnson," says Boswell, "though himself a *stern, trueborn* Englishman, and fully prejudiced against all other nations, had yet discernment enough to see, and candor enough to censure, the cold reserve among Englishmen toward strangers (of their own nation). 'Sir,' said he, 'two men of any other nation who are shown into a room together, at a house where they are both visitors, will immediately find some conversation. But two Englishmen will probably go each to a different window and remain in obstinate silence. Sir, we do not, as yet,' proceeded the Doctor, 'understand the common rights of humanity.'"

These common rights of humanity of which Dr. Johnson speaks are all summed up in the truth of man's social equality; that is, every man's joint and equal dependence with every other man upon the association of his kind for all that he himself is or enjoys. These common rights of humanity have got political ratification in England, as they have got it nowhere else in Europe out of Switzerland; but the private life of England, as Dr. Johnson charges, is shockingly indifferent to them. The moral sentiment, the sentiment of what is exceptionally due to this, that, or the other *person*, utterly dominates in that sphere the social sentiment, the sentiment of what is habitually due to every man as man. It is this unchallenged primacy of the moral life over the social life of England, this intense sensibility among her scholars to personal claims over human claims, which so exalts her Pharisaic pride and abases her true spirituality, which leaves her outwardly the greatest and inwardly the poorest of peoples, and makes the homesick because better-nurtured foreigner feel, when exposed to it, how dismal and dingy the very heaven of heavens would become if once these odiously correct and lifeless white-cravatted and black-coated respectabilities should get the run of it.

You see at a glance that this penury of England in all spiritual regards is owing to the simple fact that not *man*, but *English*-man, is the key-note of her aspirations. European thought generally and at best is peninsular,—that is, *almost* insular,—in that it regards European culture as constituting the probable limits of the human mind. But English thought is absolutely insular, in that it makes England the actual measure of human development. Every Englishman who lives and dies an Englishman, that is to say, who has not been made by God's grace a partaker in heart of the *common*-wealth of mankind, or a spiritual alien from the mother that bore him, believes that not Europe, but England itself, one of the smallest corners of Europe, as Judæa was one of the smallest corners of Asia, furnishes the real *Ultima Thule* of human progress. This being the key-note of English thought, the pitch to which all its tunes are set, you are not surprised to see the sentiment dominating the whole strain of English character, till at last you find the Englishman not only isolating himself from the general European man, but each individual Englishman becoming a bristling independent unapproachable little islet to every other Englishman, ready, as Dr. Johnson describes them, to leap out of the windows rather than hold that safe and salutary parley with each other which God and nature urge them to; so that probably a huger amount of painful plethoric silence becomes annually accumulated under English ribs than befalls the whole world beside, and an amount of spiritual numbness and imbecility generated which is not to be paralleled by anything this side of old Judæa. And it is exactly the rebound of his thought from all this social obstruction and poverty which causes the American wayfarer's heart to dance with glee when he remembers his own incorrect and exceptionable Nazareth, his own benighted but comfortable and unsuspecting fellow-sinners, who are said to sit sometimes with their tired feet as high as their head, who light their innocent unconscious pipes at everybody's fire, and who occasionally, when the sentiment of human brotherhood is at a white heat in their bosom, ask you, as a gentleman from Cape Cod once asked me at the Astor House table, the favor of being allowed to put his superfluous fat upon your plate, provided, that is, the fat is in no way offensive to you. That the forms in which human freedom expresses itself in these latitudes are open to just criticism in many respects, I cordially admit, and even insist; but he who sees the

uncouth form alone, and has no feeling for the beautiful human substance within it, for the soul of fellowship that animates and redeems it
of all malignity, would despise the shapeless embryo because it is not
the full-formed man, and burn up the humble acorn because it is not yet
the branching oak. But the letter is nothing, the spirit everything. The
letter kills, the spirit alone gives life; and it is exclusively to this undeniable spiritual difference between Europe and America, as organized
and expressed in our own constitutional polity, that all our formal differences are owing. Our very Constitution binds us, that is to say, the
very breath of our political nostrils binds us, to disown all distinctions
among men, to disregard persons, to disallow privilege the most established and sacred, to legislate only for the common good, no longer for
those accidents of birth or wealth or culture which spiritually indi-
vidualize man from his kind, but only for those great common features
of social want and dependence which naturally unite him with his kind,
and inexorably demand the organization of such unity. It is this immense constitutional life and inspiration we are under which not only
separate us from Europe, but also perfectly explain by antagonism that
rabid hostility which the South has always shown towards the admission of the North to a fair share of government patronage, and which
now provokes her to the dirty and diabolic struggle she is making to
give human slavery the sanction of God's appointment. . . .[1]

*   *   *

---

[1] The omitted portion goes on to
state, in somewhat more conventional
terms, the familiar case against slavery.
—F. O. M.

BOOK TWO

Henry James, Senior, and Henry, Junior, from the daguerreotype by Matthew Brady, 1854

THE CHILDREN'S EDUCATION

THE MUCH DISCUSSED educational experiment in Europe was finally realized, in England and France from 1855 to 1858, and then, after an interlude at Newport, in Switzerland and Germany during 1859 and 1860. In 1855 William was thirteen, and Henry twelve. Wilky—Garth Wilkinson, named for his father's notable English Swedenborgian friend—was ten, Robertson nine, and Alice seven. Their sensibilities were to be exposed, during five impressionable years, to the Europe of the tourist, to its streets and art-galleries, its cathedrals and theaters. It goes without saying that they were also immersed in its books, since they all learned to speak French and German, and in the James family a fondness for reading was taken for granted.

The uniqueness of their experience, as compared with that of other young Americans, had begun long before they left New York. No children of the experimental nineteenth century were subjected to a more premeditated system. But what differentiated theirs .from the rigors encountered by a John Stuart Mill was that their father, while "delighting ever in the truth," was, as HJ noted,[1] "generously contemptuous of the facts," and consequently "the literal played in our education as small a part as it perhaps ever played in any, and we wholesomely breathed inconsistency and ate and drank contradictions."

Years later, when WJ was attempting to sum up the impression made upon him by HJ, after that brother's long residence in England, he said: "He's really . . . a native of the James family, and has no other country." Being a native of the James family was an experience more formative than any amount of travel in foreign lands. When Henry Senior started to bring up his children, he was reacting against the conception of the family fostered in his own youth. He protested in

---

[1] To avoid countless repetition of names, I follow the example of *Notes* *of a Son and Brother* and indicate the brothers by their initials.

his autobiography [1] against the "stagnant isolation" of the self-enclosed group, and held staunchly to the belief that the family was of value only as it contributed to a more comprehending and sympathetic participation in the concerns of society. But he did not believe that such participation could be mechanically enforced through any rules. His educational watchword was "spontaneity." "I desire my child," he said, "to become an upright man, a man in whom goodness shall be induced not by mercenary motives as brute goodness is induced, but by love for it or a sympathetic delight in it. And inasmuch as I know that this character or disposition cannot be forcibly imposed upon him, but must be freely assumed, I surround him as far as possible with an atmosphere of freedom."

But freedom through exposure, freedom through choice between all varieties of sensuous, æsthetic, and religious experience, inevitably separated the James children from those of less favored families, and gave them, in this country as well as abroad, a sense of living on a kind of blissful island. To a degree that their father seems never to have realized, they became a splendid "special case," of the sort that HJ later delighted to portray in his fiction. The very fact that their father was nearly always at home, and so took an active role in their education, distinguished them from the other denizens of Fourteenth Street. HJ commented on "that almost eccentrically home-love habit in my father which furnished us with half the household humour of our childhood —besides furnishing *him* with any quantity of extravagant picture of his so prompt pangs of anguish in absence for celebration of his precipitate returns. It was traditional for us later on, and especially on the European scene, that for him to leave us in pursuit of some advantage or convenience, some improvement of our condition, some enlargement of our view, was for him breathlessly to reappear, after the shortest possible interval, with no account at all to give of the benefit aimed at, but instead of this a moving representation, a far richer recital, of his spiritual adventures at the horrid inhuman inns and amid the hard alien races which had stayed his advance. He reacted, he rebounded, in favour of his fireside, from whatever brief explorations or curiosities; these passionate spontaneities were the pulse of his life and quite some of the principal events of ours; and, as he was nothing if not expressive, whatever happened to him for inward intensity happened abundantly to us for pity and terror, as it were, as well as for an ease and a quality of amusement among ourselves that was really always to fail us among others."

A letter from Alice, written in her twelfth year, embroiders the same theme:

---

[1] P. 30 above.

"My dear Father,—We have had two dear letters from you and find you are the same dear old good-for-nothing home-sick papa as ever. Willie is in a very extraordinary state of mind, composing odes to all the family. A warlike one he addressed to Aunt Kate, in which the hero is her husband and dies for her; and he says: 'The idea of anyone dying for her!!' . . . We have all come to the conclusion that he is fit to go to the lunatic asylum, so make haste home before such an unhappy event takes place. . . . Your affectionate daughter."

Their father's immense and uncontrollable capacity for demonstrative tenderness also heightened the daily temperature above normal. Alice remembered how he "used to spoil our Christmasses so faithfully for us, by stealing in with us, when Mother was out, to the forbidden closet and giving us a peep the week or so before. I can't remember whether he used to confess to Mother after, or not, the dear, dear creature! What an ungrateful wretch I was, and how I used to wish he hadn't done it!!" And again: "When I look back upon the unrippled stream of fostering and indulgent domestic receptivity down which I have floated all my days, I wonder that I am not a more objectionable and impossible wretch than I am." HJ observed that one great consequence of their being so separated from the competitive American business world was to turn them from the outward to the inward life. In his view, such "felicities of destitution which kept us, collectively, so genially interested in almost nothing but each other . . . come over me now as one of the famous blessings in disguise." Spared from "the she-wolf of competition," they were "all gentle and generous together."

Within that family circle nothing, surely, was ever "stagnant." The father led them into fields of conversation of the widest possible range, and conflicting ideas flourished with intensity and ardor. Godkin recalled an occasion just before the group was broken up by the Civil War: "There could not be a more entertaining treat than a dinner at the James house, when all the young people were at home. They were full of stories of the oddest kind, and discussed questions of morals or taste or literature with a vociferous vigor so great as sometimes to lead the young men to leave their seats and gesticulate on the floor. I remember, in some of these heated discussions, it was not unusual for the sons to invoke humorous curses on their parent, one of which was, that 'his mashed potatoes might always have lumps in them!' "

Alice thought, in retrospect, that she and her brothers owed most gratitude for the fact that "our excellent parents had threshed out all the ignoble superstitions, and did not feel it to be their duty to fill our minds with the dry husks—leaving them *tabulæ rasæ* to receive whatever stamp our individual experience was to give them, so that we had not the bore of wasting our energy in raking over and sweeping out the rubbish." HJ, remembering that their father's "most living" word was "spiritual," was sometimes less certain about the beneficial results of their early environing. Writing to WJ's wife in 1900 about the education of her daughter, he warned against "the preoccupation (too strong, at least) of the moral and spiritual in her training and formation. *We* (father's children) were sacrificed to that too exclusive preoccupation: and you see in William and me, above all in Bob, the *funesti* consequences! Take heed in time. With her so definite Puritan heritage Peggy could afford to be raised on almost solely *cultivated* 'social' and æsthetic lines. The Devil (of the moral and spiritual) can—given her 'atmosphere'—be trusted to look out for himself."

Henry Senior would have winced at that running together of "moral" and "spiritual," those terms that he kept in paradoxical opposition. But the question naturally rises, as we watch the unfolding record of his children's extraordinary education, of how much danger was latent in an atmosphere of such excessive mental and emotional stimulation. All the children seem to have inherited some of their father's high-strung temperament, but none of them possessed anything like his robustness. Both WJ and HJ had to fight their way through years of grave nervous ill-health before reaching any kind of mature stability; and in WJ's case a spiritual crisis, very similar to the one his father had undergone, led him almost to suicide. The broken careers of Wilky and Bob may have been owing most to the prolonged strain of having had to fight through the Civil War. But Alice, whose nervous control was shattered before she was twenty and who could give expression at last to her brilliance only in a private journal when she was dying in a sanatorium, is a witness to the high tensions that being a James could involve. Yet they felt themselves bound together by an enfolding affection, which may be best symbolized by the member of the family they talked about least and who talked very little for herself—the placid, self-effacing, devoted wife and mother.

The history of their education was preserved largely by HJ, in one of the least self-centered autobiographies on record. After WJ's death had left him the sole survivor of the group, he gave himself to the task of commemoration in filial and fraternal piety. His chief problem was that his "rag-bag of memory" had stored up "too much," and, indeed, the details of their earliest years often spin out endlessly on his discursive pages. He also added that WJ had "professed amazement, and even occasionally impatience, at my reach of reminiscence—liking as he did to brush away old moral scraps in favour of new rather than to hoard and so complacently exhibit them."

They disagreed just as flatly on the value of their schooling. WJ, according to his eldest son, seldom referred to it "with anything but contempt," or dismissed it by saying that he "never had any." He often regretted the lack of exact discipline, and felt that it had handicapped him in ever achieving methods of rigorous thought. HJ, however, agreed with their father that nothing was wasted so long as it stirred the mind to reflection; and looking backward to their New York boyhood over a span of almost seventy years, he valued each experiment with governess or tutor or small school in proportion as it had stimulated the free play of curiosity and consciousness.

The very "number and succession" of their schools excited his wonder: "We couldn't have changed oftener, it strikes me as I look back, if our presence had been inveterately objected to, and yet I enjoy an inward certainty that, my brother being vividly bright and I quite blankly innocuous, this reproach was never brought home." What invariably happened was that their father, having foreseen a promised ideal only to have it blotted out by a disappointing actual, then resolved to try again. In HJ's record the schools themselves serve as the barest theme to set off his subjective variations. "It is beyond measure odd, doubtless," he reflected, "that my main association with my 'studies,' whether of the infant or the adolescent order, should be with almost anything but the fact of learning—of learning, I mean what I was supposed to learn." In evoking those days he was far more concerned with his memories of old New York. He recalled the "entrancing interest" of having been so often "an hotel child." Some critics have found a symbolic rightness in the fact that William James, the philosopher of the open universe, should have been born in the Astor House. It is equally appropriate that the novelist whose scenes are so often projected at a distance, across the wide reach of a magnificent salon or at the end of a long vista, should have formed early the habit of "dawdling and gaping" before any spectacle presented to him.

The characteristic faces of most of our mid-century American writers still showed the "ineradicable rusticity" that observers always noted in Hawthorne. But the young Jameses were almost exclusively "town-bred." This was again owing partly to their father's accident, since with his wooden leg he could not circulate easily except over smooth pavements. But his fondness for being near people would probably have drawn him to the city anyhow. So, during the very years when Walt Whitman was absorbing the sights and sounds of the streets in preparation for his affirmation—unusual for a romantic poet—of the city's beauty, young Henry James was strolling through those same streets, an incipient cosmopolite. "I first 'realised' Fourteenth Street," he remarked, "at a very tender age." He also "realised" the contrasting "quieter harmonies" of Washington Square, near which he had been born. But his impressions did not all bear the sophistication of his later vocabulary. He remembered his delight in ice cream as a sovereign remedy for a sore mouth after the dentist's, his excited visits to Barnum's

Great American Museum, and his first considered judgment that "the highest pleasure of sense" lay in "sticky waffles"—though he also had to call them, with the circumloquacious flourish that amused him in his last manner, "the oblong farinaceous compound, faintly yet richly brown, stamped and smoking, not crisp nor brittle, but softly absorbent of the syrup dabbed upon it for a finish."

The dramatic organization of his memoirs depended on a sustained contrast between WJ and himself, a contrast that he developed in many ways. He said at the outset that one of his earliest images was "that of my brother's occupying a place in the world to which I couldn't at all aspire . . . wherever it might be that there was a question of my arriving, when arriving at all, belatedly and ruefully; as if he had gained such an advance of me in his sixteen months' experience of the world before mine began that I never for all the time of childhood and youth in the least caught up with him or overtook him. He was always round the corner and out of sight, coming back into view but at his hours of extremest ease. We were never in the same schoolroom, in the same game, scarce even in step together or in the same phase at the same time; when our phases overlapped, that is, it was only for a moment—he was clean out before I had got well in. How far he had really at any moment dashed forward it is not for me now to attempt to say; what comes to me is that I at least hung inveterately and woefully back, and that this relation alike to our interests and to each other seemed proper and preappointed. I lose myself in wonder at the loose ways, the strange process of waste, through which nature and fortune may deal on occasion with those whose faculty for application is all and only in their imagination and their sensibility."

Their temperaments were extraordinarily different, the one active and participating, the other passive and observing. WJ described himself as "a 'motor,' and morally ill-adapted to the game of patience"; whereas HJ spoke of "the vivid image and the very scene" as constituting "the only terms in which life has treated me to experience." HJ was continually lost in admiration at his brother's energy and inventiveness. WJ was the hero of all their dramas, the organizing force of all their games, their "constant comic star." But in reading HJ's account one must always remember that this is a storyteller's story, and that, in a sense, both his "William" and his "Henry" are fictional creations. In playing off the hero against a willing dolt, he often attributed to himself a stupidity that went far beyond "the dreadful blight of arithmetic," and that must have been largely nonexistent. His "William," on the other hand, though possessing the immense personal charm to which all other records agree, has a kind of unswerving sureness that does not square with WJ's own account of his inner instability. Yet the most remarkable feature of HJ's lifelong admiration is that it deviated neither into envy nor into a sense of inferiority. He might speak of "my comparatively so indirect quality for what is called taking life," but whenever he contrasted their temperaments seriously, he was staunch in asserting the values inherent in his own: "One way of taking life was to go in for everything and everyone, which kept you abundantly occupied, and the other way was to be as occupied, quite as occupied, just with the sense and the image of it all, and on only a fifth of the actual immersion: a circumstance extremely strange."

The "most characteristic" image that HJ retained of WJ's boyhood was that of his "drawing, always drawing, especially under the lamplight of the Fourteenth Street back parlour; and not as with a plodding patience, which I think would less have affected me, but easily, freely and, as who should say, infallibly: always at the stage of finishing off, his head dropped from side to side and his tongue rubbing his lower lip." The contagious effect of that example upon HJ, and how he turned it to his own purposes, is recounted in a passage which bears out that each brother kept his own balance and pursued his own ends. This passage also gives the earliest glimpse of HJ's essential education, of how, stimulated by their visits to the Broadway Theater as well as by WJ's pictures, he began to seek his own combination of dramatic and pictorial form.

"I try at least to recover here, however, some closer notation of WJ's aspects—yet only with the odd effect of my either quite losing him or but apprehending him again at seated play with his pencil under the lamp. When I see him he is intently, though summarily, rapidly drawing, his head critically balanced and his eyebrows working, and when I don't see him it is because I have resignedly relinquished him. I can't have been often for him a deprecated, still less an actively rebuffed suitor, because, as I say again, such aggressions were so little in order for me; but I remember that on my once offering him my company in conditions, those of some planned excursion, in which it wasn't desired, his putting the question of our difference at rest, with the minimum of explanation, by the responsible remark: 'I play with boys who curse and swear!' I had sadly to recognize that I didn't, that I couldn't pretend to have come to that yet—and truly, as I look back, either the unadvisedness and inexpertness of my young contemporaries on all that ground must have been complete (an interesting note on our general manners after all,) or my personal failure to grasp must have been. Besides which I wonder scarce less now than I wondered then in just what company my brother's privilege was exercised; though if he had but richly wished to be discouraging he quite succeeded. It wasn't that I mightn't have been drawn to the boys in question, but that I simply wasn't qualified. All boys, I rather found, were difficult to play with—unless it was that they rather found *me;* but who would have been so difficult as these? They account but little, moreover, I make out, for WJ's eclipses; so that I take refuge easily enough in the memory of my own pursuits, absorbing enough at times to have excluded other views. I also plied the pencil, or to be more exact the pen—even if neither implement critically, rapidly or summarily. I was so often engaged at that period, it strikes me, in literary—or, to be more precise in dramatic, accompanied by pictorial composition—that I must again and again have delightfully lost myself. I had not on any occasion personally succeeded, amid our theatric strife, in reaching the footlights; but how could I have doubted, nevertheless, with our large theatrical experience, of the nature, and of my understanding, of the dramatic form? I sacrificed to it with devotion—by the aid of certain quarto sheets of ruled paper bought in Sixth Avenue for the purpose (my father's store, though I held him a great fancier of the article in general, supplied but the unruled;) grateful in particular for the happy provision by which each fourth page of the folded sheet was left blank. When the drama itself had covered three pages the last one, over which I most laboured, served for the illustration of what I had verbally presented. Every scene had thus its explanatory picture, and as each act—though I am not positively certain I arrived at acts—would have had its vivid climax. Addicted in that degree to fictive evocation, I yet recall, on my part, no practice whatever of narrative prose or any sort of verse. I cherished the 'scene' . . . I thought, I lisped, at any rate I composed, in scenes; though how much, or how far, the scenes 'came' is another affair. Entrances, exits, the indication of 'business,' the animation of dialogue, the multiplication of designated characters, were things delightful in themselves—while I panted toward the canvas on which I should fling my figures; which it took me longer to fill than it had taken me to write what went with it, but which had on the other hand something of the interest of the dramatist's casting of his *personæ,* and must have helped me to believe in the validity of my subject.

"From where on these occasions that subject can have dropped for me I am at a loss to say, and indeed have a strong impression that I didn't at any moment quite know what I was writing about: I am sure I couldn't otherwise have written so much. . . . The odd part of all of which was that whereas my cultivation of the picture was maintained my practice of the play, my addiction to scenes, presently quite dropped. I was capable of learning, though with inordinate slowness, to express ideas in scenes, and was not capable, with whatever patience, of making proper pictures; yet I aspired to this form of design to the prejudice of any other, and long after those primitive hours was still wasting time in attempts at it. I cared so much for nothing else, and that vaguely redressed, as to a point, my general failure of acuteness. I nursed the conviction, or at least I tried to, that if my clutch of the

pencil or of the watercolour brush should once become intense enough
it would make up for other weaknesses of grasp—much as that would
certainly give it to do. This was a very false scent, which had however
the excuse that my brother's example really couldn't but act upon me
—the scent was apparently so true for *him;* from the moment my small
'interest in art,' that is my bent for gaping at illustrations and exhibitions, was absorbing and genuine. There were elements in the case that
made it natural: the picture, the representative design, directly and
strongly appealed to me, and was to appeal all my days, and I was only
slow to recognise the *kind*, in this order, that appealed most. My face
was turned from the first to the idea of representation—that of the
gain of charm, interest, mystery, dignity, distinction, gain of importance in fine, on the part of the represented thing (over the thing of
accident, of mere actuality, still unappropriated;) but in the house of
representation there were many chambers, each with its own lock, and
long was to be the business of sorting and trying the keys. When I at
last found deep in my pocket the one I could more or less work, it was
to feel, with reassurance, that the picture was still after all in essence
one's aim."

The arts of the stage and of the palette were to remain the chief
stimuli to HJ's mature work; and the process recorded here of thinking
in scenes and working through them to an inclusive symbol would still
describe his process in *The Wings of the Dove* and *The Golden Bowl*.
Equally characteristic of his maturity was his preference for the represented thing, the thing reduced to its essence by form, over the loose
and accidental raw material.

Again and again during his account of their schooling, HJ pulls himself up with a reflection on the odd quality of their situation, which
"could suffer such elements as those I have glanced at to take so considerably the place of education as more usually and conventionally
understood, and by that understanding more earnestly mapped out; a
deficiency, in the whole thing, that I fail at all consistently to deplore,
however—struck as I am with the rare fashion after which, in any small
victim of life, the inward perversity may work." He then proceeds to
elaborate his own variant of the doctrine of the conversion of waste,
and makes his most sustained justification of their unconventional rear-
ing. He also shows how thoroughly, despite appearances, their father
had directed their attention away from their own privileged group to
wider social implications.

"As I reconsider both my own and my brother's early start—even
his too, made under stronger propulsions—it is quite for me as if the
authors of our being and guardians of our youth had virtually said to
us but one thing, directed our course but by one word, though constantly repeated: Convert, convert, convert! With which I have not

even the sense of any needed appeal in us for further apprehension of the particular precious metal our chemistry was to have in view. I taste again in that pure air no ghost of a hint, for instance, that the precious metal was the refined gold of 'success'—a reward of effort for which I remember to have heard at home no good word, nor any sort of word, ever faintly breathed. It was a case of the presumption that we should hear words enough abundantly elsewhere; so that any dignity the idea might claim was in the first place not worth insisting on, and in the second might well be overstated. We were to convert and convert, success—in the sense that was in the general air—or no success; and simply everything that should happen to us, every contact, every impression and every experience we should know, were to form our soluble stuff; with only ourselves to thank should we remain unaware, by the time our perceptions were decently developed, of the substance finally projected and most desirable. That substance might be just consummately Virtue, as a social grace and value—and as a matter furthermore on which pretexts for ambiguity of view and of measure were as little as possible called upon to flourish. This last luxury therefore quite failed us, and we understood no whit the less what was suggested and expected because of the highly liberal way in which the pill, if I may call it so, was gilded: it had been made up—to emphasize my image—in so bright an air of humanity and gaiety, of charity and humour. What I speak of is the medium itself, of course, that we were most immediately steeped in—I am glancing now at no particular turn of our young attitude in it, and I can scarce sufficiently express how little it could have conduced to the formation of prigs. Our father's prime horror was of *them*—he only cared for virtue that was more or less ashamed of itself; and nothing could have been of a happier whimsicality than the mixture in him, and in all his walk and conversation, of the strongest instinct for the human and the liveliest reaction from the literal. . . . The presence of paradox was so bright among us—though fluttering ever with as light a wing and as short a flight as need have been—that we fairly grew used to allow, from an early time, for the so many and odd declarations we heard launched, to the extent of happily 'discounting' them; the moral of all of which was that we need never fear not to be good enough if we were only social enough: a splendid meaning indeed being attached to the latter term.

"Thus we had ever the amusement, since I can really call it nothing less, of hearing morality, or moralism, as it was more invidiously worded, made hay of in the very interest of character and conduct; these things suffering much, it seemed, by their association with the conscience—that is the *conscious* conscience—the very home of the literal, the haunt of so many pedantries. Pedantries, on all this ground, were anathema; and if our dear parent had at all minded his not being consistent, and had entertained about us generally less passionate an optimism (not an easy but an arduous state in him moreover,) he might have found it difficult to apply to the promotion of our studies so free a suspicion of the inhumanity of Method. Method certainly never raged among us; but it was our fortune nevertheless that everything had its turn, and that such indifferences were no more pedantic than certain rigours might perhaps have been; of all of which odd notes of our situation there would, and possibly will, be more to say—my present aim is really but to testify to what most comes up for me to-day in the queer educative air I have been trying to breathe again. That definite reflection is that if we had not had in us to some degree the root of the matter no method, however confessedly or aggressively 'pedantic,' would much have availed for us; and that since we apparently did have it, deep down and inert in our small patches of virgin soil, the fashion after which it struggled forth was an experience as intense as any other and a record of as great a dignity. It may be asked me, I recognise, of the root of 'what' matter I so complacently speak, and if I say 'Why, of the matter of our having with considerable intensity *proved* educable, or, if you like better, teachable, that is accessible to experience,' it may again be retorted: 'That won't do for a decent account of a young consciousness; for think of all the things that the failure of method, of which you make so light, didn't put into yours; think of the splendid economy of a real—or at least of a planned and attempted education, a 'regular course of instruction'—and then think of the waste involved in the so inferior substitute of which the pair of you were evidently victims.' An admonition this on which I brood, less, however, than on the still other sense, rising from the whole retrospect, of my now feeling sure, of my having mastered the particular history of just that waste—to the point of its actually affecting me as blooming with interest, to the point even of its making me ask myself how in the world, if the question is of the injection of more things into the consciousness (as would seem the case,) mine could have 'done' with more: thanks to its small trick, perhaps vicious I admit, of having felt itself from an early time almost uncomfortably stuffed."

Their father's objection to self-conscious virtue became a family joke. As HJ said, they were bred in horror of what their father was fond of calling " 'flagrant' morality." Alice remembered an anecdote of Wilky's: "Mr. George Bradford had opened a school in Newport, and one day Mr. Emerson was asking him about it in the presence of Wilky, who was paying a visit at the Emersons' in Concord. 'And what sort of a girl is Alice?' asked Mr. E. 'She has a highly moral nature,' replied Mr. B. Whereupon in great amusement, Mr. E. exclaimed: 'How in the world does her father get on with her?' "

If the key to education lay in the conversion of waste, everything

obviously depended on how much you brought to your own experience. "No education avails for the intelligence that doesn't stir in it
some subjective passion," was how HJ formulated it, whereas "almost
anything that does so act is largely educative, however small a figure
the process might make in a scheme of training." Here WJ would have
been in agreement, since one of the strongest tenets of his philosophy
was that every man must build his own world. But he might well have
failed to perceive any signs of building in the experience that gave rise
to HJ's formulation. For HJ had been reflecting on the rare freedom to
which they had all been privileged: even in his earliest memories he was
enjoying the streets by himself.

"I see myself moreover as somehow always alone in these and like New
York *flâneries* and contemplations, and feel how the sense of my being
so, being at any rate master of my short steps, such as they were,
through all the beguiling streets, was probably the very savour of each
of my chance feasts. Which stirs in me at the same time some wonder
at the liberty of range and opportunity of adventure allowed to my
tender age; though the puzzle may very well drop, after all, as I ruefully reflect that I couldn't have been judged at home reckless or adventurous. What I look back to as my infant license can only have
had for its ground some timely conviction on the part of my elders that
the only form of riot or revel ever known to me would be that of the
visiting mind. Wasn't I myself for that matter even at that time all
acutely and yet resignedly, even quite fatalistically, aware of what to
think of this? I at any rate watch the small boy dawdle and gape again,
I smell the cold dusty paint and iron as the rails of the Eighteenth Street
corner rub his contemplative nose, and, feeling him foredoomed, withhold from him no grain of my sympathy. He is a convenient little
image or warning of all that was to be for him, and he might well have
been even happier than he was. For there was the very pattern and
measure of all he was to demand: just to *be* somewhere—almost anywhere would do—and somehow receive an impression or an accession,
feel a relation or a vibration. He was to go without many things, ever so
many—as all persons do in whom contemplation takes so much the
place of action; but everywhere, in the years that came soon after, and
that in fact continued long, in the streets of great towns, in New York
still for some time, and then for a while in London, in Paris, in Geneva,
wherever it might be, he was to enjoy more than anything the so far
from showy practice of wondering and dawdling and gaping: he was
really, I think, much to profit by it. What it at all appreciably gave him
—that is gave him in producible form—would be difficult to state; but
it seems to him, as he even now thus indulges himself, an education like
another."

Little HJ as a *flâneur* of boulevards is himself a beguiling spectacle, but the essence of an educational experience for a James was something more concentrated. In HJ's case it was almost inevitably bound up with the response to a work of art. He gives no systematic account of their early reading, and what has generally been held against their upbringing are the implications of his casual remark that "all our books in that age were English"—that age, the early 1850's, being the very height of the American renaissance. But HJ's remark was obviously an overstatement, caused in part by his taking for granted his father's friendships with Emerson and George Ripley, with Washington Irving, and with several other New York writers and painters. HJ also mentions his own immediate absorption in *The Scarlet Letter* and *The House of the Seven Gables*, and how they were all "forever mounting on little platforms at our infant schools to 'speak' The Raven and Lenore and the verses in which we phrased the heroine as Annabel*lee*—falling thus into the trap the poet had so recklessly laid for us." He also reports how he "succumbed to the spell of Godey," and how *Uncle Tom's Cabin* had been, even before Hawthorne, his "first experiment in grown-up fiction."

He dated his discovery of the "free play of mind" from the family's attendance at a performance of the stage version of Mrs. Stowe's novel. Having relished the novel, they knew that its reproduction could not fail to be inferior:

"The point exactly was that we attended this spectacle just in order *not* to be beguiled, just in order to enjoy with ironic detachment and, at the very most, to be amused ourselves at our sensibility should it prove to have been trapped and caught. To have become thus aware of our collective attitude constituted for one small spectator at least a great initiation; he got his first glimpse of that possibility of a 'free play of mind' over a subject which was to throw him with force at a later stage of culture, when subjects had considerably multiplied, into the critical arms of Matthew Arnold. So he is himself at least interested in seeing the matter—as a progress in which the first step was taken, before that crude scenic appeal, by his wondering, among his companions, where the absurd, the absurd for *them*, ended and the fun, the real fun, which was the gravity, the tragedy, the drollery, the beauty, the thing itself, briefly, might be legitimately and tastefully held to begin. Uncanny though the remark perhaps, I am not sure I wasn't thus more interested in the pulse of our party, under my tiny recording thumb, than in the beat of the drama and the shock of its opposed forces— vivid and touching as the contrast was then found for instance between the tragi-comical Topsy, the slave-girl clad in a pinafore of sackcloth and destined to become for Anglo-Saxon millions the type of the absolute in the artless, and her little mistress the blonde Eva, a figure rather in the . . . tradition of pantalettes and pigtails, whom I recall as perch-

ing quite suicidally, with her elbows out and a preliminary shriek, on
that bulwark of the Mississippi steamboat which was to facilitate her
all but fatal immersion in the flood. Why should I have duly noted
that no little game on her part could well less have resembled or simu-
lated an accident, and yet have been no less moved by her reappear-
ance, rescued from the river but perfectly dry, in the arms of faithful
Tom, who had plunged in to save her, without either so much as wet-
ting his shoes, than if I had been engaged with her in a reckless romp?
I could count the white stitches in the loose patchwork, and yet could
take it for a story rich and harmonious; I could know we had all intellectually condescended and that we had yet had the thrill of an æsthetic
adventure; and this was a brave beginning for a consciousness that was
to be nothing if not mixed and a curiosity that was to be nothing if not
restless."

Some aspects of their freedom were very bewildering. Their father
sent them to church in much the same spirit that he sent them to the
theater. They were to go to all churches in turn, to appreciate and
judge for themselves. When HJ came to assess his father's character
and personality,[1] he wished that they might have been taught a more
coherent form of worship, that they "might have been either much less
religious or much more so."

"Our young liberty in respect to church-going was absolute and we
might range at will, through the great city, from one place of worship
and one form of faith to another, or might on occasion ignore them all
equally, which was what we mainly did. . . . Going forth hand in
hand into the sunshine (and I connect myself here with my next
younger, not with my elder, brother, whose orbit was other and larger)
we sampled, in modern phrase, as small unprejudiced inquirers obeying
their inspiration, any resort of any congregation detected by us; doing
so, I make out moreover, with a sense of earnest provision for any contemporary challenge. 'What church do you go to?'—the challenge took
in childish circles that searching form; of the form it took among our
elders my impression is more vague. To which I must add as well that
our 'fending' in this fashion for ourselves didn't so prepare us for invidious remark—remark I mean upon our pewless state, which involved,
to my imagination, much the same discredit that a houseless or a cook-
less would have done—as to hush in my breast the appeal to our parents,
not for religious instruction (of which we had plenty, and of the most
charming and familiar) [2] but simply for instruction (a very different

---

[1] Pp. 191–205 below.
[2] A fascinating example of the kind
of religious instruction that was carried
on in the James household is provided
by a passage in Henry Senior's "Letter
on Incarnation" (1874). To drive home

his conception of "spiritual truth" and
to contrast it with "Pantheism," he told
the following incident, which might
well have taken place years before between him and one of his sons:
"Of course whenever we truly con-

thing) as to where we should say we 'went,' in our world, under cold scrutiny or derisive comment. It was colder than any criticism, I recall, to hear our father reply that we could plead nothing less than the whole privilege of Christendom and that there was no communion, even that of the Catholics, even that of the Jews, even that of the Swedenborgians, from which we need find ourselves excluded. With the freedom we enjoyed our dilemma clearly amused him: it would have been impossible, he affirmed, to be theologically more *en règle*. How as mere detached unaccompanied infants we enjoyed such impunity of range and confidence of welcome is beyond comprehension save by the light of the old manners and conditions, the old local bonhomie, the comparatively primal innocence, the absence of complications; with the several notes of which last beatitude my reminiscence surely shines. It was the theory of the time and place that the young, were they but young enough, could take publicly no harm; to which

---

ceive of God, we think of Him not as a material but as a spiritual being; as a being of pure—which is infinite or creative—love. I remember a little boy once saying to his father at dinner-table: 'Father, you say that God is pure spirit or life, and consequently that he alone is or lives in all existence. Now I want to know if He is in this chicken on my plate?' Yes, the father replied, beyond all doubt He is there, as the specific use or power of that flesh to nourish you. 'Very well then,' said the little sceptic, hastening to cram his mouth with chicken, 'If God is in this chicken which I am eating, then I am now eating God.' Oh no, again replied the father, I did not say that God was materially in the chicken as its very flesh, for then He, like the flesh itself, would be dead, but only spiritually, i.e., as the living use or power of the flesh, so long as it exists, to nourish your body, and so empower it to serve your mind, and hence empower your mind to serve your heart, and so bring you at last into a loving or living recognition of God. Of course God *is* not the chicken, for the chicken has no existence but to a finite or sensible intelligence, but only as the creative life or force or use of the chicken to animate your body, and you don't begin to realize this creative life or force or use of the chicken until the chicken itself has been utterly consumed and done away with in your ravenous little maw. "The brave little man was silenced

but not satisfied. So after dinner he brought his cap into the library, and said to his father: 'God is in this cap, I suppose?' Not a doubt of it, the father replied, he is there not materially or as the stuff out of which the cap is made, but only spiritually or as the use of the cap to protect and adorn your foolish little head. 'So you say,' rejoined the child, and then laying the cap upon the floor and deliberately plumping his little rotundity down upon it, 'but now tell me, if you can, that I am not sitting upon God.' Why, you little goosy-gander, returned the father, do but recall what I said to you just now, namely, that God was not in the cap as its dead material but only as its living use to cover your head and protect it from the summer's heat and the winter's cold. Don't you see then that in order to your truly sitting upon God, as you say, you would have to sit not upon the cap itself but only upon its spiritual use; and as that use is active only when the cap is on your head, do you not see that you could never accomplish the first step towards sitting upon it, save by sitting upon your own head? You are now not even *using* the cap, for in that case you would have it on your head where alone it belongs as a use. You are grossly *ab*-using it by transferring it from your head to the opposite extreme of your person; and no wonder therefore you seek to degrade instead of honouring the Divine Goodness of which it is full."

adds itself moreover, and touchingly enough, all the difference of the old importances. It wasn't doubtless that the social, or call it simply the human, position of the child was higher than to-day—a circumstance not conceivable; it was simply that other dignities and values and claims, other social and human positions, were less definite and settled, less prescriptive and absolute. A rich sophistication is after all a gradual growth, and it would have been sophisticated to fear for us, before such bright and vacant vistas, the perils of the way or to see us received anywhere even with the irony of patronage. We hadn't in fact seats of honour, but that justice was done us—that is that we were placed to our advantage—I infer from my having liked so to 'go,' even though my grounds may have been but the love of the *exhibition* in general, thanks to which figures, faces, furniture, sounds, smells and colours became for me, wherever enjoyed, and enjoyed most where most collected, a positive little orgy of the senses and riot of the mind. Let me at the same time make the point that—such may be the snobbery of extreme youth—I not only failed quite to rise to the parental reasoning, but made out in it rather a certain sophistry; such a prevarication for instance as if we had habitually said we kept the carriage we observably didn't keep, kept it because we sent when we wanted one to University Place, where Mr. Hathorn had his livery-stable."

The æsthetic response to life which these early impressions induced was by no means limited to HJ. Alice might sometimes incline to WJ's view of the worthlessness of their schooling: "I wonder whether if I had had an education I should have been more or less of a fool than I am?" But she quickly added: "It would have deprived me surely of those exquisite moments of mental flatulence which every now and then inflate the cerebral vacuum with a delicious sense of latent possibilities, of stretching one's self to cosmic limits; and who would ever give up the reality of dreams for relative knowledge?" She also recalled her first dawning sense of the immense extension that is added to life when you are not just immersed in it but also intellectually detached, when you are aware not only of the immediate moment, but also of your awareness of that awareness:

"I remember so distinctly the first time I was conscious of a purely intellectual process. 'Twas the summer of '56, which we spent in Boulogne; and the parents of Mlle. Marie Boningue, our governess, had a *campagne* on the outskirts, and invited us to spend the day, perhaps Marie's fête-day. A large and shabby *calèche* came for us, into which we were packed, save William. All I can remember of the drive was a never-ending ribbon of dust, stretching in front, and the anguish, greater even than usual, of Wilky's and Bob's heels grinding into my shins. . . . But to arrive at the first flowering of me intellect! We were turned into the garden to play—a sandy, or rather dusty expanse, with nothing in it, as I remember, but two or three scrubby apple trees from one of which hung a swing. As time went on, Wilky and Bob disappeared, not to my grief, and the Boningues. Harry was sitting in the swing and I came up and stood near by, as the sun began to slant over the desolate expanse, as the dreary hours (with that endlessness which they have for infancy) passed, when Harry suddenly exclaimed: 'This might certainly be called pleasure under difficulties!' The stir of my whole being in response to the exquisite, original form of his remark almost makes my heart beat now with the sisterly pride which was then awakened, and it came to me in a flash—the higher nature of this appeal to the mind, as compared to the rudimentary solicitations which usually produced my childish explosions of laughter, and I can also feel distinctly the sense of self-satisfaction in that I could not only perceive but appreciate this subtlety, as if I had acquired a new sense, a sense whereby to measure intellectual things, wit as distinguished from giggling, for example."

When we come to HJ's account of the drama of "Europe," we must be still more on our guard against his reading back into his boyhood the thirsts and responses of his later years. Nevertheless, almost any range of response was doubtless possible for a boy who had startled his parents, even before their removal from New York, by persuading them that he remembered Paris from the only time he had previously been there, before he was two. He had detailed to them how "as a baby in long clothes, seated opposite to them in a carriage and on the lap of another person, I had been impressed with the view, framed by the clear window of the vehicle as we passed, of a great stately square surrounded with high-roofed houses and having in its centre a tall and glorious column. I had naturally caused them to marvel, but I had also, under cross-questioning, forced them to compare notes, as it were, and reconstitute the miracle. They knew what my observation of monumental squares had been—and alas hadn't; neither New York nor Albany could have offered me the splendid perspective, and, for that matter, neither could London, which moreover I had known at a younger age still. Conveyed along the Rue St.-Honoré while I waggled my small feet, as I definitely remember doing, under my flowing robe, I had crossed the Rue de Castiglione and taken in, for all my time, the admirable aspect of the Place and the Colonne Vendôme."

After such a virtuoso flight of memory it is not hard to believe that even during the New York years HJ may have felt himself continually beckoned and lured by the romantic "otherness" of Europe. Once there, the sense of romance persisted, even in the face of WJ's scorn of the little it frequently had to feed upon. They were sharply divided in their reactions to their first winter in London. "Looking back at it from after days," HJ recalled, "WJ denounced it to me, and with it the following year and more spent in Paris, as a poor and arid and lamentable time, in which, missing such larger chances and connections as we might have reached out to, we had done nothing, he and I, but walk about together, in a state of the direst propriety, little 'high' black hats and inveterate gloves, the childish costume of the place and period, to stare at grey street-scenery (that of early Victorian London had tones of a neutrality!) dawdle at shop-windows and buy water-colours and brushes with which to bedaub eternal drawing-blocks. We might, I dare say, have felt higher impulses and carried out larger plans— though indeed present to me for this, on my brother's so expressing himself, is my then quick recognition of the deeper stirrings and braver needs he at least must have known, and my perfect if rueful sense of having myself had no such quarrel with our conditions: embalmed for me did they even to that shorter retrospect appear in a sort of fatalism of patience, spiritless in a manner, no doubt, yet with an inwardly ac- tive, productive and ingenious side."

He added that such a defence could have been offered "only by a person incorrigible in throwing himself back upon substitutes for lost causes." But the fact remained that he had felt himself steeped in a denser medium than he had known before, since the streets he was walking were those he had already read about in Thackeray and Dick- ens. "I dare say our perambulations . . . in our little 'top' hats and other neatnesses must have been what WJ meant by our poverty of life —whereas it was probably one of the very things most expressive to myself of the charm and colour of history and (from the point of view of the picturesque) of society."

He did not have to conjure up much out of little when it came to what he called the most "formative, fertilising . . . 'intellectual experi- ence' our youth was to know," the experience of "the great rooms of the Louvre." Their first entrance into the Galerie d'Apollon came to symbolize for him his first conscious crossing of "that bridge over to Style," whereupon he inhaled "a general *sense* of glory."

"The beginning in short was with Géricault and David, but it went on and on and slowly spread; so that one's stretched, one's even strained, perceptions, one's discoveries and extensions piece by piece, come back, on the great premises, almost as so many explorations of the house of life, so many circlings and hoverings round the image of the world. I have dim reminiscences of permitted independent visits, uncorrectedly juvenile though I might still be, during which the house of life and the palace of art became so mixed and interchangeable—the Louvre being, under a general description, the most peopled of all scenes not less than the most hushed of all temples—that an excursion to look at pictures would have but half expressed my afternoon. I had looked at pictures, looked and looked again, at the vast Veronese, at Murillo's moon-borne

Madonna, at Leonardo's almost unholy dame with the folded hands, treasures of the Salon Carré as that display was then composed; but I had also looked at France and looked at Europe, looked even at America as Europe itself might be conceived so to look, looked at history, as a still-felt past and a complacently personal future, at society, manners, types, characters, possibilities and prodigies and mysteries of fifty sorts; and all in the light of being splendidly 'on my own,' as I supposed it, though we hadn't then that perfection of slang, and of (in especial) going and coming along that interminable and incomparable Seine-side front of the Palace against which young sensibility felt itself almost rub, for endearment and consecration, as a cat invokes the friction of a protective piece of furniture. Such were at any rate some of the vague processes—I see for how utterly vague they must show—of picking up an education; and I was, in spite of the vagueness, so far from agreeing with my brother afterwards that we didn't pick one up and that that never *is* done, in any sense not negligible, and also that an education might, or should, in particular, have picked *us* up, and yet didn't—I was so far dissentient, I say, that I think I quite came to glorify such passages and see them as part of an order really fortunate. If we had been little asses, I seem to have reasoned, a higher intention driving us wouldn't have made us less so—to any point worth mentioning; and as we extracted such impressions, to put it at the worst, from redemptive accidents (to call Louvres and Luxembourgs nothing better) why we weren't little asses, but something wholly other: which appeared all I needed to contend for. Above all it would have been stupid and ignoble, an attested and lasting dishonour, not, with our chance, to have followed our straggling clues, as many as we could and disengaging as we happily did, I felt, the gold and the silver ones, whatever the others might have been—not to have followed them and not to have arrived by them, so far as we were to arrive."

In 1857 their father, in response to distant reverberations of the American panic of that year, felt the need to economize by subletting their Paris apartment and establishing the family for the winter as well as the summer at Boulogne-sur-Mer. There for the first time WJ had an opportunity for regular instruction at the local *collège*. A letter from their father to his mother gives his view of how the whole experiment had been working out:

"Willy is very devoted to scientific pursuits, and I hope will turn out a most respectable scholar. He has been attending the Collège Impérial here all summer, and one of his professors told me the other day 'that he was an admirable student, and that all the advantages of a first-rate scientific education which Paris affords ought to be accorded him.' He is, however, much dearer to my heart for his moral worth than for his intellectual. I never knew a child of so much principle, and at the same time of a perfectly generous and conciliatory demeanour towards his younger brothers, always disposed to help them and never to oppress. Harry is not so fond of study, properly so-called, as of reading. He is a devourer of libraries, and an immense writer of novels and dramas. He has considerable talent as a writer, but I am at a loss to know whether he will ever accomplish much."

The father's perception of HJ's incipient talent may have been contributed to further by his boyish translation of some of LaFontaine's fables with a certain "felicity of idiom." WJ's scientific bent must have appeared even more positive when his father's gift of a microscope at Christmas in that year produced in him the most intense excitement he had ever shown over any present. But their father never wanted to drive any of his sons down a straight path. On the contrary, in a fashion that came to constitute another family joke, he dreaded their choice of any fixed career, on the grounds that it might narrow them prematurely and prevent other enlarging alternatives. So instead of following the natural lead to Paris for WJ to study science, the family returned to America for a year, for no clear reason that has ever been advanced. They settled in Newport, where their father's friend, the painter William Morris Hunt had his studio; and the boys experienced their first taste of New England, but, as HJ was to observe, of "a New England already comparatively subdued and sophisticated, a Samson shorn of his strength by the shears of the Southern, and more particularly of the New York, Delilah." However, he skipped over this year between the two volumes of his memoirs, and the one clear glimpse of it survives in a passage by their lifelong friend Thomas Sergeant Perry:

"The first time I saw the James boys was at the end of June or early in July 1858, shortly after their arrival in Newport for a year's stay. . . . I have often thought that the three brothers shewed that evening some of their characteristic qualities. I remember walking with Wilky hanging on my arm, talking to me as if he had found an old friend after long absence. When we got to the house and the rest of us were chattering, HJ sat on the window-seat reading Leslie's Life of Constable with a certain air of remoteness. William was full of merriment and we were soon playing a simple and childish game. In 'A Small Boy and Others' HJ speaks of Wilky's 'successful sociability, his instinct for intercourse, his genius for making friends,' and these amiable traits shewed themselves that evening as clearly as his other brother's jollity. Very soon afterwards HJ with his two younger brothers entered the school where I was studying, that of the Rev. W. C. Leverett. . . . I recall HJ as an uninterested scholar. Part of one day in a week was devoted to declaiming eloquent pieces from 'Sargent's Speaker,' and I have not forgotten his amusement at seeing in the Manual of English Literature that we were studying, in the half page devoted to Mrs.

Browning, that she had married R. Browning, 'himself no mean poet.' This compact information gave him great delight, for we were reading Browning. It was then too that he read for the first time 'The Vicar of Wakefield' and with great pleasure.

"It was at that time that we began to take long walks together almost every afternoon along the Cliffs, over the beaches to the Paradise Rocks, to the Point, or inland, wherever it might be. A thousand scrappy recollections of the strolls still remain, fragments of talk, visions of the place. Thus it was near the Lily Pond that we long discussed Fourier's plan for regenerating the world. Harry had heard his father describe the great reformer's proposal to establish universal happiness, and like a good son he tried to carry the good news further. At another time he fell under the influence of Ruskin; he devoted himself to the conscientious copying of a leaf and very faithfully drew a little rock that jutted above the surface of the Lily Pond. These artistic gropings, and those in Hunt's studio where he copied casts, were not his main interest. His chief interest was literature. We read the English magazines and reviews and the Revue des Deux Mondes with rapture. We fished in various waters, and I well remember when WJ brought home a volume of Schopenhauer and showed us with delight the ugly mug of the philosopher and read us amusing specimens of his delightful pessimism. It was WJ too who told us about Renan one cool evening of February when the twilight lingers till after six. HJ in his books speaks without enthusiasm of his school studies, but he and I read together at Mr. Leverett's school a fair amount of Latin literature."

HJ was to begin his *Notes of a Son and Brother* on the theme of the "incorrigible vagueness of current in our educational drift," as betrayed by the fact that "though we had come abroad in 1855 with an eye to the then supposedly supreme benefits of Swiss schooling, our most resolute attempt to tap that supply, after twenty distractions, waited over to the autumn of the fourth year later on, when we in renewed good faith retraced our steps to Geneva." There followed the most eccentric episode of all. WJ was entered in the Academy, but HJ, to his bewilderment and consternation—"a lost lamb, almost audibly bleating"—was sent to an institution that prepared pupils for the Zurich Polytechnic School. He could give no better explanation for this sudden enforced contact with mathematics and physics than that his parents must have "simply said to themselves, in serious concern, that I read too many novels, or at least read them too attentively—*that* was the vice. . . . It had come to me by I know not what perversity that if I couldn't tackle the smallest problem in mechanics or face without dismay at the blackboard the simplest geometric challenge I ought somehow in decency to make myself over, oughtn't really to be so inferior to almost everyone else. . . . My attempt not . . . to remain abnormal wholly broke down, however, and when I at last withdrew from the scene it was not even as a conspicuous, it was only as an obscure, a deeply hushed failure. I joined William, after what had seemed to me an eternity of woe, at the Academy, where I followed, for too short a time but with a comparative recovery of confidence, such literary *cours* as I might."

As usual HJ delighted in his brother's powers of adjustment:

"Whatever he might happen to be doing made him so interesting about it, and indeed, with the quickest concomitance, about everything else, that what I probably most did, all the while, was but to pick up, and to the effect not a bit of starving but quite of filling myself, the crumbs of his feast and the echoes of his life. His life, all this Geneva period, had been more of a feast than mine, and I recall the sense of this that I had got on the occasion of my accompanying him, by his invitation, toward the end of our stay, to a students' celebration or carouse, which was held at such a distance from the town, at a village or small bourg, up in the Vaud back-country, that we had, after a considerable journey by boat and in heterogeneous and primitive conveyances, tightly packed, to spend two nights there. The Genevese section of the Société de Zoffingue, the great Swiss students' organisation for brotherhood and beer, as it might summarily be defined, of which my brother had become a member, was to meet there certain other sections, now vague to me, but predominantly from the German-speaking Cantons, and holding a Commerce, to toast their reunion in brimming bowls. It had been thought the impression might amuse, might even interest me—for it was not denied that there were directions, after all, in which I *could* perhaps take notice; and this was doubtless what after a fashion happened, though I felt out in the cold (and all the more that the cold at the moment happened to be cruel), as the only participant in view not crowned with the charming white cap of the society, becoming to most young heads, and still less girt with the parti-coloured ribbon or complementary scarf, which set off even the shabby—for shabbiness considerably figured. I participated vaguely but not too excludedly; I suffered from cold, from hunger and from scant sleeping-space; I found the Bernese and the Bâlois strange representatives of the joy of life, some of them the finest gothic grotesques—but the time none the less very long; all of which, however, was in the day's work if I might live, by the imagination, in William's so adaptive skin. To see that he was adaptive, was initiated, and to what a happy and fruitful effect, that, I recollect, was my measure of content; which was filled again to overflowing, as I have hinted, on my finding him so launched at the Academy after our stretch of virtual separation, and just fancying, with a freedom of fancy, even if with a great reserve of expression, how much he might be living and learning, enjoying and feeling, amid work that was the right work for him and comrades, consecrated comrades, that at the worst weren't the wrong. What was not indeed, I always asked myself, the right work for him, or the right thing of any kind, that he took up or looked at or played with?—failing, as I did more than ever at the time I speak of, of the least glimpse of his being below an occasion. Whatever he played with or worked at entered at once into his intelligence, his talk, his humour, as with the action of colouring-matter dropped into water or that of the turning-on of a light within a window. Occasions waited on him, had always done so, to my view; and there he was, that spring-time, on a level with them all: the effect of which recognition had much, had more than aught else, to say to the charming silver haze just then wrapped about everything of which I was conscious."

WJ's own brief recollection of this time was that he had reached Geneva "a miserable, home-bred, obscure little ignoramus," and that the following summer he had set out to repair one of his deficiencies by working hard on German at Bonn. Some of his earliest surviving letters, which date from this summer, often effervesce into a gay irony, as he reports to their parents in Paris on the doings of Harry and Wilky:

* * * * *

Bonn, Sunday August 12, 1860

My dearest Parents,—

. . . Your hearts, I know, would have been melted if you had had a view of us this morning. I went directly after breakfast for the boys, and though Harry had an "iron stomach ache," as he called it, we went together on that low wooded hill which Aunt Kate could see from her window, and walked until dinner time, Harry being part of the time in great pain. In one part we found a platform with a stone bench commanding a view of the whole valley. We were rather tired and so we sat down upon it, Harry and Wilky each with a *Once a Week*,[1] while I tried to draw the valley in my pocket book. We wondered what our beloved parents were doing at that moment (half-past eleven), and thought that you must all have been in the parlor, Alice, the widow, with her eyes fixed on her novel, eating some rich fruit which Father has just brought in for her from the Palais Royal; and lovely Mother and Aunt Kate in arm-chairs with their hands crossed in front of them, listening to Father, who is walking up and down speaking of the superiority of America to these countries, and how much better that we should go home—and we wished, oh! how we wished! we could have been with you to partake of the fruit and join in the conversation. However, there are only three weeks more,

---

[1] *Once a Week* was a London maga-   others, Charles Reade and George
zine that published stories by, among   Meredith.

and then we rush to your arms. With a heavy sigh we got up from the seat and went on, but in a way so fraternal, presenting such a sweet picture of brotherly unitedness and affection, that it would have done anyone good to have seen us. And so it is every day in our shorter walks and talks. . . .

Sunday, August 19

My dearest Father,—

. . . I wish you would, as you promise, set down as clearly as you can on paper what your idea of the nature of art is, because I do not probably understand it fully, and should like to have it presented in a form that I might think over at my leisure. . . . I wish you would do it as fully as you conveniently can, so that I may ruminate it. I will not say anything about it before I have got your next letter.

As for what your last letter did contain, what can I do but thank you for every word of it and assure you that every word went to the right spot! Having such a father with us, how can we be other than in some measure worthy of him, though not perhaps as eminently so as the distance leads his fond heart to imagine. In regard to our self-respect and purity, I hope and trust the day may never come when your wishes will be disappointed. I am sure that *I* should as deeply deplore any loss of them in myself as you possibly could for me, and I hope that with the other children the case is the same. I never value my parents (Father especially) so much as when I am away from them. At home I only see his faults and here he seems all perfection, and every night I wonder why I did not value them more when they were beside me. I beg darling old Mother's forgiveness for the cruel and dastardly way in which I snub her, and Aunt Kate's for the impatience and violence I have always shown towards her. If ever I get back I will be perfect sherry cobbler to both of them, and to the little Alice, too, for the harsh way in which I have treated her.

I have just got home from dining at the boys' house. . . . They certainly live on the fat of the land, though they do not seem as sensible of their advantages as they should be. . . . Harry studies pretty stoutly, but I do not think you need to be apprehensive about him. There has been no renewal of the stomach aches that I am aware of, and he looks fatter and fresher than when you left. He and Wilky [1] appear to get on very harmoniously together. They enliven themselves occasionally by very good-natured brotherly trials of strength in their bedroom, when study has made them dull and sleepy. In these sometimes one, sometimes the other is victor. We see each other every day. They often pay me a visit here in my room in the morning when I am

---

[1] Bob is not mentioned: somewhat too young to be on his own, he remained this summer at school in Geneva.

dressing, which is very pleasant, and I have more than once been in their room early enough to be present at Wilky's tumble out of bed and consequent awaking, and call upon the already-at-work Harry: "Why did not you stop me?" . . . We are going to put Harry through a slashing big walk daily. His old white Lordet clothes began to look so shockingly grimy that we have at last induced him to take them to be cleaned. He clung to them with such affection that it was no easy matter. I have got on very well this last week in German, am beginning to understand and to make myself tolerably understood in straight-forward matters. . . .

Thousand thanks to the cherry-lipped, apricot-nosed, double-chinned little Bal [1] for her strongly dashed-off letter, which inflamed the hearts of her lonely brothers with an intense longing to kiss and slap her celestial cheeks. . . . Mother, in her precious letter, speaks of having her photograph taken when we get there. I conjure her by all the affection she bears us and by the ties which bind her to the eldest son, not to have it done *before*. When we get there we will have a con-sultation about it. . . . Now bosom upon bosom full of love to all, from your affectionate Willy.

* * *

The opening of this second letter points to an important decision. He had learned, no less than HJ, to live by his eyes, and whether or not as a delayed response to his contact with Hunt at Newport, WJ now determined to be a painter. His father was startled, for despite his erratic aims to that end, he said that he "had always counted upon a scientific career for Willy." Moreover, he held a low view of the artistic career as practiced in existent society: "It is melancholy to see the crawling thing which society christens Art, and feeds into fawning sycophancy." Art was not, as it should be, "the gush of God's life into every form of spontaneous speech and act"; it had been reduced to the mere "trick of a good eye, or a good hand." WJ had to debate against such views, but he stuck to his decision.

Reflecting on this event, HJ was fascinated by the phenomenon of "the career of art" being deprecated not on the grounds of its uncon-ventionality, but because it was not unconventional enough. He saw this debate between their father and WJ as the leading illustration of their father's doctrine—a doctrine to be reflected by so many of the heroes of his own fiction—that the good life consisted in *being* and not in *doing*:

"My brother challenges him, with a beautiful deference, on the im-puted damage to what might be best in a man by the professional pur-suit of 'art'—which he appears to have set forth with characteristic

---

[1] One of WJ's many nicknames for Alice.

emphasis; and I take the example for probably one of the rarest in all the so copious annals of parental opposition to the æsthetic as distinguished from some other more respectable course. What was marked in our father's prime uneasiness in presence of any particular form of success we might, according to our lights as then glimmering, propose to invoke was that it bravely, or with such inward assurance, dispensed with any suggestion of an alternative. What we were to do instead was just to *be* something, something unconnected with specific doing, something free and uncommitted, something finer in short than being *that*, whatever it was, might consist of. The 'career of art' has again and again been deprecated and denounced, on the lips of anxiety or authority, as a departure from the career of business, of industry and respectability, the so-called regular life, but it was perhaps never elsewhere to know dissuasion on the very ground of its failing to uplift the spirit in the ways it most pretends to. I must in fairness add, however, that if the uneasiness I here refer to continued, and quite by exception as compared with the development of other like episodes, during the whole of my brother's fortunately but little prolonged studio season, it was really because more alternatives swarmed before our parent's eyes, in the cause, than he could bring himself to simplify it by naming. He apprehended ever so deeply and tenderly his eldest son's other genius—as to which he was to be so justified; though this indeed was not to alter the fact that when afterwards that subject went in, by a wondrous reaction, for the pursuit of science, first of chemistry and then of anatomy and physiology and medicine, with psychology and philosophy at last piling up the record, the rich *malaise* at every turn characteristically betrayed itself, each of these surrenders being, by the measure of them in the parental imagination, so comparatively narrowing. That was the nearest approach to any plea for some other application of the spirit—that they *were* narrowing. When I myself, later on, began to 'write' it was breathed upon me with the finest bewildering eloquence, with a power of suggestion in truth which I fairly now count it a gain to have felt play over me, that this too was narrowing."

The next remove bore again the unique imprint of Henry Senior. With all the studios of Europe to choose from, they returned to Newport so that WJ could study with Hunt. Perhaps a contributing factor was that their father, as HJ put it, "had gradually ceased to 'like' Europe." His isolation there was absolute, with no audience whatever for his writing. And even though the air of his native land, as HJ also noted, was "no brisk conductor at any time of his remarkable voice," still he preferred to live "rather in the thin wilderness than in the thick." For HJ, to whom the "thickness" of Europe was an ever increasing excitement, the necessity to leave was desolating.

For half a year WJ worked hard in Hunt's studio, while HJ hung around the edges, sketching shyly and, though without talent, feeling himself "at the threshold of a world." He learned far more to his purpose by coming to know John La Farge, who, then a beginning painter in his mid-twenties, had been through a Catholic college in Maryland and was able to open new vistas of Franco-American culture. He helped form some of HJ's lasting tastes by urging him to translate Mérimée's *La Vénus d'Ille*, and, most of all, by introducing him to the novels of Balzac. Then, suddenly, WJ abandoned painting as quickly as he had taken it up. When he had first decided to try this career, he had written to a school-friend in Geneva: "In a year or two I shall know definitely whether I am suited to it or not. If not, it will be easy to withdraw. There is nothing on earth more deplorable than a bad artist." He reached his conclusion with the rapidity that was to become one of his distinguishing characteristics. One reason for his decision may be suggested by a passage in his *Principles of Psychology* where he is discussing the Imagination: "I am myself a good draughtsman, and have a very lively interest in pictures, statues, architecture and decoration, and a keen sensibility to artistic effects. But I am an extremely poor visualizer. . . ." It was equally characteristic that, having once convinced himself that he was unsuited to painting, he never touched it again, even as a hobby.

With their return to America, their father began to cultivate the contacts with Concord and Boston that were to yield the chief associates of his last twenty years. He also launched his two younger sons upon another experiment by entering them in the school conducted by Frank Sanborn, who had only recently been arrested for refusing to testify concerning his aid to John Brown. Henry Senior described this school with his usual paradoxes:

"I buried two of my children yesterday—at Concord, Mass., and feel so heart-broken this morning that I shall need to adopt two more instantly to supply their place. . . . Mary and I trotted forth . . . bearing Wilky and Bob in our arms to surrender them to the famous Mr. Sanborn. The yellowest sunshine and an atmosphere of balm were all over the goodly land, while the maple, the oak and the dogwood showered such splendours upon the eye as made the Champs Elysées and the Bois appear parvenus and comical. Mrs. Clark is a graceless enough woman outwardly, but so tenderly feathered inwardly, so unaffectedly kind and motherly toward the urchins under her roof, that one was glad to leave them in that provident nest. She has three or four other school-boarders, one of them a daughter of John Brown—tall, erect, long-haired and freckled, as John Brown's daughter has a right to be. I kissed her (inwardly) between the eyes, and inwardly heard the martyred Johannes chuckle over the fat inheritance of love and tenderness he had after all bequeathed to his children in all good men's minds. An arch little Miss Plumley also lives there, with eyes full of laughter and a mouth like a bed of lilies bordered with roses. How it is going to be possible for my two boys to pursue their studies in the midst of that bewilderment I don't clearly see. I am only sure of one thing, which is that if I had had such educational advantages as that in my youth I should probably have been now far more nearly ripe for this world's business. We asked to see Miss Waterman, one of the teachers quartered in the house, in order to say to her how much we should thank her if she would occasionally put out any too lively spark she might see fall on the expectant tinder of my poor boys' bosoms; but Miss W. herself proved of so siliceous a quality on inspection—with round tender eyes, young, fair and womanly—that I saw in her only new danger and no promise of safety. My present conviction is that a general conflagration is inevitable, ending in the total combustion of all that I hold dear on that spot. Yet I can't but felicitate our native land that such magnificent experiments in education go on among us.

"Then we drove to Emerson's and waded up to our knees through a harvest of apples and pears, which, tired of their mere outward or carnal growth, had descended to the loving bosom of the lawn, there or elsewhere to grow inwardly meet for their heavenly rest in the veins of Ellen the saintly and others; until at last we found the cordial Pan himself in the midst of his household, breezy with hospitality and blowing exhilarating trumpets of welcome. Age has just the least in the world dimmed the lustre we once knew, but an unmistakable breath of the morning still encircles him, and the odour of primæval woods. Pitchpine is not more pagan than he continues to be, and acorns as little confess the gardener's skill. Still I insist that he is a voluntary Pan, that it is a condition of mere wilfulness and insurrection on his part, contingent upon a mercilessly sound digestion and an uncommon imaginative influx, and I have no doubt that even he, as the years ripen, will at last admit Nature to be tributary and not supreme. However this be, we consumed juicy pears to the diligent music of Pan's pipe, while Ellen and Edith softly gathered themselves upon two low stools in the chimney-corner, saying never a word nor looking a look, but apparently hemming their handkerchiefs; and good Mrs. Stearns, who sat by the window and seemed to be the village dress-maker, ever and anon glanced at us over her spectacles as if to say that never before has she seen this wondrous Pan so glistening with dewdrops. Then and upon the waves of that friendly music we were duly wafted to our educational Zion and carefully made over our good and promising and affectionate boys to the schoolmaster's keeping. Out into the field beside his house Sanborn incontinently took us to show how his girls

and boys perform together their worship of Hygeia. It was a glimpse
into that new world wherein dwelleth righteousness and which is full
surely fast coming upon our children and our children's children; and
I could hardly keep myself, as I saw my children's eyes drink in the
mingled work and play of the inspiring scene, from shouting out a
joyful Nunc Dimittis. The short of the story is that we left them and
rode home robbed of our plumage, feeling sore and ugly and only
hoping that they wouldn't die, any of these cold winter days, before
the parental breast could get there to warm them back to life or cheer
them on to a better."

Less than a year later the Civil War had broken out, and the adolescence of the boys was over. Their father had, in any event, about come
to the end of his educational experiments. Almost the only stubborn
stand that he took was against their becoming undergraduates at an
American college. HJ made out in him
"a great revulsion of spirit from that incurred experience in his own
history, a revulsion I think moreover quite independent of any particular or intrinsic attributes of the seat of learning involved in it.
Union College, Schenectady, New York, the scene of his personal
experiment and the natural resort, in his youth, of comparatively adja-
cent Albanians, might easily have offered at that time no very rare
opportunities—few were the American country colleges that then had
such to offer; but when, after years, the question arose for his sons
he saw it in I scarce know what light of associational or 'subjective'
dislike. He had the disadvantage—unless indeed it was much more we
who had it—of his having, after many changes and detachments, ceased
to believe in the Schenectady resource, or to revert to it sentimentally,
without his forming on the other hand, with his boys to place, any
fonder presumption or preference. There comes out to me, much be-
dimmed but recognisable, the image of a day of extreme youth on
which, during a stay with our grandmother at Albany, we achieved,
William and I, with some confused and heated railway effort, a pious
pilgrimage to the small scholastic city—pious by reason, I clearly remember, of a lively persuasion on my brother's part that to Union
College, at some indefinite future time, we should both most naturally
and delightedly repair. We invoked, I gather, among its scattered
shades, fairly vague to me now, the loyalty that our parent appeared
to have dropped by the way—even though our attitude about it can
scarce have been prematurely contentious; the whole vision is at any
rate to-day bathed and blurred for me in the air of some charmed and
beguiled dream, that of the flushed good faith of an hour of crude
castle-building. We were helped to build, on the spot, by an older
friend, much older, as I remember him, even than my brother, already
a member of the college and, as it seemed, greatly enjoying his life

and those 'society' badges and trinkets with which he reappears to me as bristling and twinkling quite to the extinction of his particular identity. This is lost, like everything else, in the mere golden haze of the little old-time autumn adventure. Wondrous to our sensibility may well have been the October glamour—if October it was, and if it was not it ought to have been!—of that big brave region of the great State over which the shade of Fenimore Cooper's Mohawks and Mohicans (if this be not a pleonasm) might still have been felt to hang.

"The castle we had built, however, crumbled—there were plenty of others awaiting erection; these too successively had their hour, but I needn't at this time stoop to pick up their pieces. I see moreover vividly enough how it might have been that, at this stage, our parents were left cold by the various appeal, in our interest, of Columbia, Harvard and Yale. Hard by, at Providence, in the Newport time, was also 'Brown'; but I recover no connection in which that mystic syllable swept our sky as a name to conjure with. Our largest licence somehow didn't stray toward Brown. It was to the same tune not conceivable that we should have been restored for educational purposes to the swollen city, the New York of our childhood, where we had then so tumbled in and out of school as to exhaust the measure, or as at least greatly to deflower the image, of our teachability on that ground. Yale, off our beat from every point of view, was as little to be thought of, and there was moreover in our father's imagination no grain of susceptibility to what might have been, on the general ground, 'socially expected.' Even Harvard, clearly—and it was perhaps a trifle odd— moved him in our interest as little as Schenectady could do; so that, for authority, the voice of social expectation would have had to sound with an art or an accent of which it had by no means up to that time learned roundabout us the trick. This indeed (it comes to saying) is something that, so far as our parents were concerned, it would never have learned. They were, from other preoccupations, unaware of any such pressure. . . . We were not at that time, when it came to such claims, in presence of persuasive, much less of impressive, social forms and precedents—at least those of us of the liberated mind and the really more curious culture were not."

There seems to have been no question of WJ's trying to be a soldier, since his eyes, with which he later had a great deal of trouble, and his general nervous tension would have prevented it. He entered directly upon professional work in the Lawrence Scientific School at Harvard. An injury to HJ's back at this time disqualified him also for the army, and he consented to still another bootless errand by attending the Harvard Law School. His docility seems in this case to have been bound up with a latent recognition that being on his own in Cambridge would give him the opportunity for trying further his skill in writing.

Wilky, who seems to have been the one staunch non-reader in the family, enlisted at seventeen, and served subsequently as adjutant with Colonel Robert Gould Shaw's Negro troops. "To me in my boyish fancy," he wrote afterwards, "to go to war seemed glorious indeed; to my parents it seemed a stern duty, a sacrifice worth any cost." The brilliant and moody Bob also joined the army before his eighteenth birthday, and was promoted to a captaincy for bravery in front of Charleston. The severe sunstroke that he underwent and the serious wound that Wilky suffered in the assault on Fort Wagner exacted heavy tolls for the rest of their lives.

A last glimpse of the family group at Newport, just before it was broken up by the war, is afforded by Edward Emerson's memory of a holiday visit:

" 'The adipose and affectionate Wilky,' as his father called him, would say something and be instantly corrected or disputed by the little cock-sparrow Bob . . . but good-naturedly defend his statement, and then, Henry (Junior) would emerge from his silence in defence of Wilky. Then Bob would be more impertinently insistent, and Mr. James would advance as Moderator, and William, the eldest, join in. The voice of the Moderator presently would be drowned by the combatants and he soon came down vigorously into the arena, and when, in the excited argument, the dinner knives might not be absent from eagerly gesticulating hands, dear Mrs. James, more conventional, but bright as well as motherly, would look at me, laughingly reassuring, saying, 'Don't be disturbed, Edward; they won't stab each other. This is usual when the boys come home.' And the quiet little sister ate her dinner, smiling, close to the combatants. Mr. James considered this debate, within bounds, excellent for the boys. In their speech, singularly mature and picturesque, as well as vehement, the Gaelic (Irish) element in their descent always showed. Even if they blundered, they saved themselves by wit."

If WJ had looked back to the ending of their adolescence, he would probably have asserted that his education had not yet begun. HJ commented on how grateful his brother later became "for his intimate experience of the laboratory and the clinic," and then added, meditating again on their father's doctrine: "I was as constantly to feel that the varieties of his application had been as little wasted for him as those of my vagueness had really been for me." The sensuous education which they had so thoroughly absorbed was, despite their father's suspicion of literary men, far more likely to have produced Henry's career than William's. The succession of boulevards and landscapes and galleries provided material more relevant to HJ's art than to WJ's philosophy. Yet WJ's thoughts, as Morris Cohen has noted, "ran in vivid pictures"; and one of his greatest assets as a psychologist was that he had mastered the artist's skill of grasping concretely the evanescent moment of experience.

At nineteen he felt that he had learned little of direct use to him except languages and the rudiments of mathematics. But the indirect results were lifelong. HJ spoke of how the family seemed afloat and "unconnected" upon their return to American surroundings; and their having been uprooted from any fixed environment bore as many consequences for the drift of WJ's thought as for that of HJ's fiction. That rootlessness has often been held against HJ by narrowly nationalistic critics, and it did involve considerable ignorance of some of the immediate factors in the American political and social scene. But in WJ's case, to an even more marked degree, it made for flexibility and resilience, qualities without which modern man can scarcely exist. Without being aware of it WJ was more cosmopolitan at nineteen than any previous American philosopher had ever been. His intimate knowledge of French and German allowed his mature work to be easily in touch with international sources. But he was to mature very slowly, another consequence of their father's delaying of all decisions, a cause also of anxiety and strain, though of ultimate abundant ripening.

How well HJ had learned their father's central lesson can be read in a single remark in the preface to his *Princess Casamassima*: "Experience, as I see it, is our apprehension and our measure of what happens to us as social creatures." WJ would have agreed, though he would have put more emphasis on the active will as an instrument in creating that experience.

A NOTE ON
THE FAMILY TONGUE

Since both WJ and HJ were lifelong writers, the most enduring influence from their father was his gift of language. In the case of most writers, the formative modes of speech to which their ears were first attuned are lost in obscurity. But there are many witnesses to how Henry Senior's extraordinary command of rhetoric induced in his children a ready emulation. Fascinated comments make clear that the family's conversations were by no means haphazard. Their father encouraged them all to talk in order to thresh out truth through combat; and they quickly became conscious of the wonderful possibilities in the medium of language itself.

Emerson's son Edward compared Henry Senior to "the representations of Socrates with the bald head, short nose, eyes humorous yet kindly (but spectacled), and beard of moderate dimensions; and, like Socrates, he delighted in starting a theme to argue with his companion to its conclusion. . . . He was not only a humorist, but master of the superlative, and, after a little almost stuttering hesitation, he, like his sons after him, would bring out an adjective or adverb or appellation that would startle the literal minded. . . . He, with no malice, chose to attach other than the usual significations to the word, and this might lead to illuminating discussion."

Years later, reading over some family letters, Alice remarked:

"The rich robustness of Father's texture is simply overpowering when you have been divorced from it for a little and I hadn't looked into the *Literary Remains* for a good while. What 'fun' it must have been to roll out his adjectives. And the curious thing is that notwithstanding the broad swing and sweeping volume of the current, his style never mastered him and degenerated into 'manner,' but in the least little note springs as from a living fountain, as unconscious as a singing bird."

As in so many other respects, WJ and HJ were to react to the same

influence with very different results. WJ was the family's readiest
speaker, and took an early delight in letting a heady rhetoric have full
play—a rhetoric that he was to subdue and pare down as he developed
his own stylistic ideal of immediate simplicity. HJ, like his father, stam-
mered a little as, far more than his father, he hesitated over his thoughts.
In the family colloquies he seems to have been the most silent. But
he was highly susceptible to the sound of the spoken word, and from
his first infant memory of Emerson he retained particularly the tone of
Emerson's voice.[1] As a young writer HJ was more preoccupied with
diction than with rhetoric, and his first mastery was one of deftness and
ease in pictorial presentation of his material. He then set his goal in
the opposite direction from WJ's: towards an ever greater elaboration
of rhetoric. But what is generally overlooked by readers who have not
discovered how well HJ's fiction reads aloud is that even his latest style
is fitted to the cadences of HJ's own sinuous and elliptical but none
the less infectious talk.

One can overhear, in WJ's earliest letters, the kind of speeches he
improvised for his favorite role of the "comic star" of their dialogues.
He loved to sustain the liveliest irony for the family's—and his own—
delectation. This is how he expressed his regret that he was unable
to get back from Cambridge to Newport for the Christmas of 1861:

"Many times and bitterly to-day have I thought of home and lamented
that I should have to be away at this merrie Christmas tide from my
rare family, and with Wilky have I wondered if our family missed us
as we them. And now as I sit under the light of my kerosene, with the
fire quietly consuming in the grate and the twilight on the snow outside
and the melancholy old-fashioned strains of the piano dimly rising from
below, I see in vision the family at home just going in to dinner, my
aged silvered Mother leaning on the arm of her stalwart yet flexible
H., merry and garrulous as ever, my blushing Aunt Kate with her old
wild beauty still hanging over her, my modest Father with his rippling
raven locks, the genial auld Rob, and the mysterious Alice, a glorified
throng, rise before me—but two other forms, one tall, intellectual,
swarthy with curved nose and eagle eye, the other having breadth
rather than depth, but a goodly morsel too, are wanting to complete the
harmonious whole. Eftsoons they vanish and I am again Alone—*Alone*
—what pathos in the word!"

Printing this in his memoirs, HJ decided that it needed the following gloss:

"Comment on the abundance, the gaiety and drollery, the generous
play of vision and fancy in all this, would seem so needless as to be
almost officious, were not the commentator constantly, were he not

---

[1] See p. 430 below.

infinitely arrested and reminded and solicited; which is at once his advantage and his embarrassment. Such a letter, at all events, read over with the general key, touches its contemporary scene and hour into an intensity of life for him; making indeed the great sign of that life my brother's signal vivacity and cordiality, his endless spontaneity of mind. Every thing in it is characteristic of the genius and expressive of the mood, and not least, of course, the pleasantry of paradox, the evocation of each familiar image by its vivid opposite. Our mother, e.g., was not at that time, nor for a good while yet, so venerably 'silvered'; our handsome-headed father had lost, occipitally, long before, all pretence to raven locks, certainly to the effect of their 'rippling'; the beauty of our admirable aunt was as happily alien either to wildness or the 'hanging' air as it could very well be; the 'mystery' of our young sister consisted all in the candour of her natural bloom, even if at the same time of her lively intelligence; and H's mirth and garrulity appear to have represented for the writer the veriest ironic translation of something in that youth, I judge, not a little mildly—though oh so mildly!—morose or anxiously mute. To the same tune the aquiline in his own nose heroically derides the slightly relaxed line of that feature; and our brother Wilky's want of physical 'depth' is a glance at a different proportion."

WJ's play with speech was at its most effervescent in his letters to Alice, for whom he let a fantastic—one should almost say Celtic—invention ride at full rein. These letters, composed sometimes to cheer her up in her periods of sickness, reveal a flair for rhetorical flourishes to rival that of their father. And those dating from WJ's student and travel days in Europe also reveal how the warm family image remained a cohesive force even after the group was dispersed.

*   *   *   *   *

Cambridge, November 14, 1866

Chérie De Jeune Balle, . . . Your first question is, "where have I been?" "To C. S. Peirce's lecture, which I could not understand a word of, but rather enjoyed the sensation of listening to for an hour." I then turned to O. W. Holmes's and wrangled with him for another hour. . . .

Your next question probably is "how are and where are father and mother?" . . . I think father seems more lively for a few days past and cracks jokes with Harry, etc. Mother is recovering from one of her indispositions, which she bears like an angel, doing any amount of work at the same time, putting up cornices and raking out the garret-room like a little buffalo.

Your next question is "wherever is Harry?" I answer: "He is to Ashburner's, to a tea-squall in favor of Miss Haggerty." I declined. He is well. We have had nothing but invitations (6) in 3 or 4 days. One, a painted one, from "Mrs. Lowell" of Pemberton Square, whoever she may be. I replied that domestic affliction prevented me from going, but I would take a pecuniary equivalent instead, viz: To 1 oyster stew 30 cts., 1 chicken salad 0.50, 1 roll 0.02, 3 ice creams at 20 cts. 0.60, 6 small cakes at 0.05, 0.30, 1 pear $1.50, 1 lb. confectionery 0.50.

6 glasses hock at 0.50	$3.00
3 glasses sherry at 30	0.90
Salad spilt on floor	5.00
Dish of do., broken	3.00
Damage to carpet & Miss Lowell's dress frm. do	75.00
3 glasses broken	1.20
Curtains set fire to in dressing-room	40.00
Other injury frm. fire in room	250.00
Injury to house frm. water pumped upon it by steam fire-engine come to put out fire	5000.00
Miscellaneous	0.35
	5300.00

I expect momentarily her reply with a check, and when it comes will take you and Aunt Kate on a tour in Europe and have you examined by the leading physicians and surgeons of that country. . . . Your af. bro. Wm. James.

Berlin, November 19, 1867

Süss Balchen!—I stump wearily up the three flights of stairs after my dinner to this lone room where no human company but a ghastly lithograph of Johannes Müller and a grinning skull are to cheer me. Out in the street the slaw and fine rain is falling as if it would never stop— the sky is low and murky, and the streets filled with water and the finely worked-up paste of mud which never is seen on our continent. For some time past I have thought with longing of the brightness and freshness of my home in New England—of the extraordinary, and in ordinary moments little appreciated, but sometimes-coming-across-you- and-striking-you-with-an-unexpected-sense-of-rich-privilege blessings of a mother's love (excuse my somewhat German style)—of the advantage of having a youthful-hearted though bald-headed father who looks at the Kosmos as if it had some life in it—of the delicious and respectable meals in the family circle with the aforesaid father telling touching horse-car anecdotes, and the serene Harry dealing his snubs around—with a clean female handmaiden to wait, and an open fire to toast one's self at afterwards instead of one of these pallid porcelain monuments here,—with a whole country around you full of friends and acquaintances in whose company you can refresh your social nature, a library of books in the house and a still bigger one over the way,—and all the rest of it. The longer I live, the more inclined am I to value the domestic affections and to be satisfied with the domestic and citizenly virtues (probably only for the reason that I am temporarily debarred from exercising any of them, I blush to think). At any rate I feel *now* and *here* the absence of any object with which to start up some sympathy, and the feeling is real and unpleasant while it lasts. . . .

The few commissions and questions I have sent home have been so unnoticed and disregarded that I hardly hope for success this time. It has always been the way with me, however, from birth upwards, and Heaven forbid that I should now begin to complain! But lo! I here send another commission. I definitely appoint by name my father H. James, Senior, author of Substance and Shadder, etc., to perform it; and solemnly charge all the rest of you to be as lions in his path, as thorns upon his side, as lumps in his mashed potatoes, until he do it or write me Nay. 'Tis to send by post Cousin's lectures on Kant, and that other French translation of a German introduction to Kant, which he bought last winter! By return of mail! . . . Adieu. 1000 kisses to all. . . . Ever your Bruder, W. J.

*   *   *

WJ's "pleasantry of paradox" was still in the ascendant when, a few years later, he reported from Rome upon HJ's habits and dress. He had been describing his own frugal diet:

"In this respect I am economical. Likewise in my total abstinence from spirituous liquors, to which Harry, I regret to say, has become an utter slave, spending a large part of his earnings in Bass's Ale and wine, and trembling with anger if there is any delay in their being brought to him. After feeding, the Angel in his old rather shabby striped overcoat, and I in my usual neat attire, proceed to walk together."

Some of the foregoing jets of energy challenge comparison with the fountainhead that gave them rise. The farthest reaches of Henry Senior's rhetoric—more formal than WJ's, and of a serious intention, but always breaking into a colloquial strain—may be sampled in a letter that he wrote during the Civil War to the editor of the *New Jerusalem Messenger*, a Swedenborgian magazine:

"You were good enough, when I called on you at Mr. Appleton's request in New York, to say among other friendly things that you would send me your paper; and I have regularly received it ever since. I think you for your kindness, but my conscience refuses any longer to sanction its taxation in this way, as I have never been able to read the paper with any pleasure, nor therefore of course with any profit. I presume its editorials are by you, and while I willingly seized upon every evidence they display of an enlarged spirit, I yet find the general drift of the paper so very poverty-stricken in a spiritual regard, as to make it absolutely the least nutritive reading I know. The old sects are notoriously bad enough, but your sect compares with these very much as a heap of dried cod on Long Wharf in Boston compares with the same fish while still enjoying the freedom of the Atlantic Ocean. I remember the manly strain of your conversation with me in New York, and I know therefore how you must suffer from the control of persons so unworthy as those who have the property of your paper. Why don't you cut the whole concern at once, as a rank offence to every human hope and aspiration? The intercourse I had some years since with the leaders of the sect, on a visit to Boston, made me fully aware of their deplorable want of manhood; but judging from your paper, the whole sect seems spiritually benumbed. Your mature men have an air of childishness and your young men have the aspect of old women. I find it hard above all to imagine the existence of a living woman in the bounds of your sect, whose breasts flow with milk instead of hardening with pedantry. I know such things are of course, but I tell you frankly that these are the sort of questions your paper forces on the unsophisticated mind. I really know nothing so sad and spectral in the shape of literature. It seems composed by skeletons and intended for readers who are content to disown their good flesh and blood, and be moved by some ghastly mechanism. It cannot but prove very unwholesome to you spiritually, to be so nearly connected with all that sadness and silence, where nothing more musical is heard than the occasional jostling of bone by bone. Do come out of it before you wither as an autumn leaf, which no longer rustles in full-veined life on the pliant bough, but rattles instead with emptiness upon the frozen melancholy earth.

"Pardon my freedom; I was impressed by your friendliness towards me, and speak to you therefore in return with all the frankness of friendship.

"Consider me as having any manner and measure of disrespect for your ecclesiastical pretensions, but as being personally, yours cordially, H. James."

Both the father's and WJ's letter-writing styles carry the electric charge of their conversation. WJ's published work was, almost inevitably, somewhat more sober, since, during the many years that he was developing his *Principles of Psychology*, he trained himself on articles for scientific journals. It was then that he established his lasting ideal: "to say a thing in one sentence as straight and explicit as it can be made, and then to drop it forever." He sought in his mature essays "the sudden word, the unmediated transition," which he believed to be keyed to the modern American temper. Those objectives also indicate how much he had also responded to Emerson's belief that in good writing "the word becomes one with the thing." But WJ was often moved by the impulse to communicate his latest ideas without waiting to give them systematic form. To any criticism of looseness of style, he was apt to respond: "I don't care how incorrect language may be if it only has fitness of epithet, energy and clearness," or, "Isn't fertility better than perfection?" No wonder that Peirce took the somewhat unfair advantage of personal acquaintance to describe some of the "idiosyncrasies of diction and tricks of language" in WJ's writing as being "such as usually spring up in households of great talent."

One is reminded of part of the criticism that Emerson had made of the father. On one of his lecture tours through the Middle West he had given his copy of Henry Senior's *The Church of Christ not an Ecclesiasticism* to a young clergyman,

"who promised to read it to all the ministers of his town. I could safely praise it to him . . . and mark the capital sentences, for I had read it well, though not enough. I told him what I had found,—that nobody accosted the truth so largely and adequately as this amateur writer, and with a sound humanity, too, which kept him from losing his way. Nay, it might be seen in this very tract, that he could take two or three consecutive steps in the same direction,—a feat scarce accomplished by another man in the century—and that, with so much wit, so much penetration, and so much right manly purpose he could only fail of being what we call a *classic*, from some apparent scorn of details and finish. I tried hard to keep my minister from too much admiration, by accusing the scholastic dress and dialect forms; but he was determined to be pleased, and I had to leave him. And by this time, I doubt not, all Rockford is impregnated."

On his part, HJ became more and more absorbed in the possibilities of his medium. He was still in his father's tradition when he wrote, near the end of his career, to a younger friend: "I'm glad you like adverbs—I adore them; they are the only qualifications I really much respect, and I agree . . . in thinking that the sense for them is *the* literary sense." He may still have been indulging, unconsciously, in the family habit of "attaching other than usual significances" when he read his peculiar catch-all meanings into such epithets as "splendid," "prodigious," and "sacred"; and, unlike his father, he certainly deviated sometimes over the line from style into mannerism. Yet, unlike both father and brother, his ideal of composition was nothing less than perfection, and he would doubtless have defended the position that fertility in literature came only through the struggle for perfection.

He was forever revising and touching up his work for each new reissue. On one occasion he startled WJ's oldest son by the length to which he carried this procedure. When this son taxed HJ with introducing occasional revisions even into the letters of WJ that he had included in *Notes of a Son and Brother,* HJ made only the defense of the dedicated artist. He had wanted to do a "Family Book," and when he "laid hands upon the letters to use as so many touches and tones in the

picture, I frankly confess I seemed to see them in a better, or at all
events in another light, here and there, than those rough and rather
illiterate copies I had from you showed at their face value. I found
myself again in such close relation with your Father, such a revival of
relation as I hadn't known since his death, and which was a passion of
tenderness for doing the best thing by him that the material allowed,
and which I seemed to feel him in the room and at my elbow asking
me for as I worked and as he listened. It was as if he had said to me
on seeing me lay my hands on the weak little relics of our common
youth, 'Oh but you're not going to give me away, to hand me over,
in my raggedness and my poor accidents, quite unhelped, unfriended;
you're going to do the very best for me you *can*, aren't you, and since
you appear to be making such claims for me you're going to let me
seem to justify them as much as I possibly may?' And it was as if I
kept spiritually replying to this that he might indeed trust me to handle
him with the last tact and devotion—that is do with him everything
I seemed to feel him *like*, for being kept up to the amenity pitch. These
were small things, the very smallest, they appeared to me all along to
be, tiny amendments in order of words, degrees of emphasis &c., to
the end that he should be more easily and engagingly readable and
thereby more tasted and liked—from the moment there was no excess
of these *soins* and no violence done to his real identity. Everything the
letters meant affected me so, in all the business, as of *our* old world
only, mine and his alone together, with every item of it intimately
known and remembered by me, that I daresay I did instinctively regard
it at last as all *my* truth, to do what I would with. . . . I am perfectly
willing . . . that the effect on the pages embodied shall be pronounced
a mistake—that I quite inevitably, by my irrepressible 'æsthetic,' lost
the right reckoning . . . and that this makes my course practically
an aberration. Yet I think I am none the less right as to the passages
hanging better together so with my own text, and 'melting' so into
my own atmosphere, than if my superstition had been . . . of the
opposite and absolutely hands-off kind. . . . My mistake will have
begun in thinking that with so literary, so compositional an obsession
as my whole book-making impulse is governed by, any more merciless
transcript might have been possible to me. I have to the last point the
instinct and the sense for fusions and interrelations, for framing and
encircling (as I think I have already called it) every part of my stuff
in every other—and that makes a danger when the frame and circle
play over too much upon the image. Never again shall I stray from
my proper work—the one in which that danger is the reverse of one
and becomes a rightness and a beauty. But strange is the 'irony of fate'
that has made the very intensity of my tenderness on your Dad's behalf a stumbling-block and an offense—for the sad thing is I think

you're right in being offended. I could only dictate my transcript . . .
with emotion and imagination, and those things betrayed me." [1]

HJ's discussion of one phrase he had changed took the whole question straight back to the family circle of half a century before:

"I may mention however that your exception that particularly caught my eye—to 'poor old Abraham' for 'poor old Abe'—was a case for change that I remember feeling wholly irresistible. Never, never, under our Father's roof did we talk of Abe, either *tout court* or as 'Abe Lincoln'—it wasn't conceivable: Abraham Lincoln he was for us, when he wasn't either Lincoln or Mr. Lincoln (the Western note and the popularization of 'Abe' were quite away from us *then*:) and the form of the name in your Dad's letter made me reflect how off, how far off in his queer other company than ours I must at the time have felt him to be. You will say that this was just a reason for leaving it so— and so in a sense it was. But I could *hear* him say Abraham and couldn't hear him say Abe, and the former came back to me as sincere, also graver and tenderer and more like ourselves, among whom I couldn't imagine any 'Abe' ejaculation under the shock of his death as possible."

For better or worse, HJ carried his devotion to the word farther than any member of the family, farther than any writer of his period in either America or England. His monologues became interior, and attempted to catch the very shape in which thoughts formed in his brain. In his latest style, when he was dictating, he often enjoyed displaying his command of rhetoric at its last conceivable intricacy. Since we have already had to reach through this highly sophisticated style to come at the account of their early education, it does no violence to chronology to place here the show-piece of virtuosity in all his correspondence, as a companion to his father's letter to the Swedenborgian editor, and as the ultimate contrast with WJ's mature style. HJ was writing, in 1912, to his Paris-American friend, Walter Berry, to thank him, with a circuity more flamboyant than that of Proust's aunts, for a

---

[1] The usual extent of HJ's changes may be seen in those he introduced into WJ's Christmas letter home (p. 102 above): "and with Wilky have I wondered if our family missed us as we them" became "wondering, with Wilky, if they were missing us as we miss them"; "under the light" became "in the light"; "the family" became "those at home"; and "a glorified throng, rise before me" became "all rise before me, a glorified throng."

Three of these four seem to have been determined by HJ's own feeling for the flow of prose rhythm. Elsewhere, as in WJ's letter from Bonn describing the brothers' walk (pp. 91–2 above), he slightly heightened the drama by altering "H. being part of the time in great pain" to "all of the time." On the other hand, he omitted the detail of Harry's "old white Lordet clothes" looking "so shockingly grimy"; and he made other slight cuts and condensations, in Henry Senior's letters as well, for the sake of a more telling pace. Consequently, in whatever quotations I have made from these letters, I have substituted the originals, whenever they still exist, for the texts given in *Notes of a Son and Brother*.

fitted leather suitcase. The effect is preposterous: it was presumably designed to be as preposterous as possible. That was the humor in it. His language has retained none of the Irish overtones of his heritage. It is splashed with French phrases that are scaled to the recipient, and weighted down by Anglicisms that had long since become habitual. But it is like no one else's English. It is still that of a native of the James family:

*   *   *   *   *

Lamb House, Rye, February 8

Très-cher et très-grand ami! How you must have wondered at my silence! But it has been, alas, inevitable and now is but feebly and dimly broken. Just after you passed through London—or rather even *while* you were passing through it—I began to fall upon evil days again; a deplorable bout of unwellness. . . . The case has really and largely been, however, all the while, dearest Walter, that of my having had to yield, just after your glittering passage in town, to that simply overwhelming *coup de massue* of your—well, of your you know what. It was *that* that knocked me down—when I was just trembling for a fall; it was that that laid me flat.

February 14th. Well, dearest Walter, it laid me after all so flat that I broke down, a week ago, in the foregoing attempt to do you, and your ineffable procédé, some manner of faint justice; I wasn't then apt for any sort of right or worthy approach to you, and there was nothing for me but resignedly to intermit and *me recoucher.* You had done it with your own mailed fist—mailed in glittering gold, speciously glazed in polished, inconceivably and indescribably sublimated, leather, and I had rallied but too superficially from the stroke. It claimed its victim afresh, and I have lain the better part of a week just languidly heaving and groaning as a result *de vos œuvres*—and forced thereby quite to neglect and ignore all letters. I am a little more on my feet again, and if this continues shall presently be able to return to town (Saturday or Monday;) where, however, the monstrous object will again confront me. That is the grand fact of the situation —that is the tawny lion, portentous creature, in my path. I can't get past him, I can't get round him, and on the other hand he stands glaring at me, refusing to give way and practically blocking all my future. I can't live with him, you see; because I can't live *up* to him. His claims, his pretensions, his dimensions, his assumptions and consumptions, above all the manner in which he causes every surrounding object (on my poor premises or within my poor range) to tell a dingy or deplorable tale—all this makes him the very scourge of my life, the very blot on my scutcheon. He doesn't regild that rusty metal—he simply takes up an attitude of gorgeous swagger, straight in front of all the rust and the rubbish, which makes me look as if I had stolen

somebody else's (regarnished *blason*) and were trying to palm it off
as my own. Cher et bon Gaultier, I simply can't *afford* him, and that is
the sorry homely truth. *He is out of the picture*—out of *mine;* and
behold me condemned to live forever with that canvas turned to the
wall. Do you know what that means?—to have to give up going about
at all, lest complications (of the most incalculable order) should ensue
from its being seen what I go about *with*. Bonne renommée vaut mieux
que sac-de-voyage doré, and though I may have had weaknesses that
have brought me a little under public notice, my modest hold-all (which
has accompanied me in most of my voyage through life) has at least,
so far as I know, never *fait jaser*. All this I have to think of—and
I put it candidly to you while yet there is time. That you shouldn't
have counted the cost—to yourself—that is after all perhaps conceivable (quoiqu'à peine!) but that you shouldn't have counted the cost to
me, to whom it spells ruin: *that* ranks you with those great lurid,
though lovely, romantic and historic figures and charmers who have
scattered their affections and lavished their favours only (as it has
presently appeared) to consume and to destroy! More prosaically,
dearest Walter (if one of the most lyric acts recorded in history—
and one of the most finely æsthetic, and one stamped with the most
matchless grace, *has* a prosaic side,) I have been truly overwhelmed
by the princely munificence and generosity of your procédé, and I
have gasped under it while tossing on the bed of indisposition. For a
beau geste, c'est le plus beau, by all odds, of any in all my life ever
esquissé in my direction, and it *has*, as such, left me really and truly
panting helplessly after—or rather quite intensely *before*—it! What is
a poor man to do, mon prince, mon bon prince, mon grand prince,
when so prodigiously practised upon? There is *nothing*, you see: for
the proceeding itself swallows at a gulp, with its open crimson jaws
(*such* a rosy mouth!) like Carlyle's Mirabeau, 'all formulas.' One doesn't
'thank,' I take it, when the heavens open—that is when the whale of
Mr. Allen's-in-the-Strand celestial shopfront does—and discharge
straight into one's lap the perfect compendium, the very burden of the
song, of just what the Angels have been raving about ever since we
first heard of them. Well *may* they have raved—but I can't, you see;
I have to take the case (the incomparable suit-case) in abject silence
and submission. Ah, Walter, Walter, why do you do these things?
they're magnificent, but they're not—well, discussable or permissible
or forgiveable. At least not all at once. It will take a long, long time.
Only little by little and buckle-hole by buckle-hole, shall I be able to
look, with you, even one strap in the face. As yet a sacred horror possesses me, and I must ask you to let me, please, though writing you at
such length, not so much as mention the subject. It's better so. Perhaps
your conscience will tell you why—tell you, I mean, that great supreme

gestes are only fair when addressed to those who can themselves gesticulate. I can't—and it makes me feel so awkward and graceless and poor.
I go about trying—so as to hurl it (something or other) back on you;
but it doesn't come off—practice *doesn't* make perfect; you are victor,
winner, master, oh irresistible one—you've done it, you've brought it
off and got me down forever, and I must just feel your weight and
bear your might to bless your name—even to the very end of the days
of yours, dearest Walter, all to abjectly and too touchedly, Henry
James.

*   *   *

Tastes will always be divided between the styles of WJ and HJ. In
their letters the warm humanity of the one is more directly appealing
than the spun-out nuances of the other. Their finished work could
serve as a basis for contrast between the organic and the artificial styles.
WJ, again like Emerson, wanted art to approach nature as closely as
possible; HJ came to realize more and more that art is not nature,
though based upon it, and that the artist must give his fullest attention
to creating his own forms. Increasing divergences inevitably grew from
the practice of their theories. The widening distance between their
styles can be charted by noting that *The Principles of Psychology* and
The Tragic Muse appeared in the same year (1890), as did *The Will
to Believe* and *The Spoils of Poynton* and *What Maisie Knew* (1897),
Human Immortality and *The Turn of the Screw* (1898), *Talks to
Students on Some of Life's Ideals* and *The Awkward Age* (1899), *The
Varieties of Religious Experience* and *The Wings of the Dove* (1902),
and, finally, *Pragmatism* and *The American Scene* and the first *Prefaces*
(1907).

FATHER TO SONS

THEIR FATHER'S fervent interest continued unabated as his two oldest sons began to find their careers. "It is a delight above all delights," he wrote to Henry in 1872, "to see one's children turn out—as ours have done—all that the heart covets in children; and my delight is so full that I sometimes fancy my heart will have to burst for its own relief." Sometimes, as we have seen, he even rebuked himself that such excessive love for his own was sinful:

* * * * *

Cambridge, December 21, 1873

My darling Harry,—

. . . Your long sickness, and Alice's, and now Willy's, have been an immense discipline for me, in gradually teaching me to universalize my sympathies. It was dreadful to see those you love so tenderly exposed to so much wearing suffering, and I fought against the conviction that it was inevitable. But when I gained a truer perception of the case, and saw that it was a zeal chiefly on behalf of my own children that animated my rebellion, and that I should perhaps scarcely suffer at all, if other people's children alone were in question, and mine were left to enjoy their wonted health and peace, I grew ashamed of myself, and consented to ask for the amelioration of their lot only as a part of the common lot. This is what we want, and this alone, for God's eternal sabbath in our nature, the reconciliation of the individual and the universal interest in humanity. . . . Ever, my darling boy, your loving Daddy.

* * *

But faced with specific cases, he failed to keep this benign detachment. HJ quoted with amusement a letter from his father to James T. Fields, the editor of the *Atlantic Monthly*, "a letter under date of May 1868 and referring clearly to some published remarks on a certain young writer which did violence to the blessedly quick paternal prejudice!":

"I had no sooner left your sanctum yesterday than I was afflicted to remember how I had profaned it by my unmeasured talk about poor H. Please forget it utterly. I don't know how it is with better men, but the parental sentiment is so fiendish a thing with me that if anyone attempt to slay my young, especially in a clandestine way, or out of a pious regard (*e.g.*) to the welfare of the souls comprised in the diocese of the Atlantic Monthly, I can't help devoting him bag and baggage with all my vows to the infernal gods. I am not aware of my animus until I catch, as yesterday, a courteous ear; then the unholy fire flames forth at such a rate as to leave me no doubt on reflection where it was originally lighted. Please pray for your sinful suffering but cordial friend Henry James."

To this HJ added the comment:

"Almost all my dear father is there, making the faded page to-day inexpressibly touching to me; his passionate tenderness, his infinite capacity for reaction on reaction, a force in him fruitful in so many more directions than any high smoothness of *parti-pris* could be, and his beautiful fresh individual utterance, always so stamped with the very whole of him. The few lines make for me, after all the years, a sort of silver key, so exquisitely fitting, to the treasure of living intercourse, of a domestic air quickened and infinitely coloured, comprised in all our younger time."

WJ wrote home from Brazil, where he had gone on the expedition with Agassiz in 1865: "I think Father is the *wisest* of all men whom I know." But there was often debate between them. WJ grew to maturity in the era of Darwin and Spencer, and whereas his father kept insisting that men of science were incapable of apprehending spiritual truths, WJ's own scientific training made him feel the need of coming to grips with the physical before trusting himself in his father's realm of the metaphysical. The distance separating them can be suggested by remembering the father's remark: "A sceptical state . . . I have never known for a moment." WJ's young manhood was ridden by skepticism. He had to fight his way through to the point where he could be aware of, and at last affirm, the limitations of science. He came to value his scientific education, as R. B. Perry has remarked, "as a means of delivering him from the spell of scientific authority"; and he strove in his maturity to justify religion without doing violence to the material world. His will to believe finally owed much to his father, but at the outset he was more aware of the differences between them. When he was studying at Heidelberg with the physicist and psychologist Helmholtz, he wrote to his father: "He is probably the greatest scientific genius extant . . . and in his company your despised child can well afford to let rebound the shafts of your ridicule." At almost the same time WJ was writing to HJ: "I have been reading *Moralism and Christianity* and *Lectures and Miscellanies*. Father is a genius certainly, —a religious genius. I feel it continually to be unfortunate that his discordance from me on other points, in which I think the fault is really his—his want or indeed absence of *intellectual* sympathies of any sort—makes it so hard for me to make him feel how warmly I respond to the positive side of him."

What he meant by his father's lack of "intellectual sympathies" was that Henry Senior reached his truths intuitively, in a way that was very hard for a doubter to cope with. Henry Senior made it, indeed, as hard as possible by affirming without hesitation that "the first requisite . . . of a man being a philosopher, is not to *think*, however comprehensively or profoundly, but *to become a living man* by the actual putting away of selfishness from his heart. For philosophy is not a system of thought reflecting the universe—this part belongs to science; it is an actual life of God in man's finite consciousness, marrying the two poles of nature indissolubly together in a way forever to baffle and humiliate the scientific understanding."

WJ was to find his own philosophy very slowly, through the disciplines of biology and psychology. One of the most remarkable tributes to the indissolubility of the family bond is the series of letters that, all their divergences notwithstanding, passed between father and son while William was in Germany in 1867. Here we see the man in his mid-fifties and the man of twenty-five each sticking tenaciously to his own set of assumptions. They hew fairly close to technicalities, and for those not yet familiar with the terms of Henry Senior's thought, the reading of these letters might follow more naturally after WJ's introduction to his father's *Literary Remains*. But they are too integral a part of the interplay of this family of minds to be omitted from their proper place in the record here—even though WJ had not yet reached the ease of diction that was to characterize his later correspondence.

*   *   *   *   *
                                                        Berlin, Sept. 5, 1867
My beloved old Dad,—

. . . I have read your article [1] which I got in Teplitz several times carefully. I must confess that the darkness which to me has always hung over what you have written on these subjects is hardly at all cleared up. Every sentence seems written from a point of view which I nowhere get within range of, and on the other hand ignores all sorts of questions which are visible from my present view. My questions, I know, belong to the Understanding, and I suppose deal

---

[1] "Swedenborg's Ontology," which had recently appeared in the *North American Review*.

entirely with the "natural constitution" of things, but I find it impossible to step out from them into relation with "spiritual" facts, and the very language you use *ontologically* is also so extensively rooted in the finite and phenomenal that I cannot avoid accepting it as it were in its mechanical sense, when it becomes to me devoid of significance. I feel myself, in fact, more and more drifting towards a sensationalism closed in by scepticism—but the scepticism will keep bursting out in the very midst of it, too, from time to time, so that I cannot help thinking I may one day get a glimpse of things through the ontological window. At present it is walled up. I can understand now no more than ever the world wide gulf you put between "Head" and "Heart"; to me they are inextricably entangled together, and seem to grow from a common stem—and *no* theory of creation seems to me to make things clearer. I cannot logically understand *your* theory. You posit first a phenomenal Nature in which the *alienation* is produced (but phenomenal to *what?* to the already unconsciously existing creature?), and from this effected alienation a *real* movement of return follows. But how *can* the real movement have its rise in the phenomenal? And if it does not, it seems to me the creation is the very arbitrary one you inveigh against; and the whole process is a mere circle of the creator described within his own being and returning to the starting-point. I cannot understand what you mean by the descent of the creator into nature; you don't explain it, and it seems to be the kernel of the whole.

You speak sometimes of our natural life as our whole conscious life; sometimes of our consciousness as composed of both elements, finite and infinite. If our *real* life is unconscious, I don't see how you can occupy in the final result a different place from the Stoics, for instance. These are points on which I have never understood your position, and they will doubtless make you smile at my stupidity; but I cannot help it. I ought not to write about them in such a hurry. . . . I arrived here late last night. My back will prevent my studying physiology this winter at Leipsig, which I rather hoped to do. I shall stay here if I can. If unable to live here and cultivate the society of the natives without a greater moral and·dorsal effort than my shattered frame will admit, I will retreat to Vienna where, knowing so many Americans, I shall find social relaxation without much expense of strength. . . . Much love from your affectionate, Wm. James.

Berlin, Sept. 26, 1867

My dearest Dad,—

. . . Many thanks for writing so often. I wrote you three weeks ago, just after my arrival, more hastily than the seriousness of the subject required perhaps, and so hastily that I cannot now remember what I said with any distinctness. Whatever I did say, however, was meant rather as a description of the natural *sag* of my mind when left to itself, than as its deliberate opinion when active. Then it becomes wholly sceptical. I do not despair, however, of finding bottom somewhere, and it may be where you stand, if I ever fully understand you. i see much better what you are driving at now than I ever did before, however. I wish you would send me to read again that article on "Faith and Science." I had somewhere among my traps the copy you sent me to Pará. Perhaps Harry can find it. I want you to feel how thorough is my personal sympathy with you, and how great is my delight in much that I do understand of what you think, and my admiration of it. You live in such mental isolation that I cannot help often feeling bitterly at the thought that you must see in even your own children strangers to what you consider the best part of yourself. But it is a matter in which one's wishes are of little influence, and until something better comes, you can feel sure of the fullest and heartiest *respect* I feel for any living person. . . .

I have sent Harry with this an ineffably flat article for the *Nation*.[1] Having just read it over it seems to me really hardly worth the postage, so don't let Harry hesitate, through fear of wounding my feelings, from sending it, if he thinks it not adapted for publication. Tell Mother I kiss her more like twice a day than once a month. Give lots of love to Bob, Alice, and all. . . . Ever your loving Wm. James.

Cambridge, Sept. 27, 1867

My dear Willy,—

I wrote you by Thursday steamer in haste, and now add what I hadn't time to say in that letter. I have no great conceit of my expository ability, and my *N. A. R.* article is full, no doubt, of incapacity, but at the same time it is very evident to me that your trouble in understanding it arises *mainly* from the purely scientific cast of your thought just at present, and the temporary blight exerted thence upon your metaphysic wit. Ontological problems seem very idle to the ordinary scientific imagination, because it is stupefied by the giant superstition we call Nature. That is to say, the man of science admits that every thing he observes by any sense is strictly phenomenal or relative to every thing else; but he is not disconcerted by this fact, because he holds instinctively to an *absolute substance* in which all these fleeting things inhere, this substance being Nature. We all *instinctively* do the same thing, but the difference between the philosopher and the man of science, between the man who *reflects* and the man who simply *observes*, is, that the former outgrows his intellectual instincts or disavows the bondage of sense, and attains to the exercise of free thought. And

---

[1] See p. 315 below.

the first postulate of free thought is that Nature—being a mere gen-
eralization of the human mind, intended to give a quasi-unity to the
divergent objects of sense—is void of absoluteness, or has no being
in se but only in the exigencies of our carnal understanding. If we believed instinctively in *creation*, we should have no need to this hypothesis of Nature. For then we should see all the various forms of sense
acknowledging a unitary human substance, and would regard any brute
unintelligible quantity like what we call Nature, a sheer superfluity or
superstition. But while we disbelieve in creation, as we do while we
are still the sport of our senses or the dupes of our scientific activity,
we must believe in Nature as the objective source or explication (instead of the subjective product or implication) of all phenomena; and
so long as this belief lasts, the mind remains puerile, and God—though
we may continuously admit his existence out of regard to tradition—
becomes a rigid superfluity, so far as the conduct of life is concerned.

Now here it seems to me is exactly where you are as yet intellectually: in this scientific or puerile stage of progress. That is, you
believe in some universal quantity called Nature, able not merely to
mother all the specific objects of sense, or give them the subjective
identity they crave to our understanding, but also to *father* them or
give them the objective individuality or character they claim in themselves. And of course while this state of mind endures, the idea of
creation is idle and superfluous to you, for if Nature is there to give
absolute being to existence, what need have we to hunt up a creator?

But let me get down to your particular difficulties. I quote: "I cannot, etc. . . . to the starting-point." I don't know what you mean by
the *"unconsciously existing* creature," as all existence implies to my
mind consciousness of some sort. Certainly when I speak of my existing
phenomenally, I mean that I *exist* or *appear to my own consciousness*,
and *to the perception of others. Reflectively* I admit that this appearance . . . has no reality out of consciousness, that is, no absolute
reality, being altogether relative or subservient to a higher spiritual and
as yet unconscious existence . . . but my reflection is utterly impotent
to control the data of sense, and I *feel* my own existence or reality to
be as absolute—feel the delivery of consciousness to be as unquestionable—if not indeed more absolute and unquestionable than all other
knowledge, sensuous and scientific both, put together. I *know* that I
am not God, that I am *other* than infinite, and nothing but disease of
my brain, or some overpowering sophistry, can ever possibly shake
that knowledge or enfeeble it, but everything on the contrary goes
forever to confirm and enhance it.

Thus my self-consciousness eternally projects or separates me from
God; stamps me essentially finite where he is infinite, imperfect where
he is perfect, contingent where he is absolute; created where He

is creative; and so of strict necessity, as it were, originates a free movement of return to Him; that is to say, an inward movement, a movement of my inward or *individual* being. The movement is a spontaneous one, and infallibly leads to that objective or spiritual conjunction with God in which my real being lies. For this separation from God which consciousness affirms as inherent in my *self*, is noway agreeable to me as a selfish being, but on the contrary every way disagreeable and painful; so that my very selfishness prompts me to unselfishness—prompts me to separate myself from myself as it were—in paying some regard to my neighbor, or learning to identify myself to some extent with others. This is that birth of my inward or spiritual and immortal life, to which my natural consciousness has been wholly subsidiary. If, as my consciousness avers, I am alienated from God, or the infinite good, *just in so far as I am myself*, then clearly my aroused self-love binds me to the utmost alertness in getting away from myself, or postponing its interests to those of my fellow-man. By this instinctive movement I begin to put on real or objective being, that being which lies in becoming conjoined actively with the Divine perfection. . . .

* * *

He turned next to William's statement, "I cannot understand what you mean by the creative descent into nature," and continued to expound his conception of God's alienation and reunion by developing the theme that "the descent of the creator is what we call Nature, or the universe of existence." He then added:

"But it is time that I put my letter in the mail, and my head aches with the fatigue of writing so much on a stretch. I will write again and doubtless more to the purpose if you answer this letter critically, I am sure I have something better to tell you than you will be able to learn from all Germany—at least all scientific Germany. So urge me hard to your own profit. . . ."

* * * * *

Berlin, October 27, 1867

My dear Father—

I acknowledged your metaphysical letter last week. I will now try as well as my feeble power will let me to reply to it. It helped to clear up many of the points on which your position was obscure to me, though I cannot say that I yet fully understand it. I think much of my difficulty has been from uncertainty as to your use of words; and from having been led astray by your *tone* to look for a *necessary* connection between propositions, where I could not find one, although there was a very intelligible empirical one. Thoughts would naturally in your mind, interwoven through and through it as they have been by long brooding, acquire a substantialness and vividness, and consequently a

positiveness and absoluteness of expression, which they would needs
be deprived of on their first reception into mine. This applies to almost
all your ontological matter. You say that such and such *must* be the
way in creation, as if there were an *a priori* logical necessity binding
on the mind. This I cannot see at all in the way you seem to, although
I may be quite ready to accept the contents of your propositions as
an *a posteriori* hypothesis; or, if you object to that word, an "unprov-
able" affirmation of the heart like those you speak of.

*   *   *

WJ proceeds to debate in detail his father's foregoing discussion of
the meaning of Creation, and then, as an ending to this interchange,
sums up their differences:

"You probably now see the state of my mind, and where the trouble
lies. Either I entirely lose sight of some vital element of the question;
or I am led by the natural zeal of your mode of expression to think
that you draw fundamental distinctions where you do not really do so.
In either case it will now be easier than before for you to set me right.
I do not think you will accuse me of wanting to 'chop logic' on these,
of all matters. Really, my tendency is entirely the other way. For
myself, I shrink from trying to image too exactly these things; but if
we are to talk about them at all, we must try to work as much clearness into our words as possible. I am sure that I understand you now
better than before, though probably still imperfectly. You know how
much depends in these matters on a natural bent of feeling, and you
probably know how sceptical I am and how little ready to *assert* anything about them. I think that spontaneously I am rather inclined to
lapse into a pantheistic mode of contemplating the world, but even if
my thoughts were worthier and more serious than they are, I doubt
if I should ever care to measure very jealously one way of considering
it against another, but would rather let each go as symbols. Your
analysis or Swedenborg's of creation into its elements seems to me a
most full and beautiful one, and I do not now think that my possible
joy in going forth to meet the Creator in the sort of marriage or equa-
tion you represent ought to be diminished by my believing that the
thing was after all a piece of 'magic' on his part. Empirically it is
different. I cannot attain to any such 'inexpugnable testimony of consciousness to my spiritual reality' as that you speak of, and that must
be a decisive moment in determining one's attitude towards such problems. *Practically*, it seems to me that *all* tendencies must nowadays
unite in philanthropy; perhaps an atheistic tendency more than any,
for sympathy is now so much developed in the human breast that
misery and undeveloped-ness would all the more powerfully call for
correction when coupled with the thought that from nowhere else

than from us could correction possibly come,—that we ourselves must be our own providence.

"I have now laid bare to you the general complexion of my mind. I cannot help thinking that to you it will appear most pitiful and bald. But I cannot help it and cannot feel responsible for it. Heaven knows I do not love it, and if in a future letter or letters you are able to sow some seed in it which may grow up and help to furnish it I shall be thankful enough. Good night, my dear old Daddy. . . . Ever your loving son, Wm. J."

Naturally there could be no such debate between Henry Senior and Henry Junior. This son's medium was never abstract discourse, but the slow imponderable development of a point of view and of the craftsmanship to present it. He felt himself at sea among his father's ideas—though a letter written in 1870, near the end of his first year on his own in Europe shows him sympathetically trying to cope with their social implications, and should help correct the notion that he was always indifferent to politics:

"Be very sure that as I live more I care none the less for these wise human reflections of yours. I turn with great satisfaction to any profession of interest in the fate of collective humanity—turn with immense relief from the wearisome European world of idlers and starers and self-absorbed pleasure seekers. I am not prepared perhaps to measure the value of your notions with regard to the amelioration of society, but I certainly have not travelled a year in this quarter of the globe without coming to a very deep sense of the absurdly flimsy and transitory organization of the actual social body. The only respectable state of mind, indeed, is to constantly express one's perfect dissatisfaction with it—and your letter was one of the most respectable things I have seen in a long time. So don't be afraid of treating me to a little philosophy."

But when it came to his own work, HJ knew instinctively that his father's usual concern with generalized humanity could not serve him, since the novelist must deal with concrete individuals. Yet he was charmed to note the loving inconsistency, for, despite Henry Senior's opposition to the artist's career, once his son had adopted it, the father was filled with nothing but encouragement. The following letter conveys the warm interest of the whole family in the activity of any one of its members:

* * * * *

Cambridge, January 14, 1873

My darling Harry:—

We had a sitting last evening, and the evening before in the library, at which were present Mother, Alice and Willy, to whom I read the proof of your *Madonna of the Future*, which I had from Howells, and which is to appear in the March *Atlantic*. . . . Willy pronounced it very *distingué*, Mother charming, Alice exquisite. I was very much struck with it as a whole, and admired it greatly also in parts. But I have a story to tell. Mr. Howells couldn't agree to give twenty-five pages of one number of the magazine to it; that was positive. And then besides he had a decided shrinking from one episode—that in which Theobald tells of his love for, and his visit from, the Titian-ic beauty, and his subsequent disgust of her worthlessness, as being risky for the magazine; and then, moreover, he objected to the interview at the end between the writer and the old English neighbor, as rubbing into the reader what was sufficiently evident without it. On both the first and second points, we all thought that while Howells *in general* is too timid, there was good ground for his timidity in the present case. Both Mother and Alice shrank from both the episodes as not helping the understanding of the story along, and as being scary rather in themselves. Willy thought the second quite unnecessary and super-fluous, and thought the first, if it had not been so much detailed but had been condensed into half a column, would perhaps do. But I thought they were both utterly uncalled for by the actual necessities of the tale, while they would both alike confer upon it a disagreeable, musky odour strikingly at war with its unworldly beauty. I went to Howells accordingly this morning, and told him that if he would consent to publish the whole tale in one piece, I would take upon me the responsibility of striking out the two episodes. He agreed, and he has made the connection of the parts perfect, so that no one would ever dream of anything stricken out. He promises me also to save the excluded pieces, and I will send them to you or keep them for you so that you may publish them, if you like, in your volume—which Howells says ought to be published forthwith.[1] I ought to say also that Howells admires the story very much, thinks it very beautiful, and only objects to these episodes as being too much fashioned upon French literature. . . . He said he would like nothing better than an article of six or seven pages from you *every month*, of whatever sort; and he was clear that you ought to publish a volume under the title of *Romances*. . . . He was very friendly, and I told him I would communicate with you at once . . . I can help you if you are disposed to publish a selection of your tales. I think it would be a good thing for you to do, and Willy also is clear about it. You have a large number of admirers, that is evident; and I suspect the volume might be remunerative. . . .

Willy is going on with his teaching. The eleven o'clock bell has just

---

[1] See p. 126 below. The omitted episodes were never restored.

tolled, and he is on his platform expounding the mysteries of Physiology. He uses himself up now and then visiting and all the rest of
it, such as debating about *Middlemarch* and other transient topics, but
on the whole he gets on very well. He often talks of you. We all do
that of course, but *he* very often initiates the talk. I needn't say that
he always talks of you in the most tenderly affectionate and ·apprecia-
tive way. Yes we are all your tender lovers darling Harry, and none
more so than your devoted Daddy.

* * *

To this HJ answered from Rome, taking cognizance of the genteel
restrictions of Anglo-Saxon magazines, as he was to have to do throughout his career:

"Dearest father—I have just received your long and most satisfactory
letter about the proof of my story and Howells' restrictions, invitations, etc. The former I regret, and as far as I can remember the
'immoral' episode don't artistically approve. With such a standard of
propriety, it makes it a bad look-out ahead for imaginative writing.
For what class of minds is it that such very timorous scruples are
thought necessary?—But of course you were quite right to make all
convenient . . . and I am much obliged to you for your trouble. Evidently, too, Howells has a better notion of the allowances of the common public than I have, and I am much obliged to him for performing
the excision personally, for of course he will have done it neatly. About
his offer to have me write monthly for the Atlantic Monthly I shall
directly write to him. I am charmed and ask nothing better. . . ."

In this same winter his father's eager desire to meet HJ on his own
ground caused him to go so far as to send him a detailed outline for
a story:

"I went to see Osgood about publishing a selection from your Tales.
He repeated what he told you: that he would give you fifteen per
cent, do all the advertising etc., you paying for the plates: or he would
pay everything and give you *ten* per cent on every copy sold after
the first thousand. I shall be willing (in case you would like to publish,
and I think it is time for you to do so) to bear the expense of stereo-
typing, and if you will pick out what you would like to be included,
we shall set to work at once, and have the book ready by next autumn.
I have got the materials of a story for you which I was telling Willy
of the other day as a regular Tourgenieff subject, and he told me to
send it off to you at once, he was so struck with it. Matthew Henry
Webster was a very cultivated and accomplished young man in Albany,
at the time I was growing up. He belonged to a respectable family,
(of booksellers and publishers) was himself bred to the law, but had
such a love of literature and, especially, of the natural sciences, that
he never devoted himself very strictly to his profession. He was the

intimate friend of Professor Henry and other distinguished men of science, corresponded with foreign scientific bodies, and his contributions to science were of so original a cast as to suggest great hopes of his future eminence. He *was a polished gentleman, of perfect address, brave as Cæsar, utterly unegotistic,* and one's wonder was how he ever grew up in Albany or reconciled himself to living in the place. One day he invested some money in a scheme much favoured by the President of the Bank in which he deposited, and his adventure proved a fortune.

"There lived also a family in Albany of the name of Kane (Mary Port's step-mother being of its members) and this family reckoned upon a great social sensation in bringing out their youngest daughter, (Lydia Sybil Kane) who had never been seen by mortal eye outside of her own family, except that of a physician, who reported that she was fabulously beautiful. She *was* the most beautiful girl I think I ever saw, at a little distance. Well, she made her sensation, and brought Mr. Webster incontinently to her feet. Her family wanted wealth above all things for her; but here was wealth and something more, very much more, and they smiled upon his suit. Everything went merrily for a while. Webster was profoundly intoxicated with his prize. Never was man so enamoured, and never was beauty better fitted to receive adoration. She was of an exquisite Grecian outline as to face, with a countenance like the tender dawn, and form and manners ravishingly graceful. But Webster was not content with his adventure—embarked again and lost all he owned almost. Mr. Oliver Kane (or Mrs., for she was the ruler of the family and as hard as the nether world in heart) gave the cue to her daughter, and my friend was dismissed. He couldn't believe his senses. He raved and cursed his fate. But it was inexorable. What was to be done? With a bitterness of heart inconceivable he plucked his revenge by marrying instantly a stout and blooming jade who in respect to Miss Kane was a peony to a violet, and who was absolutely nothing but flesh and blood. Her he bore upon his arm at fashionable hours through the streets; her he took to church, preserving his exquisite ease and courtesy to everyone, as if absolutely nothing had occurred; and her he pretended to take to his bosom in private, with what a shudder one can imagine. Everybody stood aghast. He went daily about his affairs, as serene and unconscious as the moon in the heavens. Soon his poverty showed itself in certain economies of his wardrobe which had always been very recherché. Soon again he broke his leg, and went about on crutches, but neither poverty nor accident had the *least* power to ruffle his perfect repose. He was always superior to his circumstances, met you exactly as he had always done, impressed you invariably as the best bred man you ever saw, and left you wondering what a heart and what a brain lay behind such a fortune.

"One morning we all read in the paper at breakfast that Mr. Henry

Webster had appealed the day before to the protection of the police against his wife, who had beaten him, and whom as a woman he could not degrade by striking in return: and the police responded promptly to his appeal. He went about his affairs as usual that day and every day, never saying a word to any one of his trouble, nor even indirectly asking sympathy, but compelling you to feel that here if anywhere was a novel height of manhood, a self-respect so eminent as to look down with scorn upon every refuge open to ordinary human infirmity. This lasted for five or six years. He never drank, had no vice, in fact of any kind, and lived a life of such decorum, so far as his own action was concerned, a life of such interest in science and literature as to be the most delightful and unconscious of companions even when his coat was shabby beyond compare, and you dare not look at him for fear of betraying your own vulgar misintelligence.

"Finally Sybil Kane died smitten with small pox, and all her beauty gone to hideousness. He lingered awhile, his beautiful manners undismayed still, his eye as undaunted as at the beginning, and then he suddenly died. I never knew his equal in manhood, sheer, thorough, manly force, competent to itself in every emergency, and seeking none of the ordinary subterfuges which men seek in order to hide their own imbecility. I think it a good basis for a novel."

HJ's comment upon this in his memoirs ran as follows:

"As for the recital, in such detail, of the theme of a possible literary effort . . . how could I feel this, when it had reached me, as anything but a sign of the admirable anxiety with which thought could be taken, even though 'amateurishly,' in my professional interest?—since professional I by that time appeared able to pass for being. And how above all can it not serve as an exhibition again of the manner in which all my benevolent backer's inveterate original *malaise* in face of betrayed symptoms of the impulse to 'narrow down' on the part of his young found its solution always, or its almost droll simplification, as soon as the case might reach for him a *personal* enough, or 'social' enough, as he would have said, relation to its fruits? Then the malaise might promptly be felt as changed, by a wave of that wand, to the extremity of active and expatiative confidence."

The letter he had sent home at the time shows him feeling his way to what was to be his first book:

*   *   *   *   *

Rome, March 24, 1873

Dearest Mammy—

. . . I have rejoiced in your home news when it was good—and deplored it when it was not, as for example when you touch upon your furious snows and frosts—you, dearest Mammy, upon your grievous domestic fatigues and woes, and Willy upon Alice's spoiled dinner parties.—But I hope by this time the tender grass is peeping up along the border of the Brattle Street fences, where I used to watch it so lovingly last year . . . and Alice has ornamented all the feasts to which she has been bidden. . . . I owe father [a letter], which he shall soon have. Thank him meanwhile greatly for his story of *Mr. Webster*. It is admirable material, and excellently presented. I have transcribed it in my note book with religious care, and think that some day something will come of it. It would require much thinking out. But it is a 1st class theme. Thank him also for his trouble in discussing with Osgood the matter of my bringing out a volume. He mentioned it some time since, and it has been on my mind to respond. Briefly, I don't care to do it, just now. I value none of my early tales enough to bring them forth again, and if I did, should absolutely need to give them an amount of verbal retouching which it would be very difficult out here to effect. What I desire is this: to make a volume, a short time hence, of tales on the theme of American adventurers in Europe, leading off with the *Passionate Pilgrim*. I have three or four more to write: one I have lately sent to Howells and have half finished another. They will all have been the work of the last three years and be much better and maturer than their predecessors. . . .

Farewell, farewell, dearest Mother. A smoother kitchen and many happy months ahead. . . . Your fondest H.

* * *

This letter also reveals how HJ, no less than WJ, kept, in absence, a living image of the family group. He had written WJ during that first winter on his own in Europe:

"Beloved Brother,— . . . I have had a cheery British fire made up in my dingy British bedroom and have thus sate me down to this ghastly mockery of a fraternal talk. My heart reverts across the awful leagues of wintry ocean to that blessed library in Quincy Street, and to the image of the gathering dusk, the assembled family, the possible guest, the impending—Oh! the impending, American *tea!* In fine, if I wanted I could be as homesick as you please. All the conditions are present: *rien n'y manque*. But I'll steep myself in action lest I perish with despair. I'll drive the heavy-footed pen, and brush away the importunate tear. . . ."

Those last sentences pick up WJ's own brand of irony, but a decade later HJ was still to write quite seriously that "nothing in the world gives me so much pleasure . . . as the feeling of being 'acceptable' to the little Quincy Street circle." Being a writer in the James family meant that you had an audience and a standard from the start of your career.

Mrs. Henry James, Senior, about 1880

DEATH OF THE MOTHER
AND FATHER

HJ's MEMOIRS include only a passing tribute to his mother, to her "soundless and yet absolutely all-saving service and trust." When one of his nephews expressed regret at the omission of a longer characterization, HJ responded: "Oh! my dear Boy—that memory is too sacred!"

The depth of his feeling for her shines through his letters about her death in the early winter of 1882. He wrote to Godkin: "My dearest mother died last Sunday—suddenly and tranquilly, from an affection of the heart. . . . You know my mother and you know what she was to us—the sweetest, gentlest, most natural embodiment of maternity— and our protecting spirit, our household genius." He added, in a letter to Norton, a few days later: "My mother's death is the greatest change that could befall us, but our lives are so full of her still that we scarcely yet seem to have lost her. The long beneficence of her own life remains and survives."

He had providentially been in America that winter for the first time in six years. He wrote in his notebook:

"On Sunday January 29th, as Aunt Kate sat with her in the closing dusk (she had been ill with an attack of bronchial asthma, but was apparently recovering happily,) she passed away. . . . I knew that I loved her—but I didn't know how tenderly till I saw her lying in her shroud in that cold North Room, with a dreary snowstorm outside, and looking as sweet and tranquil and noble as in life. . . . I found Father and Alice . . . extraordinarily calm—almost happy. Mother seemed still to be there—so beautiful, so full of all that we loved in her she looked in death. We buried her on Wednesday February 1st; Wilkie arrived from Milwaukee a couple of hours before. Bob had been there for a month—he was devoted to mother in her illness. It was a splendid winter's day—the snow lay deep and high. We placed her for the present in a temporary vault in the Cambridge cemetery—the part

that lies near the river. When the spring comes on we shall go and
choose a burial place. I have often walked there in the old years—in
those long, lonely rambles that I used to take about Cambridge, and I
had, I suppose, a vague idea that some of us would some day lie there,
but I didn't see just that scene.

"It is impossible for me to say—to begin to say—all that has gone
down into the grave with her. She was our life, she was the house, she
was the keystone of the arch. She held us all together, and without
her we are scattered reeds. She was patience, she was wisdom, she was
exquisite maternity. Her sweetness, her mildness, her great natural
beneficence were unspeakable, and it is infinitely touching to me to
write about her here as one that *was*. When I think of all that she had
been, for years—when I think of her hourly devotion to each and all
of us—and that when I went to Washington the last of December I
gave her my last kiss, I heard her voice for the last time,—there seemed
not to be enough tenderness in my being to register the extinction of
such a life. But I can reflect, with perfect gladness, that her work was
done—her long patience had done its utmost. She had had heavy cares
and sorrows, which she had borne without a murmur, and the weariness of age had come upon her. I would rather have lost her forever than
see her begin to suffer as she would probably have been condemned to
suffer, and I can think with a kind of holy joy of her being lifted now
above all our pains and anxieties. Her death has given me a passionate
belief in certain transcendent things—the immanence of being as
nobly created as hers—the immortality of such a virtue as that—the
reunion of spirits in better conditions than these. She is no more of an
angel today than she had always been; but I can't believe that by the
accident of her death all her unspeakable tenderness is lost to the beings
she so dearly loved. She is with us, she is of us—the eternal stillness is
but a form of her love. One can hear her voice in it—one can feel,
forever, the inextinguishable vibration of her devotion. I can't help
feeling that in those last weeks I was not tender enough with her—that
I was blind to her sweetness and beneficence. One can't help wishing
one had only known what was coming, so that one might have en-
veloped her with the softest affection.

"When I came back from Europe I was struck with her being worn
and shrunken, and now I know that she was very weary. She went
about her usual activities, but the burden of life had grown heavy for
her, and she needed rest. There is something inexpressibly touching to
me in the way in which, during these last years, she went on from year
to year without it. If she could only have lived she should have had it,
and it would have been a delight to see her have it. But she has it now,
in the most complete perfection! Summer after summer she never left

Cambridge—it was impossible that father should leave his own house. The country, the sea, the change of air and scene, were an exquisite enjoyment to her; but she bore with the deepest gentleness and patience, the constant loss of such opportunities. She passed her nights and her days in that dry, flat, hot, stale and odious Cambridge, and had never a thought while she did so but for father and Alice. It was a perfect mother's life—the life of a perfect wife. To bring her children into the world—to expend herself, for years, for their happiness and welfare—then, when they had reached a full maturity and were absorbed in the world and in their own interests—to lay herself down in her ebbing strength and yield up her pure soul to the celestial power that had given her this divine commission. Thank God one knows this loss but once; and thank God that certain supreme impressions remain!"

When HJ returned to England that spring, his father sent him off with these words:

"And now, my darling boy, I must bid you farewell. How loving a farewell it is, I can't say, but only that it is most loving. All my children have been very good and sweet from their infancy, and I have been very proud of you and Willy. But I can't help feeling that you are the one that has cost us the least trouble, and given us always the most delight. Especially do I mind mother's perfect joy in you the last few months of her life, and your perfect sweetness to her. I think in fact it is this which endears you so much to me now. No doubt the other boys in the same circumstances would have betrayed the same tender and playful love to her, only they were not called upon to do so. I am in no way unjust to them, therefore, but I feel that I have fallen heir to all dear mother's fondness for you, as well as my proper own, and bid you accordingly a distinctly widowed farewell. That blessed mother, what a link her memory is to us all henceforth! I think none of us who remember her natural unaffected ways of goodness, and especially her sleepless sense of justice, will ever again feel tempted to do a dishonest or unhandsome thing. She was not to me 'a liberal education,' intellectually speaking, as some one has said of his wife, but she really did arouse my heart, early in our married life, from its selfish torpor, and so enabled me to become a man. And this she did altogether unconsciously, without the most cursory thought of doing so, but solely by the presentation of her womanly sweetness and purity, which she herself had no recognition of. The sum of it all is, that I would sooner rejoin her in her modesty, and find my eternal lot in association with her, than have the gift of a noisy delirious world!

"Good-bye then again, my precious Harry! . . . We shall each rejoice in you in our several way as you plough the ocean and attain to your old rooms, where it will be charming to think of you as once more settled and at work. I wish England itself offered a less troubled residence to you than it does. A lingering good-bye, then, dearest Harry, from all of us! and above all from your loving Father."

Henry Senior survived his wife by less than a year. He continued to work on his *Spiritual Creation*, which he subtitled *"An Essay towards ascertaining the role of Evil in Divine Housekeeping"*; but he wrote to Godkin in the fall:

"The making of the book has been my only refuge against the suffering involved in the loss of my wife. . . . For four or five months I didn't see how I was going to live without her. I had actually run down to death's door when we moved to the country, and I have been slowly pulling up since. But even now I am miserably feeble, and look forward to nothing with so much desire as to a reunion beyond the skies with my adorable wife."

When he died, the week before Christmas, WJ was on a much-needed year's leave of absence in Europe, and HJ was on shipboard, trying vainly to get home before the end. Among their father's last recorded utterances was: "I stick by Almighty God—He alone *is*, all else is death. Don't call this dying; I am just entering upon life." Alice was to recall in her journal:

"A week before Father died, I asked him one day whether he had thought what he should like to have done about his funeral. He was immediately very much interested, not having apparently thought of it before; he reflected for some time, and then said, with the greatest solemnity and looking so majestic: 'Tell him to say only this: "Here lies a man, who has thought all his life that the ceremonies attending birth, marriage, and death were all damned nonsense." Don't let him say a word more!' But there was no Unitarian even elastic enough for this. What a washed-out, cowering mess humanity seems beside a creature like that!"

HJ had found at the pier a letter from Alice:

"Darling Father's weary longings were all happily ended on Monday at 3 P.M. The last words on his lips being 'There is my Mary!' For the last two hours he had said perpetually 'My Mary.' He had no suffering but was very devotedly thankful when the rest came to him, he so longed to go. The last thing he said before he lost consciousness was, 'I am going with great joy!' The end of life had come for him and he went, and I am sure you will feel as thankful as I do that the weary burden of life is over for him. I have no terrors for the future, for I know I shall have strength to meet all that is in store for me. With a heart full of love and counting the minutes till you get here, Always your devoted A.

"The funeral is to be to-morrow . . . at 11 A.M. There seemed no use in waiting for you, the uncertainty was so great."

HJ wrote in great detail to WJ on the day after Christmas:

"You will already have heard the circumstances under which I arrived at New York on Thursday 21st, at noon, after a very rapid and prosperous, but painful passage. Letters from Alice and Katherine Loring were awaiting me at the dock, telling me that dear father was to be buried that morning. I reached Boston at 11 that night; there was so much delay in getting up-town. I found Bob at the station here. He had come on for the funeral only, and returned to Milwaukee the next morning. Alice, who was in bed, was very quiet and Aunt Kate was perfect. They told me everything—or at least they told me a great deal—before we parted that night, and what they told me was deeply touching, and yet not at all literally painful. Father had been so tranquil, so painless, had died so easily and, as it were, deliberately, and there had been none—not the least—of that anguish and confusion which we imagined in London. . . . It appears to have been most strange, most characteristic, above all, and as full of beauty as it was void of suffering. There was none of what we feared—no paralysis, no dementia, no violence. He simply, after the 'improvement' of which we were written before I sailed, had a sudden relapse—a series of swoons—after which he took to his bed not to rise again. He had no visible malady—strange as it may seem. The 'softening of the brain' was simply a gradual refusal of food, because he *wished* to die. There was no dementia except a sort of exaltation of his belief that he had entered into 'the spiritual life.' Nothing could persuade him to eat, and yet he never suffered, or gave the least sign of suffering, from inanition. All this will seem strange and incredible to you, but told with all the details, as Aunt Kate has told it to me, it becomes real—taking Father as he was—almost natural. He prayed and longed to die. He ebbed and faded away, though in spite of his strength becoming continually less, he was able to see people and to talk. He wished to see as many people as he could, and he talked with them without effort. . . . Alice says he said the most picturesque and humorous things. He knew I was coming and was glad, but not impatient. He was delighted when he was told that you would stay in my rooms in my absence, and seemed much interested in the idea. He had no belief apparently that he should live to see me, but was perfectly cheerful about it. He slept a great deal, and, as Aunt Kate says, there was 'so little of the sick-room' about him. He lay facing the windows, which he would never have darkened—never pained by the light.

"I sit writing this in his room upstairs, and a cast which Alice had taken from his head, but which is very unsatisfactory and represents him as terribly emaciated, stands behind me on that high chest of drawers. . . . He spoke of everything—the disposition of his things, made all arrangements of every kind. Aunt Kate repeats again and again, that he *yearned* unspeakably to die. . . . The house is so *empty*

—I scarcely know myself. Yesterday was such a Christmas as you may imagine—with Alice at K. Loring's, me ill in bed here, and Aunt Kate sitting alone downstairs, not only without a Christmas dinner but without any dinner, as she doesn't eat, according to her wont! . . . All our wish here is that you should remain abroad the next six months. Ever your H. J."

Four days before his father died, WJ had written to him from London. This letter and HJ's reply to it are among the most remarkable contributions to the family's annals:

*   *   *   *   *

London, December 14, 1882

Darling old Father . . . We have been so long accustomed to the hypothesis of your being taken away from us, especially during the past ten months, that the thought that this may be your last illness conveys no very sudden shock. You are old enough, you've given your message to the world in many ways and will not be forgotten; you are left alone, and on the other side, let us hope and pray, dear, dear old Mother is waiting for you to join her. If you go, it will not be an inharmonious thing. Only, if you are still in possession of your normal consciousness, I should like to see you once again before we part. I stayed here only in obedience to the last telegram, and am waiting now for Harry—who knows the exact state of my mind, and who will know yours—to telegraph again what I shall do. Meanwhile, my blessed old Father, I scribble this line (which may reach you though I should come too late), just to tell you how full of the tenderest memories and feelings about you my heart has for the last few days been filled. In that mysterious gulf of the past into which the present soon will fall and go back and back, yours is still for me the central figure. All my intellectual life I derive from you; and though we have often seemed at odds in the expression thereof, I'm sure there's a harmony somewhere, and that our strivings will combine. What my debt to you is goes beyond all my power of estimating,—so early, so penetrating and so constant has been the influence. You need be in no anxiety about your literary remains. I will see them well taken care of, and that your words shall not suffer for being concealed. At Paris I heard that Milsand, whose name you may remember in the *Revue des Deux Mondes* and elsewhere, was an admirer of the *Secret of Swedenborg*, and Hodgson told me your last book had deeply impressed him. So will it be; especially, I think, if a collection of *extracts* from your various writings were published, after the manner of the extracts from Carlyle, Ruskin, & Co. I have long thought such a volume would be the best monument to you.

As for us; we shall live on each in his way,—feeling somewhat unprotected, old as we are, for the absence of the parental bosoms as a refuge, but holding fast together in that common sacred memory. We will stand by each other and by Alice, try to transmit the torch in our off-spring as you did in us, and when the time comes for being gathered in, I pray we may, if not all, some at least, be ripe as you. As for myself, I know what trouble I've given you at various times through my peculiarities; and as my own boys grow up, I shall learn more and more of the kind of trial you had to overcome in superintending the development of a creature different from yourself, for whom you felt responsible. I say this merely to show how my *sympathy* with you is likely to grow much livelier, rather than to fade—and not for the sake of regrets.

As for the other side, and Mother, and our all possibly meeting, I *can't* say anything. More than ever at this moment do I feel that if that *were* true, all would be solved and justified. And it comes strangely over me in bidding you good-bye how a life is but a day and expresses mainly but a single note. It is so much like the act of bidding an ordinary good-night. Good-night, my sacred old Father! If I don't see you again—Farewell! a blessed farewell! Your William.

> Boston, January 1, 1883
>
> Dear William . . . I went out yesterday (Sunday) morning to the Cambridge cemetery. . . . I stood beside his grave a long time and read him your letter of farewell—which I am sure he heard somewhere out of the depths of the still bright winter air. He lies extraordinarily close to Mother, and as I stood there and looked at this last expression of so many years of mortal union, it was difficult not to believe that they were not united again in some consciousness of my belief. . . . Ever yours H. James.

* * *

WJ's answer to HJ's detailed account of the end rounds out this cycle:

"Your eagerly awaited letter came yesterday. . . . What would I not give if I could have seen the dear old man lying there as you describe him, culminating his life by this drama of complete detachment from it. I must now make amends for my rather hard non-receptivity of his doctrines as he urged them so absolutely during his life, by trying to get a little more public justice done them now. As life closes, all a man has done seems like one cry or sentence. Father's cry was the single one that religion is real. The thing is so to 'voice' it that other ears shall hear,—no easy task, but a worthy one, which in some shape I shall attempt."

As WJ's mind continued to play over the past, there welled up a steady flow of reminiscence. He wrote to his wife:

"Father's boyhood up in Albany, Grandmother's house, the father and brothers and sister, with their passions and turbulent histories, his burn-

ing, amputation and sickness, his college days and ramblings, his theological throes, his engagement and marriage and fatherhood, his finding
more and more of the truths he finally settled down in, his travels in
Europe, the days of the old house in New York and all the men I used
to see there, at last his quieter motion down the later years of life in
Newport, Boston and Cambridge, with his friends and correspondents
about him, and his books more and more easily brought forth—how
long, how long all these things were in the living, but how short their
memory now is! What remains is a few printed pages, us and our children and some incalculable modifications of other people's lives, influenced this day or that by what he said or did. For me, the humor,
the good spirits, the humanity, the faith in the divine, and the sense of
his right to have a say about the deepest reasons of the universe, are
what will stay by me. I wish I could believe I should transmit some of
them to our babes. We all of us have some of his virtues and some of
his shortcomings. Unlike the cool, dry thin-edged men who now
abound, he was full of the fumes of the ur-sprünglich human nature;
things turbid, more than he could formulate, wrought within him and
made his judgments or rejection of so much of what was brought [be-
fore him] seem like revelations as well as knock-down blows. . . . I
hope that rich soil of human nature will not become more rare!"

Two months after his father's death WJ added in a letter to his
mother-in-law:

"It is singular how I'm learning every day now how the thought of
his comment on my experiences has hitherto formed an integral part of
my daily consciousness, without my having realized it at all. I interrupt
myself incessantly now in the old habit of imagining what he will say
when I tell him this or that thing I have seen or heard."

In 1890, when Alice was in England, she had her old desk sent from
home. She was deeply stirred to find that her letters were in it:

"I fell upon Father's and Mother's and could not tear myself away
from them for two days,—one of the most intense, exquisite and profoundly interesting experiences I ever had. I think if I try to give it
form its vague intensity will take limits to itself, and the 'divine anguish'
of the myriad memories stirred grow less. Although they were as the
breath of life to me, as the years have passed they have always been as
present as they were at first, and will be for the rest of my numbered
days (with their little definite portion of friction and serenity, so short
a span), until we three are blended together again, if such should be our
spiritual necessity. But as I read it seemed as if I had opened up a postscript of the past and that I had had, in order to find them truly, really
to lose them. It seems now incredible to me that I should have drank as
a matter of course at that ever springing fountain of responsive love,
and bathed all unconscious in that flood of human tenderness. The

letters are made of the daily events of their pure, simple lives, with souls unruffled by the ways of men, like special creatures, spiritualized and remote from coarser clay,—Father ringing the changes upon the Mother's perfections, he not being of the order of 'charming man who hangs up his fiddle outside his own front door,' for his fireside inspired his sweetest music; and Mother's words breathing her extraordinary selfless devotion, as if she simply embodied the unconscious essence of wife-and-motherhood. What a beautiful picture do they make for the thoughts of their children to dwell upon. How the emotions of those two dreadful years when I was wrenching myself away from them surge through me,—the first haunted by the terror that I should fail him, as I watched the poor old man fade, day by day,—'his fine fibre,' William said, 'wearing and burning itself out at things too heavy for it,'—until the longing cry of his soul was answered and the dear old shrunken body was 'lying beside Mary on the hilltop in Cambridge.' Mother died Sunday Evening, January 29, 1882; Father on Monday mid-day December 18, 1882; and now I am shedding the tears I didn't shed then."

THE TRIBUTES OF THE SONS
TO THE FATHER

WJ's Introduction
to Henry Senior's Literary Remains

WILLIAM'S EFFORT to get "public justice" done to their father's doc-trines took the shape of a long introduction to a volume containing the unfinished *Spiritual Creation* as well as his father's *Autobiography* and his *Recollections of Carlyle*. As long as his father was alive, they had all, as HJ said, taken his writing "infinitely for granted." They had also treated it with the uninhibited freedom that they brought to the family discussions of everything. When their father was about to publish *Substance and Shadow; or Morality and Religion in Their Relation to Life: An Essay on the Physics of Creation* (1863), WJ amused them all, as T. S. Perry remembered, "by designing a small cut to be put on the title-page, representing a man beating a dead horse." Sometimes such freedom struck outsiders as a constraint upon Henry Senior. As Howells remarked, after an evening at the house: "Now and then he'd break out and say something that each of the others had to modify and explain away, and then he'd be clapped back into durance again." But Henry Senior no doubt took all such sallies in the spirit of high comedy in which they were meant.

A year or two after he had debated his father's ideas in his letters from Germany, WJ wrote to HJ:

"Father's book is out, *The Secret of Swedenborg*, and is selling very fast, partly I suppose by virtue of the title, to people who won't read it. I read it, and am very much enlightened as to his ideas and as to his intellectual rank thereby. I am going slowly through his other books. I will write you more when I have read more. Suffice it that many points which before were incomprehensible to me because doubtfully fallacious, I now definitely believe to be entirely fallacious; but as this pile accumulates on one side there is left a more and more definite residuum on the other of great and original ideas, so that my respect for him is on the whole increased rather than diminished. But his ignorance of the way of thinking of other men, and his cool neglect of their difficulties, is fabulous in a writer on such subjects. It is pure theology, and not philosophy commonly so-called, that he deals with."

At that point WJ's own evolving empiricism had taken him about as far away from his father's position as he was ever to go. His letters at the time of the old gentleman's death reveal WJ's consciousness of a much greater debt and kinship. The Introduction that he undertook as a labor of love lives up to its title. It is an admirable piece of exposition, a real *leading into* his father's truths, with copious and judicious quotation from his chief religious works. WJ realizes that he is writing for a positivistic age, in a climate of opinion very different from that which gave rise to his father's theological system; but only at the close does he indicate briefly his own divergences. He thereby produces a very rare document for our intellectual history: an objective portrayal by the leading philosopher of one generation of the dominant philosophy of the generation preceding him, and, at the same time, a record of exactly why and how and where he crossed the divide that separated him from his forebears.

It is interesting to note how in this earliest publication of WJ's own in volume form, and long before he had come before the world with his philosophy, he begins to use the terms that are to be characteristic of him. He concludes that his father's conception of God, though essentially monistic, is "yet warm and living and dramatic enough to speak to the heart of the common pluralistic man." He allies himself with pluralism on the characteristic grounds that "apart from analytic and intellectual arguments, pluralism is a view to which we all practically incline when in the full and successful exercise of our moral energy." He takes his stand against his father's commitment to idealism and absolutism, and even more strongly against his father's opposition to moralism. WJ is already a convinced moralist, and believes in *doing*, not merely in *being*. Very typically he finds this attitude an integral part of "healthy-mindedness," thus introducing the term that he was to illustrate at great length in his *Varieties of Religious Experience*. But even though he contends that any thoroughgoing moralism "must needs be such a healthy-minded pluralism," he grants the validity of another view—the view of religion, the view of those whom he was to call the "sick souls," those to whom all unaided human effort is vanity in the face of our nothingness and of the abyss of evil over which even the best of men always hover. He perceived thereby the depth of his father's religious insight, and spoke also out of the knowledge gained from his own psychological crisis, when he added: "Well, we are all *potentially* such sick men. The sanest and best of us are of one clay with lunatics and prison-inmates."

Half a dozen years after finishing his exposition of his father's work, WJ wrote to Alice: "Father would find in me to-day a much more receptive listener—all *that* philosophy has got to be brought in." Half a dozen years later again he announced: "Religion is the great interest of my life." But he remained fundamentally opposed to his father's attitude towards evil. For Henry Senior evil was not an accident, but a part of God's beneficent plan for the universe: "We have walked the weary road we have walked, and suffered the bitter things we have suffered, not because God hated or condemned us, or had even the faintest shadow of a quarrel with us, but solely because He loved us with unspeakable love, and wooed us in that unsuspected way out of the death we have in ourselves to the embrace of His own incorruptible life." Henry Senior could write in that way because he believed that there could be no good unless there was also evil, no heaven without hell. In his eyes Creation was a drama of love, the drama of man's fall and potential rise. Adam's disobedience was even "fortunate," in that "it made experience possible."

WJ understood what his father meant by experience. In placing Henry Senior among the small group who keep religion "forever alive," he said: "The experience in question has always been an acute despair, passing over into an equally acute optimism, through a passion of renunciation of the self and surrender to the higher power." Charles Saunders Peirce was to hold that "the true solution of the problem of evil is precisely that of *Substance and Shadow*. . . . The real is composed of the potential and actual *together*." But as R. B. Perry has said, WJ "was too sensitive to ignore evil, too moral to tolerate it, and too ardent to accept it as inevitable." He may have suffered more from the existence of evil than his father did. He spoke of the power with which his sense of that existence had haunted him in his youth. Once Henry Senior had passed through his psychological crisis, he remained largely confident, and could hold pessimistic views of the actual evil of mankind along with the most radiant optimism regarding its transformation. But WJ felt, as a young man, the need to rescue himself from what he called his father's "non-optimistic view of nature," and found solace in Goethe's naturalistic pantheism. And despite his growing interest in religion as his life advanced, he always stated that his own personal religious experience was not abundant. His most characteristic role was that of the intense moral champion of many causes, eager to do battle by pitting his will against whatever specific evils he encountered. Yet despite that fundamental difference from his father, the human warmth that radiated from them both was very similar. The "spontaneity" that they both loved and lived by could often leap the gap between the spiritual and the moral. And one of the paternal traits commemorated by WJ at his father's death, "the sense of his right to have a say about the deepest reasons of the universe," endured also as the leading impulse to WJ's philosophy.

* * * * *

. . . It has seemed to me not only a filial but a philosophic duty, in giving these posthumous pages to the world, to prefix to them some such account [1] of their author's ideas as might awaken, in readers hitherto strangers to his writings, the desire to become acquainted with them. I wish a less unworthy hand than mine were there to do the work. As it is, I must screen my own inadequacy under the language of the original, and let my father speak, as far as possible, for himself. It would indeed be foolish to seek to paraphrase anything once directly said by him. The matter would be sure to suffer; for, from the very outset of his literary career, we find him in the effortless possession of that style with which the reader will soon become acquainted, and which, to its great dignity of cadence and full and homely vocabulary, united a sort of inward palpitating human quality, gracious and tender, precise, fierce, scornful, humorous by turns, recalling the rich vascular temperament of the old English masters, rather than that of an American of to-day.

With all the richness of style, the ideas are singularly unvaried and few. Probably few authors have so devoted their entire lives to the monotonous elaboration of one single bundle of truths. Whenever the eye falls upon one of Mr. James's pages,—whether it be a letter to a newspaper or to a friend, whether it be his earliest or his latest book,— we seem to find him saying again and again the same thing; telling us what the true relation is between mankind and its Creator. What he had to say on this point was the burden of his whole life, and its only burden. When he had said it once, he was disgusted with the insufficiency of the formulation (he always hated the sight of his old books), and set himself to work to say it again. But he never analyzed his terms or his data beyond a certain point, and made very few fundamentally new discriminations; so the result of all these successive re-editings was repetition and amplification and enrichment, rather than reconstruction. The student of any one of his works knows, consequently, all that is *essential* in the rest. I must say, however, that the later formulations are philosophically, if not always rhetorically, the best. In "Society the Redeemed Form of Man," which was composed while the lingering

---

[1] I have omitted from WJ's Introduction a little of the prefatory material, and some of the notes containing longer illustrative quotations.—F. O. M.

effects of an apoplectic stroke had not passed away, there are passages unsurpassed in any former writing. And in the work herewith published, although most of it was written when my father's *general* mental powers were visibly altered by a decay of strength that ended with his death, I doubt if his earlier readers will discover any signs of intellectual decrepitude. His truths were his life; they were the companions of his death-bed; and when all else had ebbed away, his grasp of them was still vigorous and sure.

As aforesaid, they were truths theological. This is anything but a theological age, as we all know; and so far as it permits itself to be theological at all, it is growing more and more to distrust all systems that aim at abstract metaphysics in dogma, or pretend to rigor in their terms. The conventional and traditional acquiescence we find in the older dogmatic formularies is confined to those who are intellectually hardly vitalized enough either to apprehend or discuss a novel and rival creed; whilst those of us who have intellectual vitality are either apt to be full of bias against theism in any form, or if we are theistic at all, it is in such a tentative and supplicating sort of way that the sight of a robust and dogmatizing theologian sends a shiver through our bones. A man like my father, lighting on such a time, is wholly out of his element and atmosphere, and is soon left stranded high and dry. His effectiveness as a missionary is null; and it is wonderful if his voice, crying in the wilderness and getting no echo, do not soon die away for sheer discouragement. That my father should not have been discouraged, but should have remained serene and active to the last, is a proof both of the stoutness of his heart and of the consolations of his creed. How many unknown persons may have received help and suggestion from his writings it is impossible to say. Of out-and-out disciples he had very few who ever named themselves. Few as they were, his correspondence with them was perhaps his principal solace and recreation.

I have often tried to imagine what sort of a figure my father might have made, had he been born in a genuinely theological age, with the best minds about him fermenting with the mystery of the Divinity, and the air full of definitions and theories and counter-theories, and strenuous reasonings and contentions, about God's relations to mankind. Floated on such a congenial tide, furthered by sympathetic comrades, and opposed no longer by blank silence but by passionate and definite resistance, he would infallibly have developed his resources in many ways which, as it was, he never tried; and he would have played a prominent, perhaps a momentous and critical, part in the struggles of his time, for he was a religious prophet and genius, if ever prophet and genius there were. He published an intensely positive, radical, and fresh conception of God, and an intensely vital view of our connection with him. And nothing shows better the altogether lifeless and unintellectual character of the professional theism of our time, than the fact that this view, this conception, so vigorously thrown down, should not have stirred the faintest tremulation on its stagnant pool.

The centre of his whole view of things is this intense conception of God as a creator. Grant it, accept it without criticism, and the rest follows. He nowhere attempts by metaphysical or empirical arguments to make the existence of God plausible; he simply assumes it as something that must be confessed. As has been well said in a recent little work,[1] "Mr. James looks at creation instinctively from the creative side; and this has a tendency to put him at a remove from his readers. The usual problem is,—given the creation, to find the creator. To Mr. James it is,—given the creator, to find the creation. God is; of His being there is no doubt; but who and what are *we?*"

To sceptics of theism in any possible form, this fundamental postulate may naturally prove a barrier. But it is difficult to see why it should be an obstacle to professedly Christian students. They also confess God's existence; and the way in which Mr. James took it *au grand sérieux,* and the issues he read in it, ought, one would suppose, to speak to them with some accent of reality. Like any early Jewish prophet, like the Luther described in a recent work of genius,[2] he went back so far and so deep as to find the religious sentiment in its purest and most unsophisticated form. He lived and breathed as one who knew he had not made himself, but was the work of a power that let him live from one moment to the next, and could do with him what it pleased. His intellect reacted on his sense of the presence of this power, so as to form a *system* of the most radical and self-consistent, as well as of the most simple, kind. I will essay to give the reader a preliminary notion of what its main elements and outlines were, and then try to build up a more adequate representation of it by means of quotations from the author's own pen.

It had many and diverse affinities. It was optimistic in one sense, pessimistic in another. Pantheistic, idealistic, hegelian, are epithets that very naturally arise on the reader's lips to describe it; and yet some part there is of the connotation of each of these epithets that made my father violently refuse to submit to their imposition. The ordinary empirical ethics of evolutionary naturalism can find a perfect *permis de séjour* under the system's wings; and yet close alongside is an insistence on the need of the death of the natural man and of a supernatural redemption, more thorough-going than what we find in the most evangelical protestantism. Dualism, yet monism; antinomianism, yet restraint; atheism (as we might almost name it,—that is, the swallowing up of God in

---

[1] *Philosophy of Henry James: A Digest.* By J. A. Kellogg. New York, 1883.

[2] J. Milsand: *Luther et le Serf-Arbitre.* Paris, 1884. *Passim.*

Humanity) as the last result of God's achievement,—such are some of
the first aspects of this at bottom very simple and harmonious view of
the world.

It all flowed from two perceptions, insights, convictions, whatever
one pleases to call them, in its author's mind. In the first place, he felt
that the individual man, as such, is nothing, but owes all he is and has to
the race nature he inherits, and to the society into which he is born.
And, secondly, he scorned to admit, even as a possibility, that the great
and loving Creator, who has all the being and the power, and has
brought us as far as *this*, should not bring us *through*, and *out*, into the
most triumphant harmony.

I beseech the reader from now onwards to listen to my stammering
exposition in a very uncritical mood of mind. Do not *squeeze* the terms
or the logic too hard! And if you are a positivist, do not be too prompt
to throw the book down with an ejaculation of disgust at Alexandrian
theosophizing, and of wonder that such brain-spinning should find a
printer at the present day. My father's own disgust at any abstract statement of his system could hardly be excelled by that of the most positivistic reader. I will not say that the logical relations of its terms were
with him a mere afterthought; they were more organic than that. But
the core and centre of the thing in him was always instinct and attitude,
something realized at a stroke, and felt like a fire in his breast; and all
attempts at articulate verbal formulations of it were makeshifts of a
more or less desperately impotent kind. This is why he despised every
formulation he made as soon as it was uttered, and set himself to the
Sisyphus-labor of producing a new one that should be less irrelevant. I
remember hearing him groan, when struggling in this way, "Oh, that
I might thunder it out in a single interjection that would tell the *whole*
of it, and never speak a word again!" But he paid his tribute to necessity; and few writers in the end were more prolix than he.

To begin then,—trying to think the matter in as simple, childlike, and
empirical a fashion as possible,—the negativity and dearth of the creature (which is surely a part of the truth we livingly feel every day of
our lives) [1] is an elementary and primitive factor in the creative prob-

---

[1] Empirically, we know that we are
creatures with a lack, a destitution, a
death, an ultimate helplessness. Which
of us but sometimes "lifts a pallid face
in prayer to God, lest some hideous
calamity engulf his fairest hopes? . . .
We are all without real selfhood, without the selfhood which comes from
God alone. We have only a showy and
fallacious one . . . which is wholly inadequate to guarantee us against calamity. We shiver in every breeze, and
stand aghast at every cloud that passes
over the sun. When our ships go down
at sea, what shrieks we hear from
blanched and frenzied lips peopling the
melancholy main, perturbing the sombre
and sympathetic air for months afterwards! When our children die, and take
back to heaven the brimming innocence
which our corrupt manhood feels no
use for, and therefore knows not how
to shelter; when our friends drop off;
when our property exhales; when our

lem. It plays an active and dynamic part through Mr. James's pages, and is the feature which made me say, a moment back, that "hegelian" would be a very natural epithet to use in describing the doctrine they set forth. Hegel sometimes speaks of the Divinity making an illusion first, in order to remove it; setting up his own antithesis in order to the subsequent neutralization thereof. And this will also very well describe the creative drama as pictured by Mr. James, provided one bear in mind that the preliminary production of an illusory stage of being is *forced* upon the Creator by the character of that *positively yawning emptiness* which is the opposite of himself, and with which he has to deal.

The ordinary orthodox view of creation is that Jehovah explodes the universe absolutely out of what was previously pure blank; his *fiat* whacks it down upon the *tabula rasa* of time and space, and there it remains. Such simple, direct, and "magical" creation is always derided by Mr. James as a childish idea. The *real* nothingness cannot become thus promptly the seat of real being; it must taint with its own "abysmal destitution" whatever first comes to fill it, and reduce it to the status of a sham, or unreal magic-lantern picture projected on the dark inane.

This first result of the intercourse of the creative energy with the void may *become* however, by decaying unto itself, a surface of rebound for *another* movement, of which the result is real. Creation is thus made up of two stages, the first of which is mere scaffolding to the second, which is the final work. Mr. James's terminology is a little vacillating with regard to these two stages. On the whole, "formation" is the word he oftenest applies to the first stage, and "redemption" to the second. His view of the matter is obviously entirely different from the simple, direct process taught by natural theology and by the Jewish Scripture; and it as obviously agrees in point of form with the composite movement of the Christian scheme.

All this is verbally simple enough; but what are the facts it covers? To speak very oracularly, *Nature* is for Mr. James the movement of formation, the first quickening of the void unto itself; and *Society* is the movement of redemption, or the finished spiritual work of God.

Now, both "Nature" and "Society" are words of peculiar and com-

---

reason totters on its throne, and menaces us with a downfall,—who then is strong? Who in fact, if he were left in these cases for a moment to himself,—that is, if he were not steadied in his own despite by the mere life of routine and tradition,—but would be ready to renounce God and perish? So too our *ennui* and prevalent disgust of life, which lead so many suffering souls every year to suicide, which drive so many tender and yearning and angel-freighted natures to drink, to gambling, to fierce and ruinous excess of all sorts, —what are these things but the tacit avowal (audible enough, however, to God!) that we are nothing at all and vanity; that we are absolutely without help in ourselves; and that we can never be blessed and tranquil until God take compassion on us, and conjoin us livingly and immortally with himself?"— *Christianity the Logic of Creation*, p. 133.

plex meaning in Mr. James's writings, so that much explanation is needed of the assertions just laid down.

"Nature" and "Society," if I understand our author correctly, do not differ from each other at all in substance or material. Their substance is the Creator himself, for he is the sole positive substance in the universe, all else being nothingness.[1] But they differ in form; for while Nature is the Creator immersed and lost in a nothingness self-affirming and obstructive, Society is the same Creator, with the nothingness saved, determined to transparency and self-confession, and traversed from pole to pole by his life-giving rays.

The *matter* covered by both these words is Humanity and the totality of its conditions, nothing short of the entire world of phenomenal experience,—mineral, vegetable, animal, and human,—"Nature" culminating in, whilst "Society" starts from, the moral and religious consciousness of man. This is why I said the system could hospitably house anything that naturalistic evolutionism might ever have to say about man; for, according to both doctrines, man's morality and religion, his consciousness of self and his moral conscience, are natural products like everything else we see. Now, for Mr. James, the consciousness of self and the conscience are the hinges on which the process of creation turns, as it slowly revolves from its formative and natural to its redeemed and spiritual position of equilibrium. What I say will still be dark and unreal enough to those who know nothing of the original; but the exercise of a little patience will erelong make things clear.

What is self-consciousness or morality? and what is conscience or religion?—for our author uses synonymously the terms within each pair. The terminology is at first bewildering, and the metaphysical results confounding; for whilst the *stuff* of both morality and religion is, so to speak, the very energy, the very being, of God himself, yet in morality that being takes wholly, and in religion it takes partly, the form of a lie. Let us consider the matter *naïvely* and mythically, so as to understand. Remember, that for Mr. James a mere resistless "bang" is no creative process at all, and that a *real* creation means nothing short of a real *bringing to life* of the essential nothingness, which is the eternal antithesis to God,—a *work*, therefore, upon that nothingness actually performed. Well, then, God must work upon the void; but how can the trackless void be wrought upon? It must first be vivified and quick-

---

[1] This is why I said one might call the system pantheistic. Mr. James denounces pantheism, however; for he supposes it to exclude a dualism even of *logical* elements, and to represent the Divine as manifesting itself in phenomena by a simple outward movement without subsequent recoil. It is a matter of verbal definition after all. One might say that the gist of his differences, both with pantheism and with ordinary theism, is that while the latter represent creation to be essentially the formation of Two out of an original One, to Mr. James it is something more like the union into One of an original Two.

ened into some kind of substantiality of its own, and made existential and phenomenal instead of merely logical and essential that it was, before any further fashioning of it can take place. God then must, *in the first instance*, make a being that has the void for its other parent, and *involves* nothingness in itself. To make a long story short, then, God's first product is a Nature *subject to self-consciousness or selfhood*,—that is, a Nature essentially good, as being divine, but the several members whereof *appropriate* the goodness, and egoistically and atheistically [1] seek to identify it with their private selves. This selfishness of the several members is the trail of the serpent over creation, the coming to life of the ancestral void. It negates, because it entirely inverts, God's own energy, which is undiluted altruistic love; it intercepts the truth of his impartial flowing tides; it is an utter lie, and yet a lie under the dense and unsuspecting mask of which alone "the great and sincere Creator of men" is able gradually to conciliate our instincts, and win us over to the truth.

This happens whenever we are weaned from the lie; for the abandoning of the lie in this instance coalesces in the same conscious act with the confessing of the truth. "I am nothing as substantive,—I am everything as recipient"; this is a thought in which both I and the Creator figure, but in which we figure in perfectly harmonious and truthful guise. It is accordingly the threshold of spiritual life; and instead of obstructing and striving to intercept, it welcomes and furthers all that the divine Love may have in store for every member of the created family.

The agents of the *weaning* are conscience and religion. In the philosophy before us, these faculties are considered to have no other function than that of being ministers of death to the fallacious selfhood. They have no positive worth or character, and are mere clearers of the way. They bring no new content upon the scene; they simply permit the pre-existing content to settle into a new and truer form. The facts of our nature with every man in it blinded with pride and jealousy, and stiffened in exclusiveness and self-seeking, are one thing,—that thing whose destinies Church and State are invoked to control, and whose

---

[1] "That is to say, the only hindrance to men's believing in God as a creator is their inability to believe in *themselves* as created. Self-consciousness, the sentiment of personality, the feeling I have of life in myself, absolute and underived from any other save in a natural way, is so subtly and powerfully atheistic, that, no matter how loyally I may be taught to insist upon creation as a mere traditional or legendary fact, I never feel inclined personally to believe in it, save as the fruit of some profound intellectual humiliation or hopeless inward vexation of spirit. My inward *afflatus* from this cause is so great, I am conscious of such superabounding personal life, that I am satisfied, for my own part at least, that my sense of selfhood must in some subtle exquisite way find itself wounded to death—find itself *become death* in fact, *the only death I am capable of believing in*—before any genuine spiritual resuscitation is at all practicable for me."—*Society the Redeemed Form of Man*, p. 185.

tragic and discordant history we partly know. Those very same facts, after conscience and religion have played their part, and undermined the illusion of the self, so that men acknowledge their life to come from God, and love each other as God loves, having no exclusive private cares, will form the kingdom of heaven on earth, the regenerate social order which none of us yet know. In a word, God will be fully incarnated at last in a form that no longer contradicts his character, in what Mr. James calls, with Swedenborg, the Divine-Natural Humanity. God's real creature is this aggregate Humanity. He cannot be partial to one fractional unit of us more than to another. And the only difference between the unredeemed and the regenerate social form lies in the simple fact, that in the former the units *will* not fall into relations accordant with this truth, while in the latter, such an attitude is the one they most spontaneously assume. One Substance, extricating itself by finding at last a true form,—such is the process, once begun! And no one *part* is either "lost" or "saved" in any other sense than that it either arrests or furthers the transmission through itself to others of God's life-giving tides.

This probably sounds to most ears thin and cold and mythical enough,—the "Divine-Natural Humanity" especially, with its abolition of selfishness, appearing quite as shallow and insipid a dream as any other paradise excogitated by imaginative man. This is the inevitable result of trying to express didactically and articulately, in the form of a story, what in its origin is more like an intuition, sentiment, or attitude of the soul. The matter shall be immediately thickened and filled out to the reader's understanding by quotations from Mr. James himself, touching successively the various elements of the scheme. But if I may be permitted an opinion here, I should say that in no such successive shape as this did the scheme have *authority* over Mr. James's own mind. I fancy that his belief in its truth was strongest when the dumb sense of human life, sickened and baffled as it is forever by the strange unnatural fever in its breast of unreality and dearth struggling with infinite fulness and possession, became a sort of voice within him, and cried out, "This *must* stop! The good, the good, is really *there*, and *must* see to its own! Who is its own? Is it this querulous usurping, jealous *me*, sickened of defeat and done to death, and glad never to raise its head again? Never more! It is some sweeter, larger, more innocent and generous receptacle of life than that cadaverous and lying thing can ever be.[1] Let *that* but be removed, and the other may come

---

[1] "Just in proportion, accordingly, as a man's spiritual knowledge improves, will his contempt for himself, as an unmixed spiritual tramp and irredeemable vagabond, increase and abound. We might very well bear with an uninstructed or inexperienced child, who, shut up to the companionship of its doll, constructed all of sawdust and prunella, looks upon it as spiritually alive; but one has no patience with an experienced, instructed man or churchman,

in. And there must be a way to remove it, for God himself is there, and cannot be frustrated forever of his aim,—least of all by such an obstacle as that! He must *somehow*, and by eternal necessity he *shall*, bring the kingdom of heaven about!"

I may as well say here, once for all, that the kingdom of heaven postulated in this deep and simple way, and then more articulately formulated as the "Divine-Natural Humanity," remained to the end a mere postulate or programme in my father's pages, and never received at his hands any concrete filling out. It was what *must* come to be, if God truly exist,—an assumption we *owe* to his power and his love, and that any man with a sense of God's reality will scorn to hesitate to make. That, moreover, the kingdom was to be made of no other stuff than the actual stuff of human nature, was but another tribute,—a tribute of manly loyalty to the real divinity of the Good existing in the human bosom now. In his earlier years, between 1842 and 1850, when Mr. James's ideas were being settled by the reading of Swedenborg, he also became interested in the socialistic fermentations then so rife, and in particular in the writings of Fourier. His first two works shadow forth the Divine-Natural Humanity as about to be born, through the yoking of the passions into harmonious social service, by the growth of socialistic organization, in place of the old régime of Church and State, among men. Since then, there have been many disappointments, in which he shared; and although Fourier's system was never displaced from his mind as at least a provisional representation of possible redeemed life, I think that at the last he cared little to dispute about matters of detail, being willing to cast the whole burden upon God, who would be sure to order it rightly when all the conditions were fulfilled.

I will now let the author speak as much as possible for himself. And perhaps the best way to begin is to cull a few of the numerous passages in which he succinctly states the necessities which, by its own intrinsic logic, the problem of creation involves.

"Nothing can be so intensely antagonistic to the conception of a creator as that of a creature. To create is one thing; to be created is the total and exact opposite of that thing. For what is one's *nature* as a creature? It is abject want or destitution. To be created is to be void of all things in one's self, and to possess them only in another; and if I am the creature accordingly of an infinite creator, my want of course must be infinite. The nature of a thing is what the thing is in itself, and apart from foreign interference. And evidently what the creature is in him-

---

who undergoes precisely the same hallucination with regard to his own worthless doll of a selfhood,—which is destitute even of so much as a sawdust and prunella reality,—and conceives that the Divine being has nothing better to do than literally to bestow divine and immortal life upon that dead, corrupt, and stinking thing."—*New Church Independent*, September, 1879, p. 413.

self, and apart from the creator, is sheer nothingness; that is to say, sheer want or destitution,—destitution of all things, whether of life, of existence, or even of being. So that to give the creature natural form or selfhood, is merely to vivify the infinite void he is in himself; is merely to organize in living form the universal destitution he is under with respect to the creative fulness." [1]

"If, accordingly, the creative love should scruple to permit *proprium* or selfhood to its creature, scruple to endow him with moral consciousness, it would withhold from him all conscious life or joy, and leave him a mere form of vegetative existence. Creation, to allow of any true fellowship or equality between creator and creature, demands that the creature be *himself*,—that is, be *naturally* posited to his own consciousness. And he cannot be thus posited save in so far as the creative love vivifies his essential destitution, organizes it in living form, and by the experience thus engendered in the created bosom lays a basis for any amount of free or spiritual reaction in the creature towards the uncreated good.

"One sees at a glance, then, how very discreditable a thing creation would be to the creator, and how very injurious to the creature, if it stopped short in itself,—that is, contented itself with simply giving the creature natural selfhood, or antagonizing him with the creator. Nothing could be more hideous to conceive of than a creation which should end by exhibiting the subjective antagonism of its two factors, without providing for their subsequent objective reconciliation; which should show every cupidity incident to the abstract *nature* of the creature inflamed to infinitude, while the helpless creature *himself* at the same time was left to be the unlimited prey of his nature." [2]

"I attempt no apology, accordingly, for Swedenborg's doctrine on this subject, but applaud it with all my heart. I perfectly agree with him that *redemption* and not creation avouches the proper glory of the Divine name. Creation is not, and cannot be, the final word of the Divine dealings with us. It has at most a rigidly subjective efficacy as affording us self-consciousness, and not the least objective value as affording us any spiritual fellowship of the Divine perfection. To be naturally created indeed—to be created an image of God—is to be anything except a spiritual likeness of him. The law of the image is subjectively to invert the lineaments of its original. . . . And to be spiritually *like* God is inwardly to undo this subjective inversion of the divine perfection to which we find ourselves naturally born or created, and put on that direct or objective presentation of it to which we are historically reborn or re-created." [3]

"You see, in short, how infinitely remote from spiritual sonship to

---

[1] *Secret of Swedenborg*, p. 47.   [3] Ibid., p. 48.
[2] Ibid., p. 132.

God our natural creation leaves us, and how obligatory it is upon him therefore, if he would ever spiritually affiliate us to himself, to give us redemption from our own nature. And this great redemption, how shall it ever be able to come about? By the very nature of the case, *the sphere of its evolution is restricted to the limits of the created consciousness,* so that the creator can command absolutely no enginery to effect it which is not supplied exclusively by the resources of that consciousness." [1]

The tragic evolution of the selfhood itself, "a limitation upon human life which *on its face* is one of inconceivable malignity," is the only enginery required. But of its tragedy anon. Meanwhile—

"In truth, this altogether unobtrusive fact of selfhood or natural life which we are all born to, and which we therefore think nothing of, but accept as a mere matter of course, is itself the eternal marvel of creation. We ourselves can modify existence almost at pleasure; we can change the form of existing things,—that is, can convert natural forms into artificial ones. But we cannot confer life; cannot make these artificial forms self-conscious or living. We can turn a block of wood into a table, a block of stone into a statue; but our work in no wise reflects the vivacity of Nature, because we not being life in ourselves cannot possibly communicate life to the work of our hands. We frame a beautiful effigy of life; but the effigy remains forever uninhabited, forever irresponsive to the love which fashions it; in short, forever unconscious or dead.

"Now, the splendor of the creative activity is that it makes even this effigy of itself alive with the amplest life; its product being no cold inanimate statue, but a living, breathing, exulting person. In short, the everlasting miracle is that God is able, in giving us himself, to endow us with our own finite selfhood as well; leaving us thereby so unidentified with himself, so utterly free and untrammelled to our own consciousness, as to be able very often seriously to doubt, and not seldom permanently to deny, his own existence. And this miracle, I say, is utterly inexplicable upon any *datum* but that I have alleged; namely, that God is so truly infinite in love as not to shrink from shrouding his uncreated splendor in his creature's lineaments, from eternally humiliating himself to the lowest possibilities of creaturely imbecility and iniquity, in order that the creature may thus become freely or spiritually elevated to the otherwise impracticable heights of his majestic wisdom and goodness.

"I ask no indulgence of my reader for this language. I literally mean what I say, that creation is absolutely contingent upon the Divine ability to humble himself to the creature's level, to diminish himself to the creature's *natural* dimensions. Language is incapable of painting too

---

[1] Ibid., p. 57.

vividly the strength of my convictions on this subject. If the creature by the bare fact of his creatureship be demonstrably void of life in himself, then the creator can only succeed in rescuing him from this intrinsic death, and elevating him to himself by first abasing himself to the creature; that is, allowing his proper infinitude or perfection to be so swallowed up in the other's proper finiteness or imperfection, as never by any possibility to come into the least overt collision with it. Thus, whenever I draw a breath or perform any automatic function; when I see or hear or smell or taste or touch; when I hunger or thirst; when I think or take cognizance of any truth; when I glow with passion; when I do good or evil to my fellow-man,—my ability in all these cases is due exclusively to the great truth that God's love to me is so truly *infinite* (that is, untainted by the least admixture of love to himself) as to permit him, within the entire periphery of my consciousness, physical, intellectual, and moral, to veil himself so effectually from sight, to obscure and as it were annihilate himself so completely on my behalf, that I cannot help *feeling* myself to exist absolutely or irrespectively of him, and enjoy a conscious ability not only to do what is congruous with his ultimate good pleasure in me, but to abound, if I please, at any moment in all manner of profane, injurious, and filthy behavior." [1]

"There is no alternative if creation is really to take place. The creative love must either disavow its infinitude, and so renounce creation, or else it must frankly submit to all the degradation the created nature imposes upon it,—that is, it must consent to be converted from infinite love in itself to an altogether finite love in the creature," namely, the love of self. "This is the only true or philosophic conception of creation,—namely, the abandonment of yourself to what is not yourself in a manner so intimate and hearty, as that you thenceforth shall utterly disappear within the precincts of its existence; shall become phenomenally extinct within the entire realm of its personality, while it alone shall appear to be." The divine creation is no exception to this law, which "necessitates that the creature shall not even appear to be save by the creator's actual or objective disappearance within all the field of his subjective consciousness; save by the creator's becoming objectively merged, obscured, drowned out, so to speak, in the created subjectivity."

Elsewhere the same truth is expressed in a way which to ordinary ears might sound almost revoltingly paradoxical, but which can alone bring out the full depth of its meaning.

"Creator and creature, then, are strictly correlated existences,—the latter remorselessly implicating or involving the former; the former in

---

[1] *Substance and Shadow,* pp. 83, 84.

his turn assiduously explicating or evolving the latter. The Creator is in truth the inferior term of the relation, and the creature its superior term; although in point of appearance the relationship is reversed,—the Creator being thought to be primary and controlling, while the creature is thought secondary and subservient. The truth incurs this humiliation, undergoes this falsification, on *our* behalf exclusively, who, because we have by nature no perception of God as a spirit, but only as a person like ourselves, are even brutally ignorant of the divine power and ways. But it *is* a sheer humiliation nevertheless; for in very truth it is the Creator alone who gives subjective constitution to us, only that we, appearing to ourselves thereupon absolutely to be, may ever after give objective reality to him.[1] Thus creation is not a something outwardly achieved by God in space and time, but a something inwardly wrought by him within the compass exclusively of human nature or human consciousness; a something subjectively conceived by his love, patiently borne or elaborated by his wisdom, and painfully brought forth by his power,—just as the child is subjectively conceived, patiently borne, and painfully brought forth by the mother. Creation is no brisk activity on God's part, but only a long patience or suffering. It is no ostentatious self-assertion, no dazzling parade of magical, irrational, or irresponsible power; it is an endless humiliation or prorogation of himself to all the lowest exigencies of the created consciousness. In short, it is no finite divine action, as we stupidly dream, giving the creature objective or absolute projection from his creator; it is in truth and exclusively an infinite divine passion, which, all in giving its creature subjective or phenomenal existence, contrives to convert this provisional existence of his into objective or real being, by freely endowing the created nature with all its own pomp of love, of wisdom, and of power."

These two conceptions, of God's unendingly patient self-surrender to us, and of our intrinsic nothingness, formed the deepest springs of Mr. James's view of life. He has no words of scorn too deep for the venerable notion of Christian theology that God creates for his own glory; and when he vindicates his own idea of the divine character, it is in language by whose passionate fervor all must be impressed.

Here are some passages in point:—

"It is an easy enough thing to find a holiday God who is all too selfish to be touched with the infirmities of his own creatures,—a God, for example, who has nought to do but receive assiduous court for a work of creation done myriads of ages ago, and which is reputed to have cost him in the doing neither pains nor patience, neither affection nor

---

[1] As *effective* Creator, namely. A few redundant words have been omitted from the passage, which will be found in the *Secret of Swedenborg*, pp. 185, 186.

thought, but simply the utterance of a dramatic word; and who is willing, accordingly, to accept our decorous Sunday homage in ample
quitance of obligations so unconsciously incurred on our part, so lightly
rendered and so penuriously sanctioned on his. Every sect, every nation, every family almost, offers some pet idol of this description to our
worship. But I am free to confess that I have long outgrown this loutish
conception of deity. I can no longer bring myself to adore a characteristic activity in the God of my worship, which falls below the
secular average of human character. In fact, what I crave with all my
heart and understanding,—what my very flesh and bones cry out for,
—is no longer a Sunday but a week-day divinity, a working God,
grimy with the dust and sweat of our most carnal appetites and passions, and bent not for an instant upon inflating our worthless pietistic
righteousness, but upon the patient, toilsome, thorough cleansing of our
physical and moral existence from the odious defilement it has contracted, until we each and all present at last in body and mind the
deathless effigy of his own uncreated loveliness." [1]

"Accordingly, when orthodoxy commends God, the universal creator, to our rational reverence and affection, under the guise of a great
melodramatic being so essentially heartless as to live for untold eterni-
ties without feeling any desire for companionship, so essentially irrational that it cost him no effort of thought to summon the universe into
absolute being"; when "natural religion represents creation as an act of
pure will on God's part, a movement of simple caprice, involving not
one particle of the honest labor and sweat which go to the execution of
any humane enterprise,—say, the growing or the making or the baking
of a loaf of bread,"—"I will not acknowledge a God so void of human
worth, so every way level to the character of a mere ostentatious showman or conjuror. It is just such a childish caricature of deity as Byron
might paint to match those childish caricatures of manhood with which
his purulent imagination runs riot. I am constrained by every inspiration of true manhood to demand for my worship a perfectly human
deity; that is to say, a deity who is so intent upon rescuing every creature he has made, from the everlasting death and damnation he bears
about in himself *as finitely constituted*, as not to shrink if need be from
humbling himself to every patient form of ignominy, and feeding contentedly year in and year out, century after century, and millennium
after millennium, upon the literal breath of our self-righteous contempt." [2]

"We laugh, as I said awhile ago, at an inventor who should ask us to
take his genius on trust, or without any evidence of its reality. And
there can be no more offensive tribute to the divine name than to show

---

[1] *Secret of Swedenborg*, pp. 6, 7.   [2] *Substance and Shadow*, pp. 72, 73.

him a deference we deny to the rankest charlatan. How infinitely unworthy of God it would be to exact or expect of the absolute and
unintelligent creatures of his power a belief out of all proportion to
their sensible knowledge, or unbacked by anything but tradition! . . .
I am free to confess for my own part that I have no belief in God's
absolute or irrelative and unconditional perfection. I have not the least
sentiment of worship for his name, the least sentiment of awe or reverence towards him, considered as a perfect person sufficient unto himself. That style of deity exerts no attraction either upon my heart or
understanding. Any mother who suckles her babe upon her own breast,
any bitch in fact who litters her periodical brood of pups, presents to
my imagination a vastly nearer and sweeter divine charm. What do I
care for a goodness which boasts of a hopeless aloofness from my own
nature, except to hate it with a manly inward hatred? And what do I
care for a truth which professes to be eternally incommunicable to its
own starving progeny, but to avert myself from it with a manly outward contempt? Let men go on to cherish under whatever name of
virtue, or wisdom, or power they will the idol of self-sufficiency; I for
my part will cherish the name of him alone whose insufficiency to himself is so abject that he is incapable *of realizing himself except in others.*
In short, I neither can nor will spiritually confess any deity who is not
essentially *human,* and existentially thence exclusively *natural;* that is to
say, devoid of all distinctively personal or limitary pretensions." [1]
    It is plain enough that a God like this can be neither a judge, nor a
respecter, of persons; that every creature, as such, must be as dear to
him as every other; and that private differences must be melted down
in the warmth of his charity, as dust disappears in a furnace blast. *Our*
desperate clinging to private differences is what makes us the great enemies we are to the Creator, and is the next point it will be well to
take up.
    Mr. James uses the words "proprium" and "selfhood" to designate
what more properly should be called selfishness or self-love; for the
faculty in question is evidently not the mere cognitive awareness of
one's self as a special part of all existence,—which would be self-consciousness merely,—but an active emotional interest in the part so sin-
gled out, to the exclusion of the rest. Mr. James calls it sometimes the
deliverance of our "consciousness," sometimes that of our "sense."
Sometimes he calls it our "morality,"—a very unusual use of the word,
but one which has deep reasons in his system. On the whole, however,
he has no properly psychological doctrine on the subject, but merely
takes his stand upon the empirical fact that this surly and jealous principle exists within us, and then proceeds to tell its function and its fate.

---

[1] *Society the Redeemed Form of Man,* pp. 333, 334.

"Morality expresses the sentiment I have of my own absoluteness, the feeling I have of a selfhood strictly independent of that of any other man. . . . It gives us that ample individual development and nursing, that affluent preliminary experience of our finite selves, which is necessary to base or engender our subsequent unlimited social expansion. It lifts us out of the mud of animality, out of the mire of mere natural passion and appetite, and endows us with selfhood or soul,—that is, with the sense of a life so much more intimate and near than that of the body, as to lead us to identify ourselves with it or to cleave to it alone, cheerfully forsaking all things for it, . . . so allying us to our own inexperienced imaginations with God; giving us that sentiment of individual power and glory which is unknown to the animal nature, and which is the coarse rude germ of all our subsequent conceptions of spiritual things; whispering in short in our fondest hearts, *Ye shall be as God, knowing good and evil.* . . .

"Self-assertion is thus so clearly the fundamental law, the vital breath, of our moral life, that it is no wonder we cling to that life as the true end of our being, and require an internal divine quickening, or the denunciatory voice of conscience, before we consent to regard it simply as a means to an infinitely higher end,—which is our unity with all mankind. The inspiration of the moral sentiment, the sentiment of selfhood, is so powerful within us; it is so sweet to feel this delicious bosom inmate disengage itself from its gross carnal envelope, and come forth a radiant white-armed Eve, full-formed in all divine vigor and beauty, —that we cannot help clasping it to our bosoms as thenceforth bone of our bone and flesh of our flesh, cheerfully forsaking for it father and mother, or all we have traditionally loved and traditionally believed, and cleaving undismayed to its fortunes though it lead us through the gloom of death and the fires of hell. . . .

"Self-love is the vital atmosphere of morality, and there can be no extrication from it but by honest conflict with it,—conflict if need be even unto death. Some men have been more grievously lacerated in this conflict than others, going down to their graves scourged by the contempt of the proud and unthinking, with banners once so lofty now all trailing in the dust of men's reproach. But this is not because they were spiritually any worse than other men; probably the exact contrary. It is only because they had fifty times the ordinary amount of moral or self-righteous force to start with, and it could only become spiritually weakened and overcome by this terrific personal humiliation." [1]

If the creature's *nature* were anything other than the mere provisional scaffolding it is, there would be no need of extrication, of conflict, of the quickening within it of a self doomed to humiliation and defeat. In that case there might be no consciousness of self at all. All

---

[1] *Substance and Shadow*, pp. 137–40.

flesh might "*sensibly* perceive God to be the sole life of the universe. But were this so, we should sit like stocks and stones, leaving him who obviously was life to the exclusive appropriation and enjoyment of it." On the other hand, we might imagine ourselves endowed with a prosperous and harmonious self from the start, and creation beginning and ending with the Garden of Eden,[1]—"a state of blissful infantile delight, unperturbed as yet by those fierce storms of the intellect which are soon to envelop and sweep it away, but also unvisited by a single glimpse of that divine and halcyon calm of heart in which these hideous storms will finally rock themselves to sleep. Nothing can indeed be more remote (except in pure imagery) from distinctively *human* attributes, or from the spontaneous life of man, than this sleek and comely Adamic condition, provided it should turn out an abiding one; because man in that case would prove a mere dimpled nursling of the skies, without ever rising into the slightest divine communion or fellowship, without ever realizing a truly divine manhood and dignity,—mere unfermented dough, insipid and impracticable. . . . He would have mineral body and consequent inertia, no doubt; he would have vegetable form, and consequent growth; he would have animal life and consequent motion,—but he would be without all power of human action, because he would lack that constant permeation and interpenetration of his spirit by the living spirit of God, which weaves his pallid natural annals into the purple tissue of history, and separates man from Nature by all the plenitude and power of incarnate deity." [2]

But the consciousness of self *cannot* be innocent and prosperous. Being, as it is, a mere magic-lantern-phantom cast by the divine love upon essential nothingness, it must reveal the void on which it is based, and have a *tragic* history, if it have a history at all. The experience of the working out of the tragedy of the self is called by our author sometimes "conscience," and sometimes "religion."

"By religion I mean—what is invariably meant by the term where the thing itself still exists—such a conscience on man's part of a forfeiture of the divine favor, as perpetually urges him to make sacrifices of his ease, his convenience, his wealth, and if need be his life, in order to restore himself, if so it be possible, to that favor. This is religion in its literal form; natural religion; religion as it stands authenticated by the universal instincts of the race, before it has undergone a spiritual conversion into life, and while claiming still a purely ritual embodiment." [3]

---

[1] Mr. James, following Swedenborg, often calls the creature abstracted from moral consciousness, the Adam; the moral consciousness being the Eve. *Homo* and *vir* are terms symbolizing the same distinction.

[2] *Christianity the Logic of Creation,* p. 120.

[3] Mr. James scorned to apply the word religion to any experience whose starting point was not pessimistic. Our modern optimism made him complain that "religion in the old virile sense of the word has disappeared from sight

"Every man who has reached even his intellectual teens begins to suspect this; begins to suspect that life is no farce; that it is not genteel comedy even; that it flowers and fructifies on the contrary out of the profoundest tragic depths,—the depths of the essential dearth in which its subject's roots are plunged. . . . The natural inheritance of every one who is capable of spiritual life, is an unsubdued forest where the wolf howls and every obscene bird of night chatters.[1] The only valid natural superiority I can claim to the animal, lies in the fact that I have *conscience* and he has not. And the only valid moral superiority I can claim to my fellow-man is, that I am more hearty in my allegiance to

---

and become replaced by a feeble Unitarian sentimentality. The old religion involved a conscience of the profoundest antagonism between God and the worshipper, which utterly refused to be placated by anything short of an unconditional pledge of the utmost divine mercy. The ancient believer felt himself sheerly unable to love God, or do anything else towards his salvation, were it only the lifting of a finger. To un-love was his only true loving; to un-learn, his only true learning; to un-do, his only true doing. The modern religionist is at once amused and amazed at these curious archæological beginnings of his own history. He feels towards them as a *virtuoso* does towards what is decidedly *rococo* in fashion, and not seldom bestows a word of munificent Pharisaic patronage upon them, such as the opulent Mr. Ruskin dispenses to uncouth specimens of early religious art. He has not the slightest conception of himself as a spiritual form inwardly enlivened by all God's peace and innocence. On the contrary, he feels himself to be a strictly moral or self-possessed being, vivified exclusively by his own action, or the relations he voluntarily assumes with respect to human and divine law. The modern believer aspires to be a saint; the ancient one abhorred to be anything but a sinner. The former looks back, accordingly, to some fancied era of what he calls conversion,—that is, when he passed from death to life. The latter was blissfully content to forget himself, and looked forward exclusively to his Lord's promised spiritual advent in all the forms of a redeemed nature. The one is an absolutely changed man, no longer to be confounded with the world, and meet for the divine approba-

tion. The other was a totally unchanged one, only more dependent than he ever was before upon the unmitigated divine mercy. The one feels sure of going to heaven if the Lord observes the distinctions which his own grace ordains in human character. The other felt sure of going to hell unless the Lord was blessedly indifferent to those distinctions."—*Substance and Shadow*, pp. 14, 15.

Again: "Religion has undergone so sheer a demoralization since her pure and holy prime,—has sunk into such a brazen handmaid to worldliness, such a painted and bedizened courtesan and street-walker, proffering her unstinted favors to every sentimental fop, or clerical *beau diseur*, who has the smallest change of self-conceit in his pocket wherewith to pay for them,—that one finds himself secretly invoking the advent of some grand social renovation in order to blot it *as a profession* out of remembrance, and leave it extant only as a spiritual life. Religion was once a spiritual life in the earth, though a very rude and terrible one; and her conquests were diligently authenticated by the divine spirit. Then she meant terror and amazement to all devout self-complacency in man; then she meant rebuke and denial to every form of distinctively *personal* hope and pretension towards God; then she meant discredit and death to every breath of a Pharisaic or Quaker temper in humanity, by which a man could be led to boast of a 'private spirit' in his bosom, giving him a differential character and aspect in God's sight to that of other men, especially the great and holy and unconscious mass of his kind."—*Secret of Swedenborg*, p. 221.

[1] *Substance and Shadow*, p. 75.

it, and he less hearty. Thus deeper than my intellect, deeper than my heart, deeper in fact than aught and all that I recognize as myself, or am wont to call emphatically *me*, is this dread omnipotent power of conscience, which now soothes me with the voice and nurses me with the milk of its tenderness, as the mother soothes and nurses her child, and anon scourges me with the lash of its indignation, as the father scourges his refractory heir.

"But this is only telling half the story. It is very true that conscience is the sole arbiter of good and evil to man; and that persons of a literal and superficial cast of mind—persons of a good hereditary temperament—may easily fancy themselves in spiritual harmony with it, or persuade themselves and others that they have fully satisfied every claim of its righteousness. But minds of a deeper quality soon begin to suspect that the demands of conscience are not so easily satisfied; soon discover in fact that it is a ministration of death exclusively, and not of life, to which they are abandoning themselves. For what conscience inevitably teaches all its earnest adepts erelong is, to give up the hopeless effort to reconcile good and evil in their own practice, and learn to identify themselves, on the contrary, with the evil principle alone, while they assign all good exclusively to God. Thus no man of a sincere and honest intellectual make has ever set himself seriously to cultivate conscience with a view to its spiritual emoluments,—that is, with a view to placate the divine righteousness,—without speedily discovering that every such hope is illusory; that peace flees from him just in proportion to the eagerness with which he covets it. In other words, no man not a fool, since the beginning of history, has ever deliberately set himself 'to eat of the tree of the knowledge of good and evil,'—that is, *to prosecute his moral instincts until he should become inwardly assured of God's personal complacency in him*,—without finding death and not life to his soul; without his inward and spiritual obliquity being sooner or later made to abound in the exact ratio of his moral or outward rectitude. I have no idea, of course, that a man may not be beguiled by the insinuating breath of sense into believing himself spiritually, or in the depths, just what he appears to be morally, or in the shallows. Vast numbers of persons, indeed, are to be found in every community, who, having as yet attained to no spiritual insight or understanding, are entirely content with—nay, proud of—the moral 'purple and fine linen' with which they are daily decked out in the favorable esteem of their friends, and are meanwhile at hearty peace with themselves. All this in fact is strictly inevitable to our native and cultivated fatuity in spiritual things; but I am not here concerned with the fact in the way either of denial or of confirmation. What I here mean specifically to say is, that every one in whom, to use a common locution of Swedenborg, 'the spiritual degree of the mind has been opened,' finds conscience no friend, but an impassioned foe to his moral righteousness or complacency in himself, and hence to his personal repose in God. . . . A stream cannot mount above its source, and . . . when I earnestly aspire to fulfil the divine law,—when I earnestly strive after moral or personal excellence,—my aim unquestionably is to lift myself above the level of human nature, or attain to a place in the divine regard unshared by the average of my kind; unshared by the liar, the thief, the adulterer, the murderer. But the same law which discountenances false-witness, theft, adultery, and murder binds me also *not to covet,*—that is, *not to desire for myself what other men do not enjoy;* so that the law which I fondly imagined was designed to give me life turns out a subtle ministry of death, and in the very crisis of my moral exaltation fills me with the profoundest spiritual humiliation and despair. It is an instinct doubtless of the divine life in me to hate false-witness, theft, adultery, and murder, and actually to avert myself from these evils whenever I am naturally tempted to do them. But then I must hate them *for their own sake* exclusively, or because of their contrariety to infinite goodness and truth, and not with a base view to tighten my hold upon God's personal approbation. I grossly pervert the spirit of the law, and betray its infinite majesty to shame, if I suppose it capable of ratifying in any degree my private and personal cupidity towards God, or lending even a moment's sanction to the altogether frivolous and odious separation which I devoutly hope to compass between myself and other men in his sight.

"The entire historic function of conscience has been to operate an effectual check upon our gigantic natural pride and cupidity in spiritual things, by avouching a total contrariety between God and ourselves, so long as we remain indifferent to the truth of our essential society, fellowship, or equality with our kind, and are moved only by selfish or personal considerations in the devout overtures we make to the divine regard. . . . The only respect it ever pays to the private votary is to convince him of sin through a conviction of God's wholly *impersonal* justice, . . . and make him frankly disavow every title to the divine esteem which is not quite equally shared by publican and harlot." [1]

Selfhood and conscience, then, or "morality and religion, together, constitute the subject-earth of self-love, which revolves now in light, now in shade,—morality being the illuminated side of that love, religion its obscured side; the one constituting the splendor of its day, the other the darkness of its night. Morality is the summer lustihood and luxuriance of self-love, clothing its mineral ribs with vegetable grace, permeating its rigid trunk with sap, decorating its gnarled limbs with foliage, glorifying every reluctant virgin bud and every modest wifely blossom into rich, ripe motherly fruit. Religion is the icy winter which blights this summer fertility, which arrests the ascent of its vivifying sap, and

---

[1] *Secret of Swedenborg,* pp. 161–65.

humbles its superb life to the ground, in the interests of a spring that shall be perennial, and of autumns bursting with imperishable fruit. In other words, religion has no substantive force. Her sole errand on earth has been to dog the footsteps of morality, to humble the pride of selfhood which man derives from nature, and so soften his interiors to the reception of divine truth, as that truth shall stand fulfilled in the organization of human equality or fellowship." [1]

"Self-conceit and self-reproach, pride and penitence, thus make up the fever and the chill into which that great intermittent, which we call our moral and religious experience, ordinarily resolves itself." My father seems in his early years to have had an unusually lively and protracted visitation of this malady, and his philosophy indeed is but the statement of his cure. In the autobiographic pages to be found further on, there is a full account of his boyish evolution in this respect. And here and there in his other writings we get glimpses of later states of mind which it will be profitable now to transcribe. Here is one of them:

"I had never for a moment *intellectually* realized my moral consciousness to be that mere steward or servant of the divine inheritance in our nature which Swedenborg showed it to be. On the contrary, with the intellect, and in spite of the heart's misgiving, I had always quietly allowed it to be the undeniable lord of the inheritance, and beheld it accordingly whipping the men-servants and the maid-servants at its pleasure, without a suspicion. Far from supposing my natural selfhood or *proprium* to constitute a strictly *negative* token, an essentially *inverse* attestation, of God's spiritual and infinite presence in our nature, I habitually viewed it as the Church taught me to view it,— that is, as the only direct and positive manifestation of his power; and my religious life accordingly became one of incessant conflict and perturbation.

"How could it have been otherwise? Having as I supposed a purely moral *status* by creation,—never dreaming that my selfhood possessed only a formal or subjective validity,—I attributed to myself an objective or substantial reality in God's sight, and of course sought to attract his approbation to me by the unswerving pursuit of moral excellence, by studiously cultivating every method of personal purity. It was all in vain. The more I strove to indue myself in actual righteousness, the wider gaped the jaws of hell within me; the fouler grew its fetid breath. A conviction of inward defilement so sheer took possession of me, that death seemed better than life. I soon found my conscience, once launched in this insane career, acquiring so infernal an edge, that I could no longer indulge myself in the most momentary deviation from an absurd and pedantic literal rectitude; could not, for example, bestow

[1] *Substance and Shadow*, p. 10.

a sulky glance upon my wife, a cross word upon my child, or a petulant objurgation on my cook, without tumbling into an instant inward frenzy of alarm lest I should thereby have provoked God's personal malignity to me. There is indeed no way of avoiding spiritual results so belittling, but by ceasing to regard morality as a direct, and looking upon it as an inverse, image of God's true life in us. If my moral consciousness constitute the true and eternal bond of intercourse between me and God; that is to say, if he attribute to me all the good and evil which I in my insane pride attribute to myself,—then it will be impossible for me to avoid all eternity either a most conceited and disgusting conviction of his personal complacency in me, or else a shuddering apprehension of his personal ill-will. If I have a naturally complacent temper, my religious life will reflect it, and array me spiritually in all manner of nauseous Pharisaism and flunkeyism. If I have what is called a 'morbid' natural temperament, on the other hand, leading me to self-distrust and self-depreciation, my religious life will deepen these things into despair, by making my self-condemnation confess itself a feeble reflection of God's profounder vindictiveness." [1]

In a couple of long passages of his latest published work, he tells as follows of the manner in which he became acquainted with the writings of Swedenborg, and began to get relief:—

"In the spring of 1844 I was living with my family in the neighborhood of Windsor, England, much absorbed in the study of the Scriptures. Two or three years before this period I had made an important discovery, as I fancied; namely, that the book of Genesis was not intended to throw a direct light upon our natural or race history, but was an altogether mystical or symbolic record of the laws of God's *spiritual* creation and providence. I wrote a course of lectures in exposition of this idea, and delivered them to good audiences in New York. The preparation of these lectures, while it did much to confirm me in the impression that I had made an interesting discovery and one which would extensively modify theology, convinced me, however, that a much more close and studious application of my idea than I had yet given to the illustration of the details of the sacred letter was imperatively needed. During my residence abroad, accordingly, I never tired in my devotion to this aim; and my success seemed so flattering at length, that I hoped to be finally qualified to contribute a not insignificant mite to the sum of man's highest knowledge. I remember I felt especially hopeful in the prosecution of my task all the time I was at Windsor; my health was good, my spirits cheerful, and the pleasant scenery of the great Park and its neighborhood furnished us a constant temptation to long walks and drives.

---

[1] *Substance and Shadow*, pp. 125–27.

"One day, however, towards the close of May, having eaten a comfortable dinner, I remained sitting at the table after the family had dispersed, idly gazing at the embers in the grate, thinking of nothing, and feeling only the exhilaration incident to a good digestion, when suddenly—in a lightning-flash as it were—'fear came upon me, and trembling, which made all my bones to shake.' To all appearance it was a perfectly insane and abject terror, without ostensible cause, and only to be accounted for, to my perplexed imagination, by some damnèd shape squatting invisible to me within the precincts of the room, and raying out from his fetid personality influences fatal to life. The thing had not lasted ten seconds before I felt myself a wreck; that is, reduced from a state of firm, vigorous, joyful manhood to one òf almost helpless infancy. The only self-control I was capable of exerting was to keep my seat. I felt the greatest desire to run incontinently to the foot of the stairs and shout for help to my wife,—to run to the roadside even, and appeal to the public to protect me; but by an immense effort I controlled these frenzied impulses, and determined not to budge from my chair till I had recovered my lost self-possession. This purpose I held to for a good long hour, as I reckoned time, beat upon meanwhile by an ever-growing tempest of doubt, anxiety, and despair, with absolutely no relief from any truth I had ever encountered save a most pale and distant glimmer of the divine existence, when I resolved to abandon the vain struggle, and communicate without more ado what seemed my sudden burden of inmost, implacable unrest to my wife.

"Now, to make a long story short, this ghastly condition of mind continued with me, with gradually lengthening intervals of relief, for two years, and even longer. I consulted eminent physicians, who told me that I had doubtless overworked my brain,—an evil for which no remedy existed in medicine, but only in time and patience, and growth into improved physical conditions. They all recommended by way of hygiene a resort to the water-cure treatment, a life in the open air, cheerful company, and so forth, and thus quietly and skilfully dismissed me to my own spiritual medication. At first, when I began to feel a half-hour's respite from acute mental anguish, the bottomless mystery of my disease completely fascinated me. The more, however, I worried myself with speculations about the cause of it, the more the mystery deepened, and the deeper also grew my instinct of resentment at what seemed so needless an interference with my personal liberty. I went to a famous water-cure, which did nothing towards curing my malady but enrich my memory with a few morbid specimens of English insularity and prejudice; but it did much to alleviate it by familiarizing my senses with the exquisite and endless charm of English landscape, and giving me my first full rational relish of what may be called England's pastoral beauty. To be sure, I had spent a few days in Devonshire when I was young; but my delight then was simple enthusiasm, was helpless æsthetic intoxication in fact. The 'cure' was situated in a much less lovely but still beautiful country, on the borders of a famous park, to both of which, moreover, it gave us unlimited right of possession and enjoyment. At least this was the way it always struck my imagination. The thoroughly disinterested way the English have of looking at their own hills and vales, the indifferent, contemptuous, and as it were *disowning* mood they habitually put on towards the most ravishing pastoral loveliness man's sun anywhere shines upon, gave me always the sense of being a discoverer of these things, and of a consequent right to enter upon their undisputed possession. At all events, the rich light and shade of English landscapé, the gorgeous cloud-pictures that forever dimple and diversify her fragrant and palpitating bosom, have awakened a tenderer chord in me than I have ever felt at home almost; and time and again while living at this dismal water-cure, and listening to its endless 'strife of tongues' about diet, and regimen, and disease, and politics, and parties, and persons, I have said to myself, *The curse of mankind, that which keeps our manhood so little and so depraved, is its sense of self-hood, and the absurd, abominable opinionativeness it engenders. How sweet it would be to find oneself no longer man, but one of those innocent and ignorant sheep pasturing upon that placid hillside, and drinking in eternal dew and freshness from Nature's lavish bosom!*

"But let me hasten to the proper upshot of this incident. My stay at the water-cure, unpromising as it was in point of physical results, made me conscious erelong of a most important change operating in the sphere of my will and understanding. It struck me as very odd, soon after my breakdown, that I should feel no longing to resume the work which had been interrupted by it; and from that day to this (nearly thirty-five years) I have never once cast a retrospective glance, even of curiosity, at the immense piles of manuscript which had erewhile so absorbed me. I suppose if any one had designated me previous to that event as an earnest seeker after truth, I should myself have seen nothing unbecoming in the appellation. But now, within two or three months of my catastrophe, I felt sure I had never caught a glimpse of truth. My present consciousness was exactly that of an utter and plenary destitution of truth. Indeed, an ugly suspicion had more than once forced itself upon me that I had never really wished the truth, but only to ventilate my own ability in discovering it. I was getting sick to death in fact with a sense of my downright intellectual poverty and dishonesty. My studious mental activity had served manifestly to base a mere 'castle in the air'; and the castle had vanished in a brief bitter moment of time, leaving not a wrack behind. I never felt again the most passing impulse, even, to look where it stood, having done with it forever. Truth, indeed! How should a beggar like me be expected to discover it? How should any man of woman born pretend to such ability? Truth must *reveal itself* if it would be known; and even then how imperfectly known at best! For truth is God, the omniscient and omnipotent God; and who shall pretend to comprehend that great and adorable perfection? And yet who that aspires to the name of man, would not cheerfully barter all he knows of life for a bare glimpse of the hem of its garment?

"I was calling one day upon a friend (since deceased) who lived in the vicinity of the water-cure,—a lady of rare qualities of heart and mind, and of singular personal loveliness as well,—who desired to know what had brought me to the water-cure. After I had done telling her in substance what I have told you, she replied: 'It is, then, very much as I had ventured from two or three previous things you have said, to suspect: you are undergoing what Swedenborg calls a *vastation;* and though, naturally enough, you yourself are despondent or even despairing about the issue, I cannot help taking an altogether hopeful view of your prospects.' In expressing my thanks for her encouraging words, I remarked that I was not at all familiar with the Swedenborgian technics, and that I should be extremely happy if she would follow up her flattering judgment of my condition by turning into plain English the contents of the very handsome Latin word she had used. To this she again modestly replied, that she only read Swedenborg as an *amateur,* and was ill-qualified to expound his philosophy; but there could be no doubt about its fundamental postulate, which was, that a new birth for man, both in the individual and the universal realm, is the secret of the Divine creation and providence; that the other world, according to Swedenborg, furnishes the true sphere of man's spiritual or individual being, the real and immortal being he has in God; and he represents *this* world, consequently, as furnishing only a preliminary theatre of his natural formation or existence in subordination thereto,—so making the question of human regeneration, both in grand and in little, the capital problem of philosophy; that, without pretending to dogmatize, she had been struck with the philosophic interest of my narrative in this point of view, and had used the word *vastation* to characterize one of the stages of the regenerative process, as she had found it described by Swedenborg. And then, finally, my excellent friend went on to outline for me, in a very interesting manner, her conception of Swedenborg's entire doctrine on the subject.

"Her account of it, as I found on a subsequent study of Swedenborg, was neither quite as exact nor quite as comprehensive as the facts required; but at all events I was glad to discover that any human being had so much even as proposed to shed the light of positive knowledge upon the soul's history, or bring into rational relief the alternate dark and bright or infernal and celestial phases of its finite constitution. For

I had an immediate hope, amounting to an almost prophetic instinct, of finding in the attempt, however rash, some diversion to my cares; and I determined instantly to run up to London and procure a couple of Swedenborg's volumes, of which, if I should not be allowed on sanitary grounds absolutely to read them, I might at any rate turn over the leaves, and so catch a satisfying savor, or at least an appetizing flavor, of the possible relief they might in some better day afford to my poignant need. From the huge mass of tomes placed by the bookseller on the counter before me, I selected two of the least in bulk,—the treatise on the 'Divine Love and Wisdom,' and that of the 'Divine Providence.' I gave them, after I brought them home, many a random but eager glance; but at last my interest in them grew so frantic under this tantalizing process of reading, that I resolved, in spite of the doctors, that instead of standing any longer shivering on the brink, I would boldly plunge into the stream, and ascertain, once for all, to what undiscovered sea its waters might bear me.

"I read from the first with palpitating interest. My heart divined, even before my intelligence was prepared to do justice to the books, the unequalled amount of truth to be found in them. Imagine a fever patient, sufficiently restored of his malady to be able to think of something beside himself, suddenly transported where the free airs of heaven blow upon him, and the sound of running waters refreshes his jaded senses; and you have a feeble image of my delight in reading. Or, better still, imagine a subject of some petty despotism condemned to die, and with (what is more and worse) a sentiment of death pervading all his consciousness, lifted by a sudden miracle into felt harmony with universal man, and filled to the brim with the sentiment of indestructible life instead; and you will have a true picture of my emancipated condition. For while these remarkable books familiarized me with the angelic conception of the Divine being and providence, they gave me at the same time the amplest *rationale* I could have desired of my own particular suffering, as inherent in the profound unconscious death I bore about in my *proprium* or selfhood." [1]

"I had always, from childhood, conceived of the Creator as bearing an outside relation to the creature, and had attributed to the latter, consequently, the power of provoking his unmeasured hostility. Although these crude traditional views had been much modified by subsequent reflection, I had nevertheless on the whole been in the habit of ascribing to the Creator, so far as my own life and actions were concerned, an outside discernment of the most jealous scrutiny, and had accordingly put the greatest possible alertness into his service and worship, until my will, as you have seen,—thoroughly fagged out as it were with the

---

[1] *Society the Redeemed Form of Man*, pp. 43-54.

formal, heartless, endless task of conciliating a stony-hearted Deity,—
actually collapsed. This was a catastrophe far more tragic to my feelings, and far more revolutionary in its intellectual results, than the actual violation of any mere precept of the moral law could be. It was the
practical abrogation of the law itself, through the unexpected moral
inertness of the subject. It was to my feeling not only an absolute decease of my moral or voluntary power, but a shuddering recoil from
my conscious activity in that line. It was an actual acute loathing of
the moral pretension itself as so much downright charlatanry. No idiot
was ever more incompetent, practically, to the conduct of life than I, at
that trying period, felt myself to be. It cost me, in fact, as much effort
to go out for a walk, or to sleep in a strange bed, as it would an ordinary man to plan a campaign or write an epic poem. I have told you
how, in looking out of my window at the time at a flock of silly sheep
which happened to be grazing in the green park opposite, I used to
envy them their blissful, stupid ignorance of any law higher than their
nature, their deep unconsciousness of self, their innocence of all private
personality and purpose, their intense moral incapacity, in short, and indifference. I would freely—nay, gladly—have bartered the world at
the moment for one breath of the spiritual innocence which the benign
creatures outwardly pictured or stood for to my imagination; and all
the virtue, or moral righteousness, consequently, that ever illustrated
our specific human personality seemed simply foul and leprous in comparison with the deep Divine possibilities and promise of our common
nature, as these stood symbolized to my spiritual sight in all the gentler
human types of the merely animate world. There seemed, for instance,
—lustrously represented to my inward sense,—a far more heavenly
sweetness in the soul of a patient, overdriven cab-horse, or misused
cadger's donkey, than in all the voluminous calendar of Romish and
Protestant hagiology, which, sooth to say, seemed to me, in contrast
with it, nothing short of infernal.

"You may easily imagine, then, with what relish my heart opened to
the doctrine I found in these most remarkable books, *of the sheer and
abject phenomenality of selfhood in man;* and with what instant alacrity
my intellect shook its canvas free to catch every breeze of that virgin,
unexplored sea of Being, to which this doctrine, for the first time, furnished me the clew. Up to this very period I had lived in the cheerful
faith, nor ever felt the slightest shadow of misgiving about it,—any
more, I venture to say, than you at this moment feel a shadow of similar
misgiving in your own mind,—that my being or substance lay absolutely in myself, was in fact identical with the various limitations implied in that most fallacious but still unsuspected quantity. To be sure,
I had no doubt that this being or self of mine (whether actually burdened, or not burdened, with its limitations I did not stop to inquire,

but unquestionably with a capacity of any amount of burdensome limitation) came originally as a gift from the hand of God; but I had just as little doubt that the moment the gift had left God's hand, or fell into my conscious possession, it became as essentially independent of him in all spiritual or subjective regards as the soul of a child is of its earthly father, however much in material or objective regards it might be expedient for me still to submit to his external police. My moral conscience, too, lent its influence to the same profound illusion; for all the precepts of the moral law being objectively so good and real, and intended in the view of an unenlightened conscience to make men righteous in the sight of God, I could never have supposed, even had I been tempted on independent grounds to doubt my own spiritual or subjective reality, that so palpably divine a law contemplated, or even tolerated, a wholly infirm and fallacious subject; much less that it was, in fact, altogether devised for the reproof, condemnation, and humiliation of such a subject. I had no misgiving, therefore, as to the manifest purpose of the law. The divine intent of it at least was as clear to me as it ever had been to the Jew,—namely, to serve as a ministry of plain moral life or actual righteousness among men, so constructing an everlasting heaven out of men's warring and divided personalities: and not at all, as the apostles taught, a ministry of death, *to convince those who stood approved by it of* SIN, thereby shutting up all men, good and evil alike, but especially the good, to unlimited dependence upon the sheer and mere mercy of God.

"It was impossible for me, after what I have told you, to hold this audacious faith in selfhood any longer. When I sat down to dinner on that memorable chilly afternoon in Windsor, I held it serene and unweakened by the faintest breath of doubt; before I rose from table, it had inwardly shrivelled to a cinder. One moment I devoutly thanked God for the inappreciable boon of selfhood; the next, that inappreciable boon seemed to me the one thing damnable on earth, seemed a literal nest of hell within my own entrails." [1]

The reader who shall have persevered as far as this, is now well emerged from the *apriori* logical atmosphere in which our quotations concerning the creative process began. He sees that those cold accounts were but a garb, a vehicle of introduction to the intellect, of experiences of the heart of the most living kind. He sees, if he be of a generalizing turn of mind, that Mr. James was one member of that band of saints and mystics, whose rare privilege it has been, by the mere example and recital of their own bosom-experience, to prevent religion from becoming a fossil conventionalism, and to keep it forever alive. The experience in question has always been an acute despair, passing

---

[1] *Society the Redeemed Form of Man,*   Moral Death and Burial."
pp. 70–74. These pages are headed, "My

over into an equally acute optimism, through a passion of renunciation of the self and surrender to the higher power. Doubtless it would be easy enough to muster pages of quotations from spiritual literature,— pagan, catholic, and protestant,—which would tally in all essential respects with what my father felt and said about the relation of the Self and the Divine. But every man carries his signature stamped upon him, and my father's was, I think, very peculiar indeed.

The common run of mystics seem less to let their Self expire than to get it calmed and appeased and made innocent on their hands, so that it still remains extant to taste the delights of God's renewed conversation with it. This gives to much of their writing that voluptuous tinge, that perfume of spiritual sensuality, which makes it impossible to many readers, even religious ones, to get any edification from their pages. One feels rebuked and distanced, and kept out of the pale. It is the *I*, and not the *we*, that speaks. Now, my father, with all the mystical depth of experience, and all the mystical unction, had not a trace of the mystical egotism or voluptuousness, but was as drastic and unsenti- mental as old Epictetus or even Diogenes himself. A calm and clarified and triumphantly peaceful self was still a self, as much as a bitter and grievous one. And not if he could help it, would he dally and toy with the enemy in any shape. Universal Man is God's one creature: only in Man and through Man would he be saved. "When Swedenborg called the selfhood the realm of our *uncreation*, he by that unexpected word sent a breath of health to the deepest heart of hell." Uncreated then shall *my* self become! Accordingly it was a strange thing to see him, when in a depressed mood, murmur the psalms of David to him- self by the hour, apparently without a feeling of personal application. He fairly revelled in the emotion of humanity, and lost himself in the sentiment of unity with his kind, like a river in the sea.

The following passage may be quoted here:

"All the science or knowledge of life to which I am begotten, born, and bred by our existing civilization tells me, with an undeviating per- sistency, that there is nothing so divinely true, because so divinely sweet and sufficing, as selfhood; and the consequence is that I actually succeed in giving the real divinity in my great race or nature only a scant and drowsy recognition. Indeed, if I should freely yield to instinct within me, or abandon myself to the current inspiration of cul- ture about me, I doubt not I should end by altogether sacrificing that patient divinity to the unscrupulous idol and counterfeit enshrined in myself. For then my senses, authenticated and unchecked, would be free to tell me that my life or being is strictly identical with my finite personality, and that the only death and hell I shall ever have to dread is one which menaces that personality with desolation; namely, the death and hell wrapped up in my intimate Divine-Natural innocence, truth, and chastity. I confess, though, that when once one's eyes are opened to a glimmer of eternal truth on the subject, one has no hesitation in hoping that ere he is caught hearkening to this gospel of an atheistic and drunken self-conceit he may actually perish out of life, and the great lord of life know him no more forever. I for one should distinctly prefer forfeiting my self-consciousness altogether, to being found capable, in ever so feeble a degree, of identifying my being with it. My being lies utterly outside of my*self*, lies in utterly forgetting my*self*, lies in utterly unlearning and disusing all its elaborately petty schemes and dodges now grown so transparent that a child is not deceived by them; lies, in fact, *in honestly identifying myself with others.* I know it will never be possible for me to do this perfectly,—that is, attain to self-extinction,—because being created, I can never hope actually to become Divine; but at all events I shall become through eternal years more and more intimately one in nature, and I hope in spirit, with a being who *is* thoroughly destitute of this finiting principle,—that is, a being who is without selfhood save in His creatures. And certainly the next best thing to being God is to know Him, for this knowledge makes one content with any burden of personal limitation." [1]

Nothing so endlessly besotted in Mr. James's eyes, as the pretension to possess personally any substantive merit or advantage whatever, any worth other than your unconscious uses to your kind! Nothing pleased him like exploding the bubbles of conventional dignity, unless it was fraternizing on the simplest and commonest plane with all lowly persons whom he met. To exalt humble and abase proud things was ever the darling sport of his conversation,—a conversation the somewhat reckless invective humor of which, when he was in the *abasing* mood, often startled the good people of Boston, who did not know him well enough to see the endlessly genial and humane intuition from which the whole mood flowed. A friend, in a private letter received during this writing, says of him: "He was of such an immense temperament, that when you took him to task for violating the feelings of others in his talk, he would score you black and blue for your distinctions; and all the while he made you feel that the origin of the matter was his divine rage with *himself* at still being so dominated by his natural selfhood which would not be shaken off. I have felt in him at times, away down at bottom of the man, so sheer a humility and self-abasement as to give me an idea of infinity."

The theology that went with all this was the passionate conviction that the *real* creature of God—human *nature* at large, *minus* the preposterous claims of the several selves—must be wholly good. For is it

---

[1] *Society the Redeemed Form of Man*, p. 361.

not the work of the good God, or rather the very substance of the good God, there *being* nought beside?

"What sort of a creator would he be who could allow, for a single moment, such an imputation to rest upon his creative power as that his creature was *really* bad? Evidently a most beggarly sort. For if God's creature were *really* bad,—that is, if his badness be, as the philosophers say, not only *subjective*, spiritual, formal, but *objective*, natural, substantial,—why, then, no man can even begin to form an estimate of how much worse than the creature the creator himself must be, in order simply to account for the devilish atrocity of such a creation! The creature, you know, by the hypothesis of his creation, is absolute nought *in himself;* and if therefore he be *really* evil, where does this evil reality of his come from, if not from him in whom alone he lives and moves and has his being?"

In another autobiographic passage he defends the rights of our nature as being the very incarnation of God:—

"As well as I can remember, in fact, the spring of all my intellectual activity in the past was to know for certain whether our felt finiteness was a necessity of our spiritual creation, or simply an incident of our natural constitution; whether, for example, it was to be interpreted as having been arbitrarily imposed upon us by the Divine will, or as inherent merely in the sentiment we so inordinately cherish of personal independence. For in the former case, my hope in God necessarily dies out by the practical decease of his infinitude, while in the latter case it is not only left unimpaired, but is revived and invigorated. . . .

"Here, in fact, was the veritable secret source of all my intellectual unrest. During all my early intellectual existence I was haunted by so keen a sense of God's *natural* incongruity with me—of his *natural* and therefore invincible alienation, otherness, externality, distance, remoteness to me—as to breed in my bosom oftentimes a wholly unspeakable heartsickness or homesickness. The sentiment, to be sure, masked its ineffable malignity from my perception under the guise of an alleged *super*natural limitation on God's part; but it none the less filled my soul with the tremor and pallor of death. I have no doubt, indeed, that if it had not been for my excessive 'animal spirits' as we say, or the extreme good-will I felt towards sensuous pleasure of every sort, which alternated with my morbid conscientiousness and foiled its corrosive force, I should have turned out a flagrant case of arrested intellectual development. I could have borne very well, mind you, a conviction of God's *personal* antipathy to me, carried to any pitch you please, for my person does not go with my nature as man; and a personal condemnation, therefore, which should not cut me off from a natural resurrection, would not deprive me of hope toward God. But my conviction of God's personal alienation had been hopelessly saddled, through the incompetency of my theologic sponsors, with the senseless tradition of his inveterate estrangement also from *human nature*. Thus, unhappily, though my person did not go with human nature, they made human nature to go with my person, or managed so perfectly to confound the two things to my unpractised sense, that, whenever I felt a superficial or intrinsically evanescent pang of mere personal remorse, it was sure to pass, by a quick diabolical chemistry, into a sense of the deadliest *natural* hostility between me and the source of my life.

"It is in fact this venomous tradition of a natural as well as a personal disproportion between man and his maker,—speciously cloaked as it is under the ascription of a *super*natural being and existence to God,— that alone gives its intolerable odium and poignancy to men's other-wise healthful and restorative conscience of sin. That man's personality should utterly alienate him from God,—that is to say, make him in-finitely other and opposite to God,—this I grant you with all my heart; since if God were the least like me personally, all my hope in him would perish. . . . But that God should be also an infinitely alien *substance* to me,—an infinitely other or foreign *nature*,—this wounds my spontaneous faith in him to its core, or leaves it a mere mercenary and servile homage. I perfectly understand how he should disown all private or personal relation to me, because I am, . . . to all the extent of my distinctively personal interests and ambitions, the impassioned foe and rival of universal man. This is one thing. But it is quite a different and most odious thing that he should feel an envenomed animosity also to my innocent nature, or what binds me in indissoluble unity with every man of woman born." [1]

Some sort of antinomianism, or indifference to outward human con-trasts, is the logical outcome of every creed which makes the Deity's love so impartial, and lays such stress upon the prominence of the *whole* to his regard. I cannot say that my father succeeded in practice in keeping faithful to this consequence; but in theory he did; and great was his delight in those pages of Swedenborg in which he found the doctrine of indifference clearly set down. First, concerning the angels:—

"The angel would be incontinently overcome of hell, if he were not seduously preserved by the Divine power, vanquishing his incessant natural gravitation towards it. Swedenborg affirms that he found no angel in any heaven, however elevated, who was not in himself, or intrinsically, of a very shabby pattern, and who did not, therefore, cordially refer all his goodness and wisdom to the Lord; and he sets it down as the fundamental principle of their intelligence, that they ascribe all their good to the Lord, and all their evil to the devil. No

---

[1] *Society the Redeemed Form of Man*, pp. 314–318.

matter what heights of manly virtue the angel may have reached; no matter what depths of Divine peace and contentment he may have sounded,—Swedenborg invariably reports that in himself, or intrinsically, he is replete with every selfish and worldly lust, being in fact utterly undistinguishable from the lowest devil. Was ever testimony so loyal as this? Was ever honest heart or seeing eye so unseduced before by the most specious shows of things? I confess the wonder to me is endless. What other man in that rotten and degraded generation was capable of such devotion to humanity? Of which one of his contemporaries could you allege, that, being admitted to the most lustrous company in the universe, he would never for an instant lose his balance, or duck his servile head in homage, but steadfastly maintain his invincible faith in the great truth of human equality? George Washington is doubtless an unblemished name to all the extent of his commerce with the world; but how puny that commerce was, compared with this grand interior commerce of the soul; and how juvenile and rustic his virtue seems beside the profound, serene, unconscious humanity of this despised old soldier of truth! To gaze undazzled upon the solar splendors of heaven; to gaze undismayed upon the sombre abysses of hell; to preserve one's self-respect, or one's fidelity to the Divine name, unbribed by the subtlest attractions of the one sphere, and unchilled by the nakedest horrors of the other,—implies a heroism of soul which in no wise belongs to the old Church, even in its highest sanctities, and which leaves the old State, even as to its most renowned illustrations, absolutely out of sight." [1]

Here are a couple of soberer passages:—

"The true or spiritual creation ignores the sentiment of morality in its subjects,—that is, disallows the distinction of good and evil among men, as at all pertinent to the Divine mind. No angel that Swedenborg encountered was ever so foolish as to attribute the good which was visible in him to himself; and no devil was ever wise enough not to do so. The fundamental difference, in short, between Swedenborg's angels and devils was the difference between humility and loftiness,—the latter always cherishing an unsubdued selfhood, or pride of character; the former being always more or less cultivated out of it." [2]

"Swedenborg shows, accordingly, throughout all his books, from their beginning to their close, that God has no joy in the angel, nor any grief in the devil, save as they tend to enforce or enfeeble the universality and the particularity of his presence and providence throughout the earth. The Lord's love, as Swedenborg invariably reports it, is a universal love, being the salvation of the whole human race; and no form of his church, therefore, can satisfy his regard, which

---

[1] *Christianity the Logic of Creation,* p. 17.
[2] *Secret of Swedenborg,* p. 107.

is not practically identical with the interests of human society,—that is, which does not in itself structurally reproduce and avouch the intimate and indissoluble fellowship, equality, brotherhood of universal man." [1]

And here is an abstract statement about good and evil:—

"Good and evil, heaven and hell, are not facts of creative, but of purely constitutive, order. They bear primarily upon man's natural destiny, and have no relation to his spiritual freedom save through that. They are the mere geology of our natural consciousness; and this is all they are. They have no distinctively supernatural quality nor efficacy whatever. They have a simply constitutional relevancy to the earth of man's associated consciousness, and disavow therefore any properly creative or controlling relation to his spiritual or individual freedom. We have been traditionally taught that good and evil, heaven and hell, were objective realities, having an absolute ground of being in the creative perfection. But this is the baldest, most bewildering nonsense. They have not a grain of objective reality in them, and are no way vitalized by the absolute Divine perfection. They are purely subjective appearances, vitalized exclusively by the created imperfection, or the uses they subserve to our provisional moral and rational consciousness. When, accordingly, this consciousness—having more than fulfilled its legitimate office, and become, as it now is, a mere stumbling-block or rock of offence to the regenerate mind of the race—finally expires in its own stench, or else frankly allows itself to be taken up and disappear in our advancing social and æsthetic consciousness, good and evil, heaven and hell, will cease to be appearances even. For angel and devil, saint and sinner, will then find themselves perfectly fused or made over in a new or comprehensive race-manhood, which will laugh to scorn our best empirical or tentative manhood,—that is, our existing civic and ecclesiastic manhood so-called." [2]

One more quotation may conclude our illustrations of this aspect of Mr. James's philosophy:

"There are no fundamental differences in men. All men have one and the same Creator, one and the same essential being; and what formally differences one man from another, what distinguishes hell from heaven, is that they are differently related to the Divine-*natural* humanity, or to the life of God in nature, which is a life of perfect freedom or spontaneity. In that life self-love freely subordinates itself to neighborly love, or promotes its own ends by promoting the welfare of all mankind. But so long as this life is wholly unsuspected by men; so long

[1] Ibid., p. 78.
[2] *Society the Redeemed Form of Man,* p. 251.

as no man dreams of any other social destiny for the race than that which it has already realized, and which leaves one man out of all fellowship or equality with another,—self-love is completely unprovided for, except in subtle and hypocritical forms, and is consequently driven to these disorderly assertions of itself by way of actually keeping itself alive. . . . The liar, the thief, the adulterer, the murderer, no doubt utterly perverts the divine life which is latent in every human form; he degrades and defiles self-love, in lifting it out of that free subordination which it will evince to brotherly love in the Divine-*natural* man: but he nevertheless does all this in the way of a mute, unconscious protest against an overwhelming social tyranny, which would otherwise crush out the distinctive life of man under the machinery of government and caste. Accordingly, I am profoundly convinced that if it had not been for these men; if we had not had some persons of that audacious make which would qualify them to throw off their existing social subjection, and so ventilate, even by infernal airs, the underlying life and freedom of humanity,—that life and freedom would have been utterly stifled, and we should now be a race of abject slaves, without hope towards God, without love to our fellow-man, contentedly kissing the feet of some infallible Pope of Rome, contentedly doing the bidding of some unquestionable Emperor of all the Russias. These men have been, unknown to themselves, the forlorn hope of humanity, plunging headlong into the unfathomable night only that we by the bridge of their desecrated forms might eventually pass over its hideous abysses into the realms of endless day. Let us, then, at least manfully acknowledge our indebtedness to them; let us view them as the unconscious martyrs of humanity, dying for a cause so divinely high as to accept no conscious or voluntary adhesion, and yet so divinely sure and sweet and human as ultimately to vindicate even their dishonored memory, and rehabilitate them in the love and tenderness of eternal ages. In short, let us agree with Swedenborg, that odious and fearful as these men have seemed in merely celestial light, they have yet borne the unrecognized livery of the Divine-NATURAL humanity, and will not fail in the end to swell the triumphs of his majestic patience. And this, simply because by an undying divine instinct, under every depth of degradation celestially viewed, they have always been true to themselves,—feeling themselves to be men and not devils,— and over their scarred and riven legions have ever indestructibly waved the banner of a conscious freedom and rationality." [1]

Such being Mr. James's intellectual destiny, there was no fending off the catastrophe that had to occur in his relations with the church in which he was born. For the church, the particular person is the unit,

---

[1] *Christianity the Logic of Creation*, pp. 104–7.

wherewith, in the last resort, God deals. Whatever theological formulas the sects may use, whatever reasons for the damning, whatever means for the saving, they may assign, still it is always *one* of us who becomes God's vessel of honor, and another who is lost from out his sight. He thus stands over against us, an *imputer*, an outward and eventually a hostile power, consecrating, by the absolute distinctions he makes, that whole seething life of private jealousy and exclusion which is the bane of this world's estate.

Here is an autobiographic passage which may usher in some of the drastic remarks on the bad stewardship of the church which our author scatters about with so profuse a hand: [1]—

"I never questioned the absoluteness of all the *data*, good and evil, of my moral experience. I never doubted the infinite and eternal consequences which seemed to me to be wrapped up in my consciousness of personality, or the sentiment I habitually cherished of my individual relations and responsibility to God. I had never, to my own suspicion, been arrayed in any overt hostility to the Divine name. On the contrary, I reckoned myself an unaffected friend of God, inasmuch as I was a most eager and conscientious aspirant after moral perfection. And yet the total unconscious current of my religious life was so egotistic, the habitual color of my piety was so bronzed by an inmost selfishness and indifference to all mankind, save in so far as my action towards them bore upon my own salvation, that I never reflected myself to myself, never was able to look back upon any chance furrow my personality had left upon the sea of time, without a shuddering conviction of the abysses of spiritual profligacy over which I perpetually hovered, and towards which I incessantly gravitated. . . . From the day of my birth I had not only never known what it was to have an honest want, a want of my nature, ungratified, but I had also been able to squander, upon the will of my personal caprice, an amount of sustenance equal to the maintenance of a virtuous household. And yet thousands of persons directly about me, in all respects my equals, in many respects my superiors, had never in all their lives enjoyed an honest meal, an honest sleep, an honest suit of clothes, save at the expense of their own personal toil or of that of some parent or child, and had never once been able to give the reins to their personal caprice without an ignominious exposure to severe social penalties. It is, to be sure, perfectly just that I should be conveniently fed and lodged

---

[1] His earlier writings were largely taken up with negative criticisms on Orthodoxy in its practice as well as its teaching. The essay entitled "The Old and the New Theology" (in the volume of "Lectures and Miscellanies"), and the work called the "Church of Christ not an Ecclesiasticism," are masterpieces in this vein. The last named work seems to have been written in a peculiarly happy hour, and is distinguished by a charming freshness and geniality of tone.

and clad, and that I should be educated out of my native ignorance; but it is a monstrous affront to the divine justice or righteousness that I should be guaranteed, by what calls itself society, a lifelong career of luxury and self-indulgence, while so many other men and women, my superiors, go all their days miserably fed, miserably lodged, miserably clothed, and die at last in the same ignorance and imbecility, though not, alas! in the same innocence, that cradled their infancy.

"Now, I had long felt this deep spiritual damnation in myself growing out of an outraged and insulted divine justice, had long been pent up in spirit to these earthquake mutterings and menaces of a violated conscience, without seeing any clear door of escape open to me. That is to say, I perceived with endless perspicacity, that, if it were not for the hand of God's providence visiting with constant humiliation and blight every secret aspiration of my pride and vanity, I should be more than any other man reconciled to the existing most atrocious state of things. I knew no outward want; I had the amplest social recognition; I enjoyed the converse and friendship of distinguished men; I floated in fact on a sea of unrighteous plenty; and I was all the while so indifferent, if not inimical in heart, to the divine justice, that save for the spiritual terrors it ever and anon supplied to my lethargic sympathies, to my swinish ambition, I should have dragged out all my days in that complacent sty, nor have ever so much as dreamed that the outward want of my fellows—their want with respect to nature and society—was in truth but the visible sign and fruit of my own truer want, my own more inward destitution with respect to God. Thus my religious conscience was one of poignant misgiving toward God, if not of complete practical separation; and it filled my intellect with all manner of perplexed speculation and gloomy foreboding. Do what I might, I never could attain to the least religious self-complacency, or push my devout instincts to the point of actual fanaticism. Do what I would, I could never succeed in persuading myself that God Almighty cared a jot for me in my personal capacity,—that is, as I stood morally individualized from, or consciously antagonized with, my kind; and yet this was the identical spiritual obligation imposed upon me by the Church. Time and again I consulted my spiritual advisers to know how it might do for me to abandon myself to the simple joy of the truth as it was in Christ, without taking any thought for the Church, or the interests of my religious character. And they always told me that it would not do at all; that my Church sympathies, or the demands of my religious character, were everything comparatively, and my mere belief in Christ comparatively nothing, since devils believed just as much as I did. The retort was as apt as it was obvious, that the devils believed and trembled, while I believed and rejoiced; and that this joy on my part could not be helped, but only hindered, whenever it was allowed to be complicated with any question about myself. But, no; the evidently foregone conclusion to be forced upon me in every case was, that a man's religious standing, or the love he bears the Church, takes the place under the gospel of his moral standing, or the love he bore the State under the law; hence that no amount of delight in the truth, for the truth's sake alone, could avail me spiritually, unless it were associated with a scrupulous regard for a sanctified public opinion.

"Imagine, then, my glad surprise, my cordial relief, when in this state of robust religious nakedness, with no wretchedest fig-leaf of ecclesiastical finery to cover me from the divine inclemency, I caught my first glimpse of the spiritual contents of revelation, or discerned the profoundly philosophic scope of the Christian truth. This truth at once emboldened me to obey my own regenerate intellectual instincts without further parley, in throwing the Church overboard, or demitting all care of my religious character to the devils, of whom alone such care is an inspiration. The Christian truth, indeed, . . . teaches me to look upon the Church's heartiest malison as God's heartiest benison, inasmuch as whatsoever is most highly esteemed among men—namely, that private or personal righteousness in man, of which the Church is the special protagonist and voucher—is abomination to God. . . . In other words, spiritual Christianity means the complete secularization of the Divine name, or its identification henceforth only with man's common or natural want,—that want in which all men are absolutely one,—and its consequent utter estrangement from the sphere of his private or personal fulness, in which every man is consciously divided from his neighbor; so that I may never aspire to the Divine favor, and scarcely to the Divine tolerance, save in my social or redeemed natural aspect,— that is, as I stand morally identified with the vast community of men of whatever race or religion, cultivating no consciousness of antagonist interests to any other man, but on the contrary frankly disowning every personal hope towards God which does not flow exclusively from his redemption of human nature, or is not based, purely and simply, upon his indiscriminate love to the race." [1]

"Deism," as I have already said, was Mr. James's name for the doctrine that represents God as external to a plurality of absolute and substantial subject beings.

"If the Church could have sincerely felt to be true what she always formally professed,—namely, that God was the sole real and active life of our nature,—she might perhaps have put herself at the head of human affairs, and victoriously led man's forlorn hope against the sullen and sodden Deity that everywhere affects of right to bestride the world.

---

[1] Secret of Swedenborg; pp. 170–175 (abridged).

"The sincere, uncommitted mass of men are spiritually and intellectually incompetent to recognize any 'slough of despond' half so fatal or frightful to them as that of deism, which is the conception of God as a power essentially outside of man, and therefore both inimical and hateful to him. Deism is out and out the only doctrine that has power logically to fill the human heart with despair towards God, *in making man's person a reality*. But this vile deistic doctrine is the very most cherished doctrine of the Church itself, without which indeed to inspire it, it would be ready to confess itself a mere lunatic organization, without further business upon the earth. And there is no chance, consequently, of the Church's again leading the human mind, in ministering to men's higher interests, unless she at once renounces the very doctrine by which she lives, and returns *ex animo* to the early faith which was once *literally* her only possession,—namely, that God, the only true God, the only God worthy to inspire the devotion of the human heart, is not any God of the nations, or foreign supernatural deity at all, but is all simply the Lord; that is, God-*man* figuratively made known to us in the Christ,—thus a most domestic deity, partaker of our own nature to the very brim, making the very grave a farce by virtue of it, essential source and purveyor in fact of this nature, and constant spiritual redeemer of it from the defilement and limitation imposed upon it by our own most absurd and dishonest personality.

"But it is idle, and worse than idle, to expect any revival of the Church. The Bible would have to be written over again, before that stale mother of harlots could ever presume again to put on the dew of her infancy, and aspire to head human hope in its patient, ever enduring battle against deistic oppression and tyranny. The Church is absolutely identified with the deistic name and fame throughout history, so that no honest human cause, nor any sincere zeal for humanity, has ever been ecclesiastically born or ecclesiastically propagated. The visible Church is altogether dead in fact, *sans* teeth, *sans* eyes, *sans* taste, *sans* everything. Unknown to, and even unfelt by, itself consequently, it has providentially been replaced by a new and subtler, because living or invisible, Church, which will neither itself be, nor of itself breed, any hindrance to human hope and aspiration." [1]

The treacherous part played by "professional religion" is thus described:—

"The only danger to the spirit of religion comes from the effort of the soul to assume and cherish a devout *self*-consciousness; or so to *abound* in a religious sense, as to incur the imputation of religiosity or superstition. This is the inalienable vice of professional religion, the only sincere fruit it is capable of bringing forth. The evil spirit which

---

[1] *The New Church Independent*, August, 1881, pp. 373, 374.

religion is primarily intended to exorcise in us is the spirit of selfhood, based upon a most inadequate apprehension of its strictly *provisional* uses to our spiritual nurture. The gradual conquest or slaying of this unholy spirit of self in man is the sole function which religion proposes to itself during his natural life; and without taxing our co-operation too severely, it yet gives us enough to do before its benignant mission is fully wrought out. Such being the invariable office of the religious instinct, *professional* religion steps in to simulate its sway; and with an air all the while of even canting deference, proceeds to build again the things which were destroyed, by reorganizing man's selfhood on a more specious or consecrated basis, and so authenticating all its unslain lusts in a way of devotion to the conventicle, at least, if not to the open, undisguised world.

"Professional religion thus stamps itself the devil's subtlest device for keeping the human soul in bondage. Religion says death—*inward or spiritual death*—to the selfhood in man. Professional religion says: 'Nay, not death, above all not inward or spiritual—because this would be *living*—death, and obviously the selfhood must live in order to be vivified of God. By no means, therefore, let us say an *inward* or *living* death to selfhood, but an outward or *quasi* death, *professionally or ritually enacted*, and so operating a change of base for the selfhood. Selfhood doubtless has been hitherto based upon a most unrighteous enmity on the part of the world to God, and has of itself shared the enmity. Let man then only acknowledge, professionally or ritually, this wicked enmity of the world to God, and he may keep his selfhood unimpaired and unchallenged, to expand and flourish *in secula seculorum.*'

"Professional religion, I repeat, is the devil's masterpiece for ensnaring silly, selfish men. The ugly beast has two heads: one called Ritualism, intended to devour a finer and fastidious style of men,—men of sentiment and decorum, cherishing scrupulously moderate views of the difference between man and God; the other called Revivalism, with a great red mouth intended to gobble up a coarser sort of men,—men for the most part of a fierce carnality, of ungovernable appetite and passion, susceptible at best only of the most selfish hopes and the most selfish fears towards God. I must say, we are not greatly devastated here in Boston—though occasionally vexed—by either head of the beast; on the contrary, it is amusing enough to observe how afraid the great beast himself is of being pecked to pieces on our streets by a little indigenous bantam-cock which calls itself Radicalism, and which struts and crows and scratches gravel in a manner so bumptious and peremptory, that I defy any ordinary barnyard chanticleer to imitate it." [1]

Even the possession of the Bible has been unavailing to us, since its official interpreters have reversed its spiritual sense:—

---

[1] *Society the Redeemed Form of Man*, p. 42.

"The letter of Revelation has doubtless proved inestimably advanta-geous to our civilization; but the most orderly citizenship is as remote from spontaneous or spiritual manhood as baked apples are from ripe ones. Compared with heathen nations, we are indeed as baked apples to green; but I do not see that apples plucked green from the tree and assiduously cooked, as we have been, are near so likely to ripen in the long run as those which are still left hanging upon the boughs, exposed to God's unstinted sun and air. We manage to maintain our egregious self-complacency unperturbed, by vehemently compassionating the heathen, and sending out missionaries to convert them to our foolish ecclesiastical habits,—precisely as if a baked apple should grudge its fellows their natural ripening, and beg them also to come and sputter their indignant life away under the burning summer of the oven, under the blackening autumn of the bake-pan. In fact, the heathen, I suspect, find it difficult to regard us yet even as baked fruit. Our ungenerous overbearing and polluting intercourse with them fits them rather to regard us only as very rotten fruit. Whether baked or rotten, however, we are in either case, so far as our ecclesiastical and political manners are concerned, past the chance of any inward or spiritual ripening. So far as our ecclesiastical conscience is concerned especially, there does not seem one drop of honest native unsophisticated juice left in us. If there were, could we be so content year in and year out to see our clergy, heterodox and orthodox, alternately cuff and clout God's sacred word,—which is inwardly all alive and leaping with spiritual or universal meaning,—as if it were some puny brat of man's begetting, some sickly old-wives' tale, some vapid and senile tradition, destitute even of a fabulous grace and tenderness?" [1]

As one of the appendices to "Substance and Shadow," Mr. James gives us an apologue and its moral,—both of them too good sense and too good literature not to be copied here:—

"I knew a gentleman some years ago of exemplary religiosity and politeness, but of a seasoned inward duplicity, who failed in business, as was supposed, fraudulently. He was in the habit of meeting one of the largest of his creditors every Sunday on his way to church, where his own voice was always among the most melodious to confess any amount of abstract sins and iniquities; and he never failed to raise his hat from his head as he passed, and testify by every demonstrative flourish how much he would still do for the bare forms of friendship, when its life or substance was fled. The creditor was long impatient, but at last grew frantic under this remorseless courtesy, and stopping his debtor one day, told him that he would cheerfully abandon to him the ten thousand dollars he had robbed him of, provided he would forego the exhibition of so much nauseous politeness. 'Sir,' replied the

---

[1] *Substance and Shadow*, p. 503.

imperturbable scamp, 'I would not forego the expression of my duty to you, when we meet, for twice ten thousand dollars!' This is very much our case religiously; whereas, if we would only give over our eternal grimacing and posturing, only leave off our affable but odious ducking and bowing to our great creditor, long enough to see the real truth of the case, and frankly acknowledge bankruptcy utter and fraudulent, nothing could be so hopeful. The supreme powers are infinitely above reckoning with us for our shortcomings, if we would only have the manliness to confess spiritual insolvency, and not seek any longer to hide it from their eyes and our own under these transparent monkey-shines of a mock devotion, under this perpetual promise to pay which never comes to maturity, but gets renewed from Sunday to Sunday *in secula seculorum*. God does not need our labored civility, and must long ere this have sickened of our vapid doffing of the hat to him as we pass. He seeks our solid advantage, not our ridiculous patronage. He desires our living, not our professional, humility; and he desires it only for our sakes, not his own. He would fashion us into the similitude of his perfect love, only that we might enjoy the unspeakable delights of his sympathetic fellowship. If he once saw us to be thus spontaneously disposed towards him, thus genuinely qualified for the immortal participation of his power and blessedness, he would I am sure be more than content never to get a genuflexion from us again while the world lasted, nor hear another of our dreary litanies while sheep bleat and calves bellow." [1]

On the principle of *corruptio optimorum pessima*, it was natural that if the churches in general should in Mr. James's eyes have sold themselves to the devil, the arch-sinners in this respect should be the Swedenborgian congregations, who, if any, might be expected to know better. He accordingly never fails to lash them with his heartiest invective,—with what degree of justice or injustice, it is beyond my power to say. In the larger work in the present volume they have a chapter devoted to themselves. And here is a shorter extract, which will show the writer in his best denunciatory vein:—

"The Swedenborgian sect assumes to be the New Jerusalem, which is the figurative name used in the Apocalypse to denote God's perfected spiritual work in human nature; and under this tremendous designation it is content to employ itself in doing—what? why, in pouring new wine into old bottles, with such a preternatural solicitude for the tenacity of the bottles as necessitates an altogether comical indifference to the quality of the wine. New wine cannot safely go into old bottles but upon one condition, which is that the wine had previously become swipes, or was originally very small beer. In fact, the Swedenborgian sect, viewed as to its essential aims, though of course not as to its

---

[1] *Substance and Shadow*, p. 520.

professed ones, is only on the part of its movers a strike for higher wages,—that is, for higher ecclesiastical consideration than the older sects enjoy at the popular hands. And like all strikes, it will probably succumb at last to the immense stores of fat (or popular respect) traditionally accumulated under the ribs of the old organizations, and enabling them to hybernate through any stress of cold weather merely by sucking their thumbs, or without assimilating any new material. No doubt the insurgents impoverish the older sects to the extent of their own bulk; but they do not substantially affect them in popular regard, because the people, as a rule, care little for truth, but much for the good that animates it; very little for dogmas, but very much for that undeniably human substance which underlies all dogmas, and makes them savory, whether technically sound or unsound. And here the new sect is at a striking disadvantage with all its more ancient competitors; for these are getting ashamed of their old narrowness, and are gradually expanding into some show of sympathy with human want. The sect of the *soi-disant* New Jerusalem, on the other hand, deliberately empties itself of all interest in the hallowed struggle which society is everywhere making for her very existence against established injustice and sanctified imposture, in order to concentrate its energy and prudence upon the washing and dressing, upon the larding and stuffing, upon the embalming and perfuming, of its own invincibly squalid little *corpus*. This Pharisaic spirit, the spirit of separatism or sect, is the identical spirit of hell; and to attempt compassing any consideration for oneself at the Divine hands by making oneself to differ from other people, or claiming a higher divine sanctity than they enjoy, is to encounter the only sure damnation. . . . Let the reader, whatever else he may fairly or foolishly conclude against Swedenborg, acquit him point-blank of countenancing this abject ecclesiastical drivel." [1]

Thus did the sentiment of God's impartial indwelling in all humanity harden Mr. James's heart against all places where the "foolish babble of individual moralism" is preached, and make him unforgiving to whatever bore the name of Church. In setting forth his philosophy up to this point, I have made no reference to Christianity at all. Yet a Christian he was, and a most devout one, after his own fashion,—an *abject* Christian, as a clergyman in Boston called him at the time of his death. I confess, though, that I am myself unable to see any radical and essential necessity for the mission of Christ in his scheme of the universe. A "fall" there is, and a redemption; but with his view of the solidarity of man, we are *all* redeemers of the total order so far as we open ourselves each in his little measure to the spirit of God. Our state reverberates through the whole spiritual world, and helps the construction of that "society" which is the race's redeemed form. All the ac-

---

[1] *Secret of Swedenborg*, p. 209.

counts he gives of Christ do but represent him in this function, in which in lesser degree all may share. I cannot help thinking that if my father had been born outside the pale of Christendom, he might perfectly well have brought together all the other elements of his system, much as it stands now, yet laid comparatively little stress on Christ. Still, the point is an obscure one, and I will let the author speak for himself.

He speaks of Christ in a great many places,—always with the following tenor:—

"To suppose that the universal Father of mankind cared for the Jew one jot more than for the Gentile, and that he cared for one Jew also more than for another, actually intending to give both the former and the latter an endless earthly dominion, was manifestly to blacken the Divine character, and pervert it to the inflammation of every diabolic ambition. And yet this was that literal form of the Jewish hope to which Christ was born. The innocent babe opened his eyes upon mother and father, brother and sister, neighbor and friend, ruler and priest, stupidly agape at the marvels which heralded his birth; [1] and no doubt, as his intelligence dawned, he lent a naturally complacent ear to the promises of personal advancement and glory they showered upon him.

---

[1] A word about Mr. James's attitude towards Biblical criticism is here not out of place. With the education he had, and with the tenacity of his feelings, it was quite impossible he should ever have ceased to regard the Scriptures as inspired books. And yet the atmosphere of *Aufklärung* in which he lived forbade him to keep unaltered that simple mode of regarding these writings which had satisfied his youth. He finally drifted into a state of mind on the subject which was neither credulous nor rationalistic, and not easy for another person to defend. There is a chapter *ad hoc* in the work to which this is an introduction; and this quotation will meanwhile stop the gap:—

"I confess for my part that I should as soon think of spitting upon my mother's grave, or offering any other offence to her stainless memory, as of questioning any of the Gospel facts. And this, not because I regard them as literally or absolutely true,—for the whole realm of fact is as far beneath that of truth as earth is beneath heaven,—but simply because they furnish the indispensable WORD, or master-key, to our interpretation of God's majestic revelation of himself in human nature. When,

accordingly, I am asked whether I believe in the literal facts of Christ's birth from a virgin, his resurrection from death, his ascension into heaven, and so forth, I feel constrained to reply that I neither believe in them nor disbelieve, because the sphere of fact is the sphere of men's knowledge exclusively, and therefore invites neither belief nor disbelief; but that I have a most profound, even a heartfelt conviction of the truth which they, and they alone, reveal,— namely, *the truth of God's essentially human perfection, and,* as implied in that, *the amazing truth of His natural or adventitious manhood;* which conviction keeps me blessedly indifferent to, and utterly unvexed by, the cheap and frivolous scepticism with which so many of our learned modern pundits assail them. I have not the least reverence nor even respect for the facts in question, save as basing or ultimating this grand creative or spiritual truth; and while the truth stands to my apprehension, I shall be serenely obdurate to the learned reasonings of any of my contemporaries in regard to the facts, whether *pro* or *con.*"—*Society the Redeemed Form of Man,* p. 293.

He sucked in the subtlest spiritual poison with every swallow of his mother's milk; and his very religion bound him, so far as human probabilities went, to become an unmitigated devil. I find no trace of any man in history being subject to the temptations that beset this truest of men. I find no trace of any other man who felt himself called upon by the tenderest human love to loathe and disavow the proud and yearning bosom that bore him. I find no other man in history whose profound reverence for infinite goodness and truth drove him to renounce the religion of his fathers, simply because that religion contemplated as its issue his own supreme aggrandizement; and whose profound love to man drove him to renounce every obligation of patriotism, simply because these obligations were plainly coincident with the supremest and subtlest inspirations of his own self-love. No doubt many a man has renounced his traditional creed because it associated him with the obloquy and contempt of his nation, or stood in the way of his personal ambition; and so no doubt many a man has abjured his country, because it disclaimed his title and ability to rule. In short, a thousand men can be found every day who do both of these things from the instinct of self-love. But the eternal peculiarity of the Christian fact is, that Christ did them utterly without the aid of that tremendous lever, actually while it was undermining his force, and subjecting him to ceaseless death. He discredited his paternal gods simply because they were bent upon doing him unlimited honor; and shrank from kindred and countrymen, only because they were intent upon rendering him unparalleled gratitude and benediction. What a mere obscenity every great name in history confesses itself beside this spotless Judean youth, who in the thickest night of time,—unhelped by priest or ruler, by friend or neighbor, by father or mother, by brother or sister; helped, in fact, if we may so consider it, only by the dim expectant sympathy of that hungry rabble of harlots and outcasts who furnished his inglorious retinue, and still further drew upon him the ferocious scorn of all that was devout and honorable and powerful in his nation,—yet let in eternal daylight upon the soul, by steadfastly expanding in his private spirit to the dimensions of universal humanity, so bringing, for the first time in history, the finite human bosom into perfect experimental accord with the infinite Divine love. For my part, I am free to declare that I find the conception of any Divinity superior to this radiant human form inexpressibly treasonable to my own manhood. In fact, I do not hesitate to say that I find the orthodox and popular conception of Deity to be in the comparison a mere odious stench in the nostrils, against which I here indite my exuberant and eternal protest. I shall always cherish the most hearty and cheerful atheism towards every deity but him who has illustrated my own nature with such resplendent power as to make me feel that *Man* henceforth is the only name of honor, and that any God out of the strictest human proportions, any God with essentially disproportionate aims and ends to man, is an unmixed superfluity and nuisance."

The reader ought now to be able to judge for himself whether the works of Henry James deserve further study on his part. For myself, nothing could be so agreeable as to believe that this unpretending introduction might lead a larger public to open the writings of which it treats. Although their author, as will have been noted, gives such ample credit to Swedenborg as the source of his opinions, I have all along spoken of him as an original thinker, whose philosophy was underived. Many disciples of Swedenborg, wielding high authority, say there is no warrant in the master's pages for Mr. James's views. It is certain, to say the very least, that Mr. James has given to the various elements in Swedenborg's teaching an extremely different accentuation and perspective relation to each other, from anything other readers have been able to find. In Swedenborg, as in other writers, much must count for *slag*, and the question "what is the *real* Swedenborg," will naturally be solved by different students in different ways. Such being the case, and I being personally entitled to no opinion, I have thought it best to ignore the name of Swedenborg altogether in the previous pages; not meaning by this to prejudge the question, or attribute to my father an originality he would have disclaimed, but wishing merely to keep the exposition as short and uncomplicated as I could.

A word of comment after so much exposition may not be out of place. Common-sense theism, the popular religion of our European race, has, through all its apparent variations, remained essentially faithful to pluralism, one might almost say to polytheism. Neither Judaism nor Christianity could tend to alter this result, or make us generally see the world in any other light than as a collection of beings which, however they might have arisen, are now severally and substantively there, and the important thing about whom is their practical relations with each other. God, the Devil, Christ, the Saints, and we, are some of these beings. Whatever monistic and pantheistic metaphysics may have crept into the history of Christianity has been confined to epochs, sects, and individuals. For the great mass of men, the practical fact of pluralism has been a sufficient basis for the religious life, and the ultra-phenomenal unity has been nothing more than a lip-formula.

And *naïve* as in the eyes of metaphysics such a view may seem, finite and short of vision and lacking dignity from the intellectual point of view, no philosopher, however subtle, can afford to treat it with disdain; unless, perhaps, he be ready to say that the spirit of Europe is all wrong, and that of Asia right. God, treated as a principle among others,—*primus inter pares*,—has warmth and blood and personality;

is a concrete being whom it does not take a scholar to love and make sacrifices and die for, as history shows. Being almost like a personage in a drama, the lightning of dramatic interest can play from him and about him, and rivet human regard.

The "One and Only Being," however, the Universal Substance, the Soul and Spirit of Things, the First Principle of monistic metaphysics, call it by names as theological and reverential as we will, always seems, it must be confessed, a pale, abstract, and impersonal conception compared with that of the eternal living God, worshipped by the incalculable majority of our race. Such a monistic principle never can be worshipped by a majority of our race until the race's mental constitution change.

Now, the great peculiarity of Mr. James's conception of God is, that it is monistic enough to satisfy the philosopher, and yet warm and living and dramatic enough to speak to the heart of the common pluralistic man. This double character seems to make of this conception an entirely fresh and original contribution to religious thought. I call it monistic enough to satisfy the metaphysician, for although Mr. James's system is anything but a *bald* monism, yet it makes of God the one and only *active* principle; and that is practically all that monism demands. Our experience makes us, it is true, acquainted with an *other* of God, in our own selfhood; but for Mr. James, that other, that selfhood, has no positive existence, being really *naught*, a provisional phantom-soul breathed by God's love into mere logical negation. And that a monism, thus mitigated, can speak to the common heart, a perusal of those pages in which Mr. James portrays creation on God's part as an infinite passion of self-surrender to his opposite, will convince any reader. Anthropomorphism and metaphysics seem for the first time in these pages to go harmoniously hand in hand. The same sun that lights up the frozen summits of abstraction, lights up life's teeming plain,—and no chasm, but an open highway lies between.

The extraordinary power and richness of this conception of the Deity ought, one would say, to make Mr. James's writings indispensable to students of religious thought. Within their compass, each old element receives a fresh expression, each old issue a startling turn. It is hard to believe, that, when they are better known, they will not come to be counted among the few truly original theological works which our language owns. So that even those who think that no theological thought can be *conclusive* will, for this reason, perhaps, not refuse to them a lasting place in literature.

Their most serious enemy will be the *philosophic* pluralist. The naïf practical pluralism of popular religion ought, as I have said, to have no quarrel with the monism they teach. There is however a pluralism hardened by reflection, and deliberate; a pluralism which, in face of the

old mystery of the One and the Many, has vainly sought peace in identification, and ended by taking sides against the One. It seems to me that
the deepest of all philosophic differences is that between this pluralism
and all forms of monism whatever. Apart from analytic and intellectual
arguments, pluralism is a view to which we all practically incline when
in the full and successful exercise of our moral energy. The life we then
feel tingling through us vouches sufficiently for itself, and nothing
tempts us to refer it to a higher source. Being, as we are, a match for
whatever evils actually confront us, we rather prefer to think of them
as endowed with reality, and as being absolutely alien, but, we hope,
subjugable powers. Of the day of our possible impotency we take no
thought; and we care not to make such a synthesis of our weakness
and our strength, and of the good and evil fortunes of the world, as
will reduce them all to fractions, with a common denominator, of some
less fluctuating Unity, enclosing some less partial and more certain
form of Good. The feeling of *action*, in short, makes us turn a deaf
ear to the thought of *being;* and this deafness and insensibility may be
said to form an integral part of what in popular phrase is known as
"healthy-mindedness." Any absolute moralism must needs be such a
healthy-minded pluralism; and in a pluralistic philosophy the healthy-
minded moralist will always feel himself at home.

But healthy-mindedness is not the whole of life; and the *morbid*
view, as one by contrast may call it, asks for a philosophy very different
from that of absolute moralism. To suggest personal will and effort to
one "all sicklied o'er" with the sense of weakness, of helpless failure,
and of fear, is to suggest the most horrible of things to him. What he
craves is to be consoled in his very impotence, to feel that the Powers
of the Universe recognize and secure him, all passive and failing as he
is. Well, we are all *potentially* such sick men. The sanest and best of us
are of one clay with lunatics and prison-inmates. And whenever we
feel this, such a sense of the vanity of our voluntary career comes over
us, that all our morality appears but as a plaster hiding a sore it can
never cure, and all our well-doing as the hollowest substitute for that
well-*being* that our lives ought to be grounded in, but, alas! are not.
This well-being is the object of the *religious* demand,—a demand so
penetrating and unassuageable that no consciousness of such occasional
and outward well-doing as befalls the human lot can ever give it satisfaction. On the other hand, to satisfy the religious demand is to deny
the demands of the moralist. The latter wishes to feel the empirical
goods and evils, on the recognition of which his activity proceeds, to
be *real* goods and evils, with their distinction absolutely preserved. So
that of religion and moralism, the morbid and the healthy view, it may
be said that what is meat to the one is the other's poison. Any absolute

moralism is a pluralism; any absolute religion is a monism. It shows the
depth of Mr. James's religious insight that he first and last and always
made moralism the target of his hottest attack, and pitted religion and
it against each other as enemies, of whom one must die utterly, if the
other is to live in genuine form. The accord of moralism and religion is
superficial, their discord radical. Only the deepest thinkers on both
sides see that one must go. Popular opinion gets over the difficulty by
compromise and contradiction, and the shifting, according to its convenience, of its point of view. Such inconsistency cannot be called a
solution of the matter, though it practically seems to work with most
men well enough. Must not the more radical ways of thinking, after all,
appeal to the same umpire of practice for corroboration of their more
consistent views? Is the religious tendency or the moralistic tendency
on the whole the most serviceable to man's life, taking the latter in the
largest way? By their fruits ye shall know them. *Solvitur ambulando;*
for the *decision* we must perhaps await the day of judgment. Meanwhile, the battle is about us, and we are its combatants, steadfast or
vacillating, as the case may be. It will be a hot fight indeed if the friends
of philosophic moralism should bring to the service of their ideal, so
different from that of my father, a spirit even remotely resembling the
life-long devotion of his faithful heart.

*   *   *

HJ was delighted with what WJ had done for their father's reputation, and wrote him at once:

*   *   *   *   *

London, January 2, 1885

. . . Three days ago . . . came the two copies of Father's (and
your) book, which have [given] me great filial and fraternal joy. All
I have had time to read as yet is the introduction—your part of which
seems to me admirable, perfect. It must have been very difficult to do,
and you couldn't have done it better. And how beautiful and extraordinarily individual (some of them magnificent) all the extracts from
Father's writings which you have selected so happily. It comes over
me as I read them (more than ever before,) how intensely original and
personal his whole system was, and how indispensable it is that those
who go in for religion should take some heed of it. I can't enter into
it (much) myself—I can't be so theological, nor grant his extraordinary
premises, nor throw myself into conceptions of heavens and hells, nor
be sure that the keynote of nature is humanity, etc. But I can enjoy
greatly the spirit, the feeling, and the manner of the whole thing (full as
this last is of things that displease me too,) and feel really that poor
Father, struggling so alone all his life, and so destitute of every worldly
or literary ambition, was yet a great writer. At any rate your task is

beautifully and honourably done—may it be as great or even half as great a service as it deserves to be, to his memory! The book came at a bad time for Alice, as she has had an upset . . . but though she has been able to have it in her hand but for a moment it evidently gives her great pleasure. She burst into tears when I gave it to her, exclaiming "How beautiful it is that William should have done it! Isn't it, isn't it beautiful? And how good William is, how good, how good!" And we talked of poor Father's fading away into silence and darkness, the waves of the world closing over this system which he tried to offer it, and of how we were touched by this act of yours which will (I am sure) do so much to rescue him from oblivion. . . . But the newspapers and reviews are so grim and philistine and impenetrable and stupid, that I can scarcely think of any to which it isn't almost an act of untenderness to send it.

* * *

Copies sold very slowly, and WJ was immensely gratified when his friend the English empiricist Shadworth Hodgson wrote thanking him for the book, although Hodgson had added: "What a pity that all this deep and true insight into the moral and spiritual nature and wants and aspirations and faiths of man—man collectively—should be unaccompanied with a correspondingly complete framework of ideas . . . about the universe of things logically worked out and organised. . . . The *whole* thinking is done with the sole aid of *theological* terminology."

To this WJ answered:

"Your letter . . . was most welcome. Anything responsive about my poor old father's writing falls most gratefully upon my heart. For I fear he found *me* pretty unresponsive during his lifetime; and that through my means any post-mortem response should come seems a sort of atonement. You would have enjoyed knowing him. I know of no one except Carlyle who had such a smiting *Ursprünglichkeit* of intuition, and such a deep sort of humor where human nature was concerned. He bowled one over in such a careless way. He was like Carlyle in being no *reasoner* at all, in the sense in which philosophers are reasoners. Reasoning was only an unfortunate necessity of exposition for them both. His *ideas*, however, were the exact inversion of Carlyle's; and he had nothing to correspond to Carlyle's insatiable learning of historic facts and memory. As you say, the world of his thought had a few elements and no others ever troubled him. *Those* elements were very deep ones, and had theological names. Under 'Man' he would willingly have included all flesh, even that resident in Sirius or ethereal worlds. But he felt no need of positively looking so far. He was the humanest and most genial being in his impulses whom I have ever personally known, and had a bigness and power of nature that everybody felt. I thank you heartily for your interest. I wish that somebody could *take up* something from his system into a system more articulately scientific. As it is, most people will feel the *presence* of something real and true for the while they read, and go away and presently, unable to dovetail [it] into their own framework, forget it altogether."

THE TRIBUTES OF THE SONS
TO THE FATHER

HJ's Notes of a Son

Long after his father's work had been forgotten by any public, HJ produced his impression of him. The difference between what he said and what WJ had said may be partly due to the fact that WJ wrote near the beginning of his career, and HJ at the very end of his. But it is due far more to their inevitably different angles of approach. WJ faced his father as a thinker whose thought must be appraised by other thinkers; whereas HJ retained the memory of an absorbing character whose essence he wanted to suggest. Like WJ, he had responded to his father's immense humanity. He also respected the firmness of his idealism and its grounding in solid intelligence. He even tried to cope with the meaning of his "idea of the Revolution." But he frankly admits that he had to apprehend all his father's ideas "indirectly." He speaks of "assisting" at "intellectual 'scenes' " between Father and William just as though he had been watching a play. It is very revelatory of their relationship that he says he felt his father most completely through the intermediacy of his mother.

As a consequence, even in the chapter where he sums up his impressions, Henry Junior writes about Henry Senior in his most elliptical vein. He is grateful for his father's rare forbearance in never making demands for allegiance from his own "total otherness" of mind. But he also recurs to his belief that as children they enjoyed too much license in religion, and regrets the absence of any coherent form. Not considering himself a thinker, he attempts no assessment of his father's thought beyond what he said to WJ, that he could not enter much into any system of religion. He phrases, very modestly and devotedly withal, his own chief reaction—the reaction he had felt while listening

as a boy to his father reading his work aloud. HJ had sensed a monotony
in its dialectic, and had longed for a greater variety of images—
"Variety, variety—*that* sweet ideal, *that* straight contradiction of any
dialectic."

What had separated him from his father's universals was that he himself, as an incipient storyteller, had been " 'after' persons so much more
than after anything else." It would be interesting to know what he
would have said in response to one of his father's leading contentions,
that "the evil of human nature is subjective consciousness." For the
characters in HJ's fiction are endowed with the fullest play of such
consciousness. It is equally true, however, that his evil characters are
those who are selfishly grasping and blind to the rich play of consciousness in others. He showed himself his father's son in that he was always
concerned not merely with personal but also with social values.

* * * * *

We took his "writing" infinitely for granted—we had always so
taken it, and the sense of him, each long morning, at his study table
either with bent considering brow or with a half-spent and checked
intensity, a lapse backward in his chair and a musing lift of perhaps
troubled and baffled eyes, seems to me the most constant fact, the most
closely interwoven and underlying, among all our breaks and variations. He applied himself there with a regularity and a piety as little
subject to sighing abatements or betrayed fears as if he had been working under pressure for his bread and ours and the question were too
urgent for his daring to doubt. This play of his remarkable genius
brought him in fact throughout the long years no ghost of a reward in
the form of pence, and could proceed to publicity, as it repeatedly
did, not only by the copious and resigned sacrifice of such calculations,
but by his meeting in every single case all the expenses of the process.
The untired impulse to this devotion figured for us, comprehensively
and familiarly, as "Father's Ideas," of the force and truth of which in
his own view we were always so respectfully, even though at times
so bewilderedly and confoundedly persuaded, that we felt there was
nothing in his exhibition of life that they didn't or couldn't account
for. They pervaded and supported his existence, and very considerably
our own; but what comes back to me, to the production of a tenderness and an admiration scarce to be expressed, is the fact that though
we thus easily and naturally lived with them and indeed, as to their
more general effects, the colour and savour they gave to his talk,
breathed them in and enjoyed both their quickening and their embarrassing presence, to say nothing of their almost never less than
amusing, we were left as free and unattacked by them as if they had
been so many droppings of gold and silver coin on tables and chimney-
pieces, to be "taken" or not according to our sense and delicacy, that

is our felt need and felt honour. The combination in him of his different vivacities, his living interest in his philosophy, his living interest in
us and his living superiority to all greed of authority, all overreaching
or everemphasising "success," at least in the heated short run, gave
his character a magnanimity by which it was impossible to us not to
profit in all sorts of responsive and in fact quite luxurious ways. It was
a luxury, I to-day see, to have all the benefit of his intellectual and
spiritual, his religious, his philosophic and his social passion, without
ever feeling the pressure of it to our direct irritation or discomfort.
It would perhaps more truly figure the relation in which he left us to
these things to have likened our opportunities rather to so many scattered glasses of the liquor of faith, poured-out cups stood about for
our either sipping or draining down or leaving alone, in the measure
of our thirst, our curiosity or our strength of head and heart. If there
was much leaving alone in us—and I freely confess that, so far as the
taking any of it all "straight" went, my lips rarely adventured—this
was doubtless because we drank so largely at the source itself, the personally overflowing and irrigating. What it then comes to, for my
present vision, was that he treated us most of all on the whole, as he in
fact treated everything, by his saving imagination—which set us, and
the more as we were naturally so inclined, the example of living as
much as we might in some such light of our own. If we had been asked
in our younger time for instance what *were* our father's ideas, or to
give an example of one of them, I think we should promptly have answered (I should myself have hastened to do so) that the principal was
a devoted attachment to the writings of Swedenborg; as to whom we
were to remember betimes, with intimate appreciation, that in reply to
somebody's plea of not finding him credible our parent had pronounced
him, on the contrary, fairly "insipid with veracity." We liked that
partly, I think, because it disposed in a manner, that is in favour of
our detachment, of the great Emanuel, but when I remember the part
played, so close beside us, by this latter's copious revelation, I feel
almost ashamed for my own incurious conduct. The part played consisted to a large extent in the vast, even though incomplete, array of
Swedenborg's works, the old faded covers of which, anciently red,
actually apt to be loose, and backed with labels of impressive, though
to my sense somewhat sinister London imprint, Arcana Cœlestia,
Heaven and Hell and other such matters—they all had, as from other
days, a sort of black emphasis of dignity—ranged themselves before us
wherever, and however briefly, we disposed ourselves, forming even
for short journeys the base of our father's travelling library and perhaps at some seasons therewith the accepted strain on our mother's
patience. I recall them as inveterately part of our very luggage, requiring proportionate receptacles; I recall them as, in a number con-

siderable even when reduced, part of their proprietor's own most particular dependence on his leaving home, during our more agitated years, for those speculative visits to possible better places (than whatever place of the moment) from which, as I have elsewhere mentioned, he was apt to return under premature, under passionate nostalgic, reaction. The Swedenborgs were promptly out again on their customary shelves or sometimes more improvised perches, and it was somehow not till we had assured ourselves of this that we felt *that* incident closed.

Nothing could have exceeded at the same time our general sense—unless I all discreetly again confine myself to the spare record of my own—for our good fortune in never having been, even when most helpless, dragged by any approach to a faint jerk over the threshold of the inhabited temple. It stood there in the centre of our family life, into which its doors of fine austere bronze opened straight; we passed and repassed them when we didn't more consciously go round and behind; we took for granted vague grand things within, but we never paused to peer or penetrate, and none the less never had the so natural and wistful, perhaps even the so properly resentful, "Oh I say, do look in a moment for manners if for nothing else!" called after us as we went. Our admirable mother sat on the steps at least and caught reverberations of the inward mystic choir; but there were positive contemporary moments when I well-nigh became aware, I think, of something graceless, something not to the credit of my aspiring "intellectual life," or of whatever small pretensions to seriousness I might have begun to nourish, in the anything but heroic impunity of my inattention. William, later on, made up for this not a little, redeeming so, to a large extent, as he grew older, our filial honour in the matter of a decent sympathy, if not of a noble curiosity: distinct to me even are certain echoes of passages between our father and his eldest son that I assisted at, more or less indirectly and wonderingly, as at intellectual "scenes," gathering from them portents of my brother's independent range of speculation, agitations of thought and announcements of difference, which could but have represented, far beyond anything I should ever have to show, a gained and to a considerable degree an enjoyed, confessedly an interested, acquaintance with the paternal philosophic *penetralia*. That particular impression refers indeed to hours which at the point I have reached had not yet struck; but I am touched even now, after all the years, with something exquisite in my half-grasped premonitory vision of their belonging, these belated discussions that were but the flowering of the first germs of such *other*, doubtless already such opposed, perceptions and conclusions, to that order of thin consolations and broken rewards which long figured as the most and the best of what was to have been waited for on our companion's part without the escape of a plaint. Yet I feel I may claim that our aware-

ness of all that was so serenely dispensed with—to call it missed would
have been quite to falsify the story and reflect meanly on the spirit—
never in the least brutally lapsed from admiration, however unuttered
the sentiment itself, after the fashion of raw youth; it is in fact quite
distinct to me that, had there been danger of this, there came to us
from our mother's lips at intervals long enough to emphasise the final
sincerity and beauty a fairly sacred reminder of that strain of almost
solely self-nourished equanimity, or in other words insuperable gaiety,
in her life's comrade, which she had never seen give way. This was the
very gaiety that kept through the years coming out for us—to the
point of inviting free jokes and other light familiarities from us at its
expense. The happiest household pleasantry invested our legend of
our mother's fond habit of address, "Your father's *ideas*, you know—!"
which was always the signal for our embracing her with the last responsive finality (and, for the full pleasure of it, in his presence).
Nothing indeed so much as his presence encouraged the licence, as I may
truly call it, of the legend—that is of our treatment *en famille* of any
reference to the attested public weight of his labours; which, I hasten to
add, was much too esoteric a ground of geniality, a dear old family
joke, not to be kept, for its value, to ourselves. But there comes back to
me the impression of his appearing on occasion quite moved to the
exuberance of cheer—as a form of refreshment he could draw on for
a stronger and brighter spurt, I mean—by such an apology for resonance of reputation as our harmless, our of course utterly edgeless,
profanity represented. It might have been for him, by a happy stretch,
a sign that the world *did* know—taking us for the moment, in our
selfish young babble, as a part of the noise of the world. Nothing, at the
same time, could alter the truth of his case, or can at least alter it to me
now: he had, intellectually, convictionally, passionally speaking, a selfless detachment, a lack of what is called the eye for effect—always I
mean of the elated and interested order—which I can but marvel at in
the light of the rare aptitude of his means to his end, and in that of the
beauty of both, though the stamp was doubtless most vivid, for so
differing, so gropingly "esthetic" a mind as my own, in his unfailingly
personal and admirable style. We knew he had thoroughly his own
"unconventional" form, which, by the unspeakable law of youth, we
managed to feel the distinction of as not platitudinous even while we
a bit sneakingly felt it as quotable, on possible occasions, against our
presence of mind; the great thing was at all events that we couldn't
live with him without the sense that if his books resembled his talk and
his character—as we moreover felt they couldn't help almost violently
doing—they might want for this, that or the other which kept the
conventional true to its type, but could as little fail to flush with the
strong colour, colour so remarkably given and not taken, projected

and not reflected, colour of thought and faith and moral and expressional atmosphere, as they could leave us without that felt side-wind of their strong composition which made after all so much of the air we breathed and was in the last resort the gage of something perpetually fine going on.

It is not too much to say, I think, that our religious education, so far as we had any, consisted wholly in that loose yet enlightening impression: I say so far as we had any in spite of my very definitely holding that it would absolutely not have been possible to us, in the measure of our sensibility, to breathe more the air of that reference to an order of goodness and power greater than any this world by itself can show which we understand as the religious spirit. Wondrous to me, as I consider again, that my father's possession of this spirit, in a degree that made it more deeply one with his life than I can conceive another or a different case of its being, should have been unaccompanied with a single one of the outward or formal, the theological, devotional, ritual, or even implicitly pietistic signs by which we usually know it. The fact of course was that his religion was nothing if not a philosophy, extraordinarily complex and worked out and original, intensely personal as an exposition, yet not only susceptible of application, but clamorous for it, to the whole field of consciousness, nature and society, history, knowledge, all human relations and questions, every pulse of the process of our destiny. Of this vast and interesting conception, as striking an expression of the religious spirit surely as ever was put forth, his eldest son has given an account [1]—so far as this was possible at once with brevity and with full comprehension—that I should have been unable even to dream of aspiring to, and in the masterly clearness and justice of which the opportunity of the son blends with that of the critic, each character acting in perfect felicity, after a fashion of which I know elsewhere no such fine example. It conveys the whole sense of our father's philosophic passion, which was theologic, by my direct impression of it, to a degree fairly outdistancing all theologies; representing its weight, reproducing its utterance, placing it in the eye of the world, and making for it the strong and single claim it suggests, in a manner that leaves nothing to be added to the subject. I am not concerned with the intrinsic meaning of these things here, and should not be even had they touched me more directly, or more converted me from what I can best call, to my doubtless scant honour, a total otherness of contemplation, during the years when my privilege was greatest and my situation for inquiry and response amplest; but the active, not to say the obvious, moral of them, in all our younger time, was that a life of the most richly consequent flowed straight out of them, that

[1] *Literary Remains of Henry James,* Boston, 1885. The portrait accompanying the volume gave us, alas, but the scantest satisfaction.

in this life, the most abundantly, and above all naturally, communicated *as* life that it was possible to imagine, we had an absolutely equal share, and that in fine I was to live to go back with wonder and admiration to the quantity of secreted thought in our daily medium, the quality of intellectual passion, the force of cogitation and aspiration, as to the explanation both of a thousand surface incoherences and a thousand felt felicities. A religion that was so systematically a philosophy, a philosophy that was so sweepingly a religion, being together, by their necessity, as I have said, an intensity of relation to the actual, the consciousness so determined was furnished forth in a way that met by itself the whole question of the attitude of "worship" for instance; as I have attempted a little to show that it met, with a beautiful good faith and the easiest sufficiency, every other when such came up: those of education, acquisition, material vindication, what is called success generally. In the beauty of the whole thing, again, I lose myself—by which I mean in the fact that we were all the while partaking, to our most intimate benefit, of an influence of direction and enlargement attended with scare a single consecrated form and which would have made many of these, had we been exposed to intrusion from them, absurdly irrelevant. My father liked in our quite younger period to read us chapters from the New Testament and the Old, and I hope we liked to listen to them—though I recall their seeming dreary from their association with school practice; but that was the sole approach to a challenge of our complete freedom of inward, not less than our natural ingenuity of outward, experience. No other explicit address to us in the name of the Divine could, I see, have been made with any congruity—in face of the fact that invitations issued in all the vividest social terms, terms of living appreciation, of spiritual perception, of "human fellowship," to use the expression that was perhaps oftenest on his lips and his pen alike, were the very substance of the food supplied in the parental nest.

The freedom from pressure that we enjoyed in every direction, all those immunities and exemptions that had been, in protracted childhood, positively embarrassing to us, as I have already noted, before the framework, ecclesiastical and mercantile, squared at us as with reprobation from other households, where it seemed so to conduce to their range of resource—these things consorted with our yet being yearned over or prescribed for, by every implication, after a fashion that was to make the social organisation of such invidious homes, under my subsequent observation of life, affect me as so much bleak penury or domestic desert where these things of the spirit, these genialities of faith were concerned. Well do I remember, none the less, how I was troubled all along just by this particular crookedness of our being so extremely religious without having, as it were, anything in the least classified or striking to show for it; so that the measure of other-worldliness pervading our premises was rather a waste, though at the same time oddly enough a congestion—projecting outwardly as it did no single one of those usual symptoms of propriety any of which, gathered at a venture from the general prospect, might by my sense have served: I shouldn't have been particular, I thought, as to the selection. Religion was a matter, by this imagination, to be worked off much more than to be worked in, and I fear my real vague sentiment to have been but that life would under the common equipment be somehow more amusing; and this even though, as I don't forget, there was not an item of the detail of devotional practice that we had been so much as allowed to divine. I scarce know why I should have wanted anything more amusing, as most of our coevals would have regarded it, than that we had from as far back as I could remember indulged in no shade of an approach to "keeping Sunday"; which is one of the reasons why to speak as if piety could have borne for us any sense but the tender human, or to speak at all of devotion, unction, initiation, even of the vaguest, into the exercises or professions, as among our attributes, would falsify altogether our mere fortune of a general liberty of living, of making ourselves as brightly at home as might be, in that "spiritual world" which we were in the habit of hearing as freely alluded to as we heard the prospect of dinner or the call of the postman. The oddity of my own case, as I make it out so far as it involved a confused criticism, was that my small uneasy mind, bulging and tightening in the wrong, or at least in unnatural and unexpected, places, like a little jacket ill cut or ill sewn, attached its gaping view, as I have already more than enough noted, to things and persons, objects and aspects, frivolities all, I dare say I was willing to grant, compared with what-ever manifestations of the serious, these being by need, apparently, the abstract; and that in fine I should have been thankful for a state of faith, a conviction of the Divine, an interpretation of the universe—anything one might have made bold to call it—which would have supplied more features or appearances. Feeling myself "after" persons so much more than after anything else—to recur to that side of my earliest and most constant consciousness which might have been judged most de-plorable—I take it that I found the sphere of our more nobly sup-positious habitation too imperceptibly peopled; whereas the religious life of every other family that could boast of any such (and what family didn't boast?) affected my fancy as with a social and material crowdedness. That faculty alone was affected—this I hasten to add; no directness of experience ever stirred for me; it being the case in the first place that I scarce remember, as to all our young time, the crossing of our threshold by any faint shade of an ecclesiastical presence, or the lightest encounter with any such elsewhere, and equally of the essence, over and above, that the clerical race, the pre-eminently restrictive tribe, as I apprehended them, couldn't very well have agreed less with the general colour of my fondest vision: if it be not indeed more correct to say that I was reduced to *supposing* they couldn't. We knew in truth nothing whatever about them, a fact that, as I recover it, also flushes for me with its fine awkwardness—the social scene in general handsomely bristling with them to the rueful view I sketch, and they yet remaining for us, or at any rate for myself, such creatures of pure hearsay that when late in my teens, and in particular after my twentieth year, I began to see them portrayed by George Eliot and Anthony Trollope the effect was a disclosure of a new and romantic species. Strange beyond my present power to account for it this anomaly that amid a civilisation replete with "ministers"—for we at least knew the word—actively, competitively, indeed as would often appear quite violently, ministering, so little sense of a brush against approved examples was ever to attend me that I had finally to draw my nearest sufficiency of a true image from pictures of a social order largely alien to our own. All of which, at the same time, I allow myself to add, didn't mitigate the simple fact of my felt—my indeed so luxuriously permitted—detachment of sensibility from everything, everything, that is, in the way of great relations, as to which our father's emphasis was richest. *There* was the dim dissociation, there my comparative poverty, or call it even frivolity, of instinct: I gaped imaginatively, as it were, to such a different set of relations. I couldn't have framed stories that would have succeeded in involving the least of the relations that seemed most present to *him;* while those most present to myself, that is more complementary to whatever it was I thought of as humanly most interesting, attaching, inviting, were the ones his schemes of importances seemed virtually to do without. Didn't I discern in this from the first a kind of implied snub to the significance of mine?—so that, in the blest absence of "pressure" which I just sought here passingly to celebrate, I could brood to my heart's content on the so conceivable alternative of a field of exposure crammed with those objective appearances that my faculty seemed alone fitted to grasp. In which there was ever the small torment of the fact—though I don't quite see to-day why it should not have been of a purely pleasant irritation—that what our parent most overflowed with was just the brave contradiction or opposition between all his parts, a thing which made for perfect variety, which he carried ever so easily and brightly, and which would have put one no less in the wrong had one accused him of knowing only the abstract (as I was so complacently and invidiously disposed to name it) than if one had foolishly remarked on his living and concluding without it. But I have already made clear his great mixed range—which of course couldn't *not* have been the sign of a mind conceiving our very own breathing humanity in its every fibre the absolute expression of a resident Divinity. No element of character, no spontaneity of life, but instantly seized his attention and incurred his greeting and his comment; which things could never possibly have been so genially alert and expert—as I have, again, before this, super-abundantly recorded—if it had not fairly fed on active observation and contact. He could answer one with the radiant when one challenged him with the obscure, just as he could respond with the general when one pulled at the particular; and I needn't repeat that this made for us, during all our time, anything but a starved actuality.

None the less, however, I remember it as savouring of loss to me—which is my present point—that our so thoroughly informal scene of susceptibility seemed to result from a positive excess of familiarity, in his earlier past, with such types of the shepherd and the flock, to say nothing of such forms of the pasture, as might have met in some degree my appetite for the illustrational. This was one of the things that made me often wish, as I remember, that I might have caught him sooner or younger, less developed, as who should say; the matters that appeared, however confusedly, to have started his development being by this measure stranger and livelier than most of those that finally crowned it, marked with their own colour as many of these doubtless were. Three or four strongest pages in the fragment of autobiography gathered by his eldest son into the sheaf of his Literary Remains describe the state of soul undergone by him in England, in '44, just previous to the hour at which Mrs. Chichester, a gentle lady of his acquaintance there, brought to his knowledge, by a wondrous chance, the possibility that the great Swedenborg, from whom she had drawn much light, might have something to say to his case; so that under the impression of his talk with her he posted at once up to London from the neighbourhood of Windsor, where he was staying, possessed him-self of certain volumes of the writings of the eminent mystic (so-called I mean, for to my father this description of him was grotesque), and passed rapidly into that grateful infinitude of recognition and applica-tion which he was to inhabit for the rest of his days. I saw him move about there after the fashion of the oldest and easiest native, and this had on some sides its own considerable effect, tinged even on occasion with romance; yet I felt how the *real* right thing for me would have been the hurrying drama of the original rush, the interview with the ad-mirable Mrs. Chichester, the sweet legend of his and my mother's charmed impression of whom had lingered with us—I admired her very name, there seeming none other among us at all like it; and then the return with the tokens of light, the splendid agitation as the light deepened, and the laying in of that majestic array of volumes which were to form afterward the purplest rim of his library's horizon and

which I was thus capable, for my poor part, of finding valuable, in
default of other values, as coloured properties in a fine fifth act. It was
all a play I hadn't "been to," consciously at least—that was the trouble;
the curtain had fallen while I was still tucked in my crib, and I assisted but on a comparatively flat home scene at the echo of a great
success. I could still have done, for the worst, with a consciousness
of Swedenborg that should have been graced at least with Swedenborgians—aware as I was of the existence of such enrolled disciples,
ornaments of a church of their own, yet known to us only as persons
rather acidly mystified by the inconvenience, as we even fancied them
to feel it, of our father's frankly independent and disturbingly irregular
(all the more for its being so expressive) connection with their in-
spirer. In the light or the dusk of all this it was surely impossible to
make out that he professed any faint shade of that clerical character
as to his having incurred which we were, "in the world," to our bewilderment, not infrequently questioned. Those of the enrolled order,
in the matter of his and their subject of study, might in their way too
have raised to my regard a fretted vault or opened a long-drawn aisle,
but they were never at all, in the language of a later day, to materialise
to me; we neither on a single occasion sat in their circle, nor did one
of them, to the best of my belief, ever stray, remonstrantly or in-
vitingly, into ours; where Swedenborg was read not in the least as the
Bible scarce more than just escaped being, but even as Shakespeare or
Dickens or Macaulay was content to be—which was without our
arranging or subscribing for it. I seem to distinguish that if a fugitive or
a shy straggler from the pitched camp did turn up it was under cover
of night or of curiosity and with much panting and putting off of the
mantle, much nervous laughter above all—this safe, however, to become
on the shortest order amusement easy and intimate. That *figured*
something in a slight way—as at least I suppose I may infer from the
faint adumbration I retain; but nothing none the less much attenuated
what I suppose I should have denounced as the falsity of our position
(meaning thereby of mine) had I been constitutionally at all voluble
for such flights. Constructionally we had all the fun of licence, while
the truth seemed really to be that fun in the religious connection
closely depended on bondage. The fun was of course that I wanted
in this line of diversion something of the coarser strain; which came
home to me in especial, to cut the matter short, when I was present,
as I yielded first and last to many an occasion for being, at my father's
reading out to my mother with an appreciation of that modest grasp of
somebody's attention, the brief illusion of publicity, which has now
for me the exquisite grace of the touching, some series of pages from
among his "papers" that were to show her how he had this time at last
done it. No touch of the beautiful or the sacred in the disinterested life

can have been absent from such scenes—I find every such ideally there; and my memory rejoices above all in their presentation of our mother at her very perfectest of soundless and yet absolutely all-saving service and trust. To have attempted any projection of our father's aspect without an immediate reference to her sovereign care for him and for all of us as the so widely open, yet so softly enclosing, lap of all his liberties and all our securities, all our variety and withal our harmony, the harmony that was for nine-tenths of it our sense of her gathered life in us, and of her having no other—to have so proceeded has been but to defer by instinct and by scruple to the kind of truth and of beauty before which the direct report breaks down. I may well have stopped short with what there would be to say, and yet what account of us all can pretend to have gone the least bit deep without coming to our mother at every penetration? We simply lived by her, in pro-portion as we lived spontaneously, with an equanimity of confidence, an independence of something that I should now find myself think of as decent compunction if I didn't try to call it instead morbid delicacy, which left us free for detachments of thought and flights of mind, ex-periments, so to speak, on the assumption of our genius and our intrinsic interest, that I look back upon as to a luxury of the un-worried that is scarce of this world. This was a support on which my father rested with the absolute whole of his weight, and it was when I felt her listen with the whole of her usefulness, which needed no other force, being as it was the whole of her tenderness and amply sufficing by itself, that I understood most what it was so to rest and so to act. When in the fulness of the years she was to die, and he then to give us time, a few months, as with a beatific depth of design, to marvel at the manner of his acceptance of the stroke, a shown triumph of his philosophy, he simply one day consciously ceased, quietly declined to continue, as an offered measure of his loss of interest. Nothing—he had enabled himself to make perfectly sure—was in the least worth while without her; this attested, he passed away or went out, with entire simplicity, promptness and ease, for the definite reason that his support had failed. His philosophy had been not his support but his suspension, and he had never, I am sure, felt so lifted as at that hour, which splendidly crowned his faith. It showed us more intimately still what, in this world of cleft components, one human being can yet be for another, and how a form of vital aid may have operated for years with such perfection as fairly to have made recognition seem at the time a sort of excess of reaction, an interference or a pedantry. All which is imaged for me while I see our mother listen, at her work, to the full music of the "papers." She could do that by the mere force of her complete availability, and could do it with a smoothness of sur-render that was like an array of all the perceptions. The only thing that

I might well have questioned on these occasions was the possibility on the part of a selflessness so consistently and unabatedly active of its having anything ever left *acutely* to offer; to abide so unbrokenly in such inaptness for the personal claim might have seemed to render difficult such a special show of it as any particular pointedness of hospitality would propose to represent. I dare say it was our sense of this that so often made us all, when the explicit or the categoric, the impulse of acclamation, flowered out in her, find our happiest play of filial humour in just embracing her for the sound of it; than which I can imagine no more expressive tribute to our constant depths of indebtedness. She lived in ourselves so exclusively, with such a want of use for anything in her consciousness that was not about us and for us, that I think we almost contested her being separate enough to be proud of us—it was too like our being proud of ourselves. We were delightedly derisive with her even about pride in our father—it was the most domestic of our pastimes; for what really could exceed the tenderness of our fastening on her that she *was* he, *was* each of us, was our pride and our humility, our possibility of *any* relation, and the very canvas itself on which we were floridly embroidered? How can I better express what she seemed to do for her second son in especial than by saying that even with her deepest delicacy of attention present I could still feel, while my father read, why it was that I most of all seemed to wish we might have been either much less religious or much more so? Was not the reason at bottom that I so suffered, I might almost have put it, under the impression of his style, which affected me as somehow too philosophic for life, and at the same time to living, as I made out, for thought?—since I must weirdly have opined that by so much as you were individual, which meant personal, which meant monotonous, which meant limitedly allusive and verbally repetitive, by so much you were not literary or, so to speak, *largely* figurative. My father had terms, evidently strong, but in which I presumed to feel, with a shade of irritation, a certain narrowness of exclusion as to images otherwise—and oh, since it was a question of the pen, so multitudinously!—entertainable. Variety, variety—*that* sweet ideal, *that* straight contradiction of any dialectic, hummed for me all the while as a direct, if perverse and most unedified, effect of the parental concentration, with some of its consequent, though heedless, dissociations. I heard it, felt it, saw it, both shamefully enjoyed and shamefully denied it as form, though as form only; and I owed thus supremely to my mother that I could, in whatever obscure levity, muddle out some sense of my own preoccupation under the singular softness of the connection that she kept for me, by the outward graces, with that other and truly much intenser which I was so little framed to share.

. . . A less vague or vain idealist couldn't, I think, have been encountered; it was given him to catch in the fact at almost any turn right or left some flagrant assurance or promise of the state of man transfigured. . . . In which light it is that I recognise, and even to elation, how little, practically, of the idea of the Revolution in the vulgar or violent sense was involved in his seeing so many things, in the whole social order about him, and in the interest of their being more or less immediately altered, as lamentably, and yet at the same time and under such a coloured light, as amusingly and illustratively, wrong—wrong, that is, with a blundering helpless human salience that kept criticism humorous, kept it, so to speak, sociable and almost "sympathetic" even when readiest. The case was really of his rather feeling so vast a rightness close at hand or lurking immediately behind actual arrangements that a single turn of the inward wheel, one real response to pressure of the spiritual spring, would bridge the chasms, straighten the distortions, rectify the relations and, in a word, redeem and vivify the whole mass— after a far sounder, yet, one seemed to see, also far subtler, fashion than any that our spasmodic annals had yet shown us. It was of course the old story that we had only to *be* with more intelligence and faith—an immense deal more, certainly—in order to work off, in the happiest manner, the many-sided ugliness of life; which was a process that might go on, blessedly, in the quietest of all quiet ways. *That* wouldn't be blood and fire and tears, or would be none of these things stupidly precipitated; it would simply have taken place by *enjoyed* communication and contact, enjoyed concussion or convulsion even—since pangs and agitations, the very agitations of perception itself, are of the highest privilege of the soul and there is always, thank goodness, a saving sharpness of play or complexity of consequence in the intelligence completely alive. The meaning of which remarks for myself, I must be content to add, is that the optimists of the world, the constructive idealists, as one has mainly known them, have too often struck one as overlooking more of the aspects of the real than they recognise; whereas our indefeasible impression, William's and mine, of our parent was that he by his very constitution and intimate heritage recognised many more of those than he overlooked. What was the finest part of our intercourse with him—that is the most nutritive—but a positive record of that? Such a matter as that the factitious had absolutely no hold on him was the truest thing about him, and it was all the while present to us, I think, as backing up his moral authority and play of vision that never, for instance, had there been a more numerous and candid exhibition of all the human susceptibilities than in the nest of his original nurture. I have spoken of the fashion in which I still see him, after the years, attentively bent over those much re-written "papers," that we had, even at our stupidest, this warrant for going in vague admiration of that they caught the eye, even the most filially detached, with a final face of wrought clarity, and thereby of beauty, that there *could* be no thinking unimportant—and see him also fall back from the patient posture, again and again, in long fits of remoter consideration, wondering, pondering sessions into which I think I was more often than not moved to read, for the fine interest and colour of it, some story of acute inward difficulty amounting for the time to discouragement. If one wanted drama *there* was drama, and of the most concrete and most immediately offered to one's view and one's suspense; to the point verily, as might often occur, of making one go roundabout it on troubled tiptoe even as one would have held one's breath at the play.

These opposed glimpses, I say, hang before me as I look back, but really fuse together in the vivid picture of the fond scribe separated but by a pane of glass—his particular preference was always directly to face the window—from the general human condition he was so devoutly concerned with. He *saw* it, through the near glass, saw it in such detail and with a feeling for it that broke down nowhere—that was the great thing; which truth it confirmed that his very fallings back and long waits and stays and almost stricken musings witnessed exactly to his intensity, the intensity that would "come out," after all, and make his passionate philosophy and the fullest array of the appearances that couldn't be blinked fit together and harmonise. Detached as I could during all those years perhaps queerly enough believe myself, it would still have done my young mind the very greatest violence to have to suppose that any plane of conclusion for him, however rich and harmonious he might tend to make conclusion, could be in the nature of a fool's paradise. Small vague outsider as I was, I couldn't have borne *that* possibility; and I see, as I return to the case, how little I really could ever have feared it. This would have amounted to fearing it on account of his geniality—a shocking supposition; as if his geniality had been thin and *bête*, patched up and poor, and not by the straightest connections, nominal and other, of the very stuff of his genius. No, I feel myself complacently look back to *my* never having, even at my small poorest, been so *bête*, either, as to conceive he might be "wrong," wrong as a thinker-out, in his own way, of the great mysteries, because of the interest and amusement and vividness his attesting spirit could fling over the immediate ground. What he saw *there* at least could be so enlightening, so evocatory, could fall in so—which was to the most inspiring effect within the range of perception of a scant son who was doubtless, as to the essential, already more than anything else a novelist *en herbe*. If it didn't sound in a manner patronising I should say that I saw that my father saw; and that I couldn't but have given my own case away by not believing, however obscurely, in the virtue of his consequent and ultimate synthesis. Of course I never dreamed of any such

name for it—I only thought of it as something very great and fine
founded on those forces in him that came home to us and that touched
us all the while. As these were extraordinary forces of sympathy and
generosity, and that yet knew how to be such without falsifying any
minutest measure, the structure raised upon them might well, it would
seem, and even to the uppermost sublime reaches, be as valid as it was
beautiful. If he so endeared himself wasn't it, one asked as time went on,
through his never having sentimentalised or merely meditated away, so
to call it, the least embarrassment of the actual about him, and having
with a passion peculiarly his own kept together his stream of thought,
however transcendent and the stream of life, however humanised?
There was a kind of experiential authority in his basis, as he felt his basis
—there being no human predicament he couldn't by a sympathy more
like direct experience than any I have known enter into; and this
authority, which concluded so to a widening and brightening of the
philosophic—for him the spiritual—sky, made his character, as intercourse disclosed it, in a high degree fascinating.

*   *   *

BOOK THREE

BOOK THREE

FORMULATIONS

WJ

WILLIAM JAMES came to maturity extremely slowly. One consequence of his father's insistence on *being* was that WJ did not even find the sort of work he wanted to be *doing* until he was past thirty. His temperament did not allow him to take such uncertainty easily. He wrote to Wendell Holmes from Germany in 1868: "Much would I give for a constructive passion of some kind."

HJ's picture of their education stops at the threshold of WJ's professional training. His rapt admiration for WJ's seemingly endless capabilities, and for his growing interest, from the time of boyish experiments, "in the 'queer' or the incalculable effects of things," led him to falsify the actual pattern by adding: "There was apparently for him no possible effect whatever that mightn't be more or less rejoiced in as such." For between spurts of enthusiasm WJ's young manhood knew not only boredom but the gravest sort of anxiety. He had his father's excitable nature without the steady lodestar of his father's faith. The strain upon him can be observed in the succession of neurotic symptoms that oppressed him so severely that it was for some years doubtful whether he would ever be able to adjust to a normal career. The general frailty that had kept him out of the Civil War grew far more marked during the latter half of his twenties. As his oldest son summed up the record of these years, "Insomnia, digestive disorders, eye-troubles, weakness of the back, and sometimes deep depression of spirits followed each other or afflicted him simultaneously."

During his first year in Cambridge, before his twentieth birthday, he had written home a mock-serious "resumé of his future history": "One year study chemistry, then spend one term at home, then one year with Wyman, then a medical education, then five or six years with Agassiz, then probably death, death, death with inflation and plethora of knowledge." He carried out that scheme to the extent that he moved with brilliant but restless versatility from chemistry under Eliot to anatomy under Wyman to natural history under Agassiz. He went off on the expedition to Brazil even before taking his degree at the Medical School, and said in later years: "The hours I spent with Agassiz so taught me the difference between all possible abstractionists and all livers in the light of the world's concrete fulness that I have never been able to forget it."

He resumed his studies at Harvard in the spring of 1866, only to conclude that he had not enough stamina for regular work, and to leave for eighteen months in Germany. From there he wrote back, with the candor which always distinguished his self-scrutiny, that he was not fitted for laboratory work. He also added that he had a "bad memory," and "slack interest in the details" of physiology. He became increasingly burdened with the misery of insecurity, and poured out in his journal his "unspeakable disgust for the dead drifting of my own life for some time past. . . . Oh God! an end to the idle, idiotic sinking into *Vorstellungen* disproportionate to the object. Every good experience ought to be interpreted in practice. . . . Keep sinewy all the while,—and work at present with a mystical belief in the reality, interpreted somehow, of humanity!" That last sentence indicates how, despite his skepticism, he clung instinctively to his father's core of belief. The "ought" in the sentence before also suggests how he was to find the way out of his pit of despondency—through the force of a resolute will.

From this time forward to the end of his life we can follow each successive stage of WJ's thought by means of an abundant variety of formulations. His greatest natural gift, as much an artist's as a psychologist's, was for seizing upon and describing the qualities of the "fugitive sequences" of consciousness. His formulations have none of the pompousness or the dessication of the usual professorial philosopher. He was, indeed, forever warning his friends against the "earnest search for coherency in a mind that is but a jumble of fragments." He often scandalized colleagues by what Perry has called "a pathological repugnance to the processes of exact thought." But this repugnance rose from his ever living sense of "the gaping contrast between the richness of life and the poverty of all possible formulas." He was thus a philosopher in Emerson's sense. He was Man Thinking, as a result of the impact of life and of the need to find his directions.

Even during the intermittences of his worst period of depression he remained the vivid personality who, as Alice said, seemed "to be born afresh every morning." The stages of his career take on, therefore, a widely representative value, since the directions that he found were those of the liberal mind when, particularly in America, the choices all

WJ at 18

Pencil portrait of WJ,
by himself, about 1866

HJ at 17

seemed free, and liberalism meant primarily liberation. WJ wrote on one of the final pages of his *Principles of Psychology*: "A thing is important if any one *think* it important," and he was able to remain confident in that belief. He dedicated *Pragmatism* in 1907 "to the Memory of John Stuart Mill, from whom I first learned the pragmatic openness of mind, and whom my fancy likes to picture as our leader were he alive to-day."

He broke with his father's metaphysics and became an empiricist because he began to work during the era of evolutionary science, when both psychology and philosophy had close connections with biology. He was greatly impressed by Shadworth Hodgson's dictum that "realities are only what they are 'known as.'" But he soon began to choose for himself. Though greatly influenced by Darwin, he showed his own bent by taking issue, in the mid-1870's, with Spencer's "spectator theory of knowledge," and by affirming that "the knower is not simply a mirror floating with no foot-hold anywhere, and passively reflecting an order that he comes upon and finds simply existing. The knower is an actor. . . . Mental interests, hypotheses, postulates, so far as they are bases for human action—action which to a great extent transforms the world—help to *make* the truth which they declare. In other words, there belongs to mind from its birth upwards, a spontaneity, a vote." Here was the beginning of his pragmatism.

Further summary is unnecessary in the face of the amplitude of James' own statements. Each one of the following could be extended by many variants; but taken together they are designed, not to catalogue all the tenets of his philosophy, but to immerse the reader in the main currents of an American mind in action. We may start with one of his strongest protests against his want of formal education, a deficiency which John Dewey believes to have been among James' greatest assets since it protected his mind from academic deadening.

* * * * *

Berlin, November 7, 1867

. . . If six years ago I could have felt the same satisfied belief in the worthiness of a life devoted to simple, patient, monotonous, scientific labor day after day (without reference to its results) and at the same time have had some inkling of the importance and nature of *education* (i.e., getting orderly habits of thought, and by intense exercise in a variety of different subjects, getting the mind supple and delicate and firm), I might be now on the path to accomplishing something some day, even if my health had turned out no better than it is. But my habits of mind have been so bad that I feel as if the greater part of the last ten years had been worse than wasted, and now have so little surplus of physical vigor as to shrink from trying to retrieve them. Too late! too late! If I had been *drilled* further in mathematics, physics, chemistry, logic, and the history of metaphysics, and had established, even if only in my memory, a firm and thoroughly familiar *basis* of knowledge in all these sciences (like the basis of human anatomy one gets in study- ing medicine), to which I should involuntarily refer all subsequently acquired facts and thoughts,—instead of having now to keep going back and picking up loose ends of these elements, and wasting whole hours in looking to see how the new facts are related to them, or whether they are related to them at all,—I might be steadily advancing. —But enough! Excuse the damned whine of this letter; I had no idea whatever of writing it when I sat down, but I am in a mood of indi- gestion and blueness.

* * *

Tom Ward, to whom this letter and the next were addressed, was one of the close friends of WJ's youth, who, after being a member of the Brazilian expedition, turned from science to banking. Wendell Holmes presented more of a challenge to WJ's mind, but it is char- acteristic of WJ that his feeling that Ward needed help drew from him the following intimate disclosure of his own problems. It is equally characteristic that although WJ respected Holmes throughout his life, he was gradually repelled by a certain cold impersonality in Holmes' nature and particularly by his skepticism. For once James had out- grown his own doubts, he found such an attitude inadequate.

* * * * *

Berlin, January 1868

. . . It made me feel quite sad to hear you talk about the inward deadness and listlessness into which you had again fallen in New York. Bate not a jot of heart nor hope, but steer right onward. Take for granted that you've got a temperament from which you must make up your mind to expect twenty times as much anguish as other people need to get along with. Regard it as something as external to you as possible, like the curl of your hair. Remember when old December's darkness is everywhere about you, that the world is really in every minutest point as full of life as in the most joyous morning you ever lived through; that the sun is whanging down, and the waves dancing, and the gulls skimming down at the mouth of the Amazon, for in- stance, as freshly as in the first morning of creation; and the hour is just as fit as any hour that ever was for a new gospel of cheer to be preached. I am sure that one can, by merely thinking of these matters of fact, limit the power of one's evil moods over one's way of looking at the Kosmos.

I am very glad that you think the methodical habits you must stick to in book-keeping are going to be good discipline to you. I confess to having had a little feeling of spite when I heard you had gone back on science; for I had always thought you would one day emerge into deep and clear water there—by keeping on long enough. But I really don't think it so *all*-important what our occupation is, so long as we do respectably and keep a clean bosom. Whatever we are *not* doing is pretty sure to come to us at intervals, in the midst of our toil, and fill us with pungent regrets that it is lost to us. I have felt so about zoölogy whenever I was not studying it, about anthropology when studying physiology, about practical medicine lately, now that I am cut off from it, etc., etc., etc.; and I conclude that that sort of nostalgia is a necessary incident of our having imaginations, and we must expect it more or less whatever we are about. I don't mean to say that in some occupations we should not have less of it though.

My dear old Thomas, you have always sardonically greeted me as the man of calm and clockwork feelings. The reason is that your own vehemence and irregularity was so much greater, that it involuntarily, no matter what my private mood might have been, threw me into an outwardly antagonistic one in which I endeavored to be a clog to your mobility, as it were. So I fancy you have always given me credit for less sympathy with you and understanding of your feelings than I really have had. All last winter, for instance, when I was on the continual verge of suicide, it used to amuse me to hear you chaff my animal contentment. The appearance of it arose from my reaction against what seemed to me your unduly *noisy* and demonstrative despair. The fact is, I think, that we have both gone through a good deal of similar trouble; we resemble each other in being both persons of rather wide sympathies, not particularly logical in the processes of our minds, and of mobile temperament; though your physical temperament being so much more tremendous than mine makes a great quantitative difference both in your favor, and against you, as the case may be.

Well, neither of us wishes to be a mere loafer; each wishes a work which shall by its mere *exercise* interest him and at the same time allow him to feel that through it he takes hold of the reality of things—whatever that may be—in some measure. Now the first requisite is hard for us to fill, by reason of our wide sympathy and mobility; we can only choose a business in which the evil of feeling restless shall be at a minimum, and then go ahead and make the best of it. That minimum will grow less every year.—In this connection I will again refer to a poem you probably know: "A Grammarian's Funeral," by R. Browning, in "Men and Women." It always strengthens my backbone to read it, and I think the feeling it expresses of throwing upon eternity the responsibility of making good your one-sidedness somehow or other ("Leave *now* for dogs and apes, Man has forever") is a gallant one, and fit to be trusted if one-sided activity is in itself at all respectable.

The other requirement is hard theoretically, though practically not so hard as the first. All I can tell you is the thought that with me outlasts all others, and onto which, like a rock, I find myself washed up when the waves of doubt are weltering over all the rest of the world; and that is the thought of my having a will, and of my belonging to a brotherhood of men possessed of a capacity for pleasure and pain of different kinds. For even at one's lowest ebb of belief, the fact remains empirically certain (and by our will we can, if not *absolutely* refrain from looking beyond that empirical fact, at least practically and *on the whole* accept it and let it suffice us)—that men suffer and enjoy. And if we have to give up all hope of seeing into the purposes of God, or to give up theoretically the idea of final causes, and of God anyhow as vain and leading to nothing for us, we can, by our will, make the enjoyment of our brothers stand us in the stead of a final cause; and through a knowledge of the fact that that enjoyment on the whole depends on what individuals accomplish, lead a life so active, and so sustained by a clean conscience as not to need to fret much. Individuals can add to the welfare of the race in a variety of ways. You may delight its senses or "taste" by some production of luxury or art, comfort it by discovering some moral truth, relieve its pain by concocting a new patent medicine, save its labor by a bit of machinery, or by some new application of a natural product. You may open a road, help start some social or business institution, contribute your mite in *any* way to the mass of the work which each generation subtracts from the task of the next; and you will come into *real* relations with your brothers— with some of them at least.

I know that in a certain point of view, and the most popular one, this seems a cold activity for our affections, a stone instead of bread. We long for sympathy, for a purely *personal* communication, first with the soul of the world, and then with the soul of our fellows. And happy are they who think, or know, that they have got them! But to those who must confess with bitter anguish that they are perfectly isolated from the soul of the world, and that the closest human love incloses a potential germ of estrangement or hatred, that all *personal* relation is finite, conditional, mixed (*vide* in Dana's "Household Book of Poetry," stanzas by C. P. Cranch,[1] "Thought is deeper than speech," etc., etc.), it may not prove such an unfruitful substitute. At least, when you have added to the property of the race, even if no one knows your name, yet it is certain that, without what you have done,

---

[1] Cranch's "Gnosis," a typical poem of the transcendental movement, remained one of WJ's favorites. Its opening stanzas run:

Thought is deeper than all speech,
　Feeling deeper than all thought;
Souls to souls can never teach
　What unto themselves was taught.

We are spirits clad in veils;
　Man by man was never seen;
All our deep communing fails
　To remove the shadowy screen.

Heart to heart was never known;
　Mind with mind did never meet;
We are columns left alone,
　Of a temple once complete.

some individuals must needs be acting now in a somewhat different manner. You have modified their life; you are in *real* relation with them; you have in so far forth entered into their being. And is that such an unworthy stake to set up for our good, after all? Who are these men anyhow? Our predecessors, even apart from the physical link of generation, have made us what we are. Every thought you now have and every act and intention owes its complexion to the acts of your dead and living brothers. *Everything* we know and are is through men. We have no revelation but through man. Every sentiment that warms your gizzard, every brave act that ever made your pulse bound and your nostril open to a confident breath was a man's act. However mean a man may be, man is *the best we know;* and your loathing as you turn from what you probably call the vulgarity of human life—your homesick yearning for a *Better,* somewhere—is furnished by your manhood; your ideal is made up of traits suggested by past men's words and actions. Your manhood shuts you in forever, bounds all your thoughts like an overarching sky—and all the Good and True and High and Dear that you know by virtue of your sharing in it. They are the Natural Product of our Race. So that it seems to me that a sympathy with men as such, and a desire to contribute to the weal of a species, which, whatever may be said of it, contains All that we acknowledge as good, may very well form an external interest sufficient to keep one's moral pot boiling in a very lively manner to a good old age. The idea, in short, of becoming an accomplice in a sort of "Mankind its own God or Providence" scheme is a *practical* one.

I don't mean, by any means, to affirm that we must come to that, I only say it is *a* mode of envisaging life; which is capable of affording moral support—and may at any rate help to bridge over the despair of skeptical intervals. I confess that, in the lonesome gloom which beset me for a couple of months last summer, the only feeling that kept me from giving up was that by waiting and living, by hook or crook, long enough, I might make my *nick,* however small a one, in the raw stuff the race has got to shape, and so assert my reality. The stoic feeling of being a sentinel obeying orders without knowing the general's plans is a noble one. And so is the divine enthusiasm of moral culture (Channing, etc.), and I think that, successively, they may all help to ballast the same man.

What a preacher I'm getting to be! I had no idea when I sat down to begin this long letter that I was going to be carried away so far. I feel like a humbug whenever I endeavor to enunciate moral truths, because I am at bottom so skeptical. . . . I had no idea this morning that I had so many of the elements of a Pascal in me. Excuse the presumption.— But to go back. I think that in business as well as in science one can

have this philanthropic aspiration satisfied. I have been growing lately
to feel that a great mistake of my past life—which has been prejudicial
to my education, and by telling me which, and by making me understand it some years ago, some one might have conferred a great benefit
on me—is an impatience of *results*. Inexperience of life is the cause of
it, and I imagine it is generally an American characteristic. I think you
suffer from it. Results should not be too voluntarily aimed at or too
busily thought of. They are *sure* to float up of their own accord, from
a long enough daily work at a given matter; and I think the work as a
mere occupation ought to be the primary interest with us. At least, I
am sure this is so in the intellectual realm, and I strongly suspect it is
the secret of German prowess therein. Have confidence, even when
you seem to yourself to be making no progress, that, if you but go on
in your own uninteresting way, they must bloom out in their good
time. Ouf, my dear old Tom! I think I must pull up. I have no time or
energy left to gossip to thee of our life here. . . .

*　*　*

On his return to America, WJ completed his medical course in the
the winter and spring of 1869, but seems never to have had any intention of practicing medicine. His health was now at its most critical
stage, but though he did not feel up to the demands of any regular occupation for the next three years, he continued to absorb an immense
amount of miscellaneous reading in all fields. But he felt that he had
little to sustain him. He wrote in his diary on February 1, 1870:

"Today I about touched bottom, and perceive plainly that I must
face the choice with open eyes: shall I *frankly* throw the moral business overboard, as one unsuited to my innate aptitudes, or shall I follow
it, and it alone, making everything else merely stuff for it? I will give
the latter alternative a fair trial. Who knows but the moral interest may
become developed. . . . Hitherto I have tried to fire myself with the
moral interest, as an aid in the accomplishing of certain utilitarian ends."

He felt himself up against the primal forces, and wrote to HJ that
spring:

"It seems to me that all a man has to depend on in this world, is, in
the last resort, mere brute power of resistance. I can't bring myself, as
so many men seem able to, to blink the evil out of sight, and gloss it
over. It's as real as the good, and if it is denied, good must be denied
too. It must be accepted and hated, and resisted while there's breath in
our bodies."

But he could not always be so deliberate in formulating his problems, nor so resolute in his determination to face them. At about this
time he underwent the terrifying hallucination that he was to describe
in his chapter on "The Sick Soul" as an instance of "the worst kind of
melancholy . . . which takes the form of panic fear." He purported to

have translated his description from the French, and said that for permission to print it, he had to "thank the sufferer." Only towards the end of his life did he admit that the case was really his own.

"Whilst in this state of philosophic pessimism and general depression of spirits about my prospects, I went one evening into a dressing-room in the twilight to procure some article that was there; when suddenly there fell upon me without any warning, just as if it came out of the darkness, a horrible fear of my own existence. Simultaneously there arose in my mind the image of an epileptic patient whom I had seen in the asylum, a black-haired youth with greenish skin, entirely idiotic, who used to sit all day on one of the benches, or rather shelves against the wall, with his knees drawn up against his chin, and the coarse gray undershirt, which was his only garment, drawn over them inclosing his entire figure. He sat there like a sort of sculptured Egyptian cat or Peruvian mummy, moving nothing but his black eyes and looking absolutely non-human. The image and my fear entered into a species of combination with each other. *That shape am I*, I felt, potentially. Nothing that I possess can defend me against that fate, if the hour for it should strike for me as it struck for him. There was such a horror of him, and such a perception of my own merely momentary discrepancy from him, that it was as if something hitherto solid within my breast gave way entirely, and I became a mass of quivering fear. After this the universe was changed for me altogether. I awoke morning after morning with a horrible dread at the pit of my stomach, and with a sense of the insecurity of life that I never knew before, and that I have never felt since. It was like a revelation; and although the immediate feelings passed away, the experience has made me sympathetic with the morbid feelings of others ever since. It gradually faded, but for months I was unable to go out into the dark alone.

"In general I dreaded to be left alone. I remember wondering how other people could live, how I myself had ever lived, so unconscious of the pit of insecurity beneath the surface of life. My mother in particular, a very cheerful person, seemed to me a perfect paradox in her unconsciousness of danger, which you may well believe I was very careful not to disturb by revelations of my own state of mind. I have always thought that this experience of melancholia of mine had a religious bearing. I mean that the fear was so invasive and powerful that if I had not clung to scripture-texts like 'The eternal God is my refuge,' etc., 'Come unto me, all ye that labor and are heavy-laden,' etc., 'I am the resurrection and the life,' etc., I think I should have grown really insane."

At this point WJ added a footnote: "For another case of fear equally sudden, see Henry James: *Society the Redeemed Form of Man*, . . . pp. 43ff." The reference is to the passage describing his father's crisis, which had manifested many of the same symptoms. Although it had not been preceded by the debilitations of gnawing skepticism, Henry Senior's "vastation" had also come during the time when he had been very uncertain what career he should follow. WJ found his way back to life, not through religious conversion, but through a philosophic challenge to his will. He made this diary-entry the week before he wrote HJ about the necessity of fighting evil:

"I think that yesterday was a crisis in my life. I finished the first part of Renouvier's second 'Essais' and see no reason why his definition of Free Will—'the sustaining of a thought *because I choose to* when I might have other thoughts'—need be the definition of an illusion. At any rate, I will assume for the present—until next year—that it is no illusion. My first act of free will shall be to believe in free will. For the remainder of the year, I will abstain from the mere speculation and contemplative *Grüblei* in which my nature takes most delight, and voluntarily cultivate the feeling of moral freedom, by reading books favorable to it, as well as by acting. After the first of January, my callow skin being somewhat fledged, I may perhaps return to metaphysical study and skepticism without danger to my powers of action. For the present then remember: care little for speculation; much for the *form* of my action; recollect that only when habits of order are formed can we advance to really interesting fields of action—and consequently accumulate grain on grain of willful choice like a very miser; never forgetting how one link dropped undoes an indefinite number. *Principiis obsta*—To-day has furnished the exceptionally passionate initiative which Bain posits as needful for the acquisition of habits. I will see to the sequel. Not in maxims, not in *Anschauungen*, but in accumulated *acts* of thought lies salvation. *Passer outre*. Hitherto, when I have felt like taking a free initiative, like daring to act originally, without carefully waiting for contemplation of the external world to determine all for me, suicide seemed the most manly form to put my daring into; now, I will go a step further with my will, not only act with it, but believe as well; believe in my individual reality and creative power. My belief, to be sure, *can't* be optimistic—but I will posit life (the real, the good) in the self-governing *resistance* of the ego to the world. Life shall [be built in] doing and suffering and creating."

Years later WJ summed up the beginning of his career: "I originally studied medicine in order to be a physiologist, but I drifted into psychology and philosophy from a sort of fatality. I never had any philosophic instruction, the first lecture on psychology I ever heard being the first I ever gave." In the spring of 1872 he received an offer from President Eliot—who remembered him as "a very interesting and agreeable pupil"—to instruct in anatomy and physiology at Harvard. He wrote to HJ:

"My eyes serve from three to four hours daily. . . . My other symptoms are gradually modifying themselves,—I can hardly say for the better, except that all change is of good omen, and suggests a possible turn of the wheel into the track of soundness. The fits of languor have become somewhat rarer, but what were the healthy intervals have been assuming since your departure more and more of a morbid character, namely, just the opposite, nervousness, wakefulness, uneasiness. Perhaps the whole thing will soon smooth itself out. The appointment to teach physiology is a perfect godsend to me just now. An external motive to work, which yet does not strain me, a dealing with men instead of my own mind, and a diversion from those introspective studies which had bred a sort of philosophical hypochondria in me of late and which it will certainly do me good to drop for a year."

Their father wrote to HJ the following winter:

"Willy goes on swimmingly with his teaching. The students (fifty-seven) are elated with their luck in having such a professor, and next year he will have no doubt a larger class still, attracted by his fame. He came in here the other afternoon when I was sitting alone, and after walking the floor in an animated way for a moment, exclaimed 'Dear me! what a difference there is between me now and me last spring this time: then so hypochondriacal' (he used that word, though perhaps in substantive form) 'and now feeling my mind so cleared up and restored to sanity. It is the difference between death and life.' He had a great effusion. I was afraid of interfering with it, or possibly checking it, but I ventured to ask what specially in his opinion had promoted the change. He said several things: the reading of Renouvier (specially his vindication of the freedom of the will) and Wordsworth, whom he has been feeding upon now for a good while; but especially his having given up the notion that all mental disorder required to have a physical basis. This had become perfectly untrue to him. He saw that the mind did act irrespectively of material coercion, and could be dealt with therefore at first-hand, and this was health to his bones. It was a splendid confession, and though I knew the change had taken place, from unerring signs, I never was more delighted than to hear it from his own lips so unreservedly. He has been shaking off his respect for men of mere science as such, and is even more universal and impartial in his mental judgments than I have ever known him before. . . . Good-bye, my lovely Harry. Words can't tell how dear you are to my heart; how proud I am of your goodness and truth; of what Mr. Arnold calls your 'sweet reasonableness.' Truly I am a happy and grateful father at every remembrance of you."

WJ's discovery of the mental rather than necessarily physical basis for neurotic oppression was to be crucial to his psychology. But at this time he was still racked by uncertainty. When the question of his reappointment was about to come up, he wrote in his diary: "I decide today to stick to biology for a profession in case I am not called to a chair of philosophy, rather than to try to make the same amount of money by literary work, while carrying on more *general* or philosophic study. Philosophy I will nevertheless regard as my vocation and never let slip a chance to do a stroke at it." But when faced with an offer of reappointment in anatomy, his first instinct was to refuse. He now resolved "to fight it out on the line of mental science," since he felt that "with such arrears of lost time . . . and such curtailed power of work," he could no longer "afford to make so considerable an expedition into the field of anatomy."

A few days later he had changed his mind again:

"Yesterday I told Eliot I would accept the anatomical instruction for next year, if well enough to perform it, and would probably stick to that department. I came to this decision mainly from the feeling that philosophical activity as a *business* is not normal for most men, and not for me. To be responsible for a complete conception of things is beyond my strength. To make the *form* of all possible thought the prevailing *matter* of one's thought breeds hypochondria. Of course my deepest interest will as ever lie with the most general problems. But as my strongest moral and intellectual craving is for some stable reality to lean upon, and as a professed philosopher pledges himself publicly never to have done with doubt on these subjects, but every day to be ready to criticize afresh and call in question the grounds of his faith of the day before, I fear the constant sense of instability generated by this attitude would be more than the voluntary faith I can keep going is sufficient to neutralize. . . . That gets reality for us in which we place our responsibility, and the concrete facts in which a biologist's responsibilities lie form a fixed basis from which to aspire as much as he pleases to the mastery of the universal questions when the gallant mood is on him; and a basis, too, upon which he can passively float, and tide over times of weakness and depression, trusting all the while blindly in the beneficence of nature's forces and the return of higher opportunities. A 'philosopher' has publicly renounced the privilege of trusting *blindly*, which every simple man owns as a right—and my sight is not always clear enough for such constant duty. Of course one may say, you could make of psychology proper just such a basis; but not so, you can't divorce psychology from introspection, and immense as is the work demanded by its purely objective physiologic part, yet it is the other part rather for which a professor thereof is expected to make himself publicly responsible."

He added, in a letter to HJ:

"I believe I told you in my last that I had determined to stick to psychology or die. I have changed my mind, and for the present give myself to biology, *i.e.*, accept the tuition here for next year with its six hundred dollars; and this is virtually tantamount to my clinging to those subjects for the next ten or twelve years, if I linger so long. On the whole this is the wiser, if the tamer decision. The fact is, I'm not a strong enough man to choose the other and nobler lot in life, but I can in a less penetrating way work out a philosophy in the midst of the other duties."

He did not rest at all easy in that decision. As his first year of teaching drew to its close, he felt himself worn out by it. He wrote again to HJ:

"This is the point I want you to answer; from your experience of killing time in Rome and elsewhere, should you think the experiment would be a safe one for a man in my state to try? Your being there and with me (if you are willing) would of course help it through amazingly. Answer as soon as you can, so as to let me have the datum to help my decision. I confess it's not an easy one to make anyhow. On the one hand the everlasting postponement of active life, on the other the reality of my sickness, and the misery of being ever knocked back by it from the work I burn to do from each day to the morrow."

By the end of the summer he had postponed his appointment for a year: "My dear H.—The die is cast! The 600 dollars salary fall into the pocket of another! And for a year I am adrift again and free. I feel the solemnity of the moment, and that I *must* get well now or give up. It seems to me as if I should too—for nothing remains but this g— d—d weakness of nerve now." He soon sailed to join his brother in Italy.

After this recuperation he began at last to settle down. His mother observed him anxiously after his return in the spring of 1874, and wrote to HJ: "The trouble with him is that he *must express* every fluctuation of feeling, and especially every unfavorable symptom; without reference to the effect upon those about him. . . . He keeps his good looks, but whenever he speaks of himself, says he is no better. This I cannot believe to be the true state of the case, but his temperament is a morbidly hopeless one, and with this he has to contend all the time, as well as with his physical disability." She also said: "If, dear Harry, you could only have imparted to him a few grains of your own blessed hopefulness, he would have been well long ago."

Once he had fitted into the harness of regular professional work, his health became far more stable, and the symptoms of hypochondria gradually diminished. For several consecutive years he offered a course on "The Comparative Anatomy and Physiology of Vertebrates," and soon added one on "The Relations between Physiology and Psychology." He was promoted assistant professor of physiology in 1876, and to a professorship of philosophy a decade later. He undertook, at the outset, the pioneering work of setting up a laboratory in experimental psychology, one of the earliest anywhere in the world. But he never felt himself confined to any one field. Up to the time of his first promotion he had written only a handful or reviews and notes, mostly for the *Nation,* to which he sent a short piece on "The Teaching of Philosophy in Our Colleges," as he saw it in the mid-1870's. In outlining an ideal, to the realization of which his own lively efforts were to contribute much, he also revealed why philosophy rather than psychology was finally to beckon him as her own.

"The philosophical teaching, as a rule, in our higher seminaries is in the hands of the president, who is usually a minister of the Gospel, and, as he more often owes his position to general excellence of character and administrative faculty than to any speculative gifts or propensities, it usually follows that 'safeness' becomes the main characteristic of his tuition; that his classes are edified rather than awakened, and leave college with the generous youthful impulse, to reflect on the world and our position in it, rather dampened and discouraged than stimulated by the lifeless discussions and flabby formulas they have had to commit to memory. . . .

"Let it not be supposed that we are prejudging the question whether the final results of speculation will be friendly or hostile to the formulas of Christian thought. All we contend for is that we, like the Greeks and the Germans, should now attack things as if there were no official answer preoccupying the field. At present we are bribed beforehand by our reverence or dislike for the official answer; and the free-thinking tendency which the *Popular Science Monthly,* for example, represents, is condemned to an even more dismal shallowness than the spiritualistic systems of our text-books of 'Mental Science.' We work with one eye on our problem, and with the other on the consequences to our enemy or to our lawgiver, as our case may be; the result in both cases alike is mediocrity.

"If the best use of our colleges is to give young men a wider openness of mind and a more flexible way of thinking than special technical training can generate, then we hold that philosophy (taken in the broad sense . . .) is the most important of all college studies. However skeptical one may be of the attainment of universal truths (and to make our position more emphatic, we are willing here to concede the extreme Positivistic position), one can never deny that philosophic study means the habit of always seeing an alternative, of not taking the usual for granted, of making conventionalities fluid again, of imagining foreign states of mind. In a word, it means the possession of mental perspective. Touchstone's question, 'Hast any philosophy in thee, shepherd?' will never cease to be one of the tests of well-born nature. It says, Is there space and air in your mind, or must your companions gasp for breath whenever they talk with you? And if our colleges are to make men, and not machines, they should look, above all things, to this aspect of their influence. . . .

"As for philosophy, technically so called, or the reflection of man on his relations with the universe, its educational essence lies in the quickening of the spirit to its *problems*. What doctrines students take from their teachers are of little consequence provided they catch from them the living, philosophic attitude of mind, the independent, personal look at all the data of life, and the eagerness to harmonize them. . . .

"In short, philosophy, like Molière, claims her own where she finds it. She finds much of it today in physics and natural history, and must and will educate herself accordingly. . . . Meanwhile, when we find announced that the students in Harvard College next year may study any or all of the following works under the guidance of different professors,—Locke's 'Essay,' Kant's 'Kritik,' Schopenhauer and Hartmann, Hodgson's 'Theory of Practice,' and Spencer's 'Psychology,'—we need not complain of *universal* academic stagnation, even today."

In 1878 he gave two important hostages to his future fortune. The family had long been amused at his propensity to fall in love with every pretty girl he met, but now, after a brief engagement, he married Alice Gibbens. He also signed a publisher's contract for a volume on Psychology. He originally expected that this book, the first to which he had set himself, would be finished "inside of two years." It was not ready until after a dozen, when he was forty-eight, an age at which, under the publish-or-perish demand of subsequent American academic life, he might long since have found his university connections severed. To be sure he had staked out his claims by printing several parts of his leading chapters in learned journals; but until he had a volume to show, he must still have appeared very indecisive to an administrative eye.

The formulation by which he is probably best known, "What is an Emotion?" was in print in 1884, before he was acquainted with the work of Lange. His equally famous analogy between the constantly changing "stream of thought" and a river anticipated Bergson's independent "*durée réelle*" by a few years. James' exhaustive treatment of the emotions and the will, as well as of the functions of the brain and the perception of time and space, are naturally not subject to brief illustration.[1] But to keep in touch with him at this stage of his development, we may note that in the chapter on "The Stream of Thought," he believed that he was launching on his "study of the mind from within." He likened this chapter to "a painter's first charcoal sketch upon his canvas." He began it by insisting that "the only states of consciousness that we naturally deal with are found in personal consciousnesses, minds, selves, concrete particular I's and you's." He developed

---

[1] The so-called James-Lange thesis appears below at pp. 373–8, among the examples of the work of WJ's "characteristic maturity."

his theme that "thought is in constant change" with the characteristic concreteness that gives us also a glimpse of his own evolving state:

"It is obvious and palpable that our state of mind is never precisely the same. Every thought we have of a given fact is, strictly speaking, unique, and only bears a resemblance of kind with our other thoughts of the same fact. When the identical fact recurs, we *must* think of it in a fresh manner, see it under a somewhat different angle, apprehend it in different relations from those in which it last appeared. And the thought by which we cognize it is the thought of it-in-those-relations, a thought suffused with the consciousness of all that dim context. Often we are ourselves struck at the strange differences in our successive views of the same thing. We wonder how we ever could have opined as we did last month about a certain matter. We have outgrown the possibility of that state of mind, we know not how. From one year to another we see things in new lights. What was unreal has grown real, and what was exciting is insipid. The friends we used to care the world for are shrunken to shadows; the women, once so divine, the stars, the woods, and the waters, how now so dull and common! the young girls that brought an aura of infinity, at present hardly distinguishable existences; the pictures so empty; and as for the books, what *was* there to find so mysteriously significant in Goethe, or in John Mill so full of weight? Instead of all this, more zestful than ever is the work, the work; and fuller and deeper the import of common duties and of common goods."

He followed this with the contention that, despite all change, "within each personal consciousness, thought is sensibly continuous." He arrived thus at his central definition:

"When Peter and Paul wake up in the same bed, and recognize that they have been asleep, each one of them mentally reaches back and makes connection with but *one* of the two streams of thought which were broken by the sleeping hours. As the current of an electrode buried in the ground unerringly finds its way to its own similarly buried mate, across no matter how much intervening earth; so Peter's present instantly finds out Peter's past, and never by mistake knits itself on to that of Paul. Paul's thought in turn is as little liable to go astray. The past thought of Peter is appropriated by the present Peter alone. He may have a *knowledge*, and a correct one too, of what Paul's last drowsy states of mind were as he sank into sleep, but it is an entirely different sort of knowledge from that which he has of his own last states. He *remembers* his own states, whilst he only *conceives* Paul's. Remembrance is like direct feeling; its object is suffused with a warmth and intimacy to which no object of mere conception ever attains. This quality of warmth and intimacy and immediacy is what Peter's *present* thought also possesses for itself. So sure as this present is me, is mine, it says, so sure is anything else that comes with the same warmth and intimacy and immediacy, me and mine. What the qualities called warmth and intimacy may in themselves be will have to be matter for future consideration. But whatever past feelings appear with those qualities must be admitted to receive the greeting of the present mental state, to be owned by it, and accepted as belonging together with it in a common self. This community of self is what the time-gap cannot break in twain, and is why a present thought, although not ignorant of the time-gap, can still regard itself as continuous with certain chosen portions of the past.

"Consciousness, then, does not appear to itself chopped up in bits. Such words as 'chain' or 'train' do not describe it fitly as it presents itself in the first instance. It is nothing jointed; it flows. A 'river' or a 'stream' are the metaphors by which it is most naturally described. *In talking of it hereafter, let us call it the stream of thought, of consciousness, or of subjective life.*"

WJ's expert concern with "the consciousness of self" (the title of another chapter), and his gift for self-definition can be seen in a letter he wrote to his wife near the time of their marriage:

"I have often thought that the best way to define a man's character would be to seek out the particular mental or moral attitude in which, when it came upon him, he felt himself most deeply and intensely active and alive. At such moments there is a voice inside which speaks and says: '*This* is the real me!' And afterwards, considering the circumstances in which the man is placed, and noting how some of them are fitted to evoke this attitude, whilst others do not call for it, an outside observer may be able to prophesy where the man may fail, where succeed, where be happy and where miserable. Now as well as I can describe it, this characteristic attitude in me always involves an element of active tension, of holding my own, as it were, and trusting outward things to perform their part so as to make it a full harmony, but without any *guaranty* that they will. Make it a guaranty—and the attitude immediately becomes to my consciousness stagnant and stingless. Take away the guaranty, and I feel (provided I am *überhaupt* in vigorous condition) a sort of deep enthusiastic bliss, of bitter willingness to do and suffer anything, which translates itself physically by a kind of stinging pain inside my breast-bone (don't smile at this—it is to me an essential element of the whole thing!), and which, although it is a mere mood or emotion to which I can give no form in words, authenticates itself to me as the deepest principle of all active and theoretic determination which I possess."

He had now reached the point where he could talk about his tensions and his instability with humor, as in this letter to his sister:

"I have been paying ten or eleven visits to a mind-cure doctress, a sterling creature, resembling the 'Venus of Medicine,' Mrs. Lydia E. Pinkham, made solid and veracious-looking. I sit down beside her and presently drop asleep, whilst she disentangles the snarls out of my mind. She says she never saw a mind with so many, so agitated, so restless, etc. She said my *eyes*, mentally speaking, kept revolving like wheels in front of each other and in front of my face, and it was four or five sittings ere she could get them *fixed*. I am now, *unconsciously to myself*, much better than when I first went, etc. I thought it might please you to hear an opinion of my mind so similar to your own."

Alice recorded her opinion of his mind: "William expressed himself and his environment to perfection when he replied to my question about his house at Chocorua, 'Oh, it's the most delightful house you ever saw; it has fourteen doors, all opening outwards.' His brain isn't limited to fourteen, perhaps unfortunately." Everyone was struck with the variety of WJ's interests. In his determination to neglect no source where psychological truth might be found, however shady or disreputable its antecedents might appear to the conventional, he experimented with hypnotism and mescal, faith-cures and Yoga and mental telepathy. His hospitality to spiritualistic mediums would have horrified his father, who shared Hawthorne's digust with "spiritual rappings" as a degradation of "true spirituality." But WJ was also to prove hospitable to the possibilities in the new therapy introduced by Freud.[1]

If during the 1880's James' energy was almost entirely absorbed in working out his psychology, in the 1890's he began to come before the public as a popular philosopher. Subsequent to his *Principles*, all his published work originated either as lectures or as special articles. In making a collection of these in *The Will to Believe* (1896), he defined what it meant to be a "radical empiricist." By defending faith, he showed that his interest in religion was no less enduring than his interest in science. At the same time, he articulated his belief that truth is arrived at by a free competition between points of view in an open market:

---

[1] In one of his Lowell lectures on psychopathology, in 1896, WJ said: "In the relief of certain hysterias by handling the buried idea, whether as in Freud or in Janet, we see a portent of the possible usefulness of these new discoveries. The awful becomes relatively trivial." In the year before his death WJ recorded his mixed impression upon meeting Freud, who had come to America for a psychological congress at Clark University in Worcester: "I went there for one day in order to see what Freud was like, and met also Jung of Zürich, who . . . made a very pleasant impression. I hope that Freud and his pupils will push their ideas to the utmost limits, so that we may learn what they are. They can't fail to throw light on human nature; but I confess that he made on me personally the impression of a man obsessed with fixed ideas. I can make nothing in my own case with his dream theories, and obviously 'symbolism' is a most dangerous method. A newspaper report of the congress said that Freud had condemned American religious therapy (which has such extensive results) as very 'dangerous' because so 'unscientific.' Bah!"

"At most of our American Colleges there are Clubs formed by the students devoted to particular branches of learning; and these clubs have the laudable custom of inviting once or twice a year some maturer scholar to address them, the occasion often being made a public one. I have from time to time accepted such invitations, and afterwards had my discourse printed in one or other of the Reviews. It has seemed to me that these addresses might now be worthy of collection in a volume, as they shed explanatory light upon each other, and taken together express a tolerably definite philosophic attitude in a very untechnical way.

"Were I obliged to give a short name to the attitude in question, I should call it that of *radical empiricism,* in spite of the fact that such brief nicknames are nowhere more misleading than in philosophy. I say 'empiricism,' because it is contented to regard its most assured conclusions concerning matters of fact as hypotheses liable to modification in the course of future experience; and I say 'radical,' because it treats the doctrine of monism itself as an hypothesis, and, unlike so much of the half-way empiricism that is current under the name of positivism or agnosticism or scientific naturalism, it does not dogmatically affirm monism as something with which all experience has got to square. The difference between monism and pluralism is perhaps the most pregnant of all the differences in philosophy. *Primâ facie* the world is a pluralism; as we find it, its unity seems to be that of any collection; and our higher thinking consists chiefly of an effort to redeem it from that first crude form. Postulating more unity than the first experiences yield, we also discover more. But absolute unity, in spite of brilliant dashes in its direction, still remains undiscovered, still remains a *Grenzbegriff*. 'Ever not quite' must be the rationalistic philosopher's last confession concerning it. After all that reason can do has been done, there still remains the opacity of the finite facts as merely given, with most of their peculiarities mutually unmediated and unexplained. To the very last, there are the various 'points of view' which the philosopher must distinguish in discussing the world; and what is inwardly clear from one point remains a bare externality and datum to the other. The negative, the alogical, is never wholly banished. Something—'call it fate, chance, freedom, spontaneity, the devil, what you will'—is still wrong and other and outside and unincluded, from *your* point of view, even though you be the greatest of philosophers. Something is always mere fact and *givenness;* and there may be in the whole universe no one point of view extant from which this would not be found to be the case. 'Reason,' as a gifted writer says, 'is but one item in the mystery; and behind the proudest consciousness that ever reigned, reason and wonder blushed face to face. The inevitable stales, while doubt and hope are sisters. Not unfortunately the universe is wild,—game-flavored as a hawk's wing. Nature is miracle all; the same returns not save to bring the different. The slow round of the engraver's lathe gains but the breadth of a hair, but the difference is distributed back over the whole curve, never an instant true,—ever not quite.'[1]

"This is pluralism, somewhat rhapsodically expressed. He who takes for his hypothesis the notion that it is the permanent form of the world is what I call a radical empiricist. For him the crudity of experience remains an eternal element thereof. There is no possible point of view from which the world can appear an absolutely single fact. Real possibilities, real indeterminations, real beginnings, real ends, real evil, real crises, catastrophes, and escapes, a real God, and a real moral life, just as common-sense conceives these things, may remain in empiricism as conceptions which that philosophy gives up the attempt either to 'overcome' or to reinterpret in monistic form.

"Many of my professionally trained *confrères* will smile at the irrationalism of this view, and at the artlessness of my essays in point of technical form. But they should be taken as illustrations of the radically empiricist attitude rather than as argumentations for its validity. That admits meanwhile of being argued in as technical a shape as any one can desire, and possibly I may be spared to do later a share of that work. Meanwhile these essays seem to light up with a certain dramatic reality the attitude itself, and make it visible alongside of the higher and lower dogmatisms between which in the pages of philosophic history it has generally remained eclipsed from sight.

"The first four essays[2] are largely concerned with defending the legitimacy of religious faith. To some rationalizing readers such advocacy will seem a sad misuse of one's professional position. Mankind, they will say, is only too prone to follow faith unreasoningly, and needs no preaching nor encouragement in that direction. I quite agree that what mankind at large most lacks is criticism and caution, not faith. Its cardinal weakness is to let belief follow recklessly upon lively conception, especially when the conception has instinctive liking at its back. I admit, then, that were I addressing the Salvation Army or a miscellaneous popular crowd it would be a misuse of opportunity to preach the liberty of believing as I have in these pages preached it. What such audiences most need is that their faiths should be broken up and ventilated, that the northwest wind of science should get into them and blow their sickliness and barbarism away. But academic audiences, fed already on science, have a very different need. Paralysis of their native capacity for faith and timorous *abulia* in the religious field are their

---

[1] B. P. Blood: *The Flaw in Supremacy*: Published by the Author, Amsterdam, N. Y., 1893.

[2] "The Will to Believe," "Is Life Worth Living?" "The Sentiment of Rationality," "Reflex Action and Theism."

special forms of mental weakness, brought about by the notion, carefully instilled, that there is something called scientific evidence by waiting upon which they shall escape all danger of shipwreck in regard to
truth. But there is really no' scientific or other method by which men
can steer safely between the opposite dangers of believing too little or
of believing too much. To face such dangers is apparently our duty,
and to hit the right channel between them is the measure of our wisdom
as men. It does not follow, because recklessness may be a vice in soldiers, that courage ought never to be preached to them. What *should*
be preached is courage weighted with responsibility,—such courage as
the Nelsons and Washingtons never failed to show after they had taken
everything into account that might tell against their success, and made
every provision to minimize disaster in case they met defeat. I do not
think that any one can accuse me of preaching reckless faith. I have
preached the right of the individual to indulge his personal faith at his
personal risk. I have discussed the kinds of risk; I have contended that
none of us escape all of them; and I have only pleaded that it is better
to face them open-eyed than to act as if we did not know them to be
there.

"After all, though, you will say, Why such an ado about a matter
concerning which, however we may theoretically differ, we all practically agree? In this age of toleration, no scientist will ever try actively
to interfere with our religious faith, provided we enjoy it quietly with
our friends and do not make a public nuisance of it in the market-
place. But it is just on this matter of the market-place that I think the
utility of such essays as mine may turn. If religious hypotheses about
the universe be in order at all, then the active faiths of individuals in
them, freely expressing themselves in life, are the experimental tests by
which they are verified, and the only means by which their truth or
falsehood can be wrought out. The truest scientific hypothesis is that
which, as we say, 'works' best; and it can be no otherwise with religious
hypotheses. Religious history proves that one hypothesis after another has worked ill, has crumbled at contact with a widening knowledge of the world, and has lapsed from the minds of men. Some articles
of faith, however, have maintained themselves through every vicissitude, and possess even more vitality to-day than ever before: it is for
the 'science of religions' to tell us just which hypotheses these are.
Meanwhile the freest competition of the various faiths with one another, and their openest application to life by their several champions,
are the most favorable conditions under which the survival of the fittest
can proceed. They ought therefore not to lie hid each under its bushel,
indulged-in quietly with friends. They ought to live in publicity, vying
with each other; and it seems to me that (the régime of tolerance once
granted, and a fair field shown) the scientist has nothing to fear for his

own interests from the liveliest possible state of fermentation in the religious world of his time. Those faiths will best stand the test which
adopt also his hypotheses, and make them integral elements of their
own. He should welcome therefore every species of religious agitation
and discussion, so long as he is willing to allow that some religious hypothesis *may* be true. Of course there are plenty of scientists who
would deny that dogmatically, maintaining that science has already
ruled all possible religious hypotheses out of court. Such scientists
ought, I agree, to aim at imposing privacy on religious faiths, the public
manifestation of which could only be a nuisance in their eyes. With all
such scientists, as well as with their allies outside of science, my quarrel
openly lies; and I hope that my book may do something to persuade
the reader of their crudity, and range him on my side. Religious fermentation is always a symptom of the intellectual vigor of a society;
and it is only when they forget that they are hypotheses and put on
rationalistic and authoritative pretensions, that our faiths do harm. The
most interesting and valuable things about a man are his ideals and over-
beliefs. The same is true of nations and historic epochs; and the excesses
of which the particular individuals and epochs are guilty are compen-
sated in the total, and become profitable to mankind in the long run."

If one were looking for the briefest expression of what WJ brought
to philosophy and what he sought therein, one could hardly find a more
expressive passage than the conclusion to "Is Life Worth Living?" He
demonstrated there what he had learned from the challenge to his will
that had rescued him from neurasthenia. He knew that he must fight to
keep alive. And he demonstrated again that his matured conception of
truth was at the opposite pole from his father's. Truth for Henry Senior
was something revealed: "Divine truth has first to create the intelligence it afterwards enlightens." Truth for WJ was something a man
must make for himself:

"If this life be not a real fight, in which something is eternally gained
for the universe by success, it is no better than a game of private theatricals from which one may withdraw at will. But it *feels* like a real
fight,—as if there were something really wild in the universe which
we, with all our idealities and faithfulnesses, are needed to redeem; and
first of all to redeem our own hearts from atheisms and fears. For such
a half-wild, half-saved universe our nature is adapted. The deepest
thing in our nature is this *Binnenleben* (as a German doctor lately has
called it), this dumb region of the heart in which we dwell alone with
our willingnesses and unwillingnesses, our faiths and fears. As through
the cracks and crannies of caverns those waters exude from the earth's
bosom which then form the fountain-heads of springs, so in these
crepuscular depths of personality the sources of all our outer deeds

and decisions take their rise. Here is our deepest organ of communication with the nature of things; and compared with these concrete movements of our soul all abstract statements and scientific arguments—the veto, for example, which the strict positivist pronounces upon our faith —sound to us like mere chatterings of the teeth. For here possibilities, not finished facts, are the realities with which we have actively to deal; and to quote my friend William Salter, of the Philadelphia Ethical Society, 'as the essence of courage is to stake one's life on a possibility, so the essence of faith is to believe that the possibility exists.'

"These, then, are my last words to you: Be not afraid of life. Believe that life *is* worth living, and your belief will help create the fact. The 'scientific proof' that you are right may not be clear before the day of judgment (or some stage of being which that expression may serve to symbolize) is reached. But the faithful fighters of this hour, or the beings that then and there will represent them, may then turn to the faint-hearted, who here decline to go on, with words like those with which Henry IV greeted the tardy Crillon after a great victory had been gained: 'Hang yourself, brave Crillon! we fought at Arques, and you were not there.'"

At the very period when WJ was most concerned with such essays, he also displayed the ambivalent attitude that so shocked Santayana, to whom he remarked: "What a curse philosophy would be, if we couldn't forget all about it!" In the summer of 1895 he wrote to his friend Howison, the professor of philosophy at California:

"How you *have* misunderstood the application of my word 'trivial' as being discriminatively applied to your pluralistic idealism! Quite the reverse—if there be a philosophy that I believe in, it's that. The word came out of one who is unfit to be a philosopher because at bottom he hates philosophy, especially at the beginning of a vacation, with the fragrance of the spruces and sweet ferns all soaking him through with the conviction that it is better to *be* than to define your being. I am a victim of neurasthenia and of the sense of the hollowness and unreality that goes with it. And philosophic literature *will* often seem to me the hollowest thing. My word trivial was a general reflection exhaling from this mood, vile indeed in a supposed professor. Where it will end with me, I do not know. I wish I could give it all up. But perhaps it is a grant climacteric and will pass away. At present I am philosophizing as little as possible, in order to do it the better next year, if I can do it at all. And I envy you your stalwart and steadfast enthusiasm and faith."

WJ's next large undertaking after his *Psychology* was *The Varieties of Religious Experience*, prepared in response to an invitation to deliver, in 1900, the Gifford lectures at Edinburgh. A strain to his heart while climbing in the Adirondacks necessitated instead two years of enforced idleness in Europe before he had recovered sufficient stamina to fulfill this commitment. In some preliminary notes for these lectures he declared: "A man's religion is the deepest and wisest thing in his life." He had come to believe that liberalism had preserved intellect at the cost of depriving it of the sustenance of traditional faith, and added, in another note: "Remember that the whole point lies in really *believing* that through a certain point or part in you you coalesce and are identical with the Eternal." He had become increasingly conscious of the limits of the rational, increasingly absorbed in probing the roots of the irrational. He did not care whom he scandalized by saying that "mere sanity is the most philistine and (at bottom) unessential of a man's attributes." [1]

The formulation in these lectures which has gained the widest currency is the contrast between "the religion of healthy-mindedness" and that of "the sick soul." We have observed that WJ included his own case-history to illustrate his understanding of the latter; but we have also observed that even at the time he wrote his introduction to his father's work, he had already aligned himself with "healthy-minded pluralism" against his father's acceptance of the necessity of evil. WJ took the dominant moods of Walt Whitman as "the supreme contemporary example" of healthy-mindedness. It might be said that WJ himself grew into another such example. But he was saved from the superficial optimism attendant upon that attitude (as Whitman was also) by at least an occasional recollection of the fissures always lurking beneath the smooth melioristic surfaces, by a reminder of a greater depth of spirit than that in which he habitually lived. In his summary of the two attitudes, he aimed to give an impartial account of both:

"If we admit that evil is an essential part of our being and the key to the interpretation of our life, we load ourselves down with a difficulty that has always proved burdensome in philosophies of religion. Theism, whenever it has erected itself into a systematic philosophy of the universe, has shown a reluctance to let God be anything less than All-in-All. In other words, philosophic theism has always shown a tendency to become pantheistic and monistic, and to consider the world as one unit of absolute fact; and this has been at variance with popular or practical theism, which latter has ever been more or less frankly pluralistic, not to say polytheistic, and shown itself perfectly well satisfied with a universe composed of many original principles, provided we be only allowed to believe that the divine principle remains supreme, and that the others are subordinate. In this latter case God is not necessarily responsible for the existence of evil; he would only be responsible if it were not finally overcome. But on the monistic or pantheistic view,

---

[1] A characteristic comment of WJ's was one he made about Bryce's *American Commonwealth*: "A perfect bog of reasonableness. . . . One fairly longs for a *screech* of some kind."

evil, like everything else, must have its foundation in God; and the difficulty is to see how this can possibly be the case if God be absolutely good. This difficulty faces us in every form of philosophy in which the world appears as one flawless unit of fact. Such a unit is an *Individual,* and in it the worst parts must be as essential as the best, must be as necessary to make the individual what he is; since if any part whatever in an individual were to vanish or alter, it would no longer be *that* individual at all. The philosophy of absolute idealism, so vigorously represented both in Scotland and America to-day, has to struggle with this difficulty quite as much as scholastic theism struggled in its time; and although it would be premature to say that there is no speculative issue whatever from the puzzle, it is perfectly fair to say that there is no clear or easy issue, and that the only *obvious* escape from paradox here is to cut loose from the monistic assumption altogether, and to allow the world to have existed from its origin in pluralistic form, as an aggregate or collection of higher and lower things and principles, rather than an absolutely unitary fact. For then evil would not need to be essential; it might be, and may always have been, an independent portion that had no rational or absolute right to live with the rest, and which we might conceivably hope to see got rid of at last.

"Now the gospel of healthy-mindedness, as we have described it, casts its vote distinctly for this pluralistic view. Whereas the monistic philosopher finds himself more or less bound to say, as Hegel said, that everything actual is rational, and that evil, as an element dialectically required, must be pinned in and kept and consecrated and have a function awarded to it in the final system of truth, healthy-mindedness refuses to say anything of the sort.[1] Evil, it says, is emphatically irrational, and *not* to be pinned in, or preserved, or consecrated in any final system of truth. It is a pure abomination to the Lord, an alien unreality, a waste element, to be sloughed off and negated, and the very memory of it, if possible, wiped out and forgotten. The ideal, so far from being co-extensive with the whole actual, is a mere *extract* from the actual, marked by its deliverance from all contact with this diseased, inferior, and excrementitious stuff.

"Here we have the interesting notion fairly and squarely presented to us, of there being elements of the universe which may make no rational whole in conjunction with the other elements, and which, from the point of view of any system which those other elements make up, can

---

[1] I say this in spite of the monistic utterances of many mind-cure writers; for these utterances are really inconsistent with their attitude towards disease, and can easily be shown not to be logically involved in the experiences of union with a higher Presence with which they connect themselves. The higher Presence, namely, need not be the absolute whole of things, it is quite sufficient for the life of religious experience to regard it as a part, if only it be the most ideal part.—W. J.

only be considered so much irrelevance and accident—so much 'dirt,' as it were, and matter out of place. I ask you now not to forget this notion; for although most philosophers seem either to forget it or to disdain it too much ever to mention it, I believe that we shall have to admit it ourselves in the end as containing an element of truth. The mind-cure gospel thus once more appears to us as having dignity and importance. We have seen it to be a genuine religion, and no mere silly appeal to imagination to cure disease; we have seen its method of experimental verification to be not unlike the method of all science; and now here we find mind-cure as the champion of a perfectly definite conception of the metaphysical structure of the world. . . .

"Let us now say good-by for a while to all this way of thinking, and turn towards those persons who cannot so swiftly throw off the burden of the consciousness of evil, but are congenitally fated to suffer from its presence. Just as we saw that in healthy-mindedness there are shallower and profounder levels, happiness like that of the mere animal, and more regenerate sorts of happiness, so also are there different levels of the morbid mind, and the one is much more formidable than the other."

WJ proceeded to quote from the experiences of a number of sick souls, and then concluded:

"There is no need of more examples. The cases we have looked at are enough. One of them gives us the vanity of mortal things; another the sense of sin; and the remaining one describes the fear of the universe; —and in one or other of these three ways it always is that man's original optimism and self-satisfaction get leveled with the dust.

"In none of these cases was there any intellectual insanity or delusion about matters of fact; but were we disposed to open the chapter of really insane melancholia, with its hallucinations and delusions, it would be a worse story still—desperation absolute and complete, the whole universe coagulating about the sufferer into a material of overwhelming horror, surrounding him without opening or end. Not the conception or intellectual perception of evil, but the grisly blood-freezing heart-palsying sensation of it close upon one, and no other conception or sensation able to live for a moment in its presence. How irrelevantly remote seem all our usual refined optimisms and intellectual and moral consolations in presence of a need of help like this! Here is the real core of the religious problem: Help! help! No prophet can claim to bring a final message unless he says things that will have a sound of reality in the ears of victims such as these. But the deliverance must come in as strong a form as the complaint, if it is to take effect; and that seems a reason why the coarser religions, revivalistic, orgiastic, with blood and miracles and supernatural operations, may possibly never be displaced. Some constitutions need them too much.

"Arrived at this point, we can see how great an antagonism may naturally arise between the healthy-minded way of viewing life and the way that takes all this experience of evil as something essential. To this latter way, the morbid-minded way, as we might call it, healthy-mindedness pure and simple seems unspeakably blind and shallow. To the healthy-minded way, on the other hand, the way of the sick soul seems unmanly and diseased. With their grubbing in rat-holes instead of living in the light; with their manufacture of fears, and preoccupation with every unwholesome kind of misery, there is something almost obscene about these children of wrath and cravers of a second birth. If religious intolerance and hanging and burning could again become the order of the day, there is little doubt that, however it may have been in the past, the healthy-minded would at present show themselves the less indulgent party of the two.

"In our own attitude, not yet abandoned, of impartial onlookers, what are we to say of this quarrel? It seems to me that we are bound to say that morbid-mindedness ranges over the wider scale of experience, and that its survey is the one that overlaps. The method of averting one's attention from evil, and living simply in the light of good is splendid as long as it will work. It will work with many persons; it will work far more generally than most of us are ready to suppose; and within the sphere of its successful operation there is nothing to be said against it as a religious solution. But it breaks down impotently as soon as melancholy comes; and even though one be quite free from melancholy one's self, there is no doubt that healthy-mindedness is inadequate as a philosophical doctrine, because the evil facts which it refuses positively to account for are a genuine portion of reality; and they may after all be the best key to life's significance, and possibly the only openers of our eyes to the deepest levels of truth.

"The normal process of life contains moments as bad as any of those which insane melancholy is filled with, moments in which radical evil gets its innings and takes its solid turn. The lunatic's visions of horror are all drawn from the material of daily fact. Our civilization is founded on the shambles, and every individual existence goes out in a lonely spasm of helpless agony. If you protest, my friend, wait till you arrive there yourself! To believe in the carnivorous reptiles of geologic times is hard for our imagination—they seem too much like mere museum specimens. Yet there is no tooth in any one of those museum-skulls that did not daily through long years of the foretime hold fast to the body struggling in despair of some fated living victim. Forms of horror just as dreadful to their victims, if on a smaller spatial scale, fill the world about us to-day. Here on our very hearths and in our gardens the infernal cat plays with the panting mouse, or holds the hot bird fluttering in her jaws. Crocodiles and rattlesnakes and pythons are at this moment vessels of life as real as we are; their loathsome existence fills every minute of every day that drags its length along; and whenever they or other wild beasts clutch their living prey, the deadly horror which an agitated melancholiac feels is the literally right reaction on the situation.

"It may indeed be that no religious reconciliation with the absolute totality of things is possible. Some evils, indeed, are ministerial to higher forms of good; but it may be that there are forms of evil so extreme as to enter into no good system whatsoever, and that, in respect of such evil, dumb submission or neglect to notice is the only practical resource. This question must confront us on a later day. But provisionally, and as a mere matter of program and method, since the evil facts are as genuine parts of nature as the good ones, the philosophic presumption should be that they have some rational significance, and that systematic healthy-mindedness, failing as it does to accord to sorrow, pain, and death any positive and active attention whatever, is formally less complete than systems that try at least to include these elements in their scope.

"The completest religions would therefore seem to be those in which the pessimistic elements are best developed. Buddhism, of course, and Christianity are the best known to us of these. They are essentially religions of deliverance: the man must die to an unreal life before he can be born into the real life."

In 1904 WJ summed up his philosophy for his old friend François Pillon, the editor of the *Critique Philosophique*, to whom he had dedicated his *Psychology*:

"My philosophy is what I call a radical empiricism, a pluralism, a 'tychism,' which represents order as being gradually won and always in the making. It is theistic, but not *essentially* so. It rejects all doctrines of the Absolute. It is finitist; but it does not attribute to the question of the Infinite the great methodological importance which you and Renouvier attribute to it. I fear that you may find my system too *bottomless* and romantic. I am sure that, be it in the end judged true or false, it is essential to the evolution of clearness in philosophic thought that *someone* should defend a pluralistic empiricism radically. And all that I fear is that, with the impairment of my working powers from which I suffer, the Angel of Death may overtake me before I can get my thoughts on to paper. Life here in the University consists altogether of *interruptions*."

He had never regained full health after the strain to his heart, and often wanted to resign from his professorship so that he might have enough energy to develop his philosophy at length. He wrote to HJ at this time: "I see now with absolute clearness, that greatly as I have been helped and enlarged by my University business hitherto, the time has come when the remnant of my life must be passed in a different manner, contemplatively namely, and with leisure and simplification for the one remaining thing, which is to report in one book, at least, such impression as my own intellect has received from the Universe." He knew the warring demands between teaching and writing; and upon his final resignation in 1907, he made a classic definition of the problem encountered when a man tries to be a professor: "I thank you for your congratulations on my retirement. It makes me very happy. A professor has two functions: (1) to be learned and distribute bibliographical information; (2) to communicate truth. The *1st* function is the essential one, officially considered. The *2nd* is the only one I care for. Hitherto I have always felt like a humbug as a professor, for I am weak in the first requirement. Now I can live for the second with a free conscience."

A striking fact about the list of WJ's books is that the major portion of his philosophic writing, including *Pragmatism*, *The Meaning of Truth*, and *A Pluralistic Universe*, was done after his official career was ended, and when he realized that he had not long to live. The formulation of human types with which he opened *Pragmatism* has, again, become a part of popular language:

"The philosophy which is so important in each of us is not a technical matter; it is our more or less dumb sense of what life honestly and deeply means. It is only partly got from books; it is our individual way of just seeing and feeling the total push and pressure of the cosmos. . . .

"The history of philosophy is to a great extent that of a certain clash of human temperaments. Undignified as such a treatment may seem to some of my colleagues, I shall have to take account of this clash and explain a good many of the divergencies of philosophers by it. Of whatever temperament a professional philosopher is, he tries, when philosophizing, to sink the fact of his temperament. Temperament is no conventionally recognized reason, so he urges impersonal reasons only for his conclusions. Yet his temperament really gives him a stronger bias than any of his more strictly objective premises. It loads the evidence for him one way or the other, making for a more sentimental or a more hard-hearted view of the universe, just as this fact or that principle would. He *trusts* his temperament. Wanting a universe that suits it, he believes in any representation of the universe that does suit it. He feels men of opposite temper to be out of key with the world's character, and in his heart considers them incompetent and 'not in it,' in the philosophic business, even though they may far excel him in dialectical ability.

"Yet in the forum he can make no claim, on the bare ground of his temperament, to superior discernment or authority. There arises thus a certain insincerity in our philosophic discussions: the potentest of all our premises is never mentioned. I am sure it would contribute to clearness if in these lectures we should break this rule and mention it, and I accordingly feel free to do so.

"Of course I am talking here of very positively marked men, men of radical idiosyncrasy, who have set their stamp and likeness on philosophy and figure in its history. Plato, Locke, Hegel, Spencer, are such temperamental thinkers. Most of us have, of course, no very definite intellectual temperament, we are a mixture of opposite ingredients, each one present very moderately. We hardly know our own preferences in abstract matters; some of us are easily talked out of them, and end by following the fashion or taking up with the beliefs of the most impressive philosopher in our neighborhood, whoever he may be. But the one thing that has *counted* so far in philosophy is that a man should *see* things, see them straight in his own peculiar way, and be dissatisfied with any opposite way of seeing them. There is no reason to suppose that this strong temperamental vision is from now onward to count no longer in the history of man's beliefs.

"Now the particular difference of temperament that I have in mind in making these remarks is one that has counted in literature, art, government, and manners as well as in philosophy. In manners we find formalists and free-and-easy persons. In government, authoritarians and anarchists. In literature, purists or academicals, and realists. In art, classics and romantics. You recognize these contrasts as familiar; well, in philosophy we have a very similar contrast expressed in the pair of terms 'rationalist' and 'empiricist,' 'empiricist' meaning your lover of facts in all their crude variety, 'rationalist' meaning your devotee to abstract and eternal principles. No one can live an hour without both facts and principles, so it is a difference rather of emphasis; yet it breeds antipathies of the most pungent character between those who lay the emphasis differently; and we shall find it extraordinarily convenient to express a certain contrast in men's ways of taking their universe, by talking of the 'empiricist' and of the 'rationalist' temper. These terms make the contrast simple and massive.

"More simple and massive than are usually the men of whom the terms are predicated. For every sort of permutation and combination is possible in human nature; and if I now proceed to define more fully what I have in mind when I speak of rationalists and empiricists, by adding to each of those titles some secondary qualifying characteristics, I beg you to regard my conduct as to a certain extent arbitrary. I select types of combination that nature offers very frequently, but by no means uniformly, and I select them solely for their convenience in helping me to my ulterior purpose of characterizing pragmatism. Historically we find the terms 'intellectualism' and 'sensationalism' used as synonyms of 'rationalism' and 'empiricism.' Well, nature seems to combine most frequently with intellectualism an idealistic and optimistic tendency. Empiricists on the other hand are not uncommonly materialistic, and their optimism is apt to be decidedly conditional and tremulous. Rationalism is always monistic. It starts from wholes and universals, and makes much of the unity of things. Empiricism starts from the parts, and makes of the whole a collection—is not averse therefore to calling itself pluralistic. Rationalism usually considers itself more religious than empiricism, but there is much to say about this claim, so I merely mention it. It is a true claim when the individual rationalist is what is called a man of feeling, and when the individual empiricist prides himself on being hard-headed. In that case the rationalist will usually also be in favor of what is called free-will, and the empiricist will be a fatalist—I use the terms most popularly current. The rationalist finally will be of dogmatic temper in his affirmations, while the empiricist may be more sceptical and open to discussion.

"I will write these traits down in two columns. I think you will practically recognize the two types of mental make-up that I mean if I head the columns by the titles 'tender-minded' and 'tough-minded' respectively.

THE TENDER-MINDED.	THE TOUGH-MINDED.
Rationalistic (going by 'principles'),	Empiricist (going by 'facts'),
Intellectualistic,	Sensationalistic,
Idealistic,	Materialistic,
Optimistic,	Pessimistic,
Religious,	Irreligious,
Free-willist,	Fatalistic,
Monistic,	Pluralistic,
Dogmatical.	Sceptical.

"Pray postpone for a moment the question whether the two contrasted mixtures which I have written down are each inwardly coherent and self-consistent or not. . . . It suffices for our immediate purpose that tender-minded and tough-minded people, characterized as I have written them down, do both exist. Each of you probably knows some well-marked example of each type, and you know what each example thinks of the example on the other side of the line. They have a low opinion of each other. Their antagonism, whenever as individuals their temperaments have been intense, has formed in all ages a part of the philosophic atmosphere of the time. It forms a part of the philosophic atmosphere to-day. The tough think of the tender as sentimentalists and soft-heads. The tender feel the tough to be unrefined, callous, or brutal. Their mutual reaction is very much like that that takes place when Bostonian tourists mingle with a population like that of Cripple Creek. Each type believes the other to be inferior to itself; but disdain in the one case is mingled with amusement, in the other it has a dash of fear.

"Now, as I have already insisted, few of us are tender-foot Bostonians pure and simple, and few are typical Rocky Mountain toughs, in philosophy. Most of us have a hankering for the good things on both sides of the line."

Although WJ obviously felt more attracted to "the tough-minded," he was himself a combination of both attitudes: a pluralistic empiricist who was also predominantly an optimist with a will to believe, and with such a loose mixture of materialism and idealism as to obliterate the application of either label to him. To be sure, he never made any claims to purism, and asserted the desirability of "a system that will combine both things, the scientific loyalty to facts and willingness to take account of them, the spirit of adaptation and accommodation, in short, but also the old confidence in human values and the resultant spontaneity, whether of the religious or of the romantic type."

The publication of *Pragmatism* plunged him into heated controversy, into the kind of battling for a cause that he greatly enjoyed and that called out all his latent energy. He became an enthusiast for "the pragmatistic idea." "I am all aflame with it," he wrote, "as displacing all rationalistic systems"; and again: "It is absolutely the only philosophy with *no* humbug in it." Having introduced the term "the cash-value of an idea" to symbolize the necessary test by experience, he felt that he had been misunderstood, and devoted a chapter of *The Meaning of Truth* to the refutation of eight such misunderstandings. His counter-statement to the charge that "Pragmatism is primarily an appeal to action" is typical of these:

"The name 'pragmatism,' with its suggestions of action, has been an unfortunate choice, I have to admit, and has played into the hands of this mistake. But no word could protect the doctrine from critics so blind to the nature of the inquiry that, when Dr. Schiller speaks of these ideas 'working' well, the only thing they think of is their immediate workings in the physical environment, their enabling us to make money, or gain some similar 'practical' advantage. Ideas do work thus, of course, immediately or remotely; but they work indefinitely inside of the mental world also. Not crediting us with this rudimentary insight, our critics treat our view as offering itself exclusively to engineers, doctors, financiers, and men of action generally, who need some sort of a rough and ready *weltanschauung*, but have no time or wit to study genuine philosophy. It is usually described as a characteristically American movement, a sort of bobtailed scheme of thought, excellently fitted for the man on the street, who naturally hates theory and wants cash returns immediately.

"It is quite true that, when the refined theoretic question that prag-

matism begins with is once answered, secondary corollaries of a practical sort follow. Investigation shows that, in the function called truth,
previous realities are not the only independent variables. To a certain
extent our ideas, being realities, are also independent variables, and,
just as they follow other reality and fit it, so, in a measure, does other
reality follow and fit them. When they add themselves to being, they
partly redetermine the existent, so that reality as a whole appears
incompletely definable unless ideas also are kept account of. This
pragmatist doctrine, exhibiting our ideas as complemental factors of
reality, throws open (since our ideas are instigators of our action) a
wide window upon human action, as well as a wide license to originality in thought. But few things could be sillier than to ignore the prior
epistemological edifice in which the window is built, or to talk as if
pragmatism began and ended at the window. This, nevertheless, is what
our critics do almost without exception. They ignore our primary step
and its motive, and make the relation to action, which is our secondary
achievement, primary."

But he did not succeed in persuading many of his formal opponents,
for whom he was no match in systematic logic. They continued to hold
that James' philosophy merely gave sanction to the already overdevel-
oped activism of American life. When he had finished *The Varieties of
Religious Experience*, he had declared that he had "had enough of the
squashy popular-lecture style," and wanted "if possible to write something serious, systematic, and syllogistic." Throughout the final decade
of his life he kept recurring to the resolve that he had made to Bergson
in 1902: "I am going, if I live, to write a general system of metaphysics."
But he never really set himself to it, and his final books still started as
lectures. In other moods he recognized that what he called his "intellectual higgledy-piggledyism" could "never lead" to any such system;
and in his occasional revulsion from the whole problem he would say
that "*technical* writing on *philosophical* subjects . . . is certainly a
crime against the human race."

He remained immensely hopeful about the future prospects of his
kind of truth, and wrote to Pillon in the summer of 1909:

"I believe that philosophy stands at present at the beginning of a new
sort of activity, not unlike that which began with Locke, and which
will end by defining (in ways not dreamed of till quite recently) the
limits of what the conceptual or logical method can accomplish, and
the parts of reality which escape treatment by fixed logical categories
or concepts. I am quite sure that in establishing the inadequacy of concepts, the door will be opened to much vagueness and extravagance,
and that possibly something like the excesses of the German romantic
school in philosophy may yet be in the order of the day. That will
doubtless be a pity, and must be counted to the disadvantage of the

movement. But it gives me very little anxiety, for I think that the final upshot and result will be a greater distinctness and clearness than philosophy has ever seen. . . . But, dear old friend, neither you nor I will be there!!"

The nearest he came to formal exposition was in the unfinished *Some Problems of Philosophy*. In a memorandum dated two months before his death, he directed its publication, but added: "Say it is fragmentary and unrevised. Call it 'A beginning of an introduction to philosophy.' Say that I hoped by it to round out my system, which now is too much like an arch built only on one side."

Even more characteristic of his final state of mind was one of the last pieces of writing he undertook, the essay, "A Pluralistic Mystic," in tribute to his old friend Benjamin Paul Blood. He began his appreciation of this little-known thinker by remarking that Blood's philosophy was "not dissimilar" to his own, and built up to this ending: "Let *my* last word, then, speaking in the name of intellectual philosophy, be *his* word:—'There is no conclusion. What has concluded, that we might conclude in regard to it? There are no fortunes to be told, and there is no advice to be given.—Farewell!' "

FORMULATIONS

HJ

THE IMPOSSIBILITY of representing HJ through any similar arrangement of formulations points up the fundamental contrast between the two brothers' minds and talents. It might be put as the contrast between the subjective and the objective ways of taking life. If truth for WJ was something a man must create for himself, for HJ it was something to be absorbed. So little would he have denied "the spectator theory of knowledge" that his whole artistic production might be considered an illustration of Stendhal's view of a novel as "a mirror dawdling down a road." His novels are the great monument in American fiction to the skills of detachment and observation.

That did not mean, in his case, coldness or indifference, since, as we have seen in his account of their education, every experience worthy of the name must call out an emotional response from its recipient. But HJ inclined so much farther towards being than towards doing that external existence, the world of action and competition, seemed always separated from him by an "otherness" almost absolute. That did not lessen for him the attraction of figures moving in such a world; rather, it enhanced them with glamour, as we can observe in a passage from *A Small Boy and Others* which may help define the psychological type to which HJ belonged:

"I may remark . . . that though in that early time I seem to have been constantly eager to exchange my lot for that of somebody else, on the assumed certainty of gaining by the bargain, I fail to remember feeling jealous of such happier persons—in the measure open to children of spirit. I had rather a positive lack of the passion, and thereby, I suppose, a lack of spirit; since if jealousy bears, as I think, on what one sees one's companions able to do—as against one's falling short—envy, as I knew it at least, was simply of what they *were*, or in other words of a certain sort of richer consciousness supposed, doubtless often too freely supposed, in them. They were so *other*—that was what I felt; and to *be* other, other almost anyhow, seemed as good as the probable taste of the bright compound wistfully watched in the confectioner's window; unattainable, impossible, of course, but as to which just this impossibility and just that privation kept those active proceedings in which jealousy seeks relief quite out of the question. A platitude of acceptance of the poor actual, the absence of all vision of how in any degree to change it, combined with a complacency, an acuity of perception of alternatives, though a view of them as only through the confectioner's hard glass—that is what I recover as the nearest approach to an apology, in the soil of my nature, for the springing seed of emulation. I never dreamed of competing—a business having in it at the best, for my temper, if not for my total failure of temper, a displeasing ferocity. If competing was bad snatching was therefore still worse, and jealousy was a sort of spiritual snatching. With which, nevertheless, all the while, one might have been 'like' So-and-So, who had such horizons. A helpless little love of horizons I certainly cherished, and could sometimes even care for my own. These always shrank, however, under almost any suggestion of a further range or finer shade in the purple rim offered to other eyes—and that is what I take for the restlessness of envy. It wasn't that I wished to change with everyone, with anyone at a venture, but that I saw 'gifts' everywhere but as mine and that I scarce know whether to call the effect of this miserable or monstrous. It was the effect at least of self-abandonment—I mean to visions."

The small boy who pressed his nose against the shop windows of lower Broadway grew up to be the type of artist diametrically opposed to Walt Whitman, who proclaimed his intimate identification with everything that he saw. HJ had thoroughly assimilated his father's disapproval of the selfishness of American competition, but his mode of being was also different from his father's. For Henry Senior celebrated like Blake—or Whitman—his own immediate participation in the energy that "is eternal delight." HJ's "only form of riot or revel" was, as he said, "that of the visiting mind." He could possess the external world only through recording his images, arranging them in scenes, and framing them with the permanent form of art.

His imagination soon feasted on the romantic "otherness" of Europe. It feasted all his life on other individuals, on characters who were not himself but who could be grasped by his consciousness. He rarely used fiction to dramatize his own problems. He is not Roderick Hudson or Christopher Newman any more than he is Lambert Strether or Adam Verver, and though, as he said in his preface to "The Altar of the Dead," "My attested predilection for poor sensitive gentlemen almost embarrasses me as I march," we cannot detach his characters' speeches from their context to give HJ's philosophy of life. We can come at that philosophy only as he suggested in his fable of "The Figure in the Carpet," only by apprehending the pattern of his work as a whole.

Furthermore, HJ, though projecting the drama of consciousness, is not a philosophical novelist. By no definition of the term is he an important thinker. But if that is a limitation, it could also be an asset. It meant in HJ's case, as T. S. Eliot has argued, that, undistracted by "ideas," he pursued his way to the development of "a point of view," and to the perfection of his craft; and that, as a result, he finally reflected on the art of fiction as no previous American or English novelist had done. Eliot's contrast of this process with the education of Henry Adams is again relevant: "Henry James was not, by Adams' standards, 'educated,' but particularly limited"; yet he became a critic "who preyed not upon ideas, but upon living beings. . . . James' critical genius comes out most tellingly in his mastery over, his baffling escape from, Ideas." He had an intelligence "so fine that no idea could violate it." What Eliot is describing is sensibility rather than power of mind. He is describing what differentiates the artist from the philosopher or theorist. In contrast particularly with the New England mind as represented by Adams, Eliot added—as though summing up the results of Henry Senior's primary resolve about his sons' education: "It is the sensuous contributor to the intelligence that makes the difference."

We could arrive at HJ's standards for the art of fiction by following the genetic history of his critical opinions from the time of his first reviews, but these opinions are again hardly subject to brief formulation, since they emerge for the most part indirectly, in subordination to the author he is discussing. And by the time he composed the masterly prefaces for his own novels his ideas were so deeply interfused with the text upon which he was commenting that you have to read each preface in its entirety if you are to do it justice. At this juncture, therefore, we can only indicate the final stages of his education as it continued after the outbreak of the Civil War, and wait for more extensive illustrations of his mature sensibility until we come to his important essay on "The Art of Fiction" [1] and to his estimations of some of his masters—Hawthorne or Balzac or Turgenieff.[2]

The passage in his memoirs most indicative of his own subsequent quality is the one recalling the special inwardness that was forced upon him during the immense violent outwardness of the war. He was remembering the time of Wilky's wound and the death of one of Wilky's fellow soldiers:

"I had, under stress, to content myself with knowing it in a more indirect and muffled fashion . . . which . . . was not to prevent the

[1] Pp. 353–70 below.   [2] Pp. 483–7, 553–84 below.

whole quite indescribably intensified time—intensified through all
lapses of occasion and frustrations of contact—from remaining with me
as a more constituted and sustained act of living, in proportion to my
powers and opportunities, than any other homogeneous stretch of experience that my memory now recovers. The case had to be in a
peculiar degree, alas, that of living inwardly—like so many of my other
cases; in a peculiar degree compared, that is, to the immense and prolonged outwardness, outwardness naturally at the very highest pitch,
that was the general sign of the situation. To which I may add that my
'alas' just uttered is in the key altogether of my then current consciousness, and not in the least in that of my present appreciation of the same
—so that I leave it, even while I thus put my mark against it. . . .

"My appreciation of what I presume at the risk of any apparent
fatuity to call my 'relation to' the War is at present a thing exquisite
to me, a thing of the last refinement of romance, whereas it had to be
at the time a sore and troubled, a mixed and oppressive thing—though
I promptly see, on reflection, how it must frequently have flushed with
emotions, with small scraps of direct perception even, with particular
sharpnesses in the generalised pang of participation, that were all but
touched in themselves as with the full experience. Clear as some object
presented in high relief against the evening sky of the west, at all
events, is the presence for me beside the stretcher on which my
younger brother was to lie for so many days before he could be moved,
and on which he had lain during his boat-journey from the South to
New York and thence again to Newport, of lost Cabot Russell's stricken
father, who, failing, up and down the searched field, in respect of his
own irrecoverable boy—then dying, or dead, as afterwards appeared,
well within the enemy's works—had with an admirable charity brought
Wilky back to a waiting home instead, and merged the parental ache
in the next nearest devotion he could find. Vivid to me still is one's
almost ashamed sense of this at the hurried disordered time, and of how
it was impossible not to impute to his grave steady gentleness and judgment a full awareness of the difference it would have made for him,
all the same, to be doing such things with a still more intimate pity.
Unobliterated for me, in spite of vaguenesses, this quasi-twilight vision
of the good bereft man, bereft, if I rightly recall, of his only son, as he
sat erect and dry-eyed at the guarded feast of *our* relief; and so much
doubtless partly because of the image that hovers to me across the years
of Cabot Russell himself, my brother's so close comrade—dark-eyed,
youthfully brown, heartily bright, actively handsome, and with the
arrested expression, the indefinable shining stigma, worn, to the regard
that travels back to them, by those of the young figures of the fallen
that memory and fancy, wanting, never ceasing to want, to 'do' something for them, set as upright and clear-faced as may be, each in his

sacred niche. They have each to such a degree, so ranged, the strange property or privilege—one scarce knows what to call it—of exquisitely, for all *our* time, facing us out, quite blandly ignoring us, looking through us or straight over us at something they partake of together but that we mayn't pretend to know. We walk thus, I think, rather ruefully before them—those of us at least who didn't at the time share more happily their risk."

The sense of guilt that the responsive civilian must often feel in wartime never came to direct expression in HJ's fiction. But his extraordinary power of probing to the last reaches of consciousness, and of suggesting, in late stories like "The Altar of the Dead" or "The Beast in the Jungle" or "The Jolly Corner," how the "ghosts" of the dead seem to live through and beyond us, may well date back to this time. And we could hardly have a more sensitive instance of the way his "visiting mind" worked itself into the situations it contemplated than his imaginative participation in the feelings of the stricken father.

The accident that prevented HJ from being a soldier has been magnified by recent psychological biographers to the point of its finally being referred to, in an introduction to some of his stories, as "the first large event in his life." One would have to be a very inattentive reader of his autobiographies to miss so entirely what constituted the real events for a character like his. The fact that the injury was to his back has led to the assumption that it left him sexually impotent. The fact that WJ also suffered from severe and prolonged strain in his back, and that the two brothers often discussed their symptoms in their letters as though they were similar, has, to be sure, not been reckoned with in this connection. Since HJ never married, he may have been sexually impotent, but since he seems never to have exhibited the specific anxieties or fantasies that can be diagnosed as the product of such frustration, it has not been proved that we can learn anything about his character or his art by building on that assumption.

He introduced his own account of his injury to make the point that it served in a strange way—as the inward corresponds to the outward—to involve him in the tensions of his time:

"Scarce at all to be stated . . . the queer fusion or confusion established in my consciousness during the soft spring of '61 by the firing on Fort Sumter, Mr. Lincoln's instant first call for volunteers and a physical mishap, already referred to as having overtaken me at the same dark hour, and the effects of which were to draw themselves out incalculably and intolerably. Beyond all present notation the interlaced, undivided way in which what had happened to me, by a turn of fortune's hand, in twenty odious minutes, kept company of the most unnatural—I can call it nothing less—with my view of what was happening, with the question of what might still happen, to everyone about me, to the country at large: it so made of these marked disparities a single vast visitation. One had the sense, I mean, of a huge comprehensive ache, and there were hours at which one could scarce have told whether it came most from one's own poor organism, still so young and so meant for better things, but which had suffered particular wrong, or from the enclosing social body, a body rent with a thousand wounds and that thus treated one to the honour of a sort of tragic fellowship. The twenty minutes had sufficed, at all events, to establish a relation—a relation to everything occurring round me not only for the next four years but for long afterward—that was at once extraordinarily intimate and quite awkwardly irrelevant. I must have felt in some befooled way in presence of a crisis—the smoke of Charleston Bay still so acrid in the air—at which the likely young should be up and doing or, as familiarly put, lend a hand most wanted; the willing youths, all round, were mostly starting to their feet, and to have trumped up a lameness at such a juncture could be made to pass in no light for graceful.

"Jammed into the acute angle between two high fences, where the rhythmic play of my arms, in tune with that of several other pairs, but at a dire disadvantage of position, induced a rural, a rusty, a quasi-extemporised old engine to work and a saving stream to flow, I had done myself, in face of a shabby conflagration, a horrid even if an obscure hurt; and what was interesting from the first was my not doubting in the least its duration—though what seemed equally clear was that I needn't as a matter of course adopt and appropriate it, so to speak, or place it for increase of interest on exhibition. The interest of it, I very presently knew, would certainly be of the greatest, would even in conditions kept as simple as I might make them become little less than absorbing. The shortest account of what was to follow for a long time after is therefore to plead that the interest never did fail. It was naturally what is called a painful one, but it consistently declined, as an influence at play, to drop for a single instant. Circumstances, by a wonderful chance, overwhelmingly favoured it—as an interest, an inexhaustible, I mean; since I also felt in the whole enveloping tonic atmosphere a force promoting its growth. Interest, the interest of life and of death, of our national existence, of the fate of those, the vastly numerous, whom it closely concerned, the interest of the extending War, in fine, the hurrying troops, the transfigured scene, formed a cover for every sort of intensity, made tension itself in fact contagious —so that almost any tension would do, would serve for one's share."

HJ spoke less elliptically in his letters of the results of this spinal strain. The damage was greatly increased because he neglected at first, "through crazy juvenility," to do anything about it. It prostrated him for long periods during his twenties, and made the pursuance of regular work almost as uncertain for him as it was for WJ. But he gradually regained strength and stamina sufficient for about the longest and most productive career of any artist in American fiction.

He retained, even from the war years, other memories of hopes and promises. When he returned to America in 1881, after his first half dozen years of residence in London, he wrote in his notebook:

"The feeling of that younger time comes back to me in which I sat here scribbling, dreaming, planning, gazing out upon the world in which my fortune was to seek, and suffering tortures from my damnable state of health. It was a time of suffering so keen that that fact might seem to give its dark colour to the whole period; but that is not what I think of today. When the burden of pain has been lifted, as many memories and emotions start into being as the little insects that scramble about when, in the country, one displaces a flat stone. Ill-health, physical suffering, in one's younger years is a grievous trial; but I am not sure that we do not bear it most easily then. In spite of it, we feel the joy of youth; and that is what I think of today among the things that remind me of the past. The freshness of impression and desire, the hope, the curiosity, the vivacity, the sense of the richness and mystery of the world that lies before us,—there is an enchantment in all that which it takes a heavy dose of pain to quench and which in later hours, even if *success* has come to us, touches us less nearly. Some of my doses of pain were very heavy; very weary were some of my months and years. But all that is sacred; it is idle to write of it today.

"What comes back to me freely, delightfully, is the visions of those untried years. Never did a poor fellow have more; never was an ingenuous youth more passionately and yet more patiently eager for what life might bring. Now that life has brought something, brought a measurable part of what I dreamed of then, it is touching enough to look back. I knew at least what I wanted then—to see something of the world. I have seen a good deal of it, and I look at the past in the light of this knowledge. What strikes me is the definiteness, the unerringness of those longings. I wanted to do very much what I have done, and success, if I may say so, now stretches back a tender hand to its younger brother, desire. I remember the days, the hours, the books, the seasons, the winter skies and darkened rooms of summer. I remember the old walks, the old efforts, the old exaltations and depressions. I remember more than I can say here today."

The last educational experiment induced by his family was perhaps the oddest of all. He spoke, in his autobiography, of having proceeded to Cambridge "on the very vaguest grounds that probably ever determined a residence there," by which he designated his having been, during 1862–3, "a singularly alien member" of the Harvard Law School. Of that training he recollected that he had attended all the required lectures, and that it was "quite prodigious that I should have been so systematically faithful to them without my understanding the first word of what they were about." He cast himself in his favorite comic role of the incompetent in his unique account of a "moot-court":

"I have kept to this hour a black little memory of my having attempted to argue one afternoon, by way of exercise and under what seemed to me a perfect glare of publicity, the fierce light of a 'moot-court,' some case proposed to me by a fellow-student—who can only have been one of the most benign of men unless he was darkly the designingest, and to whom I was at any rate to owe it that I figured my shame for years much in the image of my having stood forth before an audience with a fiddle and bow and trusted myself to rub them together desperately enough (after the fashion of Rousseau in a passage of the Confessions,) to make some appearance of music. My music, I recall, before the look on the faces around me, quavered away into mere collapse and cessation, a void now engulfing memory itself, so that I liken it all to a merciful fall of the curtain on some actor stricken and stammering. The sense of the brief glare, as I have called the luckless exposure, revives even on this hither side of the wide gulf of time; but I must have outlived every witness—I was so obviously there the very youngest of all aspirants—and, in truth, save for one or two minor and merely comparative miscarriages of the sacrificial act before my false gods, my connection with the temple was to remain as consistently superficial as could be possible to a relation still restlessly perceptive through all its profaneness."

He did not bother to say just how or when he terminated his connection with the Law School, but he made clear that the chief reason he had agreed to enter this blind alley was that he had gained thereby an opportunity, very reservedly and secretly, to begin to be a writer in earnest. His first review, of N. W. Senior's *Essays on Fiction*, dealing with Scott, Bulwer, Thackeray, and Mrs. Stowe, was accepted by Charles Eliot Norton for the *North American Review* in 1864. His first short story, a neatly written but fairly conventional magazine treatment of a triangle against the background of the war, appeared in the *Atlantic Monthly* the following year. He may, as he said, have given the impression, in comparison with WJ, of "playing with much thinner things." But by the measurement of external success, he had been included in the leading American magazines before he was twenty-two.

That should not imply that his talent was greatly precocious, or that he arrived soon at the level of his mature fiction. In his collected edition he preserved only half a dozen stories composed earlier than the 1880's, and only three earlier than *Daisy Miller*, which brought him his one taste of wide popularity, at thirty-five. He did not produce his first full-length novel, *Roderick Hudson*, until ten years after his first story.

At the outset he was more striking as a critic, especially in the role of the destructive young reviewer for the newly-founded *Nation*,[1] where he coined many epigrammatic sentences like the one with which he had dismissed poor N. W. Senior: "He is superficial without being lively; he is indeed so heavy, that we are induced to wonder why his own weight does not force him below the surface."

One of the current misconceptions of HJ's early years as a writer is that he was forever deploring America and pining for Europe. The record will not bear that out. Not only was he deeply moved, like the rest of the family, by the national tragedy of Lincoln's death; but in re-calling Hawthorne's death he was to cite him as proof "to what a use American matter could be put by an American hand: a consummation involving, it appeared, the happiest moral. For the moral was that an American could be an artist, one of the finest, without 'going outside' about it, as I liked to say; quite in fact as if Hawthorne had become one just by being American *enough*, by the felicity of how the artist in him missed nothing, suspected nothing, that the ambient air didn't affect him as containing." In his biography of Hawthorne, to be sure, which he wrote at the end of the 1870's, HJ dwelt more upon Haw-thorne's discovery, at the time of *The Marble Faun* and after his expe-rience of Europe, of the thinness for an imaginative writer of the American scene.[2]

When HJ went to Europe on his own for the first time, in 1869, it was, as had been the case with WJ's trip to Germany two years before, primarily to get well. His unfinished memoirs of this time, *The Middle Years*, distort considerably the actual picture. Looking back over his long accumulation of fondness for England, HJ forgets that in spite of the eager anticipation he brought, he did not always feel so ripely at home there. His account—forty-five years after the event—of his arrival in Liverpool is an instance of the later HJ's famous sensibility:

"I found myself, from the first day of March 1869, in the face of an opportunity that affected me then and there as the happiest, the most interesting, the most alluring and beguiling, that could ever have opened before a somewhat disabled young man who was about to complete his twenty-sixth year. Treasures of susceptibility, treasures not only unconscious of the remotest approach to exhaustion, but, given the dazzling possibilities, positively and ideally intact, I now recognise— I in fact long ago recognised—on the part of that intensely 'reacting' small organism; which couldn't have been in higher spirits or made more inward fuss about the matter if it had come into a property measured not by mere impressions and visions, occasions for play of perception and imagination, mind and soul, but by dollars and 'shares,'

---

[1] For an example of such a review, see his piece on Whitman's *Drum-Taps*,   pp. 490–4, below.
[2] See pp. 481–2 below.

lands and houses or flocks and herds. It is to the account of that immense fantastication that I set down a state of mind so out of proportion to anything it could point to round about save by the vaguest of
foolish-looking gestures; and it would perhaps in truth be hard to say
whether in the mixture of spirit and sense so determined the fact of
innocence or that of intelligence most prevailed. I like to recover this
really prodigious flush—as my reader, clearly, must perceive I do; I like
fairly to hang about a particular small hour of that momentous March
day . . . for the sake of the extraordinary gage of experience that it
seemed on the spot to offer, and that I had but to take straight up: my
life, on so complacently near a view as I now treat myself to, having
veritably consisted but in the prolongation of that act. I took up the
gage, and as I look back the fullest as well as simplest account of the interval till now strikes me as being that I have never, in common honour,
let it drop again. And the small hour was just that of my having landed
at Liverpool in the gusty, cloudy, overwhelmingly English morning and
pursued, with immediate intensities of appreciation, as I may call the
muffled accompaniment for fear of almost indecently overnaming it,
a course which had seated me at a late breakfast in the coffee-room
of the old Adelphi Hotel ('Radley's,' as I had to deplore its lately having ceased to be dubbed,) and handed me over without a scruple to my
fate. This doom of inordinate exposure to appearances, aspects, images,
every protrusive item almost, in the great beheld sum of things, I regard
in other words as having settled upon me once for all while I observed
for instance that in England the plate of buttered muffin and its cover
were sacredly set upon the slop-bowl after hot water had been ingenu-
ously poured into the same, and had seen that circumstance in a perfect
cloud of accompaniments. I must have had with my tea and my muffin
a boiled egg or two and a dab of marmalade, but it was from a far
other store of condiments I most liberally helped myself. I was lucidly
aware of so gorging—esoterically, as it were, while I drew out the
gustatory process; and I . . . was again and again in the aftertime to
win back the homeliest notes of the impression, the damp and darksome light washed in from the steep, black, bricky street, the crackle
of the strong draught of the British 'sea-coal' fire, much more confident
of its function, I thought, than the fires I had left, the rustle of the thick,
stiff, loudly unfolded and refolded 'Times,' the incomparable truth to
type of the waiter, truth to history, to literature, to poetry, to Dickens,
to Thackeray, positively to Smollett and to Hogarth, to every connection that could help me to appropriate him and his setting, an arrangement of things hanging together with a romantic rightness that
had the force of a revelation."

His first surviving letter home at that time, not from Liverpool but
a few days later from London, of which his memoirs present an even

more glowing evocation, makes a fascinating contrast. He already uses some of his later favorite adjectives like "portentous" and "vulgar," but he is very unsophisticated and boyish, and his surroundings remind him not of the charming aspects of the English novelists, but of the sordid and sinister:

*   *   *   *   *

My own dearest Mother—

I have been debating with myself for the past half hour as to whether my being horribly homesick this evening is a reason for or against my scribbling these few lines; but passion, not reason, has settled the question, and here I am beating with my pen at this poor blank paper as grimly as my wretched infantile heart is thumping against my breast. What is the good of having a mother—and such a mother—unless to blurt out to her your passing follies and miseries? At all events, sitting here in this dreary London lodging between my fire and my candles, I must begin a letter, or else I shall begin to *howl* and drive the poor landlord to send out for a policeman. Yes—I confess it without stint or shame—I am homesick—abjectly, fatally homesick. Tomorrow, doubt-less I shall be better—the crisis will have passed; but meanwhile, until bedtime, let me be my own dear mother's son. In old times when we were all over in this blasted Europe together and poor father used to start out on a reconnaissance and turn up the next day and with noble frankness own up to the terrible cause, we all used brutally to jeer at him; and I doubtless, as hard as the rest. But oh, how I repent of those jeers—and how I feel in my soul the same melting anguish that softened away his resolves! If to think and to feel and to long were to act and to be—wouldn't I just be lolling on that Quincy St. sofa, in conse-quence—with my head on mother's lap and my feet in Alice's!—But I gulp down my sobs and proceed to narrative. You will have received the letter I wrote . . . in Liverpool. . . . I made up my mind to . . . spend Sunday . . . in going over to Chester, looking about, dining and returning. But on rising on Sunday I found that I had overslept—or at least overlain—the train and that I must spend the day within doors at Liverpool—within doors because the rain was gushing, of course, in black torrents. The prospect appalled and my heart failed me. I found there was just time to breakfast and catch the London train. I embraced the idea and departed. It was a slow train and we spent many hours on the route; but as we lingered along and stopped at many places, and coming southwards found better weather, I saw to much advantage a goodly part of this portentous land. I suffered somewhat from having in the carriage with me a good deal of a bore in the shape of an elderly middle-class Philistine, who on learning I was an American, overwhelmed me with fatherly care and insisted on directing my attention, imparting very vulgar and rudimentary facts and making himself a very ponderous nuisance. The only refuge was to feign slumber, whereby, of course, I lost the scenery; but 'twas a choice of evils. I arrived late in the afternoon and went to Morley's Hotel, Trafalgar Square (at the recommendation of the Philistine). What terrible places are these English hotels! I think I was never so gloom-smitten as that night at Morley's: the tortuous passages—the dingy musty bedroom—the two penny candle—the stupid coffee-room—it was like a story in an old magazine at the dentist's. What strikes me here is the extraordinary fixedness and sacredness of the superfluous and the very short measure of the necessary. At Morley's you have fifty yards of curtains to your bed and of white cravat on the waiter's neck—but not a ray of gaslight (in your room) and not the slightest facility in the coffee-room for conceiving the idea of a dinner—no bill of fare—nothing sensible nor visible save the terribly genteel waiters. Still, I got along very well; and certainly considering how bad the system of their hotels is (from an American standpoint) they work them most beautifully. Only it makes me yearn for the free promiscuous snack of Parker's.

Well, yesterday I went to Baring's, and made a few little purchases —among other things of a trunk and some clothes. I don't find the prices here at all of that fabulous lowness which we have heard vaunted. Things in fact strike me as dear; but then they are wonderfully good. I also looked at three or four lodgings and was disgusted with their dinginess and rattiness. But their keepers—what a set! The race doesn't exist with us. I'm sure even the few that I saw justify every aspersion of Thackeray or Dickens: I mean the women, you know, hard-faced, garrulous, ravening creatures encrusted with a totally indescribable greasy dingy dowdiness! But fortune has led me into these quiet waters. . . .

The above, which I have just read over seems to me such wretched puling stuff that I am ashamed to send it, but as I can hardly afford to waste so much time and material I'll let it go for what it is worth. . . . My landlord is a very finished specimen and I wish you could see him. He is an old servant of some genteel family, who lets out his three floors to gentlemen and waits upon them with the most obsequious punctuality. He does everything for me—won't let me raise a finger for myself—is butler, landlord, valet, guide, philosopher and friend all at once. I am completely comfortable, save that his tremendous respectability and officiousness are somewhat oppressive. Nevertheless, in this matter of lodgings esteem me most happy and fortunate. . . .

But I have scribbled enough. Cancel, dearest mother, all the maudlinity of the beginning of my letter; the fit is over; the ghost is laid; Richard's himself again. I assure you, I shall do very well. I'm horribly impatient for the next steamer and its mails. I thought much of my

country yesterday, but the telegram in the *Times* was very meagre.[1]
I have in the *Times* every morning at breakfast for a shilling a week.
I wish you could see me sitting between my muffin and the copper
kettle on the hob. . . . Without is the brown street still further em-
browned by the wire screen in the window—and within your son.

*   *   *

HJ was a characteristic American to the extent of being a very
faithful tourist, and his spirits soon rallied as he recounted to WJ his
impressions of the National Gallery: "I admire Raphael; I enjoy
Rubens; but I passionately love Titian." The reception of his letters,
as WJ said, made quite an event in Quincy Street; and when, later in
this year, HJ let himself go on the beauty of Italy, WJ wrote: "It is a
great pity they should be born to blush unseen by the general public
and that just the matter that they contain, in a little less rambling style,
should not appear in the columns of the *Nation*." When he added that
Father had read some of them aloud to Emerson, HJ was "terrifically
agitated." A few of these appreciative sketches, which show HJ in
the first painstaking stages of developing the descriptive skills he was
to use in his *Portraits of Places*, have been printed among his letters.
For the sake of the full record, it is important to note that even after
his first homesickness had worn off, he by no means always took the
glamorous view. D. H. Lawrence believed that a man's only honest
impression of a place is his first impression. Here is HJ's first brief
grown-up impression of Paris. He had landed at Boulogne, where the
family had lived a dozen years before, and had passed through Paris
on his way to Switzerland for the summer:

"Boulogne looked as if I had left it yesterday—*rien n'y manquait*,
except that it was much smaller. Of course I saw only the little bit
from the boat to the station. At Paris I went to the Grand Hotel—a
horrible place—a little Paris within the big and a big New York inside
of that—a complication of terrors. I was obliged to stop over the
whole day as there is but one train—the night express, to Geneva. I
spent my time in walking the streets, whereby I was mostly struck with
their magnificence. The place has turned into a perfect monotony of
glaring would-be monumental splendour. Flare and glare are the only
words it suggests—the reflection of torrid asphalt and limestone by day
and the feverish torrents of gaslight by night. Napoleon has *tué la nuit*
Victor Hugo would say. Tell Willy that I spent some time at the *Salon*,
the average tone of which is much less clever than I supposed. A very
fine Courbet, tho, a hunting piece, and an immense lot of promiscuous
ability. But it did me good afterwards to stroll through the eternal
Louvre. I enjoy the masters quite as much as I hoped. They are so
respectable, in this profligate modern world. Oh the tumult, the

---

[1] This was the week in which General Grant became President.

splendor, the crazy headlong race for pleasure—and the stagnant gulfs
of misery to be seen in two great capitals like London and Paris. Mankind seems like the bedevilled herd of swine in the Bible, rushing headlong into the sea."

The dark and ugly aspects of Paris were to be pushed to the very
edges of the canvas in the jewel-like image of the city that a tourist
like Lambert Strether conjured up. But HJ's knowledge of the city's
suffering still remained, even if he suggested it in *The Ambassadors*
only as a faint but ineradicable smell in the streets: "the smell of revolution, the smell of the public temper—or perhaps simply the smell of
blood." [1] In his presentation of London in *The Princess Casamassima*
he gave fuller evidence that he never forgot the poverty he had watched
as he walked, or the heaving of violent forces just beneath the varied
surfaces that so allured his painter's eye.

If the impression left by WJ in his first maturity is of an unstable
alternation between high spirits and melancholy, that left by HJ is
more uniformly grave and often earnest. The one attribute of genius
that he displayed at this time was an unwavering dedication to his
ultimate goal. One more exchange, again with his mother, will take
us into his personal problems in a way that his later, more social
correspondence rarely permits. Among his most troublesome com-
plaints was chronic constipation, and he had found that a certain
amount of "lively travel" was a great help to this as well as to restoring
flexibility to his back. His moving about naturally added to his expenses, and brought from home some demur. The tone of his response
illustrates what he meant by saying: "There is another Atlantic Cable,
quite as stout as the telegraph, one end of which is located in Quincy
Street, and the other tied through one of the sad perforations of my
heart."

* * * * *

Switzerland, June 28, 1869

I duly noted your injunction to spend the summer quietly and
economically. I hope to do both—or that is, to circulate in so far as I
do, by the inexpensive vehicle of my own legs. . . . When you speak
of your own increased expenses, etc., I feel very guilty and selfish in

---

[1] This image in *The Ambassadors*
would seem to stem from a letter HJ
wrote to WJ from Paris in 1872 at a
time when he had still not grown into
his later appreciation of its charm:
"Paris continues to seem very pleasant,
but doesn't become interesting. You get
tired of a place which you can call nothing but *charmant*. Besides, I read the
Figaro every day religiously, and it
leaves a bad taste in my mouth. Here-
abouts, moreover, the place is totally
Americanized,—the Boulevard des Cap-
ucines and the Rue de la Paix are a
perfect reproduction of Broadway. The
want of comprehension of the real moral
situation of France leaves one unsatisfied, too. Beneath all this neatness and
coquetry, you seem to smell the Commune suppressed, but seething."

entertaining any projects which look in the least like extravagance. My beloved mother, if you but knew the purity of my motives! Reflection assures me, as it will assure you, that the only economy for me is to get thoroughly well and into such a state as that I can work. For this consummation, I will accept everything—even the appearance of mere pleasure-seeking. A winter in Italy (if I feel two months hence as I do now) enabling me to spend my time in a certain way, will help me on further than anything else I know of—more than a winter in Paris and of course, so long as the very semblance of application is denied me—than one in Germany. . . .

If before I left home I had been as certain as I have now become, that to *pay*, my visit here must at present be a real change—a real active taking hold of the matter—we could have talked over the subject far better than we can do in this way. In effect, when I consider how *completely*, during the three or four months before I sailed I was obliged to give up all reading and writing (Willy can tell you) I see that it was a very absurd extension of my hopes to fancy that mere change of place would enable me to take them up again—or that I could lead the old life with impunity in Paris more than in Cambridge. Having lost all the time I have, you see I naturally wish to economise what is left. When I think that a winter in Italy is not as you call it a winter of "recreation," but an occasion not only of physical regeneration but of serious culture too (culture of the kind which alone I have now at 26 any time left for) I find the courage to maintain my proposition even in the face of your allusions to the need of economy at home. It takes a very honest conviction thus to plead the cause of apparently gross idleness against such grave and touching facts. I have trifled so long with my trouble that I feel as if I could afford now to be a little brutal. My lovely mother, if ever I am restored to you sound and serviceable, you will find that you have not cast the pearls of your charity before a senseless beast, but before a creature with a soul to be grateful and a will to act. . . . Of course, you will be guided in your rejoinder simply by the necessities of the case, and will quite put aside any wish to please or any fear to displease me. . . . Your devoted son.

* * *

His mother's answer bears out his father's remark: "Indeed, you are always in all our hearts and thoughts, and mother, I think, loves you more than all her other progeny." WJ's dubbing of HJ with the satiric nickname "Angel" may have been in response to their mother's tenderness for this son who looked, it was often said, a good deal like her. But in this letter she casts, as always, a devoted eye upon the rest of the family as well:

* * * * *

Pomfret, July 24, 1869

My dearly beloved child:

I have been cut off from writing for several weeks, finding that the rest had got the start of me, and now although Alice wrote but two days ago I can forbear no longer. Your letter last evening opens the deepest fountains in my soul, and my bosom seems as if it would burst with its burden of love and tenderness. If you were only here for an hour, and we could talk over this subject of expense, I could, I know, exorcise all these demons of anxiety and conscientiousness that possess you, and leave [you] free as air to enjoy to the full all that surrounds you, and drink in health of body and of mind in following out your own safe and innocent attractions. Just here we desire, dear Harry, to leave you, only exacting from you the promise that you will henceforth throw away prudence and think only of your own comfort and pleasure, for our sakes as well as your own. I am sure you may confide in your prudent old mother to take care of that side of the question. You must have got my letter suggesting your going to Italy for the winter *very* soon after writing your last, so you see we are quite of one mind. Italy will be just the place for you; and do not, I pray you, cramp yourself in any way to hinder your fullest enjoyment of it. You dear reasonable over-conscientious soul! Take the fullest liberty and enjoyment your tastes and inclinations crave, and we will promise heartily to foot the bill.

Alice has doubtless told you all about Pomfret. Suffice it to say, it is a great success. Added to the comforts of the house, and the natural advantages of the place the Bootts, as father says, are a "perfect fit." I do not think Willy could possibly in his circumstances have found a more delightful and beneficial entourage. The life we live here under the pine trees, Will in his hammock, Miss B. with her easel, Alice and I with books and work, and Father and Mr. Boott occasionally riding their favorite hobbies, philosophy and music, but more frequently meeting on the common ground of literature and manners, has something quite Arcadian in it. . . .

This is a delicious warm day. . . . Lizzie Boott and Will have been all the morning under the pines. She as usual with her pencil, and Will in the hammock, with a volume of Browning in his hand. They have been discussing, as I hear their voices, a wide range of subjects—art, languages, and literature. What a striking instance she is of what a careful and thorough education can accomplish, perhaps I should add under the most favorable circumstances. Of course she never could have been formed as she is in America. . . . Look at Minny Temple in contrast with her. Minny has all the tastes and capabilities naturally in a higher degree, and look at the difference. Minny writes that she gets up at 6 o'clock every morning and takes a lesson in drawing. Perhaps she is beginning to work out her own salvation.

I hardly dare to say or predict any thing about Will's improvement. There certainly had been *no* improvement in him up to our coming here, and for some days after. But he appears to have taken a great start the last two weeks. He is in the hammock or sitting about pretty much all day. He says he gets tired, but he gets rested. He looks fifty per cent better in the face, indeed I never saw him brighter. He is the life of the party. You know Father used to say to you, that if you would only fall in love it would be the making of you. Possibly Will's susceptible heart may be coming to the rescue of his back. . . .

Now about yourself, darling Harry. How is your sleep and how is your appetite? how is your digestion? Your legs are all right, blessings upon them! They will be your salvation I have not a doubt. This entire rest of your brain and nervous system, must after a time inevitably work its effect, and the time spent in the study of art in Italy next winter will happily and profitably bridge over the interval. Give my kindest remembrances to each of the Norton household,[1] and say just the proper thing for me. . . . Father has told you all about his book and the reason why its publication is delayed. Father got the start of me again in writing, so I have delayed this until the next steamer. Adieu, my precious one. A thousand blessings on your head. Your loving Mother.

* * *

HJ passed that winter in Italy, and returned home, in better shape to work, the following spring. A few weeks before he sailed from England, he heard from his mother of the death from tuberculosis of his brilliant cousin Minny Temple. He was to devote the final chapter of his *Notes of a Son and Brother* to memorializing her as "the very heroine of our common scene," and his last sentence declared that her death marked for WJ and himself the end of their youth. He spoke far more directly in his own person in a letter to WJ at the time, a letter which may throw more light than any other he ever wrote on the qualities of human nature that he valued most and that he sought to embody in his fiction to the very end of his career.

* * * * *

Malvern, March 29, 1870

Dear Willy—

My mind is so full of poor Minny's death that altho' I immediately wrote in answer to mother's letter, I find it easier to take up my pen again than to leave it alone. A few short hours have amply sufficed to

---

[1] The Nortons were also in Switzerland this summer.

more than reconcile me to the event and to make it seem the most natural—the happiest, fact, almost in her whole career. So it seems, at least, on reflection: to the eye of feeling there is something immensely moving in the sudden and complete extinction of a vitality so exquisite and so apparently infinite as Minny's. But what most occupies me, as it will have done all of you at home, is the thought of how her whole life seemed to tend and hasten, visibly, audibly, sensibly, to this consummation. Her character may be almost literally said to have been without practical application to life. She seems a sort of experiment of nature—an attempt, a specimen or example—a mere subject without an object. She was at any rate the helpless victim and toy of her own intelligence—so that there is positive relief in thinking of her being removed from her own heroic treatment and placed in kinder hands. What a vast amount of truth appears now in all the common-places that she used to provoke—that she was restless—that she was helpless —that she was unpractical. How far she may have been considered up to the time of her illness to have achieved a tolerable happiness, I don't know: hardly at all, I should say, for her happiness like her unhappiness remained wholly incomplete. But what strikes me above all is how great and rare a benefit her life has been to those with whom she was associated. I feel as if a very fair portion of my sense of the reach and quality and capacity of human nature rested upon my experience of her character: certainly a large portion of my admiration of it. She was a case of pure generosity—she had more even than she ever had use for—inasmuch as she could hardly have suffered at the hands of others nearly as keenly as she did at her own.

Upon her limitations, now, it seems idle to dwell; the list of her virtues is so much longer than her life. My own personal relations with her were always of the happiest. Every one was supposed, I believe, to be more or less in love with her: others may answer for themselves: I never was, and yet I had the great satisfaction that I enjoyed *pleasing* her almost as much as if I had been. I cared more to please her perhaps than she ever cared to be pleased. Looking back upon the past half-dozen years, it seems as if she *represented*, in a manner, in my life several of the elements or phases of life at large—her own sex, to begin with, but even more *Youth*, with which owing to my invalidism, I always felt in rather indirect relation.

Poor Minny—what a cold thankless part it seems for her to have played—an actor and setter-forth of things in which she had so little permanent interest! Among the sad reflections that her death provokes for me, there is none sadder than this view of the gradual change and reversal of our relations: I slowly crawling from weakness and inaction and suffering into strength and health and hope: she sinking out of brightness and youth into decline and death. It's almost as if she had

passed away—as far as I am concerned—from having served her purpose, that of standing well within the world, inviting and inviting me
onward by all the bright intensity of her example. She never knew
how sick and disordered a creature I was and I always felt that she
knew me at my worst. I always looked forward with a certain eagerness to the day when I should have regained my natural lead, and one
friendship on my part, at least, might become more active and masculine. This I have especially felt during the powerful experience of the
past year. In a measure I had worked away from the old ground of
my relations with her, without having quite taken possession of the
new: but I had it constantly in my eyes. But here I am plucking all
the sweetest fruits of this Europe which was a dream among her many
dreams—while she has "gone abroad" in another sense! Every thought
of her is a singular mixture of pleasure and pain. The thought of what
either she has lost or won, comes to one as if only to enforce the idea
of *her* gain in eternal freedom and rest and ours in the sense of it.
Freedom and rest! one must have known poor Minny to feel their
value—to know what they may contain—if one can measure, that is,
the balm by the ache.

I have been hearing all my life of the sense of loss which death
leaves behind it—now for the first time I have a chance to learn what
it amounts to. The whole past—all times and places—seems full of her.
Newport especially—to my mind—she seems the very genius of the
place. I could shed tears of joy far more copious than any tears of
sorrow when I think of her feverish earthly lot exchanged for this
serene promotion into pure fellowship with our memories, thoughts
and fancies. I had imagined many a happy talk with her in years to
come—many a cunning device for cheering and consoling her illness,
many a feast on the ripened fruits of our friendship: but this on the
whole surpasses anything I had conceived. You will all have felt by this
time the novel delight of thinking of Minny without the lurking impulse of fond regret and uneasy conjecture so familiar to the minds
of her friends. She has gone where there is neither marrying nor giving
in marriage! no illusions and no disillusions—no sleepless nights and no
ebbing strength. The more I think of her the more perfectly satisfied
I am to have her translated from this changing realm of fact to the
steady realm of thought. There she may bloom into a beauty more
radiant than our dull eyes will avail to contemplate.

My first feeling was an immense regret that I had been separated
from her last days by so great a distance of time and space; but this has
been of brief duration. I am really not sorry not to have seen her
materially changed and thoroughly thankful to have been spared the
sight of her suffering. Of this you must all have had a keen realization.
There is nevertheless something so appealing in the pathos of her final

weakness and decline that my heart keeps returning again and again to the scene, regardless of its pain. When I went to bid Minny farewell at Pelham before I sailed, I asked her about her sleep. "Sleep," she said, "Oh, I don't sleep. *I've given it up*." And I well remember the laugh with which she made this sad attempt at humor. And so she went on, sleeping less and less, waking wider and wider, until she awaked absolutely!

I asked mother to tell me what she could about her last weeks and to repeat me any of her talk or any chance incidents, no matter how trivial. This is a request easier to make than to comply with, and really to talk about Minny we must wait till we meet. But I *should* like one of her last photos, if you can get one. You will have felt for yourself, I suppose, how little is the utmost one can *do*, in a positive sense, as regards her memory. Her presence was so much, so intent—so strenuous —so full of human exaction: her absence is so modest, content with so little. A little decent passionless grief—a little rummage in our little store of wisdom—a sigh of relief—and we begin to live for ourselves again. If we can imagine the departed spirit cognizant of our action in the matter, we may suppose it much better pleased by our perfect acceptance of the void it has left than by our quarreling with it and wishing it filled up again. What once was life is always life, in one form or another, and speaking simply of this world I feel as if in effect and influence Minny had lost very little by her change of state. She lives as a steady unfaltering luminary in the mind rather than as a flickering wasting earth-stifled lamp. Among all my thoughts and conceptions I am sure I shall never have one of greater sereneness and purity: her image will preside in my intellect, in fact, as a sort of measure and standard of brightness and repose.

But I have scribbled enough. While I sit spinning my sentences, she is *dead*: and I suppose it is partly to defend myself from too direct a sense of her death that I indulge in this fruitless attempt to transmute it from a hard fact into a soft idea. Time, of course, will bring almost even-handedly the inevitable pain and the inexorable cure. I am willing to leave life to answer for life; but meanwhile, thinking how small at greatest is our change as compared with her change and how vast an apathy goes to our little measure of sympathy, I take a certain satisfaction in having simply written twelve pages.

I have been reading over the three or four letters I have got from her since I have been abroad: they are full of herself—or at least of a fraction of herself: they would say little to strangers. Poor little Minny! It's the *living* ones that die; the writing ones that survive.

One thought there is that moves me much—that I should be here delving into this alien England in which it was one of her fancies that she had a kind of property. It was not, I think, one of the happiest.

Every time that I have been out during the last three days, the aspect of things has perpetually seemed to enforce her image by simple contrast and difference. The landscape assents stolidly enough to her death; it would have ministered but scantly to her life. She was a breathing protest against English grossness, English compromises and conventions—a plant of pure American growth. None the less tho' I had a dream of telling her of England and of her immensely enjoying my stories. But it's only a half change: instead of my discoursing to her, I shall have her forever talking to me. Amen, Amen to all she may say! Farewell to all that she was! How much this was, and how sweet it was! How it comes back to one, the charm and essential grace of her early years. We shall all have known something! How it teaches, absolutely, tenderness and wonder to the mind. But it's all locked away, incorruptibly, within the crystal walls of the past. And there is my youth—and anything of yours you please and welcome! turning to gold in her bright keeping. In exchange, for you, dearest Minny, we'll all keep your future. Don't fancy that your task is done. Twenty years hence we shall be living with your love and longing with your eagerness and suffering with your patience.

30th p.m. So much I wrote last evening, but it has left me little to add, incomplete as it is. In fact it is too soon to talk of Minny's death or to pretend to feel it. This I shall not do till I get home. Every now and then the thought of it stops me short, but it's from the life of home that I shall really miss her. With this European world of associations and art and studies, she has nothing to do: she belongs to the deep domestic moral affectional realm. I can't put away the thought that just as I am beginning life, she has ended it. But her rare death is an answer to all the regrets it provokes. You remember how largely she dealt in the future—how she considered and planned and arranged. Now it's to haunt and trouble her no longer. She has her present and future in one.

To you, I suppose, her death must have been an unmitigated relief—you must have suffered keenly from the knowledge of her sufferings. Thank heaven they lasted no longer. When I first heard of her death I could think only of them: now I can't think of them even when I try.

* * *

Minny Temple was to continue to speak to him for much longer than twenty years. He tried to suggest some of her traits in Isabel Archer. The exquisite charm and radiance of Milly Theale were less veiledly hers. She gave him the elements in the human drama to which he could respond most keenly, and thus became his quintessential heroine, whose suffering was transmuted into grace. Why loss and renunciation was such a compelling theme for HJ could be probed both to psychological and to social roots. He remained aware of his passive observer's tendency to transmute "a hard fact" into "a soft idea," and we think in compelling contrast of how WJ wrote to him, while working on his *Psychology*: "I have to forge every sentence in the teeth of irreducible and stubborn facts." Such transmutation reduced even his most poignant tragedy, *The Wings of the Dove*, to the minor key its title suggests, to the realm of suffering and pathos rather than to that of heroic action. It involved a contraction of experience from the sphere of the masculine protagonist to that of the feminine deuteragonist, but not an evasion of the crucial facts of pain or of love.

Why so much of our late nineteenth-century American literature fell into the mood of elegy is too large a question to enter upon here,[1] but we can observe the causes that operated upon HJ. Minny Temple was not merely a personal symbol. She spoke to him also of the America he cared for most, typified by the old Newport of leisure and culture, which, like so much else of the past, was soon to be obliterated by the post Civil War money-world. The international contrasts, which soon became a leading theme in HJ's fiction, are also foreshadowed in this letter. The American innocence that he often pitted against European experience retained its human substance by virtue of its deep tap-root in the "moral affectional realm." As a result, his American characters are usually his most living. But HJ himself grew restive at always being bracketed as an international novelist. His deepest sense of life transcended national traits altogether, as it gave renewed voice to his father's belief in the conversion of waste. The most recurrent theme in HJ's work is that of inner victory in the face of outer defeat. He passed to the ultimate verge of the drama of consciousness as he continued to reflect upon the translation from "the changing realm of fact" to "the steady realm of thought." At this point HJ became, if hardly a philosopher, an authentic though remote descendent of Plato, and a participator with Proust in affirming the immortal essences of æsthetic idealism.[2]

---

[1] See the end of my chapter dealing with *The Wings of the Dove* in *Henry James: The Major Phase*, for further discussion of this tendency. Even Mark Twain, when he wrote about the Mississippi, celebrated a disappearing America.

[2] For HJ's further development of such ideas, see his essay, "Is There a Life after Death?" at pp. 602–14 below.

FORMULATIONS

The Younger Sons

THE "free and uncommitted" world of their youth was closed for Wilky and Bob by the war. The "successful sociability," which HJ noted as GWJ's outstanding gift, made him a good officer. But he was severely wounded in the side only a few months after he had marched out of Boston with Colonel Shaw, and his father wrote: "Poor Wilky cries aloud for his friends gone and missing, and I could hardly have supposed he might be educated so suddenly up to serious manhood." By the end of the war Wilky had taken several more steps in this kind of education, but he tried to square Lincoln's death with his father's teachings:

* * * * *

Headquarters, Department of the South, April 27, 1865
My darling Father: My heart is overflowing tonight with mingled sorrow and hope at the frightful calamity which has stricken down the magnanimous people of the North. I have never felt in all my born days before the same sentiment of grief and consternation that tonight possesses almost completely my soul. The effect of poor Lincoln's death has given a life-long lesson to those who watch it, and the effect that his death has made upon the army is truly very touching. Every man feels that his own well being has been trampled on, that his own honor has been violated. . . .

Excuse these expressions of my innermost heart, but if I have ever felt sad it is tonight. We have been talking him over and over ever since we heard of his death, and such a crowd of heart-broken young men you would never see again. We have had meetings and subscriptions all over the Department to raise a monument immediately, and I hope that his memory may in some degree impersonate himself for a little while longer. You no doubt see something a great deal higher and better than I do in this murder, yet I see something a good deal higher than I ever thought I should. I see God's wise Providence and justice ridding the sinner of a too pure-minded and clement judge, and putting over him a less worthy and more competent and timely one. He knew that Lincoln never would give the hell to these men that they had been preparing themselves for, and consequently arranged this aright. It is nearly 12 o'clock P.M., I ought to go to bed, but I feel for you and Mother tonight the same feeling I did when you were nursing me in my bed in the summer of 1863. Do write as often as possible. . . . Most affectionately, Garth W. James.

* * *

Even more severe strains were in store for both these younger brothers after the war. Their thoroughgoing abolitionism had led them to ask their father to buy them a cotton plantation in Florida, so that they might run it with free Negro labor. They embarked on this venture before either of them was twenty-one, and though GWJ was very hopeful at first, he had to write home near the close of 1868:

"I have been rebaptized in the faith of my father of late, and it has come about through trouble and anguish. The fact is, affairs here have assumed such a change that I no longer feel that safety which I once felt, and to tell the plain truth I feel that any moment I may be called upon to give up my life for the faith of the principle I professed when I was a soldier in the open field. I was insulted grossly in Gainesville the other day, and if the man who insulted me had not been a crippled drunkard, I should have knocked him down. It is well perhaps I did not. Dennis wrote me from Gordon the other day, that he could hardly hold out any longer; that a body of armed men five in number were prowling nightly around the plantation to take his life, that these threats were openly made and that any moment he might be killed. Today one of the best friends I thought I had in the whole country called upon me and informed me that hereafter I was his enemy. He had recently learned that I was an officer of the 54th Mass. and that hereafter all our intercourse must cease. If this man who represents the intelligence, the culture and the refinement of the South, as he certainly does, and one who has one of the warmest hearts I ever knew, feels that it is a matter of principle to wake up old issues, we had thought were settled by the war, then all I can say is, that it becomes me to stand as firmly as I did in 1863 and to give up everything else in so doing.

"Do not understand me as backing out of the enterprise. On the contrary, I say I have been rebaptized in my faith, and that if all goes with me, my example if it is a worthy one remains behind to attest the strength of my convictions. I am still hopeful though that good sense will eventually prevail. My political opinions which have been growing more conservative of late upon the subject of these detestable and mistakable Carpetbag governments, are not budged one iota by such occurrences as these. On the contrary these are the effect of just such causes.

"There is not much virtue compatible with a government administered by greedy office-seekers, who have already taxed the state beyond its material power of reproduction. I may be North in a week or two on business. If I come it will be for a few days only.

"I am more determined than ever to stick to this, and this I consider my duty, clearly laid out and defined to me. Do not read this letter to a soul. Remember this request I make most religiously of you. So few people who are not on the spot can appreciate my position, that I do not wish to have it even thought over, by curious outsiders, who rant and rage about matters they cannot even be made to think of with coolness and moderation."

But despite GWJ's resolve, the experiment could not be made to succeed financially, and had to be given up. Neither of these brothers prospered thereafter. They both went out to Milwaukee and, apparently through the influence of John Murray Forbes, whose son had married Emerson's daughter, secured minor positions with the railroad. But GWJ's health never became robust again, and he died of Bright's disease in his late thirties.

RJ seems to have been the most nakedly sensitive of the whole family. They spoke of the high-strung agitation and the morbid self-distrust that lurked behind his animation and his gift for talk. He was the first of the brothers to be married, in 1872, and was followed by GWJ the year after. But he never managed to settle down in Wisconsin, and finally returned to live at Concord. Impressed by Howells' analysis of industrial tension in *A Hazard of New Fortunes* (1890), he poured out his own sharp objections to the advance of capitalism, objections that still ring with his father's voice:

"God bless you forever for the work you are doing in these Books to keep alive that flame of innocence within us which the Fate of Dollars is in such danger of extinguishing. . . . Someday I would like to tell you of the true inwardness of a great Western Railway for which I worked for fifteen years. It was a great (and is) tomb to which the young men go down and in which the many bury and have to bury every emotion and desire which can glorify life. I was the confidential clerk for a long while of one of the most successful and unscrupulous Railway Barons this continent has ever seen—the Manager of the St. Paul Railway. I knew all his inner history and his outer—(He is now dead). I can tell you chapter and verse of every business motive and maxim which enabled a poor New Hampshire Stable Boy to go West and die forty years later worth five million of dollars on a salary which could never have enabled him to *save* more than $100,000.

"When we parted after fifteen years of intimacy it was because not even penniless ill health and self-contempt which association with him and his kind had brought me to could be bought by them any longer. I had never been required *to do* the felonious things this management fattened on, but I was obliged *to know it* and keep still."

Unlike GWJ, for whom, in HJ's terms, "the act of reading was inhuman and repugnant," RJ shared the family interest in writing and also in painting, and tried both intermittently. He became enthusiastic for a time about the possibility of being an actor, but could not stand "the wear and tear of city life." As his life advanced, his periods of moody depression caused him to drink heavily. He had also a strain of self-pity that made him talk sometimes as though he had been neglected as a child, whereas he would seem to have known the indulgent affection given to the smallest son. Affected for a time by his father's Swedenborgianism, he later showed some of WJ's concern with spiritualistic mediums. Still later he became deeply interested in Catholicism. He discussed his spiritual dilemma and his glimpsed solution in another letter to Howells: "After all my reading of Swedenborg I can never believe his books will become the staff of life save to the few—the complicated and ecstatic. I don't know what I would do without them. But they have only been of use to me since I have kicked myself into acquiescence with destiny. One unselfish emotion of the human heart—one act of self-sacrifice done in the darkness of doubt can open heaven wider I think than all the most finished possession of the 'illumined seer' as his disciples term him."

RJ had come to feel for himself the necessity of passing beyond abstract truth to love: "So at night when one lies awake and thinks of the things, or perhaps the one thing you've wanted on earth and couldn't get, the soft sense of a melting heart comes upon you and you begin to dimly feel for the first time the *truth of love*. Truth has no existence apart from love. . . . Oh the bliss of having lost every shred of trust in everything save the knowledge of the heart which aches. . . . Since father died, who was the only being on earth I ever cared for deeply, that loss has built up in me out of the ignominy of drink and debauchery what seems to me of late to be becoming one long day in which I see nothing but the faces of Seraphs smiling. Dead affections and decencies long long forgotten seem to be calling from afar off, and there are moments in which my heart is wrung, as if with a sort of pain of bliss—a pain at the thought of all the glory which God will give to them who will wait, and *will not* surrender to the passing darkness. Forgive this burst, but for the most part my lips are mute."

In the late 1880's, after her own long discipline of suffering, Alice spoke of RJ's excessive emotions as "superficial," and thought that he must have "progressive nervous degeneracy" as a result of his drinking. HJ was more lenient in remarking that this brother was "an extraordinary instance of a man's nature constituting his profession, his whole stock in trade." HJ was also impressed by some of RJ's fugitive verses, and found them full of "real beauty, in spite of their . . . irregularity of form. . . . They are as soft as moonbeams in a room at night—so strangely pure in feeling." He included one religious poem by RJ in his *Notes of a Son and Brother*:

* * * * *

> Although I lie so low and still
> Here came I by the Master's will;
> He smote at last to make me free,
> As He was smitten on the tree
> And nailed there. He knew of old
> The human heart, and mine is cold;
> And I know now that all we gain
> Until we come to Him is vain.
> Thy hands have never wrought a deed,
> Thy heart has never known a need,
> That went astray in His great plan
> Since far-off days when youth began.
> For in that vast and perfect plan
> Where time is but an empty span
> Our Master waits. He knows our want,
> We know not his—till pale and gaunt
> With weariness of life we come
> And say to Him, What shall I be?
> Oh Master, smite, but make me free
> Perchance in these far worlds to know
> The better thing we sought to be.
>
> And then upon thy couch lie down
> And fold the hands which have not sown;
> And as thou liest there alone
> Perhaps some breath from seraph blown
> As soft as dew upon the rose
> Will fall upon thee at life's close.
> So thou wilt say, At last, at last!
> All pain is love when pain is past!
> And to the Master once again:
> Oh keep my heart too weak to pray;
> I ask no longer questions vain
> Of life and love, of loss and gain—

These for the living are and strong;
I go to Thee, to Thee belong.
Once was I wakened by Thy light,
But years have passed, and now the night
Takes me to Thee. I am content;
So be it in Thy perfect plan
A mansion is where I am sent
To dwell among the innocent.

* * *

This younger brother's fragile talent shows to best advantage in a fragment of an autobiography that he started in his early fifties. Responding to a suggestion from WJ's wife, he returned for a brief sojourn into the one free world he had known:

"You speak of an autobiography. Would that I could write one—for —curiously enough memory of days gone by lightens up again with me—now that I have little save memory to live with. But the facts of it are so meaningless. Down the palm of my left hand runs the so called line of Fortune and of Luck. Sufficiently defined is the line of the left hand, but badly broken. On the right palm the line not half so distinct and badly broken—which signifies that Destiny of itself gave me bad fortune and that with my own right hand I made that Destiny worse. It would have to be the biography of broken fortunes. Still the lines show this in both hands. At the beginning and the ends the lines are both well marked and straight—the breaks are all in middle life. More and more I take comfort in omens and portents and go to swell the ranks of those who lean on oracles. It is the return to childhood—which word brings me back to 54 West 14th St. in N. Y. What a troop of figures come out of the shadows. Alice James and the nursery there and scarlet fever, measles, the Irish nurse whom I have never yet forgotten, and the precious brooch she wore with a green crystal in which came to me the first wonder and mystery of color. When the light struck it first, something wondrous and from heaven awoke in my stomach—so lasting that today the effect of a green crystal is to make me weep inwardly. There are no end of figures which come and go in that New York house. Uncle William from Albany who throws his nightgown, night cap, brushes etc. from the omnibus window *en passant* from the Albany train to the lower Broadway from which he is to return late in the day—signalling to the awe-struck servant on the steps that these things are his and that he will return for the night. "Tell Henry and Mary" is lost in the rumble of the wheels on the high cobbles of the roadway. Charles Dana at Saturday dinners. George Ripley, Mr. Bayard Taylor who tells of his frozen nose in the north. Mr. Bryant's son in law—name forgotten—but not forgotten the homeliest countenance in America which was his. Uncle Edward . . .

and Uncle Gus . . . Grandma James—her silk dress—peppermints, lace mittens and gentle smile. . . . Then also my mother who walked down Sixth Avenue to Washington Market *with a basket on her arm* (*of this I am sure*)—every morning—for I tagged after her, aged six years, and held to her shawl [1] . . . I might go on indefinitely writing you of these memories. Some of them are very plain like the sight of Gen. Kossuth seen in a procession of welcome on Broadway. There are plenty of others left in New York. But on the other side they come thick and fast . . . Mr. Thackeray who carried me on his shoulder, and then Boulogne-sur-mer and the Collège Municipale and its stone vaulted ceiling where Wilky and I went and failed to take prizes. But the day when the Mayor of the City distributed these I do remember, and somehow I think that tho' it was not a prize we both had souvenirs or a reward of some kind—for I recall a beautiful book with gold figures. But around the mayor who stood on a platform with great civic splendor and officials in uniform, I see yet the fortunate scholars ascend the steps of his throne, kneel at his feet, and receive crown or rosettes, or some symbol of merit which *we* did not get. The luck had begun to break early!

"The only thing to say of it is that it was a beautiful and splendid childhood for any child to have had, and I remember it all now as full of indulgence and light and color and hardly a craving unsatisfied."

RJ's fortunes did not improve at the end. He did not die until 1910, only a few weeks before WJ. But then HJ, to whom he had always remained "the genial Bob," spoke with relief that death had cleared this youngest brother "of all the darkness and pain of his stormy life."

---

[1] Another fugitive glimpse of their mother comes in Alice's comment to WJ's wife on one of the letters that she found when her old desk was sent her in England: "How inestimable this . . . from the blessed Mother, written to me in '66 when I was spending the winter at Dr. Taylor's in N. Y., at my life-long occupation of 'improving,'— 'I am so sorry to hear that round waists are coming in, they are so unbecoming to my figure, and Miss Washington has just made my new rep with very long points!'—giving instantly that which the wisdom of the sages is inadequate for, body to her ghost! For doesn't your feminine soul immediately picture to itself *your* 'new rep' coming home, at this long-drawn out, pancake moment, with a huge *Bustle*? Such are the real tragedies of life!"

FORMULATIONS

Alice

"OH, WOE, woe is me!" Alice James wrote in her journal: "I have not only stopped thinning but I am taking unto myself gross fat. All hopes of peace and rest are vanishing—nothing but the dreary snail-like climb up a little way, so as to be able to run down again! And then these doctors tell you that you will die or *recover!* But you *don't* recover. I have been at these alternations since I was nineteen, and I am neither dead nor recovered. As I am now forty-two, there has surely been time for either process. I suppose one has a greater sense of intellectual degradation after an interview with a doctor than from any other human experience." Her special tone is there, with her quizzical self-mockery and her complete lack of self-pity, and the detachment with which she has schooled herself to observe her body as a bad experiment for which she is not responsible, and in which she refuses to let her mind become implicated.

Since AJ died just prior to the development of the psychoanalytical techniques which might have been of some use to her, it is not possible to be sure to what extent her ailments were physical and to what extent purely psychic. She died finally of cancer, after a long succession of other complications, which were variously diagnosed as "rheumatic gout," "spinal neurosis," "cardiac complications," and "nervous hyperæsthesia." But her first breakdown as a girl would seem to have been brought on by the imponderable strain of being the youngest child and the only girl in such an extraordinary family.

After a seemingly normal, if delicate, girlhood of parties and friends, the pressures of mature existence proved too much for her, and, to her great consternation, she found that whenever she became particularly interested and stimulated by a conversation, she was likely to faint. Only a few glimpses survive into her deeper troubles. Hardly a month

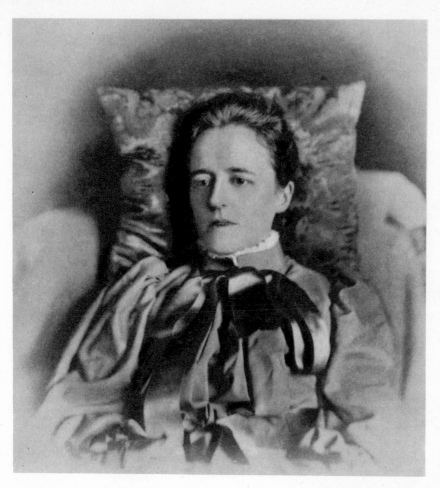

Alice James in 1891

Alice James' JOURNAL, *September 3, 1891: "Like a sheep to the shambles, I have been led by Katherine Loring to the camera. Owing to some curious cerebral condition, Annie Richards was heard to say, 'Alice has fine features.' K. seized the 'psychic moment' of titillated vanity and brought the one-eyed monster to bear upon me; such can be a woman's inhumanity to woman."*

September 7: "Mes beaux restes have returned from the photographer in refulgent beauty! so very much flattered that my heart now overflows with mansuetude for that admirable Katherine, so wise of counsel, so firm of purpose, so gentle in action."

before her death she wrote: "The fact is, I have been dead so long, and it has been simply such a grim shoving of the hours behind me as I faced a ceaseless possible horror since that hideous summer of '78 when I went down to the deep sea, and its dark waters closed over me, and I knew neither hope nor peace, that now it's only the shrivelling of an empty pea-pod that has to be completed." Her father had written Bob at the time of her crisis: "She asked me if suicide, to which at times she felt strongly tempted, was a sin. . . . I told her that so far as I was concerned she had my full permission to end her life whenever she pleased. She then remarked that . . . she could never do it now I had given her freedom . . . she was more than content to stay by my side and battle in concert with me against the evil that is in the world. I don't fear suicide much since this conversation."

She may not have thought actively thereafter of ending her own life, but she was to write of the hushed-up suicide of a friend:

"What a pity to hide it; every educated person who kills himself does something towards lessening the superstition. It's bad that it's so untidy. There is no denying that, for one bespatters one's friends morally as well as physically, taking them so much more into one's secret than they want to be taken. But how heroic to be able to suppress one's vanity to the extent of confessing that the game is too hard. The most comic and apparently the chief argument used against it is that because you were born without being consulted, you would be very sinful should you cut short your blissful career. This had been said to me a dozen times, and they never can see how they have turned things topsy-turvy."

One of the most remarkable things about her was her ability to entertain such thoughts without allowing them to become obsessive. Long after she had come to be regarded as a hopeless invalid, WJ wrote: "Alice met all attempts at sympathy with jeers and laughter, having her own brave philosophy, which was to keep her attention turned to things outside her sick-room and away from herself." The secret of her philosophy was not unlike the belief in will that sustained WJ, though the only world in which she could deploy her force was the inner world of HJ's typical heroines. She seems to have found that secret very young:

"How I recall the low grey Newport sky in that winter of '62–63; as I used to wander about over the cliffs, my young soul struggling out of its swaddling-clothes, as the knowledge crystallized within me of what life meant for me, a knowledge simple, single, and before which all mystery vanished. A spark then kindled, which every experience, great and small, has fed into a steady flame which has illuminated my little journey, and which, although it may have burned low as the waters rose, has never flickered out,—'une pensée unique, éternelle, toujours mêlée à l'heure presente.' How profoundly grateful I am for the temperament which saves me from the wretched fate of those poor creatures who never find their bearings, but are tossed like dried leaves hither, thither and yon, at the mercy of every event which o'ertakes them; who feel no shame at being vanquished, or at crying out at the common lot of pain and sorrow; who never dimly suspect that the only thing which survives is the resistance we bring to life and not the strain life brings to us."

She continued to live at home, with occasional oases of fair health, until her parents' deaths. It seemed best for her then to join HJ in England, but her six or seven years there were spent almost entirely in private sanatoriums. In one of these, at Leamington, she undertook the one formulation that gives her a permanent place in this family of minds. Though her letters were lively, they moved, for the most part, within the orbit of the more usual women's letters of her time. It was to be very different with the journal which she started with one sentence in May 1889: "I think that if I get into the habit of writing a bit about what happens, or rather doesn't happen, I may lose a little of the sense of loneliness and desolation which abides with me." Later in that month she made her second entry: "My circumstances allowing of nothing but the ejaculation of one-syllabled reflections, a written monologue by that most interesting being, myself, may have its yet to be discovered consolations. I shall, at least, have it all my own way, and it may bring relief as an outlet to that geyser of emotions, sensations, speculations and reflections which ferments perpetually within my poor old carcass for its sins; so here goes,—my first journal."

She reveled, like Emily Dickinson, in being a private writer, since all the inhibitions induced by an audience were thereby removed. It is interesting that the one stanza she quoted from Miss Dickinson's poems—which had just reached posthumous publication—was:

> How dreary to be somebody;
>   How public, like a frog,
> To tell your name, the livelong day
>   To an admiring bog!

But her latent desire for publicity is betrayed, in her very next entry after these lines, by her excessive reaction against it: "Dr. Tuckey asked me the other day whether I had written for the press, I vehemently disclaimed the imputation. How sad it is that the purely innocuous should always be supposed to have the trail of the family serpent upon them." As a matter of strict fact, she had written for the press— once. She had sent off to the *Nation* the following not very remarkable sample of the American speech that always delighted her:

"Sir: For several years past I have lived in provincial England. Although so far from home, every now and then a trans-Atlantic blast, pure and undefiled, fans to a white heat the fervour of my patriotism. This morning, most appropriately to the day, a lady from one of our eastern cities applied to my landlady for apartments. In the process of telling her that she had no rooms to let, the landlady said that there was an invalid in the house; whereupon the lady exclaimed: 'In that case perhaps it is just as well that you cannot take us in, for my little girl, who is thirteen, likes to have plenty of liberty and to *scream* through the house.' Yours very truly, INVALID.
England, July 4, 1890."

WJ recognized at once the source of this, and wrote from amidst the proofs of his *Psychology*: "You must continue to contribute now that you've made the plunge. I am entirely certain that you've got a book inside you about England, which will come out yet." Her letter was reprinted in an English paper, and HJ gaily called it her "Swan Song." AJ herself added: "Imagine my entertainment in getting . . . the Daily News extracts; a *European reputation* at the first go off! How fortunate for the male babes that I am physically so debile!" Despite all jests and disclaimers, it could not have been easy to be "Nobody" among such notable brothers.

The quality that distinguishes AJ's journal—also comparable to Emily Dickinson's quality—is her wealth of inner resources. Beleaguered by the indignity and pain of her dying body, she writes:

"If the aim of life is the accretion of fat, the consumption of food unattended by digestive disorganization, there is no doubt that I am a failure; for as an animal form my insatiable vanity must allow that my existence doesn't justify itself. But every fibre protests at being taken simply as a sick carcass, as foolish friends so flatteringly insist; for what power have dissolving flesh and aching bones to undermine a satisfaction made of imperishable things? The winter has been rich beyond compare; the heart all aglow with the affectionate demonstration of friend and brother; the mind deeply stirred by most varied and interesting events, public and private; the spirit broadened and strengthened, let us hope, by a clearer perception of the significance of experience; while from the whole has flowed perpetually these succulent juices which exude, at the slightest pressure, from the human comedy."

She noted with satisfaction that "William says in his *Psychology*: 'Genius, in truth, is little more than the faculty of perceiving in an unhabitual way.'" Of such genius she had her full share. HJ observed that she remained the most Irish of the family, and that trait asserted itself in a thoroughgoing independence. Like both her famous brothers she had developed a gift for psychological analysis, and what she saw was wholly her own. Stimulated, as so often, by WJ, she was able to recount her early hysteria in language almost clinical in its accuracy and yet imaginative in its range:

"William uses an excellent expression when he says in his paper on the *Hidden Self*, that the nervous victim 'abandons' certain portions of his consciousness. It may be the word commonly used by his kind; it is just the right one at any rate, although I have never unfortunately been able to abandon my consciousness and get five minutes rest. I have passed through an infinite succession of conscious abandonments, and, in looking back now, I see how it began in my childhood, although I wasn't conscious of the necessity until '67 or '68, when I broke down first, acutely, and had violent turns of hysteria. As I lay prostrate after the storm, with my mind luminous and active, and susceptible of the clearest, strongest impressions, I saw so distinctly that it was a fight simply between my body and my will—a battle in which the former was to be triumphant to the end. Owing to some physical weakness, excess of nervous susceptibility, the moral power *pauses*, as it were, for a moment, and refuses to maintain muscular sanity, worn out with the strain of its constabulary functions. As I used to sit immovable, reading in the library, with waves of violent inclination suddenly invading my muscles, taking some one of their varied forms, such as throwing myself out of the window or knocking off the head of the benignant Pater, as he sat, with his silver locks, writing at his table, it used to seem to me that the only difference between me and the insane was that I had only all the horrors and suffering of insanity, but the duties of doctor, nurse, and strait-jacket imposed upon me too. Conceive of never being without the sense that if you let yourself go for a moment, your mechanism will fall into pie, and that at some given moment you must abandon it all, let the dykes break and the flood sweep in, acknowledging yourself abjectly impotent before the immutable laws. When all one's moral and natural stock-in-trade is a temperament forbidding the abandonment of an inch or the relaxation of a muscle, 'tis a never-ending fight. When the fancy took me of a morning at school to *study* my lessons by way of variety instead of shrieking or wiggling through the most impossible sensations of upheaval, violent revolt in my head overtook me, so that I had to 'abandon' my brain as it were. So it has always been. Anything that sticks of itself is free to do so; but conscious and continuous cerebration is an impossible exercise, and from just behind the eyes my head feels like a dense jungle into which no ray of light has ever penetrated. So, with the rest, you abandon the pit of your stomach, the palms of your hands, the soles of your feet, and refuse to keep them sane, when you find in turn one moral impression after another producing despair in the one, terror in the other, anxiety in the third, and so on, until life becomes one long flight from remote suggestion and complicated eluding of the multifold traps set for your undoing."

The next entry, ten days later: "I must 'abandon' the rhetorical part of me, and forget the eloquent peroration with which I meant to embellish the above, on the ignorant asininity of the medical profession in its treatment of nervous disorders. The settling part of me has also give out, and had to be abandoned."

Her occasional comments on literature, and her trenchant attacks on British social organization, which sometimes disturbed HJ, will find their proper place below.[1] Her best writing was called forth by the subjects closest to her heart, and consequently appears in her characterizations of WJ and of HJ:

"August 4, 1889. I must try and pull myself together, and record the somewhat devastating episode of July 18, when Harry, after a much longer absence than usual, presented himself. . . . We had just finished luncheon, and were talking of something or other, when H. suddenly said, with a queer look upon his face, 'I must tell you something.' 'You're not going to be married!' shrieked I. 'No, but William is here; he has been lunching upon Warwick Castle, and is waiting now in the Holly Walk for the news to be broken to you; and if you survive, I'm to tie my handkerchief to the balcony.' Enter W., not à la Romeo, by the balcony; the prose of our century, to say nothing of that of our consanguinity, making it supererogatory. The beforehand having been so cleverly suppressed by the devoted H., 'it came out so much easier than could have been expected,' as they say to infants in the dental chair. I always sympathized so with Ellen Gurney when she told of how she ran and slammed the drawing room door when she heard, in the old war days, her brother Edward's voice suddenly in the hall downstairs, he having come home unexpectedly, as they always did in those days. Poor H. over whom the moment had impended for two months, looked as white as a ghost before they went; and well he may, in his anxiety as to which 'going off' in my large repertory would 'come on'; but, with the assistance of two hundred grains of bromide, I think I behaved with extreme propriety. W. had gone to London only the day before, having been for three weeks in Ireland and Scotland. He doesn't look much older for the three years, and all that there is to be said of him, of course, is that he is simply himself; a creature who speaks in another language, as H. says, from the rest of mankind, and who would lend life and charm to a treadmill. What a strange experience it was, to have what had seemed so dead and gone all these years suddenly bloom before one, a flowering oasis in the alien desert, redolent with the exquisite family perfume of the days gone by, made of

---

[1] Pp. 532–3, 536–7, 648–51 below.

the allusions and the point of view in common, so that my floating-particle sense was lost for an hour or so in the illusion that what is forever shattered had sprung anew, and existed outside of our memories, where it is forever green."

"November 18, 1889. I mustn't let other episodes vanish unrecorded . . . for the summer turned out a giddy whirl for me! First, William, instead of going to Switzerland, came suddenly back from Paris and went home, having, as usual, exhausted Europe in a few weeks, finding it stale, flat, and unprofitable. The only necessity being to get home, the first letter after his arrival was, of course, full of plans for his return plus wife and infants; he is just like a blob of mercury, you can't put a mental finger upon him. H. and I were laughing over him and recalling Father, and William's resemblance (in their ways) to him. Though the results are the same, they seem to come from a different nature in the two; in W., an entire inability or indifference 'to stick to a thing for the sake of sticking,' as some one said of him once, whilst Father, the delicious infant! couldn't submit even to the thraldom of his own whim; and then the dear being was such a prey to the demon homesickness. H. says that certain places on the Continent bring up the old scenes so vividly; Father's sudden return at the end of thirty-six hours,—having left to be gone a fortnight,—with Mother beside him holding his hand, and we five children pressing close round him 'as if he had just been saved from drowning,' and he pouring out as he alone could the agonies of desolation through which he had come. But to return to our mutton, William; he came with H. on August 14, on his way to Liverpool. He told all about his Paris experience, where he was a delegate to the Psychological Congress, which was a most brilliant success. The French most polite and hospitable; they invited W. to open the Congress, and they always had a foreigner in the chair at the different meetings. I extracted with great difficulty from him that 'Monsieur Will-yam Jams' was frequently referred to by the speakers. H. suggested that he might become another case of the great 'William.' He liked the Henry Sidgwicks and Fred Myers. . . . Mrs. Myers paid him the following enigmatic compliment: 'We are so glad that you are as you are.' This reminds me of what Mrs. Kemble said to H. about me after her first call, which was more enigmatic still. She arrived, poor lady, dreadfully out of breath from the stairs. I was greatly distressed, but my perturbation, which had been prospectively great, vanished, for Mrs. Kemble without breath was a much less alarming quantity. H. told her afterwards that I had been so troubled about the stairs; she said it was nothing more than what befell her always, and added: 'Most fortunately your sister is an American lady, a very different thing from an English lady, I assure you.' When I have seen her since, I have always been in such an agony to be the right kind of a lady.

"In the pursuit of knowledge I asked Nurse one day whether K. and I were different from English ladies in any way. 'Entirely different Miss.' 'Why how are we different?' 'Not so 'aughty, Miss.' Truly discouraging."

"March 25, 1890. Henry came on the 10th to spend the day; Henry, the Patient, I should call him. Five years ago, in November, I crossed the water and suspended myself like an old woman of the sea, round his neck, where to all appearances I shall remain for all time. I have given him endless care and anxiety, but notwithstanding this and the fantastic nature of my troubles, I have never seen an impatient look upon his face or heard an unsympathetic or misunderstanding sound cross his lips. He comes at the slightest sign, and 'hangs on' to whatever organ may be in eruption, and gives me calm and solace by assuring me that my nerves are his nerves, and my stomach his stomach—this last a pitch of brotherly devotion never before approached by the race. He has never remotely hinted that he expected me to be well at any given moment—that burden which fond friend and relative so inevitably imposes upon the cherished invalid. But he has always been the same since I can remember, and has almost as strongly as Father that personal susceptibility, what can one call it,—it seems as if it were a matter of the scarfskin, as if they perceived through that your mood, and were saved thereby from rubbing you raw with their theory of it or blindness to it.

"I was so pleased to come a little while ago across the following in a letter of William's to Wilky, in February, '66, after his return from Brazil: 'Harry, I think much improved; he is a noble fellow, so true, delicate and honourable,'—all of which is as true in 1890 as then. I was, of course, much gratified to find this farther one: 'and Alice has got to be quite a nice girl,'—hasn't it the true fraternal condescension in its ring? I am afraid that I have fallen from such altitudes since at various moments.

"To give a specimen of Harry's absolute unworldliness and inability to conceive of the base, notwithstanding his living so much in the world, he writes à propos of Cousin Henry W.'s will and the fear that Albert, or rather the depraved Mrs. Albert, should contest it: 'I suppose William will get, at any rate, his $5000; there would be a baseness in Mrs. W.'s grudging that, and her having to do that sort of thing if she does contest it, that may shame her from it.' The beautiful and babe-like innocence of this view of Mrs. W., who spends all her time betting at horse-races, being so overcome by the superiorities of the adored William as to be shamed into virtue, is truly touching.

"H. seems to be cheerful about his play, and to be unable to grasp my flutterations about it. What a 'state' I was in when he told me, six months ago, as a great secret, that he had embarked. I had to tell some one about it, or have exploded; so of course there was nothing to turn

to but little Nurse. I could cry, if it were not so much better an investment to laugh, over my poverty in the way of receptacles for my overflow,—such a contrast to the vast and receptive reservoirs of the past.
Nurse undergoes it all passively, finding it a pleasant change from the
iniquities of the parson and M. Balfour, which she has in such monotonous alternation."

She often bewildered her correct English nurses, as when she made
one of them send off to WJ's wife the following dictated message on a
postcard:

"August 2, 1890. Her trouble is dreadful indigestion and she grows
very thin. Miss James wants me to say, 'That if she vanishes completely,
you mustn't be surprised but gather the family, and give three cheers
to speed the departed spirit!' She is very naughty! Yours respectfully,
Emily A. Bradfield."

When the pain in her breast was finally diagnosed as cancer, she felt
a great relief at being taken out of "the formless vague" and deposited
"within the very heart of the sustaining concrete. One would naturally
not choose such an ugly and gruesome method of progression down
the dark valley of the shadow of death, and of course many of the
moral sinews will snap by the way; but we shall bind up our loins and
the blessed peace of the end will have no shadow cast upon it."

She declared that "poor dear William, with his exaggerated sympathy for suffering, isn't to know anything about it until it is all over."
But he was, of course, kept informed, and wrote the kind of letter that
had by now become almost a family habit:

* * * * *

Chocorua, July 6, 1891

Dearest Alice . . . Of course [this medical verdict on your case may
mean] as all men know, a finite length of days; and then, good-bye
to neurasthenia and neuralgia and headache, and weariness and palpita-
tion and disgust all at one stroke—I should think you would be reconciled to the prospect with all its pluses and minuses! I know you've
never cared for life, and to me, now at the age of nearly fifty, life and
death seem singularly close together in all of us—and life a mere farce
of frustration in all, so far as the realization of the innermost ideals go
to which we are made respectively capable of feeling an affinity and
responding. Your frustrations are only rather more flagrant than the
rule; and you've been saved many forms of self-dissatisfaction and
misery which appertain to such a multiplication of responsible relations
to different people as I, for instance, have got into. Your fortitude,
good spirits and unsentimentality have been simply unexampled in the
midst of your physical woes; and when you're relieved from your post,
just *that* bright note will remain behind, together with the inscrutable
and mysterious character of the doom of nervous weakness which has

chained you down for all these years. As for that, there's more in it
than has ever been told to so-called science. These inhibitions, these
split-up selves, all these new facts that are gradually coming to light
about our organization, these enlargements of the self in trance, etc.,
are bringing me to turn for light in the direction of all sorts of despised
spiritualistic and unscientific ideas. Father would find in me today a
much more receptive listener—all *that* philosophy has got to be brought
in. And what a queer contradiction comes to the ordinary scientific
argument against immortality (based on body being mind's condition
and mind going *out* when body is gone), when one must believe (as
now, in these neurotic cases) that some infernality in the body *prevents*
really existing parts of the mind from coming to their effective rights
at all, suppresses them, and blots them out from participation in this
world's experiences, although they are *there* all the time. When that
which is *you* passes out of the body, I am sure there will be an explosion of liberated force and life till then eclipsed and kept down. I can
hardly imagine *your* transition without a great oscillation of both
"worlds" as they regain their new equilibrium after the change! Everyone will feel the shock, but you yourself will be more surprised than
anybody else.

It may seem odd for me to talk to you in this cool way about your
end; but, my dear little sister, if one has things present to one's mind,
and I know they are present enough to *your* mind, why not speak
them out? I am sure you appreciate that best. How many times I have
thought, in the past year, when my days were so full of strong and
varied impression and activities, of the long unchanging hours in bed
which those days stood for with you, and wondered how you bore the
slow-paced monotony at all, as you did! You can't tell how I've pitied
you. But you *shall* come to your rights erelong. Meanwhile take things
gently. Look for the little good in each day as if life were to last a
hundred years. Above all things, save yourself from bodily pain, if it
can be done. You've had too much of that. Take all the morphia (or
other forms of opium if that disagrees) you want, and don't be afraid
of becoming an opium-drunkard. What was opium created for except
for such times as this? Beg the good Katherine (to whom *our* debt can
never be extinguished) to write me a line every week, just to keep the
currents flowing, and so farewell until I write again. Your ever loving, WJ.

*   *   *

Her answer, dictated to Katherine Loring, who had gone to England
to be her companion, has, with all its affectionate gratitude, just the
trace of impertinence that was called out from her whenever this oldest
brother showed signs of becoming too earnestly admonitory:

*   *   *   *   *

July 30, 1891

My dearest William,—A thousand thanks for your beautiful and fraternal letter, which came, I know not when, owing to Katherine's iron despotism. Of course I could have wanted nothing else and should have felt, notwithstanding my "unsentimentality," very much wounded and *incomprise* had you walked round and not up to my demise.

It is the most supremely interesting moment in life, the only one in fact when living seems life, and I count it the greatest good fortune to have these few months so full of interest and instruction in the knowledge of my approaching death. It is as simple in one's own person as any fact of nature, the fall of a leaf or the blooming of a rose, and I have a delicious consciousness, ever present, of wide spaces close at hand, and whisperings of release in the air.

Your philosophy of the transition is entirely mine and at this remoteness I will venture upon the impertinence of congratulating you upon having arrived "at nearly fifty" at the point at which I started at fifteen! 'Twas always thus of old, but in time, you usually, as now, caught up.

But you must believe that you greatly exaggerate the tragic element in my commonplace little journey; and so far from ever having thought that "my frustrations were more flagrant than the rule," I have always simmered complacently in my complete immunity therefrom. As from early days the elusive nature of concrete hopes shone forth, I always rejoiced that my temperament had set for my task the attainment of the simplest rudimentary ideal, which I could carry about in my pocket and work away upon equally in shower as in sunshine, in complete security from the grotesque obstructions supposed to be *life*, which have, indeed, only strengthened the sinews to whatever imperfect accomplishment I may have attained.

You must also remember that a woman, by nature, needs much less to feed upon than a man, a few emotions and she is satisfied; so when I am gone, pray don't think of me simply as a creature who might have been something else, had neurotic science been born. Notwithstanding the poverty of my outside experience, I have always had a significance for myself, and every chance to stumble along my straight and narrow little path, and to worship at the feet of my Deity, and what more can a human soul ask for?

This year has been one of the happiest I have ever known, surrounded by such affection and devotion, but I won't enter into details, as I see the blush mantle the elderly cheek of my scribe, already. . . .

Give much love to Alice and to all the household, great and small. . . .

Your always loving and grateful sister, Alice James

P.S. I have many excellent and kind letters, but the universal tendency "to be reconciled" to my passing to the summer-land might cause confusion in the mind of the uninitiated!

* * *

Katherine Loring added at the foot of the page:

"Alice tried to write to you for three days but had finally to take refuge in dictation. Since I wrote you Dr. Baldwin made another inspiring visit,—with no new results. Alice discussed her case and her demise with him as if she were talking about Queen Elizabeth. . . ."

She was to live several months longer, and, at WJ's suggestion, tried still another medical experiment, and dictated one more letter to him about the results:

". . . Supposing that your being is vibrating with more or less curiosity about the great hypnotic experiment on Camden Hill, I report progress. As far as pain goes the result is nil, save on four occasions the violent resuscitation of a dormant toothache, a wretched dying nerve which demands an agony of its own, impatient of waiting for, or too vain to lose itself in the grand mortuary moment so near at hand. What I *do* experience, is a calming of my nerves and a quiescent passive state, during which I fall asleep, without the sensations of terror which have accompanied that process for so many years, and I sleep for five or six hours, uninterruptedly. But then, I slept like a dormouse all last year before taking morphia. Katherine has very much better results than Tuckey, that is as long as she remains silent and operates only by the gesture; but when she with solemn majesty addresses herself to the digestive Boreas and with persuasive accents suggests calmness and serenity of demeanour, cachinnation is the sole recourse.

"We were fortunate in our ignorance to have fallen upon an experienced doctor as well as hypnotist. He seems to be much penetrated with my abnormal susceptibility and says that to put me actually asleep would be a very risky experiment. He seems to look upon the reckless use of it as absolutely criminal. He is only coming once this week and then he will die of course, a natural death. My pains are too much a part of my substance to have any modifications before the spirit and the flesh fall asunder. But I feel as if I had gained something in the way of a nerve pacifier and one of the most intense intellectual experiences of my life. Too tired for another word. Love to all. . . ."

She continued till the end to dictate entries in her journal, sometimes occupying her mind for several hours with shaping a few sentences exactly as she wanted them. She followed vicariously every step of HJ's first venture in the London theater, and recorded at the close of December: "*The American* died an honorable death on the seventy-sixth night. . . . I have to thank the beautiful play for all the interest and expectancy with which it has filled the last two years." She thought out her sentences about Emily Dickinson a week later: "It is reassuring to hear the English pronouncement that Emily Dickinson is fifth-rate

—they have such a capacity for missing quality; the robust evades them equally with the subtle. Her being sicklied o'er with T. W. Higginson makes one quake lest there be a latent flaw which escapes one's vision."

On March 5, 1892 she cabled WJ: "Tenderest love to all. Farewell. Am going soon. Alice."

The next day it was HJ who cabled: "Alice just passed away. Painless. Wire Bob. Henry."

Two years later, after her journal had been set up in print for the immediate family, HJ wrote to WJ and his wife an appreciation that will never be surpassed:

"As regards the life, the power, the temper, the humour and beauty and expressiveness of the Diary in itself—these things were partly 'discounted' to me in advance by so much of Alice's talk during her last years—and my constant association with her—which led me often to reflect about her extraordinary force of mind and character, her whole way of taking life—and death—in very much the manner in which the book does. I find in its pages, for instance, many things I heard her say. None the less I have been immensely impressed with the thing as a revelation of a moral and personal picture. It is heroic in its individuality, its independence—its face-to-face with the universe for and by herself —and the beauty and eloquence with which she often expresses this, let alone the rich irony and humour, constitute (I wholly agree with you) a new claim for the family renown. This last element—her style, her power to write—are indeed to me a delight. . . .

"Also it brings back to me all sorts of things I am glad to keep—I mean things that happened, hours, occasions, conversations—brings them back with a strange, living richness. But it also puts before me what I was tremendously conscious of in her lifetime—that the extraordinary intensity of her will and personality really would have made the equal, the reciprocal life of a 'well' person—in the usual world— almost impossible to her—so that her disastrous, her tragic health was in a manner the only solution for her of the practical problem of life —as it suppressed the element of equality, reciprocity, etc. The violence of her reaction against her British *ambiente*, against everything English, engenders some of her most admirable and delightful passages—but I feel in reading them, as I always felt in talking with her, that inevitably she simplified too much, shut up in her sick room, exercised her wondrous vigour of judgment on too small a scrap of what really surrounded her. It would have been modified in many ways if she had *lived* with them (the English) more—seen more of the men, etc. But doubtless it is fortunate for the fun and humour of the thing that it wasn't modified—as surely the critical emotion (about them,) the essence of much of their nature, was never more beautifully expressed. As for her allusions to H.—they fill me with tears and cover me with blushes. . . . I find an immense eloquence in her passionate 'radicalism' —her most distinguishing feature almost—which, in her, was absolutely direct and original (like everything that was in her,) unreflected, uncaught from entourage or example. It would really have made her, had she lived in the world, a feminine 'political force.' But had she lived in the world and seen things nearer she would have had disgusts and disillusions. However, what comes out in the book—as it came out to me in fact—is that she was really an Irishwoman; transplanted, transfigured —but none the less fundamentally national—in spite of her so much larger and finer than Irish intelligence. She felt the Home Rule question absolutely as only an Irishwoman (not anglicised) could. It was a tremendous emotion with her—inexplicable in any other way—but perfectly explicable by 'atavism.' What a pity she wasn't born there—and had her health for it. She would have been (if, always, she had not fallen a victim to disgust—a large 'if'!) a national glory!"

EUROPE AND/OR AMERICA?

One of the most engaging manifestations of the family mind in action is on their favorite theme of the differences between America and Europe. They responded to it almost as though they had assumed roles in a debate. Father almost invariably gave voice to the promise of American life. HJ, after he had settled abroad, became the family Anglophile; whereas Alice was no less passionately pro-American than she was pro-Irish. WJ was enthusiastic about Europe when he was in America, and eager for America when he was in Europe. He in particular, in the excitement of the debate, was perfectly capable of shifting his position and coming up with unexpected arguments for the other side. The question was naturally of the greatest moment for HJ, since his final decision to live in England involved the nature and qualities of his work. While assisting at the debate we may, therefore, see farther into his career than we could by noting his largely indirect formulations.

Henry Senior summed up his position after reading Emerson's *English Traits* in Paris in 1856:

"I am somewhat disappointed now that I have read it; the appreciation is so overdone. The study has been too conscientious. The manners —the life—he was investigating, haven't the depth either for good or evil he attributes to them. His own stand-point is too high to do justice to the English. They are an intensely vulgar race, high and low; and their qualities, good or evil, date not from any divine or diabolic *depths* whatever, but from most obvious and superficial causes. They are the abject slaves of routine, and no afflatus from above or below ever comes, apparently, to ruffle the surface of their self-complacent quietude. They are not worth studying. The prejudices one has about them, even when they are unjust, are scarcely worth correcting. There is nothing better supplied by the actual truth of the case, to put in the place of them. They belong, all their good and their evil, to the past humanity, to the infantile development of the mind, and they don't deserve, more than any other European nation, the least reverence from a denizen of the new world. They are a solider, manlier race than the French, according to the old ideas of manhood: that is, they do not lie, cheat, commit adultery and murder with half so much good-will: but of the spiritual causes out of which these evil things proceed, pride and self-love and the love of domineering, they have their full share, and perhaps more than most other people. They lack heart. Their love is clannish. They love all that wear their own livery, but they don't even *see* anyone outside of that boundary.

"Mrs. Cranch wondered the other day, upon some new experiences of French perfidy, 'what the Lord *would* do with these French people.' I wonder what He will do with any European people. Or rather, I don't wonder: for I see that they are all destined to be recast and remoulded into the form of a new and *de-nationalized humanity*, a universal form which, being animated by God's own infinite spirit, the spirit of human fellowship, will quickly shed all the soils it has contracted in the past. Thackeray was in here yesterday, and told Mary that he had just heard of an atrocious thing that happened to two American friends of his, by the name of Duncan, two very handsome women he said, or at least one was so: they had been invited to dine the day before with some English grandee living in Paris, and when they entered the drawing-room they were introduced to nobody, nor was any person requested by host or hostess to see them to the table, in consequence of which they were left, when the company were summoned to dinner, swinging their feet upon a sofa, until two good-natured fellows, looking back at them, and pitying their desolate state, returned and escorted them to the table. They ought to have left the house instead, for no milder hint will penetrate either Mr. Bull's or Mrs. Cow's hide, and bad manners will consequently maintain the ascendant. American disorder is sweet beside European order: it is so full of promise."

When WJ went abroad to study in 1867, HJ was very lonely and began to feel the tug of Europe:

"I very much enjoy your Berlin letters. Don't try to make out that America and Germany are identical, and that it is as good to be here as there. It can't be done. Only let me go to Berlin and I will say as much. Life here in Cambridge—or in this house, at least—is about as lively as the inner sepulchre . . . you have already heard of Wilkie's . . . chills and fever. It finally became so bad that he had to come home. He arrived here ten days ago and is now much better; but he must have had a fearfully hard time of it. He eats, sleeps and receives his friends, but still looks very poorly and will not be able to return for some time. Bob went a few days ago out to his old railroad place at Burlington. He was very impatient to get something to do, but nothing else turned up, although he moved heaven and earth. . . . It is plain that I shall have a very long row to hoe before I am fit for anything, for either work or play. I mention this, not to discourage you—for you have no right to be discouraged, when I am not myself—but because it occurs to me that I may have given you an exaggerated notion of the extent of my improvement during the past six months. An important element in my recovery, I believe, is to strike a happy medium between reading, etc., and social relaxation. The latter is not to be obtained in Cambridge—or only a ghastly simulacrum of it. There are no 'distractions' here. How in Boston, when the evening arrives, and I am tired of reading, and know it would be better to do something else, can I go to the theatre? I have tried it *ad nauseam*. Likewise 'calling.' Upon whom? . . . Going into town on the winter nights puts a chill on larger enterprises. I say this not in a querulous spirit—for in spite of these things I wouldn't for the present leave Cambridge,—but in order that you may not at distance falsify your reminiscences of this excellent place. Tonight, *par exemple*, I am going into town to see the French actors, who are there for a week, give *Mme. Aubray*. Dickens has arrived for his readings. It is impossible to get tickets. At seven o'clock, A.M., on the first day of the sale there were two or three hundred people at the office, and at nine when *I* strolled up, nearly a thousand. So I don't expect to hear him."

During this year and a half abroad WJ often realized how much HJ was missing, and wrote to Alice: "I somehow feel as if I were cheating Harry of his birthright." To HJ himself he added, while spending the summer of 1868 in the French Savoy: "You must have been envying me within the last few weeks, hearing that I was revisiting the sacred scenes of our youth, the shores of Léman. . . . The only pang I have felt has been caused by your absence, or rather by my presence instead of yours, for I think that your abstemious and poetic soul would have got infinitely more good out of the things I have seen than my hardening and definite growing nature."

In the following year their locations were reversed, and WJ was writing from Cambridge to HJ in Italy:

"Within ten days we have received two letters from you—one from Como, t'other from Brescia, and most luscious epistles were they indeed. It does one's heart good to think of you at last able to drink in full gulps the beautiful and the antique. As Mother said the other day, it seems as if your whole life had but been a preparation for this. . . . I am very much run down in nervous force and have resolved to read as little as I possibly can this winter, and absolutely not study, *i.e.*, read nothing which I can get interested and *thinking* about. . . . I cannot tell you, my dear brother, how my admiration of the silent pluck you have exhibited during those long years has risen of late. I never realized till within three or four months the full amount of endurance it must have needed to go through all that literary work, and especially all that unshirking social activity, which you accomplished. I give up like a baby in comparison, though occasionally I find my heart fired and my determination *retrempé'd* by a sudden wave of recollection of your behavior."

Though HJ had been homesick in England and appalled by his first glimpses of the sordidness in London and Paris, he took fire instantly in Rome:

"My dearest William . . . Here I am then in the Eternal City. . . . From midday to dusk I have been roaming the streets. Que vous en dirai-je? At last—for the first time—I live! It beats everything: it leaves the Rome of your fancy—your education—nowhere. It makes Venice —Florence—Oxford—London—seem like little cities of pasteboard. I went reeling and moaning thro' the streets, in a fever of enjoyment. In the course of four or five hours I traversed almost the whole of Rome and got a glimpse of everything—the Forum, the Coliseum (stupendissimo!), the Pantheon, the Capitol, St. Peter's, the Column of Trajan, the Castle of St. Angelo—all the Piazzas and ruins and monuments. The effect is something indescribable. For the first time I know what the picturesque is. . . . In fine I've seen Rome, and I shall go to bed a wiser man than I last rose—yesterday morning. . . . A toi, H. J. jr."

Henry Senior's reaction to such a letter was quite in character:

"It is very good to get your first impressions of Rome, and I can sympathize with you very fully. I feel that I myself should be horribly affected there by the historical picturesque. I should be extremely sensitive to it objectively, and would therefore all the more revolt from it subjectively, as hearing underneath it all the pent-up moaning and groaning soul of the race, struggling to be free or to come to consciousness. I am glad on the whole that my lot is cast in a land where life doesn't wait on death, and where consequently no natural but only an artificial picturesque is possible. The historical consciousness rules to such a distorted excess in Europe that I have always been restless there, and ended by pining for the land of the future exclusively. Condemned to *remain* there I should stifle in a jiffy."

After a couple of months of wallowing in Italian art, and having successively declared Tintoretto and Michelangelo each to be the very greatest of all painters, even HJ had had enough—for a time: "I'm sick unto death of priests and churches. Their 'picturesqueness' ends by making me want to go strongly into political economy or the New England school system. I conceived at Naples a tenfold deeper loathing than ever of the hideous heritage of the past, and felt for a moment as if I should like to devote my life to laying railroads, and erecting blocks of stores on the most classic and romantic sites. The age has a long row to hoe."

During the next few years, HJ, having tasted Europe, began to find complications, with his education and equipment, in being an American writer. He believed that civilization in the United States would "yield its secrets only to a really *grasping* imagination. . . . To write well and worthily of American things one need even more than elsewhere to be a *master*. But unfortunately one is less!" [1] At the same time, knowing as much as he now did about other countries, he noted: "It's a complex fate, being an American, and one of the responsibilities it entails is fighting against a superstitious valuation of Europe."

He took Alice abroad for a summer's trip in 1872, but, with a commission to do some "Transatlantic Sketches" for the *Nation*, he decided to stay longer. He wrote to WJ in the fall: "You have learned, by my recent letters, that I mean to try my luck at remaining abroad. I have little doubt that I shall be able to pull through. I want to spend a quiet winter, with a chance to read a good deal and to write enough. I shall be able to write enough, and well enough, I think: my only question is how to dispose of my wares. But in this, too, I shall not fail."

He still had spells of being homesick, and wrote his father after settling in Paris: "I am fast becoming a regular Parisian *badaud;* though, indeed, I led a far madder and merrier life in Cambridge than I am likely to do here. The waiters at the restaurants are as yet my chief society." This called forth a challenge from WJ: "But can't you find out a way of knowing any good French people? It seems preposterous that a man like you should be condemned to the society of washer-women and café waiters. I envy you, however, even the sight of such. Massive and teeming Paris, with its sights, sounds and smells, is so huge and real in the world, that from this insubstantial America one longs occasionally for it with a mighty yearn. Just about nightfall at this season with drizzle above and mud-paste beneath, and gas-blazing streets and restaurants, is the time that particularly appeals to me with thick-wafted associations." In another letter WJ proceeded to express sentiments that might seem far more characteristic of HJ: "Happy wretch! I hope you appreciate your lot, to spend the winter in an environment whose impression thickly assails your every sense and interest, instead of this naked vacuous America."

At this point HJ's health had settled to the fair equilibrium which he was to know, with a few exceptions, for the rest of his life, and which was to enable him to carry through such an immense amount of production. WJ, as we have seen, was still very uncertain of his direc-

---

[1] For the context of this remark, in a discussion of Howells, see below p. 499.

tion, and joined HJ in Italy the following autumn. He had his own reaction to "the picturesque":

"My dearest old Dad,—We left Florence day before yesterday and had splendid weather for the extremely picturesque railroad ride to this settlement—passing on the way by a set of little towns perched on hill spurs which would have brought from your moral consciousness certain hearty and picturesque expletives that I would have been glad to hear; so wicked and venomous did they look, huddled together and showing their teeth as it were to the world, without a ray of anything visible externally but the search for shelter and security. The 'picturesque'-ness that *we* now find there was the last thing present to the utilitarian minds of those who built them, and they make one realize how man's life is based historically on sheer force and will and fight, and how the inner world only grows up inside and under the shelter of these brute tendencies. It was a cloudless night lit by a half-moon, and after partaking of supper at the Hôtel de Rome, Harry's old abode, he proposed that we should stroll along to the Coliseum, etc. I had arrived at Rome with no more sentiment or expectation than if I were going to East Boston, and when in ten minutes after having left the modern shop-lit street, I found myself passing the old wreck-strewed Forum, and advancing under a line of trees in what seemed a common country road with a few distant lamps against the sides of houses, and right and left huge looming shapes of tumbled walls and ruins, not a living being, biped or quadruped, to be seen or heard—and finally when we entered under the mighty Coliseum wall and stood in its mysterious midst, with that cold sinister half-moon and hardly a star in the deep blue sky—it was all so strange, and, I must say, inhuman and horrible, that it felt like a nightmare. Again would I have liked to hear the great curses which you would have spoken. Anti-Christian as I generally am, I actually derived a deep comfort from the big black cross that had been planted on that damned blood-soaked soil. I think if Harry had not been with me I should have fled howling from the place."

He followed this up with a letter to Alice:

"Italy is a very *delightful* place to dip into but no more. I can't imagine how, unless one is earnestly studying history in some way, it can in the long run help injuring all one's active powers. The weight of the past world here is fatal,—one ends by becoming its mere parasite instead of its equivalent. This worship, this dependence on other men is abnormal. The ancients did things by doing the business of their own day, not by gaping at their grandfathers' tombs,—and the normal man of today will do likewise. Better fifty years of Cambridge, than a cycle of Cathay! Adieu. Your brutal and philistine Brother."

The following year when HJ set himself to dramatizing, in *Roderick Hudson*, the problems encountered by a young American artist in

Rome, he also dwelt on the weight of the past there—as Hawthorne had in *The Marble Faun*. But while traveling with WJ, he was soon able to supplement that brother's first impression in another letter home: "Willy, who at first hung fire over Rome, has now quite ignited, and confesses to its sovereign influence. But he enjoys all the melancholy of antiquity under a constant protest, which pleases me as a symptom of growing optimism and elasticity in his own disposition. His talk, as you may imagine, on all things, is most rich and vivacious. My own more sluggish perceptions can hardly keep pace with it."

WJ left HJ in Florence when he sailed for America in the spring. He was hardly home before he was writing:

"Any gossip about Florence you can still communicate will be greedily sucked in by me, who feel towards it as I do towards the old Albany of our childhood, with afternoon shadows of trees, etc. Not but that I am happy here,—more so than I ever was there, because I'm in a permanent path, and it shows me how for our type of character the thought of the *whole* dominates the particular moments. All my moments here are inferior to those in Italy, but they are parts of a long plan which is good, so they content me more than the Italian ones which only existed for themselves. . . . My short stay abroad has given me quite a new sense of what you used to call the provinciality of Boston, but that is no harm. What displeases me is the want of stoutness and squareness in the people, their ultra quietness, prudence, slyness, intellectualness of gait. Not that their intellects amount to anything, either. You will be discouraged, I remain happy!

"But this brings me to the subject of your return, of which I have thought much. It is evident that you will have to eat your bread in sorrow for a time here; it is equally evident that time (but it may take years) will prove a remedy for a great deal of the trouble, and you will attune your at present coarse senses to snatch a fearful joy from wooden fences and commercial faces, a joy the more thrilling for being so subtly extracted. Are you ready to make the heroic effort? It is a fork in the path of your life, and upon your decision hangs your whole future. If you are not persuaded enough of the importance of living at home to wade through perhaps three years slough of despond, I see no particular reason why you should come at all just now—and its extravagance is against it. This is your dilemma: The congeniality of Europe, on the one hand, plus the difficulty of making an entire living out of original writing, and its abnormality as a matter of mental hygiene . . . on the other hand, the dreariness of American conditions of life plus a mechanical, routine occupation possibly to be obtained, which from day to day is *done* when 'tis done, mixed up with the writing into which you distil your essence. . . . In short, don't come unless with a *resolute* intention. If you come, your worst years will be the first. If you stay, the bad years may be the later ones, when, moreover, you can't change. And I have a suspicion that if you come, too, and *can* get once acclimated, the quality of what you write will be higher than it would be in Europe. . . . It seems to me a very critical moment in your history. But you have several months to decide."

The issue raised here had already occupied HJ's mind. He had written to Grace Norton some months before:

"The great fact for us all . . . is that, relish Europe as we may, we belong much more to that [i.e., America] than to this, and stand in a much less factitious and artificial relation to it. I feel forever how Europe keeps holding one at arm's length, and condemning one to a meagre scraping of the surface. . . . This, you'll say, is my own stupidity; but granting this gladly, it proves that even a creature addicted as much to sentimentalizing as I am over the whole *mise en scène* of Italian life, doesn't find an easy initiation into what lies behind it. Sometimes I am overwhelmed with the pitifulness of this absurd want of reciprocity between Italy itself and all my rhapsodies about it. There is certainly, however, terribly little doubt that, practically, for those who have been happy in Europe even Cambridge the Brilliant is not an easy place to live in."

He responded to WJ's challenge to a decision by writing to his mother:

"Tell Willy I thank him greatly for setting before me so vividly the question of my going home or staying. I feel equally with him the importance of the decision. I have been meaning, as you know, for some time past to return in the autumn, and I see as yet no sufficient reason for changing my plan. I shall go with the full prevision that I shall not find life at home *simpatico*, but rather painfully, and, as regards literary work, obstructively the reverse, and not even with the expectation that time will make it easier; but simply on sternly practical grounds; i.e. because I can find more abundant literary occupation by being on the premises and relieve you and Father of your burdensome financial interposition. But I shrink from Willy's apparent assumption that going now is to pledge myself to stay forever. I feel as if my three years in Europe (with much of them so maladif) were a very moderate allowance for one who gets so much out of it as I do; and I don't think I could really hold up my head if I didn't hope to eat a bigger slice of the pudding (with a few more social plums in it, especially) at some future time. If at the end of a period at home I don't feel an overwhelming desire to come back, it will be so much gained; but I should prepare myself for great deceptions if I didn't take the possibility of such desire into account. One oughtn't, I suppose, to bother too much about the future, but arrange as best one can with the present; and the present bids me go home and try and get more things published. . . .

If I knew any one in England I should be tempted to go there for a year, for there I could work to advantage—i.e. get hold of new books to review. But I can't face, as it is, a year of British solitude. What I desire now more than anything else, and what would do me more good, is a *régal* of intelligent and suggestive society, especially male. But I don't know how or where to find it. It exists, I suppose, in Paris and London, but I can't get at it. I chiefly desire it because it would, I am sure, increase my powers of work. These are going very well, however, as it is, and I have for the present an absorbing task in my novel. Consider then that if nothing extremely unexpected turns up, I shall depart in the autumn."

His mother, whose decisions were of the heart rather than of the head, had already sent him a letter which crossed with his:

"Although I have not written to you so much of late, I believe I have never thought so much about you as since Willy came home. I feel so often that I want to throw around you the mantle of the family affection, and fold you in my own tenderest embrace. It seems to me, darling Harry, that your life must need this succulent, fattening element more than you know yourself. That notwithstanding the charm and beauty that surrounds you, and that so inspires and vivifies your intellectual and esthetic life, your social life, the life of your affection, must need the moisture and sunshine which only home, or the intercourse of a circle of familiar friends can give. I know only one thing that could solve the difficulty, and harmonize the discordant elements in your life. You would make, dear Harry, according to my estimate, the most loving and lovable and happiest of husbands. I wish I could see you in a favorable attitude of heart towards the divine institution of marriage. In the atmosphere of a happy home of your own you would thrive in every way, especially if your tent were pitched in Europe; but even in your own less favored land, it would be a blessing to you. You will doubtless exclaim after getting thus far, What on earth has got into mother! the dear old soul is getting childish, what does it all mean! It means simply that I see so much in favor of your staying abroad, and I *feel* so much in favor of your coming home, that I am blindly feeling about for some way of reconciling the difficulty—that is all it means, and we will say no more about it."

On the question of marriage HJ was to sum up his usual attitude when congratulating WJ on his engagement: "I had long wished to see you married. I believe almost as much in matrimony for most other people as I believe in it little for myself." He added to Grace Norton, in 1881: "I am unlikely ever to marry. . . . One's attitude toward marriage is a fact—the most characteristic part doubtless of one's general attitude toward life. . . . If I were to marry I should be guilty in my own eyes of inconsistency—I should pretend to think quite a little better of life than I really do."

But on the question of being a writer in America, he tried another experiment, with no commitment of finality. He spent the winter of 1874–5 mainly in New York, finishing *Roderick Hudson.* He was to describe this as "a bright cold unremunerative uninteresting winter," and in the following fall Howells wrote to a friend: "Harry James is gone abroad again not to return, I fancy, even for visits."

Once again he sampled Paris, and began to know Turgenieff, and to have at least an *entrée* to Flaubert's circle. But he still hated the boulevards and couldn't escape "the little American set—the American village encamped *en plein* Paris." He became an absorbed habitué of the Comédie Française, but the more he saw of the literary world of the Goncourts and of Zola, the less at home he felt with it. He concluded that he would remain "an eternal outsider," and went over to London in the fall of 1876. There at last he was to find the kind of milieu for which he believed himself best fitted. He wrote his mother on Christmas eve:

"I take very kindly indeed to London, and am immensely contented at having come here. I must be a born Londoner for the place to stand the very severe test to which I am putting it: leaving Paris and its brilliancies and familiarities, its easy resources and the abundant society I had there, to plunge into darkness, solitude and sleet, in mid winter, to say nothing of the sooty, wooly desolation of a London lodging—to do this, and to like this murky Babylon really all the better, is to feel that one is likely to get on here. I like the place, I like feeling in the midst of the English world, however lost in it I may be. I find it interesting, inspiring, even exhilarating."

He could have felt no longing to return home when he read WJ's brief account of an "æsthetic tea in Chestnut Street": "Certain individuals read poetry, whilst others sat and longed for them to stop so that they might begin to talk. The room was full of a decidedly goodlooking set of people, especially women—but New England all over! Give me a human race with some *guts* to them, no matter if they do belch at you now and then."

HJ reported to WJ in the spring of 1878:

"I expect to spend many a year in London—I have submitted myself without reserve to that Londonizing process of which the effect is to convince you that, having lived here, you may, if need be, abjure civilization and bury yourself in the country, but may not, in pursuit of civilization, live in any smaller town. I am still completely an outsider here, and my only chance for becoming a little of an insider (in the limited sense in which an American can ever do so) is to remain here for the present. After that—a couple of years hence—I shall go home for a year, embrace you all, and see everything of the country I can. . . . Meanwhile, if one will take what comes, one is by no means cut off from getting impressions here. . . . I know what I am about, and I have always my eyes on my native land."

After sending Alice a full account of a country estate, he added:

"I have said enough, dear sister, to make you see that I continue to see the world with perhaps even enviable profit. But don't envy me too much; for the British country-house has at moments, for a cosmopolitanised American, an insuperable flatness. On the other hand, to do it justice, there is no doubt of its being one of the ripest fruits of time —and here in Scotland, where you get the conveniences of Mayfair dovetailed into the last romanticism of nature—of the highest results of civilization."

He carried out his plan of coming home for a visit, in the fall of 1881. Upon arrival, he felt himself to be markedly different from the still somewhat indecisive young man who had left America six years before. He was impelled to sit down at a marble-topped table in the Hotel Brunswick in Boston to record in his notebook what he had learned about himself:

"I have made my choice, and God knows that I have now no time to waste. My choice is the old world—my choice, my need, my life. There is no need for me today to argue about this, it is an inestimable blessing to me, and a rare good fortune, that the problem was settled long ago, and that I have now nothing to do but to act on the settlement.—My impressions here are exactly what I expected they would be, and I scarcely see the place and feel the manners, the race, the tone of things, now that I am on the spot, more vividly than I did while I was still in Europe. My work lies there—and with this vast new world, je n'ai que faire. One can't do both—one must choose. No European writer is called upon to assume that terrible burden, and it seems hard that I should be. The burden is necessarily greater for an American— for he *must* deal, more or less, even if only by implication, with Europe; whereas no European is obliged to deal in the least with America. No one dreams of calling him less complete for not doing so. (I speak of course of people who do the sort of work that I do; not of economists, of social science people.) The painter of manners who neglects America is not thereby incomplete as yet; but a hundred years hence —fifty years hence perhaps—he will doubtless be accounted so. . . .

"The history of the five years I have spent in London—a pledge, I suppose, of many future years—is too long, and too full to write. I can only glance at it here. I took a lodging at 3 Bolton St. Piccadilly; and there I have remained till today—there I have left my few earthly possessions, to await my return. I have *lived* much there, felt much, thought much, learned much, produced much; the little shabby furnished apartment ought to be sacred to me. I came to London as a complete stranger, and today I know much too many people. J'y suis absolument chez moi. Such an experience is an education—it fortifies the character and embellishes the mind. It is difficult to speak adequately or justly of London. It is not a pleasant place; it is not agreeable, or cheerful, or easy, or exempt from reproach. It is only magnificent. You can draw up a tremendous list of reasons why it should be insupportable. The fogs, the smoke, the dirt, the darkness, the wet, the distances, the ugliness, the brutal size of the place, the horrible numerosity of society, the manner in which this senseless bigness is fatal to amenity, to convenience, to conversation, to good manners—all this and much more you may expatiate upon. You may call it dreary, heavy, stupid, dull, inhuman, vulgar at heart and tiresome in form. I have felt these things at times so strongly that I have said—'Ah London, you too then are impossible?' But these are occasional moods; and for one who takes it as I take it, London is on the whole the most possible form of life. I take it as an artist and as a bachelor; as one who has the passion of observation and whose business is the study of human life. It is the biggest aggregation of human life—the most complete compendium of the world. The human race is better represented there than anywhere else, and if you learn to know your London you learn a great many things. I felt all this in that autumn of 1876, when I first took up abode in Bolton St. I had very few friends, the season was of the darkest and wettest; but I was in a state of deep delight. I had complete liberty, and the prospect of profitable work. I used to take long walks in the rain. I took possession of London; I felt it to be the right place."

HJ was never substantially to alter those views, though he sometimes dwelt more on the obverse side, as when he summed up for Norton, in the mid-1880's, his impression of the English upper class:

"The condition of that body seems to me to be in many ways very much the same rotten and *collapsible* one as that of the French aristocracy before the revolution—minus cleverness and conversation; or perhaps it's more like the heavy, congested and depraved Roman world upon which the barbarians came down. In England the Huns and Vandals will have to come *up*—from the black depths of the (in the people) enormous misery, though I don't think the Attila is quite yet found —in the person of Mr. Hyndman. At all events, much of English life is grossly materialistic and wants blood-letting."

When HJ was back in America again at the time of his father's death, and as the shadows lifted after that event, there followed one of the most animated exchanges between the two brothers—HJ anxiously urging WJ not to break into his sabbatical leave by returning prematurely to an unrewarding Cambridge; WJ, already restless, flaring up at HJ's letter to pronounce his preference for Cambridge beyond "any place in the known world."

*   *   *   *   *

Boston, January 11, 1883

Dear William . . . You speak of being "determined to sail at latest in the *Servia* of Feb. 11th." This determination makes me really so sad. . . . I think that I must do what I can to keep you from breaking loose from Europe and giving up your stay there as a failure, prematurely. The *pity* of it almost brings tears to my eyes, and when I look upon the barren scene (bating your wife and babes) that awaits you here, I feel as if I were justified in doing almost anything to keep you on the other side. I left you so comfortably established in London with such promise of improvement and stability (as far as the fundamentals or rather, materials of life could give it), that it seems a kind of "irony of fate" that will bring you back in the midst of this harsh and rasping winter to narrow and, as it were, accidental accommodation in Mrs. Gibbens' small house,[1] where I think that for these coming months you would greatly lack space and quiet. For you to return before the summer seems a melancholy confession of failure (as regards your projects of absence), and sort of proclamation of want of continuity of purpose. . . .

It is, of course, very disappointing that you have not been able to get well at work—that you continue to feel seedy—that the London winter should not be more helpful. But there is the general fact that your being in Europe is a valuable thing, and that your undertaking there oughtn't to be abandoned—to set against these things. It is a *long, long change for you* and as that, even as that alone, it seems to me you would do well to hold on to it. It is a chance, an opportunity, which may not come to you again for years. All this came over me much as this morning I went out to poor *nudified* and staring Cambridge, and thought that *that* and your life there is what you are in such a hurry to get back to! At furthest you will take up that life soon enough; *interpose*, therefore, as much as you can before that day—continue to interpose the Europe that you are already in possession of. Do this even at the cost of sacrifices. You thought it well to make a great point of going there, and you were surely not altogether wrong. You don't know when it will be possible for you to go again—therefore don't drop the occasion from your grasp. Even if you don't do your psychology, you will do something else that is good . . . and you will escape the depressing effect of seeing yourself (and being seen by others) simply *retomber* here, to domestic worries and interruptions and into circumstances from which you had undertaken to abstract yourself. It seems to Alice,

---

[1] WJ had rented his own house when he had planned to be away for the winter.

of course (as well as to me), that your idea of going to live in some
other house (*i.e.*, take a room somewhere in Garden St.) would give a
dreary and tragic completeness to such a collapse, and have the air of
your having committed yourselves to inconstant and accidental (not
to say shiftless) ways. Therefore I say, stick to Europe till the summer, in spite of everything, in the faith that you are getting a great deal
out of it and that it is a good and valuable thing. . . . Ever your
brother, H. James.

London, January 23, 1883

My dear Harry,—On my return from a little dinner party at Hodgson's
half an hour ago, I found your long letter . . . waiting for me. . . .
Your solicitude is natural enough, but it certainly flows from a great
misconception of all the premises that are operative in the case. . . .
As far as the opinion of outsiders and their exclamations of "failure"
(which you seem so much to dread) go, I took great pains to say to
everyone that I did not think I could stay the winter. . . . The horror
you seem to feel at Cambridge is something with which I have no sympathy, preferring it as I do to any place in the known world. Quite as
little do I feel the infinite blessing of simply being in London, or in
Europe *überhaupt*. The truth is, we each of us speak from the point of
view of his own work; the place where a man's work is best done
seems and ought to seem the place of places to him. I feel tempted to
go back now just to show you how happy a man can be in the wretched
circumstances that so distress your imagination. . . .

When I decided on returning, a few weeks ago, things seemed less
hopeful here than they do now. . . . The last two days I have written
some psychology; and since yesterday noon a dry east wind and cold
air has made me feel like a different man,—I should not have supposed
that change of weather could effect such a revolution. . . . The fact is
that although from a moral point of view your sympathy commands
my warmest thanks, from the intellectual point of view, it seems, first,
to suppose that I am a bachelor, and second, that I am one who suffers
intensely from the skinniness and aridity of America. I should perhaps
suffer were I not at work there, but as it is I don't. . . . If the psychology only keeps on as it has now started, and more than all, if the
air either of Paris or of an improved London—they tell me that never
in the memory of man has there been so uninterruptedly depressing a
winter here—starts up my eyes and sleep again, I certainly shall not
think of coming home for a good many weeks to come.

(24th A.M.) I have half a mind to tear up this over-solemn reply and
write you a single page. But I can't do any more writing on the subject. It was drawn from me in the first flash of indignation at being
treated like a small child who didn't know what his own motives or in-

terests were. Your feeling evidently comes from comparing Cambridge at large with Europe at large, and then supposing that any human being must be worse off in one than in the other. Whereas it all depends on which place the human being has *business* in. I'm sure I've heard you complain enough of having to live where all your time went in futilities and your serious affairs were irreparably lost. Your working power is about three times mine; and what is lost this year on my psychology can perhaps never, or not for eight years to come, be made up. *All* that I see or do here is futility compared to that. . . . With many thanks . . . for your sympathy and trouble, believe me always your loving brother, William.

* * *

One cause of WJ's restlessness was his dissatisfaction with England:

"The complete absence of any aggregate and outward expression of pure and direct intelligence is what is so striking here. After Paris, London seems like a mediæval village, with nothing but its blanket of golden dirt to take the place of style, beauty, and rationality. At times one feels as if the former were a poor substitute. And then one does grow impatient at times with the universal expression of aggregate stupidity—stupidity heavy and massive, with a sort of voluntary self-corroboration, the like whereof exists nowhere else under the sun. Germany is the abode of the purest grace and lucency compared with this life, clogged with every kind of senseless unnecessariness, and moving down the centuries under its thick swathings, all unconscious of its load. It appeals to me as a physical image, with which doubtless the meteorological conditions of my stay here have something to do: England under a filthy, smeary, smoky fog, lusty and happy, hale and hearty, with the eternal sunlit ether outside, and she not suspecting, or not caring to think that with a puff of her breath she might rend the veil and be there.

"You ought to have seen the Rossetti exhibition,—the work of a boarding-school girl, no color, no drawing, no cleverness of any sort, nothing but feebleness incarnate, and a sort of refined intention of an extremely narrow sort, with no technical power to carry it out. Yet such expressions of admiration as I heard from the bystanders! Then the theatres, and the hippopotamus-like satisfaction of their audiences! Bad as our theatres are, they are not so massively hopeless as that. It makes Paris seem like a sort of Athens. Then the determination on the part of all who write—to do it as amateurs, and never to use the airs and language of a professional; to be first of all a layman and a gentleman, and to pretend that your ideas came to you accidentally as it were, and are things you care nothing about. As I said, it makes one impatient at times; and one finds himself wondering whether England can afford forever, when her rivals are living by the light of pure rationality to so great an extent, to go blundering thus unsystematically along, and trusting to mere luck to help her to find what is good, a fragment at a time. It's a queer mystery. She never *has* failed to find it hitherto in perhaps richer measure than they, by her method of blundering into it. But will it always last? and can she *always* fight without stripping? Won't the general clearness and keenness of a rational age force her to throw some of her nonsense away, or to fall behind the rest? I thus vomit out my bile into your in part sympathizing, in part indifferent ear. . . ."

HJ acknowledged that this letter contained
"two or three pages of remark and reflection upon England and the English, which, although rather gloomy and splenetic, are so admirably felt and admirably expressed that they have given me extraordinary pleasure. They put into much more vigorous form than I have ever been able to give them, the thoughts and impressions which have again and again arisen within me during all these years that I have lived in London, and which have finally landed me in the consciousness that if it is good to have one foot in England, it is still better, or at least as good, to have the other out of it. I haven't time to answer all you say at present, but of course you know, true as it all is, it is only part of the statement. There is more beside, and it is this *more beside* that I have been living on in London. Every now and then you will feel it (though as you are not a 'story writer' you will feel it less than I) much as you have felt the stupidity, the dowdiness and darkness. England always seems to me like a man swimming with his clothes on his head."

The last letter in this sequence came from WJ in February, for though he had put off his return for a while, he sailed early in March:
"You say you enjoyed the outpouring of my bile upon England: you will ere this have learned from my other letters that I see 'the other side' as well. They are a delectable brood, and only the slow considerings of a Goethe could do them plenary justice. The great point about them seems their good-humor and *cheerfulness;* but their civilization is *stuffy.* In spite of that, *it* is, and their whole nature is, one of the most exquisite *Kunstwerke* that the womb of time has ever brought forth. It might have failed to ripen so smoothly, but fortune seconded them without a break, and they grew into the set of customs and traditions and balancing of rights that now rolls so elastically along.
". . . Your allusions to my return continue by their solemn tone to amuse me extremely. Especially are the expressions 'confession of failure' and 'appearance of vacillation' comical. The only possible 'failure' would be to stay here longer than the refreshment, which was the only motive, either tacit or avowed, of my coming, lasted. . . . However, my reply to your first letter will have opened your eyes to all that; meanwhile the strength of your sympathy does equal credit to your

head and heart. For some reason or other London does thoroughly disagree with me. I am in a state of acute brain-fag, although I've done a mere minimum of work. . . . I feel as if the darkness of your quarters must have something to do with it; and I can't bear to think of you yourself being permanently here."

HJ went back to England that summer, and, as the years advanced, he remained generally confident of the rightness of his course. When he was working on *The Tragic Muse* (1889), he said: "I am getting to know English life better than American . . . and to understand the English character, or at least the mind, as well as if I had invented it—which indeed, I think I could have done without any very extraordinary expenditure of ingenuity." But he sometimes felt the strain of his "international theme," as when he wrote to WJ from a vacation in Geneva in the fall of 1888:

"I enjoy the easier, lighter feeling of being out of England. I suppose if one lived in one of these countries one would take its problems to one's self, also, or be oppressed and darkened by them—even as I am, more or less, by those which hang over me in London. But as it is, the Continent gives one a refreshing sense of getting *away*—away from Whitechapel and Parnell and a hundred other constantly thickening heavinesses. . . . It is always a great misfortune, I think, when one has reached a certain age, that if one is living in a country not one's own and one is of anything of an ironic or critical disposition, one mistakes the inevitable reflections and criticisms that one makes, more and more as one grows older, upon life and human nature etc., for a judgment of that particular country, its natives, peculiarities, etc., to which, really, one has grown exceedingly accustomed. For myself, at any rate, I am deadly weary of the whole 'international' state of mind—so that I *ache*, at times, with fatigue at the way it is constantly forced upon me as a sort of virtue or obligation. I can't look at the English-American world, or feel about them, any more, save as a big Anglo-Saxon total, destined to such an amount of melting together that an insistence on their differences becomes more and more idle and pedantic; and that melting together will come the faster the more one takes it for granted and treats the life of the two countries as continuous or more or less convertible, or at any rate as simply different chapters of the same general subject. Literature, fiction in particular, affords a magnificent arm for such taking for granted, and one may so do an excellent work with it. I have not the least hesitation in saying that I aspire to write in such a way that it would be impossible to an outsider to say whether I am at a given moment an American writing about England or an Englishman writing about America (dealing as I do with both countries,) and so far from being ashamed of such an ambiguity I should be exceedingly proud of it, for it would be highly civilized."

He has rarely persuaded anyone that he lived up to that last aspiration. In his detachment from both countries he remained the questioning, analyzing American who scrutinized aspects of behavior that English writers took for granted and barely noted or ignored. During the decade inaugurated by *The Tragic Muse* he confined himself almost exclusively to dealing with English life, for, as he said to Howells,[1] he felt then that his American impressions were fading. But for the three great novels of his ripest period he returned to variations upon the theme of the American in Europe. As he meditated on some of the consequences of expatriation for the sculptor William Wetmore Story, whom he had known in Rome, and as he observed the emergence of his disciple Edith Wharton, HJ was by no means sure that his course would prove right for anyone else. Indeed, he was to write to Mrs. Wharton in 1912: "Your only drawback is not having the homeliness and the inevitability and the happy limitation and the affluent poverty, of a Country of your Own." But he added the ironic flourish: "*comme moi, par exemple!*" That phrase is omitted by those who quote this remark as solemn proof that HJ came to regard his own career as a mistake. He saw its limitations, as there are limitations in any choice, but he grew ever stronger in his belief that every novelist must have "a particular window" through which to view life and bring it into form. He never really doubted that, given his upbringing and interests, he had chosen the right window.

When WJ visited him in London in 1889, he recorded an impression of his character that has been much quoted:

"Harry is as nice and simple and amiable as he can be. He has covered himself, like some marine crustacean, with all sorts of material growths, rich sea-weeds and rigid barnacles and things, and lives hidden in the midst of his strange heavy alien manners and customs; but these are all but 'protective resemblances,' under which the same dear old, good, innocent and at bottom very powerless-feeling Harry remains, caring for little but his writing, and full of dutifulness and affection for all gentle things."

On the very same day WJ filled out the picture more intimately in a letter to their sister:

"I have enjoyed being with Harry very much, but of London itself I'm thoroughly sated, and never care to see its yellow-brownness and stale spaciousness again. . . . Harry has been delightful,—easier and freer than when I was here before, and beneath all the accretions of years and the world, is still the same dear, innocent old Harry of our youth. His anglicisms are but 'protective resemblances,'—he's really, I won't say a Yankee, but a native of the James family, and has no other country."

---

[1] P. 508 below.

Alice, an expatriate now herself, was beginning to have occasion to enter the debate. She had taken stock of their situation in a letter to WJ the year before about the education of his children: "What enrichment of mind and memory can children have without continuity and if they are torn up by the roots every little while as we were! Of all things don't make the mistake which brought about our rootless and accidental childhood. Leave Europe for them until they are old enough to have *the* Grand Emotion, undiluted by vague memories."

Presently she was letting her feelings go in her journal, in accents startlingly like her father's:

"I had an almost Gallic sense of the injustice of Fate the other day, unusual with me, for I am not rebellious by temperament and have trampled down as much as possible all boresome insurrections—having fortunately early perceived that the figure of abortive rebel lent itself much more to the comic than the heroic in the eye of the cold-blooded observer, and that for practical purposes surrender, smiling if possible, is the only attainable surface which gives no hold to the scurvy tricks of Fortune. I was awfully tired one afternoon, and was going to bed when Constance Maud's name was brought up, asking if I would not see her for a moment, as she was going to America the next day. I scrambled into bed, and she, tall, straight and handsome, with shining eyes and glowing cheeks, told me that she was going to my land,— whilst my highest privilege, shrivelled and rickety, was to go to bed in hers! What a tide of homesickness swept me under for a moment! What a longing to see a shaft of sunshine shimmering through the pines, breathe in the resinous air, and throw my withered body upon my mother earth, bury my face in the coarse grass, worshipping all that the ugly, raw emptiness of the blessed land stands for,—the embodiment of a huge chance for hemmed-in humanity; its flexible conditions stretching and lending themselves to all sizes of man; pallid and naked of necessity; undraped by the illusions and mystery of a moss-grown, cobwebby past, but overflowing with a divine good-humour and benignancy, a helping hand for the faltering, an indulgent thought for the discredited, a heart of hope for every outcast of tradition."

WJ also had a vivid eye for the American landscape, but one could never be quite sure in what mood he would respond to it. He declared, as though to exorcise his upbringing: "One should not be a cosmopolitan—one's soul becomes 'disaggregated,' as Janet would say. Parts of it remain in different places, and the whole of it is nowhere. One's native land seems foreign. It is not a wholly good thing, and I think I suffer from it." His "divided soul" was very evident when, shortly after his return from another sabbatical year in Europe, he wrote HJ from Chocorua in the fall of 1893:

"I am up here for a few days with Billy, to close our house for the

winter, and get a sniff of the place. The Salters have a noble hill with
such an outlook! and a very decent little house and barn. But oh! the
difference from Switzerland, the thin grass and ragged waysides, the
poverty-stricken land, and sad American sunlight over all—sad because
so empty. There is a strange thinness and femininity hovering over all
America, so different from the stoutness and masculinity of land and
air and everything in Switzerland and England, that the coming back
makes one feel strangely sad and hardens one in the resolution never to
go away again unless one can go to end one's days. Such a divided soul
is very bad. To you, who now have such real practical relations and a
place in the old world, I should think there was no necessity of ever
coming back again. But Europe has been made what it is by men staying in their homes and fighting stubbornly generation after generation
for all the beauty, comfort and order that they have got—we must
abide and do the same. As England struck me newly and directly last
time, so America now—force and directness in the people, but a terrible grimness, more ugliness than I ever realized in things, and a greater
weakness in nature's beauty, such as it is. One must pitch one's whole
sensibility first in a different key—then gradually the quantum of personal happiness of which one is susceptible fills the cup—but the moment of change of key is lonesome."

But when HJ ventured to say, in 1896: "Strange how practically all
one's sense of news from the U. S. . . . is huge Horrors and Catastrophes. It's a terrible country *not* to live in," he brought forth from his
brother a reaction that might have been inspired by Emerson's essay on
"Compensation":

"The horrors of *not* living in America, as you so well put it, are not
shared by those who do live here. All that the telegraph imparts are the
shocks; the 'happy homes,' good husbands and fathers, fine weather,
honest business men, neat new houses, punctual meetings of engagements, etc., of which the country mainly consists, are never cabled
over. Of course, the Saint Louis disaster is dreadful, but it will very
likely end by 'improving' the city. The really bad thing here is the
silly wave that has gone over the public mind—protection humbug,
silver, jingoism, etc. It is a case of 'mob-psychology.' Any country is
liable to it if circumstances conspire, and our circumstances have con-
spired. It is very hard to get them out of the rut. It *may* take another
financial crash to get them out—which, of course, will be an expensive
method. It is no more foolish and considerably less damnable than the
Russo-phobia of England, which would seem to have been responsible
for the Armenian massacres. That to me is the biggest indictment 'of
our boasted civilization'!! It *requires* England, I say nothing of the
other powers, to maintain the Turks at that business."

When HJ heard of a camping trip being planned for WJ's sons in the last summer of the century, he took vicarious satisfaction. But though his soul was also "divided" on such occasions, and caused him to regret many things in his past, he as characteristically came out with a relish for a "classic" landscape as WJ did for a "romantic" one:

"Nothing you tell me gives me greater pleasure than what you say of the arrangements made for Harry and Billy in the forest primeval and the vision of their drawing therefrom experiences of a sort that I too miserably lacked (poor Father!) in my own too casual youth. What I most of all feel, and in the light of it conjure you to keep doing for them, is their being *à même* to contract local saturations and attachments in respect to their *own* great and glorious country, to learn, and strike roots into, its infinite beauty, as I suppose, and variety. Then they won't, as I do now, have to assimilate, but half-heartedly, the alien splendours—inferior ones too, as I believe—of the indigestible *midi* of Bourget and the Vicomte Melchior de Vogüé, kindest of hosts and most brilliant of *commensaux* as I am in the act of finding both these personages. The beauty here is, after my long stop at home [i.e., England], admirable and exquisite; but make the boys, none the less, stick fast and sink up to their necks in everything their *own* countries and climates can give *de pareil et de supérieur*. Its being that 'own' will double their *use* of it. . . . This little estate (two houses—near together—in a 25-acre walled 'parc' of dense pine and cedar, along a terraced mountainside, with exquisite views inland and to the sea) is a precious and enviable acquisition. The walks are innumerable, the pleasant 'wildness' of the land (universally accessible) only another form of sweetness, and the light, the air, the noble, graceful lines &c, all of the first order. It's classic—Claude—Virgil."

Only a couple of months later WJ strained his heart when he lost his way in the Adirondacks, and had to spend the summer taking the cure at Bad-Nauheim. He visited his brother that fall in his recently acquired place at Rye, and wrote home to a friend:

"HJ has a real little *bijou* of a house and garden, and seems absolutely adapted to his environment, and very well and contented in the leisure to write and to read which the place affords. . . . I am very glad . . . to be in an English atmosphere again. Of course it will conspire better with my writing tasks [than the Continent], and after all it is more congruous with one's nature and one's inner ideals. Still, one loves America above all things, for her youth, her greenness, her plasticity, innocence, good intentions, friends, everything. Je veux que mes cendres reposent sur les bords du Charles, au milieu de ce bon peuple de Harvarr Squerre que j'ai tant aimé. That is what I say, and what Napoleon B. would have said, had his life been enriched by your and my educational and other experiences—poor man, he knew too little of life, had never even heard of us, whilst we have heard of him!"

WJ's condition took a long time mending, and two years went by before he was able to deliver his first Gifford lectures and go home. He wrote out of his homesickness:

"When we return I shall go straight up to Chocorua to the Salters'. What I *crave* most is some wild American country. It is a curious organic-feeling need. One's social relations with European landscape are entirely different, everything being so fenced or planted that you can't lie down and sprawl. Kipling, alluding to the 'bleeding raw' appearance of some of our outskirt settlements, says, 'Americans don't mix much with their landscape as yet.' But we mix a darned sight more than Europeans, so far as our individual organisms go, with our camping and general wild-animal personal relations. Thank Heaven that our Nature is so much less 'redeemed'!"

In other moods he was more concerned with the need of some kinds of "redemption":

"I should like to return to America with the certainty that I might finish my days there and never be obliged to leave it again. These absences from one's native country break up the adhesions of the rootlets of one's being in the soil, and I have made too many absences, first and last. I should like to stay at home, and see my children grow up successfully and establish themselves in life; and *write*, myself in a way which, if possible, might slightly help to influence American ideals. But successfully to do so one must live very close to them. Otherwise one's voice sounds foreign. There are splendid things about America, but the old human leaven of national adventure and aggrandizement is threatening to substitute its brute instinctive power for our historic and hereditary principles, and liberal Americans will have a hard fight to keep the country on the happier and more beneficent track."

In the spring of 1903, HJ, having been away from America for twenty years, dispatched what he might well have considered one of his most "portentous" missives:

"The desire to go 'home' for six months (not less) daily grows in me. . . . I should wish to write a book of 'impressions' (for much money), and to that end get quite away from Boston and New York —really *see* the country at large. On the other hand I don't see myself prowling alone in Western cities and hotels or finding my way about by myself, and it is all darksome and tangled. Some light may break— but meanwhile next Wednesday (awful fact) is my 60th birthday."

To this WJ replied:

"Your . . . *inhaltsvoll* letter of April 10th arrived duly, and constituted, as usual an 'event' . . . and . . . made Alice [1] positively overflow with joyous anticipations. On my part they are less unmixed, for

---

[1] This Alice is, of course, WJ's wife.

I feel more keenly a good many of the *désagréments* to which you will inevitably be subjected, and imagine the sort of physical loathing with which many features of our national life will inspire you. It takes a long time to notice such things no longer. One thing, for example, which would reconcile *me* most easily to abandoning my native country forever would be the certainty of immunity, when traveling, from the sight of my fellow beings at hotels and dining-cars having their boiled eggs brought to them, broken by a negro, two in a cup, and eaten with butter. How irrational this dislike is, is proved both by logic, and by the pleasure taken in the custom by the élite of mankind over here. . . . Yet of such irrational sympathies and aversions (quite conventional for the most part) does our pleasure in a country depend, and in your case far more than in that of most men. The *vocalization* of our countrymen is really, and not conventionally, so ignobly awful that the process of hardening oneself thereto is very slow, and would in your case be impossible. It is simply incredibly loathsome. I should hate to have you come and, as a result, feel that you had now *done* with America forever, even in an ideal and imaginative sense, which after a fashion you can still indulge in. . . . Alice foresees Lowell lectures; but lectures have such an awful side (when not academic) that I myself have foresworn them—it is a sort of prostitution of one's person. This is rather a throwing of cold water; but it is well to realize both sides, and I think I can realize certain things for you better than the sanguine and hospitable Alice does.

"Now for the other side, there are things in the American out-of-door nature, as well as comforts indoors that can't be beat, and from which *I* get infinite pleasure. If you avoided the *banalité* of the Eastern cities, and traveled far and wide, to the South, the Colorado, over the Canadian Pacific to that coast, possibly to the Hawaiian Islands, etc., you would get some reward, at the expense, it is true, of a considerable amount of cash. . . . The hot summer months you could pass in an absolutely quiet way—if you wished to—at Chocorua with us, where you could do as much writing as you liked, continuous, and undisturbed, and would (I am sure) grow fond of, as you grew more and more intimate with, the sweet rough country there."

This brotherly opposition had the effect of sharpening all HJ's arguments for coming, and he poured them out in an immense slow flood. With the passage of time America had taken on for him the romantic "otherness" once possessed by Europe. Then, too, there were the economic reasons, though he won't say right out that he is hoping to give lectures as well as to gather material for a book on the American scene:

"There is—and there *was* when I wrote—no conceivability of my doing this for a year at least to come—before August 1904, at nearest; but it kind of eases my mind to thresh the idea out sufficiently to have

a direction to *tend* to meanwhile, and an aim to work at. It is in fact
a practical necessity for me, *dès maintenant*, to know whether or not I
absolutely want to go if, and when, I *can*. . . . Luckily, for myself,
I do already (as I feel) quite adequately remain convinced that I *shall*
want to whenever I can: that is [if] I don't put it off for much *more*
than a year—after which period I certainly shall *lose* the impulse to
return to my birth-place under the mere blight of incipient senile
decay. If I go at all I must go before I'm too old, and, above all,
before I mind being older. You are very dissuasive—even more than I
expected; but I think it comes from your understanding even less than
I expected the motives, considerations, advisabilities etc., that have
gradually, cumulatively, and under much study of the question, much
carefully invoked *light* on it, been acting upon me. . . .

"It is, roughly—and you will perhaps think too cryptically—speaking, a situation for which 6 or 8 months in my native land shine before
me as a very possible and profitable remedy: and I don't speak *not* by
book. Simply and supinely to shrink—on mere grounds of general fear
and encouraged shockability—has to me all the air of giving up,
chucking away without a struggle, the one chance that remains to me
in life of anything that can be called a *movement*: my one little ewe-
lamb of possible exotic experience, such experience as may convert itself, through the senses, through observation, imagination and reflection
now at their maturity, into vivid and solid *material*, into a general renovation of one's too monotonised grab-bag. You speak of the whole
matter rather, it seems to me, 'à votre aise'; you make, comparatively,
and have always made, so many movements; you have travelled and
gone to and fro—always comparatively!—so often and so much. I have
practically never travelled at all—having never been economically able
to; I've only gone, for short periods, a few times—so much fewer than
I've wanted—to Italy: never anywhere else that I've seen every one
about me here (who is, or was, anyone) perpetually making for. These
visions I've had, one by one, all to give up—Spain, Greece, Sicily, any
glimpse of the East, or in fact of anything; even to the extent of
rummaging about in France; even to the extent of trudging about, a
little, in Switzerland. Counting out my few dips into Italy, there has
been no time at which *any* 'abroad' was financially convenient or possible. And now, more and more, all such adventures present themselves
in the light of mere agreeable *luxuries*, expensive and supererogatory,
inasmuch as not resolving themselves into new material or assimilating
with my little acquired stock, my accumulated capital of (for convenience) 'international' items and properties. There's nothing to be
done by me, any more, in the way of writing, *de chic*, little worthless,
superficial, *poncif* articles about Spain, Greece, or Egypt. They are the
sort of thing that doesn't work in at all to what now most interests

me: which is human Anglo-Saxonism, with the American extension, or opportunity for it, so far as it may be given me still to work the same. If I *shouldn't*, in other words, bring off going to the U. S., it would simply mean giving up, for the remainder of my days, all chance of such experience as is represented by interesting 'travel.' . . . I should settle down to a mere mean oscillation from here to London and from London here—with nothing (to speak of) left, more, to happen to me in life in the way of (the poetry of) motion. That spreads before me as for mind, imagination, special, 'professional' labour, a thin, starved, lonely, defeated, beaten, prospect: in comparison with which your own circumgyrations have been as the adventures of Marco Polo or H. M. Stanley. I *should* like to think of going once or twice more again, for a sufficient number of months, to Italy, where I know my ground suffi- ciently to be able to plan for such quiet work there as might be need- fully involved. But the day is past when I can 'write' stories about Italy with a mind otherwise pre-occupied. My native land, which time, absence and change have, in a funny sort of way, made almost as ro- mantic to me as 'Europe,' in dreams or in my earlier time here, used to be—the actual bristling (as fearfully bristling as you like) U. S. A. have the merit and the precious property that they meet and fit into my ('creative') preoccupations; and that the period there which should represent the poetry of motion, the one big taste of travel not supremely missed, would carry with it also possibilities of the prose of *production* (that is of the production of prose) such as no other mere bought, paid for, sceptically and half-heartedly worried-through adventure, by land or sea, would be able to give me. My primary idea in the matter is absolutely economic—and on a basis that I can't make clear to you now, though I probably shall be able to later on if you demand it: that is if you also are accessible to the impression of my having *any* 'pro- fessional standing' là-bas big enough to be improved on. I am not think- ing (I'm sure) vaguely or blindly (but recognising direct intimations) when I take for granted some such Chance as my personal presence there *would* conduce to improve: I don't mean by its beauty or bril- liancy, but simply by the benefit of my managing for once in my life not to fail to be on the spot. . . .

"It isn't in the least a question of my trying to make old copy-rights pay better or look into arrangements actually existing; it's a question— well, of too much more than I can go into the detail of now (or, much rather, into the general and comprehensive truth of); or even than I can ever do, so long as I only have from you Doubt. What you say of the Eggs (!!!), of the Vocalisation, of the Shocks in general, and of every- thing else, is utterly beside the mark—it being absolutely *for* all that class of phenomena, and every other class, that I nurse my infatuation. I want to see them, I want to see everything. I want to see the Country (scarcely a bit New York and Boston, but intensely the Middle and Far West and California and the South)—in *cadres* as complete and immeasurably more mature than those of the celebrated Taine when he went, early in the sixties, to Italy for six weeks, in order to write his big book. . . . But enough of all this—I am saying, *have* said, much more than I meant to say at the present date. Let it, at any rate, simmer in your mind, if your mind has any room for it, and take *time*, above all, if there is any danger of your still replying adversely. . . ."

When HJ was in such a mood, WJ could only respond with delight:

"Your long and excitingly interesting type-written letter about coming hither arrived yesterday, and I hasten to retract all my dampening remarks, now that I understand the motives fully. The only ones I had imagined, blindling that I am, were fraternal piety and patriotic duty. Against those I thought I ought to proffer the thought of 'eggs' and other shocks, so that when they came I might be able to say that you went not unwarned. But the moment it appears that what you crave is millions of just such shocks, and that a new lease of artistic life, with the lamp of genius fed by the oil of twentieth-century American life, is to be the end and aim of the voyage, all my stingy doubts wither and are replaced by enthusiasm that you are still so young-feeling, receptive and hungry for raw material and experience. It cheers me immensely, and makes me feel more so myself. It is pathetic to hear you talk so about your career and its going to seed without the contact of new material; but feeling as you do about the new material, I augur a great revival of energy and internal effervescence from the execution of your project. Drop your English ideas and take America and Americans as they take themselves, and you will certainly experience a rejuvenation. That is all I have to say *today*—merely to let you see how the prospect exhilarates us."

As though anticipating what HJ *might* say of Chocorua, WJ wrote to his daughter that same spring: "Poverty-stricken this New Hampshire country may be—weak in a certain sense, shabby, thin, pathetic —say all that, yet, like 'Jenny,' it *kissed* me; and it is not *vulgar*—even HJ can't accuse it of that—or of 'stodginess,' especially at this emaciated season. It remains pure, and clear and distinguished—Bless it!" His anxieties seem to have been needless. To be sure, there is the family legend that HJ, after going for a walk at Chocorua, reported that he had seen "a peasant gathering faggots." But WJ wrote just after his visit there: "My brother Henry stayed a delightful fortnight, and seemed to enjoy nature here intensely—found so much *sentiment* and feminine delicacy in it all. It is a pleasure to be with anyone who takes in things through the eyes. Most people don't." It is wonderful to observe how, to the end of their lives, each could always find his gift of seeing stimulated by the other. HJ reflected, after this same visit:

"Whenever one is with William one receives such an immense accession of suggestion and impression that the memory of the episode remains bathed for one in the very liquidity of his extraordinary play of mind."

Some of HJ's published impressions of America will be included below,[1] but here we may bring the lifelong debate to a close by putting side by side a few of the brothers' final offhand responses to various parts of this country. Their reactions to California were not dissimilar. HJ declared at Coronado Beach in the spring of 1905:

"California, on these terms, when all is said (Southern C. at least— which, however, the real C, I believe, much repudiates,) has completely bowled me over—such a delicious difference from the rest of the U. S. do I find in it. (I speak of course all of nature and climate, fruits and flowers; for there is absolutely nothing else, and the sense of the shining social and human inane is utter.)"

While lecturing at Stanford the following winter, WJ commented to HJ:

"You've seen this wonderful spot, so I needn't describe it. It is really a miracle; and so simple the life and so benign the elements, that for a young ambitious professor who wishes to leave his mark on Pacific civilization while it is most plastic, or for *any one* who wishes to teach and work under the most perfect conditions for eight or nine months, and *who is able to get to the East, or Europe, for the remaining three*, I can't imagine anything finer. It is Utopian. Perfection of weather. Cold nights, though above freezing. Fire pleasant until 10 o'clock A.M., then unpleasant. In short, the 'simple life' with all the essential higher elements thrown in as communal possessions. The drawback is, of course, the great surrounding human vacuum—the historic silence fairly rings in your ears when you listen—and the social insipidity. I'm glad I came, and with God's blessing I may pull through."

HJ had given his lectures on "The Lesson of Balzac" and "The Question of our Speech" in many different places, with considerable success and acclaim. But when he had returned to England, he summed up his recent experience for a friend:

"I found my native land, after so many years, interesting, formidable, fearsome and fatiguing, and much more difficult to see and deal with in any extended and various way than I had supposed. I was able to do with it far less than I had hoped, in the way of visitation—I found many of the conditions too deterrent; but I did what I could, went to the far South, the Middle West, California, the whole Pacific coast &c, and spent some time in the Eastern cities. It is an extraordinary world, an altogether huge 'proposition,' as they say there, giving one, I think,

---

[1] Pp. 651–67 below.

an immense impression of material and political power; but almost cruelly charmless, in effect, and calculated to make one crouch, ever afterwards, as cravenly as possible, at Lamb House, Rye—if one happens to have a poor little L.H., R., to crouch in."

WJ would, no doubt, have taken exception to some of that, since he wrote in 1907 of the new New York:

"The first impression . . . if you stay there not more than 36 hours, which has been my limit for twenty years past, is one of repulsion at the clangor, disorder, and permanent earthquake conditions. But this time, installed as I was at the Harvard Club (44th St.) in the centre of the cyclone, I caught the pulse of the machine, took up the rhythm, and vibrated *mit*, and found it simply magnificent. I'm surprised at you, Henry, not having been more enthusiastic, but perhaps that superbly powerful and beautiful subway was not opened when you were there. It is an *entirely* new New York, in soul as well as in body, from the old one, which looks like a village in retrospect. The courage, the heaven-scaling audacity of it all, and the *lightness* withal, as if there was nothing that was not easy, and the great pulses and bounds of progress, so many in directions all simultaneous that the coordination is indefinitely future, give a kind of *drumming background* of life that I never felt before. I'm sure that once *in* that movement, and at home, all other places would seem insipid. . . . I got such an impression of easy efficiency in the midst of their bewildering conditions of speed and complexity of adjustment."

Yet, upon his return from still another trip to Europe, to deliver at Oxford the lectures that formed *A Pluralistic Universe*, WJ again confessed himself partly unreconciled to the American scene:

"We're a thousand years behindhand in so many things; and the *attained* social character of European civilizations generally is more *erfreulich* than those mere suggestions and possibilities of good, that are perhaps more abundant here. After five months spent mainly in rural England, both my wife and I were sickened by the shock of the scurviness and *decay* which the face of things presented when we landed here. In 500 years we may hope for polish, but hardly in less, with the West wide-open to drain off every rise of the water-level of civilization in the older parts of the country. *Tight fit* is what shapes things definitely; with a loose fit you get no results, and America is redolent of loose fits everywhere."

On the other hand, HJ did recall, in retrospect, some glimpses of charm, particularly as he envisaged the countryside in the summer of 1909, the year before WJ died:

"I like to think of your tranquil—if the word be the least applicable! —Chocorua summer; and as the time of year comes round again of my sole poor visit there (my mere fortnight from September 1st 1904), the yearning but baffled thought of being with you on that woodland scene and at the same season once more tugs at my sensibilities and is almost too much for me. I have the sense of my then leaving it all un-sated, after a beggarly snatch only, and of how I might have done with so much more of it. But I shall pretty evidently have to do with what I got. The very smell and sentiment of the American summer's end there and of Alice's beautiful 'rustic' hospitality of overflowing milk and honey, to say nothing of squash pie and ice-cream in heroic pro-portions, all mingle for me with the assault of forest and lake and of those delicious orchardy, yet rocky vaguenesses and Arcadian 'no-wheres,' which are the note of what is sweetest and most attaching in the dear old American, or particularly New England, scenery. It comes back to me as with such a magnificent beckoning looseness—in relieving contrast to the consummate tightness (a part, too, oddly, of the very wealth of effect) *du pays d'ici*. It isn't however, luckily, that I have really turned 'agin' my landscape portion here, for never so much as this summer, e.g., have I felt the immensely noble, the truly aristocratic, beauty of this splendid county of Sussex, especially as the winged car of offence has monstrously unfolded it to me."

There the debaters rested.

WJ AND HJ:

ON EACH OTHER'S WORK

ANOTHER lifelong interchange between the brothers dealt with each other's work. At the outset it was mainly HJ's work that was under discussion, since HJ was a professional writer, with an impressive list of stories, travel sketches, and critical essays behind him when WJ was just beginning to be an instructor at Harvard. Half a dozen years before WJ brought out his *Psychology*, HJ had already issued a fourteen-volume collection of his novels and tales. Then, as WJ advanced in his career as a writer, HJ admired him enormously, but felt that much of his brother's production was too technical for him to judge, whereas WJ always had opinions about fiction. So most frequently it is WJ who is the critic and adviser, though one who had the highest respect for his brother's skills, and who even relied on them to improve his own first attempts. He preserved this respect to the end, though by then his imperfect sympathy would have liked to make HJ's style over into something else.

The record begins in the spring of 1865, when their father noted: "Harry has a story in the current number (March) of the *Atlantic*. Considered good. . . . *The Story of a Year* by H.J. Jr." WJ wrote home from Brazil: "I pine for Harry's literary *efforts* and to see a number or so of the *Nation*."

Two years later, in Berlin, WJ tried his first review—of Herman Grimm's *Unüberwindliche Mächte,* a "German-American" novel:

"Beloved 'Arry—I hope you will not be severely disappointed on opening this fat envelope to find it is not all *letter*. I will first explain to you the nature of the enclosed document and then proceed to personal matters. The other day, as I was sitting alone with my deeply breached letter of credit, beweeping my outcast state, and wondering what I could possibly do for a living, it flashed across me that I might write a 'notice' of H. Grimm's novel which I had just been reading.

315

To conceive with me is to execute, as you well know. And after sweating fearfully for three days, erasing, tearing my hair, copying, recopying, etc., etc., I have just succeeded in finishing the enclosed. I want you to read it, and if, after correcting the style and thoughts, with the aid of Mother, Alice, and Father, and rewriting it if possible, you judge it to be capable of interesting in any degree anyone in the world but H. Grimm, himself, to send it to the *Nation*. . . .

"I feel that a living is hardly worth being gained at this price. Style is not my forte, and to strike the mean between pomposity and vulgar familiarity is indeed difficult. Still, an the rich guerdon accrue, an but ten beauteous dollars lie down on their green and glossy backs within the family treasury in consequence of my exertions, I shall feel glad that I have made them. . . . The notice was mere taskwork. I could not get up a spark of interest in it, and I should not think it would be *d'actualité* for the *Nation*. Still, I could think of nothing else to do, and was bound to do something."

To this HJ responded: "I received about a fortnight ago your letter with the review of Grimm's novel. . . . I liked your article very much and was delighted to find you attempting something of the kind. It struck me as neither dull nor flat, but very readable. I copied it forthwith and sent it to the *Nation*." WJ's next rejoinder ran: "I got a letter from you and one from Wilky last week, with the *Nation* and its contemptible contents. I perceived the tracks of your repairing hand, and thank you for them. I sent you another notice last week of Quatrefage's 'Anthropology'; but feel so ashamed of merely writing against space without having anything to say, that I think you had better either not give it, or cut it down to a mere page or two. I really have no respect for this unprincipled literary wash that floods the world and don't see why I should be guilty of augmenting it." [1]

That same year in Germany WJ undertook several analyses of HJ's stories, beginning with "The Story of a Masterpiece" and "The Romance of Certain Old Clothes":

"Both stories show a certain neatness and airy grace of touch which is characteristic of your productions (I suppose you want to hear in an unvarnished manner what is exactly the impression they make on me). And both show a greater suppleness and freedom of movement in the composition; although the first was unsympathetic to me from being one of those male *vs.* female subjects you have so often treated, and besides there was something cold about it, a want of heartiness or unction. It seems to me that a story must have rare picturesque elements of some sort, or much action, to compensate for the absence of heartiness, and the elements of yours were those of everyday life.

---

[1] This review likewise appeared in the *Nation*, under the title: "The Prog- ress of Anthropology."

It can also escape by the exceeding 'keen'ness of its analysis and thoroughness of its treatment, as in some of Balzac's (but even there the result is disagreeable, if valuable); but in yours the moral action was very lightly touched, and rather indicated than exhibited. I fancy this rather dainty and disdainful treatment of yours comes from a wholesome dread of being sloppy and gushing and over-abounding in power of expression, like the most of your rivals in the *Atlantic* . . . and that is excellent, in fact it is the instinct of truth against humbug and twaddle, and when it governs the treatment of a rich material it produces first class works. But the material in your stories (except 'Poor Richard') has been *thin* (and even in P. R., relatively to its length), so that they give a certain impression of the author clinging to his gentlemanliness though all else be lost, and dying happy provided it be *sans déroger*. That, to be sure, is expressed rather violently, but . . . I feel something of a . . . want of blood in your stories, as if you did not fully fit them, and I tell you so because I think the same thing would strike you if you read them as the work of another. . . . If you see what I mean perhaps it may put you on the track of some useful discovery about yourself, which is my excuse for talking to you thus unreservedly. So far I think 'Poor Richard' the best of your stories because there is warmth in the material, and I should have read it and enjoyed it very much indeed had I met it anywhere. The story of 'Old Clothes' is in a different tone from any of yours, seems to have been written with the mind more unbent and careless, is very pleasantly done, but is, as the *Nation* said, 'trifling' for you. . . .

"I have uttered this long rigmarole in a dogmatical manner, as one speaks to himself, but of course you will use it merely as a mass to react against in your own way, so that it may serve you some good purpose. It must be almost impossible to get anyone's real, whole feeling about what one has written. I wish I could say it *viva voce*. If I were you I'd select some particular problem, literary or historical, to study on. There's no comfort to the mind like having some special task, and then you could write stories by the way for pleasure and profit. I don't suppose *your literarisches Selbstgefühl* suffers from what I have said; for I really think my taste is rather incompetent in these matters, and as beforesaid, only offer these remarks as the impressions of an individual for you to philosophize upon yourself."

A month later WJ added:

"Exactly what escaped me in the ardor of composition I cannot now remember, but I have the impression I assumed a rather law-giving tone. I hope it did not hurt you in any way, or mislead you as to the opinion I may have of you as a whole, for I feel as if you were one of the two or three sole intellectual and moral companions I have. If you could have known how I have ached at times to have you by and hear your opinion on different matters, or see how things would strike you, you would not think I thought lightly of the evolutions of your mind."

He now perceived what was to remain a distinguishing feature of HJ's structures:

"I have got your last *Atlantic* story ('Extraordinary Case'), and read it with much satisfaction. It makes me think I may have partly mis-understood your aim heretofore, and that one of the objects you had had in view has been to give an impression like that we often get of people in life: Their orbits come out of space and lay themselves for a short time along of ours, and then off they whirl again into the un-known, leaving us with little more than an impression of their reality and a feeling of baffled curiosity as to the mystery of the beginning and end of their being, and of the intimate character of that segment of it which we have seen. Am I right in guessing that you had a conscious intention of this sort here? . . . You seem to acknowledge that you can't exhaust any character's feelings or thoughts by an articulate dis-playing of them. You shrink from the attempt to drag them all reeking and dripping and raw upon the stage, which most writers make and fail in. You expressly restrict yourself, accordingly, to showing a few external acts and speeches, and by the magic of your art making the reader *feel* back of these the existence of a body of being of which these are casual features. You wish to suggest a mysterious fulness which you do not lead your reader through. It seems to me this is a very legitimate method, and has a great effect when it succeeds. . . . Only it must succeed. The gushing system is better to fail in, since that admits of a warmth of feeling and generosity of intention that may reconcile the reader. . . . Your style grows easier, firmer and more concise as you go on writing. The tendency to return on an idea and over-refine it, becomes obsolete,—you hit it the first lick now. The face of the whole story is bright and sparkling, no dead places, and on the whole the scepticism and, as some people would say, impudence im-plied in your giving a story which is no story at all, is not only a rather *gentlemanly* thing, but has a deep justification in nature, for we know the beginning and end of nothing. Still, while granting your success here, I must say that I think the thorough and passionate con-ception of a story is the highest, as of course you think yourself."

HJ's answers to these letters do not seem to have survived, but on this question of structure he was to persevere in the method he had used in "A Most Extraordinary Case." When working out his ending for *The Portrait of a Lady*, he observed that "the obvious criticism of course will be that it is not finished—that I have not seen the heroine to the end of her situation—that I have left her *en l'air*. This is both true and false. The whole of anything is never told; you can only take what groups together. What I have done has that unity—it groups to-gether. It is complete in itself—and the rest may be taken up or not, later." He was to make his final, confident formulation on this matter in the preface to *Roderick Hudson*: "Really, universally, relations stop nowhere, and the exquisite problem of the artist is eternally but to draw, by a geometry of his own, the circle within which they shall happily *appear* to do so."

In 1869 WJ wrote from Cambridge to HJ in London:

"On account of my back I will write but one sheet, though I fain would write more. I have missed your conversation bad, but not your services as errand-boy, coal-heaver, etc., at all. . . . I wrote a notice of a book on spiritualism (*Planchette*) for the *Advertiser* and got $10.00!! *Galaxy* for April advertised this magazine with your dialogue [*Pyramus and Thisbe: A Farce*]. . . . Your thing reads very well. Better than when you read it to me. Father says, 'Harry has decidedly got a gift.' "

The correspondence continued:

*   *   *   *   *

Cambridge, January 19, 1870

Dear Harry . . . Father has been writing a couple of articles on woman and marriage in the *Atlantic*.[1] I can't think he shows himself to most advantage in this kind of speculation. I will send you . . . the January number . . . with a long and good poem by Lowell ["The Cathedral"]. . . . I enjoyed last week the great pleasure of reading *The House of the Seven Gables*. I little expected so *great* a work. It's like a great symphony with no touch alterable without injury to the harmony. It made a deep impression on me and I thank heaven that Hawthorne was an American. It also tickled my national feeling not a little to note the resemblance of Hawthorne's style to yours and Howells's, even as I had earlier noted the converse. That you and Howells with all the models in English literature to follow, should needs involuntarily have imitated (as it were) this American, seems to point to the existence of some real American mental quality. But I must spare my eyes and stop.

Great Malvern, February 13, 1870

Beloved Brother . . . I received your *Atlantic* with Lowell's poem, which I enjoyed largely, though it seems to be lacking in the real poetic element through excess of cleverness—the old story. I enjoyed unmiti-gatedly Howells's little paper ["By Horse-Car to Boston"]. I have en-joyed all his things, more even since being abroad than at home. They

[1] These articles, highly personal spec-ulations on free love, were called "The Woman Thou Gavest Me," "Is Mar-riage Holy?" and "The Logic of Mar-riage and Murder."

are really American. I'm glad you've been liking Hawthorne. But I mean to write as good a novel one of these days (perhaps) as *The House of the Seven Gables*.

* * *

Shortly after WJ had accepted his first teaching appointment, he felt a characteristic revulsion, which he expressed to HJ:

"I envy ye the world of art. Away from it, as we live, we sink into a flatter, blanker kind of consciousness, and indulge in an ostrich-like forgetfulness of all our richest potentialities; and they startle us now and then when by accident some rich human product, pictorial, literary, or architectural slaps us with its tail. . . . I have been of late so sickened and sceptical of philosophic activity as to regret much that I did not stick to painting, and to envy those like you to whom the æsthetic relations of things were the real world. Surely they reveal a deeper part of the universal life than all the mechanical and logical abstractions do, and if I were you I would never repine that my life had got cast among them rather than elsewhere."

At the same time he discussed HJ's *Transatlantic Sketches*:

"Your letters to the *Nation*, of which I have as yet seen three, have been very exquisite, and both I and others . . . have got great refreshment from them. But as one gets more appreciative one's self for fineness of perception and fineness of literary touch either in poetry or prose, one also finds how few there are to sympathize with one. I suppose, moreover, that descriptive writing is on the whole not a popular kind. Your own tendency is more and more to over-refinement, and elaboration. Recollect that for newspaporial purposes, a broader treatment hits a broader mark; and keep bearing that way as much as you can with comfort."

HJ answered from Paris:

"Your criticism of my *Nation* letters was welcome and just: their tendency is certainly to over-refinement. Howells wrote to me to the same effect and you are both right. But I am not afraid of not being able on the whole, and in so far as this is deeply desirable, to work it off with practice. Beyond a certain point, this would not be desirable I think—for me at least, who must give up the ambition of ever being a free-going and light-paced enough writer to please the multitude. The multitude, I am more and more convinced, has absolutely no taste— none at least that a thinking man is bound to defer to. To write for the few who have is doubtless to lose money—but I am not afraid of starving. . . . All writing not really leavened with thought of some sort or other is terribly unprofitable, and to try and work one's material closely is the only way to form a manner on which one can keep afloat —without intellectual bankruptcy at least. I have a mortal horror of seeming to write thin—and if I ever feel my pen beginning to scratch, shall consider that my death-knell has rung. . . . I read your Taine [1] and admired, though I but imperfectly understood it."

WJ continued the charge:

"Your letters to the *Nation* have been rather too few, and very much enjoyed by me, and by a number of other people so large that I confess it has rather surprised me; as I thought the style ran a little more to *curliness* than suited the average mind, or in general the newspaper reader. In my opinion what you should *cultivate* is directness of style. Delicacy, subtlety and ingenuity will take care of themselves. . . .

"I send you today the last *Nation* with your letter about Chambéry, etc.,—a very delightful light bit of work, and perhaps the best of all for commercial newspaporial purposes. I must, however, still protest against your constant use of French phrases. There is an order of taste, and certainly a respectable one, to which they are simply maddening. I have said nothing to you about 'Guest's Confession' which I read and enjoyed, admiring its cleverness though not loving it exactly. I noted at the time a couple of blemishes, one of the French phrase *les indifférents* at the end of one of [the] sentences which suddenly chills one's very marrow. The other the expression: 'to whom I had dedicated a sentiment.' . . . Of the people who experience a personal dislike, so to speak, of your stories, the most I think will be repelled by the element which gets expression in these two phrases, something cold, thin-blooded and priggish suddenly popping in and freezing the genial current. And I think that is the principal defect you have now to guard against. In flexibility, ease, and light power of style you clearly continue to gain—'Guest's Confession' and this last letter in the *Nation* are proofs of it; but I think you should fight shy of that note of literary reminiscence in the midst of what ought to be pure imagination absorbed in the object, which keeps every now and then betraying itself, as in these French phrases. I criticize you so much as perhaps to seem a mere caviler, but I think it ought to be of use to you to have any detailed criticism from even a wrong judge, and you don't get much from anyone else. I meanwhile say nothing of the great delight which all your pieces give me by their insight into the shades of being, and their exquisite diction and sense of beauty."

In the following year WJ suggested an idea that was to eventuate in *French Poets and Novelists*:

"I take up my pen once more . . . to converse with my in many respects twin brother. We have not heard from you in a fortnight and

---

[1] This review of Taine, "On Intelligence," is, according to Perry, "the first of William James's publications that can be said to afford any hint of his philosophical tendencies."

eagerly expect a letter today, describing new sensual delights and luxuries in which your body and soul shall have alike been wallowing. Alice and I keep up a rather constant fire of *badinage,* etc., of which you furnish the material; she never speaking of you except as 'that angel'—and I sarcastically calling you the 'angel-hero-martyr.' Usually towards bedtime I wander into the parlor where the three are sitting and say 'I suppose that angel is now in such and such an attitude,' drawing on my imagination for something very 'oriental,' to which Alice generally finds no better reply than a tirade upon the petty jealousies of *men.* Long may you have the power of enjoying what luxuries you can get! . . . Another event for us has been the reception of a proof . . . of your article on Gautier. It is admirable, delightful, as good as Gautier himself at his best; and when one considers that it was written impromptu, *i.e.,* from memory, it shows after all that the power one contains in his skin at a given moment does accumulate insensibly by years and experience. When one sees you doing that sort of thing so well, it makes one curse every day that passes without your trying your hand on Turgenieff, Balzac, George Sand, Dumas *fils* and others. Collected, they would make a standard book. You must come to it some day, for no talent can escape its destiny."

*   *   *   *   *

Perugia, May 19, 1873

Dearest William . . . Looking over your letter, I perceive your adjuration to prepare articles, etc., on the French, George Sand, Balzac, etc. I may come to it, some day, but there are various things I want to do first. Just at present I shall write a few more notes of travel, for two reasons: first, that a few more joined with those already published and written will make a decent little volume; and second, that now or never (I think) is my time. The *keen* love and observation of the picturesque is ebbing away from me as I grow older, and I doubt whether a year or two hence I shall have it in me to describe houses and mountains, or even cathedrals and pictures. I don't know whether I shall do anything better, but I shall have been spoiled for this. The real, natural time,—if I *could,* would have been when I was abroad before. Mysterious and incontrollable (even to one's self) is the growth of one's mind. Little by little, I trust, my abilities will catch up with my ambitions.

I am glad to hear you have decided on the physiology and anatomy place for next year. Father mentioned it in a letter received about the same time with Alice's . . . I hope you will go on from success to success.

*   *   *

When he received WJ's essay in the *Nation* about the over-strenuousness of the American temperament and the need for leisure and relaxation, he added: "I read with great pleasure your *Vacations*. It was all very well worth saying, and was very well said."

After finishing *Roderick Hudson* in America, HJ went back to Europe again before it came out. WJ wrote him near the close of 1875: "*Roderick Hudson* seems to be a very common theme of conversation. . . . In looking through the volume it seems to me even better than it did, but I must tell you that I am again struck unfavorably by the tendency of the personages to reflect on themselves and give an acute critical scientific introspective classification of their own natures and states of mind, *à la* George Sand. Take warning once more."

WJ worried about the effect that living in France seemed to be having on HJ's writing:

"Keep watch and ward lest in your style you become too Parisian and lose your hold on the pulse of the great American public, to which after all you must pander for support. In your last *Tribune* letter . . . there were too many traces of Gallicism in manner. It will be a good thing for you to resolve never to use the word 'supreme,' and to take great care not to use 'delicate' in the French sense of a 'cultured and fastidious' person." But he then added: "Your second instalment of *The American* is prime. The morbid little clergyman is worthy of Ivan Sergeitch [Turgenieff]. I was not a little amused to find some of my own attributes in him.—I think you found my 'moral reaction' excessive when I was abroad."

*　*　*　*　*

Etretat, July 29, 1876

Dear Wm. . . . I am much obliged to you for your literary encouragement and advice—glad especially you like my novel. I can't judge it. Your remarks on my French tricks in my letters are doubtless most just, and shall be heeded. But it's an odd thing that such tricks should grow at a time when my last layers of resistance to a long-encroaching weariness and satiety with the French mind and its utterance has fallen from me like a garment. I have done with 'em, forever, and am turning English all over. I desire only to feed on English life and the contact of English minds—I wish greatly I knew some. Easy and smooth-flowing as life is in Paris, I would throw it over tomorrow for an even very small chance to plant myself for a while in England. If I had but a single good friend in London I would go thither. I have got nothing important out of Paris nor am likely to. My life there makes a much more succulent figure in your letters, my mention of its thin ingredients as it comes back to me, than in my own consciousness. A good deal of Boulevard and third-rate Americanism: few retributive relations otherwise. I know the Théâtre Français by heart!

*　*　*

To London he shortly went, and from there he discussed WJ's opinion of his next novel: [1]

"I was much depressed on reading your letter by your painful reflections on *The Europeans;* but now, an hour having elapsed, I am beginning to hold up my head a little; the more so as I think I myself estimate the book very justly and am aware of its extreme slightness. I think you take these things too rigidly and unimaginatively—too much as if an artistic experiment were a piece of conduct, to which one's life were somehow committed; but I think also that you're quite right in pronouncing the book 'thin' and empty. I don't at all despair, yet, of doing something fat. Meanwhile I hope you will continue to give me, when you can, your free impression of my performances. It is a great thing to have some one write to one of one's things as if one were a third person, and you are the only individual who will do this. I don't think however you are always right, by any means. . . . I don't trust your judgment altogether (if you will permit me to say so) about *details;* but I think you are altogether right in returning always to the importance of subject. I hold to this strongly; and if I don't as yet seem to proceed upon it more, it is because, being 'very artistic,' I have a constant impulse to try experiments of form, in which I wish to not run the risk of wasting or gratuitously using big situations. But to these I am coming now. It is something to have learned how to write, and when I look round me and see how few people (doing my sort of work) know how (to my sense,) I don't regret my step-by-step evolution."

HJ wrote to their mother, at the opening of 1879: "I have just been reading his two articles—the *Brute and Human Intellect* and the one in *Mind,* which have given me a very elevated idea of his abilities. Tell him I perused them with great interest, sufficient comprehension, and extreme profit." The second essay referred to was "Are We Automata?" in which WJ developed his conception of the "essentially selective or interested character" of consciousness.

In discussing *Confidence,* the weakest of his novels, HJ carried farther his developing conception of the relation between subject-matter and form:

"Only a line to acknowledge your note . . . acknowledging my return of your manuscript, and containing strictures on *Confidence,* etc. The latter were, I think, just (as regards the lightness of the tale), but I also think that, read as a whole, the thing will appear more grave. I have got (Heaven knows!) plenty of gravity within me, and I don't know why I can't put it more into the things I write. It comes from modesty and delicacy (to drop these qualities for the moment); or at

---

[1] WJ's letters to HJ between 1876 and 1881, the period of the latter's first residence in London, do not appear to have been preserved.

least from the high state of development of my artistic conscience, which is so greatly attached to *form* that it shrinks from believing that it can supply it properly for *big* subjects, and yet is constantly studying the way to do so; so that at last, I am sure, it will arrive. I am determined that the novel I write this next year shall be 'big.' "

The novel he was then planning was *The Portrait of a Lady*, his first masterpiece. WJ seems to have thought well of it, as, to a lesser extent, of *Washington Square*, if we can judge from HJ's answer:

"Thank you for what you say about my two novels. The young man in *Washington Square* is not a portrait—he is sketched from the outside merely, not *fouillé*. The only good thing in the story is the girl. The other book increases, I think, in merit and interest as it goes on, and being told in a more spacious, expansive way than its predecessors, is inevitably more human, more sociable. It was the constant effort at *condensation* (which you used always to drum into my head, apropos of Mérimée etc., and when I was young you bullied me) that has deprived my former things of these qualities. I shall read what Grant Allen and Fiske reply to you in the *Atlantic*, but shall be sure not to enter into what they say as I did into your article, which I greatly appreciated."

WJ's article was "Great Men, Great Thoughts, and Their Environment." Here he insisted on the importance of individuals in shaping history, taking issue thereby with the school of Spencer, and particularly with Grant Allen. HJ always delighted in watching his brother's mind in action. He wrote to their father after a visit from WJ in London this same year:

"It is very delightful to see him again, and we have had much interesting talk, which as well as most other things, he seems to enjoy. . . . I find him very little changed, looking no older and with the same tendency to descant on his sensations—but with all his vivacity and Williamcy of mind undimmed."

Since the next years were broken up for HJ by his visit in America, and then by the deaths of their parents, he did not start on another big piece of work until 1884. He wrote WJ that fall: "It is a better subject than I have ever had before, and I think will be much the best thing I have done yet. It is called *The Bostonians*. I shall be much abused for the title, but it exactly and literally fits the story, and is much the best, simplest and most dignified I could have chosen."

WJ's reaction, upon reading the first installment in the *Century*, has again unfortunately been lost, but HJ's answer makes clear his point of attack. Elizabeth Peabody, Hawthorne's sister-in-law, had outlived her generation, but remained true to it by still continuing to attend every lecture. WJ himself had gaily declared that her perennial curiosity made her "the most dissolute woman" in Boston. In disclaiming any intention of basing his Miss Birdseye upon her, HJ provides a detailed description of the way in which he evolved his characters:

"I am quite appalled by your note . . . in which you assault me on the subject of my having painted a 'portrait from life' of Miss Peabody! I was in some measure prepared for it by Lowell's (as I found the other day) taking for granted that she had been my model, and an allusion to the same effect in a note from Aunt Kate. Still, I didn't expect the charge to come from you. I hold that I have done nothing to deserve it, and think your tone on the subject singularly harsh and unfair. I care not a straw what people in general may say about Miss Birdseye—they can say nothing more idiotic and insulting than they have already said about all my books in which there has been any attempt to represent things or persons in America; but I should be very sorry—in fact deadly sick, or fatally ill—if I thought Miss Peabody *herself* supposed I intended to represent her. I absolutely had no shadow of such an intention. I have not seen Miss P. for twenty years, I never had but the most casual observation of her, I didn't know whether she was alive or dead, and she was not in the smallest degree my starting-point or example. Miss Birdseye was evolved entirely from my moral consciousness, like every other person I have ever drawn, and originated in my desire to make a figure who should embody in a sympathetic, pathetic, picturesque, and at the same time grotesque way, the humanitary and *ci-devant* transcendental tendencies which I thought it highly probable I should be accused of treating in a contemptuous manner in so far as they were otherwise represented in the tale. I wished to make this figure a woman, because so it would be more touching, and an old, weary, battered and simple-minded woman because that deepened the same effect. I elaborated her in my mind's eye—and after I had got going reminded myself that my creation would perhaps be identified with Miss Peabody—*that* I freely admit. So I have in mind the sense of being careful, at the same time that I didn't see what I could do but go my way, according to my own fancy, and make my image as living as I saw it. The one definite thing about which I had a scruple was some touch about Miss Birdseye's spectacles—I remembered that Miss Peabody's were always in the wrong place; but I didn't see, really, why I should deprive myself of an effect (as regards this point) which is common to a thousand old people. So I thought no more about Miss P. *at all*, but simply strove to realize my vision. If I have made my old woman *live* it is my misfortune, and the thing is doubtless a rendering, a vivid rendering, of my idea. If it is at the same time a rendering of Miss P. I am absolutely irresponsible—and extremely sorry for the accident. If there is any chance of its being represented to *her* that I have undertaken to reproduce her in a novel I will immediately write to her, in the most respectful manner, to say that I have done nothing of the kind, that an old survivor of the New England Reform period was an indispensable personage in my story, that my paucity of data and not my repletion is the faulty side of the whole picture, that, as I went, I had no sight or thought of her, but only of an imaginary figure which was much nearer to me, and that in short I have the vanity to claim that Miss Birdseye is a creation. You may think I protest too much: but I am alarmed by the sentence in your letter—'It is really a pretty bad business,' and haunted by the idea that this may apply to some rumour you have heard of Miss Peabody's feeling *atteinte*. I can imagine no other reason why you should call the picture of Miss Birdseye a 'bad business,' or indeed any business at all. . . . Miss Birdseye is a subordinate figure in *The Bostonians*, and after appearing in the first and second numbers vanishes till toward the end, where she re-enters, briefly, and pathetically and honourably dies. But though subordinate, she is, I think, the best figure in the book; she is treated with respect throughout, and every virtue of heroism and disinterestedness is attributed to her. She is represented as the embodiment of pure, the purest philanthropy. The story is, I think, the best fiction I have written, and I expected you, if you said anything about it, would intimate that you thought as much—so that I find this charge on the subject of Miss Peabody a very cold douche indeed."

When WJ, some months later, added more relevant criticism, HJ sadly agreed:

"I concur absolutely in all you say, and am more conscious than any reader of the redundancy of the book in the way of descriptive psychology, etc. There is far too much of the sort of thing you animadvert upon, though there is in the public mind at the same time a truly ignoble levity and puerility and aversion to any attempt on the part of a novelist to establish his people solidly. All the same, I have overdone it—for reasons I won't take time to explain. It would have been much less the case if I had ever seen a proof of *The Bostonians;* but not a page had I before me till the magazine was out. It is the same with the *Princess Casamassima*, though that story will be found probably less tedious, owing to my having made to myself all the reflections your letter contains, several months ago, and never ceased to make them since. The *Princess* will, I trust, appear more 'popular.' I fear *The Bostonians* will be, as a finished work, a fiasco, as not a word, echo or comment on the serial (save your remarks) have come to me (since the row about the first number) from any quarter whatever. The deathly silence seems to indicate that it has fallen flat. I hoped much of it, and shall be disappointed—having got no money for it, I hoped for a little glory. . . . But how can one murmur at one's success not being what one would like when one thinks of the pathetic, tragic ineffectualness of poor Father's lifelong effort, and the silence and oblivion that seem to have swallowed it up? Not a person to whom I sent of copy of your book [i.e., *Literary Remains*] in London, has given me a sign or sound in consequence, and not a periodical appears to have taken the smallest notice of it. It is terribly touching and when I think of the evolution of his productions and ideas, fills me with tears."

At this point WJ felt he had gone too far: "Your letter from Paris in reply to my 'strictures' on *The Bostonians* showed you in such an attitude of angelic humility that I wished I had ne'er been born rather than have written such things. The best advice I can give you as an author, and the last I shall now ever give you, is to imitate your own method in your shorter stories, and in *The American* and *Roderick Hudson*. No better models are possible." WJ also wrote to Alice at this time, in relation to his enthusiasm for Stevenson: "He is simply to me the most delightful of living writers,—except Harry."

When WJ had gone through the book in volume form the next spring, he gave his final judgment:

"I seize my pen the first leisure moment I have had for a week to tell you that I have read *The Bostonians* in the full flamingness of its bulk, and consider it an exquisite production. My growling letter was written to you before the end of Book I had appeared . . . and the suspense of narrative in that region, to let the relation of Olive and Verena grow, was enlarged by the vacant months between the numbers of the magazine, so that it seemed to me so slow a thing had ne'er been writ. Never again shall I attack one of your novels in the magazine. I've only read one number of *The Princess Casamassima*—though I hear all the people about me saying it is the best thing you've done yet. To return to *The Bostonians;* the last two books are simply sweet. There isn't a hair wrong in Verena, you've made her neither too little nor too much—but absolutely *liebenswürdig*. It would have been so easy to spoil her picture by some little excess or false note. Her moral situation, between Woman's rights and Ransom, is of course deep, and her discovery of the truth on the Central Park day, etc., inimitably given. Ransom's character, which at first did not become alive to me, does so, handsomely, at last. . . . I hear very little said of the book, and I imagine it is being less read than its predecessors. The truth about it, combining what I said in my previous letter with what I have just written, seems to be this, that it is superlatively well done, provided one admits that method of doing such a thing at all. Really the *datum* seems to me to belong rather to the region of fancy, but the treatment to that of the most elaborate realism. One can easily imagine the story cut out and made into a bright, short, sparkling thing of a hundred pages, which would have been an absolute success. But you have worked it up by dint of descriptions and psychologic commentaries into near 500—charmingly done for those who have the leisure and the peculiar mood to enjoy that amount of miniature work—but perilously near to turning away the great majority of readers who crave more matter and less art. I can truly say, however, that as I have lain on my back after dinner each day for ten days past reading it to myself, my enjoyment has been complete. I imagine that the inhabitants of other parts of the country have read it more than natives of these parts. They have bought it for the sake of the information. The way you have touched off the bits of American nature, Central Park, the Cape, etc., is exquisitely true and calls up just the feeling. Knowing you had done such a good thing makes the meekness of your reply to me last summer all the more wonderful."

But now HJ went ahead to point out what he had come to believe were weaknesses in the method of this novel:

"Thank you for your letter . . . on the subject of *The Bostonians*. Everything you said in it gratified me extremely—and very superfluous was your retraction of what you wrote before (last autumn while the thing was going on in the magazine and before you had more than dipped into it.) I myself subscribe just as much to those strictures now as I did then—and find 'em very just. All the middle part is too diffuse and insistent—far too describing and explaining and expatiating. The whole thing is too long and dawdling. This came from the fact (partly) that I had the sense of knowing terribly little about the kind of life I had attempted to describe—and felt a constant pressure to make the picture substantial by thinking it out—pencilling and 'shading.' I was afraid of the reproach (having *seen* so little of the whole business treated of,) of being superficial and cheap—and in short I should have been much more rapid, and had a lighter hand, with a subject concerned with people and things of a nature more near to my experience. Let me also say that if I have displeased people, as I hear, by calling the book *The Bostonians*—this was done wholly without invidious intention. I hadn't a dream of generalizing—but thought the title simple and handy, and meant only to designate Olive and Verena by it, as they appeared to the mind of Ransom, the southerner and outsider looking at them from New York. I didn't even *mean* it to cover Miss Birdseye and the others, though it might very well. I shall write another: *The Other Bostonians*. However, this only by the way, for after one of my productions is finished and cast upon the waters it has, for me, quite sunk beneath the surface—I cease to care for it and transfer my interest to the one I am next trying to float."

In the meantime WJ was continuing to do the massive ground-work for his long delayed *Psychology*, which for a decade he was always hoping to finish "next year." A note to HJ in the spring of 1885 is typical of many others: "I have made a start with my psychology which I shall work at, temperately, through the vacation and hope to get finished a year from next fall, *sans faute*. Then shall the star of your romances be eclipst."

Two years later he was saying:

"I have been writing with something more like continuity this winter, and shall to all appearance have the book finished a year from now. . . . How you produce volume after volume the way you do is more than I can conceive, but you haven't to forge every sentence in the teeth of irreducible and stubborn facts as I do. It is like walking through the densest brushwood. Howells told me the other night that he had written a rousing eulogy of your *Princess* for the next *Harper*, and he hadn't a fault to find with it. Rev. John Brooks, a good man, interested in Socialism, was here this morning and called it 'a superb book.' It certainly has left a good taste in the mouth of both of *us*."

HJ, always encouraging, wrote that fall: "I hope indeed you may finish your *Psychology* by the date you desire. It will be a tough morsel for me to chew, but I don't despair of nibbling it slowly up." In the same letter he outlined his own future aims: "I have tried for a good while now to get *out* of society, as hard as certain people are supposed to try to get into it, and I am happy to say I am perceptibly succeeding. I have very large accumulations (of 'observation of the world,' etc.) and I now simply want elbow-room for the exercise, as it were, of my art. I have during the next ten years to do some things of a certain importance: if I don't, it won't be that I haven't tried hard or that I am wanting in an extreme ambition."

This drew a response from WJ on Thanksgiving day, 1887:

"Your last letter was too good to answer promptly. It gave a better impression of your heartiness than any letter you ever writ, and I have been *im Stillen* living on that remembrance. . . . I am glad you write so sanguinely of your work. That's the way to feel. If only one *can* feel so. A strange coldness has come over me with reference to all my deeds and productions, within the past six months. I don't know whether it be the passage under the meridian of forty-five years, or due to a more reparable cause, but everything I've done and shall do seems so *small*. Meanwhile I'm very well again as to eyes, sleep, and working and walking power."

He continued to find time for HJ's new work, though they seem now to have agreed that he had better not try to read any more stories in serial form:

"I have followed your advice and not looked at *The Aspern Papers*. But I have taken great satisfaction in the Stevenson and Maupassant articles. . . . In your Maupassant . . . you used that author's own directness more than is your wont, and I think with great good effect. If you keep on writing like that I'll never utter another cavil as long as I live. Did you work over it more than over other things, or did it *couler de source* in that form? . . . I rejoice in your obesity and your fencing. As for me, chest-weights are as high as I can fly. . . .

"I must also thank for *Partial Portraits* and *The Reverberator*. The former, I of course knew (except the peculiarly happy Woolson one), but have read several of 'em again with keen pleasure, especially the Turgenieff. *The Reverberator* is masterly and exquisite. I quite squealed through it, and all the household has amazingly enjoyed it. It shows the technical ease you have attained, that you can handle so delicate and difficult a fancy so lightly. It is simply delicious. . . . How you can keep up such a productivity and live, I don't see. All your time is your own, however, barring dinner-parties, and that makes a great difference."

The Reverberator, one of HJ's lightest-paced novels, a charming *jeu d'esprit* about Americans in Paris, was in the vein that WJ liked best. He mentioned it again that autumn:

"I hunger and thirst for more of those short stories which I have purposely avoided reading in their periodical shape. *The Reverberator* is immortal. Aldrich told me that you had a splendid serial for next year's *Atlantic*. I don't see how you can produce at such a rate, or how you find time for a line of reading or anything else. I should think you'd feel all hollowed out inwardly, and absolutely need to fill up. I am to have lots of reading and no writing to speak of this year, and expect to enjoy it hugely. It does one good to read classic books. For months past I've done nothing else, in behalf of my ethics class—Plato, Aristotle, Adam Smith, Butler, Paley, Spinoza, etc.—no book is celebrated without deserving it for some quality, and recenter books, certain never to be celebrated, have an awfully squashy texture."

On the question of the relation between reading and writing HJ replied:

"You are right in surmising that it must often be a grief to me not to get more time for reading—though not in supposing that I am 'hollowed out inside' by the limitations my existence has too obstinately attached to that exercise, combined with the fact that I produce a great deal. At times I do read almost as much as my wretched little *stomach* for it literally will allow, and on the whole I get much more time for it as the months and the years go by. I touched bottom, in the way of missing time, during the first half of my long residence in London—and traversed then a sandy desert, in that respect—where, however, I took on board such an amount of human and social information that if the same necessary alternatives were presented to me again I should make the same choice. One can read when one is middle-aged or old; but one can mingle in the world with fresh perceptions only when one is young.

The great thing is to be *saturated* with something—that is, in one way
or another, with life; and I chose the form of my saturation. Moreover
you exaggerate the degree to which my writing takes it out of my
mind, for I try to spend only the interest of my capital. . . . I am full
of gratulation on your enlarged classes, chances of reading, etc. . . .
You are entering the period of keen suspense about Cleveland, and I
share it even here. I have lately begun to receive and read the *Nation*
after a long interval—and it seems to me very rough. Was it *ever* so?"

In the summer of 1890 WJ could finally write:

"My dear Harry . . . The great event for me is the completion at
last of my tedious book. I have been at my desk with it every day since
I got back from Europe [last autumn], and up at four in the morning
with it for many a day of the last month. I have written every page four
or five times over, and carried it 'on my mind' for nine years past, so
you may imagine the relief. Besides, I am glad to appear at last as a man
who has done something more than make phrases and projects. I will
send you a copy, in the fall, I trust, though [the printer] is so inert
about starting the proofs that we may not get through till midwinter or
later. As 'Psychologies' go, it is a good one, but psychology is in such
an ante-scientific condition that the whole present generation of them
is predestined to become unreadable old medieval lumber, as soon as the
first genuine tracks of insight are made. The sooner the better, for me!"

Three weeks later he added:

"At last you've done it and no mistake. *The Tragic Muse* caps the
climax. It is a most original, wonderful, delightful and admirable production. It must make you feel jolly to have so masterfully and effort-
lessly answered the accusation that you could do nothing but the international and cosmopolitan business; for cosmopolitan as the whole atmosphere of the book is, yet the people and setting are most easily and
naturally English, and the perfect air of good society which reigns
through the book is one of its most salient characteristics. It leaves a
good taste in one's mouth, everyone in it is human and good, and although the final winding up is, as usual with you, rather a losing of the
story in the sand, yet that is the way in which things lose themselves in
real life. The only thing I positively find to object to in the book is the
length of the chapter on Mr. Nash's portrait, which is a little too much
in the Hawthornian allegorizing vein for you.

"I have nothing to say in detail. The whole thing hangs together
most intimately and well; and it is truly a spectacle for rejoicing to see
that by the sort of practice a man gives himself he attains the plenitude
and richness which you have at last got. Your sentences are straighter
and simpler than before, and your felicities of observation are on every
page. . . . The whole thing is an exquisite mirage which remains afloat
in the air of one's mind. I imagine that that sort of thing is extremely

educative to a certain 'section' of the community. As for the question of the size of your public, I tremble. The work is too refined, too elaborate and minute, and requires to be read with too much leisure to appeal to any but the select few. But you mustn't mind that. It will *always* have its audience. No reason, however, for not doing less elaborate things for wider audiences; which I hope ere long to have direct testimony that you have done.

". . . My proofs have only just begun coming in; but they promise to come thick and fast. I take little pride or pleasure in the accursed book, which has clung to me so long, but I shall be glad to have it out, just to show that I *can* write one book."

HJ answered from Vallombrosa where, for the first time in years, he had been drinking in nature, or rather "wandering through dusky woods and lying with a book on warm, breezy hillsides."

"I had from you some ten days ago a most delightful letter written just after the heroic perusal of my interminable novel. . . . It has plunged me into a glow of satisfaction which is far, as yet, from having faded. I can only thank you tenderly for seeing so much good in the clumsy thing. . . . I have no illusions of any kind about the book, and least of all about its circulation and 'popularity.' From these things I am quite divorced and never was happier than since the dissolution has been consecrated by (what seems to me) the highest authorities. One must go one's way and know what one's about and have a general plan and a private religion—in short have made up one's mind as to *ce qui en est* with a public the draggling after which simply leads one in the gutter. One has always a 'public' enough if one has an audible vibration —even if it should only come from one's self. I shall never make my fortune—nor anything like it; but—I know what I shall do, and it won't be bad."

This drew forth a warm reaction from Chocorua:

"It gave me great pleasure to get your letter from Vallombrosa about a fortnight ago. . . . You see now why I have been urging you all these years to take more of your vacation in the face of nature. Your last two letters have breathed a spirit of youth, a sort of *Lebenslust*, which has long been absent from them, and which nothing but mother earth can give. Alternation between her and the gas-lit life of corrupt capitals is the optimum for man here below. Neither element alone will do, but both must be there. I'm glad you've had such a vacation from writing. I don't see how either you or Howells can keep it up at such a rate. I am just now in the middle of his *Hazard of New Fortunes*, which is an extraordinarily vigorous production, quite up to Dickens I should say, in humor, detail of observation and geniality, with flexible human beings on the stage instead of puppets. With that work, your *Tragic Muse*, and last *but by no means least*, my *Psychology*, all appearing in it, the year 1890 will be known as the great epochal year in American literature."

That fall, just after his epoch-making work had appeared, WJ wrote to HJ:

"College begins with many changes in the Philosophical courses and a much smaller number of men to be dealt with than usual by me, though the subjects I have to treat are rather more arduous than heretofore, and my standard of what is good is so much higher that it is difficult to be satisfied with my work. I wish it were possible for me to make a living by my pen, as you do, but I can't, so there's an end. My book appeared two days since, and I've ordered the publishers to send a copy to you. Most of it is quite unreadable, but you may find some pages in the second volume that will go. Also the earlier pages of the chapter on *Consciousness of Self*. The infernal thing is too long to sell well, I'm afraid."

Alice, whose journal shows that she was a very alert reader of the *Psychology*, had her own version of this year in the family annals. In the course of discussing HJ's prospects in the theater, she noted: "Within the year he has published *The Tragic Muse*, brought out *The American*, and written a play, *Mrs. Vibert* (which Hare accepted), and his admirable comedy; combined with William's *Psychology*, not a bad show for one family!—especially if I get myself dead, the hardest job of all."

During the distraction of bringing *The American* finally to the stage, HJ wrote to WJ early in 1891:

"I blush to say that I haven't had freedom of mind or cerebral freshness (I find the drama much more *obsédant* than the novel) to tackle— more than dipping in just here and there—your mighty and magnificent book, which requires a stretch of leisure and an absence of 'crisis' in one's own egotistical little existence. As this is essentially a year of crisis, or of epoch-making, for me, I shall probably save up the great volumes till I can recline upon roses, the fruits of my production fever, and imbibe them like sips of sherbet, giving meanwhile all my cerebration to the condensation of masterpieces."

But once the first occasion had slipped, HJ seems never to have got round to writing WJ about his *Psychology*. His brotherly ardor was all aroused, however, by what he pronounced "the idiotic review" in the *Nation*. That was the review by Charles Saunders Peirce,[1] who began by remarking that WJ's work was probably "the most important contribution that has been made to the subject for many years." But HJ may well have overlooked this beginning in his indignation at the charges that WJ indulged in "idiosyncrasies of diction and tricks of

---

[1] See p. 107 above.

language," and that in his reckless scorn of rigorous logic, "it is his *métier* to subject to severe investigation any doctrine whatever that smells of intelligibility."

The 1890's were the years in which the brothers wrote least to each other about their work. This may have been due partly to the fact that they saw each other somewhat more, WJ being in Europe in 1892–3, and again for two years at the close of the decade. He was not in London, however, at the time of the performance of *Guy Domville*, the only one of HJ's new plays to be produced; and since HJ was mainly preoccupied with the stage until that play's failure in 1895, there was little during those years for WJ to comment upon. For his own part, WJ was increasingly taken up with the public lectures that finally composed both *The Will to Believe* (1897) and *Talks to Teachers on Psychology and to Students upon Some of Life's Ideals* (1899), upon neither of which have comments from HJ survived. The only mention of either comes from WJ in the spring of 1897: "A good letter . . . from you the other day . . . announcing the completion of a heavy job of work, and the arrival of my Essays, which *pray* don't read except for pleasure—they may well not give you much of that, being so abstract."

WJ, however, seldom passed by any of HJ's publications. No sooner had HJ put in print, in 1894, his still unproduced plays, than WJ commented:

"Your *Theatricals* came duly and were eagerly read—I regret to say with a certain type of disappointment by most of us. The last one [*Disengaged*] is entirely for acting purposes. . . . I should think it might be effective enough with Mrs. Jasper embodied in Rehan flesh and dimples; but for reading, the *matter* is so slight, that my only wonder is that you could have carried it through with such nerve, being on the whole in a line so unlike the spontaneous bent of your genius. *Tenants* has more body, and well acted would I think be very effective indeed. But Mrs. Vibert doesn't show her inside nature enough, and her relation to Lurcher is too positive a thing to be left merely indicated. In other words, the stuff is of too weighty a nature to be so sketchily treated, and a curious unsympathetic and uncanny impression remains on the reader. But these are my first crude personal reactions. You know the real defects and merits more than I ever can; and meanwhile I can't enough admire the transposition, so complete, of your composing attitude, to the requirements of the orchestra stalls and away from those of the library. It *must* bear fruit sometime, only give up everything for *emotionality and breadth*, and make your repartees turn less on the verbal suggestions of the previous sentence!"

After the catastrophic first night of *Guy Domville*, HJ turned naturally to his brother:

* * * * *

London, January 9, 1895

My dear William,—I never cabled to you on Sunday 6th (about the first night of my play,) because, as I daresay you will have gathered from some despatches or newspapers (if there have been any, and you have seen them,) the case was too complicated. Even now it's a sore trial to me to have to write about it—weary, bruised, sickened, disgusted as one is left by the intense, the cruel ordeal of a first night that —after the immense labour of preparation and the unspeakable tension of suspense—has, in a few brutal moments, not gone well. In three words the delicate, picturesque, extremely human and extremely artistic little play was taken profanely by a brutal and ill-disposed gallery which had shown signs of malice prepense from the first and which, held in hand till the end, kicked up an infernal row at the fall of the curtain. There followed an abominable quarter of an hour during which all the forces of civilization in the house waged a battle of the most gallant, prolonged and sustained applause with the hoots and jeers and catcalls of the roughs, whose *roars* (like those of a cage of beasts at some infernal "zoo") were only exacerbated (as it were) by the conflict. It was a cheering scene, as you may imagine, for a nervous, sensitive, exhausted author to face—and you must spare my going over again the horrid hour, or those of disappointment and depression that have followed it; from which last, however, I am rapidly and resolutely, thank God, emerging. The "papers" have, into the bargain, been mainly ill-natured and densely stupid and vulgar; but the only two dramatic critics who count, W. Archer and Clement Scott, have done me more justice. Meanwhile all *private* opinion is apparently one of extreme admiration—I have been flooded with letters of the warmest protest and assurance. . . . Everyone who was there has either written to me or come to see me—I mean every one I know and many people I don't. Obviously the little play, which I strove to make as broad, as simple, as clear, as British, in a word, as possible, is over the heads of the *usual* vulgar theatre-going London public—and the chance of its going for a while (which is too early to measure) will depend wholly on its holding on long enough to attract the *unusual*. I was there the second night (Monday, 7th) when, before a full house—a remarkably good "money" house Alexander told me—it went singularly well. But it's soon to see or to say, and I'm prepared for the worst. The thing fills me with horror for the abysmal vulgarity and brutality of the theatre and its regular public, which God knows I have had intensely even when working (from motives as "pure" as pecuniary motives *can* be) against it; and I feel as if the simple freedom of mind thus begotten to return to one's legitimate form would be simply by itself a divine solace for everything. Don't worry about me: I'm a Rock. If the play has no life on the stage I shall publish it; it's altogether the best thing I've done. You would understand better the elements of the case if you had seen the thing it followed (*The Masqueraders*) and the thing that is now succeeding at the Haymarket—the thing of Oscar Wilde's. On the basis of *their* being plays, or successes, my thing is necessarily neither. Doubtless, moreover, the want of a roaring actuality, simplified to a few big *familiar* effects, in my subject—an episode in the history of an old English Catholic family in the last century—militates against it, with all usual theatrical people, who don't want plays (from variety and nimbleness of fancy) of different *kinds*, like books and stories, but only of one kind, which their stiff, rudimentary, clumsily-working vision recognizes as the kind they've had before. And yet I had tried so to meet them! But one can't make a sow's ear out of a silk purse.—I can't write more—and don't ask for more details. This week will probably determine the fate of the piece. If there is increased advance-booking it will go on. If there isn't, it will be withdrawn, and with it all my little hope of profit. The time one has given to such an affair from the very first to the very last represents in all—so inconceivably great, to the uninitiated, is the amount—a pitiful, tragic bankruptcy of hours that might have been rendered retroactively golden. But I am not plangent —one must take the thick with the thin—and I have such possibilities of another and better sort before me. I am only sorry for your and Alice's having to be so sorry for yours forever, Henry.

* * *

WJ believed that he knew the reason for HJ's failure as a dramatist when he spoke to Ellen Emmet of HJ's having "been weaned" from "the vital facts of human character . . . for fifteen years at least." He was growing less sympathetic with HJ's style, and what he said in 1896 foreshadowed the disagreement that was to come to a head over *The Golden Bowl*: "I got and have just read *Embarrassments* [1]—I wish I could say hurrah with a whole heart, but this recent manner of yours of using such an excessively small bit of *matter*, and that so fanciful, to show a great deal of art by, seems to me to be full of peril, if you get deeper into it." But unlike later nationalist critics, WJ did not blame HJ's expatriation for such attenuation. He had, in fact, written him, during his own trip abroad in 1893: "You have done the best thing, in putting yourself in the strongest *milieu* to be found on earth." Furthermore he liked some of HJ's *nouvelles* of this period, particularly *The Spoils of Poynton* (1897)—"which I think one of your best recent things"; and he remarked a few years later of *The Better Sort*: [2] "You certainly excel in stories of that size. It is hard enamel finish."

---

[1] This volume contained, among other stories, "The Next Time" and "The Figure in the Carpet."

[2] Including "The Story in It," "The Birthplace," and "The Beast in the Jungle."

But after visiting at Rye at the turn of the century, WJ felt that they had been drifting apart: "He and I are so utterly different in all our observances and springs of action, that we can't rightly judge each other. I even feel great shrinking from urging him to pay us a visit, fearing it might yield him little besides painful shocks." Meanwhile HJ had been anxious about WJ's prolonged trouble with his heart, and wrote that he "could howl with sympathy" at the thought that WJ had not even felt himself up to doing the reading for his Gifford lectures. When these had finally been delivered and published, HJ wrote, in the midst of entertaining: "I am reading *The Varieties of Religious Experience* with such rapturous deliberation as so many Emmets in the air . . . permit."

That fall came another important exchange:

"I have read *The Wings of the Dove* (for which all thanks!) but what shall I say of a book constructed on a method which so belies everything that *I* acknowledge as law? You've reversed every traditional canon of story-telling (especially the fundamental one of *telling* the story, which you carefully avoid) and have created a new *genre littéraire* which I can't help thinking perverse, but in which you nevertheless *succeed*, for I read with interest to the end (many pages, and innumerable sentences twice over to see what the dickens they could possibly mean) and all with unflagging curiosity to know what the upshot might become. It's very *distingué* in its way, there are touches unique and inimitable, but it's a 'rum' way; and the worst of it is that I don't know whether it's fatal and inevitable with you, or deliberate and possible to put off and on. At any rate it is your own, and no one can drive you out or supplant you, so pray send along everything else you do, whether in this line or not, and it will add great solace to our lives.

" 'In its way' the book is most *beautiful*—the great thing is the way —I went fizzling about concerning it, and expressing my wonder all the while I was reading it."

To this HJ rejoined at once:

"Your reflections on *The Wings of the Dove* greatly interest me. Yet, after all, I don't know that I can very explicitly *meet* them. Or rather, really, there is too much to say. One writes as one *can*—and also as one sees, judges, feels, thinks, and I feel and think so much on the ignoble state to which in this age of every cheapness I see the novel as a form, reduced, that there is doubtless greatly, with me, the element of what I would as well as of what I 'can.' At any rate my stuff, such as it is, is inevitable for me. Of that there is no doubt. But I should think you might well fail of joy in it—for I certainly feel that it is, in its way, more and more positive. Don't despair, however, even yet, for I feel that in its way, as I say, there may be still other variations of way that will more or less *donner le change*."

No comment from WJ about *The Ambassadors* remains among his letters. In the spring of its appearance HJ opened the correspondence that led to his trip to America. He was occupied, almost until sailing, with *The Golden Bowl*: "I have been pressing hard toward the finish of a long book, still *un*finished (but not very much thank heaven!) which I am doing with such perfection that every inch is done over and over: which makes it come expensive in the matter of time. It has also emptied me, daily, of nervous fluid and shy of the sight, after 2 p.m., of quarto paper." WJ did not read this novel until his brother was back in Europe again, but while HJ was still in America, WJ said that he had been hearing "the most extravagant opinions about the charm of your lectures. *There's* a new profession for you, any day, if you can stand it!—and me, who warned you that you never could do it!" When he had seen one of these lectures he added: "I read your Balzac yesterday. It is fine, and shows I think that you should in general be read *aloud*."

He was much less happy about *The Golden Bowl*:

"It put me, as most of your recenter long stories have put me, in a very puzzled state of mind. I don't enjoy the kind of 'problem,' especially when, as in this case, it is treated as problematic (*viz.*, the adulterous relations between Charlotte and the Prince), and the method of narration by interminable elaboration of suggestive reference (I don't know what to call it, but you know what I mean) goes agin the grain of all my own impulses in writing; and yet in spite of it all, there is a brilliancy and cleanness of effect, and in this book especially a high-toned social atmosphere that are unique and extraordinary. Your methods and my ideals seem the reverse, the one of the other—and yet I have to admit your extreme success in this book. But why won't you, just to please Brother, sit down and write a new book, with no twilight or mustiness in the plot, with great vigor and decisiveness in the action, no fencing in the dialogue, no psychological commentaries, and absolute straightness in the style? Publish it in my name, I will acknowledge it, and give you half the proceeds. Seriously, I wish you *would*, for you *can*; and I should think it would tempt you, to embark on a 'fourth manner.' You of course know these feelings of mine without my writing them down, but I'm 'nothing if not' outspoken. Meanwhile you can despise me and fall back on such opposite emotions as Howells's, who seems to admire you without restriction, as well as on the records of the sale of the book."

Quickened perhaps by the newspaper flurry over HJ's return to America, the sales of *The Golden Bowl* had been considerably greater here than those of his other later books, but he did not resort to that argument in answering:

"I mean (in response to what you write me of your having read *The Golden B.*) to try to produce some uncanny form of thing, in fiction, that will gratify you, as Brother—but let me say, dear William, that I shall greatly be humiliated if you *do* like it, and thereby lump it, in your affection, with things, of the current age, that I have heard you express admiration for and that I would sooner descend to a dishonoured grave than have written. Still I *will* write you your book, on that two-and-two-make-four system on which all the awful truck that surrounds us is produced, and *then* descend to my dishonoured grave—taking up the art of the slate pencil instead of, longer, the art of the brush (*vide* my lecture on Balzac.) But it is, seriously, too late at night, and I am too tired, for me to express myself on this question—beyond saying that I'm always sorry when I hear of your reading anything of mine, and always hope you won't—you seem to me so constitutionally unable to 'enjoy' it, and so condemned to look at it from a point of view remotely alien to mine in writing it, and to the conditions out of which, *as* mine, it has inevitably sprung—so that all the intentions that have been its main reason for being (with *me*) appear never to have reached you at all—and you appear even to assume that the life, the elements forming its subject-matter, deviate from felicity in not having an impossible analogy with the life of Cambridge. I see nowhere about me done or dreamed of the things that alone for me constitute the *interest* of the doing of the novel—and yet it is in a sacrifice of them on their very own ground that the thing you suggest to me evidently consists. It shows how far apart and to what different ends we have had to work out (very naturally and properly!) our respective intellectual lives. And yet I can read *you* with rapture—having three weeks ago spent three or four days with Manton Marble at Brighton and found in his hands ever so many of your recent papers and discourses, which, having margin of mornings in my room, through both breakfasting and lunching there (by the habit of the house,) I found time to read several of—with the effect of asking you earnestly, to address me some of those that I so often, in Irving St., saw you address to others who were not your brother. I had no time to read them there. Philosophically, in short, I am 'with' you, almost completely, and you ought to take account of this and get me over altogether."

To this WJ responded, from California:

"Your last was your delightful reply to my remarks about your 'third manner,' wherein you said that you would consider your bald head dishonored if you ever came to pleasing *me* by what you wrote, so shocking was my taste. Well! only write *for* me, and leave the question of pleasing open! I have to admit that in *The Golden Bowl* and *The Wings of the Dove*, you have succeeded *in getting there* after a fashion, in spite of the perversity of the method and its *longness*, which I am not the only one to deplore."

A few months later, after visiting San Francisco on the day after its great disaster in order to gather material for a paper on "Some Mental

Effects of the Earthquake," WJ returned to Cambridge. He found waiting for him there one of the first installments of *The American Scene*:

"I have just read your paper on Boston in the *North American Review*. I am glad you threw away the scabbard and made your critical remarks so straight. What you say about 'pay' here being the easily won 'salve' for privations, in view of which we cease to 'mind' them, is as true as it is strikingly pat. *Les intellectuels*, wedged between the millionaires and the handworkers, are the really pinched class here. They feel the frustrations and they can't get the salve. *My* attainment of so much pay in the past few years brings home to me what an all-benumbing salve it is. That whole article is of your best."

In the spring of 1907, when he had read the whole volume, WJ expressed his most detailed reaction to his brother's latest style:

"Dearest H. . . . I've been so overwhelmed with work, and the mountain of the *Unread* has piled up so, that only in these days . . . have I been able to settle down to your *American Scene*, which in its peculiar way seems to me *supremely great*. You know how opposed your whole 'third manner' of execution is to the literary ideals which animate my crude and Orson-like breast, mine being to say a thing in one sentence as straight and explicit as it can be made, and then to drop it forever; yours being to avoid naming it straight, but by dint of breathing and sighing all round and round it, to arouse in the reader who may have had a similar perception already (Heaven help him if he hasn't!) the illusion of a solid object, made (like the 'ghost' at the Polytechnic) wholly out of impalpable materials, air, and the prismatic interferences of light, ingeniously focused by mirrors upon empty space. But you *do* it, that's the queerness! And the complication of innuendo and associative reference on the enormous scale to which you give way to it does so *build out* the matter for the reader that the result is to solidify, by the mere bulk of the process, the like perception from which *he* has to start. As air, by dint of its volume, will weigh like a corporeal body; so his own poor little initial perception, swathed in this gigantic envelopment of suggestive atmosphere, grows like a germ into something vastly bigger and more substantial. But it's the rummest method for one to employ systematically as you do nowadays; and you employ it at your peril. In this crowded and hurried reading age, pages that require such close attention remain unread and neglected. You can't skip a word if you are to get the effect, and 19 out of 20 worthy readers grow intolerant. The method seems perverse: 'Say it *out*, for God's sake,' they cry, 'and have done with it.' And so I say now, give us *one* thing in your older directer manner, just to show that, in spite of your paradoxical success in this unheard-of method, you *can* still write according to accepted canons. Give us that interlude;

and then continue like the 'curiosity of literature' which you have become. For gleams and innuendoes and felicitous verbal insinuations you are unapproachable, but the *core* of literature is solid. Give it to us *once* again! The bare perfume of things will not support existence, and the effect of solidity you reach is but perfume and simulacrum.

"For God's sake don't *answer* these remarks, which (as Uncle Howard used to say of Father's writings) are but the peristaltic belchings of my own crabbed organism. For one thing, your account of America is largely one of its omissions, silences, vacancies. You work them up like solids, for those readers who already germinally perceive them (to others you are *totally* incomprehensible). I said to myself over and over in reading: 'How much greater the triumph, if instead of dwelling thus only upon America's vacuities, he could make positive suggestion of what in "Europe" or Asia may exist to fill them.' That would be nutritious to so many American readers whose souls are only too ready to leap to suggestion, but who are now too inexperienced to know what is meant by the contrast-effect from which alone your book is written. If you could supply the background which is the foil, in terms more full and positive! At present it is supplied only by the abstract geographic term 'Europe.' But of course anything of that kind is excessively difficult; and you will probably say that you *are* supplying it all along by your novels. Well, the verve and animal spirits with which you can keep your method going, first on one place then on another, through all those tightly printed pages is something marvelous; and there are pages surely doomed to be immortal, those on the 'drummers,' *e.g.*, at the beginning of 'Florida.'[1] They are in the best sense Rabelaisian.

"But a truce, a truce! I had no idea, when I sat down, of pouring such a bath of my own subjectivity over you. Forgive! forgive! and don't reply, don't at any rate in the sense of defending yourself, but only in that of attacking *me*, if you feel so minded. I have just finished the proofs of a little book called *Pragmatism* which even you *may* enjoy reading. It is a very 'sincere' and, from the point of view of ordinary philosophy-professorial manners, a very unconventional utterance, not particularly original at any one point, yet, in the midst of the literature of the way of thinking which it represents, with just that amount of squeak or shrillness in the voice that enables one book to *tell*, when others don't, to supersede its brethren, and be treated later as 'representative.' I shouldn't be surprised if ten years hence it should be rated as 'epoch-making,' for of the definitive triumph of that general way of thinking I can entertain no doubt whatever—I believe it to be something quite like the protestant reformation.

---

[1] See pp. 662–7 below.

"You can't tell how happy I am at having thrown off the nightmare of my 'professorship.' As a 'professor' I always felt myself a sham, with its chief duties of being a walking encyclopedia of erudition. I am now at liberty to be a *reality*, and the comfort is unspeakable—literally unspeakable, to be my own man, after 35 years of being owned by others. I can now live for truth pure and simple, instead of for truth accommodated to the most unheard-of requirements set by others. . . . Your affectionate W. J."

HJ was greatly interested by the news of WJ's retirement: "I enter immensely into the deep joy of your liberation from the long incubus of your lectures and the real possession of your time and genius. It's magnificent and oh so grandly auspicious, to think of!—altogether worth having so wearily waited for. Nothing is good that one *hasn't* waited for—nothing." On the subject of *The American Scene* he said simply: "You shall have, after a little more patience, a reply to your so rich and luminous reflections on my book—a reply almost as interesting as, and far more illuminating than, your letter itself." He seems not to have got to that reply before WJ had added, a few months later: "I have just been reading to Mrs. Bryce, with great gusto on her part and renewed gusto on mine, the first few pages of your chapter on Florida in *The American Scene. Köstlich* stuff! I had just been reading to myself almost 50 pages of the New England part of the book, and fairly melting with delight over the Chocorua portion. Evidently that book will last, and bear reading over and over again—a few pages at a time, which is the right way for 'literature' fitly so called. It all makes me wish that we had you here again, and you will doubtless soon come."

To this HJ answered:

"Why the devil I didn't write to you after reading your *Pragmatism* —how I kept from it—I can't now explain save by the very fact of the spell itself (of interest and enthralment) that the book cast upon me; I simply sank down, under it, into such depths of submission and assimilation that *any* reaction, very nearly, even that of acknowledgment, would have had almost the taint of dissent or escape. Then I was lost in the wonder of the extent to which all my life I have (like M. Jourdain) unconsciously pragmatised. You are immensely and universally *right*, and I have been absorbing a number more of your followings-up of the matter in the American (Journal of Psychology?) which your devouring devotee Manton Marble . . . plied, and always on invitation does ply, me with. I feel the reading of the book, at all events to have been really the event of my summer. In which connection (that of 'books'), I am infinitely touched by your speaking of having read parts of my *American Scene* . . . to Mrs. Bryce—paying them the tribute of that test of their value. Indeed the tribute of your calling the whole thing '*köstlich* stuff' and saying it will remain to *be* read so and really gauged, gives me more pleasure than I can say, and quickens my regret and pain at the way the fates have been all against (all finally and definitely now) my having been able to carry out my plan and do a second instalment, embodying more and complimentary impressions. Of course I *had* a plan—and the second vol. would have attacked the subject (and my general mass of impression) at various *other* angles, thrown off various other pictures, in short *contributed* much more. But the thing was not to be."

After reading *A Pluralistic Universe*, HJ again professed himself a disciple:

"All this time I'm not thanking you in the competent way for your *Pluralistic* volume—which now I can effusively do. I read it, while in town, with a more thrilled interest than I can say; with enchantment, with pride, and almost with comprehension. It may sustain and inspire you a little to know that I'm *with* you, all along the line—and can conceive of no sense in any philosophy that is not yours! As an artist and a 'creator' I can catch on, hold on, to pragmatism and can work in the light of it and apply it; finding, in comparison, everything else (so far as I know the same!) utterly irrelevant and useless—vainly and coldly parallel!"

In the fall of 1909, when WJ's prolific final period had added *The Meaning of Truth*, HJ declared again that he had embraced pragmatism, without ever making clear quite what he implied thereby:

"I have beautiful communications from you all too long unacknowledged and unrequited. . . . To these I add the arrival, still more recently, of your brave new book, which I fell upon immediately and have quite passionately absorbed—to within 50 pages of the end; a great number previous to which I have read this evening—which makes me late to begin this. I find it of thrilling interest, triumphant and brilliant, and am lost in admiration of your wealth and power. I palpitate as you make out your case (since it seems to me you so utterly do,) as I under no romantic spell ever palpitate now; and into that case I enter intensely, unreservedly, and I think you would allow almost intelligently. I find you nowhere as difficult as you surely make everything for your critics. Clearly you are winning a great battle and great will be your fame. . . .

"I broke this off last night and went to bed—and now add a few remarks after a grey soft windless and miraculously rainless day (under a most rainful sky,) which has had rather a sad hole made in it by a visitation from a young person from New York, addressed to me by poor Ida Smalley there as her bosom friend . . . who, arriving from town at 1:30, to luncheon, remained New Yorkily conversing till 6:30, when I got her off to Hastings, where she was—and I trust *is*—to sleep.

She stole from me the hour or two before my small evening feed in which I hoped to finish *The Meaning of Truth;* but I have done much toward this since that repast, and with a renewed eagerness of inglutition. You surely make philosophy more interesting and living than anyone has *ever* made it before, and by a real creative and undemolishable making; whereby all you write plays into *my* poor 'creative' consciousness and artistic vision and pretension with the most extraordinary suggestiveness and force of application and inspiration. Thank the powers —that is thank *yours!*—for a relevant and assimilable and *referable* philosophy, which is related to the rest of one's intellectual life otherwise and more conveniently than a fowl is related to a fish. In short, dearest William, the effect of these collected papers of your present volume—which I had read all individually before—seems to me exquisitely and adorably cumulative and, so to speak, consecrating; so that I, for my part feel Pragmatic invulnerability constituted. Much will this *suffrage* help the cause!"

The following summer HJ wrote from Chocorua, where he had escorted his ailing brother back from an abortive trip to Europe:

"I sit heavily stricken and in darkness—for from far back in dimmest childhood he had been my ideal Elder Brother, and I still, through all the years, saw in him, even as a small timorous boy yet, my protector, my backer, my authority and my pride. His extinction changes the face of life for me—besides the mere missing of his inexhaustible company and personality, originality, the whole unspeakably vivid and beautiful presence of him. And his noble intellectual vitality was still but at its climax—he had two or three ardent purposes and plans. He had cast them away, however, at the end—I mean that, dreadfully suffering, he wanted only to die."

BOOK FOUR

BOOK FOUR

WJ as a camper

HJ as a tourist

WJ as a camper

HJ as a tourist

CHARACTERISTIC MATURITY

In "The Art of Fiction" and "What is an Emotion?"—both produced in the same year (1884)—HJ and WJ each made one of his most searching pronouncements upon mind and character. HJ condensed into his essay what he had learned from twenty years of practicing his craft. Twenty-five years later again he was to distill into his prefaces his further subtle reflections. Those prefaces constitute, as he hoped they would, "a sort of comprehensive manual or *vademecum* for aspirants in our arduous profession." Indeed, there is nothing else quite like them in the art of criticism. But his earlier essay outlines his leading assumptions, and is the place where any reading of his criticism should start.

Composed three or four years after he had brought his method to maturity with *The Portrait of a Lady*, many of its passages, particularly those on the interrelation between character and action, seem surely to have been written with that novel in mind. The immediate stimulus was a lecture at the Royal Institution by Walter Besant, a novelist well known at that time, on "Fiction as One of the Fine Arts." HJ, who had learned from the example of France the necessary dependence, for a serious art, of practice upon theory, was delighted that fiction should at last be taken seriously in official English quarters. But he found Besant's blueprint for a novel somewhat standard and unimaginative. HJ by now believed the novel to be "the most magnificent form of art," a claim that had seldom been advanced, and a sign of the times in that it could hardly have been entertained if the drama or the larger forms of poetry had been thriving.

But the age in which HJ had grown up had been that of the great novelists, and in one of his earliest reviews he had spoken of the man "who of all novelists is certainly the most of one—Balzac." He based that opinion on the fact that the author of the *Comédie Humaine* "looked upon French society in the nineteenth century as a great

349

whole." But HJ also owed allegiance to the standards of a very different school, and for several years believed the author of *Felix Holt* and *Middlemarch* to be the most absorbing of philosophical novelists. Hawthorne's moral preoccupations were even more deeply interwoven with HJ's own background, but Hawthorne had written romances, and HJ's first conscious aim was to emulate the new school and be a realist.

By the time he produced "The Art of Fiction" he had assimilated many other models as well, and was a disciple neither of Balzac nor of George Eliot. He had responded most intimately to Turgenieff, and it is in keeping with his matured tastes that he singles out in his essay a story by Turgenieff to prefer over one by Flaubert. He expresses a similar preference for his friend Stevenson's *Treasure Island* over Edmond de Goncourt's *Chérie*. For though James took his stand for the psychological novel against that of adventure, and though Goncourt's subject, the development of a child's consciousness, was to become one of James' recurrent themes, he was always uneasy with the French realists' want of moral discrimination. Believing, with their master Balzac, that a great novelist writes the moral history of his age, he was none the less incisive in his objections to Besant's blunt insistence on "a conscious moral purpose."

He was to arrive at his most masterly formulation on this difficult question in his preface to *The Portrait of a Lady*, where, after reflecting on what he had learned from Turgenieff, he added: "There is, I think, no more nutritive or suggestive truth . . . than that of the perfect dependence of the 'moral' sense of a work of art on the amount of felt life concerned in producing it." With that formulation WJ would have been in hearty agreement, since he had himself declared: "It is the amount of life which a man feels that makes you value his mind." HJ had doubtless long since forgotten that sentence, but it had been in a letter to him in 1876, and in description of Turgenieff, whom WJ had been reading as a result of HJ's suggestion.

When WJ came to formulate his definitive conception of an emotion, he had developed greatly as a writer from the time when he had remarked of his first review: "Style is not my forte." In fact, when his *Principles of Psychology* appeared, it was adjudged even more of a literary than a scientific masterpiece. Howells, reviewing it for *Harper's*, noted at once that WJ took "an artistic pleasure" in the presentation of his facts, and that he wrote with an informality that could not fail to win the average reader. Several psychologists, on the other hand, were suspicious of his making the subject so lively. Stanley Hall was typical in deploring his mixture of science and philosophy, particularly in his "yearning" for the traditional conception of the soul. The best that Hall could say for him was that he "might be described as an *impressionist* in psychology."

WJ did not pretend that his volumes were based on much original experimental work, and for the most part he devoted himself to an interpretation of the whole range of extant knowledge in the field. His leading function may have been to give a wider currency to ideas rather than to be himself a coiner of many. But, as has often been said, if he was not the father of modern psychology, he was at all events present at the birth.

No other psychologist had anything like his equipment as a writer. He refused to make a separation between the scientist and the artist. He drew copiously upon philosophy and literature for his illustrations, and he realized instinctively that he must develop artistic skills of presentation if he was to fulfill his aim of keeping the reader in contact "with the actual conscious unity which each of us at all times feels himself to be." As a result, his *Psychology* has made a lasting place for itself in general literature, though the reader of other works in its field may be astonished by how much of it is obviously written by an ardent moralist who produces Emersonian essays on the conservative value of Habit or on the power of the enlisted Will. WJ gave the clue to what to expect from him in his chapter on "The Perception of Reality," where he said that, among rival theories, the one most generally believed will "appeal most urgently to our æsthetic, emotional, and active needs." His own appeal is that of the individualist who believes that the command: "Son of Man, *stand upon thy feet* and I will speak unto thee!" is "the only revelation of truth to which the solving epochs have helped the disciple."

The psychologist who wrote this is no different from the popular philosopher who wrote "The Will to Believe." That title-essay, which is probably the one by which WJ will continue to be most widely known, is a justification of faith by a man who holds that "the willing department of our nature . . . dominates both the conceiving department and the feeling department; or, in plainer English, perception and thinking are only there for behavior's sake." The title got him into trouble with more careful philosophers, and was parodied as "The Will to Make-Believe" and even as "The Will to Deceive." One critic pointed out that "it does not follow, because we cannot prove everything, because in the last resort we can prove nothing, that we are free to assume what we choose." In the face of such opposition, WJ came to wish that he had selected the less provocative title "The Right to Believe," which he said would have been more accurately descriptive of his contention.

Some of the other essays in this first collection of his shorter pieces may be examples of solider thinking, "The Dilemma of Determinism" perhaps, and "The Sentiment of Rationality," which at the time he produced it, at the end of the 1870's, he declared to be "the only decent thing I have ever written." But the mature WJ was most concerned with challenges to the individual will, with *Talks to Students on Some of Life's Ideals*. Since two of these talks, "On a Certain Blindness in Human Beings" and "What Makes a Life Significant?" are storehouses of his most familiar quotations, they both must be included in any representation of his mind. The seeming disproportion in this section between examples from WJ and from HJ will be redressed when we come to the essays in criticism, which are of course primarily by the latter.

WJ once described "On a Certain Blindness" as containing "the perception on which my whole individualistic philosophy is based." It is also a good example of his essay method. Again following Emerson, he weaves in ample passages from his reading in order to illustrate his theme. The tenor of his taste may be observed in his choices: Stevenson's "The Lantern-Bearers," Royce's *The Religious Aspect of Philosophy*, De Sénancour's *Obermann*, Wordsworth's *The Prelude*, Richard Jefferies' *The Story of My Heart*, Walt Whitman's "Crossing Brooklyn Ferry" and a letter to Pete Doyle, Benvenuto Cellini's *Autobiography*, Tolstoy's *War and Peace*, Emerson's *Nature*, and W. H. Hudson's *Idle Days in Patagonia*. Such an essay is inevitably discursive. It also presents a problem in tone that very definitely dates it. Despite WJ's unorthodox liveliness as a professor, despite the fact that he cried "Ouf! what a relief!" upon escaping after a week at Chautauqua, his essays were meant to be "helpful" to students, and they occasionally emanate a faint aroma of the audiences for whom they were first designed, the graduate students' Philosophical Club, or the Young Men's Christian Association. They sound a little earnest and parochial, and, in contrast with Henry Senior's untrammeled flights into communism and free love, a little vitiated—albeit unwittingly—by the deadly atmosphere of Academia. Yet WJ was always concerned with major issues, and he believed his plea for tolerance of other lives to be especially needful in the face of our incipient domineering imperialism at the time of the Spanish-American War.

"What Makes a Life Significant?" shows why he responded to Whitman, as it celebrates the heroic aspect of the common workingman. But WJ falls short of Whitman's unswerving allegiance in his rather too easy solution of "the labor question." The dominant theme of both these talks serves, none the less, to bring out the most attractive quality in WJ's personality, his own "enormous capacity" for what he celebrates—the capacity "for friendship and for taking delight in other people's lives."

CHARACTERISTIC MATURITY

Henry James: The Art of Fiction

* * * * *

I SHOULD not have affixed so comprehensive a title to these few remarks, necessarily wanting in any completeness upon a subject the full consideration of which would carry us far, did I not seem to discover a pretext for my temerity in the interesting pamphlet lately published under this name by Mr. Walter Besant. Mr. Besant's lecture at the Royal Institution—the original form of his pamphlet—appears to indicate that many persons are interested in the art of fiction, and are not indifferent to such remarks, as those who practise it may attempt to make about it. I am therefore anxious not to lose the benefit of this favourable association, and to edge in a few words under cover of the attention which Mr. Besant is sure to have excited. There is something very encouraging in his having put into form certain of his ideas on the mystery of story-telling.

It is a proof of life and curiosity—curiosity on the part of the brotherhood of novelists as well as on the part of their readers. Only a short time ago it might have been supposed that the English novel was not what the French call *discutable*. It had no air of having a theory, a conviction, a consciousness of itself behind it—of being the expression of an artistic faith, the result of choice and comparison. I do not say it was necessarily the worse for that: it would take much more courage than I possess to intimate that the form of the novel as Dickens and Thackeray (for instance) saw it had any taint of incompleteness. It was, however, *naïf* (if I may help myself out with another French word); and evidently if it be destined to suffer in any way for having lost its *naïveté* it has now an idea of making sure of the corresponding advantages. During the period I have alluded to there was a comfortable, good-humoured feeling abroad that a novel is a novel, as a pudding is a pudding, and that our only business with it could be to swallow it. But within a year or two, for some reason or other, there have been signs of returning animation—the era of discussion would appear to have been to a certain extent opened. Art lives upon discussion, upon experiment, upon curiosity, upon variety of attempt, upon the exchange of views and the comparison of standpoints; and there is a presumption that those times when no one has anything particular to say about it, and has no reason to give for practice or preference, though they may be times of honour, are not times of development—are times, possibly even, a little of dulness. The successful application of any art is a delightful spectacle, but the theory too is interesting; and though there is a great deal of the latter without the former I suspect there has never been a genuine success that has not had a latent core of conviction. Discussion, suggestion, formulation, these things are fertilising when they are frank and sincere. Mr. Besant has set an excellent example in saying what he thinks, for his part, about the way in which fiction should be written, as well as about the way in which it should be published; for his view of the "art," carried on into an appendix, covers that too. Other labourers in the same field will doubtless take up the argument, they will give it the light of their experience, and the effect will surely be to make our interest in the novel a little more what it had for some time threatened to fail to be—a serious, active, inquiring interest, under protection of which this delightful study may, in moments of confidence, venture to say a little more what it thinks of itself.

It must take itself seriously for the public to take it so. The old superstition about fiction being "wicked" has doubtless died out in England; but the spirit of it lingers in a certain oblique regard directed toward any story which does not more or less admit that it is only a joke. Even the most jocular novel feels in some degree the weight of the proscription that was formerly directed against literary levity: the jocularity does not always succeed in passing for orthodoxy. It is still expected, though perhaps people are ashamed to say it, that a production which is after all only a "make-believe" (for what else is a "story"?) shall be in some degree apologetic—shall renounce the pretension of attempting really to represent life. This, of course, any sensible, wide-awake story declines to do, for it quickly perceives that the tolerance granted to it on such a condition is only an attempt to stifle it disguised in the form of generosity. The old evangelical hostility to the novel, which was as explicit as it was narrow, and which regarded it as little less favourable to our immortal part than a stage-play, was in reality far less insulting. The only reason for the existence of a novel is that it does attempt to represent life. When it relinquishes this attempt, the same attempt that we see on the canvas of the painter, it will have arrived at a very strange pass. It is not expected of the picture that it will make itself humble in order to be forgiven; and the analogy between the art of the painter and the art of the novelist is, so far as I am able to see, complete. Their inspiration is the same, their process (allowing for the different quality of the vehicle), is the same, their success is the same. They may learn from each other, they may explain and sustain each other. Their cause is the same, and the honour of one is the honour of another. The Mahometans think a picture an unholy thing, but it is a long time since any Christian did, and it is therefore the more odd that in the Christian mind the traces (dissimulated though they may be) of a suspicion of the sister art should linger to this day. The only effectual way to lay it to rest is to emphasise the analogy to which I have just alluded—to insist on the fact that as the picture is reality, so the novel is history. That is the only general description (which does it justice) that we may give of the novel. But history also is allowed to represent life; it is not, any more than painting, expected to apologise. The subject-matter of fiction is stored up likewise in documents and records, and if it will not give itself away, as they say in California, it must speak with assurance, with the tone of the historian. Certain accomplished novelists have a habit of giving themselves away which must often bring tears to the eyes of people who take their fiction seriously. I was lately struck, in reading over many pages of Anthony Trollope, with his want of discretion in this particular. In a digression, a parenthesis or an aside, he concedes to the reader that he and this trusting friend are only "making believe." He admits that the events he narrates have not really happened, and that he can give his narrative any turn the reader may like best. Such a betrayal of a sacred office seems to me, I confess, a terrible crime; it is what I mean by the attitude of apology, and it shocks me every whit as much in Trollope as it would have shocked me in Gibbon or Macaulay. It implies that the novelist is less occupied in looking for the truth (the truth, of course I mean, that he assumes, the premises that we must grant him, whatever they may be), than the historian, and in doing so it deprives him at a stroke of all his standing-room. To represent and illustrate the past, the actions of men, is the task of either writer, and the only difference that I can see is, in proportion as he succeeds, to the honour of the novelist, consisting as it does in his having more difficulty in collecting his evidence, which is so far from being purely literary. It seems to me to give him a great character, the fact that he has at once so much in common with the philosopher and the painter; this double analogy is a magnificent heritage.

It is of all this evidently that Mr. Besant is full when he insists upon the fact that fiction is one of the *fine* arts, deserving in its turn of all the honours and emoluments that have hitherto been reserved for the successful profession of music, poetry, painting, architecture. It is impossible to insist too much on so important a truth, and the place that Mr.

Besant demands for the work of the novelist may be represented, a trifle less abstractly, by saying that he demands not only that it shall be reputed artistic, but that it shall be reputed very artistic indeed. It is excellent that he should have struck this note, for his doing so indicates that there was need of it, that his proposition may be to many people a novelty. One rubs one's eyes at the thought; but the rest of Mr. Besant's essay confirms the revelation. I suspect in truth that it would be possible to confirm it still further, and that one would not be far wrong in saying that in addition to the people to whom it has never occurred that a novel ought to be artistic, there are a great many others who, if this principle were urged upon them, would be filled with an indefinable mistrust. They would find it difficult to explain their repugnance, but it would operate strongly to put them on their guard. "Art," in our Protestant communities, where so many things have got so strangely twisted about, is supposed in certain circles to have some vaguely injurious effect upon those who make it an important consideration, who let it weigh in the balance. It is assumed to be opposed in some mysterious manner to morality, to amusement, to instruction. When it is embodied in the work of the painter (the sculptor is another affair!) you know what it is: it stands there before you, in the honesty of pink and green and a gilt frame; you can see the worst of it at a glance, and you can be on your guard. But when it is introduced into literature it becomes more insidious—there is danger of its hurting you before you know it. Literature should be either instructive or amusing, and there is in many minds an impression that these artistic preoccupations, the search for form, contribute to neither end, interfere indeed with both. They are too frivolous to be edifying, and too serious to be diverting; and they are moreover priggish and paradoxical and superfluous. That, I think, represents the manner in which the latent thought of many people who read novels as an exercise in skipping would explain itself if it were to become articulate. They would argue, of course, that a novel ought to be "good," but they would interpret this term in a fashion of their own, which indeed would vary considerably from one critic to another. One would say that being good means representing virtuous and aspiring characters, placed in prominent positions; another would say that it depends on a "happy ending," on a distribution at the last of prizes, pensions, husbands, wives, babies, millions, appended paragraphs, and cheerful remarks. Another still would say that it means being full of incident and movement, so that we shall wish to jump ahead, to see who was the mysterious stranger, and if the stolen will was ever found, and shall not be distracted from this pleasure by any tiresome analysis or "description." But they would all agree that the "artistic" idea would spoil some of their fun. One would hold it accountable for all the description, another would see it revealed in the absence of sympathy. Its hostility to a happy ending would be evident, and it might even in some cases render any ending at all impossible. The "ending" of a novel is, for many persons, like that of a good dinner, a course of dessert and ices, and the artist in fiction is regarded as a sort of meddlesome doctor who forbids agreeable aftertastes. It is therefore true that this conception of Mr. Besant's of the novel as a superior form encounters not only a negative but a positive indifference. It matters little that as a work of art it should really be as little or as much of its essence to supply happy endings, sympathetic characters, and an objective tone, as if it were a work of mechanics: the association of ideas, however incongruous, might easily be too much for it if an eloquent voice were not sometimes raised to call attention to the fact that it is at once as free and as serious a branch of literature as any other.

Certainly this might sometimes be doubted in presence of the enormous number of works of fiction that appeal to the credulity of our generation, for it might easily seem that there could be no great character in a commodity so quickly and easily produced. It must be admitted that good novels are much compromised by bad ones, and that the field at large suffers discredit from overcrowding. I think, however, that this injury is only superficial, and that the superabundance of written fiction proves nothing against the principle itself. It has been vulgarised, like all other kinds of literature, like everything else to-day, and it has proved more than some kinds accessible to vulgarisation. But there is as much difference as there ever was between a good novel and a bad one: the bad is swept with all the daubed canvases and spoiled marble into some unvisited limbo, or infinite rubbish-yard beneath the back-windows of the world, and the good subsists and emits its light and stimulates our desire for perfection. As I shall take the liberty of making but a single criticism of Mr. Besant, whose tone is so full of the love of his art, I may as well have done with it at once. He seems to me to mistake in attempting to say so definitely beforehand what sort of an affair the good novel will be. To indicate the danger of such an error as that has been the purpose of these few pages; to suggest that certain traditions on the subject, applied *a priori*, have already had much to answer for, and that the good health of an art which undertakes so immediately to reproduce life must demand that it be perfectly free. It lives upon exercise, and the very meaning of exercise is freedom. The only obligation to which in advance we may hold a novel, without incurring the accusation of being arbitrary, is that it be interesting. That general responsibility rests upon it, but it is the only one I can think of. The ways in which it is at liberty to accomplish this result (of interesting us) strike me as innumerable, and such as can only suffer from being marked out or fenced in by prescription. They are as various as the temperament of man, and they are successful in proportion as they

reveal a particular mind, different from others. A novel is in its broadest definition a personal, a direct impression of life: that, to begin with,
constitutes its value, which is greater or less according to the intensity
of the impression. But there will be no intensity at all, and therefore no
value, unless there is freedom to feel and say. The tracing of a line to be
followed, of a tone to be taken, of a form to be filled out, is a limitation
of that freedom and a suppression of the very thing that we are most
curious about. The form, it seems to me, is to be appreciated after the
fact: then the author's choice has been made, his standard has been indicated; then we can follow lines and directions and compare tones and
resemblances. Then in a word we can enjoy one of the most charming
of pleasures, we can estimate quality, we can apply the test of execution. The execution belongs to the author alone; it is what is most personal to him, and we measure him by that. The advantage, the luxury,
as well as the torment and responsibility of the novelist, is that there is
no limit to what he may attempt as an executant—no limit to his possible experiments, efforts, discoveries, successes. Here it is especially
that he works, step by step, like his brother of the brush, of whom we
may always say that he has painted his picture in a manner best known
to himself. His manner is his secret, not necessarily a jealous one. He
cannot disclose it as a general thing if he would; he would be at a loss to
teach it to others. I say this with a due recollection of having insisted
on the community of method of the artist who paints a picture and the
artist who writes a novel. The painter *is* able to teach the rudiments of
his practice, and it is possible, from the study of good work (granted
the aptitude), both to learn how to paint and to learn how to write. Yet
it remains true, without injury to the *rapprochement*, that the literary
artist would be obliged to say to his pupil much more than the other,
"Ah, well, you must do it as you can!" It is a question of degree, a
matter of delicacy. If there are exact sciences, there are also exact arts,
and the grammar of painting is so much more definite that it makes the
difference.

I ought to add, however, that if Mr. Besant says at the beginning of
his essay that the "laws of fiction may be laid down and taught with as
much precision and exactness as the laws of harmony, perspective, and
proportion," he mitigates what might appear to be an extravagance by
applying his remark to "general" laws, and by expressing most of these
rules in a manner with which it would certainly be unaccommodating
to disagree. That the novelist must write from his experience, that his
"characters must be real and such as might be met with in actual life";
that "a young lady brought up in a quiet country village should avoid
descriptions of garrison life," and "a writer whose friends and personal
experiences belong to the lower middle-class should carefully avoid introducing his characters into society"; that one should enter one's notes

in a common-place book; that one's figures should be clear in outline;
that making them clear by some trick of speech or of carriage is a bad
method, and "describing them at length" is a worse one; that English
Fiction should have a "conscious moral purpose"; that "it is almost impossible to estimate too highly the value of careful workmanship—that
is, of style"; that "the most important point of all is the story," that "the
story is everything": these are principles with most of which it is surely
impossible not to sympathise. That remark about the lower middle-class
writer and his knowing his place is perhaps rather chilling; but for the
rest I should find it difficult to dissent from any one of these recom-
mendations. At the same time, I should find it difficult positively to
assent to them, with the exception, perhaps, of the injunction as to entering one's notes in a common-place book. They scarcely seem to me
to have the quality that Mr. Besant attributes to the rules of the novelist
—the "precision and exactness" of "the laws of harmony, perspective,
and proportion." They are suggestive, they are even inspiring, but they
are not exact, though they are doubtless as much so as the case admits
of: which is a proof of that liberty of interpretation for which I just
contended. For the value of these different injunctions—so beautiful
and so vague—is wholly in the meaning one attaches to them. The
characters, the situation, which strike one as real will be those that
touch and interest one most, but the measure of reality is very difficult
to fix. The reality of Don Quixote or of Mr. Micawber is a very delicate shade; it is a reality so coloured by the author's vision that, vivid as
it may be, one would hesitate to propose it as a model: one would expose one's self to some very embarrassing questions on the part of a
pupil. It goes without saying that you will not write a good novel unless you possess the sense of reality; but it will be difficult to give you a
recipe for calling that sense into being. Humanity is immense, and
reality has a myriad forms; the most one can affirm is that some of the
flowers of fiction have the odour of it, and others have not; as for telling you in advance how your nosegay should be composed, that is
another affair. It is equally excellent and inconclusive to say that one
must write from experience; to our suppositious aspirant such a declaration might savour of mockery. What kind of experience is intended,
and where does it begin and end? Experience is never limited, and it is
never complete; it is an immense sensibility, a kind of huge spider-web
of the finest silken threads suspended in the chamber of consciousness,
and catching every air-borne particle in its tissue. It is the very atmosphere of the mind; and when the mind is imaginative—much more
when it happens to be that of a man of genius—it takes to itself the
faintest hints of life, it converts the very pulses of the air into revelations. The young lady living in a village has only to be a damsel upon
whom nothing is lost to make it quite unfair (as it seems to me) to de-

clare to her that she shall have nothing to say about the military. Greater miracles have been seen than that, imagination assisting, she should speak the truth about some of these gentlemen. I remember an English novelist, a woman of genius, telling me that she was much commended for the impression she had managed to give in one of her tales of the nature and way of life of the French Protestant youth. She had been asked where she learned so much about this recondite being, she had been congratulated on her peculiar opportunities. These opportunities consisted in her having once, in Paris, as she ascended a staircase, passed an open door where, in the household of a *pasteur*, some of the young Protestants were seated at table round a finished meal. The glimpse made a picture; it lasted only a moment, but that moment was experience. She had got her direct personal impression, and she turned out her type. She knew what youth was, and what Protestantism; she also had the advantage of having seen what it was to be French, so that she converted these ideas into a concrete image and produced a reality. Above all, however, she was blessed with the faculty which when you give it an inch takes an ell, and which for the artist is a much greater source of strength than any accident of residence or of place in the social scale. The power to guess the unseen from the seen, to trace the implication of things, to judge the whole piece by the pattern, the condition of feeling life in general so completely that you are well on your way to knowing any particular corner of it—this cluster of gifts may almost be said to constitute experience, and they occur in country and in town, and in the most differing stages of education. If experience consists of impressions, it may be said that impressions *are* experience, just as (have we not seen it?) they are the very air we breathe. Therefore, if I should certainly say to a novice, "Write from experience and experience only," I should feel that this was rather a tantalising monition if I were not careful immediately to add, "Try to be one of the people on whom nothing is lost!"

I am far from intending by this to minimise the importance of exactness—of truth of detail. One can speak best from one's own taste, and I may therefore venture to say that the air of reality (solidity of specification) seems to me to be the supreme virtue of a novel—the merit on which all its other merits (including that conscious moral purpose of which Mr. Besant speaks) helplessly and submissively depend. If it be not there they are all as nothing, and if these be there, they owe their effect to the success with which the author has produced the illusion of life. The cultivation of this success, the study of this exquisite process, form, to my taste, the beginning and the end of the art of the novelist. They are his inspiration, his despair, his reward, his torment, his delight. It is here in very truth that he competes with life; it is here that he competes with his brother the painter in *his* attempt to render the look of things, the look that conveys their meaning, to catch the colour, the relief, the expression, the surface, the substance of the human spectacle. It is in regard to this that Mr. Besant is well inspired when he bids him take notes. He cannot possibly take too many, he cannot possibly take enough. All life solicits him, and to "render" the simplest surface, to produce the most momentary illusion, is a very complicated business. His case would be easier, and the rule would be more exact, if Mr. Besant had been able to tell him what notes to take. But this, I fear, he can never learn in any manual; it is the business of his life. He has to take a great many in order to select a few, he has to work them up as he can, and even the guides and philosophers who might have most to say to him must leave him alone when it comes to the application of precepts, as we leave the painter in communion with his palette. That his characters "must be clear in outline," as Mr. Besant says—he feels that down to his boots; but how he shall make them so is a secret between his good angel and himself. It would be absurdly simple if he could be taught that a great deal of "description" would make them so, or that on the contrary the absence of description and the cultivation of dialogue, or the absence of dialogue and the multiplication of "incident," would rescue him from his difficulties. Nothing, for instance, is more possible than that he be of a turn of mind for which this odd, literal opposition of description and dialogue, incident and description, has little meaning and light. People often talk of these things as if they had a kind of internecine distinctness, instead of melting into each other at every breath, and being intimately associated parts of one general effort of expression. I cannot imagine composition existing in a series of blocks, nor conceive, in any novel worth discussing at all, of a passage of description that is not in its intention narrative, a passage of dialogue that is not in its intention descriptive, a touch of truth of any sort that does not partake of the nature of incident, or an incident that derives its interest from any other source than the general and only source of the success of a work of art—that of being illustrative. A novel is a living thing, all one and continuous, like any other organism, and in proportion as it lives will it be found, I think, that in each of the parts there is something of each of the other parts. The critic who over the close texture of a finished work shall pretend to trace a geography of items will mark some frontiers as artificial, I fear, as any that have been known to history. There is an old-fashioned distinction between the novel of character and the novel of incident which must have cost many a smile to the intending fabulist who was keen about his work. It appears to me as little to the point as the equally celebrated distinction between the novel and the romance—to answer as little to any reality. There are bad novels and good novels, as there are bad pictures and good pictures; but that is the only distinction in which I see any meaning, and I can as little imagine speaking of a novel of character as I can imagine speaking of a picture of character. When one says picture one says of character, when one says novel one says of incident, and the terms may be transposed at will. What is character but the determination of incident? What is incident but the illustration of character? What is either a picture or a novel that is *not* of character? What else do we seek in it and find in it? It is an incident for a woman to stand up with her hand resting on a table and look out at you in a certain way; or if it be not an incident I think it will be hard to say what it is. At the same time it is an expression of character. If you say you don't see it (character in *that—allons donc!*), this is exactly what the artist who has reasons of his own for thinking he *does* see it undertakes to show you. When a young man makes up his mind that he has not faith enough after all to enter the church as he intended, that is an incident, though you may not hurry to the end of the chapter to see whether perhaps he doesn't change once more. I do not say that these are extraordinary or startling incidents. I do not pretend to estimate the degree of interest proceeding from them, for this will depend upon the skill of the painter. It sounds almost puerile to say that some incidents are intrinsically much more important than others, and I need not take this precaution after having professed my sympathy for the major ones in remarking that the only classification of the novel that I can understand is into that which has life and that which has it not.

The novel and the romance, the novel of incident and that of character—these clumsy separations appear to me to have been made by critics and readers for their own convenience, and to help them out of some of their occasional queer predicaments, but to have little reality or interest for the producer, from whose point of view it is of course that we are attempting to consider the art of fiction. The case is the same with another shadowy category which Mr. Besant apparently is disposed to set up—that of the "modern English novel"; unless indeed it be that in this matter he has fallen into an accidental confusion of standpoints. It is not quite clear whether he intends the remarks in which he alludes to it to be didactic or historical. It is as difficult to suppose a person intending to write a modern English as to suppose him writing an ancient English novel: that is a label which begs the question. One writes the novel, one paints the picture, of one's language and of one's time, and calling it modern English will not, alas! make the difficult task any easier. No more, unfortunately, will calling this or that work of one's fellow-artist a romance—unless it be, of course, simply for the pleasantness of the thing, as for instance when Hawthorne gave this heading to his story of *Blithedale*. The French, who have brought the theory of fiction to remarkable completeness, have but one name for the novel, and have not attempted smaller things in it, that I can see, for that. I can think of no obligation to which the "romancer" would not be held equally with the novelist; the standard of execution is equally high for each. Of course it is of execution that we are talking—that being the only point of a novel that is open to contention. This is perhaps too often lost sight of, only to produce interminable confusions and cross-purposes. We must grant the artist his subject, his idea, his *donnée*: our criticism is applied only to what he makes of it. Naturally I do not mean that we are bound to like it or find it interesting: in case we do not our course is perfectly simple—to let it alone. We may be-lieve that of a certain idea even the most sincere novelist can make nothing at all, and the event may perfectly justify our belief; but the failure will have been a failure to execute, and it is in the execution that the fatal weakness is recorded. If we pretend to respect the artist at all, we must allow him his freedom of choice, in the face, in particular cases, of innumerable presumptions that the choice will not fructify. Art derives a considerable part of its beneficial exercise from flying in the face of presumptions, and some of the most interesting experiments of which it is capable are hidden in the bosom of common things. Gustave Flaubert has written a story about the devotion of a servant-girl to a parrot, and the production, highly finished as it is, cannot on the whole be called a success. We are perfectly free to find it flat, but I think it might have been interesting; and I, for my part, am extremely glad he should have written it; it is a contribution to our knowledge of what can be done—or what cannot. Ivan Turgénieff has written a tale about a deaf and dumb serf and a lap-dog, and the thing is touching, loving, a little masterpiece. He struck the note of life where Gustave Flaubert missed it—he flew in the face of a presumption and achieved a victory.

Nothing, of course, will ever take the place of the good old fashion of "liking" a work of art or not liking it: the most improved criticism will not abolish that primitive, that ultimate test. I mention this to guard myself from the accusation of intimating that the idea, the sub-ject, of a novel or a picture, does not matter. It matters, to my sense, in the highest degree, and if I might put up a prayer it would be that artists should select none but the richest. Some, as I have already hastened to admit, are much more remunerative than others, and it would be a world happily arranged in which persons intending to treat them should be exempt from confusions and mistakes. This fortunate condition will arrive only, I fear, on the same day that critics become purged from error. Meanwhile, I repeat, we do not judge the artist with fairness unless we say to him, "Oh, I grant you your starting-point, because if I did not I should seem to prescribe to you, and heaven forbid I should take that responsibility. If I pretend to tell you what you must not take, you will call upon me to tell you then what you must take; in which case I shall be prettily caught. Moreover, it isn't till I have accepted your data that I can begin to measure you. I have the standard, the pitch; I have no right to tamper with your flute and then criticise your music. Of course I may not care for your idea at all; I may think it silly, or stale, or unclean; in which case I wash my hands of you altogether. I may content myself with believing that you will not have succeeded in being interesting, but I shall, of course, not attempt to demonstrate it, and you will be as indifferent to me as I am to you. I needn't remind you that there are all sorts of tastes: who can know it better? Some people, for excellent reasons, don't like to read about carpenters; others, for reasons even better, don't like to read about courtesans. Many object to Americans. Others (I believe they are mainly editors and publishers) won't look at Italians. Some readers don't like quiet subjects; others don't like bustling ones. Some enjoy a complete illusion, others the consciousness of large concessions. They choose their novels accordingly, and if they don't care about your idea they won't, *a fortiori*, care about your treatment."

So that it comes back very quickly, as I have said, to the liking: in spite of M. Zola, who reasons less powerfully than he represents, and who will not reconcile himself to this absoluteness of taste, thinking that there are certain things that people ought to like, and that they can be made to like. I am quite at a loss to imagine anything (at any rate in this matter of fiction) that people *ought* to like or to dislike. Selection will be sure to take care of itself, for it has a constant motive behind it. That motive is simply experience. As people feel life, so they will feel the art that is most closely related to it. This closeness of relation is what we should never forget in talking of the effort of the novel. Many people speak of it as a factitious, artificial form, a product of ingenuity, the business of which is to alter and arrange the things that surround us, to translate them into conventional, traditional moulds. This, however, is a view of the matter which carries us but a very short way, condemns the art to an eternal repetition of a few familiar *clichés*, cuts short its development, and leads us straight up to a dead wall. Catching the very note and trick, the strange irregular rhythm of life, that is the attempt whose strenuous force keeps Fiction upon her feet. In proportion as in what she offers us we see life *without* rearrangement do we feel that we are touching the truth; in proportion as we see it *with* rearrangement do we feel that we are being put off with a substitute, a compromise and convention. It is not uncommon to hear an extraordinary assurance of remark in regard to this matter of rearranging, which is often spoken of as if it were the last word of art. Mr. Besant seems to me in danger of falling into the great error with his rather unguarded talk about "selection." Art is essentially selection, but it is a selection whose main care is to be typical, to be inclusive.

For many people art means rose-coloured window-panes, and selection means picking a bouquet for Mrs. Grundy. They will tell you glibly that artistic considerations have nothing to do with the disagreeable, with the ugly; they will rattle off shallow commonplaces about the province of art and the limits of art till you are moved to some wonder in return as to the province and the limits of ignorance. It appears to me that no one can ever have made a seriously artistic attempt without becoming conscious of an immense increase—a kind of revelation—of freedom. One perceives in that case—by the light of a heavenly ray— that the province of art is all life, all feeling, all observation, all vision. As Mr. Besant so justly intimates, it is all experience. That is a sufficient answer to those who maintain that it must not touch the sad things of life, who stick into its divine unconscious bosom little prohibitory in- scriptions on the end of sticks, such as we see in public gardens—"It is forbidden to walk on the grass; it is forbidden to touch the flowers; it is not allowed to introduce dogs or to remain after dark; it is requested to keep to the right." The young aspirant in the line of fiction whom we continue to imagine will do nothing without taste, for in that case his freedom would be of little use to him; but the first advantage of his taste will be to reveal to him the absurdity of the little sticks and tickets. If he have taste, I must add, of course he will have ingenuity, and my disrespectful reference to that quality just now was not meant to imply that it is useless in fiction. But it is only a secondary aid; the first is a capacity for receiving straight impressions.

Mr. Besant has some remarks on the question of "the story" which I shall not attempt to criticise, though they seem to me to contain a singular ambiguity, because I do not think I understand them. I cannot see what is meant by talking as if there were a part of a novel which is the story and part of it which for mystical reasons is not—unless indeed the distinction be made in a sense in which it is difficult to suppose that any one should attempt to convey anything. "The story," if it represents anything, represents the subject, the idea, the *donnée* of the novel; and there is surely no "school"—Mr. Besant speaks of a school—which urges that a novel should be all treatment and no subject. There must assuredly be something to treat; every school is intimately conscious of that. This sense of the story being the idea, the starting-point, of the novel, is the only one that I see in which it can be spoken of as something different from its organic whole; and since in proportion as the work is successful the idea permeates and pene- trates it, informs and animates it, so that every word and every punctua- tion-point contribute directly to the expression, in that proportion do we lose our sense of the story being a blade which may be drawn more or less out of its sheath. The story and the novel, the idea and the form, are the needle and thread, and I never heard of a guild of tailors who recommended the use of the thread without the needle, or the needle without the thread. Mr. Besant is not the only critic who may be observed to have spoken as if there were certain things in life which constitute stories, and certain others which do not. I find the same odd implication in an entertaining article in the *Pall Mall Gazette*, devoted, as it happens, to Mr. Besant's lecture. "The story is the thing!" says this graceful writer, as if with a tone of opposition to some other idea. I should think it was, as every painter who, as the time for "sending in" his picture looms in the distance, finds himself still in quest of a subject —as every belated artist not fixed about his theme will heartily agree. There are some subjects which speak to us and others which do not, but he would be a clever man who should undertake to give a rule— an index expurgatorius—by which the story and the no-story should be known apart. It is impossible (to me at least) to imagine any such rule which shall not be altogether arbitrary. The writer in the *Pall Mall* opposes the delightful (as I suppose) novel of *Margot la Balafrée* to certain tales in which "Bostonian nymphs" appear to have "rejected English dukes for psychological reasons." I am not acquainted with the romance just designated, and can scarcely forgive the *Pall Mall* critic for not mentioning the name of the author, but the title appears to refer to a lady who may have received a scar in some heroic adventure. I am inconsolable at not being acquainted with this episode, but am utterly at a loss to see why it is a story when the rejection (or accept-ance) of a duke is not, and why a reason, psychological or other, is not a subject when a cicatrix is. They are all particles of the multitudinous life with which the novel deals, and surely no dogma which pretends to make it lawful to touch the one and unlawful to touch the other will stand for a moment on its feet. It is the special picture that must stand or fall, according as it seem to possess truth or to lack it. Mr. Besant does not, to my sense, light up the subject by intimating that a story must, under penalty of not being a story, consist of "adventures." Why of adventures more than of green spectacles? He mentions a category of impossible things, and among them he places "fiction with-out adventure." Why without adventure, more than without matri-mony, or celibacy, or parturition, or cholera, or hydropathy, or Jansen-ism? This seems to me to bring the novel back to the hapless little *rôle* of being an artificial, ingenious thing—bring it down from its large, free character of an immense and exquisite correspondence with life. And what *is* adventure, when it comes to that, and by what sign is the listening pupil to recognise it? It is an adventure—an immense one—for me to write this little article; and for a Bostonian nymph to reject an English duke is an adventure only less stirring, I should say, than for an English duke to be rejected by a Bostonian nymph. I see dramas within dramas in that, and innumerable points of view. A psychological reason is, to my imagination, an object adorably pictorial; to catch the tint of its complexion—I feel as if that idea might inspire one to Titian-esque efforts. There are few things more exciting to me, in short, than a psychological reason, and yet, I protest, the novel seems to me the most magnificent form of art. I have just been reading, at the same time, the delightful story of *Treasure Island*, by Mr. Robert Louis Stevenson and, in a manner less consecutive, the last tale from M. Edmond de Goncourt, which is entitled *Chérie*. One of these works treats of murders, mysteries, islands of dreadful renown, hairbreadth escapes, miraculous coincidences and buried doubloons. The other treats of a little French girl who lived in a fine house in Paris, and died of wounded sensibility because no one would marry her. I call *Treasure Island* delightful, because it appears to me to have succeeded wonder-fully in what it attempts; and I venture to bestow no epithet upon *Chérie*, which strikes me as having failed deplorably in what it attempts —that is in tracing the development of the moral consciousness of a child. But one of these productions strikes me as exactly as much of a novel as the other, and as having a "story" quite as much. The moral consciousness of a child is as much a part of life as the islands of the Spanish Main, and the one sort of geography seems to me to have those "surprises" of which Mr. Besant speaks quite as much as the other. For myself (since it comes back in the last resort, as I say, to the prefer-ence of the individual), the picture of the child's experience has the advantage that I can at successive steps (an immense luxury, near to the "sensual pleasure" of which Mr. Besant's critic in the *Pall Mall* speaks) say Yes or No, as it may be, to what the artist puts before me. I have been a child in fact, but I have been on a quest for a buried treasure only in supposition, and it is a simple accident that with M. de Gon-court I should have for the most part to say No. With George Eliot, when she painted that country with a far other intelligence, I always said Yes.

The most interesting part of Mr. Besant's lecture is unfortunately the briefest passage—his very cursory allusion to the "conscious moral pur-pose" of the novel. Here again it is not very clear whether he be re-cording a fact or laying down a principle; it is a great pity that in the latter case he should not have developed his idea. This branch of the subject is of immense importance, and Mr. Besant's few words point to considerations of the widest reach, not to be lightly disposed of. He will have treated the art of fiction but superficially who is not prepared to go every inch of the way that these considerations will carry him. It is for this reason that at the beginning of these remarks I was careful to notify the reader that my reflections on so large a theme have no pretension to be exhaustive. Like Mr. Besant, I have left the question of the morality of the novel till the last, and at the last I find I have used up my space. It is a question surrounded with difficulties, as witness the very first that meets us, in the form of a definite question, on the threshold. Vagueness, in such a discussion, is fatal, and what is the meaning of your morality and your conscious moral purpose? Will you not define your terms and explain how (a novel being a picture) a picture can be either moral or immoral? You wish to paint a moral picture or carve a moral statue: will you not tell us how you would set about it? We are discussing the Art of Fiction; questions of art are questions (in the widest sense) of execution; questions of morality are quite another affair, and will you not let us see how it is that you find it so easy to mix them up? These things are so clear to Mr. Besant that he has deduced from them a law which he sees embodied in English Fiction, and which is "a truly admirable thing and a great cause for congratulation." It is a great cause for congratulation indeed when such thorny problems become as smooth as silk. I may add that in so far as Mr. Besant perceives that in point of fact English Fiction has addressed itself preponderantly to these delicate questions he will appear to many people to have made a vain discovery. They will have been positively struck, on the contrary, with the moral timidity of the usual English novelist; with his (or with her) aversion to face the difficulties with which on every side the treatment of reality bristles. He is apt to be extremely shy (whereas the picture that Mr. Besant draws is a picture of boldness), and the sign of his work, for the most part, is a cautious silence on certain subjects. In the English novel (by which of course I mean the American as well), more than in any other, there is a traditional difference between that which people know and that which they agree to admit that they know, that which they see and that which they speak of, that which they feel to be a part of life and that which they allow to enter into literature. There is the great difference, in short, between what they talk of in conversation and what they talk of in print. The essence of moral energy is to survey the whole field, and I should directly reverse Mr. Besant's remark and say not that the English novel has a purpose, but that it has a diffidence. To what degree a purpose in a work of art is a source of corruption I shall not attempt to inquire; the one that seems to me least dangerous is the purpose of making a perfect work. As for our novel, I may say lastly on this score that as we find it in England to-day it strikes me as addressed in a large degree to "young people," and that this in itself constitutes a presumption that it will be rather shy. There are certain things which it is generally agreed not to discuss, not even to mention, before young people. That is very well, but the absence of discussion is not a symptom of the moral passion. The purpose of the English novel —"a truly admirable thing, and a great cause for congratulation"— strikes me therefore as rather negative.

There is one point at which the moral sense and the artistic sense lie very near together; that is in the light of the very obvious truth that the deepest quality of a work of art will always be the quality of the mind of the producer. In proportion as that intelligence is fine will the novel, the picture, the statue partake of the substance of beauty and truth. To be constituted of such elements is, to my vision, to have purpose enough. No good novel will ever proceed from a superficial mind; that seems to me an axiom which, for the artist in fiction, will cover all needful moral ground: if the youthful aspirant take it to heart it will illuminate for him many of the mysteries of "purpose." There are many other useful things that might be said to him, but I have come to the end of my article, and can only touch them as I pass. The critic in the *Pall Mall Gazette,* whom I have already quoted, draws attention to the danger, in speaking of the art of fiction, of generalising. The danger that he has in mind is rather, I imagine, that of particularising, for there are some comprehensive remarks which, in addition to those embodied in Mr. Besant's suggestive lecture, might without fear of misleading him be addressed to the ingenuous student. I should remind him first of the magnificence of the form that is open to him, which offers to sight so few restrictions and such innumerable opportunities. The other arts, in comparison, appear confined and hampered; the various conditions under which they are exercised are so rigid and definite. But the only condition that I can think of attaching to the composition of the novel is, as I have already said, that it be sincere. This freedom is a splendid privilege, and the first lesson of the young novelist is to learn to be worthy of it. "Enjoy it as it deserves," I should say to him; "take possession of it, explore it to its utmost extent, publish it, rejoice in it. All life belongs to you, and do not listen either to those who would shut you up into corners of it and tell you that it is only here and there that art inhabits, or to those who would persuade you that this heavenly messenger wings her way outside of life altogether, breathing a superfine air, and turning away her head from the truth of things. There is no impression of life, no manner of seeing it and feeling it, to which the plan of the novelist may not offer a place; you have only to remember that talents so dissimilar as those of Alexandre Dumas and Jane Austen, Charles Dickens and Gustave Flaubert have worked in this field with equal glory. Do not think too much about optimism and pessimism; try and catch the colour of life itself. In France to-day we see a prodigious effort (that of Emile Zola, to whose solid and serious work no explorer of the capacity of the novel can allude without respect), we see an extraordinary effort vitiated by a spirit of pessimism on a narrow basis. M. Zola is magnificent, but he strikes an English reader as ignorant; he has an air of working in the dark; if he had as much light as energy, his results would be of the highest value.

As for the aberrations of a shallow optimism, the ground (of English fiction especially) is strewn with their brittle particles as with broken glass. If you must indulge in conclusions, let them have the taste of a wide knowledge. Remember that your first duty is to be as complete as possible—to make as perfect a work. Be generous and delicate and pursue the prize."

* * *

CHARACTERISTIC MATURITY

William James: The Emotions

WJ to his publisher, Henry Holt, on *The Principles of Psychology*, May 9, 1890:

"No one could be more disgusted than I at the sight of the book. *No* subject is worth being treated of in 1000 pages! Had I ten years more, I could rewrite it in 500; but as it stands it is this or nothing—a loathsome, distended, tumefied, bloated, dropsical mass, testifying to nothing but two facts: *1st*, that there is no such thing as a *science* of psychology, and *2nd*, that WJ is an incapable."

To his wife, May 24, 1890:

"I came home very weary, and lit a fire, and had a delicious two hours all by myself, thinking of the big *étape* of my life which now lay behind me (I mean that infernal book done), and of the possibilities that the future yielded of reading and living and loving out from the shadow of that interminable black cloud. . . . At any rate, it does give me some comfort to think that I don't live *wholly* in projects, aspirations and phrases, but now and then have something done to show for all the fuss. The joke of it is that I, who have always considered myself a thing of glimpses, of discontinuity, of *aperçus*, with no power of doing a big job, suddenly realize at the *end* of this task that it is the biggest book on psychology in any language except Wundt's, Rosmini's and Daniel Greenleaf Thompson's! Still, if it burns up at the printing-office, I shan't much care, for I shan't ever write it again!!"

To the English philosopher and psychologist James Sully, July 8, 1890:

"It seems to me that psychology is like physics before Galileo's time—not a single elementary law yet caught a glimpse of. A great chance for some future psychologue to make a greater name than

Newton's; but who then will read the books of this generation? Not
many, I trow. Meanwhile they must be written."

From the preface:

"I have kept close to the point of view of natural science throughout
the book. Every natural science assumes certain data uncritically, and
declines to challenge the elements between which its own 'laws' obtain, and from which its own deductions are carried on. Psychology,
the science of finite individual minds, assumes as its data (1) *thoughts
and feelings*, and (2) *a physical world* in time and space with which
they coexist and which (3) *they know*. Of course these data themselves are discussable; but the discussion of them (as of other elements)
is called metaphysics and falls outside the province of this book. This
book, assuming that thoughts and feelings exist and are vehicles of
knowledge, thereupon contends that psychology when she has ascertained the empirical correlation of the various sorts of thought or
feeling with definite conditions of the brain, can go no farther—can go
no farther, that is, as a natural science. If she goes farther she becomes
metaphysical. All attempts to *explain* our phenomenally given thoughts
as products of deeper-lying entities (whether the latter be named 'Soul,'
'Transcendental Ego,' 'Ideas,' or 'Elementary Units of Consciousness')
are metaphysical. This book consequently rejects both the associationist
and the spiritualist theories; and in this strictly positivistic point of
view consists the only feature of it for which I feel tempted to claim
originality. Of course this point of view is anything but ultimate. Men
must keep thinking; and the data assumed by psychology, just like those
assumed by physics and other natural sciences, must some time be over-
hauled. The effort to overhaul them clearly and thoroughly is metaphysics; but metaphysics can only perform her task well when distinctly
conscious of its great extent. Metaphysics fragmentary, irresponsible,
and half-awake, and unconscious that she is metaphysical, spoils two
good things when she injects herself into a natural science. And it seems
to me that the theories both of a spiritual agent and of associated
'ideas' are, as they figure in psychology-books, just such metaphysics
as this. Even if their results be true, it would be as well to keep them,
as thus presented, out of psychology as it is to keep the results of
idealism out of physics.

"I have therefore treated our passing thoughts as integers, and regarded the mere laws of their coexistence with brain-states as the
ultimate laws for our science. The reader will in vain seek for any
closed system in the book. It is mainly a mass of descriptive details,
running out into queries which only a metaphysics alive to the weight
of her task can hope successfully to deal with. That will perhaps be
centuries hence; and meanwhile the best mark of health that a science
can show is this unfinished-seeming front."

ON "THE EMOTIONS"

* * * * *

Were we to go through the whole list of emotions which have been named by men, and study their organic manifestations, we should but ring the changes on the elements which these three typical cases [1] involve. Rigidity of this muscle, relaxation of that, constriction of arteries here, dilation there, breathing of this sort or that, pulse slowing or quickening, this gland secreting and that one dry, etc., etc. We should, moreover, find that our descriptions had no absolute truth; that they only applied to the average man; that every one of us, almost, has some personal idiosyncrasy of expression, laughing or sobbing differently from his neighbor, or reddening or growing pale where others do not. We should find a like variation in the objects which excite emotion in different persons. Jokes at which one explodes with laughter nauseate another, and seem blasphemous to a third; and occasions which overwhelm me with fear or bashfulness are just what give you the full sense of ease and power. The internal shadings of emotional feeling, moreover, merge endlessly into each other. Language has discriminated some of them, as hatred, antipathy, animosity, dislike, aversion, malice, spite, vengefulness, abhorrence, etc., etc.; but in the dictionaries of synonyms we find these feelings distinguished more by their severally appropriate objective stimuli than by their conscious or subjective tone.

The result of all this flux is that the merely descriptive literature of the emotions is one of the most tedious parts of psychology. And not only is it tedious, but you feel that its subdivisions are to a great extent either fictitious or unimportant, and that its pretences to accuracy are a sham. But unfortunately there is little psychological writing about the emotions which is not merely descriptive. As emotions are described in novels, they interest us, for we are made to share them. We have grown acquainted with the concrete objects and emergencies which call them forth, and any knowing touch of introspection which may grace the page meets with a quick and feeling response. Confessedly literary works of aphoristic philosophy also flash lights into our emotional life, and give us a fitful delight. But as far as "scientific psychology" of the emotions goes, I may have been surfeited by too much reading of classic works on the subject, but I should as lief read verbal descriptions of the shapes of the rocks on a New Hampshire farm as toil through them again. They give one nowhere a central point of view, or a deductive or generative principle. They distinguish and refine and specify *in infinitum* without ever getting on to another logical level. Whereas the beauty of all truly scientific work is to get

---

[1] WJ had just given descriptive examples of the manifestations of Grief, Fear, and Hatred.

to ever deeper levels. Is there no way out from this level of individual description in the case of the emotions? I believe there is a way out, but I fear that few will take it.

The trouble with the emotions in psychology is that they are regarded too much as absolutely individual things. So long as they are set down as so many eternal and sacred psychic entities, like the old immutable species in natural history, so long all that *can* be done with them is reverently to catalogue their separate characters, points, and effects. But if we regard them as products of more general causes (as "species" are now regarded as products of heredity and variation), the mere distinguishing and cataloguing becomes of subsidiary importance. Having the goose which lays the golden eggs, the description of each egg already laid is a minor matter. Now the general causes of the emotions are indubitably physiological. Prof. C. Lange, of Copenhagen, in the pamphlet from which I have already quoted, published in 1885 a physiological theory of their constitution and conditioning, which I had already broached the previous year in an article in Mind. None of the criticisms which I have heard of it have made me doubt its essential truth. I will therefore devote the next few pages to explaining what it is. I shall limit myself in the first instance to what may be called the *coarser* emotions, grief, fear, rage, love, in which every one recognizes a strong organic reverberation, and afterwards speak of the *subtler* emotions, or of those whose organic reverberation is less obvious and strong.

EMOTION FOLLOWS UPON THE BODILY EXPRESSION IN THE COARSER EMOTIONS AT LEAST

Our natural way of thinking about these coarser emotions is that the mental perception of some fact excites the mental affection called the emotion, and that this latter state of mind gives rise to the bodily expression. My theory, on the contrary, is that *the bodily changes follow directly the perception of the exciting fact, and that our feeling of the same changes as they occur is the emotion.* Common-sense says, we lose our fortune, are sorry and weep; we meet a bear, are frightened and run; we are insulted by a rival, are angry and strike. The hypothesis here to be defended says that this order of sequence is incorrect, that the one mental state is not immediately induced by the other, that the bodily manifestations must first be interposed between, and that the more rational statement is that we feel sorry because we cry, angry because we strike, afraid because we tremble, and not that we cry, strike, or tremble, because we are sorry, angry, or fearful, as the case may be. Without the bodily states following on the perception, the latter would be purely cognitive in form, pale, colorless, destitute of emotional warmth. We might then see the bear, and judge it best to run, receive the insult and deem it right to strike, but we should not actually *feel* afraid or angry.

Stated in this crude way, the hypothesis is pretty sure to meet with immediate disbelief. And yet neither many nor far-fetched considerations are required to mitigate its paradoxical character, and possibly to produce conviction of its truth.

To begin with, no reader of the last two chapters will be inclined to doubt the fact that *objects do excite bodily changes* by a preorganized mechanism, or the farther fact that *the changes are so indefinitely numerous and subtle that the entire organism may be called a soundingboard*, which every change of consciousness, however slight, may make reverberate. The various permutations and combinations of which these organic activities are susceptible make it abstractly possible that no shade of emotion, however slight, should be without a bodily reverberation as unique, when taken in its totality, as is the mental mood itself. The immense number of parts modified in each emotion is what makes it so difficult for us to reproduce in cold blood the total and integral expression of any one of them. We may catch the trick with the voluntary muscles, but fail with the skin, glands, heart, and other viscera. Just as an artificially imitated sneeze lacks something of the reality, so the attempt to imitate an emotion in the absence of its normal instigating cause is apt to be rather "hollow."

The next thing to be noticed is this, that *every one of the bodily changes, whatsoever it be, is* FELT, *acutely or obscurely, the moment it occurs*. If the reader has never paid attention to this matter, he will be both interested and astonished to learn how many different local bodily feelings he can detect in himself as characteristic of his various emotional moods. It would be perhaps too much to expect him to arrest the tide of any strong gust of passion for the sake of any such curious analysis as this; but he can observe more tranquil states, and that may be assumed here to be true of the greater which is shown to be true of the less. Our whole cubic capacity is sensibly alive; and each morsel of it contributes its pulsations of feeling, dim or sharp, pleasant, painful, or dubious, to that sense of personality that every one of us unfailingly carries with him. It is surprising what little items give accent to these complexes of sensibility. When worried by any slight trouble, one may find that the focus of one's bodily consciousness is the contraction, often quite inconsiderable, of the eyes and brows. When momentarily embarrassed, it is something in the pharynx that compels either a swallow, a clearing of the throat, or a slight cough; and so on for as many more instances as might be named. Our concern here being with the general view rather than with the details, I will not linger to discuss these, but, assuming the point admitted that every change that occurs must be felt, I will pass on.

I now proceed to urge the vital point of my whole theory, which is this: *If we fancy some strong emotion, and then try to abstract from our consciousness of it all the feelings of its bodily symptoms, we find we have nothing left behind*, no "mind-stuff" out of which the emotion can be constituted, and that a cold and neutral state of intellectual perception is all that remains. It is true that, although most people when asked say that their introspection verifies this statement, some persist in saying theirs does not. Many cannot be made to understand the question. When you beg them to imagine away every feeling of laughter and of tendency to laugh from their consciousness of the ludicrousness of an object, and then to tell you what the feeling of its ludicrousness would be like, whether it be anything more than the perception that the object belongs to the class "funny," they persist in replying that the thing proposed is a physical impossibility, and that they always *must* laugh if they see a funny object. Of course the task proposed is not the practical one of seeing a ludicrous object and annihilating one's tendency to laugh. It is the purely speculative one of subtracting certain elements of feeling from an emotional state supposed to exist in its fulness, and saying what the residual elements are. I cannot help thinking that all who rightly apprehend this problem will agree with the proposition above laid down. What kind of an emotion of fear would be left if the feeling neither of quickened heart-beats nor of shallow breathing, neither of trembling lips nor of weakened limbs, neither of goose-flesh nor of visceral stirrings, were present, it is quite impossible for me to think. Can one fancy the state of rage and picture no ebullition in the chest, no flushing of the face, no dilatation of the nostrils, no clenching of the teeth, no impulse to vigorous action, but in their stead limp muscles, calm breathing, and a placid face? The present writer, for one, certainly cannot. The rage is as completely evaporated as the sensation of its so-called manifestations, and the only thing that can possibly be supposed to take its place is some cold-blooded and dispassionate judicial sentence, confined entirely to the intellectual realm, to the effect that a certain person or persons merit chastisement for their sins. In like manner of grief: what would it be without its tears, its sobs, its suffocation of the heart, its pang in the breast-bone? A feelingless cognition that certain circumstances are deplorable, and nothing more. Every passion in turn tells the same story. A purely disembodied human emotion is a nonentity. I do not say that it is a contradiction in the nature of things, or that pure spirits are necessarily condemned to cold intellectual lives; but I say that for *us*, emotion dissociated from all bodily feeling is inconceivable. The more closely I scrutinize my states, the more persuaded I become that whatever moods, affections, and passions I have are in very truth constituted by, and made up of, those bodily changes which we ordinarily call their expression or consequence; and the more it seems to me that if I were to become corporeally anæsthetic, I should be excluded from the life of the affections, harsh and tender alike, and drag out an existence of merely cognitive or intellectual form. Such an existence, although it seems to have been the ideal of ancient sages, is too apathetic to be keenly sought after by those born after the revival of the worship of sensibility, a few generations ago.

Let not this view be called materialistic. It is neither more nor less materialistic than any other view which says that our emotions are conditioned by nervous processes. No reader of this book is likely to rebel against such a saying so long as it is expressed in general terms; and if any one still finds materialism in the thesis now defended, that must be because of the special processes invoked. They are *sensational* processes, processes due to inward currents set up by physical happenings. Such processes have, it is true, always been regarded by the platonizers in psychology as having something peculiarly base about them. But our emotions must always be *inwardly* what they are, whatever be the physiological ground of their apparition. If they are deep, pure, worthy, spiritual facts on any conceivable theory of their physiological source, they remain no less deep, pure, spiritual, and worthy of regard on this present sensational theory. They carry their own inner measure of worth with them; and it is just as logical to use the present theory of the emotions for proving that sensational processes need not be vile and material, as to use their vileness and materiality as a proof that such a theory cannot be true.

. If such a theory is true, then each emotion is the resultant of a sum of elements, and each element is caused by a physiological process of a sort already well known. The elements are all organic changes, and each of them is the reflex effect of the exciting object. Definite questions now immediately arise—questions very different from those which were the only possible ones without this view. Those were questions of classification: "Which are the proper genera of emotion, and which the species under each?" or of description: "By what expression is each emotion characterized?" The questions now are *causal*: "Just what changes does this object and what changes does that object excite?" and "How come they to excite these particular changes and not others?" We step from a superficial to a deep order of inquiry. Classification and description are the lowest stage of science. They sink into the background the moment questions of genesis are formulated, and remain important only so far as they facilitate our answering these. .Now the moment the genesis of an emotion is accounted for, as the arousal by an object of a lot of reflex acts which are forthwith felt, *we immediately see why there is no limit to the number of possible different emotions which may exist, and why the emotions of different individuals may vary indefinitely*, both as to their constitution and as to objects which call them forth. For there is nothing sacramental or eternally fixed in reflex action. Any sort of reflex effect is possible, and reflexes actually vary indefinitely, as we know.

"We have all seen men dumb, instead of talkative, with joy; we have seen fright drive the blood into the head of its victim, instead of making him pale; we have seen grief run restlessly about lamenting, instead of sitting bowed down and mute; etc., etc., and this naturally enough, for one and the same cause can work differently on different men's blood-vessels (since these do not always react alike), whilst moreover the impulse on its way through the brain to the vaso-motor centre is differently influenced by different earlier impressions in the form of recollections or associations of ideas." [1]

In short, *any classification of the emotions is seen to be as true and as "natural" as any other*, if it only serves some purpose; and such a question as "What is the 'real' or 'typical' expression of anger, or fear?" is seen to have no objective meaning at all. Instead of it we now have the question as to how any given "expression" of anger or fear may have come to exist; and that is a real question of physiological mechanics on the one hand, and of history on the other, which (like all real questions) is in essence answerable, although the answer may be hard to find.

*   *   *

---

[1] Lange: *Über Gemüthsbewegungen*, Leipzig 1887, p. 75.

CHARACTERISTIC MATURITY

The Will to Believe [1]

* * * * *

IN THE recently published Life by Leslie Stephen of his brother, Fitz-James, there is an account of a school to which the latter went when he was a boy. The teacher, a certain Mr. Guest, used to converse with his pupils in this wise: "Gurney, what is the difference between justification and sanctification?—Stephen, prove the omnipotence of God!" etc. In the midst of our Harvard freethinking and indifference we are prone to imagine that here at your good old orthodox College conversation continues to be somewhat upon this order; and to show you that we at Harvard have not lost all interest in these vital subjects, I have brought with me to-night something like a sermon on justification by faith to read to you,—I mean an essay in justification *of* faith, a defence of our right to adopt a believing attitude in religious matters, in spite of the fact that our merely logical intellect may not have been coerced. "The Will to Believe," accordingly, is the title of my paper.

I have long defended to my own students the lawfulness of voluntarily adopted faith; but as soon as they have got well imbued with the logical spirit, they have as a rule refused to admit my contention to be lawful philosophically, even though in point of fact they were personally all the time chock-full of some faith or other themselves. I am all the while, however, so profoundly convinced that my own position is correct, that your invitation has seemed to me a good occasion to make my statements more clear. Perhaps your minds will be more open than those with which I have hitherto had to deal. I will be as little technical as I can, though I must begin by setting up some technical distinctions that will help us in the end.

---

[1] An Address to the Philosophical Clubs of Yale and Brown Universities.

I

Let us give the name of *hypothesis* to anything that may be proposed to our belief; and just as the electricians speak of live and dead wires, let us speak of any hypothesis as either *live* or *dead*. A live hypothesis is one which appeals as a real possibility to him to whom it is proposed. If I ask you to believe in the Mahdi, the notion makes no electric connection with your nature,—it refuses to scintillate with any credibility at all. As an hypothesis it is completely dead. To an Arab, however (even if he be not one of the Mahdi's followers), the hypothesis is among the mind's possibilities: it is alive. This shows that deadness and liveness in an hypothesis are not intrinsic properties, but relations to the individual thinker. They are measured by his willingness to act. The maximum of liveness in an hypothesis means willingness to act irrevocably. Practically, that means belief; but there is some believing tendency wherever there is willingness to act at all.

Next, let us call the decision between two hypotheses an *option*. Options may be of several kinds. They may be—1, *living* or *dead;* 2, *forced* or *avoidable;* 3, *momentous* or *trivial;* and for our purposes we may call an option a *genuine* option when it is of the forced, living, and momentous kind.

1. A living option is one in which both hypotheses are live ones. If I say to you: "Be a theosophist or be a Mohammedan," it is probably a dead option, because for you neither hypothesis is likely to be alive. But if I say: "Be an agnostic or be a Christian," it is otherwise: trained as you are, each hypothesis makes some appeal, however small, to your belief.

2. Next, if I say to you: "Choose between going out with your umbrella or without it," I do not offer you a genuine option, for it is not forced. You can easily avoid it by not going out at all. Similarly, if I say, "Either love me or hate me," "Either call my theory true or call it false," your option is avoidable. You may remain indifferent to me, neither loving nor hating, and you may decline to offer any judgment as to my theory. But if I say, "Either accept this truth or go without it," I put on you a forced option, for there is no standing place outside of the alternative. Every dilemma based on a complete logical disjunction, with no possibility of not choosing, is an option of this forced kind.

3. Finally, if I were Dr. Nansen and proposed to you to join my North Pole expedition, your option would be momentous; for this would probably be your only similar opportunity, and your choice now would either exclude you from the North Pole sort of immortality altogether or put at least the chance of it into your hands. He who refuses to embrace a unique opportunity loses the prize as surely as if he tried and failed. *Per contra*, the option is trivial when the opportunity is

not unique, when the stake is insignificant, or when the decision is reversible if it later prove unwise. Such trivial options abound in the scientific life. A chemist finds an hypothesis live enough to spend a year in its verification: he believes in it to that extent. But if his experiments prove inconclusive either way, he is quit for his loss of time, no vital harm being done.

It will facilitate our discussion if we keep all these distinctions well in mind.

II

The next matter to consider is the actual psychology of human opinion. When we look at certain facts, it seems as if our passional and volitional nature lay at the root of all our convictions. When we look at others, it seems as if they could do nothing when the intellect had once said its say. Let us take the latter facts up first.

Does it not seem preposterous on the very face of it to talk of our opinions being modifiable at will? Can our will either help or hinder our intellect in its perceptions of truth? Can we, by just willing it, believe that Abraham Lincoln's existence is a myth, and that the portraits of him in McClure's Magazine are all of some one else? Can we, by any effort of our will, or by any strength of wish that it were true, believe ourselves well and about when we are roaring with rheumatism in bed, or feel certain that the sum of the two one-dollar bills in our pocket must be a hundred dollars? We can *say* any of these things, but we are absolutely impotent to believe them; and of just such things is the whole fabric of the truths that we do believe in made up,—matters of fact, immediate or remote, as Hume said, and relations between ideas, which are either there or not there for us if we see them so, and which if not there cannot be put there by any action of our own.

In Pascal's Thoughts there is a celebrated passage known in literature as Pascal's wager. In it he tries to force us into Christianity by reasoning as if our concern with truth resembled our concern with the stakes in a game of chance. Translated freely his words are these: You must either believe or not believe that God is—which will you do? Your human reason cannot say. A game is going on between you and the nature of things which at the day of judgment will bring out either heads or tails. Weigh what your gains and your losses would be if you should stake all you have on heads, or God's existence: if you win in such case, you gain eternal beatitude; if you lose, you lose nothing at all. If there were an infinity of chances, and only one for God in this wager, still you ought to stake your all on God; for though you surely risk a finite loss by this procedure, any finite loss is reasonable, even a certain one is reasonable, if there is but the possibility of infinite gain. Go, then, and take holy water, and have masses said; belief will come and stupefy your scruples,—*Cela vous fera croire et vous abêtira.* Why should you not? At bottom, what have you to lose?

You probably feel that when religious faith expresses itself thus, in the language of the gaming-table, it is put to its last trumps. Surely Pascal's own personal belief in masses and holy water had far other springs; and this celebrated page of his is but an argument for others, a last desperate snatch at a weapon against the hardness of the unbelieving heart. We feel that a faith in masses and holy water adopted wilfully after such a mechanical calculation would lack the inner soul of faith's reality; and if we were ourselves in the place of the Deity, we should probably take particular pleasure in cutting off believers of this pattern from their infinite reward. It is evident that unless there be some pre-existing tendency to believe in masses and holy water, the option offered to the will by Pascal is not a living option. Certainly no Turk ever took to masses and holy water on its account; and even to us Protestants these means of salvation seem such foregone impossibilities that Pascal's logic, invoked for them specifically, leaves us unmoved. As well might the Mahdi write to us, saying, "I am the Expected One whom God has created in his effulgence. You shall be infinitely happy if you confess me; otherwise you shall be cut off from the light of the sun. Weigh, then, your infinite gain if I am genuine against your finite sacrifice if I am not!" His logic would be that of Pascal; but he would vainly use it on us, for the hypothesis he offers us is dead. No tendency to act on it exists in us to any degree.

The talk of believing by our volition seems, then, from one point of view, simply silly. From another point of view it is worse than silly, it is vile. When one turns to the magnificent edifice of the physical sciences, and sees how it was reared; what thousands of disinterested moral lives of men lie buried in its mere foundations; what patience and postponement, what choking down of preference, what submission to the icy laws of outer fact are wrought into its very stones and mortar; how absolutely impersonal it stands in its vast augustness,—then how besotted and contemptible seems every little sentimentalist who comes blowing his voluntary smoke-wreaths, and pretending to decide things from out of his private dream! Can we wonder if those bred in the rugged and manly school of science should feel like spewing such subjectivism out of their mouths? The whole system of loyalties which grow up in the schools of science go dead against its toleration; so that it is only natural that those who have caught the scientific fever should pass over to the opposite extreme, and write sometimes as if the incorruptibly truthful intellect ought positively to prefer bitterness and unacceptableness to the heart in its cup.

> It fortifies my soul to know
> That, though I perish, Truth is so—

sings Clough, while Huxley exclaims: "My only consolation lies in the reflection that, however bad our posterity may become, so far as they hold by the plain rule of not pretending to believe what they have no reason to believe, because it may be to their advantage so to pretend [the word 'pretend' is surely here redundant], they will not have reached the lowest depth of immorality." And that delicious *enfant terrible* Clifford writes: "Belief is desecrated when given to unproved and unquestioned statements for the solace and private pleasure of the believer. . . . Whoso would deserve well of his fellows in this matter will guard the purity of his belief with a very fanaticism of jealous care, lest at any time it should rest on an unworthy object, and catch a stain which can never be wiped away. . . . If [a] belief has been accepted on insufficient evidence [even though the belief be true, as Clifford on the same page explains] the pleasure is a stolen one. . . . It is sinful because it is stolen in defiance of our duty to mankind. That duty is to guard ourselves from such beliefs as from a pestilence which may shortly master our own body and then spread to the rest of the town. . . . It is wrong always, everywhere, and for every one, to believe anything upon insufficient evidence."

III

All this strikes one as healthy, even when expressed, as by Clifford, with somewhat too much of robustious pathos in the voice. Free-will and simple wishing do seem, in the matter of our credences, to be only fifth wheels to the coach. Yet if any one should thereupon assume that intellectual insight is what remains after wish and will and sentimental preference have taken wing, or that pure reason is what then settles our opinions, he would fly quite as directly in the teeth of the facts.

It is only our already dead hypotheses that our willing nature is unable to bring to life again. But what has made them dead for us is for the most part a previous action of our willing nature of an antagonistic kind. When I say "willing nature," I do not mean only such deliberate volitions as may have set up habits of belief that we cannot now escape from,—I mean all such factors of belief as fear and hope, prejudice and passion, imitation and partisanship, the circumpressure of our caste and set. As a matter of fact we find ourselves believing, we hardly know how or why. Mr. Balfour gives the name of "authority" to all those influences, born of the intellectual climate, that make hypotheses possible or impossible for us, alive or dead. Here in this room, we all of us believe in molecules and the conservation of energy, in democracy and necessary progress, in Protestant Christianity and the duty of fighting for "the doctrine of the immortal Monroe," all for no reasons worthy of the name. We see into these matters with no more inner clearness, and probably with much less, than any disbeliever in them might possess. His unconventionality would probably have some grounds to show for its conclusions; but for us, not insight, but the *prestige* of the opinions, is what makes the spark shoot from them and light up our sleeping magazines of faith. Our reason is quite satisfied, in nine hundred and ninety-nine cases out of every thousand of us, if it can find a few arguments that will do to recite in case our credulity is criticised by some one else. Our faith is faith in some one else's faith, and in the greatest matters this is most the case. Our belief in truth itself, for instance, that there is a truth, and that our minds and it are made for each other,—what is it but a passionate affirmation of desire, in which our social system backs us up? We want to have a truth; we want to believe that our experiments and studies and discussions must put us in a continually better and better position towards it; and on this line we agree to fight out our thinking lives. But if a pyrrhonistic sceptic asks us *how we know* all this, can our logic find a reply? No! certainly it cannot. It is just one volition against another,—we willing to go in for life upon a trust or assumption which he, for his part, does not care to make.[1]

As a rule we disbelieve all facts and theories for which we have no use. Clifford's cosmic emotions find no use for Christian feelings. Huxley belabors the bishops because there is no use for sacerdotalism in his scheme of life. Newman, on the contrary, goes over to Romanism, and finds all sorts of reasons good for staying there, because a priestly system is for him an organic need and delight. Why do so few "scientists" even look at the evidence for telepathy, so called? Because they think, as a leading biologist, now dead, once said to me, that even if such a thing were true, scientists ought to band together to keep it suppressed and concealed. It would undo the uniformity of Nature and all sorts of other things without which scientists cannot carry on their pursuits. But if this very man had been shown something which as a scientist he might *do* with telepathy, he might not only have examined the evidence, but even have found it good enough. This very law which the logicians would impose upon us—if I may give the name of logicians to those who would rule out our willing nature here—is based on nothing but their own natural wish to exclude all elements for which they, in their professional quality of logicians, can find no use.

Evidently, then, our non-intellectual nature does influence our convictions. There are passional tendencies and volitions which run before and others which come after belief, and it is only the latter that are too late for the fair; and they are not too late when the previous passional work has been already in their own direction. Pascal's argu-

---

[1] Compare the admirable page 310 in S. H. Hodgson's "Time and Space," London, 1865.

ment, instead of being powerless, then seems a regular clincher, and is the last stroke needed to make our faith in masses and holy water complete. The state of things is evidently far from simple; and pure insight and logic, whatever they might do ideally, are not the only things that really do produce our creeds.

IV

Our next duty, having recognized this mixed-up state of affairs, is to ask whether it be simply reprehensible and pathological, or whether, on the contrary, we must treat it as a normal element in making up our minds. The thesis I defend is, briefly stated, this: *Our passional nature not only lawfully may, but must, decide an option between propositions, whenever it is a genuine option that cannot by its nature be decided on intellectual grounds; for to say, under such circumstances, "Do not decide, but leave the question open," is itself a passional decision,—just like deciding yes or no,—and is attended with the same risk of losing the truth.* The thesis thus abstractly expressed will, I trust, soon become quite clear. But I must first indulge in a bit more of preliminary work.

V

It will be observed that for the purposes of this discussion we are on "dogmatic" ground,—ground, I mean, which leaves systematic philosophical scepticism altogether out of account. The postulate that there is truth, and that it is the destiny of our minds to attain it, we are deliberately resolving to make, though the sceptic will not make it. We part company with him, therefore, absolutely, at this point. But the faith that truth exists, and that our minds can find it, may be held in two ways. We may talk of the *empiricist* way and of the *absolutist* way of believing in truth. The absolutists in this matter say that we not only can attain to knowing truth, but we can *know when* we have attained to knowing it; while the empiricists think that although we may attain it, we cannot infallibly know when. To *know* is one thing, and to know for certain *that* we know is another. One may hold to the first being possible without the second; hence the empiricists and the absolutists, although neither of them is a sceptic in the usual philosophic sense of the term, show very different degrees of dogmatism in their lives.

If we look at the history of opinions, we see that the empiricist tendency has largely prevailed in science, while in philosophy the absolutist tendency has had everything its own way. The characteristic sort of happiness, indeed, which philosophies yield has mainly consisted in the conviction felt by each successive school or system that by it bottom-certitude has been attained. "Other philosophies are collections of opinions, mostly false; *my* philosophy gives standing-ground forever,"—

who does not recognize in this the key-note of every system worthy of the name? A system, to be a system at all, must come as a *closed* system, reversible in this or that detail, perchance, but in its essential features never!

Scholastic orthodoxy, to which one must always go when one wishes to find perfectly clear statement, has beautifully elaborated this absolutist conviction in a doctrine which it calls that of "objective evidence." If, for example, I am unable to doubt that I now exist before you, that two is less than three, or that if all men are mortal then I am mortal too, it is because these things illumine my intellect irresistibly. The final ground of this objective evidence possessed by certain propositions is the *adæquatio intellectûs nostri cum rê*. The certitude it brings involves an *aptitudinem ad extorquendum certum assensum* on the part of the truth envisaged, and on the side of the subject a *quietem in cognitione*, when once the object is mentally received, that leaves no possibility of doubt behind; and in the whole transaction nothing operates but the *entitas ipsa* of the object and the *entitas ipsa* of the mind. We slouchy modern thinkers dislike to talk in Latin,—indeed, we dislike to talk in set terms at all; but at bottom our own state of mind is very much like this whenever we uncritically abandon ourselves: You believe in objective evidence, and I do. Of some things we feel that we are certain: we know, and we know that we do know. There is something that gives a click inside of us, a bell that strikes twelve, when the hands of our mental clock have swept the dial and meet over the meridian hour. The greatest empiricists among us are only empiricists on reflection: when left to their instincts, they dogmatize like infallible popes. When the Cliffords tell us how sinful it is to be Christians on such "insufficient evidence," insufficiency is really the last thing they have in mind. For them the evidence is absolutely sufficient, only it makes the other way. They believe so completely in an anti-christian order of the universe that there is no living option: Christianity is a dead hypothesis from the start.

VI

But now, since we are all such absolutists by instinct, what in our quality of students of philosophy ought we to do about the fact? Shall we espouse and indorse it? Or shall we treat it as a weakness of our nature from which we must free ourselves, if we can?

I sincerely believe that the latter course is the only one we can follow as reflective men. Objective evidence and certitude are doubtless very fine ideals to play with, but where on this moonlit and dream-visited planet are they found? I am, therefore, myself a complete empiricist so far as my theory of human knowledge goes. I live, to be sure, by the practical faith that we must go on experiencing and thinking over our experience, for only thus can our opinions grow more true; but to hold any one of them—I absolutely do not care which—as if it never could be reinterpretable or corrigible, I believe to be a tremendously mistaken attitude, and I think that the whole history of philosophy will bear me out. There is but one indefectibly certain truth, and that is the truth that pyrrhonistic scepticism itself leaves standing,—the truth that the present phenomenon of consciousness exists. That, however, is the bare starting-point of knowledge, the mere admission of a stuff to be philosophized about. The various philosophies are but so many attempts at expressing what this stuff really is. And if we repair to our libraries what disagreement do we discover! Where is a certainly true answer found? Apart from abstract propositions of comparison (such as two and two are the same as four), propositions which tell us nothing by themselves about concrete reality, we find no proposition ever regarded by any one as evidently certain that has not either been called a falsehood, or at least had its truth sincerely questioned by some one else. The transcending of the axioms of geometry, not in play but in earnest, by certain of our contemporaries (as Zöllner and Charles H. Hinton), and the rejection of the whole Aristotelian logic by the Hegelians, are striking instances in point.

No concrete test of what is really true has ever been agreed upon. Some make the criterion external to the moment of perception, putting it either in revelation, the *consensus gentium*, the instincts of the heart, or the systematized experience of the race. Others make the perceptive moment its own test,—Descartes, for instance, with his clear and distinct ideas guaranteed by the veracity of God; Reid with his "commonsense"; and Kant with his forms of synthetic judgment *a priori*. The inconceivability of the opposite; the capacity to be verified by sense; the possession of complete organic unity or self-relation, realized when a thing is its own other,—are standards which, in turn, have been used. The much lauded objective evidence is never triumphantly there; it is a mere aspiration or *Grenzbegriff*, marking the infinitely remote ideal of our thinking life. To claim that certain truths now possess it, is simply to say that when you think them true and they *are* true, then their evidence is objective, otherwise it is not. But practically one's conviction that the evidence one goes by is of the real objective brand, is only one more subjective opinion added to the lot. For what a contradictory array of opinions have objective evidence and absolute certitude been claimed! The world is rational through and through,—its existence is an ultimate brute fact; there is a personal God,—a personal God is inconceivable; there is an extra-mental physical world immediately known,—the mind can only know its own ideas; a moral imperative exists,—obligation is only the resultant of desires; a permanent spiritual principle is in every one,—there are only shifting states of mind; there is an endless chain of causes,—there is an absolute first cause; an eternal necessity,—a freedom; a purpose,—no purpose; a primal One,—a primal Many; a universal continuity,—an essential discontinuity in things; an infinity,—no infinity. There is this,—there is that; there is indeed nothing which some one has not thought absolutely true, while his neighbor deemed it absolutely false; and not an absolutist among them seems ever to have considered that the trouble may all the time be essential, and that the intellect, even with truth directly in its grasp, may have no infallible signal for knowing whether it be truth or no. When, indeed, one remembers that the most striking practical application to life of the doctrine of objective certitude has been the conscientious labors of the Holy Office of the Inquisition, one feels less tempted than ever to lend the doctrine a respectful ear.

But please observe, now, that when as empiricists we give up the doctrine of objective certitude, we do not thereby give up the quest or hope of truth itself. We still pin our faith on its existence, and still believe that we gain an ever better position towards it by systematically continuing to roll up experiences and think. Our great difference from the scholastic lies in the way we face. The strength of his system lies in the principles, the origin, the *terminus a quo* of his thought; for us the strength is in the outcome, the upshot, the *terminus ad quem*. Not where it comes from but what it leads to is to decide. It matters not to an empiricist from what quarter an hypothesis may come to him: he may have acquired it by fair means or by foul; passion may have whispered or accident suggested it; but if the total drift of thinking continues to confirm it, that is what he means by its being true.

VII

One more point, small but important, and our preliminaries are done. There are two ways of looking at our duty in the matter of opinion, —ways entirely different, and yet ways about whose difference the theory of knowledge seems hitherto to have shown very little concern. *We must know the truth;* and *we must avoid error,*—these are our first and great commandments as would-be knowers; but they are not two ways of stating an identical commandment, they are two separable laws. Although it may indeed happen that when we believe the truth *A*, we escape as an incidental consequence from believing the falsehood *B*, it hardly ever happens that by merely disbelieving *B* we necessarily believe *A*. We may in escaping *B* fall into believing other falsehoods, *C* or *D*, just as bad as *B*; or we may escape *B* by not believing anything at all, not even *A*.

Believe truth! Shun error!—these, we see, are two materially different laws; and by choosing between them we may end by coloring differently our whole intellectual life. We may regard the chase for truth as paramount, and the avoidance of error as secondary; or we may, on the other hand, treat the avoidance of error as more imperative, and let truth take its chance. Clifford, in the instructive passage which I have quoted, exhorts us to the latter course. Believe nothing, he tells us, keep your mind in suspense forever, rather than by closing it on insufficient evidence incur the awful risk of believing lies. You, on the other hand, may think that the risk of being in error is a very small matter when compared with the blessings of real knowledge, and be ready to be duped many times in your investigation rather than postpone indefinitely the chance of guessing true. I myself find it impossible to go with Clifford. We must remember that these feelings of our duty about either truth or error are in any case only expressions of our passional life. Biologically considered, our minds are as ready to grind out falsehood as veracity, and he who says, "Better go without belief forever than believe a lie!" merely shows his own preponderant private horror of becoming a dupe. He may be critical of many of his desires and fears, but this fear he slavishly obeys. He cannot imagine any one questioning its binding force. For my own part, I have also a horror of being duped; but I can believe that worse things than being duped may happen to a man in this world: so Clifford's exhortation has to my ears a thoroughly fantastic sound. It is like a general informing his soldiers that it is better to keep out of battle forever than to risk a single wound. Not so are victories either over enemies or over nature gained. Our errors are surely not such awfully solemn things. In a world where we are so certain to incur them in spite of all our caution, a certain lightness of heart seems healthier than this excessive nervousness on their behalf. At any rate, it seems the fittest thing for the empiricist philosopher.

VIII

And now, after all this introduction, let us go straight at our question. I have said, and now repeat it, that not only as a matter of fact do we find our passional nature influencing us in our opinions, but that there are some options between opinions in which this influence must be regarded both as an inevitable and as a lawful determinant of our choice.

I fear here that some of you my hearers will begin to scent danger, and lend an inhospitable ear. Two first steps of passion you have indeed had to admit as necessary,—we must think so as to avoid dupery, and we must think so as to gain truth; but the surest path to those ideal consummations, you will probably consider, is from now onwards to take no further passional step.

Well, of course, I agree as far as the facts will allow. Wherever the option between losing truth and gaining it is not momentous, we can throw the chance of *gaining truth* away, and at any rate save ourselves

from any chance of *believing falsehood*, by not making up our minds
at all till objective evidence has come. In scientific questions, this is
almost always the case; and even in human affairs in general, the need
of acting is seldom so urgent that a false belief to act on is better than
no belief at all. Law courts, indeed, have to decide on the best evidence
attainable for the moment, because a judge's duty is to make law as well
as to ascertain it, and (as a learned judge once said to me) few cases
are worth spending much time over: the great thing is to have them
decided on *any* acceptable principle, and got out of the way. But in our
dealings with objective nature we obviously are recorders, not makers,
of the truth; and decisions for the mere sake of deciding promptly and
getting on to the next business would be wholly out of place. Throughout the breadth of physical nature facts are what they are quite inde-
pendently of us, and seldom is there any such hurry about them that
the risks of being duped by believing a premature theory need be faced.
The questions here are always trivial options, the hypotheses are hardly
living (at any rate not living for us spectators), the choice between
believing truth or falsehood is seldom forced. The attitude of sceptical
balance is therefore the absolutely wise one if we would escape mistakes. What difference, indeed, does it make to most of us whether we
have or have not a theory of the Röntgen rays, whether we believe or
not in mind-stuff, or have a conviction about the causality of conscious
states? It makes no difference. Such options are not forced on us. On
every account it is better not to make them, but still keep weighing
reasons *pro et contra* with an indifferent hand.

I speak, of course, here of the purely judging mind. For purposes of
discovery such indifference is to be less highly recommended, and science would be far less advanced than she is if the passionate desires of
individuals to get their own faiths confirmed had been kept out of the
game. See for example the sagacity which Spencer and Weismann now
display. On the other hand, if you want an absolute duffer in an investigation, you must, after all, take the man who has no interest whatever
in its results: he is the warranted incapable, the positive fool. The most
useful investigator, because the most sensitive observer, is always he
whose eager interest in one side of the question is balanced by an
equally keen nervousness lest he become deceived.[1] Science has organized this nervousness into a regular *technique*, her so-called method of
verification; and she has fallen so deeply in love with the method that
one may even say she has ceased to care for truth by itself at all. It is
only truth as technically verified that interests her. The truth of truths
might come in merely affirmative form, and she would decline to touch
it. Such truth as that, she might repeat with Clifford, would be stolen in

---

[1] Compare   Wilfrid   Ward's   Essay,   *to the Unseen*, Macmillan & Co., 1893.
"The Wish to Believe," in his *Witnesses*

defiance of her duty to mankind. Human passions, however, are stronger than technical rules. "Le cœur a ses raisons," as Pascal says, "que la raison ne connaît pas"; and however indifferent to all but the bare rules of the game the umpire, the abstract intellect, may be, the concrete players who furnish him the materials to judge of are usually, each one of them, in love with some pet "live hypothesis" of his own. Let us agree, however, that wherever there is no forced option, the dispassionately judicial intellect with no pet hypothesis, saving us, as it does, from dupery at any rate, ought to be our ideal.

The question next arises: Are there not somewhere forced options in our speculative questions, and can we (as men who may be interested at least as much in positively gaining truth as in merely escaping dupery) always wait with impunity till the coercive evidence shall have arrived? It seems *a priori* improbable that the truth should be so nicely adjusted to our needs and powers as that. In the great boarding-house of nature, the cakes and the butter and the syrup seldom come out so even and leave the plates so clean. Indeed, we should view them with scientific suspicion if they did.

IX

Moral questions immediately present themselves as questions whose solution cannot wait for sensible proof. A moral question is a question not of what sensibly exists, but of what is good, or would be good if it did exist. Science can tell us what exists; but to compare the *worths*, both of what exists and of what does not exist, we must consult not science, but what Pascal calls our heart. Science herself consults her heart when she lays it down that the infinite ascertainment of fact and correction of false belief are the supreme goods for man. Challenge the statement, and science can only repeat it oracularly, or else prove it by showing that such ascertainment and correction bring man all sorts of other goods which man's heart in turn declares. The question of having moral beliefs at all or not having them is decided by our will. Are our moral preferences true or false, or are they only odd biological phenomena, making things good or bad for *us*, but in themselves indifferent? How can your pure intellect decide? If your heart does not *want* a world of moral reality, your head will assuredly never make you believe in one. Mephistophelian scepticism, indeed, will satisfy the head's play-instincts much better than any rigorous idealism can. Some men (even at the student age) are so naturally cool-hearted that the moralistic hypothesis never has for them any pungent life, and in their supercilious presence the hot young moralist always feels strangely ill at ease. The appearance of knowingness is on their side, of *naïveté* and gullibility on his. Yet, in the inarticulate heart of him, he clings to it that he is not a dupe, and that there is a realm in which (as Emerson says) all their wit and intellectual superiority is no better than the cunning of a fox. Moral scepticism can no more be refuted or proved by logic than intellectual scepticism can. When we stick to it that there *is* truth (be it of either kind), we do so with our whole nature, and resolve to stand or fall by the results. The sceptic with his whole nature adopts the doubting attitude; but which of us is the wiser, Omniscience only knows.

Turn now from these wide questions of good to a certain class of questions of fact, questions concerning personal relations, states of mind between one man and another. *Do you like me or not?*—for example. Whether you do or not depends, in countless instances, on whether I meet you half-way, am willing to assume that you must like me, and show you trust and expectation. The previous faith on my part in your liking's existence is in such cases what makes your liking come. But if I stand aloof, and refuse to budge an inch until I have objective evidence, until you shall have done something apt, as the absolutists say, *ad extorquendum assensum meum,* ten to one your liking never comes. How many women's hearts are vanquished by the mere sanguine insistence of some man that they *must* love him! he will not consent to the hypothesis that they cannot. The desire for a certain kind of truth here brings about that special truth's existence; and so it is in innumerable cases of other sorts. Who gains promotions, boons, appointments, but the man in whose life they are seen to play the part of live hypotheses, who discounts them, sacrifices other things for their sake before they have come, and takes risks for them in advance? His faith acts on the powers above him as a claim, and creates its own verification.

A social organism of any sort whatever, large or small, is what it is because each member proceeds to his own duty with a trust that the other members will simultaneously do theirs. Wherever a desired result is achieved by the co-operation of many independent persons, its existence as a fact is a pure consequence of the precursive faith in one another of those immediately concerned. A government, an army, a commercial system, a ship, a college, an athletic team, all exist on this condition, without which not only is nothing achieved, but nothing is even attempted. A whole train of passengers (individually brave enough) will be looted by a few highwaymen, simply because the latter can count on one another, while each passenger fears that if he makes a movement of resistance, he will be shot before any one else backs him up. If we believed that the whole car-full would rise at once with us, we should each severally rise, and train-robbing would never even be attempted. There are, then, cases where a fact cannot come at all unless a preliminary faith exists in its coming. *And where faith in a fact can help create the fact,* that would be an insane logic which should say that faith running ahead of scientific evidence is the "lowest kind of immorality" into which a thinking being can fall. Yet such is the logic by which our scientific absolutists pretend to regulate our lives!

X

In truths dependent on our personal action, then, faith based on desire is certainly a lawful and possibly an indispensable thing.

But now, it will be said, these are all childish human cases, and have nothing to do with great cosmical matters, like the question of religious faith. Let us then pass on to that. Religions differ so much in their accidents that in discussing the religious question we must make it very generic and broad. What then do we now mean by the religious hypothesis? Science says things are; morality says some things are better than other things; and religion says essentially two things.

First, she says that the best things are the more eternal things, the overlapping things, the things in the universe that throw the last stone, so to speak, and say the final word. "Perfection is eternal,"—this phrase of Charles Secrétan seems a good way of putting this first affirmation of religion, an affirmation which obviously cannot yet be verified scientifically at all.

The second affirmation of religion is that we are better off even now if we believe her first affirmation to be true.

Now, let us consider what the logical elements of this situation are *in case the religious hypothesis in both its branches be really true.* (Of course, we must admit that possibility at the outset. If we are to discuss the question at all, it must involve a living option. If for any of you religion be a hypothesis that cannot, by any living possibility be true, then you need go no farther. I speak to the "saving remnant" alone.) So proceeding, we see, first that religion offers itself as a *momentous* option. We are supposed to gain, even now, by our belief, and to lose by our non-belief, a certain vital good. Secondly, religion is a *forced* option, so far as that good goes. We cannot escape the issue by remaining sceptical and waiting for more light, because, although we do avoid error in that way *if religion be untrue,* we lose the good, *if it be true,* just as certainly as if we positively chose to disbelieve. It is as if a man should hesitate indefinitely to ask a certain woman to marry him because he was not perfectly sure that she would prove an angel after he brought her home. Would he not cut himself off from that particular angel-possibility as decisively as if he went and married some one else? Scepticism, then, is not avoidance of option; it is option of a certain particular kind of risk. *Better risk loss of truth than chance of error,* —that is your faith-vetoer's exact position. He is actively playing his stake as much as the believer is; he is backing the field against the religious hypothesis, just as the believer is backing the religious hypothesis against the field. To preach scepticism to us as a duty until "sufficient evidence" for religion be found, is tantamount therefore to telling us, when in presence of the religious hypothesis, that to yield to our fear of its being error is wiser and better than to yield to our hope that it may be true. It is not intellect against all passions, then; it is only intellect with one passion laying down its law. And by what, forsooth, is the supreme wisdom of this passion warranted? Dupery for dupery, what proof is there that dupery through hope is so much worse than dupery through fear? I, for one, can see no proof; and I simply refuse obedience to the scientist's command to imitate his kind of option, in a case where my own stake is important enough to give me the right to choose my own form of risk. If religion be true and the evidence for it be still insufficient, I do not wish, by putting your extinguisher upon my nature (which feels to me as if it had after all some business in this matter), to forfeit my sole chance in life of getting upon the winning side,—that chance depending, of course, on my willingness to run the risk of acting as if my passional need of taking the world religiously might be prophetic and right.

All this is on the supposition that it really may be prophetic and right, and that, even to us who are discussing the matter, religion is a live hypothesis which may be true. Now, to most of us religion comes in a still further way that makes a veto on our active faith even more illogical. The more perfect and more eternal aspect of the universe is represented in our religions as having personal form. The universe is no longer a mere *It* to us, but a *Thou*, if we are religious; and any relation that may be possible from person to person might be possible here. For instance, although in one sense we are passive portions of the universe, in another we show a curious autonomy, as if we were small active centres on our own account. We feel, too, as if the appeal of religion to us were made to our own active good-will, as if evidence might be forever withheld from us unless we met the hypothesis half-way. To take a trivial illustration: just as a man who in a company of gentlemen made no advances, asked a warrant for every concession, and believed no one's word without proof, would cut himself off by such churlishness from all the social rewards that a more trusting spirit would earn, —so here, one who should shut himself up in snarling logicality and try to make the gods extort his recognition willy-nilly, or not get it at all, might cut himself off forever from his only opportunity of making the gods' acquaintance. This feeling, forced on us we know not whence, that by obstinately believing that there are gods (although not to do so would be so easy both for our logic and our life) we are doing the universe the deepest service we can, seems part of the living essence of the religious hypothesis. If the hypothesis *were* true in all its parts, including this one, then pure intellectualism, with its veto on our making willing advances, would be an absurdity; and some participation of our sympathetic nature would be logically required. I, therefore, for one, cannot see my way to accepting the agnostic rules for truth-seeking, or wilfully agree to keep my willing nature out of the game. I cannot do so for this plain reason, that *a rule of thinking which would absolutely prevent me from acknowledging certain kinds of truth if those kinds of truth were really there, would be an irrational rule.* That for me is the long and short of the formal logic of the situation, no matter what the kinds of truth might materially be.

I confess I do not see how this logic can be escaped. But sad experience makes me fear that some of you may still shrink from radically saying with me, *in abstracto,* that we have the right to believe at our own risk any hypothesis that is live enough to tempt our will. I suspect, however, that if this is so, it is because you have got away from the abstract logical point of view altogether, and are thinking (perhaps without realizing it) of some particular religious hypothesis which for you is dead. The freedom to "believe what we will" you apply to the case of some patent superstition; and the faith you think of is the faith defined by the schoolboy when he said, "Faith is when you believe something that you know ain't true." I can only repeat that this is misapprehension. *In concreto,* the freedom to believe can only cover living options which the intellect of the individual cannot by itself resolve; and living options never seem absurdities to him who has them to consider. When I look at the religious question as it really puts itself to concrete men, and when I think of all the possibilities which both practically and theoretically it involves, then this command that we shall put a stopper on our heart, instincts, and courage, and *wait*—acting of course meanwhile more or less as if religion were *not* true [1]—till doomsday, or till such time as our intellect and senses working together may have raked in evidence enough,—this command, I say, seems to me the queerest idol ever manufactured in the philosophic cave. Were we scholastic absolutists, there might be more excuse. If we had an infallible intellect with its objective certitudes, we might feel ourselves disloyal to such a perfect organ of knowledge in not trusting to it exclusively, in not waiting for its releasing word. But if we are empiricists, if we believe that no bell in us tolls to let us know for certain when

---

[1] Since belief is measured by action, he who forbids us to believe religion to be true, necessarily also forbids us to act as we should if we did believe it to be true. The whole defence of religious faith hinges upon action. If the action required or inspired by the religious hypothesis is in no way different from that dictated by the naturalistic hypothesis, then religious faith is a pure superfluity, better pruned away, and controversy about its legitimacy is a piece of idle trifling, unworthy of serious minds. I myself believe, of course, that the religious hypothesis gives to the world an expression which specifically determines our reactions, and makes them in a large part unlike what they might be on a purely naturalistic scheme of belief.

truth is in our grasp, then it seems a piece of idle fantasticality to preach so solemnly our duty of waiting for the bell. Indeed me *may* wait if we will,—I hope you do not think that I am denying that,—but if we do so, we do so at our peril as much as if we believed. In either case we *act*, taking our life in our hands. No one of us ought to issue vetoes to the other, nor should we bandy words of abuse. We ought, on the contrary, delicately and profoundly to respect one another's mental freedom: then only shall we bring about the intellectual republic; then only shall we have that spirit of inner tolerance without which all our outer tolerance is soulless, and which is empiricism's glory; then only shall we live and let live, in speculative as well as in practical things.

I began by a reference to Fitz-James Stephen; let me end by a quotation from him. "What do you think of yourself? What do you think of the world? . . . These are questions with which all must deal as it seems good to them. They are riddles of the Sphinx, and in some way or other we must deal with them. . . . In all important transactions of life we have to take a leap in the dark. . . . If we decide to leave the riddles unanswered, that is a choice; if we waver in our answer, that, too, is a choice: but whatever choice we make, we make it at our peril. If a man chooses to turn his back altogether on God and the future, no one can prevent him; no one can show beyond reasonable doubt that he is mistaken. If a man thinks otherwise and acts as he thinks, I do not see that any one can prove that *he* is mistaken. Each must act as he thinks best; and if he is wrong, so much the worse for him. We stand on a mountain pass in the midst of whirling snow and blinding mist, through which we get glimpses now and then of paths which may be deceptive. If we stand still we shall be frozen to death. If we take the wrong road we shall be dashed to pieces. We do not certainly know whether there is any right one. What must we do? 'Be strong and of a good courage.' Act for the best, hope for the best, and take what comes. . . . If death ends all, we cannot meet death better." [1]

* * *

---

[1] Liberty, Equality, Fraternity, p. 353, 2d edition. London, 1874.

CHARACTERISTIC MATURITY

On a Certain Blindness in Human Beings [1]

From the preface to *Talks to Teachers on Psychology, and to Students on Some of Life's Ideals* (1899):

"I wish I were able to make . . . 'On a Certain Blindness in Human Beings,' more impressive. It is more than the mere piece of sentimentalism which it may seem to some readers. It connects itself with a definite view of the world and of our moral relations to the same. Those who have done me the honor of reading my volume of philosophic essays will recognize that I mean the pluralistic or individualistic philosophy. According to that philosophy, the truth is too great for any one actual mind, even though that mind be dubbed 'the Absolute,' to know the whole of it. The facts and worths of life need many cognizers to take them in. There is no point of view absolutely public and universal. Private and uncommunicable perceptions always remain over, and the worst of it is that those who look for them from the outside never know *where*.

"The practical consequence of such a philosophy is the well-known democratic respect for the sacredness of individuality, is, at any rate the outward tolerance of whatever is not itself intolerant. These phrases are so familiar that they sound now rather dead in our ears. Once they had a passionate inner meaning. Such a passionate inner meaning they may easily acquire again if the pretension of our nation to inflict its own inner ideals and institutions *vi et armis* upon Orientals should meet with a resistance as obdurate as so far it has been gallant and spirited. Religiously and philosophically, our ancient national doctrine of live and let live may prove to have a far deeper meaning than our people now seem to imagine it to possess."

[1] For the sake of space, I have omitted the bulk of the illustrative quotations, which make up more than half of this essay.—F. O. M.

* * * * *

Our judgments concerning the worth of things, big or little, depend
on the *feelings* the things arouse in us. Where we judge a thing to be
precious in consequence of the *idea* we frame of it, this is only because
the idea is itself associated already with a feeling. If we were radically
feelingless, and if ideas were the only things our mind could entertain,
we should lose all our likes and dislikes at a stroke, and be unable to
point to any one situation or experience in life more valuable or significant than any other.

Now the blindness in human beings, of which this discourse will
treat, is the blindness with which we all are afflicted in regard to the
feelings of creatures and people different from ourselves.

We are practical beings, each of us with limited functions and duties
to perform. Each is bound to feel intensely the importance of his own
duties and the significance of the situations that call these forth. But this
feeling is in each of us a vital secret, for sympathy with which we
vainly look to others. The others are too much absorbed in their own
vital secrets to take an interest in ours. Hence the stupidity and injustice
of our opinions, so far as they deal with the significance of alien lives.
Hence the falsity of our judgments, so far as they presume to decide in
an absolute way on the value of other persons' conditions or ideals.

Take our dogs and ourselves, connected as we are by a tie more intimate than most ties in this world; and yet, outside of that tie of friendly
fondness, how insensible, each of us, to all that makes life significant for
the other!—we to the rapture of bones under hedges, or smells of trees
and lamp-posts, they to the delights of literature and art. As you sit
reading the most moving romance you ever fell upon, what sort of a
judge is your fox-terrier of your behavior? With all his good will toward you, the nature of your conduct is absolutely excluded from his
comprehension. To sit there like a senseless statue, when you might be
taking him to walk and throwing sticks for him to catch! What queer
disease is this that comes over you every day, of holding things and
staring at them like that for hours together, paralyzed of motion and
vacant of all conscious life? The African savages came nearer the truth;
but they, too, missed it, when they gathered wonderingly round one of
our American travellers who, in the interior, had just come into possession of a stray copy of the New York *Commercial Advertiser*, and
was devouring it column by column. When he got through, they offered him a high price for the mysterious object; and, being asked for
what they wanted it, they said: "For an eye medicine,"—that being the
only reason they could conceive of for the protracted bath which he
had given his eyes upon its surface.

The spectator's judgment is sure to miss the root of the matter, and
to possess no truth. The subject judged knows a part of the world of

reality which the judging spectator fails to see, knows more while the spectator knows less; and, wherever there is conflict of opinion and difference of vision, we are bound to believe that the truer side is the side that feels the more, and not the side that feels the less.

Let me take a personal example of the kind that befalls each one of us daily:

Some years ago, while journeying in the mountains of North Carolina, I passed by a large number of "coves," as they call them there, or heads of small valleys between the hills, which had been newly cleared and planted. The impression on my mind was one of unmitigated squalor. The settler had in every case cut down the more manageable trees, and left their charred stumps standing. The larger trees he had girdled and killed, in order that their foliage should not cast a shade. He had then built a log cabin, plastering its chinks with clay, and had set up a tall zigzag rail fence around the scene of his havoc, to keep the pigs and cattle out. Finally, he had irregularly planted the intervals between the stumps and trees with Indian corn, which grew among the chips; and there he dwelt with his wife and babes—an axe, a gun, a few utensils, and some pigs and chickens feeding in the woods, being the sum total of his possessions.

The forest had been destroyed; and what had "improved" it out of existence was hideous, a sort of ulcer, without a single element of artificial grace to make up for the loss of Nature's beauty. Ugly, indeed, seemed the life of the squatter, scudding, as the sailors say, under bare poles, beginning again away back where our first ancestors started, and by hardly a single item the better off for all the achievements of the intervening generations.

Talk about going back to nature!—I said to myself, oppressed by the dreariness, as I drove by. Talk of a country life for one's old age and for one's children! Never thus, with nothing but the bare ground and one's bare hands to fight the battle! Never, without the best spoils of culture woven in! The beauties and commodities gained by the centuries are sacred. They are our heritage and birthright. No modern person ought to be willing to live a day in such a state of rudimentariness and denudation.

Then I said to the mountaineer who was driving me, "What sort of people are they who have to make these new clearings?" "All of us," he replied. "Why, we ain't happy here, unless we are getting one of these coves under cultivation." I instantly felt that I had been losing the whole inward significance of the situation. Because to me the clearings spoke of naught but denudation, I thought that to those whose sturdy arms and obedient axes had made them they could tell no other story. But, when *they* looked on the hideous stumps, what they thought of was personal victory. The chips, the girdled trees, and the vile split rails spoke of honest sweat, persistent toil and final reward. The cabin was a warrant of safety for self and wife and babes. In short, the clearing, which to me was a mere ugly picture on the retina, was to them a symbol redolent with moral memories and sang a very pæan of duty, struggle, and success.

I had been as blind to the peculiar ideality of their conditions as they certainly would also have been to the ideality of mine, had they had a peep at my strange indoor academic ways of life at Cambridge.

Wherever a process of life communicates an eagerness to him who lives it, there the life becomes genuinely significant. Sometimes the eagerness is more knit up with the motor activities, sometimes with the perceptions, sometimes with the imagination, sometimes with reflective thought. But, wherever it is found, there is the zest, the tingle, the excitement of reality; and there *is* "importance" in the only real and positive sense in which importance ever anywhere can be. . . .

Yet so blind and dead does the clamor of our own practical interests make us to all other things, that it seems almost as if it were necessary to become worthless as a practical being, if one is to hope to attain to any breadth of insight into the impersonal world of worths as such, to have any perception of life's meaning on a large objective scale. Only your mystic, your dreamer, or your insolvent tramp or loafer, can afford so sympathetic an occupation, an occupation which will change the usual standards of human value in the twinkling of an eye, giving to foolishness a place ahead of power, and laying low in a minute the distinctions which it takes a hard-working conventional man a lifetime to build up. You may be a prophet, at this rate; but you cannot be a worldly success.

Walt Whitman, for instance, is accounted by many of us a contemporary prophet. He abolishes the usual human distinctions, brings all conventionalisms into solution, and loves and celebrates hardly any human attributes save those elementary ones common to all members of the race. For this he becomes a sort of ideal tramp, a rider on omnibus-tops and ferry-boats, and, considered either practically or academically, a worthless, unproductive being. His verses are but ejaculations —things mostly without subject or verb, a succession of interjections on an immense scale. He felt the human crowd as rapturously as Wordsworth felt the mountains, felt it as an overpoweringly significant presence, simply to absorb one's mind in which should be business sufficient and worthy to fill the days of a serious man. . . .

And, if you wish to see what this hoary loafer considered the most worthy way of profiting by life's heaven-sent opportunities, read the delicious volume of his letters to a young car-conductor who had become his friend:

"NEW YORK, Oct. 9, 1868.

"*Dear Pete*,—It is splendid here this forenoon—bright and cool. I was out early taking a short walk by the river only two squares from where I live. . . . Shall I tell you about [my life] just to fill up? I generally spend the forenoon in my room writing, etc., then take a bath fix up and go out about twelve and loafe somewhere or call on someone down town or on business, or perhaps if it is very pleasant and I feel like it ride a trip with some driver friend on Broadway from 23rd Street to Bowling Green, three miles each way. (Every day I find I have plenty to do, every hour is occupied with something.) You know it is a never ending amusement and study and recreation for me to ride a couple of hours on a pleasant afternoon on a Broadway stage in this way. You see everything as you pass, a sort of living, endless panorama —shops and splendid buildings and great windows: on the broad sidewalks crowds of women richly dressed continually passing, altogether different, superior in style and looks from any to be seen anywhere else —in fact a perfect stream of people—men too dressed in high style, and plenty of foreigners—and then in the streets the thick crowd of carriages, stages, carts, hotel and private coaches, and in fact all sorts of vehicles and many first class teams, mile after mile, and the splendor of such a great street and so many tall, ornamental, noble buildings many of them of white marble, and the gayety and motion on every side: you will not wonder how much attraction all this is on a fine day, to a great loafer like me, who enjoys so much seeing the busy world move by him, and exhibiting itself for his amusement, while he takes it easy and just looks on and observes."

Truly a futile way of passing the time, some of you may say, and not altogether creditable to a grown-up man. And yet, from the deepest point of view, who knows the more of truth, and who knows the less, —Whitman on his omnibus-top, full of the inner joy with which the spectacle inspires him, or you, full of the disdain which the futility of his occupation excites?

When your ordinary Brooklynite or New Yorker, leading a life replete with too much luxury, or tired and careworn about his personal affairs, crosses the ferry or goes up Broadway, *his* fancy does not thus "soar away into the colors of the sunset" as did Whitman's, nor does he inwardly realize at all the indisputable fact that this world never did anywhere or at any time contain more of essential divinity, or of eternal meaning, than is embodied in the fields of vision over which his eyes so carelessly pass. There is life; and there, a step away, is death. There is the only kind of beauty there ever was. There is the old human struggle and its fruits together. There is the text and the sermon, the real and the ideal in one. But to the jaded and unquickened eye it is all dead and common, pure vulgarism, flatness, and disgust. "Hech! it is a sad sight!"

says Carlyle, walking at night with some one who appeals to him to note the splendor of the stars. And that very repetition of the scene to new generations of men in *secula seculorum*, that eternal recurrence of the common order, which so fills a Whitman with mystic satisfaction, is to a Schopenhauer, with the emotional anæsthesia, the feeling of "awful inner emptiness" from out of which he views it all, the chief ingredient of the tedium it instils. What is life on the largest scale, he asks, but the same recurrent inanities, the same dog barking, the same fly buzzing, forevermore? Yet of the kind of fibre of which such inanities consist is the material woven of all the excitements, joys, and meanings that ever were, or ever shall be, in this world.

To be rapt with satisfied attention, like Whitman, to the mere spectacle of the world's presence, is one way, and the most fundamental way, of confessing one's sense of its unfathomable significance and importance. But how can one attain to the feeling of the vital significance of an experience, if one have it not to begin with? There is no receipt which one can follow. Being a secret and a mystery, it often comes in mysteriously unexpected ways. It blossoms sometimes from out of the very grave wherein we imagined that our happiness was buried. . . .

The occasion and the experience, then, are nothing. It all depends on the capacity of the soul to be grasped, to have its life-currents absorbed by what is given. "Crossing a bare common," says Emerson, "in snow puddles, at twilight, under a clouded sky, without having in my thoughts any occurrence of special good fortune, I have enjoyed a perfect exhilaration. I am glad to the brink of fear."

Life is always worth living, if one have such responsive sensibilities. But we of the highly educated classes (so called) have most of us got far, far away from Nature. We are trained to seek the choice, the rare, the exquisite exclusively, and to overlook the common. We are stuffed with abstract conceptions, and glib with verbalities and verbosities; and in the culture of these higher functions the peculiar sources of joy connected with our simpler functions often dry up, and we grow stone-blind and insensible to life's more elementary and general goods and joys.

The remedy under such conditions is to descend to a more profound and primitive level. To be imprisoned or shipwrecked or forced into the army would permanently show the good of life to many an over-educated pessimist. Living in the open air and on the ground, the lopsided beam of the balance slowly rises to the level line; and the over-sensibilities and insensibilities even themselves out. The good of all the artificial schemes and fevers fades and pales; and that of seeing, smelling, tasting, sleeping, and daring and doing with one's body, grows and grows. The savages and children of nature, to whom we deem ourselves so much superior, certainly are alive where we are often dead, along these lines; and, could they write as glibly as we do, they would read us impressive lectures on our impatience for improvement and on our blindness to the fundamental static goods of life. "Ah! my brother," said a chieftain to his white guest, "thou wilt never know the happiness of both thinking of nothing and doing nothing. This, next to sleep, is the most enchanting of all things. Thus we were before our birth, and thus we shall be after death. Thy people, . . . when they have finished reaping one field, they begin to plough another; and, if the day were not enough, I have seen them plough by moonlight. What is their life to ours,—the life that is as naught to them? Blind that they are, they lose it all! But we live in the present." . . .

And now what is the result of all these considerations and quotations? It is negative in one sense, but positive in another. It absolutely forbids us to be forward in pronouncing on the meaninglessness of forms of existence other than our own; and it commands us to tolerate, respect, and indulge those whom we see harmlessly interested and happy in their own ways, however unintelligible these may be to us. Hands off: neither the whole of truth nor the whole of good is revealed to any single observer, although each observer gains a partial superiority of insight from the peculiar position in which he stands. Even prisons and sick-rooms have their special revelations. It is enough to ask of each of us that he should be faithful to his own opportunities and make the most of his own blessings, without presuming to regulate the rest of the vast field.

* * *

CHARACTERISTIC MATURITY

What Makes a Life Significant?

* * * * *

IN MY previous talk, "On a Certain Blindness," I tried to make you feel how soaked and shot-through life is with values and meanings which we fail to realize because of our external and insensible point of view. The meanings are there for the others, but they are not there for us. There lies more than a mere interest of curious speculation in understanding this. It has the most tremendous practical importance. I wish that I could convince you of it as I feel it myself. It is the basis of all our tolerance, social, religious, and political. The forgetting of it lies at the root of every stupid and sanguinary mistake that rulers over subject-peoples make. The first thing to learn in intercourse with others is non-interference with their own peculiar ways of being happy, provided those ways do not assume to interfere by violence with ours. No one has insight into all the ideals. No one should presume to judge them off-hand. The pretension to dogmatize about them in each other is the root of most human injustices and cruelties, and the trait in human character most likely to make the angels weep.

Every Jack sees in his own particular Jill charms and perfections to the enchantment of which we stolid onlookers are stone-cold. And which has the superior view of the absolute truth, he or we? Which has the more vital insight into the nature of Jill's existence, as a fact? Is he in excess, being in this matter a maniac? or are we in defect, being victims of a pathological anæsthesia as regards Jill's magical importance? Surely the latter; surely to Jack are the profounder truths revealed; surely poor Jill's palpitating little life-throbs *are* among the wonders of creation, *are* worthy of this sympathetic interest; and it is to our shame that the rest of us cannot feel like Jack. For Jack realizes Jill concretely, and we do not. He struggles toward a union with her inner life, divining her feelings, anticipating her desires, understanding her limits as manfully as he can, and yet inadequately, too; for he is also afflicted with some blindness, even here. Whilst we, dead clods that we are, do not even seek after these things, but are contented that that portion of eternal fact named Jill should be for us as if it were not. Jill, who knows her inner life, knows that Jack's way of taking it—so importantly—is the true and serious way; and she responds to the truth in him by taking him truly and seriously, too. May the ancient blindness never wrap its clouds about either of them again! Where would any of *us* be, were there no one willing to know us as we really are or ready to repay us for *our* insight by making recognizant return? We ought, all of us, to realize each other in this intense, pathetic, and important way.

If you say that this is absurd, and that we cannot be in love with everyone at once, I merely point out to you that, as a matter of fact, certain persons do exist with an enormous capacity for friendship and for taking delight in other people's lives; and that such persons know more of truth than if their hearts were not so big. The vice of ordinary Jack and Jill affection is not its intensity, but its exclusions and its jealousies. Leave those out, and you see that the ideal I am holding up before you, however impracticable today, yet contains nothing intrinsically absurd.

We have unquestionably a great cloud-bank of ancestral blindness weighing down upon us, only transiently riven here and there by fitful revelations of the truth. It is vain to hope for this state of things to alter much. Our inner secrets must remain for the most part impenetrable by others, for beings as essentially practical as we are are necessarily short of sight. But, if we cannot gain much positive insight into one another, cannot we at least use our sense of our own blindness to make us more cautious in going over the dark places? Cannot we escape some of those hideous ancestral intolerances and cruelties, and positive reversals of the truth?

For the remainder of this hour I invite you to seek with me some principle to make our tolerance less chaotic. And, as I began my previous lecture by a personal reminiscence, I am going to ask your indulgence for a similar bit of egotism now.

A few summers ago I spent a happy week at the famous Assembly Grounds on the borders of Chautauqua Lake. The moment one treads that sacred enclosure, one feels one's self in an atmosphere of success. Sobriety and industry, intelligence and goodness, orderliness and ideality, prosperity and cheerfulness, pervade the air. It is a serious and studious picnic on a gigantic scale. Here you have a town of many thousands of inhabitants, beautifully laid out in the forest and drained, and equipped with means for satisfying all the necessary lower and most of the superfluous higher wants of man. You have a first-class college in full blast. You have magnificent music—a chorus of seven hundred voices, with possibly the most perfect open-air auditorium in the world. You have every sort of athletic exercise from sailing, rowing, swimming, bicycling, to the ball-field and the more artificial doings which the gymnasium affords. You have kindergartens and model secondary schools. You have general religious services and special clubhouses for the several sects. You have perpetually running soda-water fountains, and daily popular lectures by distinguished men. You have the best of company, and yet no effort. You have no zymotic diseases, no poverty, no drunkenness, no crime, no police. You have culture, you have kindness, you have cheapness, you have equality, you have the best fruits of what mankind has fought and bled and striven for under the name of civilization for centuries. You have, in short, a foretaste of what human society might be, were it all in the light, with no suffering and no dark corners.

I went in curiosity for a day. I stayed for a week, held spell-bound by the charm and ease of everything, by the middle-class paradise, without a sin, without a victim, without a blot, without a tear.

And yet what was my own astonishment, on emerging into the dark and wicked world again, to catch myself quite unexpectedly and involuntarily saying: "Ouf! what a relief! Now for something primordial and savage, even though it were as bad as an Armenian massacre, to set the balance straight again. This order is too tame, this culture too second-rate, this goodness too uninspiring. This human drama without a villain or a pang; this community so refined that ice-cream and soda-water is the utmost offering it can make to the brute animal in man; this city simmering in the tepid lakeside sun; this atrocious harmlessness of all things,—I cannot abide with them. Let me take my chances again in the big outside worldly wilderness with all its sins and sufferings. There are the heights and depths, the precipices and the steep ideals, the gleams of the awful and the infinite; and there is more hope and help a thousand times than in this dead level and quintessence of every mediocrity."

Such was the sudden right-about-face performed for me by my lawless fancy! There had been spread before me the realization—on a small, sample scale of course—of all the ideals for which our civilization has been striving: security, intelligence, humanity, and order; and here was the instinctive hostile reaction, not of the natural man, but of a so-called cultivated man upon such a Utopia. There seemed thus to be a self-contradiction and paradox somewhere, which I, as a professor drawing a full salary, was in duty bound to unravel and explain, if I could.

So I meditated. And, first of all, I asked myself what the thing was that was so lacking in this Sabbatical city, and the lack of which kept one forever falling short of the higher sort of contentment. And I soon recognized that it was the element that gives to the wicked outer world all its moral style, expressiveness and picturesqueness,—the element of precipitousness, so to call it, of strength and strenuousness, intensity and danger. What excites and interests the looker-on at life, what the romances and the statues celebrate and the grim civic monuments remind us of, is the everlasting battle of the powers of light with those of darkness; with heroism, reduced to its bare chance, yet ever and anon snatching victory from the jaws of death. But in this unspeakable Chautauqua there was no potentiality of death in sight anywhere, and no point of the compass visible from which danger might possibly appear. The ideal was so completely victorious already that no sign of any previous battle remained, the place just resting on its oars. But what our human emotions seem to require is the sight of the struggle going on. The moment the fruits are being merely eaten, things become ignoble. Sweat and effort, human nature strained to its uttermost and on the rack, yet getting through alive, and then turning its back on its success to pursue another more rare and arduous still—this is the sort of thing the presence of which inspires us, and the reality of which it seems to be the function of all the higher forms of literature and fine art to bring home to us and suggest. At Chautauqua there were no racks, even in the place's historical museum; and no sweat, except possibly the gentle moisture on the brow of some lecturer, or on the sides of some player in the ball-field.

Such absence of human nature *in extremis* anywhere seemed, then, a sufficient explanation for Chautauqua's flatness and lack of zest.

But was not this a paradox well calculated to fill one with dismay? It looks indeed, thought I, as if the romantic idealists with their pessimism about our civilization were, after all, quite right. An irremediable flatness is coming over the world. Bourgeoisie and mediocrity, church sociables and teachers' conventions, are taking the place of the old heights and depths and romantic chiaroscuro. And, to get human life in its wild intensity, we must in future turn more and more away from the actual, and forget it, if we can, in the romancer's or the poet's pages. The whole world, delightful and sinful as it may still appear for a moment to one just escaped from the Chautauquan enclosure, is nevertheless obeying more and more just those ideals that are sure to make of it in the end a mere Chautauqua Assembly on an enormous scale. *Was im Gesang soll leben muss im Leben untergehn.* Even now, in our own country, correctness, fairness, and compromise for every small advantage are crowding out all other qualities. The higher heroisms and the old rare flavors are passing out of life.[1]

With these thoughts in my mind, I was speeding with the train toward Buffalo, when, near that city, the sight of a workman doing something on the dizzy edge of a sky-scaling iron construction brought me to my senses very suddenly. And now I perceived, by a flash of insight, that I had been steeping myself in pure ancestral blindness, and looking at life with the eyes of a remote spectator. Wishing for heroism and the spectacle of human nature on the rack, I had never noticed the great fields of heroism lying around about me, I had failed to see it present and alive. I could only think of it as dead and embalmed, labelled and costumed, as it is in the pages of romance. And yet there it was before me in the daily lives of the laboring classes. Not in clanging fights and desperate marches only is heroism to be looked for, but on every railway bridge and fire-proof building that is going up today. On freight-trains, on the decks of vessels, in cattle-yards and mines, on lumber-rafts, among the firemen and the policemen, the demand for courage is incessant; and the supply never fails. There, every day of the year somewhere, is human nature *in extremis* for you. And wherever a scythe, an axe, a pick, or a shovel is wielded, you have it sweating and aching and with its powers of patient endurance racked to the utmost under the length of hours of the strain.

As I awoke to all this unidealized heroic life around me, the scales seemed to fall from my eyes; and a wave of sympathy greater than anything I had ever before felt with the common life of common men began to fill my soul. It began to seem as if virtue with horny hands and dirty skin were the only virtue genuine and vital enough to take account of. Every other virtue poses; none is absolutely unconscious and simple, and unexpectant of decoration or recognition, like this. These are our soldiers, thought I, these our sustainers, these the very parents of our life.

Many years ago, when in Vienna, I had had a similar feeling of awe and reverence in looking at the peasant-women, in from the country on their business at the market for the day. Old hags many of them were, dried and brown and wrinkled, kerchiefed and short-petticoated, with thick wool stockings on their bony shanks, stumping through the glittering thoroughfares, looking neither to the right nor the left, bent on duty, envying nothing, humble-hearted, remote;—and yet at bottom, when you came to think of it, bearing the whole fabric of the splendors and corruptions of that city on their laborious backs. For where would

---

[1] This address was composed before the Cuban and Philippine wars. Such outbursts of the passion of mastery are, however, only episodes in social process which in the long run seems everywhere tending toward the Chautauquan ideals.

any of it have been without their unremitting, unrewarded labor in the fields? And so with us: not to our generals and poets, I thought, but to the Italian and Hungarian laborers in the Subway, rather, ought the monuments of gratitude and reverence of a city like Boston to be reared.

If any of you have been readers of Tolstoï, you will see that I passed into a vein of feeling similar to his, with its abhorrence of all that conventionally passes for distinguished, and its exclusive deification of the bravery, patience, kindliness, and dumbness of the unconscious natural man.

Where now is *our* Tolstoï, I said, to bring the truth of all this home to our American bosoms, fill us with a better insight, and wean us away from that spurious literary romanticism on which our wretched culture —as it calls itself—is fed? Divinity lies all about us, and culture is too hide-bound to even suspect the fact. Could a Howells or a Kipling be enlisted in this mission? or are they still too deep in the ancestral blindness, and not humane enough for the inner joy and meaning of the laborer's existence to be really revealed? Must we wait for some one born and bred and living as a laborer himself, but who, by grace of Heaven, shall also find a literary voice?

And there I rested on that day, with a sense of widening of vision, and with what it is surely fair to call an increase of religious insight into life. In God's eyes the differences of social position, of intellect, of culture, of cleanliness, of dress, which different men exhibit, and all the other rarities and exceptions on which they so fantastically pin their pride, must be so small as practically quite to vanish; and all that should remain is the common fact that here we are, a countless multitude of vessels of life, each of us pent in to peculiar difficulties, with which we must severally struggle by using whatever of fortitude and goodness we can summon up. The exercise of the courage, patience, and kindness, must be the significant portion of the whole business; and the distinctions of position can only be a manner of diversifying the phenomenal surface upon which these underground virtues may manifest their effects. At this rate, the deepest human life is everywhere, is eternal. And, if any human attributes exist only in particular individuals, they must belong to the mere trapping and decoration of the surface-show.

Thus are men's lives levelled up as well as levelled down,—levelled up in their common inner meaning, levelled down in their outer gloriousness and show. Yet always, we must confess, this levelling insight tends to be obscured again; and always the ancestral blindness returns and wraps us up, so that we end once more by thinking that creation can be for no other purpose than to develop remarkable situations and conventional distinctions and merits. And then always some new leveller in the shape of a religious prophet has to arise—the Buddha, the Christ, or some Saint Francis, some Rousseau or Tolstoï—to redispel our blindness. Yet, little by little, there comes some stable gain; for the world does get more humane, and the religion of democracy tends toward permanent increase.

This, as I said, became for a time my conviction, and gave me great content. I have put the matter into the form of a personal reminiscence, so that I might lead you into it more directly and completely, and so save time. But now I am going to discuss the rest of it with you in a more impersonal way.

Tolstoï's levelling philosophy began long before he had the crisis of melancholy commemorated in that wonderful document of his entitled "My Confession," which led the way to his more specifically religious works. In his masterpiece "War and Peace,"—assuredly the greatest of human novels,—the rôle of the spiritual hero is given to a poor little soldier named Karataïeff, so helpful, so cheerful, and so devout that, in spite of his ignorance and filthiness, the sight of him opens the heavens, which have been closed, to the mind of the principal character of the book; and his example evidently is meant by Tolstoï to let God into the world again for the reader. Poor little Karataïeff is taken prisoner by the French; and, when too exhausted by hardship and fever to march, is shot as other prisoners were in the famous retreat from Moscow. The last view one gets of him is his little figure leaning against a white birch-tree, and uncomplainingly awaiting the end.

"The more," writes Tolstoï in the work "My Confession," "the more I examined the life of these laboring folks, the more persuaded I became that they veritably have faith, and get from it alone the sense and the possibility of life. . . . Contrariwise to those of our own class, who protest against destiny and grow indignant at its rigor, these people receive maladies and misfortunes without revolt, without opposition, and with a firm and tranquil confidence that all had to be like that, could not be otherwise, and that it is all right so. . . . The more we live by our intellect, the less we understand the meaning of life. We see only a cruel jest in suffering and death, whereas these people live, suffer, and draw near to death with tranquillity, and oftener than not with joy. . . . There are enormous multitudes of them happy with the most perfect happiness, although deprived of what for us is the sole good of life. Those who understand life's meaning, and know how to live and die thus, are to be counted not by twos, threes, tens, but by hundreds, thousands, millions. They labor quietly, endure privations and pains, live and die, and throughout everything see the good without seeing the vanity. I had to love these people. The more I entered into their life, the more I loved them; and the more it became possible for me to live, too. It came about not only that the life of our society, of the learned and of the rich, disgusted me—more than that, it lost all semblance of meaning in my eyes. All our actions, our deliberations, our sciences, our arts, all appeared to me with a new significance. I understood that these things might be charming pastimes, but that one need seek in them no depth, whereas the life of the hard-working populace, of that multitude of human beings who really contribute to existence, appeared to me in its true light. I understood that there veritably is life, that the meaning which life there receives is the truth; and I accepted it."[1]

In a similar way does Stevenson appeal to our piety toward the elemental virtue of mankind.

"What a wonderful thing," he writes,[2] "is this Man! How surprising are his attributes! Poor soul, here for so little, cast among so many hardships, savagely surrounded, savagely descended, irremediably condemned to prey upon his fellow-lives,—who should have blamed him, had he been of a piece with his destiny and a being merely barbarous? . . . [Yet] it matters not where we look, under what climate we observe him, in what stage of society, in what depth of ignorance, burdened with what erroneous morality; in ships at sea, a man inured to hardship and vile pleasures, his brightest hope a fiddle in a tavern, and a bedizened trull who sells herself to rob him, and he, for all that, simple, innocent, cheerful, kindly like a child, constant to toil, brave to drown, for others; . . . in the slums of cities, moving among indifferent millions to mechanical employments, without hope of change in the future, with scarce a pleasure in the present, and yet true to his virtues, honest up to his lights, kind to his neighbors, tempted perhaps in vain by the bright gin-palace, . . . often repaying the world's scorn with service, often standing firm upon a scruple; . . . everywhere some virtue cherished or affected, everywhere some decency of thought and courage, everywhere the ensign of man's ineffectual goodness,—ah! if I could show you this! If I could show you these men and women all the world over, in every stage of history, under every abuse of error, under every circumstance of failure, without hope, without help, without thanks, still obscurely fighting the lost fight of virtue, still clinging to some rag of honor, the poor jewel of their souls."

All this is as true as it is splendid, and terribly do we need our Tolstoïs and Stevensons to keep our sense for it alive. Yet you remember the Irishman who, when asked, "Is not one man as good as another?" replied, "Yes; and a great deal better, too!" Similarly (it seems to me) does Tolstoï overcorrect our social prejudices, when he makes his love of the peasant so exclusive, and hardens his heart toward the educated man as absolutely as he does. Grant that at Chautauqua there was little

---

[1] *My Confession*, X. (condensed).
[2] *Across the Plains*: "Pulvis et Umbra" (abridged).

moral effort, little sweat or muscular strain in view. Still, deep down in the souls of the participants we may be sure that something of the sort was hid, some inner stress, some vital virtue not found wanting when required. And, after all, the question recurs, and forces itself upon us, Is it so certain that the surroundings and circumstances of the virtue do make so little difference in the importance of the result? Is the functional utility, the worth to the universe of a certain definite amount of courage, kindliness, and patience, no greater if the possessor of these virtues is in an educated situation, working out far-reaching tasks, than if he be an illiterate nobody, hewing wood and drawing water, just to keep himself alive? Tolstoï's philosophy, deeply enlightening though it certainly is, remains a false abstraction. It savors too much of that Oriental pessimism and nihilism of his, which declares the whole phenomenal world and its facts and their distinctions to be a cunning fraud.

A mere bare fraud is just what our Western common sense will never believe the phenomenal world to be. It admits fully that the inner joys and virtues are the *essential* part of life's business, but it is sure that *some* positive part is also played by the adjuncts of the show. If it is idiotic in romanticism to recognize the heroic only when it sees it labelled and dressed-up in books, it is really just as idiotic to see it only in the dirty boots and sweaty shirt of some one in the fields. It is with us really under every disguise: at Chautauqua; here in your college; in the stock-yards and on the freight-trains; and in the czar of Russia's court. But, instinctively, we make a combination of two things in judging the total significance of a human being. We feel it to be some sort of a product (if such a product only could be calculated) of his inner virtue *and* his outer place,—neither singly taken, but both conjoined. If the outer differences had no meaning for life, why indeed should all this immense variety of them exist? They *must* be significant elements of the world as well.

Just test Tolstoï's deification of the mere manual laborer by the facts. This is what Mr. Walter Wyckoff, after working as an unskilled laborer in the demolition of some buildings at West Point, writes of the spiritual condition of the class of men to which he temporarily chose to belong:—

"The salient features of our condition are plain enough. We are grown men, and are without a trade. In the labor-market we stand ready to sell to the highest bidder our mere muscular strength for so many hours each day. We are thus in the lowest grade of labor. And, selling our muscular strength in the open market for what it will bring, we sell it under peculiar conditions. It is all the capital that we have. We have no reserve means of subsistence, and cannot, therefore, stand off for a 'reserve price.' We sell under the necessity of satisfying imminent hunger. Broadly speaking, we must sell our labor or starve; and, as hunger is a matter of a few hours, and we have no other way of meeting this need, we must sell at once for what the market offers for our labor.

"Our employer is buying labor in a dear market, and he will certainly get from us as much work as he can at the price. The gang-boss is secured for this purpose, and thoroughly does he know his business. He has sole command of us. He never saw us before, and he will discharge us all when the débris is cleared away. In the meantime he must get from us, if he can, the utmost physical labor which we, individually and collectively, are capable of. If he should drive some of us to exhaustion, and we should not be able to continue at work, he would not be the loser; for the market would soon supply him with others to take our places.

"We are ignorant men, but so much we clearly see,—that we have sold our labor where we could sell it dearest, and our employer has bought it where he could buy it cheapest. He has paid high, and he must get all the labor that he can; and, by a strong instinct which possesses us, we shall part with as little as we can. From work like ours there seems to us to have been eliminated every element which constitutes the nobility of labor. We feel no personal pride in its progress, and no community of interest with our employer. There is none of the joy of responsibility, none of the sense of achievement, only the dull monotony of grinding toil, with the longing for the signal to quit work, and for our wages at the end.

"And being what we are, the dregs of the labor-market, and having no certainty of permanent employment, and no organization among ourselves, we must expect to work under the watchful eye of a gang-boss, and be driven, like the wage-slaves that we are, through our tasks.

"All this is to tell us, in effect, that our lives are hard, barren, hopeless lives."

And such hard, barren, hopeless lives, surely, are not lives in which one ought to be willing permanently to remain. And why is this so? Is it because they are so dirty? Well, Nansen grew a great deal dirtier on his polar expedition; and we think none the worse of his life for that. Is it the insensibility? Our soldiers have to grow vastly more insensible, and we extol them to the skies. Is it the poverty? Poverty has been reckoned the crowning beauty of many a heroic career. Is it the slavery to a task, the loss of finer pleasures? Such slavery and loss are of the very essence of the higher fortitude, and are always counted to its credit,—read the records of missionary devotion all over the world. It is not any one of these things, then, taken by itself,—no, nor all of them together,—that make such a life undesirable. A man might in truth live like an unskilled laborer, and do the work of one, and yet count as one of the noblest of God's creatures. Quite possibly there were some such persons in the gang that our author describes; but the current of their souls ran underground; and he was too steeped in the ancestral blindness to discern it.

If there *were* any such morally exceptional individuals, however, what made them different from the rest? It can only have been this,—that their souls worked and endured in obedience to some inner *ideal*, while their comrades were not actuated by anything worthy of that name. These ideals of other lives are among those secrets that we can almost never penetrate, although something about the man may often tell us when they are there. In Mr. Wyckoff's own case we know exactly what the self-imposed ideal was. Partly he had stumped himself, as the boys say, to carry through a strenuous achievement; but mainly he wished to enlarge his sympathetic insight into fellow-lives. For this his sweat and toil acquire a certain heroic significance, and make us accord to him exceptional esteem. But it is easy to imagine his fellows with various other ideals. To say nothing of wives and babies, one may have been a convert of the Salvation Army, and had a nightingale singing of expiation and forgiveness in his heart all the while he labored. Or there might have been an apostle like Tolstoï himself, or his compatriot Bondareff, in the gang, voluntarily embracing labor as their religious mission. Class-loyalty was undoubtedly an ideal with many. And who knows how much of that higher manliness of poverty, of which Phillips Brooks has spoken so penetratingly, was or was not present in that gang?

"A rugged, barren land," says Phillips Brooks, "is poverty to live in, —a land where I am thankful very often if I can get a berry or a root to eat. But living in it really, letting it bear witness to me of itself, not dishonoring it all the time by judging it after the standard of the other lands, gradually there come out its qualities. Behold! no land like this barren and naked land of poverty could show the moral geology of the world. See how the hard ribs . . . stand out strong and solid. No life like poverty could so get one to the heart of things and make men know their meaning, could so let us feel life and the world with all the soft cushions stripped off and thrown away. . . . Poverty makes men come very near each other, and recognize each other's human hearts; and poverty, highest and best of all, demands and cries out for faith in God. . . . I know how superficial and unfeeling, how like mere mockery, words in praise of poverty may seem. . . . But I am sure that the poor man's dignity and freedom, his self-respect and energy, depend upon his cordial knowledge that his poverty is a true region and kind of life, with its own chances of character, its own springs of happiness and revelations of God. Let him resist the characterlessness which often goes with being poor. Let him insist on respecting the condition where he lives. Let him learn to love it, so that by and by, (if) he grows rich, he shall go out of the low door of the old familiar poverty with a true pang of regret, and with a true honor for the narrow home in which he has lived so long." [1]

The barrenness and ignobleness of the more usual laborer's life consist in the fact that it is moved by no such ideal inner springs. The backache, the long hours, the danger, are patiently endured—for what? To gain a quid of tobacco, a glass of beer, a cup of coffee, a meal, and a bed, and to begin again the next day and shirk as much as one can. This really is why we raise no monument to the laborers in the Subway, even though they be our conscripts, and even though after a fashion our city is indeed based upon their patient hearts and enduring backs and shoulders. And this is why we do raise monuments to our soldiers, whose outward conditions were even brutaller still. The soldiers are supposed to have followed an ideal, and the laborers are supposed to have followed none.

You see, my friends, how the plot now thickens; and how strangely the complexities of this wonderful human nature of ours begin to develop under our hands. We have seen the blindness and deadness to each other which are our natural inheritance; and, in spite of them, we have been led to acknowledge an inner meaning which passeth show, and which may be present in the lives of others where we least descry it. And now we are led to say that such inner meaning can be *complete* and *valid for us also,* only when the inner joy, courage, and endurance are joined with an ideal.

But what, exactly, do we mean by an ideal? Can we give no definite account of such a word?

To a certain extent we can. An ideal, for instance, must be something intellectually conceived, something of which we are not unconscious, if we have it; and it must carry with it that sort of outlook, uplift, and brightness that go with all intellectual facts. Secondly, there must be *novelty* in an ideal,—novelty at least for him whom the ideal grasps. Sodden routine is incompatible with ideality, although what is sodden routine for one person may be ideal novelty for another. This shows that there is nothing absolutely ideal: ideals are relative to the lives that entertain them. To keep out of the gutter is for us here no part of consciousness at all, yet for many of our brethren it is the most legitimately engrossing of ideals.

Now, taken nakedly, abstractly, and immediately, you see that mere ideals are the cheapest things in life. Everybody has them in some shape or other, personal or general, sound or mistaken, low or high; and the

---

[1] *Sermons*, 5th Series, New York, 1893, pp. 166, 167.

most worthless sentimentalists and dreamers, drunkards, shirks and verse-makers, who never show a grain of effort, courage, or endurance, possibly have them on the most copious scale. Education, enlarging as it does our horizon and perspective, is a means of multiplying our ideals, of bringing new ones into view. And your college professor, with a starched shirt and spectacles, would, if a stock of ideals were all alone by itself enough to render a life significant, be the most absolutely and deeply significant of men. Tolstoï would be completely blind in despising him for a prig, a pedant and a parody; and all our new insight into the divinity of muscular labor would be altogether off the track of truth.

But such consequences as this, you instinctively feel, are erroneous. The more ideals a man has, the more contemptible, on the whole, do you continue to deem him, if the matter ends there for him, and if none of the laboring man's virtues are called into action on his part,—no courage shown, no privations undergone, no dirt or scars contracted in the attempt to get them realized. It is quite obvious that something more than the mere possession of ideals is required to make a life significant in any sense that claims the spectator's admiration. Inner joy, to be sure, it may *have*, with its ideals; but that is its own private sentimental matter. To extort from us, outsiders as we are, with our own ideals to look after, the tribute of our grudging recognition, it must back its ideal visions with what the laborers have, the sterner stuff of manly virtue; it must multiply their sentimental surface by the dimension of the active will, if we are to have *depth*, if we are to have anything cubical and solid in the way of character.

The significance of a human life for communicable and publicly recognizable purposes is thus the offspring of a marriage of two different parents, either of whom alone is barren. The ideals taken by themselves give no reality, the virtues by themselves no novelty. And let the orientalists and pessimists say what they will, the thing of deepest— or, at any rate, of comparatively deepest—significance in life does seem to be its character of *progress*, or that strange union of reality with ideal novelty which it continues from one moment to another to present. To recognize ideal novelty is the task of what we call intelligence. Not every one's intelligence can tell which novelties are ideal. For many the ideal thing will always seem to cling still to the older more familiar good. In this case character, though not significant totally, may be still significant pathetically. So, if we are to choose which is the more essential factor of human character, the fighting virtue or the intellectual breadth, we must side with Tolstoï and choose that simple faithfulness to his light or darkness which any common unintellectual man can show.

But, with all this beating and tacking on my part, I fear you take me to be reaching a confused result. I seem to be just taking things up and dropping them again. First I took up Chautauqua, and dropped that; then Tolstoï and the heroism of common toil, and dropped them; finally, I took up ideals, and seem now almost dropping those. But please observe in what sense it is that I drop them. It is when they pretend *singly* to redeem life from insignificance. Culture and refinement all alone are not enough to do so. Ideal aspirations are not enough, when uncombined with pluck and will. But neither are pluck and will, dogged endurance and insensibility to danger enough, when taken all alone. There must be some sort of fusion, some chemical combination among these principles, for a life objectively and thoroughly significant to result.

Of course, this is a somewhat vague conclusion. But in a question of significance, of worth, like this, conclusions can never be precise. The answer of appreciation, of sentiment, is always a more or a less, a balance struck by sympathy, insight, and good will. But it is an answer, all the same, a real conclusion. And, in the course of getting it, it seems to me that our eyes have been opened to many important things. Some of you are, perhaps, more livingly aware than you were an hour ago of the depths of worth that lie around you, hid in alien lives. And, when you ask how much sympathy you ought to bestow, although the amount is, truly enough, a matter of ideal on your own part, yet in this notion of the combination of ideals with active virtues you have a rough standard for shaping your decision. In any case, your imagination is extended. You divine in the world about you matter for a little more humility on your own part, and tolerance, reverence, and love for others; and you gain a certain inner joyfulness at the increased importance of our common life. Such joyfulness is a religious inspiration and an element of spiritual health, and worth more than large amounts of that sort of technical and accurate information which we professors are supposed to be able to impart.

To show the sort of thing I mean by these words, I will just make one brief practical illustration, and then close.

We are suffering today in America from what is called the labor-question; and, when you go out into the world, you will each and all of you be caught up in its perplexities. I use the brief term labor-question to cover all sorts of anarchistic discontents and socialistic projects, and the conservative resistances which they provoke. So far as this conflict is unhealthy and regrettable,—and I think it is so only to a limited extent,—the unhealthiness consists solely in the fact that one-half of our fellow-countrymen remain entirely blind to the internal significance of the lives of the other half. They miss the joys and sorrows, they fail to feel the moral virtue, and they do not guess the presence of the intellectual ideals. They are at cross-purposes all along the line, regarding each other as they might regard a set of dangerously gesticulating automata, or, if they seek to get at the inner motivation, making the most horrible mistakes. Often all that the poor man can think of in the rich man is a cowardly greediness for safety, luxury, and effeminacy, and a boundless affectation. What he is, is not a human being, but a pocket-book, a bank-account. And a similar greediness, turned by disappointment into envy, is all that many rich men can see in the state of mind of the dissatisfied poor. And, if the rich man begins to do the sentimental act over the poor man, what senseless blunders does he make, pitying him for just those very duties and those very immunities which, rightly taken, are the condition of his most abiding and characteristic joys! Each, in short, ignores the fact that happiness and unhappiness and significance are a vital mystery; each pins them absolutely on some ridiculous feature of the external situation; and everybody remains outside of everybody else's sight.

Society has, with all this, undoubtedly got to pass toward some newer and better equilibrium, and the distribution of wealth has doubtless slowly got to change: such changes have always happened, and will happen to the end of time. But if, after all that I have said, any of you expect that they will make any *genuine vital difference* on a large scale, to the lives of our descendants, you will have missed the significance of my entire lecture. The solid meaning of life is always the same eternal thing,—the marriage, namely, of some unhabitual ideal, however special, with some fidelity, courage, and endurance; with some man's or woman's pains.—And, whatever or wherever life may be, there will always be the chance for that marriage to take place.

Fitz-James Stephen wrote many years ago words to this effect more eloquent than any I can speak: "The 'Great Eastern,' or some of her successors," he said, "will perhaps defy the roll of the Atlantic, and cross the seas without allowing their passengers to feel that they have left the firm land. The voyage from the cradle to the grave may come to be performed with similar facility. Progress and science may perhaps enable untold millions to live and die without a care, without a pang, without an anxiety. They will have a pleasant passage and plenty of brilliant conversation. They will wonder that men ever believed at all in clanging fights and blazing towns and sinking ships and praying hands; and, when they come to the end of their course, they will go their way, and the place thereof will know them no more. But it seems unlikely that they will have such a knowledge of the great ocean on which they sail, with its storms and wrecks, its currents and icebergs, its huge waves and mighty winds, as those who battled with it for years together in the little craft, which, if they had few other merits, brought those who navigated them full into the presence of time and eternity, their maker and themselves, and forced them to have some definite view of their relations to them and to each other." [1]

In this solid and tridimensional sense, so to call it, those philosophers are right who contend that the world is a standing thing, with no progress, no real history. The changing conditions of history touch only the surface of the show. The altered equilibriums and redistributions only diversify our opportunities and open chances to us for new ideals. But, with each new ideal that comes into life, the chance for a life based on some old ideal will vanish; and he would needs be a presumptuous calculator who should with confidence say that the total sum of significances is positively and absolutely greater at any one epoch than at any other of the world.

I am speaking broadly, I know, and omitting to consider certain qualifications in which I myself believe. But one can only make one point in one lecture, and I shall be well content if I have brought my point home to you this evening in even a slight degree. *There are compensations*: and no outward changes of condition in life can keep the nightingale of its eternal meaning from singing in all sorts of different men's hearts. That is the main fact to remember. If we could not only admit it with our lips, but really and truly believe it, how our convulsive insistencies, how our antipathies and dreads of each other, would soften down! If the poor and the rich could look at each other in this way, *sub specie æternatis*, how gentle would grow their disputes! what tolerance and good humor, what willingness to live and let live, would come into the world!

* * *

---

[1] *Essays by a Barrister*, London, 1862, p. 318.

BOOK FIVE

WJ and Royce

*"Chocorua, September, 1903. One morning James and Royce
strolled into the road and sat down on a wall in earnest discussion. When James heard the camera click, as his daughter
took the upper snap-shot, he cried, 'Royce, you're being photographed! Look out! I say Damn the Absolute!'"—From the*
LETTERS OF WILLIAM JAMES, *edited by his son, Henry James.*

PARTIAL PORTRAITS

The Art of Criticism

CRITICISM was as natural to a member of the James family as breathing. Henry Senior's most pungent writing is in his partial portraits of Emerson and Carlyle, where the fact that he was held down to a concrete subject kept him from diffusing himself in the void. Although he took a low view of the artist in existent society, he believed that potentially the artist's function was great, since "to give outward form to inward substance, to give natural body to spiritual conception: such is the office of Art." His test of art, as of any other mode of action, was its spontaneity. Indeed, in his lecture on "Socialism and Civilization" he went so far as to say: "Our highest mode of action is æsthetic," since "not our physical and moral action, or what we do from the constraint of necessity and duty, but our æsthetic action, or what we do from taste, from spontaneity, expresses our true or inmost personality."

WJ would not have subscribed to that use of terms, nor to the position they upheld. Notwithstanding his flair for the concrete reality of the artist, he always believed in the necessary subordination of æsthetic to ethical experience. His reaction to art is typified by a passage in his chapter on Habit:

"Even the habit of excessive indulgence in music, for those who are neither performers themselves nor musically gifted enough to take it in a purely intellectual way, has probably a relaxing effect upon the character. One becomes filled with emotions which habitually pass without prompting to any deed, and so the inertly sentimental condition is kept up. The remedy would be, never to suffer one's self to have an emotion at a concert, without expressing it afterward in *some* active way. Let the expression be the least thing in the world—speaking genially to one's aunt, or giving up one's seat in a horse-car, if nothing more heroic offers—but let it not fail to take place."

That line of contention, phrased somewhat less naïvely, has been advanced by some Marxist critics, and would have to be reckoned with in any debate about the immediate social function of art. WJ's simple activism brought out opposition from Peirce, who saw the dangers, particularly in crassly materialistic America, in a praise of action for its own sake: "Pragmatism is correct doctrine only in so far as it is recognised that material action is the mere husk of ideas. The brute element exists, and must not be explained away, as Hegel seeks to do. But the end of thought is action only in so far as the end of action is another thought."

WJ was like his father in being a critic both of ideas and of men. He was by no means hostile to art. Indeed, when he summed up the grounds for his great admiration of Emerson, he pronounced him primarily an artist. But in most cases he was far more concerned with content than with form. He was often suspicious of perfection and finish, and relished the unformed and crude as tokens of continuing vitality. The contrast with HJ could not be put more sharply.

HJ found his father's standards in art too abstract, particularly when Henry Senior, enunciating "the Principle of Universality," declared that "in estimating a work of Art, you would seek to ascertain how far its genetic idea or mental conception had been fulfilled." It was as though in correction of such an approach that HJ wrote, in his preface to *The Ambassadors*: "Art deals with what we see, it must first contribute full-handed that ingredient; it plucks its material, otherwise expressed, in the garden of life—which material elsewhere grown is stale and uneatable." His father and Emerson had also been concerned with seeing, but HJ, no less than WJ, turned that double-edged word "seer" back to this world. Æsthetic experience, in its root sense of perception, remained his primary realm. He held, to be sure, moral values as well, but in his case those values were built upon successive layers of discernment and contemplation.

It was naturally more incumbent upon him than it was upon either his father or his brother to develop a theory of criticism. As an artist he needed a continuous sense of what constituted greatness in the art of fiction. In 1865, when he first undertook to be an arbiter of contemporary literature for the *Nation*, Matthew Arnold's *Essays in Criticism* had just appeared. Under their influence, with Goethe in the background, the young HJ was more rigorous and philosophical in his demands upon literature than he later became. He talked about the necessity of laying down "general principles," and held it as an axiom that the critic "is in the nature of his function *opposed* to his author." Nothing could be further from his mature assumption that "criticism is appreciation or it is nothing."

The course of his development led from a somewhat narrow concern with intellectual standards to an increasing openness to impressions. This is illustrated by the symptomatic shift in his opinion of Sainte-Beuve. HJ had at first an imperfect sympathy with him, pronounced him "little of a moralist," and not "overmuch of a thinker," and preferred Edmond Scherer on those grounds. But as soon as he had begun to taste Europe for himself, he wrote home, as a postscript to a letter in the fall of 1869: "I have just read of Sainte-Beuve's death. I have lost my best friend." He had, of course, never met Sainte-Beuve, but his debt to him steadily accrued. By the time he wrote "The Art of Fiction," "the measure" of his "enjoyment of a critic," as he said in a review of Arnold, was "the extent to which he resembles Sainte-Beuve." For the critic, as HJ phrased Sainte-Beuve's conception, "was not the narrow law-giver or the rigid censor that he is often assumed to be; he was the student, the inquirer, the observer, the interpreter, the active, indefatigable commentator, whose constant aim was to arrive at justness of characterization."

Here was an enthusiasm that WJ shared. Writing to HJ about the weaknesses of Paul Bourget, he observed: "The man has so much ability as a writer and such perception that it seems a ten-fold shame that he should be poisoned by the contemptible and pedantic Parisian ideal of materialism and of being scientific. How can men so deep in one way be so shallow in another, as if to turn living flesh and blood into abstract formulas were to be scientific. Sainte-Beuve's method of giving you the whole of an individual is far more scientific than this dissecting out of his abstract essence, which turns out after all only a couple of his bones."

The mature HJ, instead of being worried about Sainte-Beuve's limitations, takes delight in his free play of intelligence. He grants that "there may be something feminine in his tact, penetration, subtilty," yet the Frenchman possesses also "faculties of the masculine stamp, the solid sense, the constant reason, the copious knowledge, the passion for exactitude, and for general considerations. . . . No scholar was ever so much of an observer, of a moralist, a psychologist." In this appraisal HJ sees Sainte-Beuve's greatness as it has been generally recognized in France. He also presents a standard by which we might in turn estimate his own work as a critic. In comparison, his talent would appear more feminine, and he himself spoke of his "incurable preference for grace." He certainly possessed little of Sainte-Beuve's enormous range of knowledge of periods other than his own. Both HJ and WJ were very American in being preponderantly concerned with the contemporaneous, and, once HJ hit his stride as a critic, he confined himself to the writers and artists of his own century. He became a highly intelligent critic, but one whose concern with general ideas was very limited. He came closest to measuring up to Sainte-Beuve in the three final roles that he mentioned above.

He was in the end, to be sure, a critic of a very different kind, not a moral historian but a practicing theorist of the novelist's craft. When viewing doubtfully Victor Hugo's *Ninety-Three* (1874), he described himself as having "a conservative taste in literary matters . . . for conciseness, for elegance, for perfection of form." He later advanced to the point of declaring that questions of method "are the noblest speculations that can engage the human mind," and his successive essays on the French novelists, particularly those on Balzac and Flaubert, ranging in time from the 1870's to 1913, exhibit the inexhaustible attention that he brought to such questions. The weakness of his strength comes out on those occasions when he loses sight of everything except method. His ultimate criterion for a novel was the degree to which it demonstrated composition, and he was dissatisfied with Tolstoy's *War and Peace* because of its "flopping looseness": "He has a mighty fund of life, but the *waste*, and the ugliness and vice of waste, the vice of a not finer *doing*, are sickening." WJ's reaction was far more representative of the common reader. He pronounced it "undoubtedly the greatest novel ever written," and was absorbed in its immense vitality. He showed his own bias when he added: "I don't like his fatalism and semi-pessimism, but for infallible veracity concerning human nature, and absolute simplicity of method, he makes all other writers of novels and plays seem like children."

However blinded HJ may have been by his own preoccupations, his criticism of Tolstoy sprang from one of his cardinal beliefs about the nature of permanence in art. No matter how vast Tolstoy's greatness, HJ held him to be a far less useful model for the beginning practitioner than Turgenieff. He recognized Tolstoy's disciples in the "slice-of-life" novelists, in H. G. Wells and Arnold Bennett. From the latter's productions in particular, he said, "Our sole inference is that things, the things disclosed, *go on and on, in any given case, in spite of everything.*" His contrasting example of a contemporary novelist in whose work the center of interest lay in the design itself was Joseph Conrad.

HJ's most notorious stricture was that Tolstoy and Dostoevsky were "fluid puddings." It is only fair to look at the context, in a letter to Hugh Walpole. For however deplorably wrong HJ was in his examples, he was developing a principle upon which he had staked his entire career, and upon which he would base the very life of any work of art:

"When you ask me if I don't feel Dostoevsky's 'mad jumble, that flings things down in a heap,' nearer truth and beauty than the picking and composing that you instance in Stevenson, I reply with emphasis that I feel nothing of the sort, and the older I grow and the more I *go* the more sacred to me do picking and composing become—though I naturally don't limit myself to Stevenson's *kind* of the same. Don't let any one persuade you—there are plenty of ignorant and fatuous duffers to try to do it—that strenuous selection and comparison are not the very essence of art, and that Form *is* [not] substance to that degree that there is absolutely no substance without it. Form alone *takes*, and holds and preserves, substance—saves it from the welter of helpless verbiage that we swim in as in a sea of tasteless tepid pudding, and that makes one ashamed of an art capable of such degradations. Tolstoy and Dostoevsky are fluid puddings, though not tasteless, because the amount of their own minds and souls in solution in the broth gives it savour and flavour, thanks to the strong, rank quality of their genius and their experience. But there are all sorts of things to be said of them, and in particular that we see how great a vice is their lack of composition, their defiance of economy and architecture, directly they are emulated and imitated; *then*, as subjects of emulation, models, they quite give themselves away. There is nothing so deplorable as a work of art with a *leak* in its interest; and there is no such leak of interest as through commonness of form. Its opposite, the *found* (because the sought-for) form is the absolute citadel and tabernacle of interest."

PARTIAL PORTRAITS

Emerson

THE COMMENTS by father and sons upon Emerson compose by themselves a chapter of American intellectual history. Henry Senior's most incisive estimate was in his last work, *Spiritual Creation,* where he introduced a section on "Mr. Emerson" to contrast with his own insistence upon conscience as "a conscience of sin." The years had not softened Henry Senior's basic objections to Emerson's indifference to intellect, or to his lack of a sense of evil. He could explain him only as an embodiment of an arrested state of innocence, quite wanting in the Blakean energies of experience. This meant, to Henry Senior's view, that:

"Mr. Emerson had no spiritual insight into creative order, because he had no adequate doctrine of consciousness. He regarded the judgments of consciousness as final, and would as soon have jumped into the Merrimac as seriously have supposed that the divine kingdom on earth was vastly more indebted for its furtherance to sinners than to saints. He took a downright literal view of the reality of men's moral differences, and I have heard him tell with infinite *gusto* of some virtuous youth in college with him, who had such a gross faculty of moral effusion as actually to suppress all naughty conversation among his companions by his bare presence—which made me wonder what a pitch of spiritual idiocy this moral peacock, if left to himself, would be sure eventually to attain to. Only we are none of us left to ourselves, nor can be, fortunately."

Henry Senior had also written, a dozen years earlier, a more ceremonious essay on Emerson as a pendant to his reminiscences of Carlyle. But since he did not manage to publish the latter until after Carlyle's death, this other essay remained in manuscript until WJ finally placed it with the *Atlantic* in the year following Emerson's centenary. It makes its points less trenchantly than the piece included below, but WJ's introductory note is worth reprinting for its contrasting characterizations of his father and Emerson:

"My father was a theologian of the 'twice-born' type, an out-and-out Lutheran, who believed that the moral law existed solely to fill us with loathing for the idea of our own merits, and to make us turn to God's grace as our only opportunity. But God's grace, in Mr. James' system, was not for the individual in isolation: the sphere of redemption was *Society*. In a Society organized divinely our *natures* will not be altered, but our spontaneities, because they will then work harmoniously, will all work innocently, and the Kingdom of heaven will have come. With these ideas, Mr. James was both fascinated and baffled by his friend Emerson. The personal graces of the man seemed to prefigure the coming millennium, but the resolute individualism of his thought, and the way in which his imagination rested on superior personages, and on heroic anecdotes about them, as if these were creation's ultimates, set my father's philosophy at defiance. For him no man was superior to another in the final plan. Emerson would listen, I fancy, as if charmed, to James' talk of the 'divine natural Humanity,' but he would never *subscribe;* and this, from one whose native gifts were so suggestive of that same Humanity, was disappointing. Emerson, in short, was a 'once-born' man; he lived in moral distinctions, and recognized no need of a redemptive process."

WJ did not formulate his own estimate of Emerson until the centennial year, but HJ had opened his collection of *Partial Portraits* (1888) with a reconsideration of the Concord milieu and its central figure. The starting-point for HJ's essay was the memorial biography by Elliot Cabot, which HJ felt had neglected the very opportunity of which Sainte-Beuve would have made so much, of giving a "general picture" of the society which had been a counterpoise to Emerson's solitude. HJ was clearly emulating Sainte-Beuve by demonstrating how much you can learn of the natural history of an environment through a psychological scrutiny of its best human product.

His matured belief was that the Concord school had enacted a series of experiments in the void, but he penetrated none the less to the heart of Emerson's genius—"the genius for seeing character as a real and supreme thing." To Emerson's scorn of talent as being on a far lower plane than inspiration HJ could not subscribe any more than he could to a similar strain in his father. He could only view Emerson's work as an exception to "the general rule that writings live in the last resort by their form"—an exception that a further half century seems not to have upheld, to judge by the relative neglect of most of Emerson's work now in contrast, say, with the increasing response to the concentrated form of Thoreau's *Walden*.

HJ almost echoes his father in setting Emerson's unconsciousness of evil against Hawthorne's depth of penetration into its darkness. He draws most on his own special skills in his vignette of the Lyceum audiences struggling with their overshoes or in his glimpses of that "decidedly lean" Boston upon whose tone he was to remark in his autobiography that it "had somehow become that of the most educated of our societies without ceasing to be that of the village." He was also to include in his autobiography his earliest New York memory of Emerson, a passage that bears out, as we have noted, how much the sound of the spoken word signified for a member of the James family:

"I 'visualise' . . . the winter firelight of our back-parlour at dusk and the great Emerson—I knew he was great, greater than any of our friends—sitting in it between my parents, before the lamps had been lighted . . . and affecting me the more as an apparition sinuously and, I held, elegantly slim, benevolently aquiline, and commanding a tone alien, beautifully alien, to any we heard roundabout, that he bent this benignity upon me by an invitation to draw nearer to him, off the hearth-rug, and know myself as never yet, as I was not indeed to know myself again for years, in touch with the wonder of Boston. The wonder of Boston was above all just then and there for me in the sweetness of the voice and the finish of the speech—this latter through a sort of attenuated emphasis which at the same time made sounds more important, more interesting in themselves, than by any revelation yet vouchsafed us. Was not this my first glimmer of a sense that the human tone *could*, in that independent and original way, be interesting? and didn't it for a long time keep me going, however unwittingly, in that faith, carrying me in fact more or less on to my day of recognising that it took much more than simply not being of New York to produce the music I had listened to. The point was that, however that might be, I had had given me there in the firelight an absolutely abiding measure. If I didn't know from that hour forth quite all it was to *not* utter sounds worth mentioning, I make out that I had at least the opposite knowledge. And all by the operation of those signal moments—the truth of which I find somehow reflected in the fact of my afterwards knowing one of our household rooms for the time—it must have been our only guest-chamber—as 'Mr. Emerson's room.' The evening firelight played so long for me upon the door—that is to the length probably of three days, the length of a child's impression."

He devoted a passage of *The American Scene* to Concord, which he referred to, half humorously, by its sobriquet of "the American Weimar," and then went on to this climax:

"We may smile a little as we 'drag in' Weimar, but I confess myself, for my part, much more satisfied than not by our happy equivalent, 'in American money,' for Goethe and Schiller. The money is a potful in the second case as in the first, and if Goethe, in the one, represents the gold and Schiller the silver, I find (and quite putting aside any bimetallic prejudice) the same good relation in the other between Emerson and Thoreau. I open Emerson for the same benefit for which I open Goethe, the sense of moving in large intellectual space, and that of the gush, here and there, out of the rock, of the crystalline cupful, in wisdom and poetry, in Wahrheit and Dichtung; and whatever I open Thoreau for (I needn't take space here for the good reasons) I open him oftener than I open Schiller. Which comes back to our feeling that the rarity of Emerson's genius, which has made him so, for the attentive peoples, the first, and the one really rare, American spirit in letters, couldn't have spent his career in a charming woodsy, watery place, for so long socially and typically and, above all, interestingly homogeneous, without an effect as of the communication to it of something ineffaceable. It was during his long span his immediate concrete, sufficient world; it gave him his nearest vision of life, and he drew half his images, we recognize, from the revolution of its seasons and the play of its manners. I don't speak of the other half, which he drew from elsewhere. It is admirably, to-day, as if we were still seeing these things *in* those images, which stir the air like birds, dim in the eventide, coming home to nest. If one had reached a 'time of life' one had thereby at least heard him lecture; and not a russet leaf fell for me, while I was there, but fell with an Emersonian drop."

WJ also delighted in Emerson's eye for landscapes, though he found "the hottest side" of him in his nonconformist conviction of the unsurpassable value of the individual. He quite characteristically reread all of Emerson in preparation for his fifteen-minute memorial address at Concord. He wrote HJ how much this experience had meant to him: "The reading of the divine Emerson, volume after volume, has done me a lot of good, and, strange to say, has thrown a strong practical light on my own path. The incorruptible way in which he followed his own vocation, of seeing such truths as the Universal Soul vouchsafed to him from day to day and month to month, and reporting them in the right literary form, and thereafter kept his limits absolutely, refusing to be entangled with irrelevancies however urging and tempting, knowing both his strength and its limits, and clinging unchangeably to the rural environment which he once for all found to be most propitious, seems to me a moral lesson to all men who have any genius, however small, to foster." He had been stimulated by Emerson's example to cut himself free at last from the encumbrances of his profession in order to make his own final report on the Universe.

His annotations in the nine volumes of Emerson that he owned reveal how much he implied in speaking of Emerson as his "beloved master." One knows in advance the aspects he would reject. He remarked in

The Varieties of Religious Experience that "modern transcendental idealism, Emersonianism, for instance . . . seems to let God evaporate into abstract Ideality." He also took exception to Emerson's "Platonic formulas" of monism. When Emerson said that the highest truth "shall exclude example and experience," WJ pronounced this "the tasteless water of souls." But whenever the activist element in Emerson was in the ascendant, WJ was all admiration, and found "a motto" for his own philosophy in the famous passage in "Self-Reliance" which begins: "Trust thyself: every heart vibrates to that iron string," and which ends: "we are now men . . . and not minors and invalids in a protected corner, not cowards fleeing before a revolution, but guides, redeemers, and benefactors, obeying the Almighty effort and advancing on Chaos and the Dark."

That encouraging strain must have been an enormous comfort to WJ in the years when he was oppressed by what he considered his father's pessimistic view of evil, and when he was striving desperately to escape from being an invalid himself. He seems to have held throughout life to Emerson's general conception of the philosopher. When he was outlining Pragmatism, in 1905, he repudiated the prevailing opposition between science and philosophy by asserting: "Both are just man thinking, by every means in his power." Over thirty years before, while a student in Europe, he had responded to Emerson's sweeping view of the past as summed up in the proposition that "Books are for the scholar's idle times": "I am sure that an age will come when our present devotion to history, and scrupulous care for what men have done before us merely as fact, will seem incomprehensible; when acquaintance with books will be no duty, but a pleasure for odd individuals; when Emerson's philosophy will be in our bones, not our dramatic imaginations."

The further you look in WJ, the more passages you can find with an Emersonian ring. He wrote in a copy of his shorter *Psychology*, at the head of his chapter on Habit: "Sow an action, and you reap a habit; sow a habit and you reap a character; sow a character and you reap a destiny." This epigrammatic sentence could well have been shaped by Emerson, as could also WJ's summation of the difficulties involved in being "sensitive" as well as "a motor": "Heroism is always on a precipitous edge, and only keeps alive by running. Every moment is an *escape*." But it was an escape only in the sense that life "has to be conquered every minute afresh by an act, and if writing and rhetoric help us to the act, they are also part of the function." Emerson had said: "Only life avails, not the having lived"; and again, in a passage that WJ underlined: "Words and deeds are quite indifferent modes of the divine energy. Words are also actions, and actions are a kind of words."

WJ wrote, in one of the unfinished drafts for his projected final metaphysics, that if he wanted to indicate the one kind of unity the pluralist knows, he should call his volume *The Moment of Experience*. Though he probably did not have Emerson in mind, that title might equally well have served for his philosophy, since Emerson kept re-affirming the doctrine of "each and all," of the potential fullness of life in any of its briefest manifestations. But with philosophers as expansive as Emerson and WJ, and as blithely unconcerned with logical con-sistency, it would be foolish to try to pin down too many of their correspondences. WJ owed to Emerson substantially what HJ owed to Hawthorne, not an assessable sum but rather the pervasive and in-escapable debt that a man owes to the largest figure in his immediate background who is devoted to the same pursuit.

How conscious WJ remained both of Emerson's greatness and of his own divergences from him may be read in passages from two of his letters in the wake of the centenary celebration:

"I wish you had been at Concord. It was the most harmoniously æsthetic or æsthetically harmonious thing! The weather, the beauty of the village, the charming old meeting-house, the descendants of the grand old man in such profusion, the mixture of Concord and Boston heads, so many of them of our own circle, the allusions to great thoughts and things, and the old-time New England rusticity and rurality, the silver polls and ancient voices of the *vieille garde* who did the orating (including this 'yer child), all made a matchless combina-tion, took one back to one's childhood, and made that rarely realized marriage of reality with ideality, that usually occurs only in fiction or poetry.

"It was a sweet and memorable day, and I am glad that I had an active share in it. . . . I let R. W. E. speak for himself, and I find now, hearing so much from others of him, that there are only a few things that *can* be said of him; he was so squarely and simply himself as to impress every one in the same manner. Reading the whole of him over again continuously has made me feel his real greatness as I never did before. He's really a critter to be thankful for."

"I myself believe that the orthodox theology contains elements that are permanently true, and that such writers as Emerson, by reason of their extraordinary healthy-mindedness and 'once-born'-ness, are in-capable of appreciating. I believe that they will have to be expressed in any ultimately valid religious philosophy; and I see in the temper of friendliness of such a man as you [1] for such writings as Emerson's and mine (*magnus comp. parvo*) a foretaste of the day when the abstract essentials of belief will be the basis of communion more than the par-

---

[1] Henry W. Rankin of East North-field, Massachusetts, who had suggested to WJ some of the illustrative material for *The Varieties of Religious Experience*.

ticular forms and concrete doctrines in which they articulate themselves. . . . Rereading him *in extenso*, almost *in toto*, lately, has made
him loom larger than ever to me as a human being, but I feel the distinct
lack in him of too little understanding of the morbid side of life."

*   *   *   *   *

HENRY JAMES, SENIOR: MR. EMERSON (1881)

AT ALL EVENTS, if we are still to go on cherishing any such luxury as
a private conscience towards God, I greatly prefer for my own part
that it should be an evil conscience. Conscience was always intended
as a rebuke and never as an exhilaration to the private citizen; and so
let it flourish till the end of our wearisome civilization. There are many
signs, however, that this end is near. My recently deceased friend Mr.
Emerson, for example, was all his days an arch traitor to our existing
civilized regimen, inasmuch as he unconsciously managed to set aside
its fundamental principle in doing without conscience, which was the
entire secret of his very exceptional interest to men's speculation. He
betrayed it to be sure without being at all aware of what he was doing;
but this was really all that he distinctively did to my observation. His
nature had always been so innocent, so unaffectedly innocent, that when
in later life he began to cultivate a club consciousness, and to sip a glass
of wine or smoke a cigar, I felt very much outraged by it. I felt very
much as if some renowned Boston belle had suddenly collapsed and
undertaken to sell newspapers at a street corner. "Why, Emerson, is
this *you* doing such things?" I exclaimed. "What profanation! Do
throw the unclean things behind your back!" But, no; he was actually
proud of his accomplishments! This came from his never knowing
(intellectually) what he stood for in the evolution of New England life.
He was lineally descended to begin with, from a half-score of comatose
New England clergymen, in whose behalf probably the religious instinct
had been used up. Or, what to their experience had been religion, became in that of their descendant *life*. The actual truth, at any rate, was
that he never felt a movement of the life of conscience from the day of
his birth till that of his death. I could never see any signs of such a life
in him. I remember, to be sure, that he had a great gift of friendship,
and that he was very plucky in behalf of his friends whenever they
felt themselves assailed—as plucky as a woman. For instance, whenever Wendell Phillips ventilated his not untimely wit at the expense of
our club-house politicians, Emerson, hearing his friends among these
latter complain, grew indignant, and for several days you would hear
nothing from his lips but excessive eulogies of Mr. Garrison, which
sounded like nothing else in the world but revilings of Mr. Phillips.
But, bless your heart! there was not a bit of conscience in a bushel of

such experiences, but only wounded friendship, which is a totally different and much lower thing.

The infallible mark of conscience is that it is always a subjective judgment couched in some such language as this: "God be merciful to *me* a sinner!" and never an objective judgment such as this: *God damn Wendell Phillips, or some other of my friends!* This latter judgment is always an outbreak of ungovernable temper on our part, and was never known to reach the ear of God save in this guise: *God* BLESS *W. P. or any other friend implicated!* Now Emerson was seriously incapable of a subjective judgment upon himself; he did not know the inward difference between good and evil, so far as he was himself concerned. No doubt he perfectly comprehended the outward or moral difference between these things; but I insist upon it that he never so much as dreamed of any inward or spiritual difference between them. For this difference is vitally seen only when oneself seems unchangeably evil to his own sight, and one's neighbor unchangeably good in the comparison. How could Emerson ever have known this difference? I am satisfied that he never in his life had felt a temptation *to bear false-witness* against his neighbor, *to steal, to commit adultery,* or *to murder;* how then should he have ever experienced what is technically called a conviction of sin?—that is, a conviction of himself as *evil* before God, and all other men as *good.* One gets a conviction of the evil that attaches to the natural selfhood in man in no other way than—as I can myself attest—by this growing acquaintance with his own moral infirmity, and the consequent gradual decline of his self-respect. For I myself had known all these temptations—in forms of course more or less modified—by the time I was fourteen or fifteen years old; so that by the time I had got to be twenty-five or thirty (which was the date of my first acquaintance with Emerson) I was saturated with a sense of spiritual evil—no man ever more so possibly, since I felt thoroughly *self*-condemned before God. Good heavens! how soothed and comforted I was by the innocent lovely look of my new acquaintance, by his tender courtesy, his generous laudatory appreciation of my crude literary ventures! and how I used to lock myself up with him in his bed-room, swearing that before the door was opened I would arrive at the secret of his immense superiority to the common herd of literary men! I might just as well have locked myself up with a handful of diamonds, so far as any capacity of self-cognizance existed in him. I found in fact, before I had been with him a week, that the immense superiority I ascribed to him was altogether personal or practical—by no means intellectual; that it came to him by birth or genius like a woman's beauty or charm of manners; that no other account was to be given of it in truth than that Emerson himself was an unsexed woman, a veritable fruit of almighty power in the sphere of our *nature.*

This after a while grew to be a great discovery to me; but I was always more or less provoked to think that Emerson himself should take no intellectual stock in it. On the whole I may say that at first I was greatly disappointed in him, because his intellect never kept the promise which his lovely face and manners held out to me. He was to my senses a literal divine presence in the house with me; and we cannot recognize literal divine presences in our houses without feeling sure that they will be able to say something of critical importance to one's intellect. It turned out that any average old dame in a horse-car would have satisfied my intellectual rapacity just as well as Emerson. My standing intellectual embarrassment for years had been to get at the bottom of the difference between law and gospel in humanity—between the head and the heart of things—between the great God almighty, in short, and the intensely wooden and ridiculous gods of the nations. Emerson, I discovered immediately, had never been the least of an expert in this sort of knowledge; and though his immense personal fascination always kept up, he at once lost all intellectual prestige to my regard. I even thought that I had never seen a man more profoundly devoid of spiritual understanding. This prejudice grew, of course, out of my having inherited an altogether narrow ecclesiastical notion of what spiritual understanding was. I supposed it consisted unmistakably in some doctrinal lore concerning man's regeneration, to which, however, my new friend was plainly and signally incompetent. Emerson, in fact, derided this doctrine, smiling benignly whenever it was mentioned. I could make neither head nor tail of him according to men's ordinary standards—the only thing that I was sure of being that he, like Christ, was somehow divinely begotten. He seemed to me unmistakably virgin-born whenever I looked at him, and reminded me of nothing so much as of those persons dear to Christ's heart who should come after him professing no allegiance to him—having never heard his name pronounced, and yet perfectly fulfilling his will. He never seemed for a moment to antagonize the church of his own consent, but only out of condescension to his interlocutor's weakness. In fact he was to all appearance entirely ignorant of the church's existence until you recalled it to his imagination; and even then I never knew anything so implacably and uniformly mild as his judgments of it were. He had apparently lived all his life in a world where it was only subterraneously known; and, try as you would, you could never persuade him that any the least living power attached to it. The same profound incredulity characterized him in regard to the State; and it was only in his enfeebled later years that he ever lent himself to the idea of society as its destined divine form. I am not sure indeed that the lending was ever very serious. But he was always greedy, with all a Yankee's greediness, after facts, and would at least appear to listen to you with earnest respect and sympathy whenever you plead for society as the redeemed form of our nature.

In short he was, as I have said before, fundamentally treacherous to civilization, without being at all aware himself of the fact. He himself, I venture to say, was peculiarly unaware of the fact. He appeared to me utterly unconscious of himself as either good or evil. He had no conscience, in fact, and lived by perception, which is an altogether lower or less spiritual faculty. The more universalized a man is by genius or natural birth, the less is he spiritually individualized, making up in breadth of endowment what he lacks in depth. This was remarkably the case with Emerson. In his books or public capacity he was constantly electrifying you by sayings full of divine inspiration. In his talk or private capacity he was one of the least remunerative men I ever encountered. No man could look at him speaking (or when he was silent either, for that matter) without having a vision of the divinest beauty. But when you went to him to hold discourse about the wondrous phenomenon, you found him absolutely destitute of reflective power. He had apparently no private personality; and if any visitor thought he discerned traces of such a thing, you may take for granted that the visitor himself was a man of large imaginative resources. He was nothing else than a show-figure of almighty power in our nature; and that he was destitute of all the apparatus of humbuggery that goes to eke out more or less the private pretension in humanity, only completed and confirmed the extraordinary fascination that belonged to him. He was full of living inspiration to me whenever I saw him; and yet I could find in him no trivial sign of the selfhood which I found in other men. He was like a vestal virgin, indeed, always in ministry upon the altar; but the vestal virgin had doubtless a prosaic side also, which related her to commonplace people. Now Emerson was so far *unlike* the virgin: he had no prosaic side relating him to ordinary people. Judge Hoar and Mr. John Forbes constituted his spontaneous political conscience; and his domestic one (equally spontaneous) was supplied by loving members of his own family—so that he only connected with the race at second-hand, and found all the material business of life such as voting and the payment of taxes transacted for *him* with marvellous lack of friction.

Incontestably the main thing about him, however, as I have already said, was that he unconsciously brought you face to face with the infinite in humanity. When I looked upon myself, or upon the ordinary rabble of ecclesiastics and politicians, everything in us seemed ridiculously undivine. When I looked upon Emerson, these same undivine things were what gave *him* his manifest divine charm. The reason was that in him everything seemed innocent by the transparent absence of selfhood, and in us everything seemed foul and false by its preternatural activity. The difference between us was made by innocence altogether. I never thought it was a real or spiritual difference, but only a natural or apparent one. But such as it was, it gave me my first living impression of the great God almighty who alone is at work in human affairs, avouching his awful and adorable spiritual infinitude only through the death and hell wrapped up in our·finite experience. This was Emerson's incontestable virtue to every one who appreciated him, that he recognized no God outside of himself and his interlocutor, and recognized him there only as the *liaison* between the two, taking care that all their intercourse should be holy with a holiness undreamed of before by man or angel. For it is not a holiness taught by books or the example of tiresome, diseased, self-conscious saints, but simply by one's own redeemed flesh and blood. In short, the only holiness which Emerson recognized, and for which he consistently lived, was innocence. And innocence—glory be to God's spiritual incarnation in our nature!—has no other root in us than our unconscious flesh and bones. That is to say, it attaches only to what is definitively universal or natural in our experience, and hence appropriates itself to individuals only in so far as they learn to denude themselves of personality or self-consciousness; which reminds one of Christ's mystical saying: *He that findeth his life (in himself) shall lose it, and he that loseth his life for my sake shall find it.*

HJ: EMERSON (1887)[1]

Mr. Elliot Cabot has made a very interesting contribution to a class of books of which our literature, more than other, offers admirable examples: he has given us a biography[2] intelligently and carefully composed. These two volumes are a model of responsible editing—I use that term because they consist largely of letters and extracts from letters: nothing could resemble less the manner in which the mere bookmaker strings together his frequently questionable pearls and shovels the heap into the presence of the public. Mr. Cabot has selected, compared, discriminated, steered an even course between meagreness and redundancy, and managed to be constantly and happily illustrative. And his work, moreover, strikes us as the better done from the fact that it stands for one of the two things that make an absorbing memoir a good deal more than for the other. If these two things be the conscience of the writer and the career of his hero, it is not difficult to see on which side the biographer of Emerson has found himself strongest. Ralph Waldo Emerson was a man of genius, but he led for nearly

---

[1] I have omitted a few of the longer quotations.—F. O. M.

[2] *A Memoir of Ralph Waldo Emer-son; by James Elliot Cabot. Two volumes: London, 1887.*

eighty years a life in which the sequence of events had little of the rapidity, or the complexity, that a spectator loves. There is something we miss very much as we turn these pages—something that has a kind of accidental, inevitable presence in almost any personal record—something that may be most definitely indicated under the name of colour. We lay down the book with a singular impression of paleness—an impression that comes partly from the tone of the biographer and partly from the moral complexion of his subject, but mainly from the vacancy of the page itself. That of Emerson's personal history is condensed into the single word Concord, and all the condensation in the world will not make it look rich. It presents a most continuous surface. Mr. Matthew Arnold, in his *Discourses in America*, contests Emerson's complete right to the title of a man of letters; yet letters surely were the very texture of his history. Passions, alternations, affairs, adventures had absolutely no part in it. It stretched itself out in enviable quiet—a quiet in which we hear the jotting of the pencil in the notebook. It is the very life for literature (I mean for one's own, not that of another): fifty years of residence in the home of one's forefathers, pervaded by reading, by walking in the woods and the daily addition of sentence to sentence.

If the interest of Mr. Cabot's pencilled portrait is incontestable and yet does not spring from variety, it owes nothing either to a source from which it might have borrowed much and which it is impossible not to regret a little that he has so completely neglected: I mean a greater reference to the social conditions in which Emerson moved, the company he lived in, the moral air he breathed. If his biographer had allowed himself a little more of the ironic touch, had put himself once in a way under the protection of Sainte-Beuve and had attempted something of a general picture, we should have felt that he only went with the occasion. I may overestimate the latent treasures of the field, but it seems to me there was distinctly an opportunity—an opportunity to make up moreover in some degree for the white tint of Emerson's career considered simply in itself. We know a man imperfectly until we know his society, and we but half know a society until we know its manners. This is especially true of a man of letters, for manners lie very close to literature. From those of the New England world in which Emerson's character formed itself Mr. Cabot almost averts his lantern, though we feel sure that there would have been delightful glimpses to be had and that he would have been in a position—that is that he has all the knowledge that would enable him—to help us to them. It is as if he could not trust himself, knowing the subject only too well. This adds to the effect of extreme discretion that we find in his volumes, but it is the cause of our not finding certain things, certain figures and scenes, evoked. What is evoked is Emerson's pure spirit, by a copious, sifted series of citations and comments. But we must read as much as possible between the lines, and the picture of the transcendental time (to mention simply one corner) has yet to be painted— the lines have yet to be bitten in. Meanwhile we are held and charmed by the image of Emerson's mind and the extreme appeal which his physiognomy makes to our art of discrimination. It is so fair, so uniform and impersonal, that its features are simply fine shades, the gradations of tone of a surface whose proper quality was of the smoothest and on which nothing was reflected with violence. It is a pleasure of the critical sense to find, with Mr. Cabot's extremely intelligent help, a notation for such delicacies.

We seem to see the circumstances of our author's origin, immediate and remote, in a kind of high, vertical moral light, the brightness of a society at once very simple and very responsible. The rare singleness that was in his nature (so that he was *all* the warning moral voice, without distraction or counter-solicitation), was also in the stock he sprang from, clerical for generations, on both sides, and clerical in the Puritan sense. His ancestors had lived long (for nearly two centuries) in the same corner of New England, and during that period had preached and studied and prayed and practised. It is impossible to imagine a spirit better prepared in advance to be exactly what it was—better educated for its office in its far-away unconscious beginnings. There is an inner satisfaction in seeing so straight, although so patient, a connection between the stem and the flower, and such a proof that when life wishes to produce something exquisite in quality she takes her measures many years in advance. A conscience like Emerson's could not have been turned off, as it were, from one generation to another: a succession of attempts, a long process of refining, was required. His perfection, in his own line, comes largely from the non-interruption of the process.

As most of us are made up of ill-assorted pieces, his reader, and Mr. Cabot's, envies him this transmitted unity, in which there was no mutual hustling or crowding of elements. It must have been a kind of luxury to be—that is to feel—so homogeneous, and it helps to account for his serenity, his power of acceptance, and that absence of personal passion which makes his private correspondence read like a series of beautiful circulars or expanded cards *pour prendre congé*. He had the equanimity of a result; nature had taken care of him and he had only to speak. He accepted himself as he accepted others, accepted everything; and his absence of eagerness, or in other words his modesty, was that of a man with whom it is not a question of success, who has nothing invested or at stake. The investment, the stake, was that of the race, of all the past Emersons and Bulkeleys and Waldos. There is much that makes us smile, to-day, in the commotion produced by his secession from the mild Unitarian pulpit: we wonder at a condition of opinion in which any utterance of his should appear to be wanting in superior piety—in the essence of good instruction. All that is changed: the great difference has become the infinitely small, and we admire a state of society in which scandal and schism took on no darker hue; but there is even yet a sort of drollery in the spectacle of a body of people among whom the author of *The American Scholar* and of the Address of 1838 at the Harvard Divinity College passed for profane, and who failed to see that he only gave his plea for the spiritual life the advantage of a brilliant expression. They were so provincial as to think that brilliancy came ill-recommended, and they were shocked at his ceasing to care for the prayer and the sermon. They might have perceived that he *was* the prayer and the sermon: not in the least a seculariser, but in his own subtle insinuating way a sanctifier.

Of the three periods into which his life divides itself, the first was (as in the case of most men) that of movement, experiment and selection—that of effort too and painful probation. Emerson had his message, but he was a good while looking for his form—the form which, as he himself would have said, he never completely found and of which it was rather characteristic of him that his later years (with their growing refusal to give him the *word*), wishing to attack him in his most vulnerable point, where his tenure was least complete, had in some degree the effect of despoiling him. It all sounds rather bare and stern, Mr. Cabot's account of his youth and early manhood, and we get an impression of a terrible paucity of alternatives. If he would be neither a farmer nor a trader he could "teach school"; that was the main resource and a part of the general educative process of the young New Englander who proposed to devote himself to the things of the mind. There was an advantage in the nudity, however, which was that, in Emerson's case at least, the things of the mind did get themselves admirably well considered. If it be his great distinction and his special sign that he had a more vivid conception of the moral life than any one else, it is probably not fanciful to say that he owed it in part to the limited way in which he saw our capacity for living illustrated. The plain, God-fearing, practical society which surrounded him was not fertile in variations: it had great intelligence and energy, but it moved altogether in the straightforward direction. On three occasions later—three journeys to Europe—he was introduced to a more complicated world; but his spirit, his moral taste, as it were, abode always within the undecorated walls of his youth. There he could dwell with that ripe unconsciousness of evil which is one of the most beautiful signs by which we know him. His early writings are full of quaint animadversion upon the vices of the place and time, but there is something charmingly vague, light and general in the arraignment. Almost the worst he can say is that these vices are negative and that his fellow-townsmen are not heroic. We feel that his first impressions were gathered in a community from which misery and extravagance, and either extreme, of any sort, were equally absent. What the life of New England fifty years ago offered to the observer was the common lot, in a kind of achromatic picture, without particular intensifications. It was from this table of the usual, the merely typical joys and sorrows that he proceeded to generalise—a fact that accounts in some degree for a certain inadequacy and thinness in his enumerations. But it helps to account also for his direct, intimate vision of the soul itself—not in its emotions, its contortions and perversions, but in its passive, exposed, yet· healthy form. He knows the nature of man and the long tradition of its dangers; but we feel that whereas he can put his finger on the remedies, lying for the most part, as they do, in the deep recesses of virtue, of the spirit, he has only a kind of hearsay, uninformed acquaintance with the disorders. It would require some ingenuity, the reader may say too much, to trace closely this correspondence between his genius and the frugal, dutiful, happy but decidedly lean Boston of the past, where there was a great deal of will but very little fulcrum—like a ministry without an opposition.

The genius itself it seems to me impossible to contest—I mean the genius for seeing character as a real and supreme thing. Other writers have arrived at a more complete expression: Wordsworth and Goethe, for instance, give one a sense of having found their form, whereas with Emerson we never lose the sense that he is still seeking it. But no one has had so steady and constant, and above all so natural, a vision of what we require and what we are capable of in the way of aspiration and independence. With Emerson it is ever the special capacity for moral experience—always that and only that. We have the impression, somehow, that life had never bribed him to look at anything but the soul; and indeed in the world in which he grew up and lived the bribes and lures, the beguilements and prizes, were few. He was in an admirable position for showing, what he constantly endeavoured to show, that the prize was within. Any one who in New England at that time could do that was sure of success, of listeners and sympathy: most of all, of course, when it was a question of doing it with such a divine persuasiveness. Moreover, the way in which Emerson did it added to the charm—by word of mouth, face to face, with a rare, irresistible voice and a beautiful mild, modest authority. If Mr. Arnold is struck with the limited degree in which he was a man of letters I suppose it is because he is more struck with his having been, as it were, a man of lectures. But the lecture surely was never more purged of its grossness—the quality in it that suggests a strong light and a big brush—than as it issued from Emerson's lips: so far from being a vulgarisation, it was

simply the esoteric made audible, and instead of treating the few as the
many, after the usual fashion of gentlemen on platforms, he treated the
many as the few. There was probably no other society at that time in
which he would have got so many persons to understand that; for we
think the better of his audience as we read him, and wonder where else
people would have had so much moral attention to give. It is to be
remembered however that during the winter of 1847–48, on the occasion of his second visit to England, he found many listeners in London
and in provincial cities. Mr. Cabot's volumes are full of evidence of the
satisfactions he offered, the delights and revelations he may be said to
have promised, to a race which had to seek its entertainment, its rewards and consolations, almost exclusively in the moral world. But his
own writings are fuller still; we find an instance almost wherever we
open them.

"All these great and transcendent properties are ours. . . . Let us
find room for this great guest in our small houses. . . . Where the heart
is, there the muses, there the gods sojourn, and not in any geography
of fame. Massachusetts, Connecticut River, and Boston Bay, you think
paltry places, and the ear loves names of foreign and classic topography.
But here we are, and if we will tarry a little we may come to learn that
here is best. . . . The Jerseys were handsome enough ground for
Washington to tread, and London streets for the feet of Milton. . . .
That country is fairest which is inhabited by the noblest minds."

We feel, or suspect, that Milton is thrown in as a hint that the London streets are no such great place, and it all sounds like a sort of plead-
ing consolation against bleakness.

The beauty of a hundred passages of this kind in Emerson's pages is
that they are effective, that they do come home, that they rest upon
insight and not upon ingenuity, and that if they are sometimes obscure
it is never with the obscurity of paradox. We seem to see the people
turning out into the snow after hearing them, glowing with a finer glow
than even the climate could give and fortified for a struggle with
overshoes and the east wind. . . .

I have hinted that the will, in the old New England society, was a
clue without a labyrinth; but it had its use, nevertheless, in helping the
young talent to find its mould. There were few or none ready-made:
tradition was certainly not so oppressive as might have been inferred
from the fact that the air swarmed with reformers and improvers. Of
the patient, philosophic manner in which Emerson groped and waited,
through teaching the young and preaching to the adult, for his particular vocation, Mr. Cabot's first volume gives a full and orderly account.
His passage from the Unitarian pulpit to the lecture-desk was a step
which at this distance of time can hardly help appearing to us short,
though he was long in making it, for even after ceasing to have a parish

of his own he freely confounded the two, or willingly, at least, treated
the pulpit as a platform. "The young people and the mature hint at
odium and the aversion of faces, to be presently encountered in society," he writes in his journal in 1838; but in point of fact the quiet
drama of his abdication was not to include the note of suffering. The
Boston world might feel disapproval, but it was far too kindly to make
this sentiment felt as a weight: every element of martyrdom was there
but the important ones of the cause and the persecutors. Mr. Cabot
marks the lightness of the penalties of dissent; if they were light in
somewhat later years for the transcendentalists and fruit-eaters they
could press but little on a man of Emerson's distinction, to whom, all
his life, people went not to carry but to ask the right word. There was
no consideration to give up, he could not have been one of the dingy if
he had tried; but what he did renounce in 1838 was a material profession. He was "settled," and his indisposition to administer the communion unsettled him. He calls the whole business, in writing to
Carlyle, "a tempest in our washbowl"; but it had the effect of forcing
him to seek a new source of income. His wants were few and his view
of life severe, and this came to him, little by little, as he was able to
extend the field in which he read his discourses. In 1835, upon his second
marriage, he took up his habitation at Concord, and his life fell into
the shape it was, in a general way, to keep for the next half-century.
It is here that we cannot help regretting that Mr. Cabot had not found
it possible to treat his career a little more pictorially. Those fifty years
of Concord—at least the earlier part of them—would have been a subject bringing into play many odd figures, many human incongruities:
they would have abounded in illustrations of the primitive New England character, especially during the time of its queer search for something to expend itself upon. Objects and occupations have multiplied
since then, and now there is no lack; but fifty years ago the expanse was
wide and free, and we get the impression of a conscience gasping in the
void, panting for sensations, with something of the movement of the
gills of a landed fish. It would take a very fine point to sketch Emerson's
benignant, patient, inscrutable countenance during the various phases of
this democratic communion; but the picture, when complete, would be
one of the portraits, half a revelation and half an enigma, that suggest
and fascinate. Such a striking personage as old Miss Mary Emerson,
our author's aunt, whose high intelligence and temper were much of an
influence in his earlier years, has a kind of tormenting representative
value: we want to see her from head to foot, with her frame and her
background; having (for we happen to have it), an impression that she
was a very remarkable specimen of the transatlantic Puritan stock, a
spirit that would have dared the devil. We miss a more liberal handling,
are tempted to add touches of our own, and end by convincing our-

selves that Miss Mary Moody Emerson, grim intellectual virgin and daughter of a hundred minsters, with her local traditions and her combined love of empire and of speculation, would have been an inspiration for a novelist. Hardly less so the charming Mrs. Ripley, Emerson's life-long friend and neighbour, most delicate and accomplished of women, devoted to Greek and to her house, studious, simple and dainty —an admirable example of the old-fashioned New England lady. It was a freak of Miss Emerson's somewhat sardonic humour to give her once a broomstick to carry across Boston Common (under the pretext of a "moving"), a task accepted with docility but making of the victim the most benignant witch ever equipped with that utensil.

These ladies, however, were very private persons and not in the least of the reforming tribe: there are others who would have peopled Mr. Cabot's page to whom he gives no more than a mention. We must add that it is open to him to say that their features have become faint and indistinguishable to-day without more research than the question is apt to be worth: they are embalmed—in a collective way— the apprehensible part of them, in Mr. Frothingham's clever *History of Transcendentalism in New England*. This must be admitted to be true of even so lively a "factor," as we say nowadays, as the imaginative, talkative, intelligent and finally Italianised and shipwrecked Margaret Fuller: she is now one of the dim, one of Carlyle's "then-celebrated" at most. It seemed indeed as if Mr. Cabot rather grudged her a due place in the record of the company that Emerson kept, until we came across the delightful letter he quotes toward the end of his first volume —a letter interesting both as a specimen of inimitable, imperceptible edging away, and as an illustration of the curiously generalised way, as if with an implicit protest against personalities, in which his intercourse, epistolary and other, with his friends was conducted. There is an extract from a letter to his aunt on the occasion of the death of a deeply-loved brother (his own) which reads like a passage from some fine old chastened essay on the vanity of earthly hopes: strangely unfamiliar, considering the circumstances. Courteous and humane to the furthest possible point, to the point of an almost profligate surrender of his attention, there was no familiarity in him, no personal avidity. Even his letters to his wife are courtesies, they are not familiarities. He had only one style, one manner, and he had it for everything—even for himself, in his notes, in his journals. But he had it in perfection for Miss Fuller; he retreats, smiling and flattering, on tiptoe, as if he were advancing. "She ever seems to crave," he says in his journal, "something which I have not, or have not for her." What he had was doubtless not what she craved, but the letter in question should be read to see how the modicum was administered. It is only between the lines of such a production that we read that a part of her effect upon him was to bore

him; for his system was to practise a kind of universal passive hospitality—he aimed at nothing less. It was only because he was so defer-
ential that he could be so detached; he had polished his aloofness till
it reflected the image of his solicitor. And this was not because he was
an "uncommunicating egotist," though he amuses himself with saying
so to Miss Fuller: egotism is the strongest of passions, and he was altogether passionless. It was because he had no personal, just as he had
almost no physical wants. "Yet I plead not guilty to the malice prepense. 'Tis imbecility, not contumacy, though perhaps somewhat more
odious. It seems very just, the irony with which you ask whether you
may not be trusted and promise such docility. Alas, we will all promise,
but the prophet loiters." He would not say even to himself that she
bored him; he had denied himself the luxury of such easy and obvious
short cuts. There is a passage in the lecture (1844) called "Man the
Reformer," in which he hovers round and round the idea that the practice of trade, in certain conditions likely to beget an underhand competition, does not draw forth the nobler parts of character, till the reader
is tempted to interrupt him with, "Say at once that it is impossible for a
gentleman!"

So he remained always, reading his lectures in the winter, writing
them in the summer, and at all seasons taking wood-walks and looking
for hints in old books. . . .

His observation of Nature was exquisite—always the direct, irresistible impression. . . . I have said there was no familiarity in him, but
he was familiar with woodland creatures and sounds. Certainly, too, he
was on terms of free association with his books, which were numerous
and dear to him; though Mr. Cabot says, doubtless with justice, that his
dependence of them was slight and that he was not "intimate" with his
authors. They did not feed him but they stimulated; they were not his
meat but his wine—he took them in sips. But he needed them and liked
them; he had volumes of notes from his reading, and he could not have
produced his lectures without them. He liked literature as a thing to
refer to, liked the very names of which it is full, and used them, especially in his later writings, for purposes of ornament, to dress the dish,
sometimes with an unmeasured profusion. I open *The Conduct of Life*
and find a dozen on the page. He mentions more authorities than is the
fashion to-day. He can easily say, of course, that he follows a better one
—that of his well-loved and irrepressibly allusive Montaigne. In his own
bookishness there is a certain contradiction, just as there is a latent incompleteness in his whole literary side. Independence, the return to nature, the finding out and doing for one's self, was ever what he most
highly recommended; and yet he is constantly reminding his readers of
the conventional signs and consecrations—of what other men have
done. This was partly because the independence that he had in his eye

was an independence without ill-nature, without rudeness (though he likes that word), and full of gentle amiabilities, curiosities and tolerances; and partly it is a simple matter of form, a literary expedient, confessing its character—on the part of one who had never really mastered the art of composition—of continuous expression. Charming to many a reader, charming yet ever slightly droll, will remain Emerson's frequent invocation of the "scholar": there is such a friendly vagueness and convenience in it. It is of the scholar that he expects all the heroic and uncomfortable things, the concentrations and relinquishments, that make up the noble life. We fancy this personage looking up from his book and arm-chair a little ruefully and saying, "Ah, but why *me* always and only? Why so much of me, and is there no one else to share the responsibility?" "Neither years nor books have yet availed to extirpate a prejudice then rooted in me [when as a boy he first saw the graduates of his college assembled at their anniversary], that a scholar is the favourite of heaven and earth, the excellency of his country, the happiest of men."

In truth, by this term he means simply the cultivated man, the man who has had a liberal education, and there is a voluntary plainness in his use of it—speaking of such people as the rustic, or the vulgar, speak of those who have a tincture of books. This is characteristic of his humility —that humility which was nine-tenths a plain fact (for it is easy for persons who have at bottom a great fund of indifference to be humble), and the remaining tenth a literary habit. Moreover an American reader may be excused for finding in it a pleasant sign of that prestige, often so quaintly and indeed so extravagantly acknowledged, which a connection with literature carries with it among the people of the United States. There is no country in which it is more freely admitted to be a distinction—*the* distinction; or in which so many persons have become eminent for showing it even in a slight degree. Gentlemen and ladies are celebrated there on this ground who would not on the same ground, though they might on another, be celebrated anywhere else. Emerson's own tone is an echo of that, when he speaks of the scholar—not of the banker, the great merchant, the legislator, the artist—as the most distinguished figure in the society about him. It is because he has most to give up that he is appealed to for efforts and sacrifices. "Meantime I know that a very different estimate of the scholar's profession prevails in this country," he goes on to say in the address from which I last quoted (the *Literary Ethics*), "and the importunity with which society presses its claim upon young men tends to pervert the views of the youth in respect to the culture of the intellect." The manner in which that is said represents, surely, a serious mistake: with the estimate of the scholar's profession which then prevailed in New England Emerson could have had no quarrel; the ground of his lamentation was another side of the matter. It was not a question of estimate, but of accidental practice. In 1838 there were still so many things of prime material necessity to be done that reading was driven to the wall; but the reader was still thought the cleverest, for he found time as well as intelligence. Emerson's own situation sufficiently indicates it. In what other country, on sleety winter nights, would provincial and bucolic populations have gone forth in hundreds for the cold comfort of a literary discourse? The distillation anywhere else would certainly have appeared too thin, the appeal too special. But for many years the American people of the middle regions, outside of a few cities, had in the most rigorous seasons no other recreation. A gentleman, grave or gay, in a bare room, with a manuscript, before a desk, offered the reward of toil, the refreshment of pleasure, to the young, the middle-aged and the old of both sexes. The hour was brightest, doubtless, when the gentleman was gay, like Doctor Oliver Wendell Holmes. But Emerson's gravity never sapped his career, any more than it chilled the regard in which he was held among those who were particularly his own people. It was impossible to be more honoured and cherished, far and near, than he was during his long residence in Concord, or more looked upon as the principal gentleman in the place. This was conspicuous to the writer of these remarks on the occasion of the curious, sociable, cheerful public funeral made for him in 1883 by all the countryside, arriving, as for the last honours to the first citizen, in trains, in waggons, on foot, in multitudes. It was a popular manifestation, the most striking I have ever seen provoked by the death of a man of letters.

If a picture of that singular and very illustrative institution the old American lecture-system would have constituted a part of the filling-in of the ideal memoir of Emerson, I may further say, returning to the matter for a moment, that such a memoir would also have had a chapter for some of those Concord-haunting figures which are not so much interesting in themselves as interesting because for a season Emerson thought them so. And the pleasure of that would be partly that it would push us to inquire how interesting he did really think them. That is, it would bring up the question of his inner reserves and scepticisms, his secret ennuis and ironies, the way he sympathised for courtesy and then, with his delicacy and generosity, in a world after all given much to the literal, let his courtesy pass for adhesion—a question particularly attractive to those for whom he has, in general, a fascination. Many entertaining problems of that sort present themselves for such readers: there is something indefinable for them in the mixture of which he was made—his fidelity as an interpreter of the so-called transcendental spirit and his freedom from all wish for any personal share in the effect of his ideas. He drops them, sheds them, diffuses them, and we feel as if there would be a grossness in holding him to anything so temporal as a re-

sponsibility. He had the advantage, for many years, of having the question of application assumed for him by Thoreau, who took upon himself to be, in the concrete, the sort of person that Emerson's "scholar"
was in the abstract, and who paid for it by having a shorter life than
that fine adumbration. The application, with Thoreau, was violent and
limited (it became a matter of prosaic detail, the non-payment of taxes,
the non-wearing of a necktie, the preparation of one's food one's self,
the practice of a rude sincerity—all things not of the essence), so that,
though he wrote some beautiful pages, which read like a translation of
Emerson into the sounds of the field and forest and which no one who
has ever loved nature in New England, or indeed anywhere, can fail to
love, he suffers something of the *amoindrissement* of eccentricity. His
master escapes that reduction altogether. I call it an advantage to have
had such a pupil as Thoreau; because for a mind so much made up of
reflection as Emerson's everything comes under that head which pro-
longs and reanimates the process—produces the return, again and yet
again, on one's impressions. Thoreau must have had this moderating
and even chastening effect. It did not rest, moreover, with him alone;
the advantage of which I speak was not confined to Thoreau's case. In
1837 Emerson (in his journal) pronounced Mr. Bronson Alcott the
most extraordinary man and the highest genius of his time: the sequence
of which was that for more than forty years after that he had the gentleman living but half a mile away. The opportunity for the return, as
I have called it, was not wanting.

His detachment is shown in his whole attitude toward the transcendental movement—that remarkable outburst of Romanticism on Puritan
ground, as Mr. Cabot very well names it. Nothing can be more ingenious, more sympathetic and charming, than Emerson's account and
definition of the matter in his lecture (of 1842) called "The Transcendentalist"; and yet nothing is more apparent from his letters and journals than that he regarded any such label or banner as a mere tiresome
flutter. He liked to taste but not to drink—least of all to become intoxicated. He liked to explain the transcendentalists but did not care at
all to be explained by them: a doctrine "whereof you know I am wholly
guiltless," he says to his wife in 1842, "and which is spoken of as a
known and fixed element, like salt or meal. So that I have to begin with
endless disclaimers and explanations: 'I am not the man you take me
for.'" He was never the man any one took him for, for the simple reason that no one could possibly take him for the elusive, irreducible,
merely gustatory spirit for which he took himself. . . .

It was the sense of their being "bands of competing minstrels" and
their camp being only a "measure and check," in a society too sparse
for a synthesis, that kept him from wishing to don their uniform. This
was after all but a misfitting imitation of his natural wear, and what he

would have liked was to put that off—he did not wish to button it tighter. He said the best for his friends of the Dial, of Fruitlands and Brook Farm, in saying that they were fastidious and critical; but he was conscious in the next breath that what there was around them to be criticised was mainly a negative. Nothing is more perceptible to-day than that their criticism produced no fruit—that it was little else than a very decent and innocent recreation—a kind of Puritan carnival. The New England world was for much the most part very busy, but the Dial and Fruitlands and Brook Farm were the amusement of the leisure-class. Extremes meet, and as in older societies that class is known principally by its connection with castles and carriages, so at Concord it came, with Thoreau and Mr. W. H. Channing, out of the cabin and the wood-lot.

Emerson was not moved to believe in their fastidiousness as a productive principle even when they directed it upon abuses which he abundantly recognised. Mr. Cabot shows that he was by no means one of the professional abolitionists or philanthropists—never an enrolled "humanitarian." . . . I must add that . . . there comes to me the recollection of the great meeting in the Boston Music Hall, on the first day of 1863, to celebrate the signing by Mr. Lincoln of the proclamation freeing the Southern slaves—of the momentousness of the occasion, the vast excited multitude, the crowded platform and the tall, spare figure of Emerson, in the midst, reading out the stanzas that were published under the name of the Boston Hymn. They are not the happiest he produced for an occasion—they do not compare with the verses on the "embattled farmers," read at Concord in 1857, and there is a certain awkwardness in some of them. But I well remember the immense effect with which his beautiful voice pronounced the lines—

> "Pay ransom to the owner
> And fill the bag to the brim.
> Who is the owner? The slave is owner,
> And ever was. Pay *him!*"

And Mr. Cabot chronicles the fact that the *gran' rifiuto*—the great back sliding of Mr. Webster when he cast his vote in Congress for the Fugitive Slave Law of 1850—was the one thing that ever moved him to heated denunciation. He felt Webster's apostasy as strongly as he had admired his genius. "Who has not helped to praise him? Simply he was the one American of our time whom we could produce as a finished work of nature." There is a passage in his journal (not a rough jotting, but, like most of the entries in it, a finished piece of writing), which is admirably descriptive of the wonderful orator and is moreover one of the very few portraits, or even personal sketches, yielded by Mr. Cabot's selections. It shows that he could observe the human figure and "render" it to good purpose.

"His splendid wrath, when his eyes become fire, is good to see, so intellectual it is—the wrath of the fact and the cause he espouses, and not at all personal to himself. . . . These village parties must be dishwater to him, yet he shows himself just good-natured, just nonchalant enough; and he has his own way, without offending any one or losing any ground. . . . His expensiveness seems necessary to him; were he too prudent a Yankee it would be a sad deduction from his magnificence. I only wish he would not truckle [to the slave-holders]. I do not care how much he spends."

I doubtless appear to have said more than enough, yet I have passed by many of the passages I had marked for transcription from Mr. Cabot's volumes. There is one, in the first, that makes us stare as we come upon it, to the effect that Emerson "could see nothing in Shelley, Aristophanes, Don Quixote, Miss Austen, Dickens." Mr. Cabot adds that he rarely read a novel, even the famous ones (he has a point of contact here as well as, strangely enough, on two or three other sides with that distinguished moralist M. Ernest Renan, who, like Emerson, was originally a dissident priest and cannot imagine why people should write works of fiction); and thought Dante "a man to put into a museum, but not into your house; another Zerah Colburn; a prodigy of imaginative function, executive rather than contemplative or wise." The confession of an insensibility ranging from Shelley to Dickens and from Dante to Miss Austen and taking Don Quixote and Aristophanes on the way, is a large allowance to have to make for a man of letters, and may appear to confirm but slightly any claim of intellectual hospitality and general curiosity put forth for him. The truth was that, sparely constructed as he was and formed not wastefully, not with material left over, as it were, for a special function, there were certain chords in Emerson that did not vibrate at all. I well remember my impression of this on walking with him in the autumn of 1872 through the galleries of the Louvre and, later that winter, through those of the Vatican: his perception of the objects contained in these collections was of the most general order. I was struck with the anomaly of a man so refined and intelligent being so little spoken to by works of art. It would be more exact to say that certain chords were wholly absent; the tune was played, the tune of life and literature, altogether on those that remained. They had every wish to be equal to their office, but one feels that the number was short—that some notes could not be given. Mr. Cabot makes use of a singular phrase when he says, in speaking of Hawthorne, for several years our author's neighbour at Concord and a little—a very little we gather—his companion, that Emerson was unable to read his novels—he thought them "not worthy of him." This is a judgment odd almost to fascination—we circle round it and turn it over and over; it contains so elusive an ambiguity. How highly he must have esteemed the man of whose genius *The House of the Seven Gables* and *The Scarlet Letter* gave imperfectly the measure, and how strange that he should not have been eager to read almost anything that such a gifted being might have let fall! It was a rare accident that made them live almost side by side so long in the same small New England town, each a fruit of a long Puritan stem, yet with such a difference of taste. Hawthorne's vision was all for the evil and sin of the world; a side of life as to which Emerson's eyes were thickly bandaged. There were points as to which the latter's conception of right could be violated, but he had no great sense of wrong—a strangely limited one, indeed, for a moralist —no sense of the dark, the foul, the base. There were certain complications in life which he never suspected. One asks one's self whether that is why he did not care for Dante and Shelley and Aristophanes and Dickens, their works containing a considerable reflection of human perversity. But that still leaves the indifference to Cervantes and Miss Austen unaccounted for.

It has not, however, been the ambition of these remarks to account for everything, and I have arrived at the end without even pointing to the grounds on which Emerson justifies the honours of biography, discussion and illustration. I have assumed his importance and continuance, and shall probably not be gainsaid by those who read him. Those who do not will hardly rub him out. Such a book as Mr. Cabot's subjects a reputation to a test—leads people to look it over and hold it up to the light, to see whether it is worth keeping in use or even putting away in a cabinet. Such a revision of Emerson has no relegating consequences. The result of it is once more the impression that he serves and will not wear out, and that indeed we cannot afford to drop him. His instrument makes him precious. He did something better than any one else; he had a particular faculty, which has not been surpassed, for speaking to the soul in a voice of direction and authority. There have been many spiritual voices appealing, consoling, reassuring, exhorting, or even denouncing and terrifying, but none has had just that firmness and just that purity. It penetrates further, it seems to go back to the roots of our feelings, to where conduct and manhood begin; and moreover, to us to-day, there is something in it that says that it is connected somehow with the virtue of the world, has wrought and achieved, lived in thousands of minds, produced a mass of character and life. And there is this further sign of Emerson's singular power, that he is a striking exception to the general rule that writings live in the last resort by their form; that they owe a large part of their fortune to the art with which they have been composed. It is hardly too much, or too little, to say of

Emerson's writings in general that they were not composed at all. Many and many things are beautifully said; he had felicities, inspirations, unforgettable phrases; he had frequently an exquisite eloquence.

"O my friends, there are resources in us on which we have not yet drawn. There are men who rise refreshed on hearing a threat; men to whom a crisis which intimidates and paralyses the majority—demanding not the faculties of prudence and thrift, but comprehension, immovableness, the readiness of sacrifice, come graceful and beloved as a bride. . . . But these are heights that we can scarce look up to and remember without contrition and shame. Let us thank God that such things exist."

None the less we have the impression that that search for a fashion and a manner on which he was always engaged never really came to a conclusion; it draws itself out through his later writings—it drew itself out through his later lectures, like a sort of renunciation of success. It is not on these, however, but on their predecessors, that his reputation will rest. Of course the way he spoke was the way that was on the whole most convenient to him; but he differs from most men of letters of the same degree of credit in failing to strike us as having achieved a style. This achievement is, as I say, usually the bribe or toll-money on the journey to posterity; and if Emerson goes his way, as he clearly appears to be doing, on the strength of his message alone, the case will be rare, the exception striking, and the honour great.

WJ: ADDRESS AT THE EMERSON CENTENARY IN CONCORD (1903)

THE PATHOS of death is this, that when the days of one's life are ended, those days that were so crowded with business and felt so heavy in their passing, what remains of one in memory should usually be so slight a thing. The phantom of an attitude, the echo of a certain mode of thought, a few pages of print, some invention, or some victory we gained in a brief critical hour, are all that can survive the best of us. It is as if the whole of a man's significance had now shrunk into the phantom of an attitude, into a mere musical note or phrase suggestive of his singularity—happy are those whose singularity gives a note so clear as to be victorious over the inevitable pity of such a diminution and abridgment.

An ideal wraith like this, of Emerson's personality, hovers over all Concord to-day, taking, in the minds of those of you who were his neighbors and intimates a somewhat fuller shape, remaining more abstract in the younger generation, but bringing home to all of us the notion of a spirit indescribably precious. The form that so lately moved upon these streets and country roads, or awaited in these fields and woods the beloved Muse's visits, is now dust; but the soul's note, the spiritual voice, rises strong and clear above the uproar of the times, and seems securely destined to exert an ennobling influence over future generations.

What gave a flavor so matchless to Emerson's individuality was, even more than his rich mental gifts, their singularly harmonious combination. Rarely has a man so accurately known the limits of his genius or so unfailingly kept within them. "Stand by your order," he used to say to youthful students; and perhaps the paramount impression one gets of his life is of his loyalty to his own personal type and mission. The type was that of what he liked to call the scholar, the perceiver of pure truth; and the mission was that of the reporter in worthy form of each perception. The day is good, he said, in which we have the most perceptions. There are times when the cawing of a crow, a weed, a snowflake, or a farmer planting in his field become symbols to the intellect of truths equal to those which the most majestic phenomena can open. Let me mind my own charge, then, walk alone, consult the sky, the field and forest, sedulously waiting every morning for the news concerning the structure of the universe which the good Spirit will give me.

This was the first half of Emerson, but only half; for genius, as he said, is insatiate for expression, and truth has to be clad in the right verbal garment. The form of the garment was so vital with Emerson that it is impossible to separate it from the matter. They form a chemical combination—thoughts which would be trivial expressed otherwise, are important through the nouns and verbs to which he married them. The style is the man, it has been said; the man Emerson's mission culminated in his style, and if we must define him in one word, we have to call him Artist. He was an artist whose medium was verbal and who wrought in spiritual material.

This duty of spiritual seeing and reporting determined the whole tenor of his life. It was to shield this duty from invasion and distraction that he dwelt in the country, that he consistently declined to entangle himself with associations or to encumber himself with functions which, however he might believe in them, he felt were duties for other men and not for him. Even the care of his garden, "with its stoopings and fingerings in a few yards of space," he found "narrowing and poisoning," and took to long free walks and saunterings instead, without apology. "Causes" innumerable sought to enlist him as their "worker" —all got his smile and word of sympathy, but none entrapped him into service. The struggle against slavery itself, deeply as it appealed to him, found him firm: "God must govern his own world, and knows his way out of this pit without my desertion of my post, which has none to guard it but me. I have quite other slaves to face than those Negroes, to wit, imprisoned thoughts far back in the brain of man, and which have no watchman or lover or defender but me." This in reply to the possible questions of his own conscience. To hot-blooded moralists with more objective ideas of duty, such a fidelity to the limits of his genius must often have made him seem provokingly remote and unavailable; but we, who can see things in more liberal perspective, must unqualifiably approve the results. The faultless tact with which he kept his safe limits while he so dauntlessly asserted himself within them, is an example fitted to give heart to other theorists and artists the world over.

The insight and creed from which Emerson's life followed can be best summed up in his own verses:

"So nigh is grandeur to our dust,
So near is God to man!"

Through the individual fact there ever shone for him the effulgence of the Universal Reason. The great Cosmic Intellect terminates and houses itself in mortal men and passing hours. Each of us is an angle of its eternal vision, and the only way to be true to our Maker is to be loyal to ourselves. "O rich and various Man!" he cries, "thou palace of sight and sound, carrying in thy senses the morning and the night and the unfathomable galaxy; in thy brain the geometry of the city of God; in thy heart the bower of love and the realms of right and wrong."

If the individual open thus directly into the Absolute, it follows that there is something in each and all of us, even the lowliest, that ought not to consent to borrowing traditions and living at second hand. "If John was perfect, why are you and I alive?" Emerson writes; "As long as any man exists there is some need of him; let him fight for his own." This faith that in a life at first hand there is something sacred is perhaps the most characteristic note in Emerson's writings. The hottest side of him is this non-conformist persuasion, and if his temper could ever verge on common irascibility, it would be by reason of the passionate character of his feelings on this point. The world is still new and untried. In seeing freshly, and not in hearing of what others saw, shall a man find what truth is. "Each one of us can bask in the great morning which rises out of the Eastern Sea, and be himself one of the children of the light." "Trust thyself, every heart vibrates to that iron string. There is a time in each man's education when he must arrive at the conviction that imitation is suicide; when he must take himself for better or worse as his portion; and know that though the wide universe is full of good, no kernel of nourishing corn can come to him but through his toil bestowed on that plot of ground which it was given him to till."

The matchless eloquence with which Emerson proclaimed the sovereignty of the living individual electrified and emancipated his generation, and this bugle-blast will doubtless be regarded by future critics as the soul of his message. The present man is the aboriginal reality, the Institution is derivative, and the past man is irrelevant and obliterate for present issues. "If anyone would lay an axe to your tree with a text from 1 John, v, 7, or a sentence from Saint Paul, say to him," Emerson wrote, " 'My tree is Yggdrasil, the tree of life.' Let him know by your security that your conviction is clear and sufficient, and, if he were Paul himself, that you also are here and with your Creator." "Cleave ever to God," he insisted, "against the name of God";—and so, in spite of the intensely religious character of his total thought, when he began his career it seemed to many of his brethren in the clerical profession that he was little more than an iconoclast and desecrator.

Emerson's belief that the individual must in reason be adequate to the vocation for which the Spirit of the world has called him into being, is the source of those sublime pages, hearteners and sustainers of our youth, in which he urges his hearers to be incorruptibly true to their own private conscience. Nothing can harm the man who rests in his appointed place and character. Such a man is invulnerable; he balances the universe, balances it as much by keeping small when he is small, as by being great and spreading when he is great. "I love and honor Epaminondas," said Emerson, "but I do not wish to be Epaminondas. I hold it more just to love the world of this hour than the world of his hour. Nor can you, if I am true, excite me to the least uneasiness by saying, 'He acted and thou sittest still.' I see action to be good when the need is, and sitting still to be also good. Epaminondas, if he was the man I take him for, would have sat still with joy and peace, if his lot had been mine. Heaven is large, and affords space for all modes of love and fortitude." "The fact that I am here certainly shows me that the Soul has need of an organ here, and shall I not assume the post?"

The vanity of all superserviceableness and pretence was never more happily set forth than by Emerson in the many passages in which he develops this aspect of his philosophy. Character infallibly proclaims itself. "Hide your thoughts!—hide the sun and moon. They publish themselves to the universe. They will speak through you though you were dumb. They will flow out of your actions, your manners and your face. . . . Don't say things: What you are stands over you the while and thunders so that I cannot say what you say to the contrary. . . . What a man *is* engraves itself upon him in letters of light. Concealment avails him nothing, boasting nothing. There is confession in the glances of our eyes; in our smiles; in salutations; and the grasp of hands. His sin bedaubs him, mars all his good impression. Men know not why they do not trust him, but they do not trust him. His vice glasses the eye, casts lines of mean expression in the cheek, pinches the nose, sets the mark of the beast upon the back of the head, and writes, O fool! fool! on the forehead of a king. If you would not be known to

do a thing, never do it; a man may play the fool in the drifts of a
desert, but every grain of sand shall seem to see.—How can a man be
concealed? How can he be concealed?"

On the other hand, never was a sincere word or a sincere thought
utterly lost. "Never a magnanimity fell to the ground but there is some
heart to greet and accept it unexpectedly. . . . The hero fears not that
if he withstood the avowal of a just and brave act, it will go unwit-
nessed and unloved. One knows it,—himself,—and is pledged by it to
sweetness of peace and to nobleness of aim, which will prove in the
end a better proclamation than the relating of the incident."

The same indefeasible right to be exactly what one is, provided one
only be authentic, spreads itself, in Emerson's way of thinking, from
persons to things and to times and places. No date, no position is insignificant, if the life that fills it out be only genuine:—

"In solitude, in a remote village, the ardent youth loiters and mourns.
With inflamed eye, in this sleeping wilderness, he has read the story of
the Emperor, Charles the Fifth, until his fancy has brought home to the
surrounding woods the faint roar of cannonades in the Milanese, and
marches in Germany. He is curious concerning that man's day. What
filled it? The crowded orders, the stern decisions, the foreign despatches, the Castilian etiquette? The soul answers—Behold his day here!
In the sighing of these woods, in the quiet of these gray fields, in the
cool breeze that sings out of these northern mountains; in the work-
men, the boys, the maidens you meet,—in the hopes of the morning,
the *ennui* of noon, and sauntering of the afternoon; in the disquieting
comparisons; in the regrets at want of vigor; in the great idea and the
puny execution,—behold Charles the Fifth's day; another, yet the
same; behold Chatham's, Hampden's, Bayard's, Alfred's, Scipio's, Peri-
cles's day,—day of all that are born of women. The difference of circumstance is merely costume. I am tasting the self-same life,—its sweetness, its greatness, its pain, which I so admire in other men. Do not
foolishly ask of the inscrutable, obliterated past what it cannot tell,—
the details of that nature, of that day, called Byron or Burke;—but ask
it of the enveloping Now. . . . Be lord of a day, and you can put up
your history books."

"The deep to-day which all men scorn" receives thus from Emerson
superb revindication. "Other world! there is no other world." All God's
life opens into the individual particular, and here and now, or nowhere,
is reality. "The present hour is the decisive hour, and every day is
doomsday."

Such a conviction that Divinity is everywhere may easily make of
one an optimist of the sentimental type that refuses to speak ill of anything. Emerson's drastic perception of differences kept him at the opposite pole from this weakness. After you have seen men a few times,

he could say, you find most of them as alike as their barns and pantries, and soon as musty and as dreary. Never was such a fastidious lover of significance and distinction, and never an eye so keen for their discovery. His optimism had nothing in common with that indiscriminate hurrahing for the Universe with which Walt Whitman has made us familiar. For Emerson, the individual fact and moment were indeed suffused with absolute radiance, but it was upon a condition that saved the situation—they must be worthy specimens,—sincere, authentic, archetypal; they must have made connection with what he calls the Moral Sentiment, they must in some way act as symbolic mouthpieces of the Universe's meaning. To know just which thing does act in this way, and which thing fails to make the true connection, is the secret (somewhat incommunicable, it must be confessed) of seership, and doubtless we must not expect of the seer too rigorous a consistency. Emerson himself was a real seer. He could perceive the full squalor of the individual fact, but he could also see the transfiguration. He might easily have found himself saying of some present-day agitator against our Philippine conquest what he said of this or that reformer of his own time. He might have called him, as a private person, a tedious bore and canter. But he would infallibly have added what he then added: "It is strange and horrible to say this, for I feel that under him and his partiality and exclusiveness is the earth and the sea, and all that in them is, and the axis round which the Universe revolves passes through his body where he stands."

Be it how it may, then, this is Emerson's revelation:—The point of any pen can be an epitome of reality; the commonest person's act, if genuinely actuated, can lay hold on eternity. This vision is the headspring of all his outpourings; and it is for this truth, given to no previous literary artist to express in such penetratingly persuasive tones, that posterity will reckon him a prophet, and, perhaps neglecting other pages, piously turn to those that convey this message. His life was one long conversation with the invisible divine, expressing itself through individuals and particulars:—"So nigh is grandeur to our dust, so near is God to man!"

I spoke of how shrunken the wraith, how thin the echo, of men is after they are departed. Emerson's wraith comes to me now as if it were but the very voice of this victorious argument. His words to this effect are certain to be quoted and extracted more and more as time goes on, and to take their place among the Scriptures of humanity. " 'Gainst death and all oblivious enmity, shall you pace forth," beloved Master. As long as our English language lasts men's hearts will be cheered and their souls strengthened and liberated by the noble and musical pages with which you have enriched it.

*   *   *

PARTIAL PORTRAITS

Carlyle

HENRY SENIOR's combativeness was in the ascendant in his reminiscences of Carlyle. When he first read *Past and Present*, he was impressed by how the Scotchman, unlike the American transcendentalists, had held fast to the reality of evil. But a closer view filled his mind with doubts. He wrote to Emerson from London in 1856: "Carlyle is the same old sausage, fizzing and sputtering in his own grease, only infinitely more unreconciled to the blessed Providence which guides human affairs. He names God frequently, and alludes to the highest things as if they were realities; but it almost looks as if he did it only for a picturesque effect, so completely does he seem to regard them as habitually circumvented and set at naught by the politicians." After the Civil War, when Carlyle's anti-democratic bias had expressed itself further in *Shooting Niagara*, Henry Senior declared: "Carlyle nowadays is a palpable nuisance. . . . If he holds to his present mouthing ways to the end, he will find no showman to match him on the other side, for I hold Barnum to be a much more innocent personage. I shouldn't wonder if Barnum grew regenerate in some far-off day, by force of his democracy. But Carlyle's intellectual pride is so stupid, that one can hardly imagine anything to cope with it." Still, Carlyle had made an ineradicable impression upon him as a personality, and Henry Senior's literary gifts were at their best as he recorded his memories of conversations, and suggested the very cadences and accents of Carlyle's voice.

The sons divided widely in their opinions of Carlyle. HJ referred, in an early review, to his "aggressively *earnest* tone," and although, twenty years later, when Norton had edited Carlyle's correspondence, HJ granted him to be "perhaps the very greatest of letter writers," he added: "It seems to me he remains the most disagreeable in character of

men of genius of equal magnificence." He could not help being struck
by Carlyle's rich imagination, and held that it would be "by his great
pictorial energy that he will live." But when he considered Carlyle's
style, he felt it necessary to say that "he had invented a manner" that
had "swallowed him up": "To look at realities and not at imitations is
what he constantly and sternly enjoins; but all the while he gives us
the sense that it is not at things themselves, but straight into this abysmal manner of his own that he is looking."

WJ took Carlyle far more seriously, and found him of practical help,
as he did not find his own father, in solving the problem of evil.
Whereas Henry Senior believed that "moral force was the deity of
Carlyle's unscrupulous worship—the force of unprincipled, irresponsible will," WJ felt a salutary effect in Carlyle's challenge to the individual to stand on his own feet and to rely on his own powers. Any
challenge of this sort tended to cause WJ to overlook much that he did
not like, as we can see also in his frequent quotations from Fitz-James
Stephen,[1] another Tory opponent of democracy. His enthusiastic reaction to Carlyle shows again how insecure he felt in the face of his
father's doctrine of being rather than doing. In "The Sentiment of
Rationality" WJ appealed to Carlyle's "gospel of work, of fact, of
veracity." In "The Dilemma of Determinism" he added: "The only
escape is by the practical way. And since I have mentioned the nowadays much-reviled name of Carlyle, let me mention it once more, and
say it is the way of his teaching. No matter for Carlyle's life, no matter
for a great deal of his writing. What was the most important thing he
said to us? He said: 'Hang your sensibilities! Stop your snivelling com-
plaints, and your equally snivelling raptures! Leave off your general
emotional tomfoolery, and get to WORK like men!'"

* * * * *

HENRY JAMES, SENIOR:
SOME PERSONAL RECOLLECTIONS
OF CARLYLE (1881)

THOMAS CARLYLE is incontestably dead at last, by the acknowledgment
of all newspapers. I had, however, the pleasure of an intimate intercourse with him when he was an infinitely deader man than he is now,
or ever will be again, I am persuaded, in the remotest *seculum seculorum*. I undoubtedly felt myself at the time every whit as dead
(spiritually) as he was; and, to tell the truth, I never found him averse
to admit my right of insight in regard to myself. But I could never
bring him, much as he continually inspired me so to do, to face the

---

[1] As in "The Will to Believe."

philosophic possibility of this proposition in regard to himself. On the contrary, he invariably snorted at the bare presentation of the theme, and fled away from it, with his free, resentful heels high in air, like a spirited horse alarmed at the apparition of a wheelbarrow.

However, in spite of our fundamental difference about this burly life which now is,—one insisting upon death as the properer name for it, the other bent upon maintaining every popular illusion concerning it,—we had for long years what always appeared to me a very friendly intercourse; and I can never show myself sufficiently grateful to his kindly, hospitable *manes* for the many hours of unalloyed entertainment his ungrudging fireside afforded me. I should like to reproduce from my notebook some of the recollections and observations with which those sunny hours impressed me and so amuse, if I can, the readers of "The Atlantic." These reminiscences were written many years ago, when the occurrences to which they relate were fresh in my memory; and they are exact, I need not say, almost to the letter. They will tend, I hope and am sure, to enhance the great personal prestige Carlyle enjoyed during life; for I cherish the most affectionate esteem for his memory, and could freely say or do nothing to wound that sentiment in any honest human breast. At the same time, I cannot doubt that the proper effect of much that I have to say will be to lower the estimation many persons have formed of Carlyle as a man of ideas. And this I should not be sorry for. Ideas are too divinely important to derive any consequence from the persons who maintain them; they are images or revelations, in intellectual form, of divine or infinite good, and therefore reflect upon men all the sanctity they possess, without receiving a particle from them. This estimate of Carlyle, *as a man of ideas*, always struck me as unfounded in point of fact. I think his admirers, at least his distant admirers, generally mistook the claim he made upon attention. They were apt to regard him as eminently a man of thought; whereas his intellect, as it seemed to me, except where his prejudices were involved, had not got beyond the stage of instinct. They insisted upon finding him a philosopher; but he was only and consummately a man of genius. They had the fatuity to deem him a great teacher; but he never avouched himself to be anything else than a great critic.

I intend no disparagement of Carlyle's moral qualities, in saying that he was almost sure finally to disappoint one's admiration. I merely mean to say that he was without that breadth of humanitary sympathy which one likes to find in distinguished men; that he was deficient in spiritual as opposed to moral force. He was a man of great simplicity and sincerity in his personal manners and habits, and exhibited even an engaging sensibility to the claims of one's physical fellowship. But he was wholly impenetrable to the solicitations both of your heart and your understanding. I think he felt a helpless dread and distrust of you instantly that he found you had any positive hope in God or practical love to man. His own intellectual life consisted so much in bemoaning the vices of his race, or drew such inspiration from despair, that he could not help regarding a man with contempt the instant he found him reconciled to the course of history. Pity is the highest style of intercourse he allowed himself with his kind. He compassionated all his friends in the measure of his affection for them. "Poor John Sterling," he used always to say; "poor John Mill, poor Frederic Maurice, poor Neuberg, poor Arthur Helps, poor little Browning, poor little Lewes," and so on; as if the temple of his friendship were a hospital, and all its inmates scrofulous or paralytic. You wondered how any mere mortal got legitimately endowed with a commiseration so divine for the inferior race of man; and the explanation that forced itself upon you was that he enjoyed an inward power and beatitude so redundant as naturally to seek relief in these copious outward showers of compassionate benediction. Especially did Carlyle conceive that no one could be actively interested in the progress of the species without being intellectually off his balance, and in need of tenderness from all his friends. His own sympathy went out freely to cases of individual suffering, and he believed that there was an immense amount of *specific* divine mercy practicable to us. That is to say, he felt keenly whatever appealed to his senses, and willingly patronized a fitful, because that is a picturesque, Providence in the earth. He sympathized with the starving Spitalfield weaver; and would have resented the inhumanity of the slave's condition as sharply as any one, if he had had visual contact with it, and were not incited, by the subtle freemasonry that unites aristocratic pretension in literature with the same pretension in politics, to falsify his human instincts. I remember the pleasure he took in the promise that Indian corn might be found able to supplant the diseased potato in Ireland; and he would doubtless have admitted ether and chloroform to be exquisitely ordained ministers of the Divine love. But as to any sympathy with human nature itself and its inexorable wants, or any belief in a breadth of the Divine mercy commensurate with those wants, I could never discern a flavor of either in him. He scoffed with hearty scorn at the contented imbecility of Church and State with respect to social problems, but his own indifference to these things, save in so far as they were available to picturesque palaver, was infinitely more indolent and contented. He would have been the last man formally to deny the Divine existence and providence; but that these truths had any human virtue, any living efficacy to redeem us out of material and spiritual penury, I do not think he ever dreamt of such a thing. That our knowledge of God was essentially expansive; that revelation contemplated its own spiritual enlargement and fulfil-

ment in the current facts of human history, in the growth and enlargement of the human mind itself,—so that Thomas Carlyle, if only he
had not been quite so stubborn and conceited, might have proved himself far better and not far worse posted in the principles of the Divine
administration than even Plato was, and so have freed himself from the
dismal necessity he was all his life under to ransack the graves of the
dead, in order to find some spangle, still untarnished, of God's reputed
presence in our nature,—all this he took every opportunity to assure
you was the saddest bosh. "Poor John Mill," he exclaimed one night,—
"poor John Mill is writing away there in the Edinburgh Review about
what he calls the Philosophy of History! As if any man could ever
know the road he is going, when once he gets astride of such a distracted steed as that!"

But to my note-book.

"I happened to be in Carlyle's library, the other day, when a parcel
was handed in which contained two books, a present from some American admirer. One of the books proved to be a work of singular intellectual interest, as I afterwards discovered, entitled 'Lectures on the
Natural History of Man,' by Alexander Kinmont, of Cincinnati; the
other a book of Poems. Carlyle read Mr. Kinmont's titlepage, and exclaimed: 'The natural history of man, forsooth! And from Cincinnati
too, of all places on this earth! We had a right, perhaps, to expect some
light from that quarter in regard to the natural history of the hog; and
I can't but think that if the well-disposed Mr. Kinmont would set himself to study that unperverted mystery he would employ his powers
far more profitably to the world. I am sure he would employ them
far less wearisomely to me. There!' he continued, handing me the book,
'I freely make over to you all my right of insight into the natural
history of man as that history dwells in the portentous brain of Mr.
Alexander Kinmont, of Cincinnati, being more than content to wait
myself till he condescend to the more intelligible animal.' And then
opening to the blank leaf of the volume of Poems, and without more
ado, he said, 'Permit me to write my friend Mrs. So-and-So's name here,
who perhaps may get some refreshment from the poems of her countryman; for, decidedly, I shall not.' When I suggested to him that he himself did nothing all his days but philosophize in his own way,—that is,
from the artist point of view, or ground of mere feeling,—and that
his prose habitually decked itself out in the most sensuous garniture of
poetry, he affected the air of M. Jourdain, in Molière, and protested,
half fun, half earnest, that he was incapable of a philosophic purpose or
poetic emotion."

Carlyle had very much of the narrowness, intellectual and moral,
which one might expect to find in a descendant of the old Covenanting
stock, bred to believe in God as essentially inhuman, and in man, ac-

cordingly, as exposed to a great deal of divine treachery and vindictiveness, which were liable to come rattling about his devoted ears the
moment his back was turned. I have no idea, of course, that this grim
ancestral faith dwelt in Carlyle in any acute, but only in chronic, form.
He did not actively acknowledge it; but it was latent in all his intellectual and moral personality, and made itself felt in that cynical, mock-
ing humor and those bursts of tragic pathos which set off all his abstract views of life and destiny. But a genuine pity for man as sinner
and sufferer underlay all his concrete judgments; and no thought of
unkindness ever entered his bosom except for people who believed in
God's undiminished presence and power in human affairs, and were
therefore full of hope in our social future. A moral reformer like Louis
Blanc or Robert Dale Owen, a political reformer like Mr. Cobden
or Mr. Bright, or a dietetic reformer like the late Mr. Greaves or our
own Mr. Alcott, was sure to provoke his most acrid intellectual antipathy.

Moral force was the deity of Carlyle's unscrupulous worship,—the
force of unprincipled, irresponsible will; and he was ready to glorify
every historic vagabond, such as Danton or Mirabeau, in whom that
quality reigned supreme. He hated Robespierre because he was inferior
in moral or personal force to his rivals, being himself a victim to ideas,
—or, as Carlyle phrased it, to formulas. Picturesqueness in man and
Nature was the one key to his intellectual favor; and it made little difference to his artist eye whether the man were spiritually angel or
demon. Besides, one never practically surmounts his own idea of the
Divine name; and Carlyle, inheriting and cherishing for its picturesque
capabilities this rude Covenanting conception, which makes God a
being of the most aggravated moral dimensions, of a wholly super-
human egotism or sensibility to his own consequence, of course found
Mahomet, William the Conqueror, John Knox, Frederic the Second of
Prussia, Goethe, men after God's own heart, and coolly told you that
no man in history was ever unsuccessful who deserved to be otherwise.

Too much cannot be said of Carlyle in personal respects. He was a
man of even a genial practical morality, an unexceptionable good
neighbor, friend, and citizen. But in all larger or human regards he was
a literalist of the most unqualified pattern, incapable of uttering an inspiring or even a soothing word in behalf of any struggling manifestation of human hope. It is true, he abused every recognized guide of the
political world with such hearty good-will that many persons claimed
him at once as an intelligent herald of the new or spiritual divine advent
in human nature. But the claim was absurdly unfounded. He was an
amateur prophet exclusively,—a prophet "on his own hook," or in the
interest of his own irritable cuticle,—without a glimmer of sympathy
with the distinctively public want, or a gleam of insight into its ap-

proaching divine relief; a harlequin in the guise of Jeremiah, who fed you with laughter in place of tears, and put the old prophetic sincerity out of countenance by his broad, persistent winks at the by-standers over the foot-lights.

My note-book has this record:—

"I heard Carlyle, last night, maintain his habitual thesis against Mr. Tennyson, in the presence of Mr. Moxon and one or two other persons. Carlyle rode a very high horse indeed, being inspired to mount and lavishly ply the spur by Mr. Tennyson, for whom he has the liveliest regard; and it was not long before William the Conqueror and Oliver Cromwell were trotted out of their mouldy cerements, to affront Sir Robert Peel and the Irish viceroy, whose name escapes me. 'Nothing,' Carlyle over and over again said and sung,—'nothing will ever pry England out of the slough she is in, but to stop looking at Manchester as heaven's gate, and free-trade as the everlasting God's law man is bound to keep holy. The human stomach, I admit, is a memorable necessity, which will not allow itself, moreover, to be long neglected; and political economy no doubt has its own right to be heard among all our multifarious jargons. But I tell you the stomach is not the supreme necessity our potato-evangelists make it, nor is political economy any tolerable substitute for the eternal veracities. To think of our head men believin' the stomach to be the man, and legislatin' for the stomach, and compellin' this old England into the downright vassalage of the stomach! Such men as these, forsooth, to rule England,—the England once ruled by Oliver Cromwell! No wonder the impudent knave O'Connell takes them by the beard, shakes his big fist in their faces, does his own dirty will, in fact, with England, altogether! *Oh, for a day of Duke William again!*'

"In vain his fellow Arcadian protested that England was no longer the England of Duke William, nor even of Oliver Cromwell, but a totally new England, with self-consciousness all new and unlike theirs; Carlyle only chanted or canted the more lustily his inevitable dingdong, 'Oh, for a day of Duke William again!'

"Tired out at last, the long-suffering poet cried, 'I suppose you *would* like your Duke William back, to cut off some twelve hundred Cambridgeshire gentlemen's legs, and leave their owners squat upon the ground, that they mightn't be able any longer to bear arms against him!' 'Ah!' shrieked out the remorseless bagpipes, in a perfect colic of delight to find its supreme blast thus unwarily invoked,—'ah! that *was* no doubt a very sad thing for the duke to do; but somehow he conceived he had a right to do it,—and upon the whole he had!' 'Let me tell your returning hero one thing, then,' replied his practical-minded friend, 'and that is that he had better steer clear of my precincts, or he will feel my knife in his guts very soon.' "

It was in fact this indignant and unaffected prose of the distinguished poet which alone embalmed the insincere colloquy to my remembrance, or set its colors, so to speak.

Carlyle was, in truth, a hardened declaimer. He talked in a way vastly to tickle his auditors, and his enjoyment of their amusement was lively enough to sap his own intellectual integrity. Artist like, he precipitated himself upon the picturesque in character and manners wherever he found it, and he did not care a jot what incidental interest his precipitancy lacerated. He was used to harp so successfully on one string,— the importance to men of *doing*,—and the mere artistic effects he produced so infatuated him, that the whole thing tumbled off at last into a sheer insincerity, and he no longer saw any difference between *doing* well and *doing* ill. He who best denounced a canting age became himself its most signal illustration, since even his denunciation of the vice succumbed to the prevalent usage, and announced itself at length a shameless cant.

Of course I have no intention to represent this state of things as a conscious one on Carlyle's part. On the contrary, it was a wholly unconscious one, betokening such a complete absorption of his faculties in the talking function as to render him unaffectedly indifferent to the practical action which such talk, when sincere, ought always to contemplate.

. . . Carlyle is not at all primarily the man of humanitary ideas and sympathies which many people fancy him to be. Of course he has a perfect right to be what he is, and no one has a keener appreciation of him in that real light than I have. I only insist that he has no manner of right to be reported to us in a false light, as we shall thereby lose the lesson which legitimately accrues to us from his immense personality. . . .

He was not constitutionally arrogant; he was a man of real modesty; he was even, I think, constitutionally diffident. He was a man, in short, whom you could summer and winter with, without ever having your self-respect wantonly affronted as it habitually is by mere conventional men and women. He was, to be sure, a very sturdy son of earth, and capable at times of exhibiting the most helpless natural infirmity. But he would never ignore nor slight your human fellowship because your life or opinions exposed you to the reproach of the vain, the frivolous, the self-seeking. He would of course curse your gods ever and anon in a manful way, and scoff without mercy at your tenderest intellectual hopes and aspirations; but upon yourself personally, all the while,— especially if you should drink strong tea and pass sleepless nights, or suffer from tobacco, or be menaced with insanity, or have a gnawing cancer under your jacket,—he would have bestowed the finest of his wheat. He might not easily have forgiven you if you used a vegetable diet, especially if you did so on principle; and he would surely have gnashed his teeth upon you if you should have claimed any scientific knowledge or philosophic insight into the social problem,—the problem of man's coming destiny upon the earth. But within these limits you would have felt how truly human was the tie that bound you to this roaring, riotous, most benighted, yet not unbenignant brother. Leave England, above all, alone; let her stumble on from one slough of despond to another, so that he might have the endless serene delight of walloping her chief "niggers,"—Peel, Palmerston, Russell, Brougham, and the rest,—and he would dwell forever in friendly content with you. But only hint your belief that these imbecile statesmen were the true statesmen for the time, the only men capable, *in virtue of that very imbecility*, of truly coworking with the Providence that governs the world, and is guiding it full surely to a haven of final peace and blessedness, and he would fairly deluge you with the vitriol of his wrath. No; all that can be said for Carlyle on this score is, that, having an immense eye for color, an immense genius for scenic effect, he seized with avidity upon every crazy, time-stained, dishonored rag of personality that still fluttered in the breeze of history, and lent itself to his magical tissues; and he did not like that any one should attempt to dispute his finery with him. The habit was tyrannous, no doubt, but no harm, and only amusement, could have come of it; least of all would it have pushed him to his melancholy "latter-day" drivel, had it not been for the heartless people who hang, for their own private ends, upon the skirts of every pronounced man of genius, and do their best, by stimulating his vanity, to make him feel himself a god.

I again have recourse to my note-book.

"I happened to be at Mr. Carlyle's a Sunday or two since, when a large company was present, and the talk fell upon repudiation, which Jefferson Davis and Mississippi legislation are bringing into note. Among others a New Yorker was present, to whom his friends give the title of General, for no other reason that I can discover but to signify that he is nothing in particular,—an agreeable-mannered man, however, with something of that new-born innocence of belief and expectation in his demeanor and countenance which Englishmen find it so hard to do justice to in Americans; and he was apparently defending, when I went in, our general repute for honesty from the newspaper odium which is beginning to menace it. Mr. Henry Woodman,—I will call him,—from Massachusetts, was also present; an amiable, excellent man, full of knowledge and belief in a certain way, who in former times was a Unitarian clergyman in good standing, but having made what seemed to him a notable discovery, namely, that there is no personal devil,— none, at least, who is over six feet in height, and who therefore is not essentially amenable to police discipline,—he forthwith snaps his fingers at the faded terror, drops his profession, and betakes himself to agriculture, for which he has a passion. He overflows with good feeling, and is so tickled with the discovery he has made of old Nick's long imposture, that he never makes an acquaintance without instantly telling him of it, nor ever keeps one without instantly, in season and out of season, reminding him of it. He had saturated Carlyle's outward ear with the intelligence, but to no inward profit. For Carlyle's working conception of the Deity involves so much of diabolism that the decease and sepulture of a thousand legitimate old bogies, authentically chronicled in 'The Times,' would hardly enliven his sombre imagination; and he entertains a friendly contempt and compassion, accordingly, for the emancipated Mr. Woodman, which are always touching to me to witness. The evening in question my attention was suddenly arrested by Carlyle saying somewhat loudly to General —— that we were all on our way to the devil in America, and that unless we turned a short corner we should infallibly bring up in that perilous company. Mr. Woodman was talking, at the moment, with his hostess, of whom he is a deserved favorite, at the other extremity of the room; but he would have heard the name of his vanished adversary had it been pronounced in a whisper. The grateful sound no sooner reached his ear, accordingly, than he averted himself from his companion, and cried out, delighted, 'What devil do you speak of, Mr. Carlyle?' 'What devil, do you ask?' Carlyle fairly roared back in reply. 'What devil, do you ask, Mr. Woodman? The devil, Mr. Woodman, that has been known in these parts from the beginning, and is not likely soon to become unknown,—the father of *all liars, swindlers, and repudiators,* Mr. Woodman! The devil that in this Old World boasts a very numerous though unconscious progeny, and in your New World, Mr. Woodman, seems, from all accounts, to be producing a still more numerous and still more unconscious one! That is just the devil I mean, Mr. Woodman; and woe be to you and yours the day you vote *him* lifeless!'

"Mr. Woodman was discouraged, and at once reverted to his quiet colloquy with his softer companion, while the rest of us profited by the exhilarating breeze he had so suddenly conjured up. 'Speaking of the evil one,' General —— hastened to say, 'I have been visiting to-day subterranean London, its sewers, and so forth,'—and the conversation soon fell into its ordinary undulations. But earnest as Carlyle's reply to his friend undoubtedly sounded, any listener would have very much mistaken the truth of the case if he had supposed that it meant anything more than his hopeless, helpless, and consequently irritable way of contemplating social facts and tendencies. Carlyle does not believe, of course, in the literal personality of the devil near so much as Mr. Woodman does; that is, he believes in it so little as to disdain the trouble of denying it. But he has a profound faith that there is at the head of affairs some very peremptory person or other, who will infallibly have his own will in the end, or override all other wills; and he is able, consequently, to variegate his conversation and writing with lurid lights that seem most orthodox and pious to innocent imaginations, and would make the ghost of John Knox roll up the whites of his eyes in grateful astonishment. Whatever be Carlyle's interest in any question of life or destiny, he talks so well and writes so well that it can hardly escape being all swallowed up in talk or writing; and he would regard you as a bore of the largest calibre if, talking in the same sense with him, you yet did not confine yourself to talk, but went on to organize your ideas in some appropriate action."

You would say, remembering certain passages in Carlyle's books,—notably his "Past and Present" and his pamphlet on Chartism,—that he had a very lively sympathy with reform and a profound sentiment of human fellowship. He did, indeed, dally with the divine ideas long enough to suck them dry of their rhetorical juices, but then dropped them, to lavish contempt on them ever after when anybody else should chance to pick them up and cherish them, not for their rhetorical uses, but their absolute truth. He had no belief in society as a living, organizing force in history, but only as an empirical necessity of the race. He had no conception of human brotherhood or equality as the profoundest truth of science, disclosing a hell in the bosom wherever it is not allowed to reveal a heaven, but only as an emotional or sentimental experience of happily endowed natures. On the contrary, he used to laugh and fling out his scornful heels at the bare suggestion of such a thing, much as a tropical savage would laugh and fling out his heels at the suggestion of frozen rivers. He looked at the good and evil in our nature as final or absolute quantities, and saw no way, consequently, of ever utilizing the evil element. He saw no possible way of dealing with weak races but by reducing them to slavery; no way of dealing successfully with evil men but by applying lynch law to them, and crushing them out of existence. In short he had not the least conception of history as a *divine drama, designed to educate man into self-knowledge and the knowledge of God;* and consequently could never meet you on any ground of objective truth, but only on that of your subjective whim or caprice. It was this intellectual incapacity he was under to esteem truth for its own sake, or value it except for the personal prestige it confers, that made him so impotent to help a struggling brother on to daylight, and fixed him in so intense and irritable a literary *self*-consciousness. . . .

Carlyle used to strike me as a man of genius or consummate executive faculty, and not primarily of sympathy or understanding. Every one is familiar with this discrimination. We all know some one or other who is a genius in his way, or has a power of doing certain things as no one else can do them, and as arrests our great admiration. And yet, as likely as not, this person so marvelously endowed, is a somewhat uncomfortable person apart from his particular line of action. Very possibly, and even probably, he is domineering and irritable to the pitch of insanity in his personal intercourse with others, and his judgments are apt to be purely whimsical, or reflect his own imperious will. We admire the genius in his own sphere of work or production, and feel a divine force in him that moves the world. But at the same time we are persuaded that there is something in us, not half so resplendent as genius, which is yet a vast deal better; and that is spiritual character, or a cultivated deference to the humblest forms of goodness and truth. At best, genius is only a spiritual temperament in man, and therefore, though it serves as an excellent basis for spiritual character, should yet never be confounded with it. The genius is God's spoiled child upon earth; woe be unto him, if he look upon that indulgence as consecrating him for the skies as well! Character, or spiritual manhood, is not created, but only communicated. It is not our birthright, but is only brought about with our own zealous privity, or solicitous concurrence in some sort. It is honestly wrought out of the most literal conformity to the principles of universal justice. It puts up with no histrionic piety, tramples under foot the cheap humility of the prayer-book and the pew, and insists upon the just thing at the just moment, under pain of eternal damnation,—which means, *an abandonment to the endless illusions of self-love.* Hence it is, that, while the genius cuts such a lustrous figure in the eyes of men, and wins oftentimes so loud a renown, we yet know many a nameless person whom we value more than a raft of genii, because we confide without stint in their living truth, their infinite rectitude of heart and understanding. We like the genius, or whatsoever makes life glorious, powerful, divine, on Sundays or holidays; but we prefer the ordinary, unconscious, unostentatious stuff which alone keeps it sweet and human on all other days.

It always appeared to me that Carlyle valued truth and good as a painter does his pigments,—not for what they are in themselves, but for the effects they lend themselves to in the sphere of production. Indeed, he always exhibited a contempt, so characteristic as to be comical, for every one whose zeal for truth or good led him to question existing institutions with a view to any practical reform. He himself was wont to question established institutions and dogmas with the utmost license of scepticism, but he obviously meant nothing beyond the production of a certain literary surprise, or the enjoyment of his own æsthetic power. Nothing maddened him so much as to be mistaken for a reformer, really intent upon the interests of God's righteousness upon the earth, which are the interests of universal justice. This is what made him hate Americans, and call us a nation of bores,—that we took him at his word, and reckoned upon him as a sincere well-wisher to his species. He hated us, because a secret instinct told him that our exuberant faith in him would never be justified by closer knowledge; for no one loves the man who forces him upon a premature recognition of himself. I recall the uproarious mirth with which he and Mrs. Carlyle used to recount the incidents of a visit they had received from a young New England woman, and describe the earnest, devout homage her credulous soul had rendered him. It was her first visit abroad, and she supposed—poor thing!—that these famous European writers and talkers, who so dominated her fancy at a distance, really meant all they said, were as innocent and lovely in their lives as in their books; and she no sooner crossed Carlyle's threshold, accordingly, than her heart offered its fragrance to him as liberally as the flower opens to the sun. And Carlyle, the inveterate comedian, instead of being humbled to the dust by the revelation which such simplicity suddenly flashed upon his own eyes of his essentially dramatic genius and exploits, was irritated, vexed, and outraged by it as by a covert insult. His own undevout soul had never risen to the contemplation of himself as the priest of a really infinite sanctity; and when this clear-eyed barbarian, looking past him to the substance which informed him, made him feel himself for the moment the transparent mask or unconscious actor he was, his self-consciousness took the alarm. She sat, the breathless, silly little maid, between him and Mrs. Carlyle, holding a hand of each, and feeling the while her anticipations of Paradise on earth so met in this foolish encounter that she could not speak, but barely looked the pious rapture which filled her soul.

One more extract from my note-book, and I shall have done with it, for it is getting to be time to close my paper. I mentioned a while since the name of O'Connell, and *apropos* of this name I should like to cite a reminiscence which sets Carlyle in a touchingly amiable spiritual light.

"Sunday before last I found myself seated at Carlyle's with Mr. Woodman and an aid-de-camp of Lord Castlereagh, who had just returned from India, and was entertaining Mrs. Carlyle with any amount of anecdotes about the picturesque people he left behind him. To us enter Dr. John Carlyle and a certain Mr. ——, a great burly Englishman, who has the faculty (according to an *aside* of Mrs. Carlyle, dexterously slipped in for my information) of always exciting Carlyle to frenzy by talk about O'Connell, of whom he is a thick-and-thin admirer. The weather topic and the health inquiry on both sides were soon quietly disposed of; but immediately after, Mrs. Carlyle nudged my elbow, and whispered in a tone of dread, 'Now for the deluge!' For she had heard the nasty din of politics commencing, and too well anticipated the fierce and merciless *mêlée* that was about to ensue. It speedily announced itself, hot and heavy; and for an hour poor breathless Mr. Woodman and myself, together with the awe-struck aid-de-camp, taking refuge under the skirts of outraged Mrs. Carlyle, assisted at a *lit de justice* such as we had none of us ever before imagined. At last tea was served, to our very great relief. But, no! the conflict was quite unexhausted, apparently, and went on with ever new alacrity, under the inspiration of the grateful souchong. Mrs. Carlyle had placed me at her left hand, with belligerent or bellowing Mr. Bull next to me; and as her tea-table chanced to be inadequate to the number of her guests we were all constrained to sit in very close proximity. Soon after our amiable and estimable hostess had officiated at the tea-tray, I felt her foot crossing mine to reach the feet of my infuriated neighbor and implore peace! She successfully reached them, and succeeded fully, also, in bringing about her end, without any thanks to him, however. For the ruffian had no sooner felt the gentle, appealing pressure of her foot, than he turned from Carlyle to meet her tender appeal with un-disguised savagery. 'Why don't you,' he fiercely screamed,—'why don't you, Mrs. Carlyle, touch your husband's toe? I am sure he is greatly more to blame than I am!' The whole company immediately broke forth in a burst of uncontrollable glee at this extraordinary speci-men of manners, Carlyle himself taking the lead; and his amiable *convive*, seeing, I suppose, the mortifying spectacle he had made of himself, was content to 'sing small' for the remainder of the evening.

"Anyhow, I heard nothing distressing while I remained. But happen-ing to have made an appointment with Mrs. Carlyle for the next day, I went down to Chelsea in the morning, and found my friend seated with her stocking-basket beside her, diligently mending the *gudeman's* hose. I asked her if any dead had been left on the battlefield the night before, and she replied, 'Yes; I never saw Carlyle more near to death than he is this dismal Monday morning! I must first tell you that he has been a long time in the habit of going to Mr. ——'s in —— Street, for a Sun-day dinner, protesting that, though his friends have no acquaintance with books or literary people, he never pays them a Sunday visit with-out feeling himself renovated against all the soil of the week, and never comes away without being baptized anew in unconsciousness. Now, yesterday he had gone to this friend's to dine, and when he returned, about three or four o'clock, he said to me, "Jane, I am henceforth a regenerate man, and eschew evil from this hour as the snake does its skin!" This he said with conviction and earnest purpose, as if that lovely family had inoculated him with the blessed life! What a scathing sense of weakness, then, besets the poor man this morning! Such a con-trast between the placid noon of yesterday and the horrid, hideous night!'

"To my inquiry whether anything had further occurred of disagree-able after I had left, Mrs. Carlyle replied, 'Everything went on swimmingly till about eleven o'clock, when it pleased your unfortunate countryman, Mr. Woodman, to renew the war-whoop by saying, "Let us return a moment to O'Connell." If the talk was frightful before you left, what did it now become? Altogether unbearable; and when about twelve o'clock John Carlyle got up to go, taking his friend along with him, Carlyle, lighting his candle to see the company to the door, stretched out his hand to his late antagonist, with the frank remark, "Let bygones be bygones!" The latter scorned to take it saying, "Never again shall I set foot in this house!" I knew how cruelly Carlyle would feel this rebuff, and scarcely dared to glance as him as he came upstairs after lighting his guests out; but when I did look, there he stood at the door of the room, holding the candle above his head, and laughing with bitter, remorseful laughter, as he repeated the words of the morning: Jane, I am henceforth a regenerate man, and eschew evil from this hour as the snake does its skin!' "

Alas, poor Yorick!

The main intellectual disqualification, then, of Carlyle, in my opinion, was the absoluteness with which he asserted the moral principle in the human bosom, or the finality which his grim imagination lent to the conflict of good and evil in men's experience. He never had the least idea, that I could discover, of the true or intellectually educative nature of this conflict, as being purely ministerial to a new and final evolution of *human nature itself* into permanent harmony with God's spiritual perfection. He never expressed a suspicion, in intercourse with me,—on the contrary, he always denounced my fervent conviction on the subject as so much fervent nonsense,—that out of this conflict would one day emerge a positive or faultless life of man, which would otherwise have been impracticable; just as out of the conflict of alkali and acid emerges a neutral salt which would otherwise be invisible. On the contrary, he always expressed himself to the effect that the conflict was absolutely *valid in itself;* that it constituted its own end, having no other result than to insure to good men the final dominion of evil men, and so array heaven and hell in mere chronic or fossil antagonism. The truth is, he had no idea but of a carnal or literal rectitude in human nature,—a rectitude secured by an unflinching inward submission to some commanding *outward* or *personal* authority. The law, not the gospel, was for him the true bond of intercourse between God and man, and between man and man as well. That is to say, he believed in our moral instincts, not as constituting the mere carnal body or rude husk of our spiritual manhood, but its inmost kernel or soul; and hence he habitually browsed upon "the tree of the knowledge of good and evil," as if it had been divinely commended to us for that purpose, or been always regarded as the undisputed tree of life, not of death. He was mother Eve's own darling cantankerous Thomas, in short, the child of her dreariest, most melancholy old age; and he used to bury his worn, dejected face in her penurious lap, in a way so determined as forever to shut out all sight of God's new and better creation.

Of course this is only saying in other words that Carlyle was without any sense of a *universal* providence in human affairs. He supposed that God Almighty literally saw with our eyes, and had therefore the same sympathy for strong men that we ourselves have, and the same disregard for feeble men. And he conceived that the world was governed upon the obvious plan of giving strong men sway, and hustling weak men out of sight. In the teeth of all the prophets who have ever prophesied, he held that the race *is* always to the swift, the battle always to the strong. Long before Mr. Darwin had thought of applying the principle of natural selection to the animal kingdom, Carlyle, not in words but in fact, had applied it to the spiritual kingdom, proclaiming as fundamental axioms of the divine administration, "Might makes right, and devil take the hindmost." He thought the divine activity in the world exceptional, not normal, occasional, not constant; that God worked one day out of seven, and rested the remaining six; thus, that he had a much nearer relation to holiday persons like Plato or Shakespeare or Goethe than he has to everyday people like the negro, the prison convict, the street-walker. In this shallow way the great mystery of godliness, which the angels desire to look into, became to his eyes as flat as any pancake; Deity himself being an incomparable athlete, or having an enormous weight of selfhood, so that all his legitimate children are born to rule. Ruler of men, this was Carlyle's most rustical ideal of human greatness. Rule on the one hand, obedience on the other, this was his most provincial ideal of human society or fellowship, and he never dreamt of any profounder key to the interpretation of our earthly destiny. The strong man to grow ever more strong, the feeble man to grow ever more feeble, until he is finally extinguished,—that was his very pedantic and puerile conception of the rest that remains to the people of God. The glorification of force, ability, genius, "that is the one condition," he always said, "in my poor opinion, of any much-talked-of millennial felicity for this poor planet,—the only thing which will ever rescue it from being the devil's churchyard and miserable donkey pasture it now for the most part turns out to be."

The divine hieroglyphics of human nature are never going to be deciphered in his sensuous, childish way. The divine gait is not lopsided. As his special glory is to bring good *out of evil*, one can easily see that he has never had a thought of exalting one style of man outwardly or personally above another style, but only of reducing both styles to a just humility. "The tree of knowledge of good and evil" is a tree which belongs exclusively to the garden of *our* immature, sensuous, or scientific intelligence, and it will not bear transplantation to a subtler spiritual soil. Our moral experience has always been, in purpose, intellectually educative. It is adapted, in literal or outward form, to our rude and crude or nascent scientific intelligence, and as intended to afford us, in the absence of any positive conceptions of infinitude, at least a negative spiritual conception, that so we might learn betimes a modest or humble conceit of ourselves. Now, Carlyle's precise intellectual weakness was that he never had a glimpse of any distinctively divine ends in human *nature*, but only in the more or less conflicting *persons* of that nature; and hence he was even childishly unable to justify the advance of the *social* sentiment in humanity,—the sanest, deepest, most reconciling sentiment ever known to man's bosom. To escape Carlyle's fatuity, then, and avoid the just reproach which he is fated to incur in the future, we must give up our hero-worship, or sentimental reverence for great men, and put ourselves in the frankest practical harmony with the Providence that governs the world. Nor is this half so difficult a task as our leading lazy-bones in Church and State would have us believe. Our leaders should be called our misleaders, in fact, so often do they betray us as to the principles of Divine administration. The world is not administered, as Carlyle and Louis Napoleon would have us fancy, upon the principle of making everything bend to the will of the strongest. On the contrary, the true will of the Strongest is, and always has been, to efface himself before every the meanest creature he has made, and his profoundest joy, not to have His own way, but to give way to every such creature, provided, first of all, there be nothing in that way injurious to the common weal. In fact, the one principle of Divine administration in human affairs, as we learn from Christianity, is to disregard high things, and mind only low things; to contemn whatsoever is highly esteemed among men, and exalt or utilize whatsoever they despise and reject. Henry Carey has been long and vainly showing us that a proper economy of the world's waste is all we need to inaugurate in the material sphere the long-promised millennium. And Liebig published, not many years ago, what he calls a legacy to his fellows, in which he proves, first, that European agriculture is fast becoming so fruitless by the exhaustion of soils, that, unless some remedy be provided, Europe must soon go into hopeless physical decrepitude; and, secondly, that men have the amplest remedy against this contingency in their own hands, by simply economizing the sewage of large towns, and restoring to the land the mineral wealth their food robs it of. Only think of this! Europe actually depends for her material salvation upon a divine redemption mercifully stored up for her in substances which her most pious churchmen and wisest statesmen have always disdained as an unmitigated nuisance! If any one thing be more abhorrent than another to our dainty sensual pride; if one thing more than another has been permitted to fill our selfish,

stupid life with disgust and disease,—it is this waste material of the
world, which we, in our insanity, would gladly hurry into the abyss
of oblivion! And yet in God's munificent wisdom this self-same odious
waste teems with incomparably greater renovation to human society
than all the gold, silver, and precious stones ever dug from earth to
madden human lust and enslave human weakness!

Now, what is the philosophic lesson of this surprising scientific
gospel? When science thus teaches us, beyond all possibility of cavil,
that the abject waste and offscouring of the planet, which we ourselves
are too fastidious even to name, is fuller of God's redeeming virtue,
of his intimate presence, than all its pomp of living loveliness, than all
its vivid garniture of mineral, vegetable, and animal beauty, what
philosophic bearing does the lesson exert? It is the very gospel of
Christ, mind you, reduced to the level of sense, or turned into a scientific verity. What, then, is its urgent message to men's spiritual understanding? Evidently this, and nothing else; namely, that human life is
now so full of want, so full of sorrow, so full of vice,—that human
intercourse is now so full of fraud, rapacity, and violence, only because
the truth of human society, human fellowship, human equality, which
alone reveals the infinitude of God's love, enjoys as yet so stinted a
recognition, while race continues to war with race, and sect with sect.
Society has as yet achieved only a typical or provisional existence, by
no means a real or final one. Every clergyman is the professional fellow
or equal of every other; every lawyer or physician enjoys the equal
countenance of his professional brethren,—but no man is yet sacred to
his brother man by virtue of his manhood simply, but only by virtue
of some conventional or accidental advantage. The vast majority of
our Christian population are supposed to be properly excluded from an
equal public consideration with their more fortunate compeers, by the
fact of their poverty or enforced subjection to natural want, and the
personal limitations which such want imposes; while outside of Christendom the entire mass of mankind is shut out of our respect and
sympathy, if not exposed to the incursions of our ravenous cupidity,
because they do not profess the exact faith we profess, nor practise the
literal maxims we practise. Thus, the righteousness of the letter prevails
everywhere over that of the spirit, everywhere betrays and condemns
our divinest natural manhood to dishonor and death; the inevitable
consequence being, that God's living energy in our nature, disdaining
as it does anything but a universal operation, is shut up to the narrowest, most personal and penurious dimensions,—is associated, in fact,
with the meanest, most meagre bosoms of the race; while the great
mass of men, in whose hearts and brains its infinite splendors lie seething and tumultuous for an outlet, are cast out of our Christian fellow-

ship, are dishonored and reviled, as so much worthless rubbish or noisome excrement.

It is quite time then, in my opinion, that we should cease minding Carlyle's rococo airs and affectations; his antiquated strut and heroics, reminding us now of John Knox and now of Don Quixote; his owlish, obscene hootings at the endless divine day which is breaking over all the earth of our regenerate nature. We have no need that he or any other literary desperado should enlighten us as to the principles of God's administration, for we have a more sure word of prophecy in our own hearts,—a ray of the light which illumines every man who comes into the world, and is ample, if we follow it, to scatter every cloud that rests upon the course of history. We are all of us parents, potentially or actually, and although we represent the infinite paternity most imperfectly, we do nevertheless represent it. And how do we administer our families? Do we bestow our chief solicitude upon those of our children who need it least, or upon those who need it most; upon those who are most up to the world's remorseless demands upon them, or those who fall short of those demands? I need not wait for an answer. All our base, egotistic pride may go to the former, but we reserve all our care and tenderness for those whom an unkind nature, as we say, consigns to comparative indigence and ignominy. Now, God has absolutely no pride and no egotism, being infinitely inferior to us in both those respects. But then, for that very reason, he is infinitely our superior in point of love or tenderness. I do not believe that the tenderness we bestow upon our prodigals is worthy to be named in the same day with that which he bestows upon his. I do not believe, for my part, that he ever lifts a finger, or casts a glance, to bless those of his offspring who resemble him, or are in sympathy with his perfection,—for such persons need no blessing, are themselves already their own best blessing,—but reserves all his care and tenderness for the unblessed and disorderly, for the unthankful and the evil, for those who are disaffected to his righteousness, and make a mock of his peace. I doubt not, if a celestial visitor should come to us to-morrow in the flesh, we should engage the best rooms for him at the Parker House; supply his table with the fat of the land; place a coach-and-four at his beck, whisk him off to the State House; introduce him to all the notabilities, ecclesiastic, political, scholastic, financial; give him a public dinner, a box at the opera, the most conspicuous pew in church; in short, do everything our stupidity could invent to persuade *him*, at all events, that we regarded him as an arrival from the most uncelestial corner of the universe. Well, we have in truth at this time, and all the time, no celestial visitant in the flesh among us, but a divine resident in the spirit, whom the heaven of heavens is all unmeet to contain, and who yet dwells—

awaiting there his eventual glorious resurrection—a patient, despised, discredited, spiritual form in every fibre of that starved and maddened and polluted flesh and blood which feeds our prisons and fattens our hospitals, and which we have yet the sagacity to regard as the indispensable base of our unclean and inhuman civilization. And it is my fixed conviction, that unless we speedily consent to recognize his humiliated form in that loathsome sepulchre, and give emancipation to it there, first of all, by bringing this waste life, this corrupt and outcast force of Christendom, into complete social recognition, or clothing it with the equal garments of praise and salvation that hide our own spiritual nakedness, we shall utterly miss our historic justification, and baffle the majestic Providence which is striving through us to inaugurate a free, unforced, and permanent order of human life.

*   *   *

PARTIAL PORTRAITS

Hawthorne

A FEW MONTHS after the family's return from Europe in the fall of 1860, Henry Senior attended a dinner of Boston's Saturday Club at the Parker House. He wrote Emerson his irreverent reactions, but what chiefly impelled his letter was his impression of Hawthorne's "human substance":

"I am going to Concord in the morning but shall have barely time to see you, if I do as much as that: yet I can't forbear to say a word I want to say about Hawthorne and Ellery Channing. Hawthorne isn't a handsome man nor an engaging one anyway, personally: he had the look all the time, to one who didn't know him, of a rogue who suddenly finds himself in a company of detectives. But in spite of his rusticity I felt a sympathy for him amounting to anguish and couldn't take my eyes off him all the dinner, nor my rapt attention; as that indecisive little Dr. Hedge found, I am afraid to his cost, for I hardly heard a word of what he kept on saying to me, and felt at one time very much like sending down to Mr. Parker to have him removed from the room as maliciously putting his artificial little person between me and a profitable object of study.

"Yet I feel now no ill-will to Hedge and could recommend any one (but myself) to go and hear him preach. Hawthorne, however, seemed to me to possess human substance and not to have dissipated it all away as that debauched Charles Norton, and the good, inoffensive, comforting Longfellow. He seemed much nearer the human being than any one at that end of the table, much nearer. John Forbes and yourself kept up the balance at the other end: but that end was a desert with him for its only oasis. It was so pathetic to see him, contented, sprawling Concord owl that he was and always has been, brought blindfold into that brilliant daylight, and expected to wink and be lively like any

479

little dapper Tommy Titmouse, or Jenny Wren. How he buried his
eyes in his plate, and ate with such a voracity that no person should
dare to ask him a question!

"My heart broke for him as that attenuated Charles Norton kept
putting forth his long antennæ towards him, stroking his face, and
trying whether his eyes were shut. The idea I got was, and it was very
powerfully impressed upon me, that we are all of us monstrously corrupt, hopelessly bereft of human consciousness, and that it is the intention of the Divine Providence to overrun us and obliterate us in a new
Gothic and Vandalic invasion of which this Concord specimen is a
first fruits. It was heavenly to see him persist in ignoring Charles
Norton, and shutting his eyes against his spectral smiles: eating his
dinner and doing absolutely nothing but that, and then going home to
his Concord den to fall upon his knees, and ask his heavenly Father
why it was that an owl couldn't remain an owl, and not be forced into
the dimensions of a canary. I have no doubt that all the tenderest
angels saw to his care that night, and poured oil into his wounds more
soothing than gentlemen ever know.

"William Ellery Channing, too, seemed so human and good, sweet
as summer, and fragrant as pine woods. He is more sophisticated than
the other of course, but still he was kin; and I felt the world richer by
two *men*, who had not yet lost themselves in mere members of society.
This is what I suspect; that we are fast getting so fearful one to another,
we 'members of society,' that we shall ere long begin to kill one another in self-defense, and give place in that way at last to a more
veracious state of things. The old world is breaking up on all hands: the
glimpse of the everlasting granite I caught in Hawthorne and William
Ellery, shows me that there is stock enough left for fifty better. Let the
old impostor go, bag and baggage, for a very real and substantial one
is aching to come in, in which the churl shall not be exalted to a place
of dignity, in which innocence shall never be tarnished nor trafficked
in, in which every man's freedom shall be respected down to its feeblest
filament as the radiant altar of God. To the angels, says Swedenborg,
death means resurrection to life; by that necessary rule of inversion
which keeps them separate from us and us from them, and so prevents
our being mutual nuisances.

"Let us then accept political and all other destruction that chooses
to come: because what is disorder and wrath and contention on the
surface is sure to be the deepest peace at the centre, working its way
thus to a surface that shall *never* be disorderly. Yours, H. J.

"P.S. . . . What a world! What a world! But once we get rid of
slavery and the new heavens and new earth will swim into reality."

HJ was to re-echo some of the phrases of this letter in his remark
that Hawthorne "must have been struck with the glare" of Margaret

Fuller's mind, and "mentally speaking, have scowled and blinked a good deal in conversation with her." He first read through all of Hawthorne's work while living at Newport, though WJ, otherwise occupied, did not come to *The House of the Seven Gables* until a decade later, at which time, as we have noted, he was delighted to detect a similarity between Hawthorne's style and his brother's.[1]

An account of all that HJ absorbed from Hawthorne could make a good short book.[2] Here, to HJ's eyes, was the most heartening proof that an American could be an artist. Yet it was not as a conscious disciple of Hawthorne's that he began to write, for even in his first published story he was emulating the realistic skills of Balzac. As he later observed in his preface to *Roderick Hudson*, "The art of interesting us in things . . . can *only* be the art of representing them," and he often found Hawthorne's representation a little shadowy and vague. Though HJ made a few early experiments with allegory, he had decided, by the time he wrote his critical biography of Hawthorne, that this mode of projecting spiritual truths "is apt to spoil two good things —a story and a moral, a meaning and a form."

This biography, published in 1879, is a landmark in American criticism. It was the first volume in the English Men of Letters series to be devoted to an American, and the first full-length study of a major American artist to be prepared by an artist of comparable rank. HJ tried to suggest Hawthorne's milieu in exactly the fashion that he later criticized Cabot for failing to do with Emerson's. If HJ admired Emerson as our leading philosopher and essayist, he was drawn to Hawthorne far more intimately because, as writers of fiction, they shared the same problems. In reading HJ's critical study, one must remember that he wrote it at the period when he was most conscious of being, along with Howells, one of the first American apostles of realism. It therefore throws more light on his own developing aims than it does upon Hawthorne. Notwithstanding all its appreciation, it may still underrate some of the imaginative energy in Hawthorne's romances, as it sees in his allegories, instead of their somber and pondering moral substance, only a light play of fancy.

When HJ discusses the special handicaps encountered by the artist in America, he is thinking, sometimes explicitly, of himself. Hawthorne, after living several years in Europe, entertained, in *The Marble Faun*, thoughts about this country which he had not had while composing his earlier books. "No author, without a trial," he said in the preface, "can conceive of the difficulty of writing a romance about a country where there is no shadow, no antiquity, no mystery, no pictur-

---

[1] See p. 319 above.
[2] I have tried to indicate the main influences in two sections of *American* *Renaissance*: "Hawthorne and James," pp. 295–305, and "From Hawthorne to James to Eliot," pp. 351–68.

esque and gloomy wrong, nor anything but a commonplace prosperity, in broad and simple daylight, as is happily the case with my dear native land." HJ added the comment that these words "must have lingered in the minds of many Americans who have tried to write novels, and to lay the scene of them in the Western world." He had just completed, in *The Europeans*, a novel laid in New England, and was about to try to sketch New York in *Washington Square*. But confessing himself baffled by any attempt to suggest the world of business, of which he knew so little, he returned, with *The Portrait of a Lady*, to the material that was to prove his most fertile vein—the American in Europe.

In the retrospect of HJ's whole career we can see at how many points he began where Hawthorne left off, and carried his effects further. His famous prefaces may well have received their first hint from Hawthorne's brief but telling discussions of his own works. HJ's most distinctive device, that of a narrator who, as a central consciousness, frames and interprets the events, would have found one of its sources in Miles Coverdale in *The Blithedale Romance*. By the time of his last work, HJ was no longer concerned with being a strict realist, and though he did not revert to allegory, he subordinated his immensely developed skills of representation to the inner meanings they could symbolize. The kind of moral problem he was occupied with in a story like "The Beast in the Jungle," the spiritual emptiness of the man "to whom nothing was to happen," also stemmed back to Hawthorne. By comparison it must be granted that HJ's ethical values were less firmly based in a traditional pattern than Hawthorne's, just as Hawthorne's solid grasp of New England history had been refined into HJ's somewhat attenuated "sense of the past."

In the preface to *The American*, HJ made a classic formulation of the differences between romance and realism. He was no longer rejecting one for the other as he had been when he wrote his study of Hawthorne. He declared that they were both modes of apprehending truth, and as his mind traveled back over the novel of his century, he realized that "the men of largest responding imagination before the human scene," such as Scott or Balzac or even Zola, had committed themselves to both modes; that "it would be impossible to have a more romantic temper than Flaubert's Madame Bovary, and yet nothing less resembles a romance than the record of her adventures." The one distinguishing feature of the romance was that it dealt with "experience liberated, so to speak; experience disengaged, disembroiled, disencumbered, exempt from the conditions that we usually know to attach to it." But such experience may convey none the less, as Hawthorne had affirmed, "the truth of the human heart." Indeed, HJ had grown to believe that only by breaking away from the restrictions of realism could a writer express the things "we never *can* directly know; the things that can reach us only through the beautiful circuit and subterfuge of our thought and our desire." There could hardly be a phrase more descriptive of the kind of beauty that HJ evoked through his presentation of Milly Theale. When he turned back to Hawthorne shortly after finishing *The Wings of the Dove*, in the year of Hawthorne's centenary, he dwelt on the interpenetration in his work of romance and reality. The little-known letter that he wrote for the celebration of that centenary at Salem represents his final view of the first master that he had recognized in America. It may be given here in lieu of the better-known biography, the length of which would naturally preclude it. In writing this letter HJ kept before his eyes an image of the old Salem. That image was to be considerably altered by an episode that occurred the following year when he revisited the town, and found, to his bewilderment, that he had asked his way to the House of the Seven Gables of an Italian who could not understand English.

HJ to Robert S. Rantoul, June 1904:

* * * * *

I much regret my being able to participate only in that spirit of sympathy that makes light of distance—that defies difference of latitude and hemisphere—in the honours you are paying, at his birthplace, to the beautiful genius to whom Salem owes the most precious gift perhaps that an honest city may receive from one of her sons—the gift of a literary association high enough in character to emerge thus brilliantly from the test of Time. How happily it has lasted for you, and *why* it has lasted—this flower of romantic art, never to become a mere desiccated specimen, that Hawthorne interwove with your sturdy annals,—I shall attempt, by your leave, briefly to say; but your civic pride is at any rate fortunate in being able to found your claim to have contributed to the things of the mind on a case and a career so eminent and so interesting. The spirit of such occasions is always, on the spot, communicative and irresistible; full of the amenity of each man's—and I suppose still more of each woman's—scarce distinguishing, in the general friendliness, between the *loan* of enthusiasm and the gift, between the sound that starts the echo and the echo that comes back from the sound. But being present by projection of the mind, present afar off and under another sky, *that* has its advantages too—for other distinctions, for lucidity of vision and a sense of the reasons of things. The career commemorated may perhaps so be looked at, over a firm rest, as through the telescope that fixes it, even to intensity, and helps it to become, as we say, objective—and objective not strictly to cold criticism, but to admiration and wonder themselves, and even, in a degree, to a certain tenderness of envy. The earlier scene, now smothered in flowers and eloquence and music, possibly hangs before one rather

more, under this perspective, in *all* its parts—with its relation, unconscious at the time, to the rare mind that had been planted in it as in a
parent soil, and with the relation of that mind to its own preoccupied
state, to the scene itself as enveloping and suggesting medium: a relation, this latter, to come to consciousness always so much sooner, so
much more nervously, so much more expressively, than the other! By
which I mean that there is, unfortunately for the prospective celebrity,
no short cut possible, on the part of his fellow-townsmen, to the expensive holiday they are keeping in reserve for his name. It is there,
all the while—somewhere in the air at least, even while he lives; but
they cannot get *at* it till the Fates have forced, one by one, all the locks
of all the doors and crooked passages that shut it off; and the celebrity
meantime, by good luck, can have little idea what is missing.

I at all events almost venture to say that, save for the pleasure of
your company, save for that community of demonstration which is
certainly a joy in itself, I could not wish to be better placed than at
this distance for a vision of the lonely young man that Hawthorne then
was, and that he was in fact pretty well always to remain, dreaming his
dreams, nursing his imagination, feeling his way, leading his life, intellectual, personal, economic, in the place that Salem then was, and
becoming, unwittingly and unsuspectedly, with an absence of calculation fairly precious for the final effect, the pretext for the kind of
recognition you greet him with to-day. It is the addition of all the
limitations and depressions and difficulties of genius that makes always—
with the factor of Time thrown in—the sum total of posthumous
glory. We see, at the end of the backward vista, the restless unclassified
artist pursue the *immediate*, the pressing need of the hour, the question
he is not to come home to his possibly uninspiring hearth-stone without
having met—we see him chase it, none too confidently, through quite
familiar, *too* familiar streets, round well-worn corners that don't trip
it up for him, or into dull doorways that fail to catch and hold it; and
then we see, at the other end of the century, these same streets and
corners and doorways, these quiet familiarities, the stones he trod, the
objects he touched, the air he breathed, positively and all impatiently
waiting to bestow their reward, to measure him out success, in the great,
in the almost superfluous, abundance of the eventual! This general
quest that Hawthorne comes back to us out of the old sunny and shady
Salem, the blissfully homogeneous community of the forties and fifties,
as urged to by his particular, and very individual, sense of life, is that
of man's relation to his environment seen on the side that we call, for
our best convenience, the romantic side: a term that we half the time,
nowadays, comfortably escape the challenge to define precisely because "The Scarlet Letter" and "The House of the Seven Gables" have
made that possible to us under cover of mere triumphant reference to

them. That is why, to my sense, our author's Salem years and Salem impressions are so interesting a part of his development. It was while they lasted, it was to all appearance under their suggestion, that the romantic spirit in him learned to expand with that right and beautiful felicity that was to make him one of its rarest representatives. Salem had the good-fortune to assist him, betimes, to this charming discrimination —that of looking for romance near at hand, and where it grows thick and true, rather than on the other side of the globe and in the Dictionary of Dates. We see it, nowadays, more and more, inquired and bargained for in places and times that are strange and indigestible to us; and for the most part, I think, we see those who deal in it on these terms come back from their harvest with their hands smelling, under their brave leather gauntlets, or royal rings, or whatever, of the plain domestic blackberry, the homeliest growth of our actual dusty waysides. These adventurers bring home, in general, simply what they have taken with them, the mechanical, at best the pedantic, view of the list of romantic properties. The country of romance has been for them but a particular spot on the map, coloured blue or red or yellow—they have to *take* it from the map; or has been this, that or the other particular set of complications, machinations, coincidences or escapes, this, that or the other fashion of fire-arm or cutlass, cock of hat, frizzle of wig, violence of scuffle or sound of expletive: mere accidents and outward patches, all, of the engaging mystery—no more of its essence than the brass band at a restaurant is of the essence of the dinner. What was admirable and instinctive in Hawthorne was that he saw the quaintness or the weirdness, the interest *behind* the interest, of things, as continuous with the very life we are leading, or that we were leading—you, at Salem, certainly were leading—round about him and under his eyes; saw it as something deeply within us, not as something infinitely disconnected from us; saw it in short in the very application of the spectator's, the poet's mood, in the kind of reflection the things we know best and see oftenest may make in our minds. So it is that such things as "The Seven Gables," "The Blithedale Romance," "The Marble Faun," are singularly fruitful examples of the real as distinguished from the artificial romantic note. Here "the light that never was on land or sea" keeps all the intimacy and yet adds all the wonder. In the first two of the books I have named, especially, the author has read the romantic effect into the most usual and contemporary things—arriving by it at a success that, in the Seven Gables perhaps supremely, is a marvel of the free-playing, yet ever unerring, never falsifying instinct. We have an ancient gentlewoman reduced to keep a shop; a young photographer modestly invoking fortune; a full-fed, wine-flushed "prominent citizen" asleep in his chair; a weak-minded bachelor spending his life under the shadow of an early fault that has not been in the least heroic; a fresh

New England girl of the happy complexion of thousands of others—we have, thrown together, but these gently-persuasive challenges to mystification, yet with the result that they transport us to a world in which, as in that of Tennyson's Lotus-Eaters, it seems always afternoon. And somehow this very freedom of the spell remains all the while truth to the objects observed—truth to the very Salem in which the vision was born. Blithedale is scarcely less fine a case of distinction conferred, the curiosity and anxiety dear to the reader purchased, not by a shower of counterfeit notes, simulating munificence, but by that artistic economy which understands *values* and uses them. The book takes up the parti-coloured, angular, audible, traceable Real, the New England earnest, aspiring, reforming Real, scattered in a few frame-houses over a few stony fields, and so invests and colours it, makes it rich and strange—and simply by finding a felicitous *tone* for it—that its characters and images remain for us curious winged creatures preserved in the purest amber of the imagination.

All of which leads me back to what I said, to begin with, about our romancer's having borne the test of Time. I mentioned that there is a reason, in particular, why he has borne it so well, and I think you will recognize with me, in the light of what I have tried to say, that he has done so by very simply, quietly, slowly and steadily, becoming for us a Classic. If we look at the real meaning of our celebration to-day, ask ourselves what is at the back of our heads or in the bottom of our hearts about it, we become conscious of that interesting process and eloquent plea of the years on Hawthorne's behalf—of that great benefit, that effect of benevolence, for him, from so many of the things the years have brought. We are in the presence thus of one of the happiest opportunities to see how a Classic comes into being, how three such things as the Scarlet Letter, the Gables and Blithedale—to choose only a few names where I might choose many—acquire their final value. They acquire it, in a large measure, by the manner in which later developments have worked in respect to them—and, it is scarce too much to say, acquire it in spite of themselves and by the action of better machinery than their authors could have set in motion, stronger (as well as longer!) wires than their authors could have pulled. Later developments, I think, have worked in respect to them by *contrast*—that is the point—so much more either than by a generous emulation or by a still more generous originality. They have operated to make the beauty—the other beauty—delicate and noble, to throw the distinction into relief. The scene has changed and everything with it—the pitch, and the tone, and the quantity, and the quality, above all; reverberations are gained, but proportions are lost; the distracted Muse herself stops her ears and shuts her eyes: the brazen trumpet has so done its best to deafen us to the fiddle-string. But to the fiddle-string we nevertheless return; it sounds, for our sense, with the slightest lull of the general noise—such a lull as, for reflection, for taste, a little even for criticism, and much, certainly, for a legitimate complacency, our present occasion beneficently makes. Then it is that such a mystery as that of the genius we commemorate may appear a perfect example of the truth that the state of being a classic is a *comparative* state—considerably, generously, even when blindly, brought about, for the author on whom the crown alights, by the generations, the multitudes worshipping other gods, that have followed him. He must obviously have been in himself exquisite and right, but it is not to that only, to being in himself exquisite and right, that any man ever was so fortunate as to owe the supreme distinction. He owes it more or less, at the best, to the *relief* in which some happy, some charming combination of accidents has placed his intrinsic value. This combination, in our own time, has been the contagion of the form that we may, for convenience, and perhaps, as regards much of it, even for compliment, call the journalistic—so pervasive, so ubiquitous, so unprecedentedly prosperous, so wonderful for outward agility, but so unfavourable, even so fatal, to development from within. Hawthorne saw it—and it saw him—but in its infancy, before these days of huge and easy and immediate success, before the universal, the overwhelming triumph of the monster. He *had* developed from within—as to feeling, as to form, as to sincerity and character. So it is, as I say, that he enjoys his relief, and that we are thrown back, by the sense of difference, on his free possession of himself. He lent himself, of course, to his dignity—by the way the serious, in him, flowered into the grace of art; but our need of him, almost quite alone as he stands, in one tray of the scales of Justice, would add, if this were necessary, to the earnestness of our wish to see that he be undisturbed there. Vigilance, in the matter, however, assuredly, is happily not necessary! The grand sign of being a classic is that when you have "passed," as they say at examinations, you have passed; you have become one once for all; you have taken your degree and may be left to the light and the ages.

* * *

PARTIAL PORTRAITS

Whitman

THE JAMESES were aware of Whitman almost from the start of his career. Henry Senior wrote from Geneva in 1860 to an American friend: "You ask me 'why I do not brandish my tomahawk and, like Walt Whitman, raise my barbaric yawp over the roofs of all the houses.' It is because I am not yet a 'cosmos,' as that gentleman avowedly is, but only a very dim nebula, doing its modest best, no doubt, to solidify into cosmical dimensions, but still requiring an 'awful sight' of time and pains and patience on the part of its friends."

WJ alluded, a few years later, in a letter to Wendell Holmes, to Whitman's "human energy," and kept a taste for him throughout his life. He said in his mid-forties: "I've got much good from that man's verse, if such it can be called." A dozen years later, reacting against Santayana's essay "The Poetry of Barbarism," he ejaculated: "Always things burst by the growing content of experience. Dramatic unities; laws of versification; ecclesiastical systems; scholastic doctrines. Bah! Give me Walt Whitman and Browning ten times over, much as the perverse ugliness of the latter at times irritates me, and intensely as I have enjoyed Santayana's attack. The barbarians are in the line of mental growth, and those who insist that the ideal and the real are dynamically continuous are those by whom the world is to be saved." WJ liked to weave quotations from Whitman into his essays, and discussed him as one of the exemplars of "the religion of healthy-mindedness."

HJ's most notorious review is that of *Drum Taps*. It is as wrongheaded in its judgments as a destructive piece by a self-confident reviewer of twenty-two could well be, but its peroration from the Intelligence to the Bard is a virtuoso performance in rhetoric, and its underlying contention—influenced perhaps by Flaubert—that the artist should lose himself in his work is a lesson that English and American literature could always profit by.

When HJ returned to his memories of the Civil War, in *Notes of a Son and Brother*, he had quite altered his earlier view. He spoke of his visit to an army camp: "Discriminations of the prosaic order had little to do with my first and all but sole vision of the American soldier in his multitude, and above all—for that was markedly the colour of the whole thing—in his depression, his wasted melancholy almost; an effect that somehow corresponds for memory, I bethink myself, with the tender elegiac tone in which Walt Whitman was later on so admirably to commemorate him." Exactly when HJ's taste for Whitman began to mellow would be hard to say, but he wrote in 1898 a review as astonishing as his earlier one, since it could not have been foreseen that an author who had just produced *What Maisie Knew* would value Whitman's letters to Pete Doyle. His later enjoyment of *Leaves of Grass* was described by Edith Wharton, in connection with his visit to her home at Lenox, Massachusetts, in 1905:

"I had never before heard poetry read as he read it; and I never have since. He chanted it, and he was not afraid to chant it, as many good readers are, who, though they instinctively feel that the genius of the English poetical idiom requires it to be spoken *as poetry*, are yet afraid of yielding to their instinct because the present-day fashion is to chatter high verse as though it were colloquial prose. James, on the contrary, far from shirking the rhythmic emphasis, gave it full expression. His stammer ceased as by magic as soon as he began to read, and his ear, so sensitive to the convolutions of an intricate prose style, never allowed him to falter over the most complex prosody, but swept him forward on great rollers of sound till the full weight of his voice fell on the last cadence.

"James's reading was a thing apart, an emanation of his inmost self, unaffected by fashion or elocutionary artifice. He read from his soul, and no one who never heard him read poetry knows what that soul was. . . . Some one spoke of Whitman, and it was a joy to me to discover that James thought him, as I did, the greatest of American poets. *Leaves of Grass* was put into his hands, and all that evening we sat rapt while he wandered from 'The Song of Myself' to 'When lilacs last in the dooryard bloomed' (when he read 'Lovely and soothing Death,' his voice filled the hushed room like an organ adagio), and thence let himself be lured on to the mysterious music of 'Out of the Cradle,' reading, or rather crooning it in a mood of subdued ecstasy till the fivefold invocation to Death tolled out like the knocks in the opening bars of the Fifth Symphony.

"James's admiration of Whitman, his immediate response to that mighty appeal, was a new proof of the way in which, above a certain level, the most divergent intelligences walk together like gods. We talked long that night of *Leaves of Grass*, tossing back and forth to each other treasure after treasure; but finally James, in one of his sudden humorous drops from the heights, flung up his hands and cried out with the old stammer and twinkle: 'Oh, yes, a great genius; undoubtedly a very great genius! Only one cannot help deploring his too-extensive acquaintance with the foreign languages."

* * * * *

HJ: "MR. WALT WHITMAN" (1865)[1]

IT HAS BEEN a melancholy task to read this book; and it is a still more melancholy one to write about it. Perhaps since the day of Mr. Tupper's "Philosophy" there has been no more difficult reading of the poetic sort. It exhibits the effort of an essentially prosaic mind to lift itself, by a prolonged muscular strain, into poetry. Like hundreds of other good patriots, during the last four years, Mr. Walt Whitman has imagined that a certain amount of violent sympathy with the great deeds and sufferings of our soldiers, and of admiration for our national energy, together with a ready command of picturesque language, are sufficient inspiration for a poet. If this were the case, we had been a nation of poets. The constant developments of the war moved us continually to strong feeling and to strong expression of it. But in those cases in which these expressions were written out and printed with all due regard to prosody, they failed to make poetry, as any one may see by consulting now in cold blood the back volumes of the "Rebellion Record." *Of course* the city of Manhattan, as Mr. Whitman delights to call it, when regiments poured through it in the first months of the war, and its own sole god, to borrow the words of a real poet, ceased for a while to be the millionaire, was a noble spectacle, and a poetical statement to this effect is possible. *Of course* the tumult of a battle is grand, the results of a battle tragic, and the untimely deaths of young men a theme for elegies. But he is not a poet who merely reiterates these plain facts *ore rotundo*. He only sings them worthily who views them from a height. Every tragic event collects about it a number of persons who delight to dwell upon its superficial points—of minds which are bullied by the *accidents* of the affair. The temper of such minds seems to us to be the reverse of the poetic temper; for the poet, although he incidentally masters, grasps, and uses the superficial traits of his theme, is really a poet only in so far as he extracts its latent meaning and holds it up to common eyes. And yet from such minds most of our war-verses have come, and Mr. Whitman's utterances, much as the assertion may sur-

---

[1] "Walt Whitman's Drum-Taps." New York. 1865.

prise his friends, are in this respect no exception to general fashion. They are an exception, however, in that they openly pretend to be something better; and this it is that makes them melancholy reading. Mr. Whitman is very fond of blowing his own trumpet, and he has made very explicit claims for his book. "Shut not your doors," he exclaims at the outset—

> "Shut not your doors to me, proud libraries,
>   For that which was lacking among you all, yet needed most, I bring;
>   A book I have made for your dear sake, O soldiers,
>   And for you, O soul of man, and you, love of comrades;
>   The words of my book nothing, the life of it everything;
>   A book separate, not link'd with the rest, nor felt by the intellect;
>   But you will feel every word, O Libertad! arm'd Libertad!
>   It shall pass by the intellect to swim the sea, the air,
>   With joy with you, O soul of man."

These are great pretensions, but it seems to us that the following are even greater:

> "From Paumanok starting, I fly like a bird,
>   Around and around to soar, to sing the idea of all;
>   To the north betaking myself, to sing there arctic songs,
>   To Kanada, 'till I absorb Kanada in myself—to Michigan then,
>   To Wisconsin, Iowa, Minnesota, to sing their songs (they are inimitable);
>   Then to Ohio and Indiana, to sing theirs—to Missouri and Kansas and Arkansas to sing theirs,
>   To Tennessee and Kentucky—to the Carolinas and Georgia, to sing theirs,
>   To Texas, and so along up toward California, to roam accepted everywhere;
>   To sing first (to the tap of the war-drum, if need be)
>   The idea of all—of the western world, one and inseparable,
>   And then the song of each member of these States."

Mr. Whitman's primary purpose is to celebrate the greatness of our armies; his secondary purpose is to celebrate the greatness of the city of New York. He pursues these objects through a hundred pages of matter which remind us irresistibly of the story of the college professor who, on a venturesome youth's bringing him a theme done in blank verse, reminded him that it was not customary in writing prose to begin each line with a capital. The frequent capitals are the only marks of verse in Mr. Whitman's writing. There is, fortunately, but one attempt at rhyme. We say fortunately, for if the inequality of Mr. Whitman's lines were self-registering, as it would be in the case of an anticipated syllable at their close, the effect would be painful in the extreme. As the case stands, each line starts off by itself, in resolute independence of its companions, without a visible goal. But if Mr. Whitman does not write verse, he does not write ordinary prose. The reader has seen that liberty is "libertad." In like manner, comrade is "camerado"; Americans are "Americanos"; a pavement is a "trottoir," and Mr. Whitman himself is a "chansonnier." If there is one thing that Mr. Whitman is not, it is this, for Béranger was a *chansonnier*. To appreciate the force of our conjunction, the reader should compare his military lyrics with Mr. Whitman's declamations. Our author's novelty, however, is not in his words, but in the form of his writing. As we have said, it begins for all the world like verse and turns out to be arrant prose. It is more like Mr. Tupper's proverbs than anything we have met. But what if, in form, it *is* prose? it may be asked. Very good poetry has come out of prose before this. To this we would reply that it must first have gone into it. Prose, in order to be good poetry, must first be good prose. As a general principle, we know of no circumstance more likely to impugn a writer's earnestness than the adoption of an anomalous style. He must have something very original to say if none of the old vehicles will carry his thoughts. Of course he *may* be surprisingly original. Still, presumption is against him. If on examination the matter of his discourse proves very valuable, it justifies, or at any rate excuses, his literary innovation.

But if, on the other hand, it is of a common quality, with nothing new about it but its manners, the public will judge the writer harshly. The most that can be said of Mr. Whitman's vaticinations is, that, cast in a fluent and familiar manner, the average substance of them might escape unchallenged. But we have seen that Mr. Whitman prides himself especially on the substance—the life—of his poetry. It may be rough, it may be grim, it may be clumsy—such we take to be the author's argument—but it is sincere, it is sublime, it appeals to the soul of man, it is the voice of a people. He tells us, in the lines quoted, that the words of his book are nothing. To our perception they are everything, and very little at that. A great deal of verse that is nothing but words has, during the war, been sympathetically sighed over and cut out of newspaper corners, because it has possessed a certain simple melody. But Mr. Whitman's verse, we are confident, would have failed even of this triumph, for the simple reason that no triumph, however small, is won but through the exercise of art, and that this volume is an offense against art. It is not enough to be grim and rough and careless; common sense is also necessary, for it is by common sense that we are judged. There exists in even the commonest minds, in literary matters, a certain precise instinct of conservatism, which is very shrewd in detecting wanton eccentricities. To this instinct Mr. Whitman's attitude seems monstrous. It is monstrous because it pretends to persuade the soul while it slights the intellect; because it pretends to gratify the feelings while it outrages the taste. The point is that it does this *on theory*, wilfully, consciously, arrogantly. It is the little nursery game of "open your mouth and shut your eyes." Our hearts are often touched through a compromise with the artistic sense, but never in direct violation of it. Mr. Whitman sits down at the outset and counts out the intelligence. This were indeed a wise precaution on his part if the intelligence were only submissive! But when she is deliberately insulted, she takes her revenge by simply standing erect and open-eyed. This is assuredly the best she can do. And if she could find a voice she would probably address Mr. Whitman as follows: "You came to woo my sister, the human soul. Instead of giving me a kick as you approach, you should either greet me courteously, or, at least, steal in unobserved. But now you have me on your hands. Your chances are poor. What the human heart desires above all is sincerity, and you do not appear to me sincere. For a lover you talk entirely too much about yourself. In one place you threaten to absorb Kanada. In another you call upon the city of New York to incarnate you, as you have incarnated it. In another you inform us that neither youth pertains to you nor 'delicatesse,' that you are awkward in the parlor, that you do not dance, and that you have neither bearing, beauty, knowledge, nor fortune. In another place, by an allusion to your 'little songs,' you seem to identify yourself with the third person of the Trinity. For a poet who claims to sing 'the idea of all,' this is tolerably egotistical. We look in vain, however, through your book for a single idea. We find nothing but flashy imitations of ideas. We find a medley of extravagances and commonplaces. We find art, measure, grace, sense sneered at on every page, and nothing positive given us in their stead. To be positive one must have something to say; to be positive requires reason, labor, and art; and art requires, above all things, a suppression of one's self, a subordination of one's self to an idea. This will never do for you, whose plan is to adapt the scheme of the universe to your own limitations. You cannot entertain and exhibit ideas; but, as we have seen, you are prepared to incarnate them. It is for this reason, doubtless, that when once you have planted yourself squarely before the public, and in view of the great service you have done to the ideal, have become, as you say, 'accepted everywhere,' you can afford to deal exclusively in words. What would be bald nonsense and dreary platitudes in any one else becomes sublimity in you. But all this is a mistake. To become adopted as a national poet, it is not enough to discard everything in particular and to accept everything in general, to amass crudity upon crudity, to discharge the undigested contents of your blotting-book into the lap of the public. You must respect the public which you address; for it has taste, if you have not. It delights in the grand, the heroic, and the masculine; but it delights to see these conceptions cast into worthy form. It is indifferent to brute sublimity. It will never do for you to thrust your hands into your pockets and cry out that, as the research of form is an intolerable bore, the shortest and most economical way for the public to embrace its idols—for the nation to realize its genius—is in your own person. This democratic, liberty-loving, American populace, this stern and war-tried people, is a great civilizer. It is devoted to refinement. If it has sustained a monstrous war, and practised human nature's best in so many ways for the last five years, it is not to put up with spurious poetry afterwards. To sing aright our battles and our glories it is not enough to have served in a hospital (however praiseworthy the task in itself), to be aggressively careless, inelegant, and ignorant, and to be constantly preoccupied with yourself. It is not enough to be rude, lugubrious, and grim. You must also be serious. You must forget yourself in your ideas. Your personal qualities—the vigor of your temperament, the manly independence of your nature, the tenderness of your heart—these facts are impertinent. You must be *possessed*, and you must strive to possess your possession. If in your striving you break into divine eloquence, then you are a poet. If the idea which possesses you is the idea of your country's greatness, then you are a national poet; and not otherwise."

HJ: CALAMUS (1898)

WHAT SENSE shall I speak of as affected by the series of letters published, under the title of *Calamus*, by Dr. R. M. Bucke, one of the literary executors of Walt Whitman? The democratic would be doubtless a prompt and simple answer, and as an illustration of democratic social conditions their interest is lively. The person to whom, from 1868 to 1880, they were addressed was a young laboring man, employed in rough railway work, whom Whitman met by accident—the account of the meeting, in his correspondent's own words, is the most charming passage in the volume—and constituted for the rest of life a subject of a friendship of the regular "eternal"—the legendary sort. The little book appeals, I dare say, mainly to the Whitmanite already made, but I should be surprised if it has actually failed of power to make a few more. I mean by the Whitmanite those for whom the author of *Leaves of Grass* is, with all his rags and tatters, an upright figure, a *successful* original. It has in a singular way something of the same relation to poetry that may be made out in the luckiest—few, but fine—of the writer's other pages; I call the way singular because it squeezes through the narrowest, humblest gate of prose.

There is not even by accident a line with a hint of style—it is all flat, familiar, affectionate, illiterate colloquy. If the absolute natural be, when the writer is interesting, the supreme merit of letters, these, accordingly, should stand high on the list. (I am taking for granted, of course, the interest of Whitman.) The beauty of the natural is, here, the beauty of the particular nature, the man's own overflow in the deadly dry setting, the personal passion, the love of life plucked like a flower in a desert of innocent, unconscious ugliness. To call the whole thing vividly American is to challenge, doubtless, plenty of dissent—on the ground, presumably, that the figure in evidence was no less queer a feature of Camden, New Jersey, than it would have been of South Kensington. That may perfectly be; but a thousand images of patient, homely American life, else undistinguishable, are what its queerness—however startling—happened to express. In this little book is an audible New Jersey voice, charged thick with such impressions, and the reader will miss a chance who does not find in it many odd and pleasant human harmonies. Whitman wrote to his friend of what they both saw and touched, enormities of the common, sordid occupations, dreary amusements, undesirable food; and the record remains, by a mysterious marvel, a thing positively delightful. If we ever find out why, it must be another time. The riddle meanwhile is a neat one for the sphinx of democracy to offer.

WJ: FROM "THE RELIGION OF HEALTHY-MINDEDNESS" (1901)

. . . THE supreme contemporary example of such an inability to feel evil is of course Walt Whitman. . . . [He] owes his importance in literature to the systematic expulsion from his writings of all contractile elements. The only sentiments he allowed himself to express were of the expansive order; and he expressed these in the first person, not as your mere monstrously conceited individual might so express them, but vicariously for all men, so that a passionate and mystic ontological emotion suffuses his words, and ends by persuading the reader that men and women, life and death, and all things are divinely good.

Thus it has come about that many persons to-day regard Walt Whitman as the restorer of the eternal natural religion. He has infected them with his own love of comrades, with his own gladness that he and they exist. Societies are actually formed for his cult; a periodical organ exists for its propagation, in which the lines of orthodoxy and heterodoxy are already beginning to be drawn; hymns are written by others in his peculiar prosody; and he is even explicitly compared with the founder of the Christian religion, not altogether to the advantage of the latter.

Whitman is often spoken of as a "pagan." The word nowadays means sometimes the mere natural animal man without a sense of sin; sometimes it means a Greek or Roman with his own peculiar religious consciousness. In neither of these senses does it fitly define this poet. He is more than your mere animal man who has not tasted of the tree of good and evil. He is aware enough of sin for a swagger to be present in his indifference towards it, a conscious pride in his freedom from flexions and contractions, which your genuine pagan in the first sense of the word would never show.

> I could turn and live with animals, they are so placid and self-
> contained,
> I stand and look at them long and long;
> They do not sweat and whine about their condition.
> They do not lie awake in the dark and weep for their sins.
> Not one is dissatisfied, not one is demented with the mania of owning
> things,
> Not one kneels to another, nor to his kind that lived thousands of
> years ago,
> Not one is respectable or unhappy over the whole earth.

No natural pagan could have written these well-known lines. But on the other hand Whitman is less than a Greek or Roman; for their consciousness, even in Homeric times, was full to the brim of the sad mortality of this sunlit world, and such a consciousness Walt Whitman resolutely refuses to adopt. When, for example, Achilles about to slay Lycaon, Priam's young son, hears him sue for mercy, he stops to say:—

> Ah, friend, thou too must die: why thus lamentest thou? Patroclos too is dead, who was better far than thou. . . . Over me too hang death and forceful fate. There cometh morn or eve or some noon-day when my life too some man shall take in battle, whether with spear he smite, or arrow from the string.

Then Achilles savagely severs the poor boy's neck with his sword, heaves him by the foot into the Scamander, and calls to the fishes of the river to eat the white fat of Lycaon. Just as here the cruelty and the sympathy each ring true, and do not mix or interfere with one another, so did the Greeks and Romans keep all their sadnesses and gladnesses unmingled and entire. Instinctive good they did not reckon sin; nor had they any such desire to save the credit of the universe as to make them insist, as so many of *us* insist, that what immediately appears as evil must be "good in the making," or something equally ingenious. Good was good, and bad just bad, for the earlier Greeks. They neither denied the ills of nature,—Walt Whitman's verse, "What is called good is perfect and what is called bad is just as perfect," would have been mere silliness to them,—nor did they, in order to escape from those ills, invent "another and a better world" of the imagination, in which, along with the ills, the innocent goods of sense would also find no place. This integrity of the instinctive reactions, this freedom from all moral sophistry and strain, gives a pathetic dignity to ancient pagan feeling. And this quality Whitman's outpourings have not got. His optimism is too voluntary and defiant; his gospel has a touch of bravado and an affected twist,[1] and this diminishes its effect on many readers who yet are well disposed towards optimism, and on the whole quite willing to admit that in important respects Whitman is of the genuine lineage of the prophets.

* * *

[1] "God is afraid of me!" remarked such a titanic-optimistic friend in my presence one morning when he was feeling particularly hearty and cannibal-istic. The defiance of the phrase showed that a Christian education in humility still rankled in his breast.

PARTIAL PORTRAITS

Howells

ALTHOUGH WJ was an ardent reader of Howells and greeted his novels with what their delighted author called "whoops of blessing," HJ's comments possess the additional interest of constituting successive stages in the discovery of his own capacities. Howells, half a dozen years his senior, was the one contemporary American novelist to whom he felt close; and some day, when all the letters on both sides are available, they may form a running commentary on the advance of American realism.

The first mention of HJ in Howells' printed correspondence was in 1866: "Talking of talks: young Henry James and I had a famous one last evening, two or three hours long, in which we settled the true principles of literary art. He is a very earnest fellow, and I think extremely gifted—gifted enough to do better than any one has yet done toward making us a real American novel." He accepted several of HJ's early stories for the *Atlantic*, and continued to praise and befriend his work whenever possible for the rest of their lives. After rereading several of HJ's novels in the collected edition of 1909, he wrote: "I must own to you a constantly mounting wonder in myself at your 'way,' and at the fullness, the closeness, the density of your work; my own seems so meager beside it." At the time of his death, four years after HJ's, Howells was working on an essay dealing with HJ's essential Americanism. He had just been prompted by Lubbock's edition of HJ's letters to say: "He ignores the cause of James' going to live abroad which was that he was a sick man who was less of a sufferer in Europe than in America. . . . The climate was kinder to him than ours, and the life was kinder than his native life, and his native land. In fact America was never kind to James. It was rude and harsh, unworthily and stupidly so, as we must more and more own, if we would be true to ourselves. We ought to be ashamed of our part in this; the nearest of his friends in Boston would say they liked him, but they could not bear his fiction; and from the people, conscious of culture, throughout New England, especially the women, he had sometimes outright insult."

HJ, on his side, maintained an enduring interest in Howells, and said in the late 1880's that he and Stevenson "are the only English imaginative writers today whom I can look at." Once again he had been more exacting as a young man, in writing to Norton in 1871:

"Howells edits, and observes and produces—the latter in his own particular line with more and more perfection. His recent sketches in the *Atlantic*, collected into a volume,[1] belong, I think, by the wondrous cunning of their manner, to very good literature. He seems to have resolved himself, however, [into] one who can write solely of what his fleshly eyes have seen; and for this reason I wish he were 'located' where they would rest upon richer and fairer things than this immediate landscape. Looking about for myself, I conclude that the face of nature and civilization in this our country is to a certain point a very sufficient literary field. But it will yield its secrets only to a really *grasping* imagination. This I think Howells lacks. (Of course *I* don't!) To write well and worthily of American things one need even more than elsewhere to be a *master*. But unfortunately one is less! . . . I myself have been scribbling some little tales which in the course of time you will have a chance to read. To write a series of good little tales I deem ample work for a life-time. I dream that my life-time shall have done it. It's at least a relief to have arranged one's life-time."

He was very grateful to Howells for agreeing in advance to serialize *Roderick Hudson*, and wrote him from Florence about it in the spring of 1874:

"I rec'd some days ago from my father the little note you had sent him signifying your acceptance of my story for next year's *Atlantic* and . . . I'm extremely glad that my thing is destined to see the light in the *Atlantic* rather than in t'other place and am very well satisfied with the terms. My story is to be on a theme I have had in my head a long time and once attempted to write something about. The theme is interesting, and if I do as I intend and hope, I think the tale must please. It shall, at any rate have had all my pains. The opening chapter takes place in America and the people are of our glorious race, but they are soon transported to Rome, where things are to go on famously. *Ecco.* Particulars, including name, (which, however, I incline to have simply that of the hero) on a future occasion. Suffice it that I promise you some tall writing. My only fear is that it may turn out taller than

---

[1] *Suburban Sketches.*

broad. That is, I thank you for the clause in the contract as to the numbers being less than twelve. As I desire above all things to write close, and avoid padding and prolixity, it may be that I shall have my tale by the 8th or 9th number. But there is time enough to take its measure scientifically. I don't see how in parts of the length of Aldrich's *Prudence Palfrey* (my protagonist is *not* named Publicius Parsons,) it can help stretching out a good piece." [1]

HJ to Howells, from Paris, 1876:

"Yes, I see a good deal of Turgenieff and am excellent friends with him. He has been very kind to me and has inspired me with an extreme regard. He is everything that one could desire—robust, sympathetic, modest, simple, profound, intelligent, naïf—in fine angelic. He has also made me acquainted with G. Flaubert, to whom I have likewise taken a great fancy, and at whose house I have seen the little *coterie* of the young realists in fiction. They are all charming talkers—though as editor of the austere *Atlantic* it would startle you to hear some of their projected subjects. The other day Edmond de Goncourt (the best of them) said he had been working very well on his novel—he had got upon an episode that greatly interested him, and into which he was going very far. *Flaubert*: 'What is it?' *E. de G.*: 'A whore-house de province.'"

When Howells criticized the tragic ending of *The American*, HJ made a defense which epitomizes the most deep-seated difference between their work:

"I am supposed to be busily scribbling for lucre this morning, but I must write you three lines of acknowledgment of your welcome long letter. Its most interesting portion was naturally your stricture on the close of my tale, which I accept with saintly meekness. These are matters which one feels about as one may, or as one can. I quite understand that as an editor you should go in for 'cheerful endings'; but I am sorry that as a private reader you are not struck with the inevitability of the *American* dénouement. I fancied that most folks would feel that Mme. de Cintré *couldn't*, when the finish came, marry Mr. N; and what the few persons who have spoken to me of the tale have expressed to me (e.g. Mrs. Kemble t'other day) was the fear that I should really put the marriage through. *Voyons;* it would have been impossible: they would have been an impossible couple, with an impossible problem before them. For instance—to speak very materially—where could they have lived? It was all very well for Newman to talk of giving her the whole world to choose from: but Asia and Africa being counted out, what would Europe and America have offered? Mme. de C. couldn't have lived in New York, depend upon it; and Newman, after his marriage

---

[1] *Roderick Hudson* ran in the *Atlantic* from January through December 1875.

(or rather *she*, after it) couldn't have dwelt in France. There would
have been nothing left but a farm out West. No, the interest of the
subject was, for me, (without my being at all a pessimist) its exemplifi-
cation of one of those insuperable difficulties which present themselves
in people's lives and from which the only issue is by forfeiture—by
losing something. It was cruelly hard for poor N. to lose, certainly:
but *que diable allait-il faire dans cette galère?* We are each the product
of circumstances and there are tall stone walls which fatally divide us.
I have written my story from Newman's side of the wall, and I understand so well how Mme. de Cintré couldn't really scramble over from
her side! If I had represented her as doing so I should have made a
prettier ending, certainly; but I should have felt as if I were throwing
a rather vulgar sop to readers who don't really know the world and
who don't measure the merit of a novel by its correspondence to the
same. Such readers assuredly have a right to their entertainment, but I
don't believe it is in me to give them, in a satisfactory way, what they
require.—I don't think that 'tragedies' have the presumption against
them as much as you appear to; and I see no logical reason why they
shouldn't be as *long* as comedies. In the drama they are usually allowed
to be longer—*non é vero?*—But whether the *Atlantic* ought to print
unlimited tragedy is another question—which you are doubtless quite
right in regarding as you do. Of course you couldn't have, for the
present, another evaporated marriage from me! I suspect it is the tragedies in life that arrest my attention more than the other things and say
more to my imagination."

HJ to Howells, from London, June 1879, at the time of the great
vogue of *Daisy Miller*:
"I am delighted to hear of the flourishing condition of my fame in
the U. S. and feel as if it were a great shame that I shouldn't be there
to reap a little the harvest of my glory. My fame indeed seems to do
very well everywhere—the proportions it has acquired here are a constant surprise to me; it is only my fortune that leaves to be desired.
. . . I am pledged to write a long novel as soon as possible, and am
obliged to delay it only because I can't literally afford it. Working
slowly and painfully as I do, I need for such a purpose a longish stretch
of time during which I am free to do nothing else, and such liberal
periods don't present themselves—I have always to keep the pot a-boil-
ing. The aforesaid fame, expanding through two hemispheres, is represented by a pecuniary equivalent almost grotesquely small. Your account of the vogue of *Daisy Miller* and the *International Episode*, for
instance, embittered my spirit when I reflected that it had awakened no
echo (to speak of) in my pocket. I have made $200 by the whole Amer-
ican career of *D.M.* and nothing at all by the *Episode* (beyond what
was paid—a very moderate sum—for the use of it in *Harper's Maga-*

zine). The truth is I am a very bad bargainer and was born to be victimized by the pitiless race of publishers. Excuse this sordid plaint, and don't indeed take it too hard for after all I shall have made this year much more than I have ever made before, and I shall little by little do much better still."

He was very firm in resisting the criticism that Howells made of his *Hawthorne*:

"Your review of my book is very handsome and friendly and commands my liveliest gratitude. Of course your graceful strictures seem to yourself more valid than they do to me. The little book was a tolerably deliberate and meditated performance, and I should be prepared to do battle for most of the convictions expressed. It is quite true I use the word provincial too many times—I hated myself for't, even while I did it (just as I overdo the epithet 'dusky.') But I don't at all agree with you in thinking that 'if it is not provincial for an Englishman to be English, a Frenchman French, etc., so it is not provincial for an American to be American.' So it is not provincial for a Russian, an Australian, a Portuguese, a Dane, a Laplander, to savour of their respective countries: that would be where the argument would land you. I think it is extremely provincial for a Russian to be very Russian, a Portuguese very Portuguese; for the simple reason that certain national types are essentially and intrinsically provincial. I sympathize even less with your protest against the idea that it takes an old civilization to set a novelist in motion—a proposition that seems to me so true as to be a truism. It is on manners, customs, usages, habits, forms, upon all these things matured and established, that a novelist lives—they are the very stuff his work is made of; and in saying that in the absence of those 'dreary and worn-out paraphernalia' which I enumerate as being wanting in American society, 'we have simply the whole of human life left,' you beg (to my sense) the question. I should say we had just so much less of it as these same 'paraphernalia' represent, and I think they represent an enormous quantity of it. I shall feel refuted only when we have produced (setting the present high company—yourself and me—for obvious reasons apart) a gentleman who strikes me as a novelist—as belonging to the company of Balzac and Thackeray. Of course, in the absence of this godsend, it is but a harmless amusement that we should reason about it, and maintain that if right were right he should already be here. I will freely admit that such a genius will get on *only* by agreeing with your view of the case—to do something great he must feel as you feel about it. But then I doubt whether such a genius—a man of the faculty of Balzac and Thackeray—*could* agree with you! When he does I will lie flat on my stomach and do him homage—in the very centre of the contributor's club, or on the threshold of the magazine, or in any public place you may appoint!—But I didn't mean to wrangle with you—I meant only to thank you and to express my sense of how happily you turn those things. . . .

"What is your *Cornhill* novel about? I am to precede it with a poorish story in three numbers—a tale purely American,[1] the writing of which made me feel acutely the want of the 'paraphernalia.' I *must* add, however (to return for a moment to this), that I applaud and esteem you highly for not feeling it; i.e. the want. You are certainly right—magnificently and heroically right—to do so, and on the day you make your readers—I mean the readers who know and appreciate the paraphernalia—do the same, you will be the American Balzac. That's a great mission—go in for it!"

HJ was always urging his friend to be bolder in the handling of his material, and when he wrote a resumptive essay about Howells' work up to 1886, he commented again upon his slight "perception of evil." But he was if anything overgenerous in his praise, and depreciating of his own books in comparison. Almost the only large exception he took to Howells' mature work was that he was "as little as possible of a critic," since "he talks from too small a point of view." He poured out his richest appreciation for *A Hazard of New Fortunes,* on which WJ also expressed himself with enthusiasm.

HJ to Howells, from Paris, 1884:

"I have been seeing something of Daudet, Goncourt and Zola; and there is nothing more interesting to me now than the effort and experiment of this little group, with its truly infernal intelligence of art, form, manner—its intense artistic life. They do the only kind of work, to-day, that I respect; and in spite of their ferocious pessimism and their handling of unclean things, they are at least serious and honest. The floods of tepid soap and water which under the name of novels are being vomited forth in England, seem to me, by contrast, to do little honour to our race. I say this to you, because I regard you as the great American naturalist. I don't think you go far enough, and you are haunted with romantic phantoms and a tendency to factitious glosses; but you are in the right path, and I wish you repeated triumphs there. . . . It isn't for me to reproach you . . . the said gloss being a constant defect of *my* characters; they have too much of it—too damnably much. But I am a failure!—comparatively. Read Zola's last thing: *La Joie de Vivre.* The title of course has a desperate irony: but the work is admirably solid and serious. . . . It is rather hard that as you are the only English novelist I read (except Miss Woolson),[2] I should not have more comfort with you."

---

[1] The references are to Howells' *The Undiscovered Country* and to HJ's *Washington Square.*

[2] HJ's enthusiastic admiration of Stevenson dates from shortly after this letter.

HJ on Howells, 1886:

"Mr. Howells has gone from one success to another, has taken possession of the field, and has become copious without detriment to his freshness. I need not enumerate his works in their order, for, both in America and in England (where it is a marked feature of the growing curiosity felt about American life that they are constantly referred to for information and verification), they have long been in everybody's hands. Quietly and steadily they have become better and better; one may like some of them more than others, but it is noticeable that from effort to effort the author has constantly enlarged his scope. His work is of a kind of which it is good that there should be much today—work of observation, of patient and definite notation. Neither in theory nor in practice is Mr. Howells a romancer; but the romancers can spare him; there will always be plenty of people to do their work. He has definite and downright convictions on the subject of the work that calls out to be done in opposition to theirs, and this fact is a source of much of the interest that he excites.

"It is a singular circumstance that to know what one wishes to do should be, in the field of art, a rare distinction; but it is incontestable that, as one looks about in our English and American fiction, one does not perceive any very striking examples of a vivifying faith. There is no discussion of the great question of how best to write, no exchange of ideas, no vivacity nor variety of experiment. A vivifying faith Mr. Howells may distinctly be said to possess, and he conceals it so little as to afford every facility to those people who are anxious to prove that it is the wrong one. He is animated by a love of the common, the immediate, the familiar and vulgar elements of life, and holds that in proportion as we move into the rare and strange we become vague and arbitrary; that truth of representation, in a word, can be achieved only so long as it is in our power to test and measure it. He thinks scarcely anything too paltry to be interesting, that the small and vulgar have been terribly neglected, and would rather see an exact account of a sentiment or a character he stumbles against every day than a brilliant evocation of a passion or a type he has never seen and does not even particularly believe in. He adores the real, the natural, the colloquial, the moderate, the optimistic, the domestic, and the democratic; looking askance at exceptions and perversities and superiorities, at surprising and incongruous phenomena in general. One must have seen a great deal before one concludes; the world is very large, and life is a mixture of many things; she by no means eschews the strange, and often risks combinations and effects that make one rub one's eyes. Nevertheless, Mr. Howells' standpoint is an excellent one for seeing a large part of the truth, and even if it were less advantageous, there would be a great deal to admire in the firmness with which he has planted himself. He hates a 'story,' and (this private feat is not impossible) has probably made up his mind very definitely as to what the pestilent thing consists of. In this respect he is more logical than M. Émile Zola, who partakes of the same aversion, but has greater lapses as well as greater audacities. Mr. Howells hates an artificial fable and a *dénouement* that is pressed into the service; he likes things to occur as they occur in life, where the manner of a great many of them is not to occur at all. He has observed that heroic emotion and brilliant opportunity are not particularly interwoven with our days, and indeed, in the way of omission, he *has* often practised in his pages a very considerable boldness. It has not, however, made what we find there any less interesting and less human.

"The picture of American life on Mr. Howells' canvas is not of a dazzling brightness, and my readers have probably wondered why it is that (among a sensitive people) he has so successfully escaped the imputation of a want of patriotism. The manners he describes—the desolation of the whole social prospect in *A Modern Instance* is perhaps the strongest expression of those influences—are eminently of a nature to discourage the intending visitor, and yet the westward pilgrim continues to arrive, in spite of the Bartley Hubbards and the Laphams, and the terrible practices at the country hotel in *Doctor Breen*, and at the Boston boarding-house in *A Woman's Reason*. This tolerance of depressing revelations is explained partly, no doubt, by the fact that Mr. Howells' truthfulness imposes itself—the representation is so vivid that the reader accepts it as he accepts, in his own affairs, the mystery of fate—and partly by a very different consideration, which is simply that if many of his characters are disagreeable, almost all of them are extraordinarily good, and with a goodness which is a ground for national complacency. If American life is on the whole, as I make no doubt whatever, more innocent than that of any other country, nowhere is the fact more patent than in Mr. Howells' novels, which exhibit so constant a study of the actual and so small a perception of evil. His women, in particular, are of the best—except, indeed, in the sense of being the best to live with. Purity of life, fineness of conscience, benevolence of motive, decency of speech, good nature, kindness, charity, tolerance (though, indeed, there is little but each other's manners for the people to tolerate), govern all the scene; the only immoralities are aberrations of thought, like that of Silas Lapham, or excesses of beer, like that of Bartley Hubbard. In the gallery of Mr. Howells' portraits there are none more living than the admirable, humorous images of those two ineffectual sinners. Lapham, in particular, is magnificent, understood down to the ground, inside and out—a creation which does Mr. Howells the highest honor. . . .

"There are other reflections that I might indulge in if I had more space. I should like, for instance, to allude in passing, for purposes of respectful remonstrance, to a phrase that he suffered the other day to fall from his pen (in a periodical, but not in a novel), to the effect that the style of a work of fiction is a thing that matters less and less all the while. Why less and less? It seems to me as great a mistake to say so as it would be to say that it matters more and more. It is difficult to see how it can matter either less or more. The style of a novel is a part of the execution of a work of art; the execution of a work of art is a part of its very essence, and that, it seems to me, must have mattered in all ages in exactly the same degree, and be destined always to do so. I can conceive of no state of civilization in which it shall not be deemed important, though of course there are states in which executants are clumsy. I should also venture to express a certain regret that Mr. Howells (whose style, in practice, after all, as I have intimated, treats itself to felicities which his theory perhaps would condemn) should appear increasingly to hold composition too cheap—by which I mean, should neglect the effect that comes from alternation, distribution, re-lief. He has an increasing tendency to tell his story altogether in con-versations, so that a critical reader sometimes wishes, not that the dia-logue might be suppressed (it is too good for that), but that it might be distributed, interspaced with narrative and pictorial matter. The author forgets sometimes to paint, to evoke the conditions and appearances, to build in the subject. He is doubtless afraid of doing these things in ex-cess, having seen in other hands what disastrous effects that error may have; but all the same I cannot help thinking that the divinest thing in a valid novel is the compendious, descriptive, pictorial touch, à la Daudet.

"It would be absurd to speak of Mr. Howells today in the encourag-ing tone that one would apply to a young writer who had given fine pledges, and one feels half guilty of that mistake if one makes a cheer-ful remark about his future. And yet we cannot pretend not to take a still more lively interest in his future than we have done in his past. It is hard to see how it can help being more and more fruitful, for his face is turned in the right direction, and his work is fed from sources which play us no tricks."

HJ to Howells, from Milan, May 1890:

"I have been not writing to you at a tremendous, an infamous rate, for a long time past; but I should indeed be sunk in baseness if I were to keep this pace after what has just happened. For what has just hap-pened is that I have been reading the *Hazard of New Fortunes* (I con-fess I should have liked to change the name for you,) and that it has filled me with communicable rapture. . . . To my charmed and grati-fied sense, the *Hazard* is simply prodigious. . . . I should think it would make you as happy as poor happiness will let us be, to turn off from one year to the other, and from a reservoir in daily domestic use,

such a free, full, rich flood. In fact your reservoir deluges me, altogether, with surprise as well as other sorts of effusion; by which I mean
that though you do much to empty it you keep it remarkably full. I
seem to myself, in comparison, to fill mine with a teaspoon and obtain
but a trickle. However, I don't mean to compare myself with you or
to compare you, in the particular case, with anything but life. When I
do that—with the life you see and represent—your faculty for representing it seems to me extraordinary and to shave the truth—the general truth you aim at—several degrees closer than anyone else begins to
do. You are less *big* than Zola, but you are ever so much less clumsy
and more really various, and moreover you and he don't see the same
things—you have a wholly different consciousness—*you* see a totally
different side of a different race. Man isn't at all *one* after all—it takes
so much of him to be American, to be French, &. I won't even compare you with something I have a sort of dim stupid sense you might
be and are not—for I don't in the least know that you might be it, after
all, or whether, if you were, you wouldn't cease to be that something
you are which makes me write to you thus. We don't know what people might give us that they don't—the only thing is to take them on
what they do and to allow them absolutely and utterly their conditions. This alone, for the tastes, secures freedom of enjoyment. I apply
the rule to you, and it represents a perfect triumph of appreciation;
because it makes me accept, largely, all your material from you—an
absolute gain when I consider that I should never take it from myself.
I note certain things which make me wonder at your form and your
fortune (e.g.—as I have told you before—the fatal colour in which
they let *you*, because you live at home—is it?—paint American life;
and the fact that there's a whole quarter of the heaven upon which, in
the matter of composition, you seem consciously—*is* it consciously?—
to have turned your back;) but these things have no relevancy whatever as grounds of dislike—simply because you communicate so completely *what* you undertake to communicate. The novelist is a particular *window*, absolutely—and of worth insofar as he is one; and it's
because you open so well and are hung so close over the street that I
could hang out of it all day long. Your very value is that you choose
your own street—heaven forbid I should have to choose it for you. If
I should say I mortally dislike the people who pass in it, I should seem
to be taking on myself that intolerable responsibility of selection which
is exactly such a luxury to be relieved of. Indeed I'm convinced that
no readers above the rank of an idiot—this number is moderate, I admit—really fail to take any view that is really *shown* them—any gift
(of subject) that's really given. The usual imbecility of the novel is that
the showing and giving simply don't come off—the reader never
touches the subject and the subject never touches the reader; the win-

dow is no window at all—but only childish *finta*, like the ornaments of
our beloved Italy. This is why, as a triumph of *communication*, I hold
the *Hazard* so rare and strong. You communicate in touches so close, so
fine, so true, so droll, so frequent. I am writing too much (you will
think me demented with chatter;) so that I can't go into specifications
of success. . . .

"I continue to scribble, though with relaxed continuity while abroad;
but I can't talk to you about it. One thing only is clear, that henceforth I must do, or half do, England in fiction—as the place I see most
today, and, in a sort of way, know best. I have at last more acquired
notions of it, on the whole, than of any other world, and it will serve
as well as any other. It has been growing distincter that America fades
from me, and as she never trusted me at best, I can trust *her*, for effect,
no longer. Besides I can't be doing *de chic*, from here, when you, on the
spot, are doing so brilliantly the *vécu*."

WJ to Howells, from Chocorua, August 1890:

"You've done it this time and no mistake! I've had a little leisure for
reading this summer and have just read, first your *Shadow of a Dream*,
and next your *Hazard of New Fortunes*, and can hardly recollect a
novel that has taken hold of me like the latter. Some compensations go
with being a mature man, do they not? You couldn't possibly have
done so solid a piece of work as that ten years ago, could you? The
steady unflagging flow of it is something wonderful. Never a weak
note, the number of characters, each intensely individual, the observation of detail, the everlasting wit and humor, and beneath all the bass
accompaniment of the human problem, the entire Americanness of it,
all make it a very great book, and one which will last when we shall
have melted into the infinite azure. Ah! my dear Howells, it's worth
something to be able to write such a book, and it is peculiarly *yours*
too, flavored with your idiosyncrasy. (The book is so d—d humane!)
. . . It makes one love as well as admire you, and so o'ershadows the
equally exquisite, though slighter *Shadow of a Dream* that I have no
adjectives left for that. . . . I have been in Cambridge six weeks and
corrected 1400 pages of proof. The year which shall have witnessed
the apparition of your *Hazard of New Fortunes*, of Harry's *Tragic
Muse*, and of *my Psychology* will indeed be a memorable one in American Literature!!"

Robertson James had also become strongly attracted to Howells at
this period, and wrote him in a strain that combines his father's views
of conventional society with an implicit criticism of what he does not
find in his brother's fiction—the lives of the common people:

"All the 'culture' on earth can never open this sense of heaven to us
—this sense of the relationship to the common lot with its warring
loves and passions which so slowly but grimly and surely are attaining

to final harmony. I hope you will never tire of celebrating these obscure lives, because it is only apparently in these that the great fight of destiny is taking place. It makes one reconciled to small fare, to postponed desires, to many bleak conditions—this being a sharer in the great human heart of man—no matter how base its appetites and passions, because their baseness only lingers through ignorance. I know of no more 'cleansing' process than to read *Annie Kilburn, The Undiscovered Country*, and *A Modern Instance*. If we get away from these common people all sense of humor must inevitably die in us, and humor seems to be the very citadel of saving truth. When every conventionally reputable interest on earth has crucified goodness and truth, these are always safe for they always find a safe and sane sanctuary in the worldling's wit. And I must say I think these things find a most reverend touch in the humor which makes all your books a delight.

"You are a busy man and I am an idler—therefore don't feel it necessary to respond to the effusions with which I occasionally visit you."

HJ continued intermittently to share with Howells his hopes and anxieties over his own work. Late in 1894 Howells wrote: "So far as literary standing is concerned there is no one who has your rank among us. That is, you and not I, or another, are he on whom the aspiring eyes are bent of those that hope to do something themselves; and I believe that if now you were to write a novel of the same quality as your *Lesson of the Master*, or *The Death of the Lion*, you would address a larger public than you ever have reached before."

With the failure of *Guy Domville* a few weeks later, this letter became a particularly timely solace for HJ:

"I am indebted to you for your most benignant letter of December last. It lies open before me and I read it again and am soothed and cheered and comforted again. You put your finger sympathetically on the place and spoke of what I wanted you to speak of. I *have* felt, for a long time past, that I have fallen upon evil days—every sign or symbol of one's being in the least *wanted*, anywhere or by any one, having so utterly failed. A new generation, that I know not, and mainly prize not, has taken universal possession. The sense of being utterly out of it weighed me down, and I asked myself what my future would be. All these melancholies were qualified indeed by one redeeming reflection— the sense of how little, for a good while past (for reasons very logical, but accidental and temporary,) I had been producing. I *did* say to myself 'Produce again—produce; produce better than ever, and all will yet be well'; and there was sustenance in that so far as it went. But it has meant much more to me since *you* have said it—for it *is*, practically, what you admirably say. It is exactly, moreover, what I meant to admirably do—and have meant, all along, about this time to get into the motion of. The whole thing, however, represents a great change in my life, inasmuch as what is clear is that periodical publication is practically closed to me—I'm the last hand that the magazines, in this country or in the U. S., seem to want. I won't afflict you with the now accumulated (during all these past years) evidence on which this induction rests—and I have spoken of it to no creature till, at this late day, I speak of it to you. . . . All this, I needn't say, is for your *segretissimo* ear. What it means is that 'production' for me, as aforesaid, means production of the little *book*, pure and simple—independent of any antecedent appearance; and, truth to tell, now that I wholly *see* that, and have at last accepted it, I am, incongruously, not at all sorry. I am indeed very serene. I have always hated the magazine form, magazine conditions and manners, and much of the magazine company. I hate the hurried little subordinate part that one plays in the catchpenny picture-book—and the negation of all literature that the insolence of the picture-book imposes. The money-difference will be great—but not so great after a bit as at first; and the other differences will be so all to the good that even from the economic point of view they will tend to make up for that and perhaps finally even completely do so. It is about the distinctness of one's *book-position* that you have so substantially reassured me; and I mean to do far better work than ever I have done before. I have, potentially, improved immensely and am bursting with ideas and subjects—though the act of composition is with me more and more slow, painful and difficult. I shall never again write a long novel; but I hope to write six immortal short ones—and some tales of the same quality. Forgive, my dear Howells, the cynical egotism of these remarks—the fault of which is in your own sympathy."

Five years later Howells suggested that James might interweave two of his themes by undertaking an "international" ghost-story. This resulted, ultimately, in *The Sense of the Past*, but at the moment, though impressed with the possibilities in Howells' suggestion, HJ was veering back again to the long "architectural" novel, and responded:

"Preoccupied with . . . things of the altogether human order now fermenting in my brain, I don't care for 'terror' (terror, that is, without 'pity') so much as I otherwise might. . . . The scheme to which I am *now* alluding is lovely—human, dramatic, international, exquisitely 'pure,' exquisitely everything; only absolutely condemned, from the germ up, to be workable in not less than 100,000 words. If 100,000 were what you had asked me for, I would fall back upon it ('terror' failing) like a flash; and even send you, without delay, a detailed Scenario of it that I drew up a year ago; beginning then—a year ago—to *do* the thing —immediately afterwards; and then again pausing for reasons extraneous and economic. . . . It really constitutes, at any rate, the work I

intimately want actually to be getting on with. . . . My genius, I may
even say, absolutely thrives—and I am unbrokenly yours. . . ."

The "scenario" alluded to was for *The Ambassadors,* concerning
which HJ wrote further, after its completion in the summer of 1901:

"Ever since receiving and reading your elegant volume of short tales
—the arrival of which from you was affecting and delightful to me—
I've meant to write to you, but the wish has struggled in vain with the
daily distractions of a tolerably busy summer. I should blush, however,
if the season were to melt away without my greeting and thanking you.
I read your book with joy and found in it recalls from far far away—
stray echoes and scents as from another, the American, the prehistoric
existence. The thing that most took me was that entitled *A Difficult
Case,* which I found beautiful and admirable, ever so true and ever so
done. But I fear I more, almost than anything else, lost myself in mere
envy of your freedom to do, and, speaking vulgarly, to place, things
of that particular and so agreeable dimension—I mean the dimension of
most of the stories in the volume. It is sternly enjoined upon one here
(where an agent-man does what he can for me) that everything—every
hundred—above 6 or 7 thousand words is fatal to 'placing'; so that I do
them of that length, with great care, art and time (much reboiling,)
and then, even then, can scarcely get them worked off—published even
when they've been accepted. . . . So that (though I don't know why I
inflict on you these sordid groans—except that I haven't any one else
to inflict them on—and the mere affront—of being unused so inordinately long—is almost intolerable) I don't feel incited in that direction. Fortunately, however, I am otherwise immersed. I lately finished
a tolerably long novel, and I've written a third of another—with still
another begun and two or three more subjects awaiting me thereafter
like carriages drawn up at the door and horses champing their bits.
And àpropos of the first named of these, which is in the hands of the
Harpers, I have it on my conscience to let you know that the idea of
the fiction in question had its earliest origin in a circumstance mentioned to me—years ago—in respect to no less a person than yourself.
At Torquay, once, our young friend Jon. Sturges came down to spend
some days near me, and, lately from Paris, repeated to me five words
you had said to him one day on his meeting you during a call at Whis-
tler's. I thought the words charming—you have probably quite forgotten them; and the whole incident suggestive—so far as it was an
incident; and, more than this, they presently caused me to see in them
the faint vague germ, the mere point of the *start*, of a subject. I noted
them, to that end, as I note everything; [1] and years afterwards (that is

---

[1] The beginning of HJ's notebook
entry for October 31, 1895 reads: "I
was struck last evening with something
that Jonathan Sturges . . . mentioned

three or four) the subject sprang at me, one day, out of my notebook. I don't know if it be good; at any rate it has been treated now, for whatever it is; and my point is that it had long before—it had in the very act of striking me as a germ—got away from *you* or from anything like you! had become impersonal and independent. Nevertheless your initials figure in my little note; and if you hadn't said the five words to Jonathan he wouldn't have had them (most sympathetically and interestingly) to relate, and I shouldn't have had them to work in my imagination. The moral is that you are responsible for the whole business. But I've had it, since the book was finished, much at heart to tell you so. May you carry the burden bravely!"

When Howells regaled him with an unlikely New York news item in the winter of 1902, HJ responded with delight:

"Your most kind communication . . . in respect to the miraculously-named 'uptown' apartment house has at once deeply agitated me and wildly uplifted me. The agitation, as I call it, is verily but the tremor, the intensity of hope, of the delirious dream that such a stroke may 'bring my books before the public,' or do something toward it—coupled with the reassertion of my constant, too constant, conviction that no power on earth can ever do that. They are behind, irremovably behind, the public, and fixed there for my lifetime at least; and as the public hasn't eyes in the back of its head, and scarcely even in the front, no consequences can ensue. The *Henry James,* I opine, will be a terrifically 'private' hotel, and will languish like the Lord of Burleigh's wife, under the burden of an honour 'unto which it was not born.' Refined, liveried, 'two-toiled,' it will have been a short-lived, hectic paradox, and will presently have to close in order to reopen as the Mary Johnston or the Kate Douglas Wiggin or the James Lane Allen. Best of all as the Edith Wharton!"

---

to me: it was only 10 words, but I seemed, as usual, to catch a glimpse of a *sujet de nouvelle* in it. We were talking of W. D. H. and of his having seen him during a short and interrupted stay H. had made 18 months ago in Paris—called away—back to America, when he had just come, at the end of 10 days by the news of the death—or illness—of his father. He had scarcely been in Paris, ever—in former days, and he had come there to see his domiciled and initiated son, who was at the Beaux Arts. Virtually—in the evening, as it were, of life, it was all new to him: all, all, all. Sturges said he seemed sad—rather brooding; and I asked him what gave (Sturges,) that impression. 'Oh—somewhere—I forget, when I was with

him—he laid his hand on my shoulder and said apropos of some remark of mine: 'Oh, you are young, you are young—be glad of it: be glad of it and *live*. Live all you can: it's a mistake not to. It doesn't so much matter what you do—but live. This place makes it all come over me. I see it now. I haven't done so—and now I'm old. It's too late. It has gone past me—I've lost it. You have time. You are young. Live!' I amplify and improve a little—but that was the tone. It touches me—I can see him—I can hear him. Immediately, of course, as everything, thank God, does —it suggests a little situation." Thereupon HJ proceeded to add several pages, which took the situation farther and farther from Howells.

HJ to Howells, December 1902:

"Nothing more delightful, or that has touched me more closely, even
to the spring of tears, has befallen me for years, literally, than to receive your beautiful letter . . . so largely and liberally anent *The
Wings of the Dove*. Every word of it goes to my heart and to 'thank'
you for it seems a mere grimace. The same post brought me a letter
from dear John Hay, so that my measure has been full. I haven't known
anything about the American 'notices,' heaven save the mark! any more
than about those here (which I am told, however, have been remarkably genial;) so that I have *not* had the sense of confrontation with a
public more than usually childish—I mean had it in any special way. I
confess, however, that this is my chronic sense—the more than usual
childishness of publics: and it is (has been,) in my mind, long since
discounted, and my work definitely insists upon being independent of
such phantasms and on unfolding itself wholly from its own 'innards.'
Of course, in our conditions, doing anything decent is pure disinterested, unsupported, unrewarded heroism; but that's in the day's work.
The *faculty of attention* has utterly vanished from the general anglo-
saxon mind, extinguished at its source by the big blatant *Bayadère* of
Journalism, of the newspaper and the *picture* (above all) magazine;
who keeps screaming 'Look at *me*, *I* am the thing, and I only, the thing
that will keep you in relation with me *all the time* without your having
to attend *one minute* of the time.' If you are moved to write anything
anywhere about the *W. of the D.* do say something of that—it so awfully
wants saying. But we live in a lovely age for literature or for any art but
the mere visual. Illustrations, loud simplifications and *grossissements*, the
big building (good for John,[1]) the 'mounted' play, the prose that is
careful to be in the tone of, and with the distinction of a newspaper
or bill-poster advertisement—these, and these only, meseems, 'stand a
chance.' But why do I talk of such chances? I am melted at your reading *en famille The Sacred Fount*, which you will, I fear, have found
chaff in the mouth and which is one of several things of mine, in these
last years, that have paid the penalty of having been conceived only as
the 'short story' that (alone, apparently) I could hope to work off
somewhere (which I mainly failed of,) and then *grew* by a rank force
of its own into something of which the idea had, modestly, never been
to be a book. That is essentially the case with the *S. F.*, planned, like
The Spoils of Poynton, What Maisie Knew, The Turn of the Screw,
and various others, as a story of the '8 to 10 thousand words'!! and then
having accepted its bookish necessity or destiny in consequence of becoming already, at the start, 20,000, accepted it ruefully and blush-
ingly, moreover, since, *given the tenuity of the idea*, the larger quantity

---

[1] Howells' son, the architect.

of treatment hadn't been aimed at. I remember how I would have 'chucked' *The Sacred Fount* at the 15th thousand word, if in the first place I could have afforded to 'waste' 15,000, and if in the second I were not always ridden by a superstitious terror of not finishing, for finishing's and for the precedent's sake, what I have begun. I am a fair coward about *dropping,* and the book, in question, I fear, is, more than anything else, a monument to that superstition. When, if it meets my eye, I say to myself, 'You know you might not have finished it,' I make the remark not in natural reproach, but, I confess, in craven relief."

HJ to Howells, about the prefaces, August 1908:
"My actual attitude about the Lucubrations is almost only, and quite inevitably, that they make to me, for weariness; by reason of their number and extent—I've now but a couple more to write. . . . They are, in general, a sort of plea for Criticism, for Discrimination, for Appreciation on other than infantile lines—as against the so almost universal Anglo-Saxon absence of these things; which tends so, in our general trade, it seems to me, to break the heart. However, I am afraid I'm too sick of the mere doing of them, and of the general strain of the effort to avoid the deadly danger of repetition, to say much to the purpose about them. They ought, collected together, none the less, to form a sort of comprehensive manual or *vademecum* for aspirants in our arduous profession. Still, it will be long before I shall want to collect them together for that purpose and furnish them with a final Preface. I've done with prefaces forever. As for the Edition itself, it has racked me a little that I've had to leave out so many things that would have helped to make for rather a more vivid completeness. I don't at all regret the things, pretty numerous, that I've omitted from deep-seated preference and design; but I do a little those that are crowded out by want of space and by the rigour of the 23 vols., and 23 only, which were the condition of my being able to arrange the matter with the Scribners at all. Twenty-three do seem a fairly blatant array —and yet I rather surmise that there may have to be a couple of supplementary volumes for certain too marked omissions; such being, on the whole, detrimental to an all professedly comprehensive presentation of one's stuff. Only these, I pray God, without Prefaces! And I have even, in addition, a dim vague view of reintroducing, with a good deal of titivation and cancellation, the too-diffuse but, I somehow feel, tolerably full and good *Bostonians* of nearly a quarter of a century ago; that production never having, even to my much disciplined patience, received any sort of justice. But it will take, doubtless, a great deal of artful re-doing—and I haven't, now, had the courage or time for anything so formidable as touching and re-touching it. I feel at the same

time how the series suffers commercially from its having been dropped so completely out. . . .

"I could really shed salt tears of impatience and yearning to get back, after so prolonged a blocking of traffic, to too dreadfully postponed and neglected 'creative' work; an accumulated store of ideas and reachings-out for which even now clogs my brain. . . . I never have had such a sense of almost bursting, late in the day though it be, with violent and lately too much repressed creative (again!) intention."

HJ's last extended comment on the work of his old friend was an open letter for the celebration of Howells' seventy-fifth birthday, in 1912:

* * * * *

My dear Howells,

It is made known to me that they are soon to feast in New York the newest and freshest of the splendid birthdays to which you keep treating us, and that your many friends will meet round you to rejoice in it and reaffirm their allegiance. I shall not be there, to my sorrow, and though this is inevitable I yet want to be missed, peculiarly and monstrously missed; so that these words shall be a public apology for my absence: read by you, if you like and can stand it, but better still read *to* you and in fact straight *at* you, by whoever will be so kind and so loud and so distinct. For I doubt, you see, whether any of your toasters and acclaimers have anything like my ground and title for being with you at such an hour. There can scarce be one, I think, to-day, who has known you from so far back, who has kept so close to you for so long, and who has such fine old reasons—so old, yet so well preserved—to feel your virtue and sound your praise. My debt to you began wellnigh half a century ago, in the most personal way possible, and then kept growing and growing with your own admirable growth—but always rooted in the early intimate benefit. This benefit was that you held out your open editorial hand to me at the time I began to write—and I allude especially to the summer of 1866—with a frankness and sweetness of hospitality that was really the making of me, the making of the confidence that required help and sympathy and that I should otherwise, I think, have strayed and stumbled about a long time without acquiring. You showed me the way and opened me the door; you wrote to me, and confessed yourself struck with me—I have never forgotten the beautiful thrill of *that*. You published me at once—and paid me, above all, with a dazzling promptitude; magnificently, I felt, and so that nothing since has ever quite come up to it. More than this even, you cheered me on with a sympathy that was in itself an inspiration. I mean that you talked to me and listened to me—ever so patiently and genially and suggestively conversed and consorted with me. This won me to you irresistibly and made you the most interesting person I knew—lost as I was in the charming sense that my best friend was an editor, and an almost insatiable editor, and that such a delicious being as that was a kind of property of my own. Yet how didn't that interest still quicken and spread when I became aware that—with such attention as you could spare from us, for I recognised my fellow beneficiaries—you had started to cultivate *your* great garden as well; the tract of virgin soil that, beginning as a cluster of bright, fresh, sunny and savoury patches, close about the house, as it were, was to become that vast goodly pleasaunce of art and observation, of appreciation and creation, in which you have laboured, without a break or a lapse, to this day, and in which you have grown so grand a show of—well, really of everything. Your liberal visits to *my* plot, and your free-handed purchases there, were still greater events when I began to see you handle, yourself, with such ease the key to our rich and inexhaustible mystery. Then the question of what you would make of your own powers began to be even more interesting than the question of what you would make of mine—all the more, I confess, as you had ended by settling this one so happily. My confidence in myself, which you had so helped me to, gave way to a fascinated impression of your own spread and growth; for you broke out so insistently and variously that it was a charm to watch and an excitement to follow you. The only drawback that I remember suffering from was that *I*, your original debtor, couldn't print or publish or pay you—which would have been a sort of ideal *re*payment and of enhanced credit; you could take care of yourself so beautifully, and I could (unless by some occasional happy chance or rare favour) scarce so much as glance at your proofs or have a glimpse of your "endings." I could only read you, full-blown and finished—and see, with the rest of the world, how you were doing it again and again.

That then was what I had with time to settle down to—the common attitude of seeing you do it again and again; keep on doing it, with your heroic consistency and your noble, genial abundance, during all the years that have seen so many apparitions come and go, so many vain flourishes attempted and achieved, so many little fortunes made and unmade, so many weaker inspirations betrayed and spent. Having myself to practise meaner economies, I have admired, from period to period, your so ample and liberal flow; wondered at your secret for doing positively a little—what do I say a little? I mean a magnificent deal!—of Everything. I seem to myself to have faltered and languished, to have missed more occasions than I have grasped, while you have piled up your monument just by remaining at your post. For you have had the advantage, after all, of breathing an air that has suited and nourished you; of sitting up to your neck, as I may say—or at least up

to your waist—amid the sources of your inspiration. There and so you
were at your post; there and so the spell could ever work for you,
there and so your relation to all your material grow closer and stronger,
your perception penetrate, your authority accumulate. They make a
great array, a literature in themselves, your studies of American life, so
acute, so direct, so disinterested, so preoccupied but with the fine truth
of the case; and the more attaching to me, always, for their referring
themselves to a time and an order when we knew together what American life *was*—or thought we did, deluded though we may have been!
I don't pretend to measure the effect, or to sound the depths, if they be
not the shallows, of the huge wholesale importations and so-called as-
similations of this later time; I can only feel and speak for those conditions in which, as "quiet observers," as careful painters, as sincere artists, we could still, in our native, our human and social element, know
more or less where we were and feel more or less what we had hold of.
You knew and felt these things better than I; you had learnt them
earlier and more intimately, and it was impossible, I think, to be in
more instinctive and more informed possession of the general truth of
your subject than you happily found yourself. The *real* affair of the
American case and character, as it met your view and brushed your
sensibility, that was what inspired and attached you, and, heedless of
foolish flurries from other quarters, of all wild or weak slashings of the
air and wavings in the void, you gave yourself to it with an incorruptible faith. You saw your field with a rare lucidity; you saw all it
had to give in the way of the romance of the real and the interest and
the thrill and the charm of the common, as one may put it; the character and the comedy, the point, the pathos, the tragedy, the particular
home-grown humanity under your eyes and your hand and with which
the life all about you was closely interknitted. Your hand reached out
to these things with a fondness that was in itself a literary gift, and
played with them as the artist only and always can play: freely,
quaintly, incalculably, with all the assurance of his fancy and his irony,
and yet with that fine taste for the truth and the pity and the meaning
of the matter which keeps the temper of observation both sharp and
sweet. To observe, by such an instinct and by such reflection, is to find
work to one's hand and a challenge in every bush; and as the familiar
American scene thus bristled about you, so, year by year, your vision
more and more justly responded and swarmed. You put forth A Modern Instance, and The Rise of Silas Lapham, and A Hazard of New
Fortunes, and The Landlord at Lion's Head, and The Kentons (that
perfectly classic illustration of your spirit and your form,) after having
put forth in perhaps lighter-fingered prelude A Foregone Conclusion,
and The Undiscovered Country, and The Lady of the Aroostook, and
The Minister's Charge—to make of a long list too short a one; with the

effect, again and again, of a feeling for the human relation, as the social climate of our country qualifies, intensifies, generally conditions and colours it, which, married in perfect felicity to the expression you found for its service, constituted the originality that we want to fasten upon you, as with silver nails, to-night. Stroke by stroke and book by book your work was to become, for this exquisite notation of our whole democratic light and shade and give and take, in the highest degree *documentary;* so that none other, through all your fine long season, could approach it in value and amplitude. None, let me say too, was to approach it in essential distinction; for you had grown master, by insidious practices best known to yourself, of a method so easy and so natural, so marked with the personal element of your humour and the play, not less personal, of your sympathy, that the critic kept coming on its secret connection with the grace of letters much as Fenimore Cooper's Leatherstocking—so knowing to be able to do it!—comes, in the forest, on the subtle tracks of Indian braves. However, these things take us far, and what I wished mainly to put on record is my sense of that unfailing, testifying truth in you which will keep you from ever being neglected. The critical intelligence—if any such fitful and discredited light may still be conceived as within our sphere—has not at all begun to render you its tribute. The more inquiringly and perceivingly it shall still be projected upon the American life we used to know, the more it shall be moved by the analytic and historic spirit, the more indispensable, the more a vessel of light, will you be found. It's a great thing to have used one's genius and done one's work with such quiet and robust consistency that they fall by their own weight into that happy service. You may remember perhaps, and I like to recall, how the great and admirable Taine, in one of the fine excursions of his French curiosity, greeted you as a precious painter and a sovereign witness. But his appreciation, I want you to believe with me, will yet be carried much further, and then—though you may have argued yourself happy, in your generous way and with your incurable optimism, even while noting yourself not understood—your really beautiful time will come. Nothing so much as feeling that he may himself perhaps help a little to bring it on can give pleasure to yours all faithfully,

Henry James.

*   *   *

PARTIAL PORTRAITS

A Family Miscellany

SINCE this chapter aims simply to suggest the further range of men and books upon which the family exercised their taste, it may properly start with HJ's "The Science of Criticism" (1891), an essay titled with mild irony, since HJ wanted to indicate how much criticism can be an art. In that assumption, and in his war against the philistine reviewers on behalf of French distinction, he was still a disciple of Matthew Arnold, as Arnold had been of Sainte-Beuve. Although HJ had called his first book of criticism *French Poets and Novelists* (1878), only three of the twelve essays were given to poets. Those dealing with Musset and Gautier make pleasant if not particularly original or incisive introductions for English-speaking readers, but to his treatment of Baudelaire HJ brought the rigid conception of morality which he was soon to outgrow but which made him miss entirely Baudelaire's sense of evil, and see in him hardly more than a vicious fondness for filth. Speaking of Baudelaire's translations of Poe, he added that Poe "was vastly the greater charlatan of the two, as well as the greater genius," and, furthermore, that "an enthusiasm for Poe is the mark of a decidedly primitive stage of reflection." In his subsequent criticism HJ devoted even less attention to poetry and treated it on his own ground only when he wrote his late essay on "The Novel in *The Ring and the Book*" (1912).

No member of the family appears to have had any exceptionally developed interest in music, but HJ remained concerned with painting, and often went to Paris especially for the Salon. After reading his early piece on Tintoretto in the *Nation* (1873), Ruskin declared to Norton that he would count HJ "among the men for whom he should especially work." But HJ did not develop a distinctive method as a critic of painting, and though many of the scenes in his fiction show that he could see with the eyes of an impressionist, his expressed tastes

stayed fairly conventional, and would seem to have stopped just short
of a full appreciation of this new French movement of his own day.
The most effective pieces in *Picture and Text* (1893), his one book
dealing with painters and illustrators, are those on Daumier, whom he
estimated highly as a social critic before that estimate was general, and
on his younger fellow American, Sargent. HJ recorded in his notebook that he wanted a story like "The Coxon Fund" to be "an Impression—as one of Sargent's pictures is an impression," but when writing about that painter he hardly analyzed his technique. The chief
interest still inhering in HJ's essay is his instinctive perception that an
artist who seemed to have learned everything about his craft at the
very dawn of his career might encounter a dangerous future.

It is surprising that WJ's early absorption with painting did not yield
some later essays on art, but he seems to have transmuted that absorption
into his own vivid word-impressions of the outer and inner world. He
kept up with HJ a running comment upon all the fiction he read. They
shared several enthusiasms for their contemporaries—for Stevenson
even more than for Howells, and later for Kipling, and later still for
Wells. But in the case of Kipling they both outgrew their first excitement on strikingly similar grounds. In 1899, at the time of his increasing anxiety over imperialism, WJ wrote:

"Now that by his song-making power he is the mightiest force in the
formation of the 'Anglo-Saxon' character, I wish he would hearken a
bit more to his deeper human self and a bit less to his shallower jingo
self. If the Anglo-Saxon race would drop its sniveling cant it would
have a good deal less of a 'burden' to carry. We're the most loath-
somely canting crew that God ever made. Kipling knows perfectly
well that our camps in the tropics are not college settlements or our
armies bands of philanthropists, slumming it; and I think it a shame
that he should represent us to ourselves in that light. I wish he would
try a bit interpreting the savage *soul* to us, as he *could*, instead of using
such official and conventional phrases as 'half-devil and half-child,'
which leaves the whole insides out."

A couple of years earlier HJ had concluded, even more trenchantly:
"His *Ballad* future may still be big. But my view of his prose future
has much shrunken in the light of one's increasingly observing how
little of life he can make use of. Almost nothing civilised save steam
and patriotism—and the latter only in verse, where I *hate* it so, especially mixed up with God and goodness, that that half spoils my enjoyment of his great talent. Almost nothing of the complicated soul or
of the female form or of any question of *shades*—which latter constitute, to my sense, the real formative literary discipline. In his earliest
time I thought he perhaps contained the seeds of an English Balzac; but
I have quite given that up in proportion as he has come steadily from

the less simple in subject to the more simple—from the Anglo-Indians to the natives, from the natives to the Tommies, from the Tommies to the quadrupeds, from the quadrupeds to the fish, and from the fish to the engines and screws."

In their earlier days the whole family had discussed George Eliot, about whose books HJ wrote more reviews than he devoted to any other author. The first great event of his trip abroad in 1869 was his meeting with her, and his description in a letter home at that time makes an engaging companion-piece for his reminiscences, in *The Middle Years*, of a somewhat later ill-starred visit to that formidable lady. As HJ looked back, at the end of his life, to mid-Victorian London, his humor was at its ripest, as in his account of a fantastic day at Tennyson's, when the Bard expatiated on the Marquis de Sade, without the faintest notion of the implications of what he was saying. Such passages make us realize how much we lost through the accident that HJ's autobiography of his maturity was broken off by death when it was hardly more than begun.

Alice James also interwove comments upon her contemporaries into her journal, not as detached estimates, but in immediate response to something that had engaged her quick attention. She had her view of George Eliot, and of the Darwinian mind; and her sisterly reaction to an unfavorable criticism of HJ's essay on Browning's death is in her finest vein of inner comedy.

WJ's tribute to Agassiz makes a natural companion-piece to his tribute to Emerson, for Agassiz had taught him what it meant to be a naturalist. WJ never forgot this master's recital of Goethe's lines contrasting the grayness of all theory with the green tree of life. On the expedition to Brazil young WJ had learned to declare war on abstraction, and he was still waging the same campaign when, at the close of his life, he rejoiced to think that Bergson was giving a death-blow to Intellectualism.

WJ appears in his fullest strength in some of his many comments upon other philosophers. His early refusal to contribute to a monument to Schopenhauer was in keeping with his view that pessimism and fatalism were enemies to be slain by moral force. His range of appreciation of his colleagues, of Royce and Santayana and Peirce and Bergson, even when some of them were his adversaries, reveals again the personal warmth and generosity that won him so many friends.

* * * * *

HJ: THE SCIENCE OF CRITICISM (1891)

IF LITERARY criticism may be said to flourish among us at all, it certainly flourishes immensely, for it flows through the periodical press like a river that has burst its dikes. The quantity of it is prodigious, and it is a commodity of which, however the demand may be estimated, the supply will be sure to be in any supposable extremity the last thing to fail us. What strikes the observer above all, in such an affluence, is the unexpected proportion the discourse uttered bears to the objects discoursed of—the paucity of examples, of illustrations and productions, and the deluge of doctrine suspended in the void; the profusion of talk and the contraction of experiment, of what one may call literary conduct. This, indeed, ceases to be an anomaly as soon as we look at the conditions of contemporary journalism. Then we see that these conditions have engendered the practice of "reviewing"—a practice that in general has nothing in common with the art of criticism. Periodical literature is a huge, open mouth which has to be fed—a vessel of immense capacity which has to be filled. It is like a regular train which starts at an advertised hour, but which is free to start only if every seat be occupied. The seats are many, the train is ponderously long, and hence the manufacture of dummies for the seasons when there are not passengers enough. A stuffed mannikin is thrust into the empty seat, where it makes a creditable figure till the end of the journey. It looks sufficiently like a passenger, and you know it is not one only when you perceive that it neither says anything nor gets out. The guard attends to it when the train is shunted, blows the cinders from its wooden face and gives a different crook to its elbow, so that it may serve for another run. In this way, in a well-conducted periodical, the blocks of *remplissage* are the dummies of criticism—the recurrent, regulated breakers in the tide of talk. They have a reason for being, and the situation is simpler when we perceive it. It helps to explain the disproportion I just mentioned, as well, in many a case, as the quality of the particular discourse. It helps us to understand that the "organs of public opinion" must be no less copious than punctual, that publicity must maintain its high standard, that ladies and gentlemen may turn an honest penny by the free expenditure of ink. It gives us a glimpse of the high figure presumably reached by all the honest pennies accumulated in the cause, and throws us quite into a glow over the march of civilization and the way we have organized our conveniences. From this point of view it might indeed go far towards making us enthusiastic about our age. What is more calculated to inspire us with a just complacency than the sight of a new and flourishing industry, a fine economy of production? The great business of reviewing has, in its roaring routine, many of the signs of blooming health, many of the features which beguile one into rendering an involuntary homage to successful enterprise.

Yet it is not to be denied that certain captious persons are to be met who are not carried away by the spectacle, who look at it much askance, who see but dimly whither it tends, and who find no aid to vision even in the great light (about itself, its spirit, and its purposes, among other things) that it might have been expected to diffuse. "Is there any such great light at all?" we may imagine the most restless of the sceptics to inquire, "and isn't the effect rather one of a certain kind of pretentious and unprofitable gloom?" The vulgarity, the crudity, the stupidity which this cherished combination of the off-hand review and of our wonderful system of publicity have put into circulation on so vast a scale may be represented, in such a mood, as an unprecedented invention for darkening counsel. The bewildered spirit may ask itself, without speedy answer, What is the function in the life of man of such a periodicity of platitude and irrelevance? Such a spirit will wonder how the life of man survives it, and, above all, what is much more important, how literature resists it; whether, indeed, literature does resist it and is not speedily going down beneath it. The signs of this catastrophe will not in the case we suppose be found too subtle to be pointed out—the failure of distinction, the failure of style, the failure of knowledge, the failure of thought. The case is therefore one for recognizing with dismay that we are paying a tremendous price for the diffusion of penmanship and opportunity; that the multiplication of endowments for chatter may be as fatal as an infectious disease; that literature lives essentially, in the sacred depths of its being, upon example, upon perfection wrought; that, like other sensitive organisms, it is highly susceptible of demoralization, and that nothing is better calculated than irresponsible pedagogy to make it close its ears and lips. To be puerile and untutored about it is to deprive it of air and light, and the consequence of its keeping bad company is that it loses all heart. We may, of course, continue to talk about it long after it has bored itself to death, and there is every appearance that this is mainly the way in which our descendants will hear of it. They will, however, acquiesce in its extinction.

This, I am aware, is a dismal conviction, and I do not pretend to state the case gayly. The most I can say is that there are times and places in which it strikes one as less desperate than at others. One of the places is Paris, and one of the times is some comfortable occasion of being there. The custom of rough-and-ready reviewing is, among the French, much less rooted than with us, and the dignity of criticism is, to my perception, in consequence much higher. The art is felt to be one of the most difficult, the most delicate, the most occasional; and the material on which it is exercised is subject to selection, to restriction. That is, whether or no the French are always right as to what they do notice, they strike me as infallible as to what they don't. They publish hundreds of books which are never noticed at all, and yet they are much neater book-makers than we. It is recognized that such volumes have nothing to say to the critical sense, that they do not belong to litera-

ture, and that the possession of the critical sense is exactly what makes
it impossible to read them and dreary to discuss them—places them, as
a part of critical experience, out of the question. The critical sense, in
France, *ne se dérange pas*, as the phrase is, for so little. No one would
deny, on the other hand, that when it does set itself in motion it goes
further than with us. It handles the subject in general with finer finger-
tips. The bluntness of ours, as tactile implements addressed to an exquisite process, is still sometimes surprising, even after frequent exhibition. We blunder in and out of the affair as if it were a railway station
—the easiest and most public of the arts. It is in reality the most complicated and the most particular. The critical sense is so far from frequent
that it is absolutely rare, and the possession of the cluster of qualities
that minister to it is one of the highest distinctions. It is a gift inestimably precious and beautiful; therefore, so far from thinking that
it passes overmuch from hand to hand, one knows that one has only to
stand by the counter an hour to see that business is done with baser
coin. We have too many small school-masters; yet not only do I not
question in literature the high utility of criticism, but I should be
tempted to say that the part it plays may be the supremely beneficent
one when it proceeds from deep sources, from the efficient combination of experience and perception. In this light one sees the critic as
the real helper of the artist, a torch-bearing outrider, the interpreter, the
brother. The more the tune is noted and the direction observed the
more we shall enjoy the convenience of a critical literature. When one
thinks of the outfit required for free work in this spirit, one is ready to
pay almost any homage to the intelligence that has put it on; and when
one considers the noble figure completely equipped—armed *cap-à-pie*
in curiosity and sympathy—one falls in love with the apparition. It
certainly represents the knight who has knelt through his long vigil and
who has the piety of his office. For there is something sacrificial in his
function, inasmuch as he offers himself as a general touchstone. To
lend himself, to project himself and steep himself, to feel and feel till he
understands, and to understand so well that he can say, to have perception at the pitch of passion and expression as embracing as the air, to be
infinitely curious and incorrigibly patient, and yet plastic and inflam-
mable and determinable, stooping to conquer and serving to direct—
these are fine chances for an active mind, chances to add the idea of
independent beauty to the conception of success. Just in proportion as
he is sentient and restless, just in proportion as he reacts and recipro-
cates and penetrates, is the critic a valuable instrument; for in literature
assuredly criticism *is* the critic, just as art is the artist; it being assuredly
the artist who invented art and the critic who invented criticism, and
not the other way round.

And it is with the kinds of criticism exactly as it is with the kinds

HJ, after the portrait by Sargent, 1913

of art—the best kind, the only kind worth speaking of, is the kind that springs from the liveliest experience. There are a hundred labels and tickets, in all this matter, that have been pasted on from the outside and appear to exist for the convenience of passers-by; but the critic who lives *in* the house, ranging through its innumerable chambers, knows nothing about the bills on the front. He only knows that the more impressions he has the more he is able to record, and that the more he is saturated, poor fellow, the more he can give out. His life, at this rate, is heroic, for it is immensely vicarious. He has to understand for others, to answer for them; he is always under arms. He knows that the whole honor of the matter, for him, besides the success in his own eyes, depends upon his being indefatigably supple, and that is a formidable order. Let me not speak, however, as if his work were a conscious grind, for the sense of effort is easily lost in the enthusiasm of curiosity. Any vocation has its hours of intensity that is so closely connected with life. That of the critic, in literature, is connected doubly, for he deals with life at second-hand as well as at first; that is, he deals with the experience of others, which he resolves into his own, and not of those invented and selected others with whom the novelist makes comfortable terms, but with the uncompromising swarm of authors, the clamorous children of history. He has to make them as vivid and as free as the novelist makes *his* puppets, and yet he has, as the phrase is, to take them as they come. We must be easy with him if the picture, even when the aim has really been to penetrate, is sometimes confused, for there are baffling and there are thankless subjects; and we make everything up to him by the peculiar purity of our esteem when the portrait is really, like the happy portraits of the other art, a text preserved by translation.

HJ: JOHN S. SARGENT (1887)

I was on the point of beginning this sketch of the work of an artist to whom distinction has come very early in life by saying, in regard to the degree to which the subject of it enjoys the attention of the public, that no American painter has hitherto won himself such recognition from the expert; but I find myself pausing at the start as on the edge of a possible solecism. Is Mr. Sargent in very fact an American painter? The proper answer to such a question is doubtless that we shall be well advised to pretend it, and the reason of this is simply that we have an excellent opportunity. Born in Europe, he has also spent his life in Europe, but none the less the burden of proof would rest with those who should undertake to show that he is a European. Moreover he has even on the face of it this great symptom of an American origin, that in the line of his art he might easily be mistaken for a Frenchman. It sounds like a paradox, but it is a very simple truth, that when today we look for "American art" we find it mainly in Paris. When we find it out of Paris, we at least find a great deal of Paris in it. Mr. Sargent came up to the irresistible city in his twentieth year, from Florence, where in 1856 he had been born of American parents and where his fortunate youth had been spent. He entered immediately the studio of Carolus Duran, and revealed himself in 1877, at the age of twenty-two, in the portrait of that master—a fine model in more than one sense of the word. He was already in possession of a style; and if this style has gained both in finish and assurance, it has not otherwise varied. As he saw and "rendered" ten years ago, so he sees and renders today; and I may add that there is no present symptom of his passing into another manner.

Those who have appreciated his work most up to the present time articulate no wish for a change, so completely does that work seem to them, in its kind, the exact translation of his thought, the exact "fit" of his artistic temperament. It is difficult to imagine a young painter less in the dark about his own ideal, more lucid and more responsible from the first about what he desires. In an altogether exceptional degree does he give us the sense that the intention and the art of carrying it out are for him one and the same thing. In the brilliant portrait of Carolus Duran, which he was speedily and strikingly to surpass, he gave almost the full measure of this admirable peculiarity, that perception with him is already by itself a kind of execution. It is likewise so, of course, with many another genuine painter; but in Sargent's case the process by which the object seen resolves itself into the object pictured is extraordinarily immediate. It is as if painting were pure tact of vision, a simple manner of feeling.

From the time of his first successes at the Salon, he was hailed, I believe, as a recruit of high value to the camp of the Impressionists, and today he is for many people most conveniently pigeon-holed under that head. It is not necessary to protest against the classification if this addition always be made to it, that Mr. Sargent's impressions happen to be worthy of record. This is by no means inveterately the case with those of the ingenuous artists who most rejoice in the title in question. To render the impression of an object may be a very fruitful effort, but it is not necessarily so; that will depend upon what, I won't say the object, but the impression, may have been. The talents engaged in this school lie, not unjustly, as it seems to me, under the suspicion of seeking the solution of their problem exclusively in simplification. If a painter works for other eyes as well as his own he courts a certain danger in this direction—that of being arrested by the cry of the spectator: "Ah! but excuse me; I myself take more impressions than that." We feel a synthesis not to be an injustice only when it is rich.

Mr. Sargent simplifies, I think, but he simplifies with style, and his impression is the finest form of his energy.

His work has been almost exclusively in portraiture, and it has been his fortune to paint more women than men; therefore he has had but a limited opportunity to reproduce that generalized grand air with which his view of certain figures of gentlemen invests the model, which is conspicuous in the portrait of Carolus Duran, and of which his splendid "Docteur Pozzi," the distinguished Paris surgeon (a work not sent to the Salon) is an admirable example. . . . The most brilliant of all Mr. Sargent's productions is the portrait of a young lady, the magnificent picture which he exhibited in 1881: and if it has mainly been his fortune since to commemorate the fair faces of women, there is no ground for surprise at this sort of success on the part of one who had given so signal a proof of possessing the secret of the particular aspect that the contemporary lady (of any period) likes to wear in the eyes of posterity. Painted when he was but four-and-twenty years of age, the picture by which Mr. Sargent was represented at the Salon of 1881 is a performance which may well have made any critic of imagination rather anxious about his future. In common with the superb group of the children of Mr. Edward Boit, exhibited two years later, it offers the slightly "uncanny" spectacle of a talent which on the very threshold of its career has nothing more to learn. It is not simply precocity in the guise of maturity—a phenomenon we very often meet, which deceives us only for an hour; it is the freshness of youth combined with the artistic experience, really felt and assimilated, of generations. My admiration for this deeply distinguished work is such that I am perhaps in danger of overstating its merits; but it is worth taking into account that today, after several years' acquaintance with them, these merits seem to me more and more to justify enthusiasm. The picture has this sign of productions of the first order, that its style clearly would save it if everything else should change—our measure of its value of resemblance, its expression of character, the fashion of dress, the particular associations it evokes. It is not only a portrait, but a picture, and it arouses even in the profane spectator something of the painter's sense, the joy of engaging also, by sympathy, in the solution of the artistic problem. There are works of which it is sometimes said that they are painters' pictures (this description is apt to be intended invidiously), and the production of which I speak has the good-fortune at once to belong to this class and to give the "plain man" the kind of pleasure that the plain man looks for. . . .

Two years before he exhibited the young lady in black, in 1879, Mr. Sargent had spent several months in Spain, and here, even more than he had already been, the great Velasquez became the god of his idolatry.

No scenes are more delightful to the imagination than those in which we figure youth and genius confronted with great examples, and if such matters did not belong to the domain of private life we might entertain ourselves with reconstructing the episode of the first visit to the museum of Madrid, the shrine of the painter of Philip IV, of a young Franco-American worshipper of the highest artistic sensibility, expecting a supreme revelation and prepared to fall on his knees. It is evident that Mr. Sargent fell on his knees and that in this attitude he passed a considerable part of his sojourn in Spain. He is various and experimental; if I am not mistaken, he sees each work that he produces in a light of its own, not turning off successive portraits according to some well-tried receipt which has proved useful in the case of their predecessors; nevertheless there is one idea that pervades them all, in a different degree, and gives them a family resemblance—the idea that it would be inspiring to know just how Velasquez would have treated the theme. . . .

In dividing the honor that Mr. Sargent has won by his finest work between the portrait of the young lady of 1881 and the group of four little girls which was painted in 1882 and exhibited with the success it deserved the following year, I must be careful to give the latter picture not too small a share. The artist has done nothing more felicitous and interesting than this view of a rich, dim, rather generalized French interior (the perspective of a hall with a shining floor, where screens and tall Japanese vases shimmer and loom), which encloses the life and seems to form the happy play-world of a family of charming children. The treatment is eminently unconventional, and there is none of the usual symmetrical balancing of the figures in the foreground. The place is regarded as a whole; it is a scene, a comprehensive impression; yet none the less do the little figures in their white pinafores (when was the pinafore ever painted with that power and made so poetic?) detach themselves and live with a personal life. . . . The naturalness of the composition, the loveliness of the complete effect, the light, free security of the execution, the sense it gives us as of assimilated secrets and of instinct and knowledge playing together—all this makes the picture as astonishing a work on the part of a young man of twenty-six as the portrait of 1881 was astonishing on the part of a young man of twenty-four.

It is these remarkable encounters that justify us in writing almost prematurely of a career which is not yet half unfolded. Mr. Sargent is sometimes accused of a want of "finish," but if finish means the last word of expressiveness of touch, "The Hall with the Four Children," as we may call it, may stand as a permanent reference on this point. If the picture of the Spanish dancer illustrates, as it seems to me to do, the latent dangers of the Impressionist practice, so this finer performance shows what victories it may achieve. And in relation to the latter I must repeat what I said about the young lady with the flower, that this is the sort of work which, when produced in youth, leads the attentive spectator to ask unanswerable questions. He finds himself murmuring, "Yes, but what is left?" and even wondering whether it be an advantage to an artist to obtain early in life such possession of his means that the struggle with them, discipline, *tâtonnement,* cease to exist for him. May not this breed an irresponsibility of cleverness, a wantonness, an irreverence—what is vulgarly termed a "larkiness"—on the part of the youthful genius who has, as it were, all his fortune in his pocket? Such are the possibly superfluous broodings of those who are critical even in their warmest admirations and who sometimes suspect that it may be better for an artist to have a certain part of his property invested in unsolved difficulties. When this is not the case, the question with regard to his future simplifies itself somewhat portentously. "What will he do with it?" we ask, meaning by the pronoun the sharp, completely forged weapon. It becomes more purely a question of responsibility, and we hold him altogether to a higher account. This is the case with Mr. Sargent; he knows so much about the art of painting that he perhaps does not fear emergencies quite enough, and that having knowledge to spare he may be tempted to play with it and waste it. . . .

Mr. Sargent is so young . . . that, in spite . . . of the admirable works he has already produced, his future is the most valuable thing he has to show. We may still ask ourselves what he will do with it, while we indulge the hope that he will see fit to give successors to the two pictures which I have spoken of emphatically as his finest. There is no greater work of art than a great portrait—a truth to be constantly taken to heart by a painter holding in his hands the weapon that Mr. Sargent wields. The gift that he possesses he possesses completely—the immediate perception of the end and of the means. Putting aside the question of the subject (and to a great portrait a common sitter will doubtless not always contribute), the highest result is achieved when to this element of quick perception a certain faculty of brooding reflection is added. I use this name for want of a better, and I mean the quality in the light of which the artist sees deep into his subject, undergoes it, absorbs it, discovers in it new things that were not on the surface, becomes patient with it, and almost reverent, and, in short, enlarges and humanizes the technical problem.

* * *

ON GEORGE ELIOT AND OTHERS

HJ TO his father, from London, May 10, 1869:
"The one marvel, as yet, of my stay, is having finally seen Mrs.

Lewes. . . . I was immensely impressed, interested and pleased. To
begin with she is magnificently ugly—deliciously hideous. She has a
low forehead, a dull grey eye, a vast pendulous nose, a huge mouth,
full of uneven teeth and a chin and jaw-bone *qui n'en finissent pas.* . . .
Now in this vast ugliness resides a most powerful beauty which, in a
very few minutes steals forth and charms the mind, so that you end as
I ended, in falling in love with her. Yes, behold me, literally in love
with this great horse-faced blue-stocking. I don't know in what the
charm lies, but it is thoroughly potent. An admirable physiognomy—a
delightful expression, a voice soft and rich as that of a counselling
angel—a mingled sagacity and sweetness—a broad hint of a great
underlying world of reserve, knowledge, pride and power—a great
feminine dignity and character in these massively plain features—a
hundred conflicting shades of consciousness and simpleness—shyness
and frankness—graciousness and remote independence. These are some
of the more definite elements of her personality. . . . Altogether, she
has a larger circumference than any woman I have ever seen."

HJ, in *The Middle Years* (1914), recounts a call upon George Eliot
at her country place at Witley in 1878. He had been driven there by
Mrs. Greville, whom he described in a letter at that time as "a cousin
by marriage of the Greville Papers: the queerest creature living, but a
mixture of the ridiculous and the amiable in which the amiable pre-
ponderates. . . . I can't praise her better than by saying that though
she is on the whole the greatest fool I have ever known, I like her very
much and get on with her most easily." The novel of HJ's alluded to
below is probably *The Europeans*, which, though brief, had just then
been issued in two volumes:

"Even on the way I quaked a little with my sense of what *generally*
most awaited or overtook my companion's prime proposals. What had
come most to characterise the Leweses to my apprehension was that
there couldn't be a thing in the world about which they weren't, and
on the most conceded and assured grounds, almost scientifically particular; which presumption, however, only added to the relevance of
one's learning how such a matter as their relation with Mrs. Greville
could in accordance with noble consistencies be carried on. I could
trust *her* for it perfectly, as she knew no law but that of innocent and
exquisite aberration, never wanting and never less than consecrating,
and I fear I but took refuge for the rest in declining all responsibility.
I remember trying to say to myself that, even such as we were, our
visit couldn't but scatter a little the weight of cloud on the Olympus
we scaled—given the dreadful drenching afternoon we were after all an
imaginable short solace there; and this indeed would have borne me
through to the end save for an incident which, with a quite ideal logic,
left our adventure an approved ruin. I see again our bland, benign,

commiserating hostess beside the fire in a chill desert of a room where
the master of the house guarded the opposite hearthstone, and I catch
once more the impression of no occurrence of anything at all appreciable but their liking us to have come, with our terribly trivial contribution, mainly from a prevision of how they should more devoutly like it
when we departed. It is remarkable, but the occasion yields me no
single echo of a remark on the part of any of us—nothing more than
the sense that our great author herself peculiarly suffered from the fury
of the elements, and that they had about them rather the minimum of
the paraphernalia of reading and writing, not to speak of that of tea,
a conceivable feature of the hour, but which was not provided for.
Again I felt touched with privilege, but not, as in '69, with a form of it
redeemed from barrenness by a motion of my own, and the taste of
barrenness was in fact in my mouth under the effect of our taking leave.
We did so with considerable flourish till we had passed out to the hall
again, indeed to the door of the waiting carriage, toward which G. H.
Lewes himself all sociably, *then* above all conversingly, wafted us—
yet staying me by a sudden remembrance before I had entered the
brougham and signing me to wait while he repaired his omission. I
returned to the doorstep, whence I still see him reissue from the room
we had just left and hurry toward me across the hall shaking high the
pair of blue-bound volumes his allusion to the uninvited, the verily
importunate loan of which by Mrs. Greville had lingered on the air
after his dash in quest of them; 'Ah those books—take them away,
please, away, away!' I hear him unreservedly plead while he thrusts
them again at me, and I scurry back into our conveyance, where, and
where only, settled afresh with my companion, I venture to assure myself of the horrid truth that had squinted at me as I relieved our good
friend of his superfluity. What indeed was this superfluity but the two
volumes of my own precious 'last'—we were still in the blest age of
volumes—presented by its author to the lady of Milford Cottage, and
by her, misguided votary, dropped with the best conscience in the
world into the Witley abyss, out of which it had jumped with violence,
under the touch of accident, straight up again into my own exposed
face?

"The bruise inflicted there I remember feeling for the moment only
as sharp, such a mixture of delightful small questions at once salved it
over and such a charm in particular for me to my recognising that this
particular wrong—inflicted all unawares, which exactly made it sublime
—was the only rightness of our visit. Our hosts hadn't so much as connected book with author, or author with visitor, or visitor with anything but the convenience of his ridding them of an unconsidered trifle;
grudging as they so justifiedly did the impingement of such matters on
their consciousness. The vivid demonstration of one's failure to pene-

trate there had been in the sweep of Lewes's gesture, which could
scarce have been bettered by his actually wielding a broom. I think
nothing passed between us in the brougham on revelation of the identity of the offered treat so emphatically declined—I see that I couldn't
have laughed at it to the confusion of my gentle neighbour. But I quite
recall my grasp of the *interest* of our distinguished friends' inaccessi-
bility to the unattended plea, with the light it seemed to throw on what
it was really to *be* attended. Never, never save as attended—by presumptions, that is, far other than any then hanging about one—would
one so much as desire *not* to be pushed out of sight. I needn't attempt,
however, to supply all the links in the chain of association which led
to my finally just qualified beatitude: I had been served right enough in
all conscience, but the pity was that Mrs. Greville had been. This I
never wanted for her; and I may add, in the connection, that I discover
now no grain of false humility in my having enjoyed in my own person
adorning such a tale. There was positively a fine high thrill in thinking
of persons—or at least of a person, for any fact about Lewes was but
derivative—engaged in my own pursuit and yet detached, by what I
conceived, detached by a pitch of intellectual life, from all that made
it actual to myself. *There* was the lift of contemplation, there the inspiring image and the big supporting truth; the pitch of intellectual
life in the very fact of which we seemed, my hostess and I, to have
caught our celebrities sitting in that queer bleak way wouldn't have
bullied me in the least if it hadn't been the centre of such a circle of
gorgeous creation. It was the fashion among the profane in short either
to misdoubt, before George Eliot's canvas, the latter's backing of rich
thought, or else to hold that this matter of philosophy, and even if but
of the philosophic vocabulary, thrust itself through to the confounding
of the picture. But with that thin criticism I wasn't, as I have already
intimated, to have a moment's patience; I was to become, I was to
remain—I take pleasure in repeating—even a very Derondist of Deron-
dists, for my own wanton joy: which amounts to saying that I found
the figured, coloured tapestry *always* vivid enough to brave no matter
what complication of the stitch."

Alice James, June 28, 1889:

"Read the third volume of George Eliot's letters and journal, at last.
I'm glad I made myself do so, for there is a faint spark of life and an
occasional remotely humourous touch in the last half. But what a
monument of ponderous dreariness is the book! What a lifeless, diseased, self-conscious being she must have been! Not one burst of joy,
not one ray of humour, not one living breath in one of her letters or
journals; the common-place and platitudes of these last, giving her impressions of the Continent, pictures and people, are simply incredible.
Whether it is that her dank, moaning features haunt and pursue me

through the book or not she makes the impression, morally and physically, of mildew or some morbid growth,—a fungus of a pendulous
shape, or as of something damp to the touch. I never had a stronger
impression. Then to think of those books, compact of wisdom, humour,
and the richest humanity, and of her as the creator of the immortal
Maggie; in short, what a horrible disillusion. . . . On the subject of
her marriage, it is, of course, for an outsider, criminal to say anything;
but what a shock for her to say she felt as if her life were rounded,
and for her to express her sense of complacency in the vestry and
church! What a betrayal of the much-vaunted 'perfect love' of the
past! The letter in which she announces her engagement to a friend,
and at the same time assures her that Johnnie isn't going to grab her
fortune, is deliciously English. . . . But the possession of what genius
and what knowledge could reconcile one to the supreme boredom of
having to take one's self with that superlative solemnity? What a contrast to George Sand, who, whatever her failings, never committed that
unpardonable sin; it even makes her greasy men of the moment less
repulsive."

HJ on Tennyson (1914), describing a visit to Aldworth, where he
had also been escorted by Mrs. Greville, on the morrow of their visit
to George Eliot:

"I was to breathe from beginning to end of our visit, which began
with our sitting again at luncheon, an air—so unlike that of Witley!—
in which it seemed to me frankly that nothing but the blest obvious, or
at least the blest outright, could so much as attempt to live. These elements hung sociably and all auspiciously about us—it was a large and
simple and almost empty occasion; yet empty without embarrassment,
rather as from a certain high guardedness or defensiveness of situation,
literally indeed from the material, the local sublimity, the fact of our all
upliftedly hanging together over one of the grandest sweeps of view
in England. Remembered passages again people, however, in their proportion, the excess of opportunity; each with that conclusive note of
the outright all unadorned. What could have partaken more of this
quality for instance than the question I was startled to hear launched
before we had left the table by the chance of Mrs. Greville's having
happened to mention in some connection one of her French relatives,
Mademoiselle Laure de Sade? It had fallen on my own ear—the mention at least had—with a certain effect of unconscious provocation; but
this was as nothing to its effect on the ear of our host. 'De Sade?' he at
once exclaimed with interest—and with the consequence, I may frankly
add, of my wondering almost to ecstasy, that is to the ecstasy of curiosity, to what length he would proceed. He proceeded admirably—
admirably for the triumph of simplification—to the very greatest length
imaginable, as was signally promoted by the fact that clearly no one

present, with a single exception, recognised the name or the nature of the scandalous, the long ignored, the at last all but unnameable author; least of all the gentle relative of Mademoiselle Laure, who listened with the blankest grace to her friend's enumeration of his titles to infamy, among which that of his most notorious work was pronounced. It was the homeliest, frankest, most domestic passage, as who should say, and most remarkable for leaving none of us save myself, by my impression, in the least embarrassed or bewildered; largely, I think, because of the failure—a failure the most charmingly flat—of all measure on the part of auditors and speaker alike of what might be intended or understood, of what, in fine, the latter was talking about.

"He struck me in truth as neither knowing nor communicating knowledge, and I recall how I felt this note in his own case to belong to that general intimation with which the whole air was charged of the want of proportion between the great spaces and reaches and echoes commanded, the great eminence attained, and the quantity and variety of experience supposable. So to discriminate was in a manner to put one's hand on the key, and thereby to find one's self in presence of a rare and anomalous, but still scarcely the less beautiful fact. The assured and achieved conditions, the serenity, the security, the success, to put it vulgarly, shone in the light of their easiest law—that by which they emerge early from the complication of life, the great adventure of sensibility, and find themselves determined once for all, fortunately fixed, all consecrated and consecrating. If I should speak of this impression as that of glory without history, that of the poetic character more worn than paid for, or at least more saved than spent, I should doubtless much over-emphasise; but such, or something like it, was none the less the explanation that met one's own fond fancy of the scene after one had cast about for it. For I allow myself thus to repeat that I was so moved to cast about, and perhaps at no moment more than during the friendly analysis of the reputation of M. de Sade. Was I not present at some undreamed-of demonstration of the absence of the remoter real, the real other than immediate and exquisite, other than guaranteed and enclosed, in landscape, friendship, fame, above all in consciousness of awaited and admired and self-consistent inspiration?

"The question was indeed to be effectively answered for me, and everything meanwhile continued to play into this prevision—even to the pleasant growling note heard behind me, as the Bard followed with Mrs. Greville, who had permitted herself apparently some mild extravagance of homage: 'Oh yes, you may do what you like—so long as you don't kiss me before the cabman!' The allusion was explained for us, if I remember—a matter of some more or less recent leave-taking of admirer and admired in London on his putting her down at her door after being taken to the play or wherever; between the rugged humour of which reference and the other just commemorated there wasn't a pin to choose, it struck me, for a certain old-time Lincolnshire ease or comfortable stay-at-home license. But it was later on, when, my introductress having accompanied us, I sat upstairs with him in his study, that he might read to us some poem of his own that we should venture to propose, it was then that mystifications dropped, that everything in the least dislocated fell into its place, and that image and picture stamped themselves strongly and finally, or to the point even, as I recover it, of leaving me almost too little to wonder about. He had not got a third of the way through Locksley Hall, which, my choice given me, I had made bold to suggest he should spout—for I had already heard him spout in Eaton Place—before I had begun to wonder that I didn't wonder, didn't at least wonder more consumedly; as a very little while back I should have made sure of my doing on any such prodigious occasion. I sat at one of the windows that hung over space, noting how the windy, watery autumn day, sometimes sheeting it all with rain, called up the dreary, dreary moorland or the long dun wolds; I pinched myself for the determination of my identity and hung on the reader's deep-voiced chant for the credibility of his: I asked myself in fine why, in complete deviation from everything that would have seemed from far back certain for the case, I failed to swoon away under the heaviest pressure I had doubtless ever known the romantic situation bring to bear. So lucidly all the while I considered, so detachedly I judged, so dissentingly, to tell the whole truth, I listened; pinching myself, as I say, not at all to keep from swooning, but much rather to set up some rush of sensibility. It was all interesting, it was at least all odd; but why in the name of poetic justice had one anciently heaved and flushed with one's own recital of the splendid stuff if one was now only to sigh in secret 'Oh dear, oh dear'? The author lowered the whole pitch, that of expression, that of interpretation above all; I heard him, in cool surprise, take even more out of his verse than he had put in, and so bring me back to the point I had immediately and privately made, the point that he wasn't Tennysonian. I felt him as he went on and on lose that character beyond repair, and no effect of the organ-roll, of monotonous majesty, no suggestion of the long echo, availed at all to save it. What the case came to for me, I take it—and by the case I mean the intellectual, the artistic—was that it lacked the intelligence, the play of discrimination, I should have taken for granted in it, and thereby, brooding monster that I was, born to discriminate à tout propos, lacked the interest.

"Detached I have mentioned that I had become, and it was doubtless at such a rate high time for that; though I hasten to repeat that with the close of the incident I was happily able to feel a new sense in the whole connection established. My critical reaction hadn't in the least invalidated our great man's being a Bard—it had in fact made him and left him more a Bard than ever: it had only settled to my perception as not before what a Bard might and mightn't be. The character was just a rigid idiosyncrasy, to which everything in the man conformed, but which supplied nothing outside of itself, and which above all was not intellectually wasteful or heterogeneous, conscious as it could only be of its intrinsic breadth and weight. On two or three occasions of the aftertime I was to hear Browning read out certain of his finest pages, and this exactly with all the exhibition of point and authority, the expressive particularisation, so to speak, that I had missed on the part of the Laureate; an observation through which the author of Men and Women appeared, in spite of the beauty and force of his demonstration, as little as possible a Bard. He particularised if ever a man did, was heterogeneous and profane, composed of pieces and patches that betrayed some creak of joints, and addicted to the excursions from which these were brought home; so that he had to *prove* himself a poet, almost against all presumptions, and with all the assurance and all the character he could use. Was not this last in especial, the character, so close to the surface, with which Browning fairly bristled, what was most to come out in his personal delivery of the fruit of his genius? It came out almost to harshness; but the result was that what he read showed extraordinary life. During that audition at Aldworth the question seemed on the contrary not of life at all—save, that is, of one's own; which was exactly not the question. With all the resonance of the chant, the whole thing was yet *still*, with all the long swing of its motion it yet remained where it was—heaving doubtless grandly enough up and down and beautiful to watch as through the superposed veils of its long self-consciousness. By all of which I don't mean to say that I was not, on the day at Aldworth, thoroughly reconciled to learning what a Bard consisted of; for that came as soon as I had swallowed my own mistake—the mistake of having supposed Tennyson something subtly other than one. I had supposed, probably, such an impossibility, had, to repeat my term, so absurdly fantasticated, that the long journey round and about the truth no more than served me right; just as after all it at last left me quite content."

Alice on the Darwinian mind:

"The domestic muse isn't considered very original—Mr. Cross, the Georgian widower, asking Katherine whether William got his psychology from Mr. Frederick Myers, and Mrs. Litchfield (née Darwin) speaking of having just read Miss Burney's letters, asked whether Mr. Henry James had read them, and 'was it out of those books that he got the characters for his novels?' When I held my *salon* in Bolton Row, she came to see me, and asked what was the matter with me: I said 'They call it latent gout.' 'Oh! that's what we have; does it come from drink in your parents?' It occurred to me that the Darwinian mind must be greater in science than in society."

Alice, on HJ's essay "Browning in Westminster Abbey":

"Harry came yesterday, and I had, as always, a happy day with him. I should cry hard for two hours after he goes, if I could allow myself such luxuries, but tears are undiluted poison. This is such a neat example of the abortive nature of human effort that I must give it: A few days after the first number of the *Speaker* came out, a friend who is very friendly and kind, and often writes to 'cheer me up,' wrote me one of her good letters, which she concluded thus: 'Don't embark on the "Squeaker." There is such a miserably written article on Browning; but every one thinks he ought to be emotional and obscure on this topic. It is meant for imitation, I believe.' As the said article is written by Harry, she rather failed to cheer that time! After my sisterly susceptibilities had recovered from the shock, and I had towed my stomach and heart back into harbor, they having broken loose, under the impression that they were to have a day to themselves, the comic of the situation overcame me; the disproportion and want of harmony between cause and effect was so excessive. Harry's article so bad as to wreck the *Speaker* in the present and future; the good lady, through benevolent intentions, prostrating her pallid victim; she doubtless simply bringing up the subject to use the word Squeaker (a Unionist *jeu d'esprit,* I suppose), carefully avoiding politics so as not to stir me up, and seizing upon my one vulnerable point with such energy. It is rather complete. I *think* that I do not want her to find out the mistake, or rather mis-direction, but I *know* there is a sprite within me that would be greatly gratified had she an inkling thereof,—a sprite not only much entertained by the minute illustrative complications which fall within its narrow range, but nimble to run in the follies of mankind, finding 'em so much more tonic than their virtues. How thankful I am that I never struggled to be of those 'who are not as others are,' but that I discovered at the earliest moment that my talents lay in being *more so.* Hold hard, my friend, the pride of abasement is [a] more insidious one than t'other."

* * * * *

WJ: LOUIS AGASSIZ (1896)

IT WOULD be unnatural to have such an assemblage as this meet in the Museum and Faculty Room of this University and yet have no public word spoken in honor of a name which must be silently present to the minds of all our visitors.

At some near future day, it is to be hoped some one of you who is well acquainted with Agassiz's scientific career will discourse here concerning it,—I could not now, even if I would, speak to you of that of which you have far more intimate knowledge than I. On this social occasion it has seemed that what Agassiz stood for in the way of character and influence is the more fitting thing to commemorate, and to that agreeable task I have been called. He made an impression that was unrivalled. He left a sort of popular myth—the Agassiz legend, as one might say—behind him in the air about us; and life comes kindlier to all of us, we get more recognition from the world, because we call ourselves naturalists,—and that was the class to which he also belonged.

The secret of such an extraordinarily effective influence lay in the equally extraordinary mixture of the animal and social gifts, the intellectual powers, and the desires and passions of the man. From his boyhood, he looked on the world as if it and he were made for each other, and on the vast diversity of living things as if he were there with authority to take mental possession of them all. His habit of collecting began in childhood, and during his long life knew no bounds save those that separate the things of Nature from those of human art. Already in his student years, in spite of the most stringent poverty, his whole scheme of existence was that of one predestined to greatness, who takes that fact for granted, and stands forth immediately as a scientific leader of men.

His passion for knowing living things was combined with a rapidity of observation, and a capacity to recognize them again and remember everything about them, which all his life it seemed an easy triumph and delight for him to exercise, and which never allowed him to waste a moment in doubts about the commensurability of his powers with his tasks. If ever a person lived by faith, he did. When a boy of twenty, with an allowance of two hundred and fifty dollars a year, he maintained an artist attached to his employ, a custom which never afterwards was departed from,—except when he maintained two or three. He lectured from the very outset to all those who would hear him. "I feel within myself the strength of a whole generation," he wrote to his father at that time, and launched himself upon the publication of his costly "Poissons Fossiles" with no clear vision of the quarter from whence the payment might be expected to come.

At Neuchâtel (where between the ages of twenty-five and thirty he enjoyed a stipend that varied from four hundred to six hundred dollars) he organized a regular academy of natural history, with its museum, managing by one expedient or another to employ artists, secretaries, and assistants, and to keep a lithographic and printing establishment of his own employed with the work that he put forth. Fishes, fossil and living, echinoderms and glaciers, transfigured themselves under his hand, and at thirty he was already at the zenith of his reputation, recognized by all as one of those naturalists in the unlimited sense, one of those folio copies of mankind, like Linnæus and Cuvier, who aim at nothing less than an acquaintance with the whole of animated Nature. His genius for classifying was simply marvellous; and, as his latest biographer says, nowhere had a single person ever given so decisive an impulse to natural history.

Such was the human being who on an October morning fifty years ago disembarked at our port, bringing his hungry heart along with him, his confidence in his destiny, and his imagination full of plans. The only particular resource he was assured of was one course of Lowell Lectures. But of one general resource he always was assured, having always counted on it and never found it to fail,—and that was the good will of every fellow-creature in whose presence he could find an opportunity to describe his aims. His belief in these was so intense and unqualified that he could not conceive of others not feeling the furtherance of them to be a duty binding also upon them. *Velle non discitur*, as Seneca says:—Strength of desire must be born with a man, it can't be taught. And Agassiz came before one with such enthusiasm glowing in his countenance,—such a persuasion radiating from his person that his projects were the sole things really fit to interest man as man,—that he was absolutely irresistible. He came, in Byron's words, with victory beaming from his breast, and every one went down before him, some yielding him money, some time, some specimens, and some labor, but all contributing their applause and their godspeed. And so, living among us from month to month and from year to year, with no relation to prudence except his pertinacious violation of all her usual laws, he on the whole achieved the compass of his desires, studied the geology and fauna of a continent, trained a generation of zoölogists, founded one of the chief museums of the world, gave a new impulse to scientific education in America, and died the idol of the public, as well as of his circle of immediate pupils and friends.

The secret of it all was, that while his scientific ideals were an integral part of his being, something that he never forgot or laid aside, so that wherever he went he came forward as "the Professor," and talked "shop" to every person, young or old, great or little, learned or unlearned, with whom he was thrown, he was at the same time so commanding a presence, so curious and inquiring, so responsive and expansive, and so generous and reckless of himself and of his own, that every one said immediately, "Here is no musty *savant*, but a man, a great man, a man on the heroic scale, not to serve whom is avarice and sin." He elevated the popular notion of what a student of Nature could be. Since Benjamin Franklin, we had never had among us a person of more popularly impressive type. He did not wait for students to come to him; he made injuiry for promising youthful collectors, and when he heard of one, he wrote, inviting and urging him to come. Thus there is hardly one now of the American naturalists of my generation whom Agassiz did not train. Nay, more; he said to every one that a year or two of natural history, studied as he understood it, would give the best training for any kind of mental work. Sometimes he was amusingly *naïf* in this regard, as when he offered to put his whole Museum at the disposition of the Emperor of Brazil if he would but come and labor there. And I well remember how certain officials of the Brazilian empire smiled at the cordiality with which he pressed upon them a similar invitation. But it had a great effect. Natural history must indeed be a godlike pursuit, if such a man as this can so adore it, people said; and the very definition and meaning of the word naturalist underwent a favorable alteration in the common mind.

Certain sayings of Agassiz's, as the famous one that he "had no time for making money," and his habit of naming his occupation simply as that of "teacher," have caught the public fancy, and are permanent benefactions. We all enjoy more consideration for the fact that he manifested himself here thus before us in his day.

He was a splendid example of the temperament that looks forward and not backward, and never wastes a moment in regrets for the irrevocable. I had the privilege of admission to his society during the Thayer expedition to Brazil. I well remember at night, as we all swung in our hammocks in the fairy-like moonlight, on the deck of the steamer that throbbed its way up the Amazon between the forests guarding the stream on either side, how he turned and whispered, "James, are you awake?" and continued, "*I* cannot sleep; I am too happy; I keep thinking of these glorious plans." The plans contemplated following the Amazon to its headwaters, and penetrating the Andes in Peru. And yet, when he arrived at the Peruvian frontier and learned that that country had broken into revolution, that his letters to officials would be useless, and that that part of the project must be given up, although he was indeed bitterly chagrined and excited for part of an hour, when the hour had passed over it seemed as if he had quite forgotten the disappointment, so enthusiastically was he occupied already with the new scheme substituted by his active mind.

Agassiz's influence on methods of teaching in our community was prompt and decisive,—all the more so that it struck people's imagination by its very excess. The good old way of committing printed abstractions to memory seems never to have received such a shock as it encountered at his hands. There is probably no public school teacher now in New England who will not tell you how Agassiz used to lock a student up in a room full of turtle shells, or lobster shells, or oyster shells, without a book or word to help him, and not let him out till he had discovered all the truths which the objects contained. Some found the truths after weeks and months of lonely sorrow; others never found them. Those who found them were already made into naturalists thereby—the failures were blotted from the book of honor and of life. "Go to Nature; take the facts into your own hands; look, and see for yourself!"—these were the maxims which Agassiz preached wherever he went, and their effect on pedagogy was electric. The extreme rigor of his devotion to this concrete method of learning was the natural consequence of his own peculiar type of intellect, in which the capacity for abstraction and causal reasoning and tracing chains of consequences from hypotheses was so much less developed than the genius for acquaintance with vast volumes of detail, and for seizing upon analogies and relations of the more proximate and concrete kind. While on the Thayer expedition, I remember that I often put questions to him about the facts of our new tropical habitat, but I doubt if he ever answered one of these questions of mine outright. He always said: "There, you see you have a definite problem; go and look and find the answer for yourself." His severity in this line was a living rebuke to all abstraction-ists and would-be biological philosophers. More than once have I heard him quote with deep feeling the lines from Faust:

> "Grau, theurer Freund, ist alle Theorie.
> Und grün des Lebens goldner Baum."

The only man he really loved and had use for was the man who could bring him facts. To see facts, not to argue or *raisonniren*, was what life meant for him; and I think he often positively loathed the ratiocinating type of mind. "Mr. Blank, you are *totally* uneducated!" I heard him once say to a student who propounded to him some glittering theoretic generality. And on a similar occasion he gave an admonition that must have sunk deep into the heart of him to whom it was addressed. "Mr. X, some people perhaps now consider you a bright young man; but when you are fifty years old, if they ever speak of you then, what they will say will be this: 'That X,—oh, yes, I know him; he used to be a very bright young man!'" Happy is the conceited youth who at the proper moment receives such salutary cold water therapeutics as this from one who, in other respects, is a kind friend. We cannot all escape from being abstractionists. I myself, for instance, have never been able to escape; but the hours I spent with Agassiz so taught me the difference between all possible abstractionists and all livers in the light of the world's concrete fulness, that I have never been able to forget it. Both kinds of mind have their place in the infinite design, but there can be no question as to which kind lies the nearer to the divine type of thinking.

Agassiz's view of Nature was saturated with simple religious feeling, and for this deep but unconventional religiosity he found at Harvard the most sympathetic possible environment. In the fifty years that have

sped since he arrived here our knowledge of Nature has penetrated
into joints and recesses which his vision never pierced. The causal
elements and not the totals are what we are now most passionately
concerned to understand; and naked and poverty-stricken enough do
the stripped-out elements and forces occasionally appear to us to be.
But the truth of things is after all their living fulness, and some day,
from a more commanding point of view than was possible to any one
in Agassiz's generation, our descendants, enriched with the spoils of
all our analytic investigations, will get round again to that higher and
simpler way of looking at Nature. Meanwhile as we look back upon
Agassiz, there floats up a breath as of life's morning, that makes the
world seem young and fresh once more. May we all, and especially
may those younger members of our association who never knew him,
give a grateful thought to his memory as we wander through that Museum which he founded, and through this University whose ideals he
did so much to elevate and define.

*   *   *

WJ to K. Hillebrand, who had asked him to join a committee for a
memorial to Schopenhauer (1883):

"As for what you propose, what could be more tempting to an obscure chicken like myself than to see his name printed in the company
of the Illustrious whom you enumerate. But is there no other man than
Schopenhauer on whom we can combine? I really *must* decline to stir
a finger for the glory of one who studiously lived for no other purpose
than to spit upon the lives of the like of me and all those I care for.
Isn't there something rather immoral in *publicly* doing homage to one
whose writings, if the public could but understand and heed them,
would undo whatever of simple kindliness and hope keeps its life sweet?
And isn't there something inwardly farcical in getting up a mundane
celebration and signing an 'uproar,' and what vanity more I know not,
for the personal magnification of one, the burden of whose song—however little his life may have consisted with it—was the annihilation of
personal selfhood? Isn't it like offering a fur overcoat to a sweating
equatorial African? And won't Schopenhauer's spirit, looking down
from the Isles of the Blest, make gibes at the Committee more drastic
than any of those to be found in his printed works? It seems to me that
the indiscriminate newspaper optimism of our day rather overshoots
the mark when it takes to hurrahing for pessimism itself. It is as if the
Parisians should raise a monument to Bismarck or the Count de Cham-
bord to Robespierre, because, 'after all, they are good fellows too.'

"There *are* intellectual distinctions; why should scholars, of all men,
be called on to wipe them out? If the citizens of Frankfort want to
embellish their town by monuments to the celebrated men who lived
there, merely because they were celebrated, for the country people

to gape at, without knowing which is which—well and good, that's all included in the great popular, country-fair, animal-spirit, side of life, which Schopenhauer so much loathed. But if there be any kernel of truth in Schopenhauer's system (and it seems to me there is a deep one) it ought to be celebrated in silence and in secret, by the inner lives of those to whom it speaks: taking some things seriously is incompatible with 'celebrating' them! As for Schopenhauer himself, personally, his loud-mouthed pessimism was that of a dog who would rather see the world ten times worse than it is, than lose his chance of barking at it, and whom nothing would have unsuited so completely as the removal of cause for complaint. There are pathetic pessimists and cantankerous pessimists. Schopenhauer was not pathetic—Leopardi was. Then as for his metaphysics, they seem to me to unite every bad quality. He carried Kant's *Schnorkelwerk*, and machine-shop way of representing things, to an extreme where they became simply ludicrous; he ignored most all the really fruitful tendencies of his time; his only merits were his racy and pithy style, and his refusal to 'take stock' in a platitudinarian optimism. Candidly, doesn't the monument-plan savor the least bit in the world of the latter beatific *Weltanschauung*? I know you will be more amused than offended by these *Auslassungen* of mine. I wish they might induce you to change your own mind; but conversions are not so easily made!"

WJ to Peirce, 1894:

"I am heartily glad to learn that you are preparing to publish the results of your philosophizing in a complete and connected form. Pray consider me a subscriber to the whole series. There is no more original thinker than yourself in our generation. You have personally suggested more important things to me than perhaps anyone whom I have known; and I have never given you sufficient public credit for all that you have taught me. I am sure that this systematic work will increase my debt."

WJ to Royce, 1900:

"You are still the centre of my gaze, the pole of my mental magnet. When I write, 'tis with one eye on the page, and one on you. When I compose my Gifford lectures mentally, 'tis with the design exclusively of overthrowing your system, and ruining your peace. I lead a parasitic life upon you, for my highest flight of ambitious ideality is to become your conqueror, and go down into history as such, you and I rolled in one another's arms and silent (or rather loquacious still) in one last death-grapple of an embrace. How then, O my dear Royce, can I forget you, or be contented out of your close neighborhood? Different as our minds are, yours has nourished mine, as no other social influence ever has, and in converse with you I have always felt that my life was being lived importantly. Our minds, too, are not different in the *Object* which they envisage. It is the whole paradoxical physico-moral-spiritual Fatness, of which most people single out some skinny fragment, which we both cover with our eye. We 'aim at him generally' —and most others don't. I don't believe that we shall dwell apart forever, though our formulas may."

WJ to George Herbert Palmer, on Santayana's *Interpretations of Poetry and Religion* (1900):

"The great event in my life recently has been the reading of Santayana's book. Although I absolutely reject the platonism of it, I have literally squealed with delight at the imperturbable perfection with which the position is laid down on page after page; and grunted with delight at such a thickening up of our Harvard atmosphere. If our students now could begin really to understand what Royce means with his voluntaristic-pluralistic monism, what Münsterberg means with his dualistic scientificism and platonism, what Santayana means by his pessimistic platonism (I wonder if he and Mg. have had any close mutually encouraging intercourse in this line?), what I mean by my crass pluralism, what you mean by your ethereal idealism, that these are so many religions, ways of fronting life, and worth fighting for, we should have a genuine philosophic universe at Harvard. The best condition of it would be an open conflict and rivalry of the diverse systems. (Alas! that I should be out of it, just as my chance begins!) The world might ring with the struggle, if we devoted ourselves exclusively to belaboring each other.

"I now understand Santayana, the man. I never understood him before. But what a perfection of rottenness in a philosophy! I don't think I ever knew the anti-realistic view to be propounded with so impudently superior an air. It is refreshing to see a representative of moribund Latinity rise up and administer such reproof to us barbarians in the hour of our triumph. I imagine Santayana's *style* to be entirely spontaneous. But it has curious classic echoes. Whole pages of pure Hume in style; others of pure Renan. Nevertheless, how fantastic a philosophy!—as if the 'world of values' *were* independent of existence. It is only as *being*, that one thing is better than another. The idea of darkness is as good as that of light, as ideas. There is more value in light's *being*. And the exquisite consolation, when you have ascertained the badness of all fact, in knowing that badness is inferior to the end—it only rubs the pessimism in. A man whose egg at breakfast turns out always bad says to himself, 'Well, bad and good are not the same, anyhow.'" [1]

---

[1] With his usual frankness, WJ asked Palmer to pass this letter on to Santayana, who replied on Easter Day:

"Palmer has just sent me your delightful letter, by which I see with joy that you are full of life again in this season

WJ on *The Life of Reason* (1905):

"Santayana's book is a great one, if the inclusion of opposites is a measure of greatness. I think it will probably be reckoned great by posterity. It has no *rational* foundation, being merely one man's way of viewing things: so much of experience admitted and no more, so much criticism and questioning admitted and no more. He is a paragon of Emersonianism—declare your intuitions, though no other man share them; and the integrity with which he does it is as fine as it is rare. And his naturalism, materialism, Platonism, and atheism form a combination of which the centre of gravity is, I think, very deep. But there is something profoundly alienating in his unsympathetic tone, his 'preciousness' and superciliousness. The book is Emerson's first rival and successor, but how different the reader's feeling! The same things in Emerson's mouth would sound entirely different. E. receptive, expansive, as if handling life through a wide funnel with a great indraught; S. as if through a pin-point orifice that emits his cooling spray outward over the universe like a nose-disinfectant from an 'atomizer.' . . . I fear that the real originality of the book will be lost on nineteen-twentieths of the members of the Philosophical and Psychological Associations!! The enemies of Harvard will find lots of blasphemous

---

of the resurrection. . . . What you say . . . about the value of the good lying in its *existence*, and about the continuity of the world of values with that of fact, is not different from what I should admit. Ideals would be irrelevant if they were not natural entelechies, if they were not called for by something that exists and if, consequently, their realization would not be a present and actual good. And the point in insisting that all the eggs at breakfast are rotten is nothing at all except the consequent possibility and endeavour to find good eggs for the morrow. The only thing I object to and absolutely abhor is the assertion that all the eggs indiscriminately are good because the hen has laid them.

"You tax me several times with impertinence and superior airs. I wonder if you realize the years of suppressed irritation which I have passed in the midst of an unintelligible, sanctimonious and often disingenuous Protestantism, which is thoroughly alien and repulsive to me, and the need I have of joining hands with something far away from it

and far above it. My Catholic sympathies didn't justify me in speaking out because I felt them to be merely sympathies, and not to have a rational and human backing; but the study of Plato and Aristotle has given me confidence and, backed by such an authority as they and all who have accepted them represent, I have a right to be sincere, to be absolutely objective and unapologetic, because it is not I that speak but human reason that speaks in me. Truly the Babel in which we live has nothing in it so respectable as to put on the defensive the highest traditions of the human mind. No doubt, as you say, Latinity is moribund, as Greece itself was when it transmitted to the rest of the world the seeds of its own rationalism; and for that reason there is the more need of transplanting and propagating straight thinking among the peoples who hope to be masters of the world in the immediate future. Otherwise they will be its physical masters only, and the Muses will fly over them to alight among some future race that may understand the gods better."

texts in him to injure us withal. But it is a great feather in our cap to
harbor such an absolutely free expresser of individual convictions."

WJ on *L'Évolution créatrice* (1907):

"O my Bergson, you are a magician, and your book is a marvel, a
real wonder in the history of philosophy, making, if I mistake not, an
entirely new era in respect of matter, but unlike the works of genius
of the 'transcendentalist' movement (which are so obscurely and abominably and inaccessibly written), a pure classic in point of form. You
may be amused at the comparison, but in finishing it I found the same
after-taste remaining as after finishing *Madame Bovary*, such a flavor of •
persistent *euphony*, as of a rich river that never foamed or ran thin,
but steadily and firmly proceeded with its banks full to the brim. Then
the aptness of your illustrations, that never scratch or stand out at
right angles, but invariably simplify the thought and help to pour it
along! Oh, indeed you are a magician! And if your next book proves
to be as great an advance on this one as this is on its two predecessors,
your name will surely go down as one of the great creative names in
philosophy.

"There! have I praised you enough? What every genuine philosopher
(every genuine man, in fact) craves most is *praise*—although the philosophers generally call it 'recognition'! If you want still more praise,
let me know, and I will send it, for my features have been on a broad
smile from the first page to the last, at the chain of felicities that never
stopped. I feel rejuvenated.

"As to the content of it, I am not in a mood at present to make any
definite reaction. There is so much that is absolutely new that it will
take a long time for your contemporaries to assimilate it, and I imagine
that much of the development of detail will have to be performed by
younger men whom your ideas will stimulate to coruscate in manners
unexpected by yourself. To me at present the vital achievement of the
book is that it inflicts an irrecoverable death-wound upon Intellectualism. It can never resuscitate! But it will die hard, for all the inertia of
the past is in it, and the spirit of professionalism and pedantry as well
as the æsthetic-intellectual delight of dealing with categories logically
distinct yet logically connected, will rally for a desperate defense. The
élan vital, all contentless and vague as you are obliged to leave it, will
be an easy substitute to make fun of. But the beast *has* its death-wound
now, and the manner in which you have inflicted it (interval *versus*
temps d'arrêt, etc.) is masterly in the extreme. I don't know why this
later *rédaction* of your critique of the mathematics of movement has
seemed to me so much more telling than the early statement—I suppose
it is because of the wider *use* made of the principle in the book. You will
be receiving my own little 'pragmatism' book simultaneously with
this letter. How jejune and inconsiderable it seems in comparison with

your great system! But it is so congruent with parts of your system, fits so well into interstices thereof, that you will easily understand why I am so enthusiastic. I feel that at bottom we are fighting the same fight, you a commander, I in the ranks. The position we are rescuing is 'Tychism' and a really growing world."

PARTIAL PORTRAITS

The French Novelists

IF HJ's brief visit to George Eliot was the event of his first winter in England, his friendship with Turgenieff was the richest experience of the year he lived in France. His interest in Turgenieff dated back a long time before their meeting. As early as 1869 WJ was writing to HJ: "I was much satisfied by a new volume of *Nouvelles moscovites* of your old friend Turgenieff. His mind is morbid, but he is an artist through and through. His work is solid and will bear reading over and over. In other words *style* is there—that mystery." HJ also succeeded in interesting their father, who, unlike WJ, relished the Russian's radical pessimism, and felt impelled to write him from Cambridge in 1874:

"My dear Sir—It seems a pity that you should be ignorant of the immense appreciation your books have in this region, and the unfeigned delight they give to so many good persons. I am not myself a representative reader, but I have some leisure at least, which all your readers have not got, and I may therefore without presumption perhaps, constitute myself your informant on their behalf. My son (Henry James, Jr., now in Europe) lately published a critical sketch of your writings in the *North American Review*, which I think he sent you a copy of. But this was only an individual token, and what I want to say to you is, that my son's high appreciation of your genius is shared by multitudes of very intelligent people here. . . .

"I think the verdict of the large circle of admirers you have in this place is, that the novel owns a new power in your hands, a deeper fascination than it ever before exerted. Doubtless in this realm also it is true, *vixere fortes ante Agamemnona*. Men and women of great and surprising genius have made romance an instrument second only to the drama, as an educative power over the emotions. But it must be said of the greatest of these, that the most they do is, either like Scott to give us stirring pictures of human will *aux prises* with outward circumstance, and finally victorious over it; or else, like George Sand, Thackeray and George Eliot, to give us an idea of the enervating and palsying effect of social convention upon the conscience, in rendering men sceptical, self-indulgent and immoral. But you as a general thing strike a far deeper chord in the consciousness of your reader. You sink your shaft sheer through the world of outward circumstance, and of social convention, and shew us ourselves in the fixed grasp of fate, so to speak, or struggling vainly to break the bonds of temperament. Superficial critics revolt at this tragic spectacle, and pronounce you cynical. They mistake the profound spirituality of your method, and do not see that what touches the earnest heart of man, and fills it with divinest love and pity for its fellow-man, is infinitely more educative than anything addressed to his frivolous and self-righteous head.

"Such, in a measure, is the tribute we pay your sympathetic genius, when we talk of you here in the evening on the piazza of the house, facing the setting sun. One of the young ladies present wonders whether an eye so at one with nature as yours, will ever do for American landscape what you have done for Russia; and her companion, whom I sometimes fancy is worthy to take her place beside some of your own heroines, wonders whether our humanity will ever be so defined as to justify an observer like you coming over to look at us. I can only emphasize their wonder by adding my own. But should you ever cross the ocean, you must not fail to come to Cambridge, and sit with us on the piazza in the evening, while you tell us between the fumes of your pipe what the most exercised and penetrating genius of the old world discerns, either of promise or menace for humanity in the civilization of the new.

"Please look kindly on my intrusion, and believe me, my dear Sir, with the greatest esteem and admiration, yours, Henry James."

To this Turgenieff replied from Carlsbad, modestly disclaiming his right to be ranked with the great English novelists, but adding:

"Nevertheless accept my heartfelt thanks for all the good and kind things you say to me in your letter; and let me assure you, that it would make me the greatest pleasure not to 'smoke my pipe under your verandah'—I don't use tobacco—but to enjoy a quiet and pleasant conversation with the intelligent men and women of your society. Will this pleasure be ever realized? That I cannot say with certitude. I am rather too old now and too weak in health for undertaking such long journeys—but I still cherish the idea of a visit to your new world, so different from the old one."

Two years later HJ was writing to Howells from Paris about having made Turgenieff's acquaintance.[1] The more he saw him, the more he

_____
[1] P. 500 above.

preferred him to the French "literary fraternity": "I don't like their wares, and they don't like any others; and besides, they are not *accueillants*. Turgenieff is worth the whole heap of them, and yet he himself swallows them down in a manner that excites my extreme wonder. But he is the most lovable of men and takes all things easily." Similar letters to his family that winter had caused WJ to remark: "I never heard you speak so enthusiastically of any human being. . . . I read his book which you sent home . . . and although the vein of 'morbidness' was so pronounced in the stories, yet the mysterious depths which his plummet sounds atone for all. It is the amount of life which a man feels that makes you value his mind, and Turgenieff has a sense of worlds within worlds whose existence is unsuspected by the vulgar." George Eliot suffered by comparison. Of *Daniel Deronda* WJ remarked: "Her 'sapience,' as you excellently call it, passes all decent bounds. There is something essentially womanish in the irrepressible garrulity of her moral reflections. Why is it that it makes women feel so good to moralize? Man philosophizes as a matter of business, because he must,—he does it to a purpose and then lets it rest; but women don't seem to get over being tickled at the discovery that they have the faculty; hence the tedious iteration and restlessness of George Eliot's commentary on life." Both brothers were growing beyond that early enthusiasm.

What HJ learned from Turgenieff he disclosed in the course of two essays about him, the one his father mentioned, and another in 1884, the year after the Russian's death. In the first of these he defined Turgenieff's kind of realism, and made the self-revealing remark: "He loves the old, and is unable to see where the new is drifting. American readers will peculiarly appreciate this state of mind; if they had a native novelist of a large pattern, it would probably be, in a degree, his own." HJ concluded this essay with a passage that tried to mediate, not altogether coherently, between his father's and his brother's views of Turgenieff's "gloom." HJ granted that it might sometimes be "morbid," and then bethought himself, much more characteristically, that "dogmatic optimism" would have been far less real.

HJ's memorial essay, giving a modest but informal picture of their relationship, tells us even more of his debt. Through this first close acquaintance with a Continental artist of stature, he would seem to have completed his release from too narrow adherence to "our Anglo-Saxon, Protestant, moralistic, conventional standards." But he found Turgenieff sympathetic in a way that "the grandsons of Balzac" were not, since the Russian held to the belief that a subject must be "morally interesting." Turgenieff strengthened him too in his cardinal tenet that "story" was secondary to "character." When he wrote his preface to *The Portrait of a Lady*, he alluded specifically to this debt, but also indicated that he had felt on occasion uneasy with Turgenieff's want of "architecture," and had been challenged thereby to replace conventional plot with structural composition.

HJ produced essays about several of "the grandsons of Balzac," including Zola and Daudet and Maupassant, but they were his immediate contemporaries and not his masters. Balzac remained, to the end of his life, the great figure in his background. With HJ's kinship to Turgenieff so demonstrable, it may come as a surprise to hear him saying, in "The Lesson of Balzac," the lecture he delivered in America in 1905, that he had learned more about his craft from Balzac "than from any one else." He certainly had gained much of his first and therefore most fundamental knowledge from that vast source. Since La Farge had already initiated him into the *Comédie Humaine* at Newport, Miss Upham's Cambridge boarding-house, where he took his meals in 1862, had scarcely "to wait an hour" to become a "vivid translation into American terms" of the Maison Vauquer in *Le Père Goriot*. The interplay of brotherly interest may be noted again in a journal entry of WJ's that same winter: "Read . . . or rather skipped through Balzac's *Lys dans la vallée*. Wonderful! There never was such devotion of author to subject before. I will read all Balzac."

In his second published review HJ was pointing out to the New England writer Harriet Prescott Spofford how much she could profit from Balzac's example: "He is literally real: he presents objects as they are." Lecturing on Balzac forty years later, after he had written *The Golden Bowl*, HJ still dwelt on such basic matters. "No one begins," he said, "to handle the time-element and produce the time-effect with the authority of Balzac in his amplest sweeps." No one else had so immersed his characters in the conditions and circumstances that would have produced them.

WJ kept a comparable sense of Balzac's power, and when commenting on the immensity of twentieth-century New York,[1] he added: "Balzac ought to come to life again. His Rastignac imagination sketched the possibility of it long ago." He had written HJ about an interview at which "you, Balzac, or Howells ought to have been present, to work up for a novel or the stage. There's a great comedy yet to be made out of the University newly founded by the American millionaire. In this case the millionaire had announced his desire to found a professorship of psychology applied to education. The thing was to get it for Harvard, which he mistrusted. . . . He is a real Balzackian figure— a regular porker, coarse, vulgar, vain, cunning, mendacious, etc., etc." When HJ came to write about American financial corruption in *The Ivory Tower*, he may well have remembered what he had said in his

---

[1] P. 313 above.

first full-length essay on Balzac in 1875: "Money is the most general element of Balzac's novels; other things come and go, but money is always there."

Before he was done, HJ had written four long essays about this master, and always felt that there were fresh things to say. The few pages selected here are designed to indicate HJ's own progression as a critic. In *French Poets and Novelists* he hewed fairly closely to the books he was discussing, and permitted himself only at the end a compact summary of Balzac's method, with an indication of both its strength and its weakness. In *Notes on Novelists* he demonstrated that although he had increasingly limited himself as a critic to the novel of one century, this could have its compensations. For he had become such a past master of his subject that he seemed to have all of Balzac's many volumes at his fingers' ends. While developing the theme that no other novelist had even begun to emulate Balzac's saturation in his material, he produced the work of art which he believed a critical essay could be, "the efficient combination of experience and perception."

Writing to his father about Turgenieff, HJ had added: "I had also the other day a very pleasant call upon Flaubert, whom I like personally more and more each time I see him. But I think I easily—more than easily—see all round him intellectually." What he meant by that last bold sentence he developed in a letter to WJ: "In poor old Flaubert there is something almost tragic; his big intellectual temperament, machinery, etc., and his vainly colossal attempts to press out the least little drop of *passion*. So much talent, and so much naïveté, and yet so much dryness and coldness." HJ produced in the same year the essay on Flaubert in which he made his well-known remark that "Realism seems to us with *Madame Bovary* to have said its last word." The limitation of Flaubert's method, as HJ saw it, was that it was wholly external, that it gave no scope to the vibrations of the spirit.

When he returned to Flaubert in the 1890's, he still dwelt on this limitation, but he also stated why artists would always have to return to him: Flaubert was the greatest single challenge to perfection in prose. A decade later again, when HJ was asked to write an introduction to a new edition of *Madame Bovary*, he responded with the same kind of retrospective reminiscent essay that he was presently to devote to Balzac. In discussing *L'Éducation sentimentale*, he further evinced his conviction that he could see "all around" its author. But he went on to express in his fullest and freest fashion why Flaubert was, for better or worse, "the novelist's novelist"; and he made the point, which throws once more so much light back on himself, that there are two ways in which the novelist may go about to handle his material: "The more he feels his subject the more he *can* render it—that is the first way. The more he renders it the more he *can* feel it—that is the second way. The second way was unmistakably Flaubert's." It would also seem, whatever the differences between them, to have been unmistakably HJ's, as it must be that of any writer who feels the supreme importance of form. HJ knew now what made Flaubert a classic, just as WJ, from his very different angle, was to recognize it while praising his friend Bergson.[1]

The bulk of *Notes on Novelists* was given to Continental writers, but HJ at seventy also looked at "the new novel" in English in 1914. At the opening of his lecture on Balzac he had made the same kind of plea for discrimination that he had expressed indirectly in "The Figure in the Carpet" and his other stories dealing with artists: "I do not propose for a moment to invite you to blink the fact that our huge Anglo-Saxon array of producers and readers—and especially our vast cis-Atlantic multitude—presents production uncontrolled, production untouched by criticism, unguided, unlighted, uninstructed, unashamed, on a scale that is really a new thing in the world." At the end of his career he was still eager for whatever signs of life he could recognize. He was greatly impressed by the vitality of *Tono-Bungay* and *The Old Wives' Tale*, he was disturbed by the looseness of form in D. H. Lawrence's early *Sons and Lovers*, and too hopeful about Compton Mackenzie and Hugh Walpole. But over against them all he placed the contemporary methods that seemed to him most fertile in artistic possibility, that of Conrad in *Chance* and of Edith Wharton in *The Custom of the Country*. Although that essay is too discursive to be included here, it is the latest example of the standards with which HJ practiced the art of criticism.

* * * * *

HJ ON TURGENIEFF

1874

WE KNOW of several excellent critics who to the question, Who is the first novelist of the day? would reply, without hesitation, Ivan Turgénieff. . . . The Russians, among whom fiction flourishes vigorously, deem him their greatest artist. His tales are not numerous, and many of them are very short. He gives us the impression of writing much more for love than for lucre. He is particularly a favourite with people of cultivated taste; and nothing, in our opinion, cultivates the taste more than to read him.

He belongs to the limited class of very careful writers. It is to be admitted at the outset that he is a zealous genius, rather than an abundant

---

[1] P. 546 above.

one. His line is narrow observation. He has not the faculty of rapid, passionate, almost reckless improvisation—that of Walter Scott, of Dickens, of George Sand. This is an immense charm in a story-teller; on the whole, to our sense, the greatest. Turgénieff lacks it; he charms us in other ways. To describe him in the fewest terms, he is a story-teller who has taken notes. This must have been a life-long habit. His tales are a magazine of small facts, of anecdotes, of descriptive traits, taken, as the phrase is, from the life. If we are not mistaken, he notes down an idiosyncrasy of character, a fragment of talk, an attitude, a feature, a gesture, and keeps it, if need be, for twenty years, till just the moment for using it comes, just the spot for placing it.

. . . If his manner is that of a searching realist, his temper is that of an earnestly attentive observer, and the result of this temper is to make him take a view of the great spectacle of human life more general, more impartial, more unreservedly intelligent, than that of any novelist we know. Even in this direction he proceeds with his characteristic precision of method; one thinks of him as having divided his subject-matter into categories, and as moving from one to the other—with none of the magniloquent pretensions of Balzac, indeed, to be the great showman of the human comedy—but with a deeply intellectual impulse toward universal appreciation. He seems to us to care for more things in life, to be solicited on more sides, than any novelist save George Eliot. Walter Scott cares for adventure and bravery and honour and ballad-figures and the humour of Scotch peasants; Dickens cares, in a very large and various way, for the incongruous, comic and pathetic; George Sand cares for love and mineralogy. But these writers care also, greatly, and indeed almost supremely, for their fable, for its twists and turns and surprises, for the work they have in hand of amusing the reader. Even George Eliot, who cares for so many other things besides, has a weakness for making a rounded plot, and often swells out her tales with mechanical episodes, in the midst of which their moral unity quite evaporates. The Bulstrode-Raffles episode in "Middlemarch," and the whole fable of "Felix Holt," are striking cases in point. M. Turgénieff lacks, as regards form, as we have said, this immense charm of absorbed inventiveness; but in the way of substance there is literally almost nothing he does not care for. Every class of society, every type of character, every degree of fortune, every phase of manners, passes through his hands; his imagination claims its property equally, in town and country, among rich and poor, among wise people and idiots, *dilettanti* and peasants, the tragic and the joyous, the probable and the grotesque. He has an eye for all our passions, and a deeply sympathetic sense of the wonderful complexity of our souls. . . . He has a passion for shifting his point of view, but his object is constantly the same—that of finding an incident, a person, a situation, *morally* interesting. This is his great merit, and the underlying harmony of his apparently excessive attention to detail. He believes the intrinsic value of "subject" in art; he holds that there are trivial subjects and serious ones, that the latter are much the best, and that their superiority resides in their giving us absolutely a greater amount of information about the human-mind. . . .

M. Turgénieff's themes are all Russian; here and there the scene of a tale is laid in another country, but the actors are genuine Muscovites. It is the Russian type of human nature that he depicts; this perplexes, fascinates, inspires him. His works savour strongly of his native soil, like those of all great novelists, and give one who has read them all a strange sense of having had a prolonged experience of Russia. We seem to have travelled there in dreams, to have dwelt there in another state of being. M. Turgénieff gives us a peculiar sense of being out of harmony with his native land—of his having what one may call a poet's quarrel with it. He loves the old, and he is unable to see where the new is drifting. American readers will peculiarly appreciate this state of mind; if they had a native novelist of a large pattern, it would probably be, in a degree, his own. Our author *feels* the Russian character intensely, and cherishes, in fancy, all its old manifestations—the unemancipated peasants, the ignorant, absolute, half-barbarous proprietors, the quaint provincial society, the local types and customs of every kind. But Russian society, like our own, is in process of formation, the Russian character is in solution, in a sea of change, and the modified, modernized Russian, with his old limitations and his new pretensions, is not, to an imagination fond of caressing the old, fixed contours, an especially grateful phenomenon. A satirist at all points, as we shall have occasion to say, M. Turgénieff is particularly unsparing of the new intellectual fashions prevailing among his countrymen. The express purpose of one of his novels, "Fathers and Sons," is to contrast them with the old; and in most of his recent works, notably "Smoke," they have been embodied in various grotesque figures.

It was not, however, in satire, but in thoroughly genial, poetical portraiture, that our author first made his mark. "The Memoirs of a Sportsman" were published in 1852, and were regarded, says one of the two French translators of the work, as much the same sort of contribution to the question of Russian serfdom as Mrs. Stowe's famous novel to that of American slavery. This, perhaps, is forcing a point, for M. Turgénieff's group of tales strikes us much less as a passionate *pièce de circonstance* than as a disinterested work of art. But circumstances helped it, of course, and it made a great impression—an impression that testifies to no small culture on the part of Russian readers. For never, surely, was a work with a polemic bearing more consistently low in tone, as painters say. The author treats us to such a scanty dose of flagrant horrors that the moral of the book is obvious only to attentive readers. No single episode pleads conclusively against the "peculiar institution" of Russia; the lesson is in the cumulative testimony of a multitude of fine touches—in an after-sense of sadness that sets wise readers thinking. It would be difficult to name a work that contains better instruction for those heated spirits who are fond of taking sides on the question of "art for art." It offers a capital example of moral meaning giving a sense to form and form giving relief to moral meaning. Indeed, all the author's characteristic merits are to be found in the "Memoirs," with a certain amateurish looseness of texture which will charm many persons who find his later works too frugal, as it were, in shape. Of all his productions, this is indeed the most purely delightful.

. . . M. Turgénieff's pessimism seems to us of two sorts—a spontaneous melancholy and a wanton melancholy. Sometimes in a sad story it is the problem, the question, the idea, that strikes him; sometimes it is simply the picture. Under the former influence he has produced his masterpieces; we admit that they are intensely sad, but we consent to be moved, as we consent to sit silent in a death-chamber. In the other case he has done but his second best; we strike a bargain over our tears, and insist that when it comes to being simply entertained, wooing and wedding are better than death and burial. "The Antchar," "The Forsaken," "A Superfluous Man," "A Village Lear," "Toc . . . toc . . . toc," all seem to us to be gloomier by several shades than they need have been; for we hold to the good old belief that the presumption, in life, is in favour of the brighter side, and we deem it, in art, an indispensable condition of our interest in a depressed observer that he should have at least tried his best to be cheerful. The truth, we take it, lies for the pathetic in poetry and romance very much where it lies for the "immoral." Morbid pathos is reflective pathos; ingenious pathos, pathos not freshly born of the occasion; noxious immorality is superficial immorality, immorality without natural roots in the subject. We value most the "realists" who have an ideal of delicacy and the elegiasts who have an ideal of joy.

"Pictorial gloom, possibly," a thick and thin admirer of M. Turgénieff's may say to us, "at least you will admit that it *is* pictorial." This we heartily concede, and, recalled to a sense of our author's brilliant diversity and ingenuity, we bring our restrictions to a close. To the broadly generous side of his imagination it is impossible to pay exaggerated homage, or, indeed, for that matter, to its simple intensity and fecundity. No romancer has created a greater number of the figures that breathe and move and speak, in their habits as they might have lived; none, on the whole, seems to us to have had such a masterly touch in portraiture, none has mingled so much ideal beauty with so much unsparing reality. His sadness has its element of error, but it has also its larger element of wisdom. Life *is*, in fact, a battle. On this point optimists and pessimists agree. Evil is insolent and strong; beauty enchanting but rare; goodness very apt to be weak; folly very apt to be defiant; wickedness to carry the day; imbeciles to be in great places, people of sense in small, and mankind generally, unhappy. But the world as it stands is no illusion, no phantasm, no evil dream of a night; we wake up to it again for ever and ever; we can neither forget it nor deny it nor dispense with it. We can welcome experience as it comes, and give it what it demands, in exchange for something which it is idle to pause to call much or little so long as it contributes to swell the volume of consciousness. In this there is mingled pain and delight, but over the mysterious mixture there hovers a visible rule, that bids us learn to will and seek to understand. So much as this we seem to decipher between the lines of M. Turgénieff's minutely written chronicle. He himself has sought to understand as zealously as his most eminent competitors. He gives, at least, no meagre account of life, and he has done liberal justice to its infinite variety. . . . If he were a dogmatic optimist we suspect that, as things go, we should long ago have ceased to miss him from our library. The personal optimism of most of us no romancer can confirm or dissipate and our personal troubles, generally, place fictions of all kinds in an impertinent light. To our usual working mood the world is apt to seem M. Turgénieff's hard world, and when, at moments, the strain and the pressure deepen, the ironical element figures not a little in our form of address to those short-sighted friends who have whispered that it is an easy one.

1 8 8 4

WHEN the mortal remains of Ivan Turgénieff were about to be transported from Paris for interment in his own country, a short commemorative service was held at the Gare du Nord. Ernest Renan and Edmond About, standing beside the train in which his coffin had been placed, bade farewell in the name of the French people to the illustrious stranger who for so many years had been their honoured and grateful guest. M. Renan made a beautiful speech, and M. About a very clever one, and each of them characterised, with ingenuity, the genius and the moral nature of the most touching of writers, the most lovable of men. "Turgénieff," said M. Renan, "received by the mysterious decree which marks out human vocations the gift which is noble beyond all others: he was born essentially impersonal." The passage is so eloquent that one must repeat the whole of it. "His conscience was not that of an individual to whom nature had been more or less generous: it was in some sort the conscience of a people. Before he was born he had lived for thousands of years; infinite successions of reveries had amassed themselves in the depths of his heart. No man has been as much as he the incarnation of a whole race: generations of ancestors, lost in the sleep of centuries, speechless, came through him to life and utterance."

I quote these lines for the pleasure of quoting them; for while I see what M. Renan means by calling Turgénieff impersonal, it has been my wish to devote to his delightful memory a few pages written under the impression of contact and intercourse. He seems to us impersonal, because it is from his writings almost alone that we of English, French and German speech have derived our notions—even yet, I fear, rather meagre and erroneous—of the Russian people. His genius for us is the Slav genius; his voice the voice of those vaguely-imagined multitudes whom we think of more and more to-day as waiting their turn, in the arena of civilisation, in the grey expanses of the North. There is much in his writings to encourage this view, and it is certain that he interpreted with wonderful vividness the temperament of his fellow-countrymen. Cosmopolite that he had become by the force of circumstances, his roots had never been loosened in his native soil. The ignorance with regard to Russia and the Russians which he found in abundance in the rest of Europe—and not least in the country he inhabited for ten years before his death—had indeed the effect, to a certain degree, to throw him back upon the deep feelings which so many of his companions were unable to share with him, the memories of his early years, the sense of wide Russian horizons, the joy and pride of his mother-tongue. In the collection of short pieces, so deeply interesting, written during the last few years of his life, and translated into German under the name of "Senilia," I find a passage—it is the last in the little book—which illustrates perfectly this reactionary impulse: "In days of doubt, in days of anxious thought on the destiny of my native land, thou alone art my support and my staff, O great powerful Russian tongue, truthful and free! If it were not for thee how should man not despair at the sight of what is going on at home? But it is inconceivable that such a language has not been given to a great people." This Muscovite, home-loving note pervades his productions, though it is between the lines, as it were, that we must listen for it. None the less does it remain true that he was not a simple conduit or mouthpiece; the inspiration was his own as well as the voice. He was an individual, in other words, of the most unmistakable kind, and those who had the happiness to know him have no difficulty to-day in thinking of him as an eminent, responsible figure. This pleasure, for the writer of these lines, was as great as the pleasure of reading the admirable tales into which he put such a world of life and feeling: it was perhaps even greater, for it was not only with the pen that nature had given Turgénieff the power to express himself. He was the richest, the most delightful, of talkers, and his face, his person, his temper, the thoroughness with which he had been equipped for human intercourse, make in the memory of his friends an image which is completed, but not thrown into the shade, by his literary distinction. The whole image is tinted with sadness: partly because the element of melancholy in his nature was deep and constant—readers of his novels have no need to be told of that; and partly because, during the last years of his life, he had been condemned to suffer atrociously. Intolerable pain had been his portion for too many months before he died; his end was not a soft decline, but a deepening distress. But of brightness, of the faculty of enjoyment, he had also the large allowance usually made to first-rate men, and he was a singularly complete human being. The author of these pages had greatly admired his writings before having the fortune to make his acquaintance, and this privilege, when it presented itself, was highly illuminating. The man and the writer together occupied from that moment a very high place in his affection. Some time before knowing him I committed to print certain reflections which his tales had led me to make; and I may perhaps, therefore, without impropriety give them a supplement which shall have a more vivifying reference. It is almost irresistible to attempt to say, from one's own point of view, what manner of man he was.

It was in consequence of the article I just mentioned that I found reason to meet him, in Paris, where he was then living, in 1875. I shall never forget the impression he made upon me at that first interview. I found him adorable; I could scarcely believe that he would prove—that any man could prove—on nearer acquaintance so delightful as that. Nearer acquaintance only confirmed my hope, and he remained the most approachable, the most practicable, the least unsafe man of genius it has been my fortune to meet. He was so simple, so natural, so modest, so destitute of personal pretension and of what is called the consciousness of powers, that one almost doubted at moments whether he were a man of genius after all. Everything good and fruitful lay near to him; he was interested in everything; and he was absolutely without that eagerness of self-reference which sometimes accompanies great, and even small, reputations. He had not a particle of vanity; nothing whatever of the air of having a part to play or a reputation to keep up. His humour exercised itself as freely upon himself as upon other subjects, and he told stories at his own expense with a sweetness of hilarity which made his peculiarities really sacred in the eyes of a friend. I remember vividly the smile and tone of voice with which he once repeated to me a figurative epithet which Gustave Flaubert (of whom he was extremely fond) had applied to him—an epithet intended to characterise a certain expansive softness, a comprehensive indecision, which pervaded his nature, just as it pervades so many of the characters he has painted. He enjoyed Flaubert's use of this term, good-naturedly opprobrious, more even than Flaubert himself, and recognised perfectly the element of truth in it. He was natural to an extraordinary degree; I do not think I have ever seen his match in this respect, certainly not among people who bear, as he did, at the same time, the stamp of the highest cultivation. Like all men of a large pattern, he was composed of many different pieces; and what was always striking in him was the mixture of simplicity with the fruit of the most various observation. In the little article in which I had attempted to express my admiration for his works, I had been moved to say of him that he had the aristocratic temperament: a remark which in the light of further knowledge seemed to me singularly inane. He was not subject to any definition of that sort, and to say that he was democratic would be (though his political ideal was a democracy), to give an equally superficial account of him. He felt and understood the opposite sides of life; he was imaginative, speculative, anything but literal. He had not in his mind a grain of prejudice as large as the point of a needle, and people (there are many) who think this a defect would have missed it immensely in Ivan Serguéitch. (I give his name, without attempting the Russian orthography, as it was uttered by his friends when they addressed him in French.) Our Anglo-Saxon, Protestant, moralistic, conventional standards were far away from him, and he judged things with a freedom and spontaneity in which I found a perpetual refreshment. His sense of beauty, his love of truth and right, were the foundation of his nature; but half the charm of conversation with him was that one breathed an air in which cant phrases and arbitrary measurements simply sounded ridiculous.

I may add that it was not because I had written a laudatory article about his books that he gave me a friendly welcome; for in the first place my article could have very little importance for him, and in the second it had never been either his habit or his hope to bask in the light of criticism. Supremely modest as he was, I think he attached no great weight to what might happen to be said about him; for he felt that he was destined to encounter a very small amount of intelligent appreciation, especially in foreign countries. I never heard him even allude to any judgment which might have been passed upon his productions in England. In France he knew that he was read very moderately; the "demand" for his volumes was small, and he had no illusions whatever on the subject of his popularity. He had heard with pleasure that many intelligent persons in the United States were impatient for everything that might come from his pen; but I think he was never convinced, as one or two of the more zealous of these persons had endeavoured to convince him, that he could boast of a "public" in America. He gave me the impression of thinking of criticism as most serious workers think of it—that it is the amusement, the exercise, the subsistence of the critic (and, so far as this goes, of immense use); but that though it may often concern other readers, it does not much concern the artist himself. In comparison with all those things which the production of a considered work forces the artist little by little to say to himself, the remarks of the critic are vague and of the moment; and yet, owing to the large publicity of the proceeding, they have a power to irritate or discourage which is quite out of proportion to their use to the person criticised. It was not, moreover (if this explanation be not more gross than the spectre it is meant to conjure away), on account of any esteem which he accorded to my own productions (I used regularly to send them to him) that I found him so agreeable, for to the best of my belief he was unable to read them. As regards one of the first that I had offered him he wrote me a little note to tell me that a distinguished friend, who was his constant companion, had read three or four chapters aloud to him the evening before and that one of them was written *de main de maître!* [1] This gave me great pleasure, but it was my first and last pleasure of the kind. I continued, as I say, to send him my fictions, because they were the only thing I had to give; but he never alluded to the rest of the work in question, which he evidently did not finish, and never gave any sign of having read its successors. Presently I quite ceased to expect this, and saw why it was (it interested me much), that my writings could not appeal to him. He cared, more than anything else, for the air of reality, and my reality was not to the purpose. I do not think my stories struck him as quite meat for men. The manner was more apparent than the matter; they were too *tarabiscoté*, as I once heard him say of the style of a book—had on the surface too many little flowers and knots of ribbon. . . .

Nothing that Turgénieff had to say could be more interesting than his talk about his own work, his manner of writing. What I have heard him tell of these things was worthy of the beautiful results he produced; of the deep purpose, pervading them all, to show us life itself. The germ of a story, with him, was never an affair of plot—that was the last thing he thought of: it was the representation of certain persons. The first form in which a tale appeared to him was as the figure of an individual, or a combination of individuals, whom he wished to see in action, being sure that such people must do something very special and interesting. They stood before him definite, vivid, and he wished to know, and to show, as much as possible of their nature. The first

[1] Turgénieff had written: "Nous avons commencé, Mme. Viardot et moi, à lire votre livre—nous avons lu les deux premiers chapitres—et je suis heureux de vous dire tant le plaisir que cela nous a causé. La scène (avant le départ) entre Rowland, la mère de Roderick, Miss Garland et Striker est faite de main de maître. Je ne doute pas que la continuation de la lecture nous faire le même plaisir—et je ne veux pas tarder davantage à vous envoyer mes meilleures félicitations."—F. O. M.

thing was to make clear to himself what he did know, to begin with; and to this end, he wrote out a sort of biography of each of his characters, and everything that they had done and that had happened to them up to the opening of the story. He had their *dossier*, as the French say, and as the police has of that of every conspicuous criminal. With this material in his hand he was able to proceed; the story all lay in the question, What shall I make them do? He always made them do things that showed them completely; but, as he said, the defect of his manner and the reproach that was made him was his want of "architecture"—in other words, of composition. The great thing, of course, is to have architecture as well as precious material, as Walter Scott had them, as Balzac had them. If one reads Turgénieff's stories with the knowledge that they were composed—or rather that they came into being—in this way, one can trace the process in every line. Story, in the conventional sense of the word—a fable constructed, like Wordsworth's phantom, "to startle and waylay"—there is as little as possible. The thing consists of the motions of a group of selected creatures, which are not the result of a preconceived action, but a consequence of the qualities of the actors. Works of art are produced from every possible point of view, and stories, and very good ones, will continue to be written in which the evolution is that of a dance—a series of steps the more complicated and lively the better, of course, determined from without and forming a figure. This figure will always, probably, find favour with many readers, because it reminds them enough, without reminding them too much, of life. On this opposition many young talents in France are ready to rend each other, for there is a numerous school on either side. We have not yet in England and America arrived at the point of treating such questions with passion, for we have not yet arrived at the point of feeling them intensely, or indeed, for that matter, of understanding them very well. It is not open to us as yet to discuss whether a novel had better be an excision from life or a structure built up of picture-cards, for we have not made up our mind as to whether life in general may be described. There is evidence of a good deal of shyness on this point—a tendency rather to put up fences than to jump over them. Among us, therefore, even a certain ridicule attaches to the consideration of such alternatives. But individuals may feel their way, and perhaps even pass unchallenged, if they remark that for them the manner in which Turgénieff worked will always seem the most fruitful. It has the immense recommendation that in relation to any human occurrence it begins, as it were, further back. It lies in its power to tell us the most about men and women. Of course it will but slenderly satisfy those numerous readers among whom the answer to this would be, "Hang it, we don't care a straw about men and women: we want a good story!"

And yet, after all, "Elena" is a good story, and "Lisa" and "Virgin Soil" are good stories. Reading over lately several of Turgénieff's novels and tales, I was struck afresh with their combination of beauty and reality. One must never forget, in speaking of him, that he was both an observer and a poet. The poetic element was constant, and it had great strangeness and power. It inspired most of the short things that he wrote during the last few years of his life, since the publication of "Virgin Soil," things that are in the highest degree fanciful and exotic. It pervades the frequent little reveries, visions, epigrams of the "Senilia." It was no part of my intention, here, to criticise his writings, having said my say about them, so far as possible, some years ago. But I may mention that in re-reading them I find in them all that I formerly found of two other elements—their richness and their sadness. They give one the impression of life itself, and not of an arrangement, a *réchauffé* of life. I remember Turgénieff's once saying in regard to Homais, the little Norman country apothecary, with his pedantry of "enlightened opinions," in "Madame Bovary," that the great strength of such a portrait consisted in its being at once an individual, of the most concrete sort, and a type. This is the great strength of his own representations of character; they are so strangely, fascinatingly particular, and yet they are so recognisably general. Such a remark as that about Homais makes me wonder why it was that Turgénieff should have rated Dickens so high, the weakness of Dickens being in regard to just that point. If Dickens fail to live long, it will be because his figures are particular without being general; because they are individuals without being types; because we do not feel their continuity with the rest of humanity—see the matching of the pattern with the piece out of which all the creations of the novelist and the dramatist are cut. I often meant, but accidentally neglected, to put Turgénieff on the subject of Dickens again, and ask him to explain his opinion. I suspect that his opinion was in a large measure merely that Dickens diverted him, as well he might. That complexity of the pattern was in itself fascinating. I have mentioned Flaubert, and I will return to him simply to say that there was something very touching in the nature of the friendship that united these two men. It is much to the honour of Flaubert, to my sense, that he appreciated Ivan Turgénieff. There was a partial similarity between them. Both were large, massive men, though the Russian reached to a greater height than the Norman; both were completely honest and sincere, and both had the pessimistic element in their composition. Each had a tender regard for the other, and I think that I am neither incorrect nor indiscreet in saying that on Turgénieff's part this regard had in it a strain of compassion. There was something in Gustave Flaubert that appealed to such a feeling. He had failed, on the whole, more than he had succeeded, and the great machinery of erudition,—the great polishing process,—which he brought to bear upon his productions, was not accompanied with proportionate results. He had talent without having cleverness, and imagination without having fancy. His effort was heroic, but except in the case of "Madame Bovary," a masterpiece, he imparted something to his works (it was as if he had covered them with metallic plates) which made them sink rather than sail. He had a passion for perfection of form and for a certain splendid suggestiveness of style. He wished to produce perfect phrases, perfectly interrelated, and as closely woven together as a suit of chain-mail. He looked at life altogether as an artist, and took his work with a seriousness that never belied itself. To write an admirable page—and his idea of what constituted an admirable page was transcendent—seemed to him something to live for. He tried it again and again, and he came very near it; more than once he touched it, for "Madame Bovary" surely will live. But there was something ungenerous in his genius. He was cold, and he would have given everything he had to be able to glow. There is nothing in his novels like the passion of Elena for Inssaroff, like the purity of Lisa, like the anguish of the parents of Bazaroff, like the hidden wound of Tatiana; and yet Flaubert yearned, with all the accumulations of his vocabulary, to touch the chord of pathos.

. . . I almost regret having accidentally to mix up so much of Paris with this perhaps too complacent enumeration of occasions, for the effect of it may be to suggest that Ivan Turgénieff had been Gallicised. But this was not the case; the French capital was an accident for him, not a necessity. It touched him at many points, but it let him alone at many others, and he had, with that great tradition of ventilation of the Russian mind, windows open into distances which stretched far beyond the *banlieue*. I have spoken of him from the limited point of view of my own acquaintance with him, and unfortunately left myself little space to allude to a matter which filled his existence a good deal more than the consideration of how a story should be written—his hopes and fears on behalf of his native land. He wrote fictions and dramas, but the great drama of his life was the struggle for a better state of things in Russia. In this drama he played a distinguished part, and the splendid obsequies that, simple and modest as he was, have unfolded themselves over his grave, sufficiently attest the recognition of it by his countrymen. His funeral, restricted and officialised, was none the less a magnificent "manifestation." I have read the accounts of it, however, with a kind of chill, a feeling in which assent to the honours paid him bore less part than it ought. All this pomp and ceremony seemed to lift him out of the range of familiar recollection, of valued reciprocity, into the majestic position of a national glory. And yet it is in the presence of this obstacle to social contact that those who knew and loved him must address their farewell to him now. After all, it is difficult to see how the obstacle can be removed. He was the most generous, the most tender, the most delightful, of men; his large nature overflowed with the love of justice: but he also was of the stuff of which glories are made.

HJ ON BALZAC

1875

. . . THE greatest thing in Balzac cannot be exhibited by specimens. It is Balzac himself—it is the whole attempt—it is the method. This last is his unsurpassed, his incomparable merit. That huge, all-compassing, all-desiring, all-devouring love of reality which was the source of so many of his fallacies and stains, of so much dead-weight in his work, was also the foundation of his extraordinary power. The real, for his imagination, had an authority that it has never had for any other. When he looks for it in the things in which we all feel it, he finds it with a marvellous certainty of eye, and proves himself the great novelist that he pretends to be. When he tries to make it prevail everywhere, explain everything and serve as a full measure of our imagination—then he becomes simply the greatest of dupes. He is an extraordinary tissue of contradictions. He is at once one of the most corrupt of writers and one of the most naïf; the most mechanical and pedantic, and the fullest of *bonhomie* and natural impulse. He is one of the finest of artists and one of the coarsest. Viewed in one way, his novels are ponderous, shapeless, overloaded; his touch is graceless, violent, barbarous. Viewed in another, his tales have more colour, more composition, more grasp of the reader's attention than any others. Balzac's style would demand a chapter apart. It is the least simple style, probably, that ever was written; it bristles, it cracks, it swells and swaggers; but it is a perfect expression of the man's genius. Like his genius, it contains a certain quantity of everything, from immaculate gold to flagrant dross. He was a very bad writer, and yet unquestionably he was a very great writer. We may say briefly, that in so far as his method was an instinct it was successful, and that in so far as it was a theory it was a failure. But both in instinct and in theory he had the aid of an immense force of conviction. His imagination warmed to its work so intensely that there was nothing his volition could not impose upon it. Hallucination settled upon him, and he believed anything that was necessary in the circumstances. This accounts for all his grotesque philosophies, his heroic attempts to furnish specimens of things of which he was profoundly ignorant. He believed that he was about as creative as the Deity, and that if mankind and human history were swept away the "Comédie Humaine" would be a perfectly adequate substitute for them. M. Taine says of him very happily that, after Shakespeare, he is our great magazine of documents on hu-

man nature. When Shakespeare is suggested we feel rather his differences from Shakespeare—feel how Shakespeare's characters stand out
in the open air of the universe, while Balzac's are enclosed in a peculiar
artificial atmosphere, musty in quality and limited in amount, which
persuades itself with a sublime sincerity that it is a very sufficient infinite. But it is very true that Balzac may, like Shakespeare, be treated as
a final authority upon human nature; and it is very probable that as
time goes on he will be resorted to much less for entertainment, and
more for instruction. He has against him that he lacks that slight but
needful thing—charm. To feel how much he lacked it, you must read
his prefaces, with their vanity, avidity, and garrulity, their gross revelation of his processes, of his squabbles with his publishers, their culi-
nary atmosphere. But our last word about him is that he had incomparable power.

1902

STRONGER than ever, even than under the spell of first acquaintance and
of the early time, is the sense—thanks to a renewal of intimacy and, I
am tempted to say, of loyalty—that Balzac stands signally apart, that he
is the first and foremost member of his craft, and that above all the
Balzac-lover is in no position till he has cleared the ground by saying
so. . . . The authors and the books that have, as we say, done something for us, become part of the answer to our curiosity when our
curiosity had the freshness of youth, these particular agents exist for
us, with the lapse of time, as the substance itself of knowledge: they
have been intellectually so swallowed, digested and assimilated that we
take their general use and suggestion for granted, cease to be aware of
them because they have passed out of sight. But they have passed out of
sight simply by having passed into our lives. They have become a part
of our personal history, a part of ourselves, very often, so far as we
may have succeeded in best expressing ourselves. . . .

The impression then, confirmed and brightened, is of the mass and
weight of the figure and of the extent of ground it occupies; a tract
on which we might all of us together quite pitch our little tents, open
our little booths, deal in our little wares, and not materially either diminish the area or impede the circulation of the occupant. I seem to
see him in such an image moving about as Gulliver among the pigmies,
and not less good-natured than Gulliver for the exercise of any function, without exception, that can illustrate his larger life. The first and
the last word about the author of "Les Contes Drolatiques" is that of
all novelists he is the most serious—by which I am far from meaning
that in the human comedy as he shows it the comic is an absent quantity. His sense of the comic was on the scale of his extraordinary senses
in general, though his expression of it suffers perhaps exceptionally

from that odd want of elbow-room—the penalty somehow of his close-packed, pressed-down contents—which reminds us of some designedly beautiful thing but half-disengaged from the clay or the marble. It is the scheme and the scope that are supreme in him, applying this moreover not to mere great intention, but to the concrete form, the proved case, in which we possess them. We most of us aspire to achieve at the best but a patch here and there, to pluck a sprig or a single branch, to break ground in a corner of the great garden of life. Balzac's plan was simply to do everything that could be done. He proposed to himself to "turn over" the great garden from north to south and from east to west; a task—immense, heroic, to this day immeasurable—that he bequeathed us the partial performance of, a prodigious ragged clod, in the twenty monstrous years representing his productive career, years of concentration and sacrifice the vision of which still makes us ache. He had indeed a striking good fortune, the only one he was to enjoy as an harassed and exasperated worker: the great garden of life presented itself to him absolutely and exactly in the guise of the great garden of France, a subject vast and comprehensive enough, yet with definite edges and corners. This identity of his universal with his local and national vision is the particular thing we should doubtless call his greatest strength were we preparing agreeably to speak of it also as his visible weakness. Of Balzac's weaknesses, however, it takes some assurance to talk; there is always plenty of time for them; they are the last signs we know him by—such things truly as in other painters of manners often come under the head of mere exuberance of energy. So little in short do they earn the invidious name even when we feel them as defects.

What he did above all was to read the universe, as hard and as loud as he could, *into* the France of his time; his own eyes regarding his work as at once the drama of man and a mirror of the mass of social phenomena the most rounded and registered, most organised and administered, and thereby most exposed to systematic observation and portrayal, that the world had seen. There are happily other interesting societies, but these are for schemes of such an order comparatively loose and incoherent, with more extent and perhaps more variety, but with less of the great enclosed and exhibited quality, less neatness and sharpness of arrangement, fewer categories, subdivisions, juxtapositions. Balzac's France was both inspiring enough for an immense prose epic and reducible enough for a report or a chart. To allow his achievement all its dignity we should doubtless say also treatable enough for a history, since it was as a patient historian, a Benedictine of the actual, the living painter of his living time, that he regarded himself and handled his material. All painters of manners and fashions, if we will, are historians, even when they least don the uniform: Fielding, Dickens, Thackeray, George Eliot, Hawthorne among ourselves. But the great difference between the great Frenchman and the eminent others is that, with an imagination of the highest power, an unequalled intensity of vision, he saw his subject in the light of science as well, in the light of the bearing of all its parts on each other, and under pressure of a passion for exactitude, an appetite, the appetite of an ogre, for *all* the kinds of facts. We find I think in the union here suggested something like the truth about his genius, the nearest approach to a final account of him. Of imagination on one side all compact, he was on the other an insatiable reporter of the immediate, the material, the current combination, and perpetually moved by the historian's impulse to fix, preserve and explain them. One asks one's self as one reads him what concern the poet has with so much arithmetic and so much criticism, so many statistics and documents, what concern the critic and the economist have with so many passions, characters and adventures. The contradiction is always before us; it springs from the inordinate scale of the author's two faces; it explains more than anything else his eccentricities and difficulties. It accounts for his want of grace, his want of the lightness associated with an amusing literary form, his bristling surface, his closeness of texture, so rough with richness, yet so productive of the effect we have in mind when we speak of not being able to see the wood for the trees.

A thorough-paced votary, for that matter, can easily afford to declare at once that this confounding duality of character does more things still, or does at least the most important of all—introduces us without mercy (mercy for ourselves I mean) to the oddest truth we could have dreamed of meeting in such a connection. It was certainly *a priori* not to be expected we should feel it of him, but our hero is after all not in his magnificence totally an artist: which would be the strangest thing possible, one must hasten to add, were not the smallness of the practical difference so made even stranger. His endowment and his effect are each so great that the anomaly makes at the most a difference only by adding to his interest for the critic. The critic worth his salt is indiscreetly curious and wants ever to know how and why—whereby Balzac is thus a still rarer case for him, suggesting that exceptional curiosity may have exceptional rewards. The question of what makes the artist on a great scale is interesting enough; but we feel it in Balzac's company to be nothing to the question of what on an equal scale frustrates him. The scattered pieces, the *disjecta membra* of the character are here so numerous and so splendid that they prove misleading; we pile them together, and the heap assuredly is monumental; it forms an overtopping figure. The genius this figure stands for, none the less, is really such a lesson to the artist as perfection itself would be powerless to give; it carries him so much further into the special mystery. Where it carries him, at the same time, I must not in this scant space attempt to say—which would be a loss of the fine thread of my argument. I stick to our point in putting it, more concisely, that the artist of the "Comédie Humaine" is half smothered by the historian. Yet it belongs as well to the matter also to meet the question of whether the historian himself may not be an artist—in which case Balzac's catastrophe would seem to lose its excuse. The answer of course is that the reporter, however philosophic, has one law, and the originator, however substantially fed, has another; so that the two laws can with no sort of harmony or congruity make, for the finer sense, a common household. Balzac's catastrophe—so to name it once again—was in this perpetual conflict and final impossibility, an impossibility that explains his defeat on the classic side and extends so far at times as to make us think of his work as, from the point of view of beauty, a tragic waste of effort. . . .

This is Balzac caught in the very fact of his monstrous duality, caught in his most complete self-expression. He is clearly quite unwitting that in handing over his *data* to his twin-brother the impassioned economist and surveyor, the insatiate general inquirer and reporter, he is in any sort betraying our confidence, for his good conscience at such times, the spirit of edification in him, is a lesson even to the best of us, his rich robust temperament nowhere more striking, no more marked anywhere the great push of the shoulder with which he makes his theme move, overcharged though it may be like a carrier's van. It is not therefore assuredly that he loses either sincerity or power in putting before us to the last detail such a matter as, in this case, his heroine's management of her property, her tenantry, her economic opportunities and visions, for these are cases in which he never shrinks nor relents, in which positively he stiffens and terribly towers—to remind us again of M. Taine's simplifying word about his being an artist doubled with a man of business. Balzac was indeed doubled if ever a writer was, and to that extent that we almost as often, while we read, feel ourselves thinking of him as a man of business doubled with an artist. Whichever way we turn it the oddity never fails, nor the wonder of the ease with which either character bears the burden of the other.

. . . We can never know what might have become of him with less importunity in his consciousness of the machinery of life, of its furniture and fittings, of all that, right and left, he causes to assail us, sometimes almost to suffocation, under the general rubric of *things*. Things, in this sense with him, are at once our delight and our despair; we pass from being inordinately beguiled and convinced by them to feeling that his universe fairly smells too much of them, that the larger ether, the diviner air, is in peril of finding among them scarce room to circulate. His landscapes, his "local colour"—thick in his pages at a time when it was to be found in his pages almost alone—his towns, his streets, his houses, his Saumurs, Angoulêmes, Guérandes, his great prose

Turner-views of the land of the Loire, his rooms, shops, interiors, details of domesticity and traffic, are a short list of the terms into which he
saw the real as clamouring to be rendered and into which he rendered
it with unequalled authority. . . . A born son of Touraine, it must be
said, he pictures his province, on every pretext and occasion, with filial
passion and extraordinary breadth. The prime aspect in his scene all the
while, it must be added, is the money aspect. The general money question so loads him up and weighs him down that he moves through the
human comedy, from beginning to end, very much in the fashion of a
camel, the ship of the desert, surmounted with a cargo. "Things" for
him are francs and centimes more than any others, and I give up as
inscrutable, unfathomable, the nature, the peculiar avidity of his interest in them. It makes us wonder again and again what then is the use on
Balzac's scale of the divine faculty. The imagination, as we all know,
may be employed up to a certain point in inventing uses for money;
but its office beyond that point is surely to make us forget that anything so odious exists. This is what Balzac never forgot; his universe
goes on expressing itself for him, to its furthest reaches, on its finest
sides, in the terms of the market. To say these things, however, is after
all to come out where we want, to suggest his extraordinary scale and
his terrible completeness. I am not sure that he does not see character
too, see passion, motive, personality, as quite in the order of the "things"
we have spoken of. He makes them no less concrete and palpable, handles them no less directly and freely. It is the whole business in fine—
that grand total to which he proposed to himself to do high justice—
that gives him his place apart, makes him, among the novelists, the largest weightiest presence. There are some of his obsessions—that of the
material, that of the financial, that of the "social," that of the technical,
political, civil—for which I feel myself unable to judge him, judgment
losing itself unexpectedly in a particular shade of pity. The way to
judge him is to try to walk all round him—on which we see how remarkably far we have to go. He is the only member of his order really
monumental, the sturdiest-seated mass that rises in our path.

HJ ON FLAUBERT

1876

. . . M. FLAUBERT's theory as a novelist, briefly expressed, is to begin
on the outside. Human life, we may imagine his saying, is before all
things a spectacle, an occupation and entertainment for the eyes. What
our eyes show us is all that we are sure of; so with this we will at any
rate begin. As this is infinitely curious and entertaining, if we know
how to look at it, and as such looking consumes a great deal of time
and space, it is very possible that with this also we may end. We admit

nevertheless that there is something else, beneath and behind, that belongs to the realm of vagueness and uncertainty, and into this we must occasionally dip. It crops up sometimes irrepressibly, and of course we do not positively count it out. On the whole we will leave it to take care of itself and let it come off as it may. If we propose to represent the pictorial side of life, of course we must do it thoroughly well—we must be complete. There must be no botching, no bungling, no scamping; it must be a very serious matter. We will "render" things—anything, everything, from a chimney-pot to the shoulders of a duchess —as painters render them. We believe there is a certain particular phrase, better than any other, for everything in the world, and the thoroughly accomplished writer ends by finding it. We care only for what *is*—we know nothing about what ought to be. Human life is interesting, because we are in it and of it; all kinds of curious things are taking place in it (we do not analyse the curious—for artists it is an ultimate fact); we select as many of them as possible. Some of the most curious are the most disagreeable, but the chance for "rendering" in the disagreeable is as great as anywhere else (some people think even greater), and moreover the disagreeable is extremely characteristic. The real is the most satisfactory thing in the world, and if we once fairly advance in this direction nothing shall frighten us back.

Some such words as those may stand as a rough sketch of the sort of intellectual conviction under which "Madame Bovary" was written. The theory in this case at least was applied with brilliant success; it produced a masterpiece. Realism seems to us with "Madame Bovary" to have said its last word. We doubt whether the same process will ever produce anything better. In M. Flaubert's own hands it has distinctly failed to do so. "L'Éducation Sentimentale" is in comparison mechanical and inanimate. The great good fortune of "Madame Bovary" is that here the theory seems to have been invented after the fact. The author began to describe because he had laid up a great fund of disinterested observations; he had been looking at things for years, for his own edification, in that particular way. The imitative talents in the same line, those whose highest ambition is to "do" their Balzac or their Flaubert, give us the sense of looking at the world only with the most mercenary motives—of going about to stare at things only for the sake of their forthcoming novel. M. Flaubert knew what he was describing—knew it extraordinarily well. One can hardly congratulate him on his knowledge; anything drearier, more sordid, more vulgar and desolate than the greater part of the subject-matter of this romance it would be impossible to conceive. "Mœurs de Province," the subtitle runs, and the work is the most striking possible example of the singular passion, so common among Frenchmen of talent, for disparaging their provincial life.

. . . To many people "Madame Bovary" will always be a hard book to read and an impossible one to enjoy. They will complain of the abuse of description, of the want of spontaneity, of the hideousness of the subject, of the dryness and coldness and cynicism of the tone. Others will continue to think it a great performance. They will admit that it is not a sentimental novel, but they will claim that it may be regarded as a philosophical one; they will insist that the descriptions are extraordinary, and that beneath them there is always an idea that holds them up and carries them along. We cannot but think, however, that he is a very resolute partisan who would venture to make this same plea on behalf of "L'Éducation Sentimentale." Here the form and method are the same as in "Madame Bovary"; the studied skill, the science, the accumulation of material, are even more striking; but the book is in a single word a *dead* one. "Madame Bovary" was spontaneous and sincere; but to read its successor is, to the finer sense, like masticating ashes and sawdust. "L'Éducation Sentimentale" is elaborately and massively dreary. That a novel should have a certain charm seems to us the most rudimentary of principles, and there is no more charm in this laborious monument to a treacherous ideal than there is interest in a heap of gravel. To nothing that such a writer as Gustave Flaubert accomplishes—a writer so armed at all points, so informed, so ingenious, so serious—can we be positively indifferent; but to think of the talent, the knowledge, the experience, the observation that lie buried, without hope of resurrection, in the pages of "L'Éducation Sentimentale," is to pass a comfortless half-hour. That imagination, invention, taste and science should concentrate themselves, for human entertainment, upon such a result, strikes us as the most unfathomable of anomalies. The reader feels behind all M. Flaubert's writing a large intellectual machinery. He is a scholar, a man of erudition. Of all this "Salammbô" is a most accomplished example. "Salammbô" is not easy reading, nor is the book in the least agreeable; but it displays in the highest degree what is called the historical imagination. There are passages in it in which the literary expression of that refined, subtilized and erudite sense of the picturesque which recent years have brought to so high a development, seems to have reached its highest level. The "Tentation de Saint Antoine" is, to our sense, to "Salammbô" what "L'Éducation Sentimentale" is to "Madame Bovary"—what the shadow is to the substance. M. Flaubert seems to have had in him the material of but two spontaneous works. The successor, in each case, has been an echo, a reverberation.

1893

. . . His LIFE was that of a pearl-diver, breathless in the thick element while he groped for the priceless word, and condemned to plunge again and again. He passed it in reconstructing sentences, exterminating repe-titions, calculating and comparing cadences, harmonious *chutes de phrase*, and beating about the bush to deal death to the abominable assonance. Putting aside the particular ideal of style which made a pit-fall of the familiar, few men surely have ever found it so difficult to deal with the members of a phrase. He loathed the smug face of facility as much as he suffered from the nightmare of toil; but if he had been marked in the cradle for literature it may be said without paradox that this was not on account of any native disposition to write, to write at least as he aspired and as he understood the term. He took long years to finish his books, and terrible months and weeks to deliver himself of his chapters and his pages. Nothing could exceed his endeavor to make them all rich and round, just as nothing could exceed the unetherized anguish in which his successive children were born. His letters, in which, inconsequently for one who had so little faith in any rigor of taste or purity of perception save his own, he takes everybody into his most intimate literary confidence, the pages of the publication before us are the record of everything that retarded him. The abyss of reading answered to the abyss of writing; with the partial exception of "Mad-ame Bovary" every subject that he treated required a rising flood of in-formation. There are libraries of books behind his most innocent sen-tences. The question of "art" for him was so furiously the question of form, and the question of form was so intensely the question of rhythm, that from the beginning to the end of his correspondence we scarcely ever encounter a mention of any beauty but verbal beauty. He quotes Goethe fondly as to the supreme importance of the "con-ception," but the conception remains for him essentially the plastic one.

There are moments when his restless passion for form strikes us as leaving the subject out of account altogether, as if he had taken it up arbitrarily, blindly, preparing himself the years of misery in which he is to denounce the grotesqueness, the insanity of his choice. Four times, with his *orgueil*, his love of magnificence, he condemned himself in-congruously to the modern and familiar, groaning at every step over the horrible difficulty of reconciling "style" in such cases with truth and dialogue with surface. He wanted to do the battle of Thermopylæ, and he found himself doing "Bouvard et Pécuchet." One of the sides by which he interests us, one of the sides that will always endear him to the student, is his extraordinary ingenuity in lifting without falsifying, finding a middle way into grandeur and edging off from the literal without forsaking truth. This way was open to him from the moment he could look down upon his theme from the position of *une blague supérieure*, as he calls it, the amused freedom of an observer as ir-reverent as a creator. But if subjects were made for style (as to which Flaubert had a rigid theory: the idea was good enough if the expression was), so style was made for the ear, the last court of appeal, the supreme touchstone of perfection. He was perpetually demolishing his periods in the light of his merciless *gueulades*. He tried them on every one; his *gueulades* could make him sociable. The horror, in particular, that haunted all his years was the horror of the *cliché*, the stereotyped, the thing usually said and the way it was usually said, the current phrase that passed muster. Nothing, in his view, passed muster but freshness, that which came into the world, with all the honors, for the occasion. To use the ready-made was as disgraceful as for a self-respecting cook to buy a tinned soup or a sauce in a bottle. Flaubert considered that the dispenser of such wares was indeed the grocer, and, producing his ingredients exclusively at home, he would have stabbed himself for shame like Vatel. This touches on the strange weakness of his mind, his puerile dread of the grocer, the *bourgeois*, the sentiment that in his generation and the preceding misplaced, as it were, the spirit of adventure and the sense of honor, and sterilized a whole province of French literature. That worthy citizen ought never to have kept a poet from dreaming.

He had for his delectation and for satiric purposes a large collection of those second-hand and approximate expressions which begged the whole literary question. To light upon a perfect example was his nearest approach to natural bliss. "Bouvard et Pécuchet" is a museum of such examples, the cream of that "Dictionnaire des Idées Reçues" for which all his life he had taken notes and which eventually resolved itself into the encyclopædic exactitude and the lugubrious humor of the novel. Just as subjects were meant for style, so style was meant for images; therefore as his own were numerous and admirable he would have contended, coming back to the source, that he was one of the writers to whom the significance of a work had ever been most present. This significance was measured by the amount of style and the quantity of metaphor thrown up. Poor subjects threw up a little, fine subjects threw up much, and the finish of his prose was the proof of his profundity. If you pushed far enough into language you found yourself in the embrace of thought. There are, doubtless, many persons whom this account of the matter will fail to satisfy, and there will indeed be no particular zeal to put it forward even on the part of those for whom, as a writer, Flaubert most vividly exists. He is a strong taste, like any other that is strong, and he exists only for those who have a constitutional need to feel in some direction the particular æsthetic confidence that he inspires. That confidence rests on the simple fact that he carried execution so far and nailed it so fast. No one will care for him at all who does not care for his metaphors, and those moreover who care most for these will be discreet enough to admit that even a style rich in similes is limited when it renders only the visible. The invisible Flaubert scarcely touches; his vocabulary and all his methods were unadjusted and alien to it. He could not read his French Wordsworth, M. Sully-Prudhomme; he had no faith in the power of the moral to offer a surface. He himself offers such a flawless one that this hard concretion is success. If he is impossible as a companion he is deeply refreshing as a reference; and all that his reputation asks of you is an occasional tap of the knuckle at those firm thin plates of gold which constitute the leaves of his books. This passing tribute will yield the best results when you have been prompted to it by some other prose.

In other words, with all his want of *portée*, as the psychological critics of his own country would say of him, poor Flaubert is one of the artists to whom an artist will always go back. And if such a pilgrim, in the very act of acknowledgment, drops for an instant into the tenderness of compassion, it is a compassion singularly untainted with patronage or with contempt; full, moreover, of mystifications and wonderments, questions unanswered and speculations vain. Why was he so unhappy if he was so active; why was he so intolerant if he was so strong? Why should he not have accepted the circumstance that M. de Lamartine also wrote as his nature impelled, and that M. Louis Enault embraced a convenient opportunity to go to the East? The East, if we listen to him, should have been closed to one of these gentlemen and literature forbidden to the other. Why does the inevitable perpetually infuriate him, and why does he inveterately resent the ephemeral? Why does he, above all, in his private, in other words his continuous epistolary, despair, assault his correspondents with malodorous comparisons? The bad smell of the age was the main thing he knew it by. Naturally therefore he found life a *chose hideuse*. If it was his great merit and the thing we hold on to him for that the artist and the man were welded together, what becomes, in the proof, of a merit that is so little illuminating for life? What becomes of the virtue of the beauty that pretends to be worth living for? Why feel, and feel genuinely, so much about "art," in order to feel so little about its privilege? Why proclaim it on the one hand the holy of holies, only to let your behavior confess it on the other a temple open to the winds? Why be angry that so few people care for the real thing, since this aversion of the many leaves a luxury of space? The answer to these too numerous questions is the final perception that the subject of our observations failed of happiness, failed of temperance, not through his excesses, but absolutely through his barriers. He passed his life in strange oblivion of the circumstance that, however incumbent it may be on most of us to do our duty, there is, in spite of a thousand narrow dogmatisms, nothing in the world that any one is under the least obligation to *like*—not even (one braces one's self to risk the declaration) a particular kind of writing. Particular kinds of writing may sometimes, for their producers, have the good fortune to please; but these things are windfalls, pure

luxuries, not resident even in the cleverest of us as natural rights. Let
Flaubert always be cited as one of the devotees and even, when people
are fond of the word, as one of the martyrs of the plastic idea; but let
him be still more considerately preserved and more fully presented as
one of the most conspicuous of the faithless. For it was not that he went
too far, it was on the contrary that he stopped too short. He hovered
forever at the public door, in the outer court, the splendor of which
very properly beguiled him, and in which he seems still to stand as upright as a sentinel and as shapely as a statue. But that immobility and
even that erectness were paid too dear. The shining arms were meant
to carry further, the other doors were meant to open. He should at
least have listened at the chamber of the soul. This would have floated
him on a deeper tide; above all it would have calmed his nerves.

1902

THERE are many things to say about "Madame Bovary," but an old
admirer of the book would be but half-hearted—so far as they represent reserves or puzzlements—were he not to note first of all the circumstances by which it is most endeared to him. To remember it from
far back is to have been present all along at a process of singular interest
to a literary mind, a case indeed full of comfort and cheer. The finest of
Flaubert's novels is to-day, on the French shelf of fiction, one of the
first of the classics; it has attained that position, slowly but steadily,
before our eyes; and we seem so to follow the evolution of the fate of
a classic. We see how the thing takes place; which we rarely can, for
we mostly miss either the beginning or the end, especially in the case of
a consecration as complete as this. The consecrations of the past are too
far behind and those of the future too far in front. That the production
before us *should* have come in for the heavenly crown may be a fact to
offer English and American readers a mystifying side; but it is exactly
our ground and a part moreover of the total interest. The author of
these remarks remembers, as with a sense of the way such things happen, that when a very young person in Paris he took up from the
parental table the latest number of the periodical in which Flaubert's
then duly unrecognised masterpiece was in course of publication. The
moment is not historic, but it was to become in the light of history, as
may be said, so unforgettable that every small feature of it yet again
lives for him: it rests there like the backward end of the span. The
cover of the old *Revue de Paris* was yellow, if I mistake not, like that
of the new, and "Madame Bovary: Mœurs de Province," on the inside
of it, was already, on the spot, as a title, mysteriously arresting, in-
scrutably charged. I was ignorant of what had preceded and was not to
know till much later what followed; but present to me still is the act of
standing there before the fire, my back against the low beplushed and

begarnished French chimney-piece and taking in what I might of that instalment, taking it in with so surprised an interest, and perhaps as well such a stir of faint foreknowledge, that the sunny little salon, the autumn day, the window ajar and the cheerful outside clatter of the Rue Montaigne are all now for me more or less in the story and the story more or less in them. The story, however, was at that moment having a difficult life; its fortune was all to make; its merit was so far from suspected that, as Maxime Du Camp—though verily with no excess of contrition—relates, its cloth of gold barely escaped the editorial shears. This, with much more, contributes for us to the course of things to come. The book, on its appearance as a volume, proved a shock to the high propriety of the guardians of public morals under the second Empire, and Flaubert was prosecuted as author of a work indecent to scandal. The prosecution in the event fell to the ground, but I should perhaps have mentioned this agitation as one of the very few, of any public order, in his short list. "Le Candidat" fell at the Vaudeville Theatre, several years later, with a violence indicated by its withdrawal after a performance of but two nights, the first of these marked by a deafening uproar; only if the comedy was not to recover from this accident the misprised lustre of the novel was entirely to reassert itself. It is strange enough at present—so far have we travelled since then— that "Madame Bovary" should in so comparatively recent a past have been to that extent a cause of reprobation; and suggestive above all, in such connections, as to the large unconsciousness of superior minds. . . .

And yet it is not after all that the place the book has taken is so overwhelmingly explained by its inherent dignity; for here comes in the curiosity of the matter. Here comes in especially its fund of admonition for alien readers. The dignity of its substance is the dignity of Madame Bovary herself as a vessel of experience—a question as to which, unmistakably, I judge, we can only depart from the consensus of French critical opinion. M. Faguet for example commends the character of the heroine as one of the most living and discriminated figures of women in all literature, praises it as a field for the display of the romantic spirit that leaves nothing to be desired. Subject to an observation I shall presently make and that bears heavily in general, I think, on Flaubert as a painter of life, subject to this restriction he is right; which is a proof that a work of art may be markedly open to objection and at the same time be rare in its kind, and that when it is perfect to this point nothing else particularly matters. "Madame Bovary" has a perfection that not only stamps it, but that makes it stand almost alone; it holds itself with such a supreme unapproachable assurance as both excites and defies judgment. For it deals not in the least, as to unapproachability, with things exalted or refined; it only confers on its sufficiently vulgar elements of exhibition a final unsurpassable form. The form is in *itself* as interesting, as active, as much of the essence of the subject as the idea, and yet so close is its fit and so inseparable its life that we catch it at no moment on any errand of its own. That verily is to *be* interesting—all round; that is to be genuine and whole. The work is a classic because the thing, such as it is, is ideally *done,* and because it shows that in such doing eternal beauty may dwell. A pretty young woman who lives, socially and morally speaking, in a hole, and who is ignorant, foolish, flimsy, unhappy, takes a pair of lovers by whom she is successively deserted; in the midst of the bewilderment of which, giving up her husband and her child, letting everything go, she sinks deeper into duplicity, debt, despair, and arrives on the spot, on the small scene itself of her poor depravities, at a pitiful tragic end. In especial she does these things while remaining absorbed in romantic intention and vision, and she remains absorbed in romantic intention and vision while fairly rolling in the dust. That is the triumph of the book as the triumph stands, that Emma interests us by the nature of her consciousness and the play of her mind, thanks to the reality and beauty with which those sources are invested. It is not only that they represent *her* state; they are so true, so observed and felt, and especially so shown, that they represent the state, actual or potential, of all persons like her, persons romantically determined. Then her setting, the medium in which she struggles, becomes in its way as important, becomes eminent with the eminence of art; the tiny world in which she revolves, the contracted cage in which she flutters, is hung out in space for her, and her companions in captivity there are as true as herself.

I have said enough to show what I mean by Flaubert's having in this picture expressed something of his intimate self, given his heroine something of his own imagination: a point precisely that brings me back to the restriction at which I just now hinted, in which M. Faguet fails to indulge and yet which is immediate for the alien reader. Our complaint is that Emma Bovary, in spite of the nature of her consciousness and in spite of her reflecting so much that of her creator, is really too small an affair. This, critically speaking, is in view both of the value and the fortune of her history, a wonderful circumstance. She associates herself with Frédéric Moreau in "L'Éducation" to suggest for us a question that can be answered, I hold, only to Flaubert's detriment. Emma taken alone would possibly not so directly press it, but in her company the hero of our author's second study of the "real" drives it home. Why did Flaubert choose, as special conduits of the life he proposed to depict, such inferior and in the case of Frédéric such abject human specimens? I insist only in respect to the latter, the perfection of Madame Bovary scarce leaving one much warrant for wishing anything other. Even here, however, the general scale and size of Emma, who is small even of her sort, should be a warning to hyperbole. If I say that in the matter of Frédéric at all events the answer is inevitably detrimental I mean that it weighs heavily on our author's general credit. He wished in each case to make a picture of experience—middling experience, it is true—and of the world close to him; but if he imagined nothing better for his purpose than such a heroine and such a hero, both such limited reflectors and registers, we are forced to believe it to have been by a defect of his mind. . . . He takes Frédéric Moreau on the threshold of life and conducts him to the extreme of maturity without apparently suspecting for a moment either our wonder or our protest— "Why, why *him*?" Frédéric is positively too poor for his part, too scant for his charge; and we feel with a kind of embarrassment, certainly with a kind of compassion, that it is somehow the business of a protagonist to prevent in his designer an excessive waste of faith. . . .

We meet Frédéric first, we remain with him long, as a *moyen*, a provincial bourgeois of the mid-century, educated and not without fortune, thereby with freedom, in whom the life of his day reflects itself. Yet the life of his day, on Flaubert's showing, hangs together with the poverty of Frédéric's own inward or for that matter outward life; so that, the whole thing being, for scale, intention and extension, a sort of epic of the usual (with the Revolution of 1848 introduced indeed as an episode,) it affects us as an epic without air, without wings to lift it; reminds us in fact more than anything else of a huge balloon, all of silk pieces strongly sewn together and patiently blown up, but that absolutely refuses to leave the ground. The discrimination I here make as against our author is, however, the only one inevitable in a series of remarks so brief. What it really represents—and nothing could be more curious—is that Frédéric enjoys his position not only without the aid of a single "sympathetic" character of consequence, but even without the aid of one with whom we can directly communicate. Can we communicate with the central personage? or would we really if we could? A hundred times no, and if he himself can communicate with the people shown us as surrounding him this only proves him of their kind. Flaubert on his "real" side was in truth an ironic painter, and ironic to a tune that makes his final accepted state, his present literary dignity and "classic" peace, superficially anomalous. There is an explanation to which I shall immediately come; but I find myself feeling for a moment longer in presence of "L'Éducation" how much more interesting a writer may be on occasion by the given failure than by the given success. Successes pure and simple disconnect and dismiss him; failures— though I admit they must be a bit qualified—keep him in touch and in relation. Thus it is that as the work of a "grand écrivain" "L'Éducation," large, laboured, immensely "written," with beautiful passages and a general emptiness, with a kind of leak in its stored sadness, moreover, by which its moral dignity escapes—thus it is that Flaubert's ill-starred novel is a curiosity for a literary museum. Thus it is also that it suggests a hundred reflections, and suggests perhaps most of them directly to the intending labourer in the same field. If in short, as I have said, Flaubert is the novelist's novelist, this performance does more than any other toward making him so.

. . . May it not in truth be said that we practise our industry, so many of us, at relatively little cost just *because* poor Flaubert, producing the most expensive fictions ever written, so handsomely paid for it? It is as if this put it in our power to produce cheap and thereby sell dear; as if, so expressing it, literary honour being by his example effectively secure for the firm at large and the general concern, on its whole esthetic side, floated once for all, we find our individual attention free for literary and esthetic indifference. All the while we thus lavish our indifference the spirit of the author of "Madame Bovary," in the cross-light of the old room above the Seine, is trying to the last admiration for the thing itself. That production puts the matter into a nutshell: "Madame Bovary," subject to whatever qualification, is absolutely the most literary of novels, so literary that it covers us with its mantle. It shows us once for all that there is no *intrinsic* call for a debasement of the type. . . .

It is in this assured manner that the lesson sits aloft, that the spell for the critical reader resides; and if the conviction under which Flaubert labours is more and more grossly discredited among us his compact mass is but the greater. He regarded the work of art as *existing* but by its expression, and defied us to name any other measure of its life that is not a stultification. He held style to be accordingly an indefeasible part of it, and found beauty, interest and distinction as dependent on it for emergence as a letter committed to the post-office is dependent on an addressed envelope. Strange enough it may well appear to us to have to apologise for such notions as eccentric. There are persons who consider that style comes of itself—we see and hear at present, I think, enough of them; and to whom he would doubtless have remarked that it goes, of itself, still faster. . . . It was truly a wonderful success to be so the devotee of the phrase and yet never its victim. Fine as he inveterately desired it should be he still never lost sight of the question Fine for what? It is always so related and associated, so properly part of something else that is in turn part of something other, part of a reference, a tone, a passage, a page, that the simple may enjoy it for its least bearing and the initiated for its greatest. That surely is to be a writer of the first order. . . .

I have sufficiently remarked that I speak from the point of view of his interest to a reader of his own craft, the point of view of his extraordinary technical wealth—though indeed when I think of the general power of "Madame Bovary" I find myself desiring not to narrow the ground of the lesson, not to connect the lesson, to its prejudice, with that idea of the "technical," that question of the way a thing is done, so abhorrent, as a call upon attention, in whatever art, to the wondrous Anglo-Saxon mind. Without proposing Flaubert as the type of the newspaper novelist, or as an easy alternative to golf or the bicycle, we should do him less than justice in failing to insist that a masterpiece like "Madame Bovary" may benefit even with the simple-minded by the way it has been done. It derives from its firm roundness that sign of all rare works that there is something in it for every one. It may be read ever so attentively, ever so freely, without a suspicion of how it is written, to say nothing of put together; it may equally be read under the excitement of these perceptions alone, one of the greatest known to the reader who is fully open to them. Both readers will have been transported, which is all any can ask. Leaving the first of them, however that may be, to state the case for himself, I state it yet again for the second, if only on this final ground. The book and its companions represent for us a practical solution, Flaubert's own troubled but settled one, of the eternal dilemma of the painter of life. From the moment this rash adventurer deals with his mysterious matter at all directly his desire is not to deal with it stintedly. It at the same time remains true that from the moment he desires to produce forms in which it shall be preserved, he desires that these forms, things of *his* creation, shall not be, as testifying to his way with them, weak or ignoble. He must make them complete and beautiful, of satisfactory production, intrinsically interesting, under peril of disgrace with those who know. Those who don't know of course don't count for him, and it neither helps nor hinders him to say that every one knows about life. Every one does not—it is distinctly the case of the few; and if it were in fact the case of the many the knowledge still might exist, on the evidence around us, even in an age of unprecedented printing, without attesting itself by a multiplication of masterpieces. The question for the artist can only be of doing the artistic utmost, and thereby of *seeing* the general task. When it is seen with the intensity with which it presented itself to Flaubert a lifetime is none too much for fairly tackling it. It must either be left alone or be dealt with, and to leave it alone is a comparatively simple matter.

To deal with it is on the other hand to produce a certain number of finished works; there being no other known method; and the quantity of life depicted will depend on this array. What will this array, however, depend on, and what will condition the number of pieces of which it is composed? The "finish," evidently, that the formula so glibly postulates and for which the novelist is thus so handsomely responsible. He has on the one side to feel his subject and on the other side to render it, and there are undoubtedly two ways in which his situation may be expressed, especially perhaps by himself. The more he feels his subject the more he *can* render it—that is the first way. The more he renders it the more he *can* feel it—that is the second way. This second way was unmistakably Flaubert's, and if the result of it for him was a bar to abundant production he could only accept such an incident as part of the game. He probably for that matter would have challenged any easy definition of "abundance," contested the application of it to the repetition, however frequent, of the thing not "done." What but the "doing" makes the thing, he would have asked, and how can a positive result from a mere iteration of negatives, or wealth proceed from the simple addition of so many instances of penury? We should here, in closer communion with him, have got into his highly characteristic and suggestive view of the fertilisation of subject by form, penetration of the sense, ever, by the expression—the latter reacting creatively on the former; a conviction in the light of which he appears to have wrought with real consistency and which borrows from him thus its high measure of credit. It would undoubtedly have suffered if his books had been things of a loose logic, whereas we refer to it not only without shame but with an encouraged confidence by their showing of a logic so close. Let the phrase, the form that the whole is at the given moment staked on, be beautiful and related, and the rest will take care of itself—such is a rough indication of Flaubert's faith; which has the importance that it was a faith sincere, active and inspiring. I hasten to add indeed that we must most of all remember how in these matters everything hangs on definitions. The "beautiful," with our author, covered for the phrase a great deal of ground, and when every sort of propriety had been gathered in under it and every relation, in a complexity of such, protected, the idea itself, the presiding thought, ended surely by being pretty well provided for.

These, however, are subordinate notes, and the plain question, in the connection I have touched upon, is of whether we would really wish him to have written more books, say either of the type of "Bovary" or of the type of "Salammbô," and not have written them so well. When the production of a great artist who has lived a length of years has been small there is always the regret; but there is seldom, any more than here, the conceivable remedy. For the case is doubtless predetermined by the particular kind of great artist a writer happens to be, and this even if when we come to the conflict, to the historic case, deliberation and delay may not all have been imposed by temperament. The admirable George Sand, Flaubert's beneficent friend and correspondent, is exactly the happiest example we could find of the genius constitutionally incapable of worry, the genius for whom style "came," for whom the sought effect was ever quickly and easily struck off, the book freely and swiftly written, and who consequently is represented for us by upwards of ninety volumes. If the comparison were with this lady's great contemporary the elder Dumas the disparity would be quadrupled, but that ambiguous genius, somehow never really caught by us in the *fact* of composition, is out of our concern here: the issue is of those developments of expression which involve a style, and as Dumas never so much as once grazed one in all his long career, there was not even enough of that grace in him for a fillip of the finger-nail. Flaubert is at any rate represented by six books, so that he may on that estimate figure as poor, while Madame Sand, falling so little short of a hundred, figures as rich; and yet the fact remains that I can refer the congenial mind to him with confidence and can do nothing of the sort for it in respect to Madame Sand. She is loose and liquid and iridescent, as iridescent as we may undertake to find her; but I can imagine compositions quite without virtue—the virtue I mean, of sticking together—begotten by the impulse to emulate her. She had undoubtedly herself the benefit of her facility, but are we not left wondering to what extent *we* have it? There is too little in her, by the literary connection, for the critical mind, weary of much wandering, to rest upon. Flaubert himself wandered, wandered far, went much roundabout and sometimes lost himself by the way, but how handsomely he provided for our present repose! He found the French language inconceivably difficult to write with elegance and was confronted with the equal truths that elegance is the last thing that languages, even as they most mature, seem to concern themselves with, and that at the same time taste, asserting rights, insists on it, to the effect of showing us in a boundless circumjacent waste of effort what the absence of it may mean. He saw the less of this desert of death come back to that—that everything at all saved from it for us since the beginning had been saved by a soul of elegance within, or in other words by the last refinement of selection, by the indifference on the part of the very idiom, huge quite other than "composing" agent, to the individual pretension. Recognising thus that to carry through the individual pretension is at the best a battle, he adored a hard surface and detested a soft one—much more a muddled; regarded a style without rhythm and harmony as in a work of pretended beauty no style at all. He considered that the failure of complete expression so registered made of the work of pretended beauty a work of achieved barbarity. It would take us far to glance even at his fewest discriminations; but rhythm and harmony were for example most menaced in his scheme by repetition—when repetition had not a positive grace; and were above all most at the mercy of the bristling particles of which our modern tongues are mainly composed and which make of the desired surface a texture pricked through, from beneath, even to destruction, as by innumerable thorns.

On these lines production was of course slow work for him—especially as he met the difficulty, met it with an inveteracy which shows how it *can* be met; and full of interest for readers of English speech is the reflection he causes us to make as to the possibility of success at all comparable among ourselves. I have spoken of his groans and imprecations, his interminable waits and deep despairs; but what would these things have been, what would have become of him and what of his wrought residuum, had he been condemned to deal with a form of speech consisting, like ours, as to one part, of "that" and "which"; as to a second part, of the blest "it," which an English sentence may repeat in three or four opposed references without in the least losing caste; as to a third face of all the "tos" of the infinitive and the preposition; as to a fourth of our precious auxiliaries "be" and "do"; and as to a fifth, of whatever survives in the language for the precious art of pleasing? Whether or no the fact that the painter of "life" among us has to contend with a medium intrinsically indocile, on certain sides, like our own, whether this drawback accounts for his having failed, in our time, to treat us, arrested and charmed, to a single case of crowned classicism, there is at any rate no doubt that we in some degree owe Flaubert's counterweight for that deficiency to *his* having, on his own ground, more happily triumphed. By which I do not mean that "Madame Bovary" is a classic because the "thats," the "its" and the "tos" are made to march as Orpheus and his lute made the beasts, but because the element of order and harmony works as a symbol of everything else that is preserved for us by the history of the book. The history of the book remains the lesson and the important, the delightful thing, remains above all the drama that moves slowly to its climax. It is what we come back to for the sake of what it shows us. We see—from the present to the past indeed, never alas from the present to the future—how a classic almost inveterately grows. Unimportant, unnoticed, or, so far as noticed, contested, unrelated, alien, it has a cradle round which the fairies but scantly flock and is waited on in general by scarce a hint of significance. The significance comes by a process slow and small, the fact only that one perceptive private reader after another discovers at his convenience that the book is rare. The addition of the perceptive private readers is no quick affair, and would doubtless be a vain one did they not—while plenty of other much more remarkable books come and go—accumulate and count. They count by their quality and continuity of attention; so they have gathered for "Madame Bovary," and so they are held. That is really once more the great circumstance. It is always in order for us to feel yet again what it is we are held by. Such is my reason, definitely, for speaking of Flaubert as the novelist's novelist. Are we not moreover—and let it pass this time as a happy hope!—pretty well all novelists now?

*   *   *

BOOK SIX

BOOK SIX

ON CONSCIOUSNESS AND
IMMORTALITY

HENRY JAMES, SENIOR, believed that he was living at the dawn of a new religious era. He shared with Emerson and the transcendentalists the conviction that in liberating their contemporaries from the restrictions of orthodox theology they had opened for the next generation a freer and more abundant faith. The march of events was to prove them wrong. We have already seen, in the education of WJ and HJ, two of the reactions of that next generation. WJ felt as a young man that the margins of faith had been greatly reduced, that he could affirm no belief at all until he had met and mastered the challenge of the new materialistic science. HJ found a soft and vague freedom through the way that his father had prepared for him. Feeling no need to answer theological questions, his mind drifted into absorption with this world altogether.

Henry Senior had held that "Divine truth has first to create the intelligence it afterwards enlightens." He had also held with triumphant confidence that death is the beginning of life. HJ was scarcely concerned with man's relation to God; he fixed his attention exclusively on the fact of human consciousness. WJ, although he came to feel closer to his father's interests as he grew older, still remained primarily occupied with understanding what God had created rather than with the mystery of creation. His subject-matter, like HJ's, was consciousness. They were both psychologists. The distinction between them is, as John Dewey remarked, that "the former is concerned with human nature in its broad and common features (like Walt Whitman, he gives the average of the massed effect), while the latter is concerned with the special and peculiar coloring that the mental life takes on in different individualities."

But their psychologies would not have assumed the form they did without a religious background. Their conception of the sacredness of the individual stems from their father's Christianity as well as from the Declaration of Independence. And though neither of them became a religious man in any compelling sense, they finally converged, with surprising similarity, upon the question of immortality.

WJ arrived at the germinal idea of his epistemology in giving a firm negative to the question he propounded in his essay "Are We Automata?" (1879). He took issue there with the prevailing mechanistic views of the mind as reflected in Herbert Spencer, by insisting on the efficacy of consciousness in making choices. He had already reached his conception of the primacy of will, and was to say explicitly, in "Reflex Action and Theism" (1881), that "perception and thinking are only there for behavior's sake." But he was also convinced of the value of investigating consciousness by means of introspective analysis. He was a child of his century, a descendant of Coleridge, and the brother of a psychological novelist in his belief that unlimited discoveries were still to be made by any thinker who possessed the discipline to observe and the vividness to grasp the processes of his own mind. His insight into the stream-like continuity of thought was to be his leading proof of the soundness of that belief. He developed and kept a remarkably firm hold upon mental reality, and showed where he stood by declaring: "I myself find no good warrant for even suspecting the existence of any reality of a higher denomination than that distributed and strung-along and flowing sort of reality which we finite beings swim in."

Yet he did not close his mind to the possibility of immortality, any more than he did to any other thought that had proved valuable to some portion of mankind. Moreover, as he became familiar with the variety and intricacy of mental life, he stressed how one state of consciousness shades off into another, how "every bit of us at every moment is part and parcel of a wider self . . . and the actual in it is continuously one with the possibles not yet in our present sight." He was disposed, therefore, to accept the reality of mysticism on the ground that so-called "normal" consciousness was "so small a part of actual experience." In lecturing on some "Supposed Objections" to Immortality (1898), he took issue with the scientific argument that the mind was dependent upon the body and could not outlive it. He argued rather that the brain does not necessarily produce the mind, that it may simply be a channel for letting it filter through from some primal source. He went on to ask: "May not you and I be confluent in a higher consciousness, and confluently active there, though we now know it not?" After he had meditated for some years on Frederic Myers' "subliminal consciousness" and had experimented with mediums, he declared in his "Final Impressions of a Psychical Researcher" (1909):

"Out of my experience, such as it is (and it is limited enough) one

W J, by Alice Boughton, 1907

fixed conclusion dogmatically emerges, and that is this, that we with our lives are like islands in the sea, or like trees in the forest. The maple and the pine may whisper to each other with their leaves, and Conanicut and Newport hear each other's foghorns. But the trees also commingle their roots in the darkness underground, and the islands also hang together through the ocean's bottom. Just so there is a continuum of cosmic consciousness, against which our individuality builds but accidental fences, and into which our several minds plunge as into a mother-sea or reservoir. Our 'normal' consciousness is circumscribed for adaptation to our external earthly environment, but the fence is weak in spots, and fitful influences from beyond leak in, showing the otherwise unverifiable common connection. Not only psychic research, but metaphysical philosophy, and speculative biology are led in their own ways to look with favor on some such 'panpsychic' view of the universe as this."

By then he had also reached the position expressed in "Does 'Consciousness' Exist?" the first of his *Essays in Radical Empiricism*, that consciousness itself is not an entity but a function. This is the essay Whitehead cited in *Science and the Modern World* to exemplify how WJ symbolized the inauguration of a whole new era in thought by denying the Cartesian dualism between matter and mind.

Thus, both as a psychologist and as a philosopher of religion, WJ had advanced far from the bare stoicism with which he had responded to Minny Temple's death. At that time he had recorded in his diary: "By the big part of me that's in the tomb with you, may I realize and believe in the immediacy of death! May I feel that every torment suffered here passes and is as a breath of wind,—every pleasure too. . . . Minny, your death makes me feel the nothingness of all our egotistic fury. The inevitable release is sure; wherefore take our turn kindly whatever it contain. Ascend to some sort of partnership with fate, and since tragedy is at the heart of us, go to meet it, work it in to our ends, instead of dodging it all our days, and being run down by it at last. *Use* your death (or your life, it's all one meaning), 'tut twam asi.' " [1]

In the chapter on "The Consciousness of Self" in his *Psychology* he said: "The demand for immortality is nowadays essentially teleological. We believe ourselves immortal because we believe ourselves *fit* for immortality." When presented, in 1904, with a questionnaire on the subject of religion, he answered the query: "Do you believe in personal immortality? If so, why?" by saying: "Never keenly; but more strongly as I grow older. Because I am just getting fit to live." He developed this line of thought a little farther when writing to Norton four years later:

---

[1] "Thou art that."

"I am as convinced as I can be of anything that this experience of ours is only a part of the experience that is, and with which it has something to do; but *what* or *where* the other parts are, I cannot guess. It only enables one to say 'behind the veil, behind the veil!' more hopefully, however interrogatively and vaguely, than would otherwise be the case."

He had expressed his own beliefs most extensively in the conclusion to *The Varieties of Religious Experience*. In undertaking that book, he realized how strange it would seem to other philosophers in an age of positivistic science:

"The problem I have set myself is a hard one: *first*, to defend (against all the prejudices of my 'class') 'experience' against 'philosophy' as being the real backbone of the world's religious life—I mean prayer, guidance, and all that sort of thing immediately and privately felt, as against high and noble general views of our destiny and the world's meaning; and *second*, to make the hearer or reader believe, what I myself invincibly do believe, that, although all the special manifestations of religion may have been absurd (I mean its creeds and theories), yet the life of it as a whole is mankind's most important function. A task well-nigh impossible, I fear, and in which I shall fail; but to attempt it is *my* religious act."

He defined his purpose further by saying that he regarded the finished work "as in a sense a study of morbid psychology, mediating and interpreting to the philistine much that we would otherwise despise and reject utterly." He gave it the subtitle "a Study in Human Nature," and, in a draft for his opening paragraph, said that he hoped to seize upon "the living moments" of experience: "Here or nowhere, as Emerson says, is the whole fact. The moment stands and contains and sums up all things. . . . No one knows this like your genuine professor of philosophy. For whatever glimmers and twinkles like a bird's wing in the sunshine it is his business to snatch and fix."

In his hospitality to every shade of experience, WJ included testimony not only from the great leaders and saints of all religions, but also from pathological fanatics and freaks. He had in consequence to face having his book dubbed *Wild Religions I Have Known*. When he came to the explicit statement of his own convictions, he affirmed pragmatically that "God is real since he produces real effects." He left the question of immortality open, but he was by now thoroughly convinced that "the world of our present consciousness is only one out of many worlds of consciousness that exist." He took the pluralistic view that God was not necessarily one nor infinite but simply *"something* larger than ourselves" in whose support we could find help.

His approach could hardly satisfy either the irreligious or the religious. He foresaw the attack of rationalists and skeptics when he said:

"At bottom it is the feud between a naturalism . . . and a positive supernaturalism with its center of emphasis outside the margin of this world altogether. My own solution seems to favor this latter view. . . . The moderate and reasonable men will always be in the majority, and though we may consequently say that reasonable religion is the best for the race 'on the whole' . . . yet the vitally *important work* will always be done by these latter, for it is about their contributions that all the warfare revolves." It does not seem to have occurred to him that his tolerance of every conceivable sect might have the result of making them all seem equal—one vote each for Buddha and Mrs. Besant, for Jonathan Edwards and Mary Baker Eddy—and all equally uncompelling.

In casting his vote for pluralistic mysticism, WJ made no pretense that he had ever had any active sense of divine presence. He stated that "Prayer is religion in act; that is, prayer is real religion." But as far as he himself was concerned, he was to say, in answer to the questionnaire: "I can't possibly pray—I feel foolish and artificial." He knew that the chief religious adversaries to his attitude of open-minded acceptance would be the convinced absolutists with an intense consciousness of evil. It is significant that on the last page of his book he referred back, by way of contrast, to the passage on "the sick soul" in which he had described the essence of his father's religion. In the perplexity of his youth WJ had been troubled by "a dissatisfaction with anything less than grace." His final conception of grace had departed far from his father's. For Henry Senior, grace meant man's rescue from self-enclosed despair by the irresistible radiance of God's love. For WJ it meant the spontaneity of the eager will already pledged to the cause of righteousness.

On every page of HJ's fiction one is aware of his preoccupation with consciousness, so that it is no surprise to hear him saying that if he was not constantly "carrying the field of consciousness further and further, making it lose itself in the ineffable, he shouldn't in the least feel himself an artist." He must have subscribed readily to WJ's conception of "the stream of consciousness," though his own work is markedly different from the novels generally described by that term. He suggested the chief difference when remarking that, in the creation of a central reflector like Strether, he had wanted to avoid "the terrible *fluidity* of self-revelation."

Other differences from the fictional presentation of consciousness since Freud are also apparent. HJ does not treat the compulsive eruptions of the subconscious. His characters, as has often been remarked, live almost entirely "off the tops of their minds." Gide noted that HJ "only extracts from his brain what he knows to be there, and what his intelligence alone has put there." His most sophisticated characters are often, as more than one of them says, "horribly intelligent," but that being the case, it is an odd feature of HJ's work that they rarely have anything of general significance to think about. They are no more concerned with philosophy or religion than they are with politics. They are not even readers, or if they are, they rarely discuss their reading. They seldom have any occupation in HJ's pages beyond the realm of personal relations. Even in *The Princess Casamassima*, his most ambitious effort to treat political material, his interest is solely in the personal problem, in what happens when his sensitive lower-class hero is distracted from his revolutionary convictions by his desire to establish "a social—not less than a socialist connexion."

But such relations can be all-absorbing. Henry Senior believed that spiritual evil sprang wholly from having self-consciousness instead of social-consciousness; and he would certainly have disapproved of the excessive analysis of motives engaged in by, say, the characters in *The Sacred Fount*. But HJ's conception of the value of the individual caused him to make a gradation between degrees of consciousness. The bad characters in his books are—like those WJ described in his essay "On a Certain Blindness in Human Beings"—either unaware of the qualities in others, or too crass and selfish to do them justice. The good characters are those whose consciousness is an ethical as well as an æsthetic awareness, who perceive the beauty of life in others and are devoted to its free play, even when that involves sacrifice of themselves.

It was remarked, shortly after HJ's death, that he "was in love with the next world, or the next state of consciousness; he was always exploring the borderland between the conscious and the super-conscious." That is one way of describing the final refinement of his method no less than of his content, and how he took the drama of intelligence as far from the confining body as it could be made to go. One thinks in particular of what he tried to symbolize by the eerie presences in his ghost stories, or of how he carried to its extreme, in the unfinished *Sense of the Past*, his way of suggesting what lurks just behind the words of conversation to beckon us into the realm of the unspoken. It is none the less clear that HJ is not a religious novelist as Hawthorne and Dostoevsky are. But if his characters do not wrestle with the issues of faith, if they merely hover before the altars of the dead, HJ did for once, towards the end of his career, make an explicit excursion into philosophy. He contributed, in 1910, to a symposium on Immortality, an essay which has never been reprinted and seldom read: "Is There a Life after Death?"

He aimed to speak only from his own thoughts, but when he said that the artistic consciousness springs "from immersion in the fountain of being," he was using his father's language. At the time of Minny

Temple's death he possessed a fuller sense than WJ of sources beyond an individual's existence. He ventured rarely thereafter into such direct affirmation of eternal essences as he had made then.[1] His letters tended increasingly to become graceful social gestures, and very seldom penetrated to the deep level upon which he discussed consciousness and suffering with Grace Norton in the year after his parents' deaths:

"Before the sufferings of others I am always utterly powerless, and your letter reveals such depths of suffering that I hardly know what to say to you. This indeed is not my last word—but it must be my first. You are not isolated, verily, in such states of feeling as this—that is, in the sense that you appear to make all the misery of all mankind your own; only I have a terrible sense that you give all and receive nothing—that there is no reciprocity in your sympathy—that you have all the affliction and none of the returns. However—I am determined not to speak to you except with the voice of stoicism. I don't know *why* we live—the gift of life comes to us from I don't know what source or for what purpose; but I believe we can go on living for the reason that (always of course up to a certain point) life is the most valuable thing we know anything about, and it is therefore presumptively a great mistake to surrender it while there is any yet left in the cup. In other words consciousness is an illimitable power, and though at times it may seem to be all consciousness of misery, yet in the way it propagates itself from wave to wave, so that we never cease to feel, and though at moments we appear to, try to, pray to, there is something that holds one in one's place, makes it a standpoint in the universe which it is probably good not to forsake. You are right in your consciousness that we are all echoes and reverberations of the *same*, and you are noble when your interest and pity as to everything that surrounds you, appears to have a sustaining and harmonizing power. Only don't, I beseech you, *generalize* too much in these sympathies and tendernesses—remember that every life is a special problem which is not yours but another's, and content yourself with the terrible algebra of your own. Don't melt too much into the universe, but be as solid and dense and fixed as you can. We all live together, and those of us who love and know, live so most. We help each other—even unconsciously, each in our own effort, we lighten the efforts of others, we contribute to the sum of success, make it possible for others to live. Sorrow comes in great waves—no one can know that better than you —but it rolls over us, and though it may almost smother us it leaves us on the spot, and we know that if it is strong we are stronger, inasmuch as it passes and we remain. It wears us, uses us, but we wear it and use it in return; and it is blind, whereas we after a manner see."

---

[1] Pp. 259–63 above.

There, as he said, he had deliberately restricted himself to the grounds of courage and resistance. A year or two later he was to write, once more to Grace Norton: "I am always praying for you (though I don't pray, in general, and don't understand it)." Even less than WJ did he manifest an active participation in religious experience. Nevertheless, the dramas in his fiction always involve the question of what can be salvaged from "the ugliness, the grossness, the stupidity, the cruelty," and he addressed himself to that same theme when he finally wrote about immortality.

His essay possesses the double interest of making articulate the assumptions upon which so many of his characters base their behavior, and of revealing intermingled influences from the religious thought of both his father and his brother. He argues, like WJ, from need, or rather from desire, from a sense of increasing fitness to live as he grows older and as the accumulations of consciousness become so rich that he cannot believe they exist merely to be snuffed out. His assumptions are aristocratic in a manner foreign to the other members of his family, but his elite is not one of birth or of class, but of consciousness itself, in which anyone intensely sensitive to life can share.

He draws an analogy at one point with "the theory of the spiritual discipline, the purification and preparation on earth for heaven, of the orthodox theology," but knows the likeness to be merely superficial. He was not eager, like his father, to lose his personality in God; he wanted to keep it intact for further enrichment.[1] His position was essentially that of his hero in "The Great Good Place," who, dreaming of another world, declares: "I don't speak of the putting off of one's self; I speak only—if one has a self worth sixpence—of the getting it back." This exclusive concentration upon personality and personal relations throughout HJ's life as well as his work is what struck Gide as "desperately mundane," even "profane." HJ was certainly as far removed as possible from Swedenborg's dictum, to which his father held, that to think spiritually demands that you do not think in terms of persons. Yet he was like his father in his insistence, again in this essay, upon the conversion of waste. He was like WJ in concluding that he reached "beyond the laboratory brain."

* * * * *

WJ: "CONCLUSION" TO THE VARIETIES OF RELIGIOUS EXPERIENCE

. . . As I have elsewhere written, the most interesting and valuable things about a man are usually his over-beliefs.

---

[1] For further discussion of this matter, see "The Religion of Consciousness," the final chapter in *Henry James: The Major Phase*.

Disregarding the over-beliefs, and confining ourselves to what is common and generic, we have in *the fact that the conscious person is continuous with a wider self through which saving experiences come,*[1] a positive content of religious experience which, it seems to me, *is literally and objectively true as far as it goes.* If I now proceed to state my own hypothesis about the farther limits of this extension of our personality, I shall be offering my own over-belief—though I know it will appear a sorry under-belief to some of you—for which I can only bespeak the same indulgence which in a converse case I should accord to yours.

The further limits of our being plunge, it seems to me, into an altogether other dimension of existence from the sensible and merely "understandable" world. Name it the mystical region, or the supernatural region, whichever you choose. So far as our ideal impulses originate in this region (and most of them do originate in it, for we find them possessing us in a way for which we cannot articulately account), we belong to it in a more intimate sense than that in which we belong to the visible world, for we belong in the most intimate sense wherever our ideals belong. Yet the unseen region in question is not merely ideal, for it produces effects in this world. When we commune with it, work is actually done upon our finite personality, for we are turned into new men, and consequences in the way of conduct follow in the natural world upon our regenerative change.[2] But that which produces effects within another reality must be termed a reality itself, so I feel as if we had no philosophic excuse for calling the unseen or mystical world unreal.

God is the natural appellation, for us Christians at least, for the supreme reality, so I will call this higher part of the universe by the name of God.[3] We and God have business with each other; and in opening ourselves to his influence our deepest destiny is fulfilled. The universe, at those parts of it which our personal being constitutes, takes a turn genuinely for the worse or for the better in proportion as each one of us fulfills or evades God's demands. As far as this goes I probably have you with me, for I only translate into schematic language what I may call the instinctive belief of mankind: God is real since he produces real effects.

---

[1] "The influence of the Holy Spirit, exquisitely called the Comforter, is a matter of actual experience, as solid a reality as that of electro-magnetism." W. C. Brownell, *Scribner's Magazine*, vol. xxx. p. 112.

[2] That the transaction of opening ourselves, otherwise called prayer, is a perfectly definite one for certain persons, appears abundantly in the preceding lectures.

[3] Transcendentalists are fond of the term "Over-soul," but as a rule they use it in an intellectualist sense, as meaning only a medium of communion. "God" is a causal agent as well as a medium of communion, and that is the aspect which I wish to emphasize.

The real effects in question, so far as I have as yet admitted them, are exerted on the personal centres of energy of the various subjects, but the spontaneous faith of most of the subjects is that they embrace a wider sphere than this. Most religious men believe (or "know," if they be mystical) that not only they themselves, but the whole universe of beings to whom the God is present, are secure in his parental hands. There is a sense, a dimension, they are sure, in which we are *all* saved, in spite of the gates of hell and all adverse terrestrial appearances. God's existence is the guarantee of an ideal order that shall be permanently preserved. This world may indeed, as science assures us, some day burn up or freeze; but if it is part of his order, the old ideals are sure to be brought elsewhere to fruition, so that where God is, tragedy is only provisional and partial, and shipwreck and dissolution are not the absolutely final things. Only when this farther step of faith concerning God is taken, and remote objective consequences are predicted, does religion, as it seems to me, get wholly free from the first immediate subjective experience, and bring a *real hypothesis* into play. A good hypothesis in science must have other properties than those of the phenomenon it is immediately invoked to explain, otherwise it is not prolific enough. God, meaning only what enters into the religious man's experience of union, falls short of being an hypothesis of this more useful order. He needs to enter into wider cosmic relations in order to justify the subject's absolute confidence and peace.

That the God with whom, starting from the hither side of our own extra-marginal self, we come at its remoter margin into commerce should be the absolute world-ruler, is of course a very considerable over-belief. Over-belief as it is, though, it is an article of almost every one's religion. Most of us pretend in some way to prop it upon our philosophy, but the philosophy itself is really propped upon this faith. What is this but to say that Religion, in her fullest exercise of function, is not a mere illumination of facts already elsewhere given, not a mere passion, like love, which views things in a rosier light. It is indeed that, as we have seen abundantly. But it is something more, namely, a postulator of new *facts* as well. The world interpreted religiously is not the materialistic world over again, with an altered expression; it must have, over and above the altered expression, *a natural constitution* different at some point from that which a materialistic world would have. It must be such that different events can be expected in it, different conduct must be required.

This thoroughly "pragmatic" view of religion has usually been taken as a matter of course by common men. They have interpolated divine miracles into the field of nature, they have built a heaven out beyond the grave. It is only transcendentalist metaphysicians who think that, without adding any concrete details to Nature, or subtracting any, but by simply calling it the expression of absolute spirit, you make it more divine just as it stands. I believe the pragmatic way of taking religion to be the deeper way. It gives it body as well as soul, it makes it claim, as everything real must claim, some characteristic realm of fact as its very own. What the more characteristically divine facts are, apart from the actual inflow of energy in the faith-state and the prayer-state, I know not. But the over-belief on which I am ready to make my personal venture is that they exist. The whole drift of my education goes to persuade me that the world of our present consciousness is only one out of many worlds of consciousness that exist, and that those other worlds must contain experiences which have a meaning for our life also; and that although in the main their experiences and those of this world keep discrete, yet the two become continuous at certain points, and higher energies filter in. By being faithful in my poor measure to this over-belief, I seem to myself to keep more sane and true. I *can*, of course, put myself into the sectarian scientist's attitude, and imagine vividly that the world of sensations and of scientific laws and objects may be all. But whenever I do this, I hear that inward monitor of which W. K. Clifford once wrote, whispering the word "bosh!" Humbug is humbug, even though it bear the scientific name, and the total expression of human experience, as I view it objectively, invincibly urges me beyond the narrow "scientific" bounds. Assuredly, the real world is of a different temperament,—more intricately built than physical science allows. So my objective and my subjective conscience both hold me to the over-belief which I express. Who knows whether the faithfulness of individuals here below to their own poor over-beliefs may not actually help God in turn to be more effectively faithful to his own greater tasks?

POSTSCRIPT

IN WRITING my concluding lecture I had to aim so much at simplification that I fear that my general philosophic position received so scant a statement as hardly to be intelligible to some of my readers. I therefore add this epilogue, which must also be so brief as possibly to remedy but little the defect. . . .

Originality cannot be expected in a field like this, where all the attitudes and tempers that are possible have been exhibited in literature long ago, and where any new writer can immediately be classed under a familiar head. If one should make a division of all thinkers into naturalists and supernaturalists, I should undoubtedly have to go, along with most philosophers, into the supernaturalist branch. But there is a crasser and a more refined supernaturalism, and it is to the refined division that most philosophers at the present day belong. If not regular transcendental idealists, they at least obey the Kantian direction enough to bar out ideal entities from interfering causally in the course of phenomenal events. Refined supernaturalism is universalistic supernaturalism; for the "crasser" variety "piecemeal" supernaturalism would perhaps be the better name. It went with that older theology which to-day is supposed to reign only among uneducated people, or to be found among the few belated professors of the dualisms which Kant is thought to have displaced. It admits miracles and providential leadings, and finds no intellectual difficulty in mixing the ideal and the real worlds together by interpolating influences from the ideal region among the forces that causally determine the real world's details. In this the refined supernaturalists think that it muddles disparate dimensions of existence. For them the world of the ideal has no efficient causality, and never bursts into the world of phenomena at particular points. The ideal world, for them, is not a world of facts, but only of the meaning of facts; it is a point of view for judging facts. It appertains to a different "-ology," and inhabits a different dimension of being altogether from that in which existential propositions obtain. It cannot get down upon the flat level of experience and interpolate itself piecemeal between distinct portions of nature, as those who believe, for example, in divine aid coming in response to prayer, are bound to think it must.

Notwithstanding my own inability to accept either popular Christianity or scholastic theism, I suppose that my belief that in communion with the Ideal new force comes into the world, and new departures are made here below, subjects me to being classed among the supernaturalists of the piecemeal or crasser type. Universalistic supernaturalism surrenders, it seems to me, too easily to naturalism. It takes the facts of physical science at their face-value, and leaves the laws of life just as naturalism finds them, with no hope of remedy, in case their fruits are bad. It confines itself to sentiments about life as a whole, sentiments which may be admiring and adoring, but which need not be so, as the existence of systematic pessimism proves. In this universalistic way of taking the ideal world, the essence of practical religion seems to me to evaporate. Both instinctively and for logical reasons, I find it hard to believe that principles can exist which make no difference in facts.[1]

---

[1] Transcendental idealism, of course, insists that its ideal world makes *this* difference, that facts *exist*. We owe it to the Absolute that we have a world of fact at all. "A world" of fact!—that exactly is the trouble. An entire world is the smallest unit with which the Absolute can work, whereas to our finite minds work for the better ought to be done within this world, setting in at single points. Our difficulties and our ideals are all piecemeal affairs, but the Absolute can do no piecework for us; so that all the interests which our poor souls compass raise their heads too late. We should have spoken earlier, prayed for another world absolutely, before this world was born. It is strange, I have heard a friend say, to see this blind corner into which Christian thought has

But all facts are particular facts, and the whole interest of the question of God's existence seems to me to lie in the consequences for particulars which that existence may be expected to entail. That no concrete particular of experience should alter its complexion in consequence of a God being there seems to me an incredible proposition, and yet it is the thesis to which (implicitly at any rate) refined supernaturalism seems to cling. It is only with experience *en bloc*, it says, that the Absolute maintains relations. It condescends to no transactions of detail.

I am ignorant of Buddhism and speak under correction, and merely in order the better to describe my general point of view; but as I apprehend the Buddhistic doctrine of Karma, I agree in principle with that. All supernaturalists admit that facts are under the judgment of higher law; but for Buddhism as I interpret it, and for religion generally so far as it remains unweakened by transcendentalistic metaphysics, the word "judgment" here means no such bare academic verdict or platonic appreciation as it means in Vedantic or modern absolutist systems; it carries, on the contrary, *execution* with it, is *in rebus* as well as *post rem*, and operates "causally" as partial factor in the total fact. The universe becomes a gnosticism [1] pure and simple on any other terms. But this view that judgment and execution go together is that of the crasser supernaturalist way of thinking, so the present volume must on the whole be classed with the other expressions of that creed.

I state the matter thus bluntly, because the current of thought in academic circles runs against me, and I feel like a man who must set his back against an open door quickly if he does not wish to see it closed and locked. In spite of its being so shocking to the reigning intellectual tastes, I believe that a candid consideration of piecemeal supernaturalism and a complete discussion of all its metaphysical bearings will show it to be the hypothesis by which the largest number of legitimate requirements are met. That of course would be a program for other books than this; what I now say sufficiently indicates to the philosophic reader the place where I belong.

If asked just where the differences in fact which are due to God's existence come in, I should have to say that in general I have no hypothesis to offer beyond what the phenomenon of "prayerful communion," especially when certain kinds of incursion from the subconscious region take part in it, immediately suggests. The appearance is that in this phenomenon something ideal, which in one sense is part

---

worked itself at last, with its God who can raise no particular weight whatever, who can help us with no private burden, and who is on the side of our enemies as much as he is on our own. Odd evolution from the God of David's psalms.

[1] See my Will to Believe and other Essays in Popular Philosophy, 1897, p. 165.

of ourselves and in another sense is not ourselves, actually exerts an
influence, raises our centre of personal energy, and produces regenerative effects unattainable in other ways. If, then, there be a wider world
of being than that of our every-day consciousness, if in it there be
forces whose effects on us are intermittent, if one facilitating condition
of the effects be the openness of the "subliminal" door, we have the
elements of a theory to which the phenomena of religious life lend
plausibility. I am so impressed by the importance of these phenomena
that I adopt the hypothesis which they so naturally suggest. At these
places at least, I say, it would seem as though transmundane energies,
God, if you will, produced immediate effects within the natural world
to which the rest of our experience belongs.

The difference in natural "fact" which most of us would assign as
the first difference which the existence of a God ought to make would,
I imagine, be personal immortality. Religion, in fact, for the great
majority of our own race *means* immortality, and nothing else. God
is the producer of immortality; and whoever has doubts of immortality
is written down as an atheist without farther trial. I have said nothing
in my lectures about immortality or the belief therein, for to me it
seems a secondary point. If our ideals are only cared for in "eternity,"
I do not see why we might not be willing to resign their care to other
hands than ours. Yet I sympathize with the urgent impulse to be present ourselves, and in the conflict of impulses, both of them so vague
yet both of them noble, I know not how to decide. It seems to me that
it is eminently a case for facts to testify. Facts, I think, are yet lacking
to prove "spirit-return," though I have the highest respect for the
patient labors of Messrs. Myers, Hodgson, and Hyslop, and am somewhat impressed by their favorable conclusions. I consequently leave the
matter open, with this brief word to save the reader from a possible
perplexity as to why immortality got no mention in the body of this
book.

The ideal power with which we feel ourselves in connection, the
"God" of ordinary men, is, both by ordinary men and by philosophers,
endowed with certain of those metaphysical attributes which in the
lecture on philosophy I treated with such disrespect. He is assumed as
a matter of course to be "one and only" and to be "infinite"; and the
notion of many finite gods is one which hardly any one thinks it worth
while to consider, and still less to uphold. Nevertheless, in the interests
of intellectual clearness, I feel bound to say that religious experience, as
we have studied it, cannot be cited as unequivocally supporting the
infinitist belief. The only thing that it unequivocally testifies to is that
we can experience union with *something* larger than ourselves and in
that union find our greatest peace. Philosophy, with its passion for
unity, and mysticism with its monodeistic bent, both "pass to the

limit" and identify the something with a unique God who is the all-inclusive soul of the world. Popular opinion, respectful to their authority, follows the example which they set.

Meanwhile the practical needs and experiences of religion seem to me sufficiently met by the belief that beyond each man and in a fashion continuous with him there exists a larger power which is friendly to him and to his ideals. All that the facts require is that the power should be both other and larger than our conscious selves. Anything larger will do, if only it be large enough to trust for the next step. It need not be infinite, it need not be solitary. It might conceivably even be only a larger and more godlike self, of which the present self would then be but the mutilated expression, and the universe might conceivably be a collection of such selves, of different degrees of inclusiveness, with no absolute unity realized in it at all.[1] Thus would a sort of polytheism return upon us—a polytheism which I do not on this occasion defend, for my only aim at present is to keep the testimony of religious experience clearly within its proper bounds. [Compare p. 132 above.][2]

Upholders of the monistic view will say to such a polytheism (which, by the way, has always been the real religion of common people, and is so still to-day) that unless there be one all-inclusive God, our guarantee of security is left imperfect. In the Absolute, and in the Absolute only, *all* is saved. If there be different gods, each caring for his part, some portion of some of us might not be covered with divine protection, and our religious consolation would thus fail to be complete. It goes back to what was said on pages 131–133, about the possibility of there being portions of the universe that may irretrievably be lost. Common sense is less sweeping in its demands than philosophy or mysticism have been wont to be, and can suffer the notion of this world being partly saved and partly lost. The ordinary moralistic state of mind makes the salvation of the world conditional upon the success with which each unit does its part. Partial and conditional salvation is in fact a most familiar notion when taken in the abstract, the only difficulty being to determine the details. Some men are even disinterested enough to be willing to be in the unsaved remnant as far as their persons go, if only they can be persuaded that their cause will prevail —all of us are willing, whenever our activity-excitement rises sufficiently high. I think, in fact, that a final philosophy of religion will have to consider the pluralistic hypothesis more seriously than it has hitherto been willing to consider it. For practical life at any rate, the

---

[1] Such a notion is suggested in my Ingersoll Lecture On Human Immortality, Boston and London, 1899.

[2] Pp. 131–3 of *The Varieties of Religious Experience*, in which WJ contrasts the religion of healthy-mindedness with that of the sick soul, while obviously reflecting on some of the differences between his father and himself, are given at pp. 232–4 above.—F. O. M.

chance of salvation is enough. No fact in human nature is more characteristic than its willingness to live on a chance. The existence of the chance makes the difference, as Edmund Gurney says, between a life of which the keynote is resignation and a life of which the keynote is hope.

HJ: "IS THERE A LIFE AFTER DEATH?"

PART I

I CONFESS at the outset that I think it the most interesting question in the world, once it takes on all the intensity of which it is capable. It does that, insidiously but inevitably, as we live longer and longer—does it at least for many persons; I myself, in any case, find it increasingly assert its power to attach and, if I may use the word so unjustly compromised by trivial applications, to amuse. I say "assert its power" so to occupy us, because I mean to express only its most general effect. That effect on our spirit is mostly either one of two forms; the effect of making us desire death, and for reasons, absolutely *as* welcome extinction and termination; or the effect of making us desire it as a renewal of the interest, the appreciation, the passion, the large and consecrated consciousness, in a word, of which we have had so splendid a sample in this world. Either one or the other of these opposed states of feeling is bound finally to declare itself, we judge, in persons of a fine sensibility and whose innermost spirit experience has set vibrating at all; for the condition of indifference and of knowing neither is the condition of living altogether so much below the human privilege as to have little right to pass for unjustly excluded or neglected in this business of the speculative reckoning.

That an immense number of persons should not recognize the appeal of our speculation, or even be aware of the existence of our question, is a fact that might seem to demand, in the whole connection, some particular consideration; but our anxiety, our hope, or our fear, hangs before us, after all, only because it more or less torments us, and in order to contribute in any degree to a discussion of the possibility we have to be consciously in presence of it. I can only see it, the great interrogation or the great deprecation we are ultimately driven to, as a part of our general concern with life and our general, and extremely various—because I speak of each man's general—mode of reaction under it; but to testify for an experience we must have reacted in one way or another. The weight of those who don't react may be felt, it is true, in one of the scales; for it may very well be asked on their behalf whether they are distinguishable as "living" either before or after. Only the special reaction of others, or the play of *their* speculation, however, will, in due consideration, have put it there. How *can* there be a personal and a differentiated life "after," it will then of course be asked, for those for whom there has been so little of one before?—unless indeed it be pronounced conceivable that the possibility may vary from man to man, from human case to human case, and that the quantity or the quality of our practice of consciousness may have something to say to it. If I myself am disposed to pronounce this conceivable—as verily I expect to find myself before we have done—I must glance at a few other relations of the matter first.

My point for the moment is that the more or less visibly diminishing distance which separates us at a certain age from death is, however we are affected toward the supposition of an existence beyond it, an intensifier of the feeling that most works in us, and that in the light of the lamp so held up our aggravated sense of life, as I may perhaps best call it, our impression of what we have been through, is what essentially fosters and determines, on the whole ground, our desire or our aversion. So, at any rate, the situation strikes me, and one can speak of it but for one's personal self. The subject is portentous and any individual utterance upon it, however ingenious or however grave, but comparatively a feeble pipe or a pathetic quaver; yet I hold that as we can scarce have too many visions, too many statements or pictures of the conceived social Utopia that the sincere fond dreamer, the believer in better things, may find glimmer before him, so the sincere and struggling son of earth among his fellow-strugglers reports of the positive or negative presumption in the savor of his world, that is not to be of earth, and thus drops his testimony, however scant, into the reservoir. It all depends, in other words, the weight or the force or the interest of this testimony does, on what life has predominantly said to us. And there are those—I take them for the constant and vast majority—to whom it in the way of intelligible suggestion says nothing. Possibly immortality itself—or another chance at least, as we may freely call it—will say as little; which is a fair and simple manner of disposing of the idea of a new start in relation to them. Though, indeed, I must add, the contemplative critic scarce—save under one probability—sees why the universe should be at the expense of a new start for those on whom the old start appears (though but to our purblind sight, it may, of course, be replied) so to have been wasted. The probability is, in fact, that what we dimly discern as waste the wisdom of the universe may know as a very different matter. We don't think of slugs and jellyfish as the waste, but rather as the amusement, the attestation of wealth and variety, of gardens and sea-beaches; so why should we, under stress, in respect to the human scene and its discussable sequel, think differently of dull people?

This is but an instance, or a trifle, however, among the difficulties with which the whole case bristles for those on whom the fact of the

lived life has insisted on thrusting it, and which it yet leaves them tor-
mentedly to deal with. The question is of the *personal* experience, of
course, of another existence; of its being I my very self, and you,
definitely, and he and she, who resume and go on, and not of unthink-
able substitutes or metamorphoses. The whole interest of the matter is
that it is my or your sensibility that is involved and at stake; the thing
figuring to us as momentous just because that sensibility and its tasted
fruits, as we owe them to life, are either remunerative enough and
sweet enough or too barren and too bitter. Only because posthumous
survival in some other conditions involves what we know, what we
have enjoyed and suffered, as our particular personal adventure, does
it appeal to us or excite our protest; only because of the *associations* of
consciousness do we trouble and consult ourselves—do we wish the
latter prolonged and wonder if it may not be indestructible, or decide
that we have had enough of it and invoke the conclusion that we have
so had it once for all. We pass, I think, through many changes of impression, many shifting estimates, as to the force and value of those
associations; and there is no single, there is no decisive sense of them in
which, throughout our earthly course, it is easy or needful to rest.

Whatever we may begin with we almost inevitably go on, under the
discipline of life, to more or less resigned acceptance of the grim fact
that "science" takes no account of the soul, the principle we worry
about, and that, as however nobly thinking and feeling creatures, we are
abjectly and inveterately shut up in our material organs. We flutter
away from that account of ourselves, on sublime occasion, only to
come back to it with the collapse of our wings, and during much of
our life the grim view, as I have called it, the sense of the rigor of our
physical basis, is confirmed to us by overwhelming appearances. The
mere spectacle, all about us, of personal decay, and of the decay, as
seems, of the whole being, adds itself formidably to that of so much
bloom and assurance and energy—the things we catch in the very fact
of their material identity. There are times when *all* the elements and
qualities that constitute the affirmation of the personal life here affect
us as making against any apprehensible other affirmation of it. And that
general observation and evidence abide with us and keep us company;
they reinforce the verdict of the dismal laboratories and the confident
analysts as to the interconvertibility of our genius, as it comparatively is
at the worst, and our brain—the poor palpable, ponderable, probeable,
laboratory-brain that we ourselves see in certain inevitable conditions—
become as naught.

It brings itself home to us thus in all sorts of ways that we are even
at our highest flights of personality, our furthest reachings out of the
mind, of the very stuff of the abject actual, and that the sublimest idea
we can form and the noblest hope and affection we can cherish are but

flowers sprouting in that eminently and infinitely diggable soil. It may be as favorable to them—as well as to quite other moral growths—as we are free to note; but we see its power to put them forth break down and end, and ours to receive them from it to do the same—we watch the relentless ebb of the tide on which the vessel of experience carries us, and which to our earthly eyes never flows again. It is to the personality that the idea of renewed being attaches itself, and we see nothing so much written over the personalities of the world as that they are finite and precarious and insusceptible. All the ugliness, the grossness, the stupidity, the cruelty, the vast extent to which the score in question is a record of brutality and vulgarity, the so easy nonexistence of consciousness, round about us as to most of the things that make for living desirably at all, or even for living once, let alone on the enlarged chance—these things fairly rub it into us that to *have* a personality need create no presumption beyond what this remarkably mixed world is by itself amply sufficient to meet. A renewal of being, we ask, for people who understand being, even here, where renewals, of sorts, are possible, that way, and that way, apparently, alone?—leaving us vainly to wonder, in presence of such obvious and offensive matter for decay and putrescence, what there is for renewal to take hold of, or what element may be supposed fine enough to create a claim for disengagement. The mere fact in short that so much of life as we know it dishonors, or at any rate falls below, the greater part of the beauty and the opportunity even of this world, works upon us for persuasion that none other can be eager to receive it.

With which all the while there co-operates the exhibited limitation of our faculty for persistence, for not giving way, for not doing more than attest the inextinguishable or extinguishable spark in the mere minimum of time. The thinkable, the possible, we are fairly moved to say, in the way of the resistances and renewals of our conceded day, baffle us and are already beyond our command; I mean in the sense that the spirit even still in activity never shows as recovering, before our present eyes, an inch of the ground the body has once fairly taken from it. The personality, the apparently final eclipse of which by death we are discussing, fails, we remark, of any partial victory over partial eclipses, and keeps before us, once for all, the same sharp edge of blackness on the compromised disk of light. Even while "we" nominally go on those parts of us that have been overdarkened become as dead; our extinct passions and faculties and interests, that is, refuse to revive; our personality, by which I mean our "soul," declining in many a case, or in most, by inches, is aware of itself at any given moment as it is, however contracted, and not as it *was*, however magnificent; we may die piecemeal, but by no sign ever demonstrably caught does the "liberated" spirit react from death piecemeal. The answer to that may of course be that such reactions as can be "caught" are not claimed for it even by the fondest lovers of the precarious idea; the most that is claimed is that the reaction takes place *somewhere*—and the farther away from the conditions and circumstances of death the more probably. The apparently significant thing is none the less that during slow and successive stages of material extinction *some* nearness—of the personal quantity departing to the personal quantity remaining, and in the name of personal association and personal affection, and to the abatement of utter personal eclipse—might be supposable; and that this is what we miss.

Such, at least, is one of the faces, however small, that life puts on to persuade us of the utterly contingent nature of our familiar inward ease—ease of being—and that, to our comfort or our disconcertment, this familiarity is a perfectly restricted thing. And so we go on noting, through our time and amid the abundance of life, everything that makes, to our earthly senses, for the unmistakable absoluteness of death. Every hour affords us some fresh illustration of it, drawn especially from the condition of others; but one, if we really heed it, recurs and recurs as the most poignant of all. How can we not make much of the terrible fashion in which the universe takes upon itself to emphasize and multiply the disconnectedness of those who vanish from our sight? —or they perhaps not so much from ours as we from theirs; though indeed if once we lend ourselves to the hypothesis of posthumous renovation at all, the fact that our ex-fellow-mortals would appear thus to have taken up some very much better interest than the poor world they have left might pass for a positively favorable argument. On the basis of their enjoying another state of being, we have certainly to assume that this is the case, for to the probability of a quite different case the inveteracy of their neglect of the previous one, through all the ages and the spaces, the grimness of their utter refusal, so far as we know it, of a retrospective personal sign, would seem directly to point. (I can only treat here as absolutely not established the value of those personal signs that ostensibly come to us through the trance medium. These often make, I grant, for attention and wonder and interest—but for interest above all in the medium and the trance. Whether or no they may in the given case seem to savor of another state of being on the part of those from whom they profess to come, they savor intensely, to my sense, of the medium and the trance, and, with their remarkable felicities and fitnesses, their immense call for explanation, invest that personage, in that state, with an almost irresistible attraction.)

Here it is, at any rate, that we break ourselves against that conception of immortality *as* personal which is the only thing that gives it meaning or relevance. That it shall be personal and yet shall so entirely and relentlessly have yielded to dissociation, this makes us ask if such terms for it are acceptable to thought. Is to be as dissociated as that consistent with personality as we understand *our* share in the condition?—since on any contingency save *by* that understanding of it our interest in the subject drops. I practically know what I am talking about when I say, "I," hypothetically, for my full experience of another term of being, just as I know it when I say "I" for my experience of this one; but I shouldn't in the least do so were I not *able* to say "I"—had I to reckon, that is, with a failure of the signs by which I know myself. In presence of the great question I cling to these signs more than ever, and to conceive of the actual achievement of immortality by others who may have had like knowledge I have to impute to such others a clinging to similar signs. Yet with that advantage, as it were, for any friendly reparticipation, whether for our sake or for their own, in that consciousness in which they bathed themselves on earth, they yet appear to find no grain of relief to bestow on our anxiety, no dimmest spark to flash upon our ignorance. This fact, as after middle life we continue to note it, contributes to the confirmation, within us, of our seeming awareness of extinct things *as* utterly and veritably extinct, with whatever splendid intensity we may have known them to live; an awareness that settles upon us with a formidable weight as time and the world pile up around us all their affirmation of *other* things, and all importunate ones—which little by little acts upon us as so much triumphant negation of the past and the lost; the flicker of some vast sardonic, leering "Don't you see?" on the mask of Nature.

We tend so to feel *that* become for us the last word on the matter that all Nature and all life and all society and all so-called knowledge, with everything these huge, grim indifferences strive to make, and to some degree succeed in making, of ourselves, take the form and have the effect of a mass of machinery for ignoring and denying, the universe through, everything that is not of their own actuality. So it is, therefore, that we keep on and that we reflect; we begin by pitying the remembered dead, even for the very danger of our indifference to them, and we end by pitying ourselves for the final demonstration, as it were, of their indifference to us. "They must be dead, indeed," we say; "they must be as dead as 'science' affirms, for this consecration of it on such a scale, and with these tremendous rites of nullification, to take place." We think of the particular cases of those who could have been backed, as we call it, not to fail, on occasion, of somehow reaching us. We recall the forces of passion, of reason, of personality, that lived in them, and what such forces had made them, to our sight, capable of; and then we say, conclusively, "Talk of triumphant identity if *they*, wanting to triumph, haven't done it!"

Those in whom we saw consciousness, to all appearance, the consciousness of *us*, slowly *déménager*, piece by piece, so that they more or less consentingly parted with it—of *them* let us take it, under stress, if we must, that their ground for interest (in us and in other matters) "unmistakably" reached its limit. But what of those lights that went out in a single gust and those life passions that were nipped in their flower and their promise? Are these spirits thinkable as having emptied the measure the services of sense could offer them? Do we feel capable of a brutal rupture with registered promises, started curiosities, waiting initiations? The mere acquired momentum of intelligence, of perception, of vibration, of experience in a word, would have carried them on, we argue, to *something*, the something that never takes place for us, if the laboratory-brain were *not* really all. What it comes to is then that our faith or our hope may to some degree resist the fact, once accomplished, of watched and deplored death, but that they may well break down before the avidity and consistency with which everything insufferably *continues* to die.

PART II

I have said "we argue" as we take in impressions of the order of those I have glanced at and of which I have pretended to mention only a few. I am not, however, putting them forward for their direct weight in the scale; I speak of them but as the inevitable obsession of those who with the failure of the illusions of youth have had to learn more and more to reckon with reality. For if I referred previously to their bearing us increase of company I mean this to be true with the qualification that applies to our whole attitude, or that of many of us, on our question—the fact that it is subject to the very shifting admonitions of that reality, which may seem to us at times to mean one thing and at times quite another. Yet rather than attempt to speak, to this effect, even for "many of us," I had best do so simply for myself, since it is only for one's self that one can positively answer. It is a matter of individual experience, which I have seen multiply, to satiety, the obsessions I have named and then suffer them to be displaced by others—only once more to reappear again and once more to give way. I speak as one who has had time to take many notes, to be struck with many differences, and to see, a little typically perhaps, what may eventually happen; and I contribute thus, and thus only, my grain of consideration to the store.

I began, I may accordingly say, with a distinct sense that our question didn't appeal to me—as it appeals, in general, but scantly to the young—and I was content for a long time to let it alone, only asking that it should, in turn, as irrelevant and insoluble, let *me*. This it did, in abundance, for many a day—which is, however, but another way of saying that death remained for me, in a large measure, unexhibited and unaggressive. The exhibition, the aggression of life was quite ready to cover the ground and fill the bill, and to my sense of that balance still inclined even after the opposite pressure had begun to show in the scale. Resented bereavement is all at first—and may long go on appearing more than anything else—one of the exhibitions of life; the various forms and necessities of our resentment sufficiently meet then the questions that death brings up. That aspect changes, however, as we seem to see what it is to die—and to have died—in contradistinction to suffering (which means to warmly *being*) on earth; and as we so see what it is the difficulties involved in the thought of its not being absolute tend to take possession of us and rule us. Treating my own case, again, as a "given" one, I found it long impossible not to succumb —so far as one began to yield at all to irresistible wonder—to discouragement by the mere pitiless dryness of all the appearances. This was for years quite blighting to my sensibility; and the appearances, as I have called them—and as they make, in "science" particularly, the most assured show—imposed themselves; the universe, or all of it that I could make out, kept proclaiming in a myriad voices that I and my poor form of consciousness were a quantity it could at any moment perfectly do without, even in what I might be pleased to call our very finest principle. If without me then just so without others; all the more that if it was not so dispensing with them the simply *bête* situation of one's forever and forever failing of the least whiff of a positive symptom to the contrary would not so ineffably persist.

During which period, none the less, as I was afterward to find, the question subtly took care of itself for me—waking up as I did gradually, in the event (very slowly indeed, with no sudden start of perception, no bound of enthusiasm), to its facing me with a "mild but firm" refusal to regard itself as settled. That circumstance once noted, I began to inquire—mainly, I confess, of myself—why it should be thus obstinate, what reason it could at all clearly give me; and this led me in due course to my getting, or at least framing my reply: a reply not perhaps so multitudinous as those voices of the universe that I have spoken of as discouraging, but which none the less, I find, still holds its ground for me. What had happened, in short, was that all the while I had been practically, though however dimly, trying to take the measure of my consciousness—on this appropriate and prescribed basis of its being so finite—I had learned, as I may say, to live in it more, and with the consequence of thereby not a little undermining the conclusion most unfavorable to it. I had doubtless taken thus to increased living in it by reaction against so grossly finite a world—for it at least *contained* the world, and could handle and criticise it, could play with it and deride it; it had *that* superiority: which meant, all the while, such successful living that the abode itself grew more and more interesting to me, and with this beautiful sign of its character that the more and the more one asked of it the more and the more it appeared to give. I should perhaps rather say that the more one turned it, as an easy reflector, here and there and everywhere over the immensity of things, the more it appeared to take; which is but another way of putting, for "interest," the same truth.

I recognize that the questions I have come after this fashion to ask my consciousness are questions embarrassed by the conditions of this world; but it has none the less left me at last with a sense that, beautiful and adorable thing, it is capable of sorts of action for which I have not as yet even the wit to call upon it. Of what I suggestively find in it, at any rate, I shall speak; but I must first explain the felt connection between this enlarged impression of its quality and *portée* and the improved discussibility of a life hereafter. I hope, then, I shall not seem to push the relation of that idea to the ampler enjoyment of consciousness beyond what it will bear when I say that the ground is gained by the great extension so obtained for one's precious inward "personality" —one's personality not at all in itself of course, or on its claims of general importance, but as conceivably hanging together for survival. It is not that I have found in growing older any one marked or momentous line in the life of the mind or in the play and the freedom of the imagination to be stepped over; but that a process takes place which I can only describe as the accumulation of the very treasure itself of consciousness. I won't say that "the world," as we commonly refer to it, grows more attaching, but will say that the universe increasingly does, and that this makes us present at the enormous multiplication of our possible relations with it; relations still vague, no doubt, as undefined as they are uplifting, as they are inspiring, to think of, and on a scale beyond our actual use or application, yet filling us (through the "law" in question, the law that consciousness gives us immensities and imaginabilities wherever we direct it) with the unlimited vision of being. This mere fact that so small a part of one's visionary and speculative and emotional activity has even a traceably indirect bearing on one's doings or purposes or particular desires contribute strangely to the luxury—which is the magnificent waste—of thought, and strongly reminds one that even should one cease to be in love with life it would be difficult, on such terms, not to be in love with living.

Living, or feeling one's exquisite curiosity about the universe fed and fed, rewarded and rewarded—though I of course don't say definitely answered and answered—becomes thus the highest good I can conceive of, a million times better than not living (however *that* comfort may at bad moments have solicited us); all of which illustrates what I mean by the consecrated "interest" of consciousness. It so peoples and animates and extends and transforms itself; it so gives me the chance to take, on behalf of my personality, these inordinate intellectual and irresponsible liberties with the idea of things. And, once more—speaking for myself only and keeping to the facts of my experience—it is above all as an artist that I appreciate this beautiful and enjoyable independence of thought and more especially this assault of the boundlessly multiplied personal relation (my own), which carries me beyond even any "profoundest" observation of this world whatever, and any mortal adventure, and refers me to realizations I am condemned as yet but to dream of. For the artist the sense of our luxurious "waste" of postulation and supposition is of the strongest; of him is it superlatively true that he knows the aggression as of infinite numbers of modes of being. His case, as I see it, is easily such as to make him declare that if he were not constantly, in his commonest processes, carrying the field of consciousness further and further, making it lose itself in the ineffable, he shouldn't in the least feel himself an artist. As more or less of one myself, for instance, I deal with being, I invoke and evoke, I figure and represent, I seize and fix, as many phases and aspects and conceptions of it as my infirm hand allows me strength for; and in so doing I find myself—I can't express it otherwise—in communication with *sources;* sources to which I owe the apprehension of far more and far other combinations than observation and experience, in their ordinary sense, have given me the pattern of.

The truth is that to live, to this tune, intellectually, and in order to do beautiful things, with questions of being as such questions may for the man of imagination aboundingly come up, is to find one's view of one's share in it, and above all of its appeal to *be* shared, in an infinite variety, enormously enlarged. The very provocation offered to the artist by the universe, the provocation to him to *be*—poor man who may know so little what he's in for!—an artist, and thereby supremely serve it; what do I take that for but the intense desire of being to get itself personally shared, to show itself for personally sharable, and thus foster the sublimest faith? If the artist's surrender to invasive floods is accordingly nine-tenths of the matter that makes his consciousness, that makes mine, so persuasively interesting, so I should see people of our character peculiarly victimized if the vulgar arrangement of our fate, as I have called it, imputable to the power that produced us, should prove to be the true one. For I think of myself as enjoying the very maximum reason to desire the renewal of existence—existence the forms of which I have had admirably and endlessly to *cultivate*—and as therefore embracing it in thought as a possible something that shall be better than what we have known here; only then to ask myself if it be credible that the power just mentioned is simply enjoying the unholy "treat" or brutal amusement of encouraging that conviction in us in order to say with elation: "Then you shall have it, the charming confidence (for I shall wantonly let it come to that), only so long as that it shall beautifully mature; after which, as soon as the prospect has vividly and desirably opened out to you, you shall become as naught."

"Well, you *will* have had them, the sense and the vision of existence," the rejoinder on that may be; to which I retort in turn: "Yes, I shall have them exactly for the space of time during which the question of my appetite for what they represent may clear itself up. The complete privation, as a more or less prompt sequel to that clearance, is worthy but of the wit of a sniggering little boy who makes his dog jump at a morsel only to whisk it away; a practical joke of the lowest description, with the execrable taste of which I decline to charge our prime orginator."

I do not deny of course that the case may be different for those who have had another experience—there are so many different experiences of consciousness possible, and with the result of so many different positions on the matter. Those to whom such dreadful things have happened that they haven't even the refuge of the negative state of mind, but have been driven into the exasperated positive, so that they but long to lay down the burden of being and never again take it up— these unfortunates have an equal chance of expressing their attitude and of making it as eloquent and as representative as they will. Their testimony may easily be tremendous and their revelation black. Will they belong, however, to the class of those the really main condition of whose life is to work and work their inner spirit to a productive or illustrative end, and so to feel themselves find in it a general warrant for anything and everything, in the way of particular projections and adventures, that they may dream that spirit susceptible of? This comes again to asking, doubtless, whether it has been their fate to perceive themselves, in the fulness of time, and for good or for ill, living preponderantly by the imagination and having to call upon it at every turn to see them through. By which I don't mean to say that no sincere artist has ever been overwhelmed by life and found his connections with the infinite cut, so that his history may *seem* to represent for him so much evidence that this so easily awful world is the last word to us, and a horrible one at that: cases confounding me could quite too promptly be adduced. The point is, none the less, that in proportion as we (of the class I speak of) enjoy the greater number of our most characteristic inward reactions, in proportion as we do curiously and lovingly, yearningly and irrepressibly, interrogate and liberate, try and test and explore, our general productive and, as we like conveniently to say, creative awareness of things—though the individual, I grant, may pull his job off on occasion and for a while and yet never have done so at all—in that proportion does our function strike us as establishing sublime relations. It is this effect of working it that is exquisite; it is the character of the response it makes, and the merest fraction or dimmest shade of which is ever reported again in what we "have to show"; it is in a word the artistic consciousness and privilege in itself that thus shines as from immersion in the fountain of being. Into that fountain, to depths immeasurable, our spirit dips—to the effect of feeling itself, *quâ* imagination and aspiration, all scented with universal sources. What is that but an adventure of our personality, and how can we after it hold complete disconnection likely?

I do not so hold it, I profess, for my own part, and, above all, I freely concede, do not in the least want to. Consciousness has thus arrived at interesting me too much and on too great a scale—that is all my revelation or my secret; on too great a scale, that is, for me not to ask myself what she can mean by such blandishments—to the altogether normally hampered and benighted random individual that I am. Does she mean nothing more than that I shall have found life, by her enrichment, the more amusing here? But I find it, at this well-nigh final pass, mainly amusing in the light of the possibility that the idea of an exclusively present world, with all its appearances wholly dependent on our physical outfit, may represent for us but a chance for experiment in the very interest of our better and freer being and to its very honor and reinforcement; but a chance for the practice and initial confidence of our faculties and our passions, of the precious personality at stake—precious to *us* at least—which shall have been not unlike the sustaining frame on little wheels that often encases growing infants, so that, dangling and shaking about in it, they may feel their assurance of walking increase and teach their small toes to know the ground. I like to think that we here, as to soul, dangle from the infinite and shake about in the universe; that this world and this conformation and these senses are our helpful and ingenious frame, amply provided with wheels and replete with the lesson for us of how to plant, spiritually, our feet. That conception of the matter rather comes back, I recognize, to the theory of the spiritual discipline, the purification and preparation on earth for heaven, of the orthodox theology—which is a resemblance I don't object to, all the more that it is a superficial one, as well as a fact mainly showing, at any rate, how neatly extremes may sometimes meet.

My mind, however that may be, doesn't in the least resent its association with all the highly appreciable and perishable matter of which the rest of my personality is composed; nor does it fail to recognize the beautiful assistance—alternating indeed frequently with the extreme inconvenience—received from it; representing, as these latter forms do, much ministration to experience. The ministration may have sometimes affected my consciousness as clumsy, but has at other times affected it as exquisite, and it accepts and appropriates and consumes everything the universe puts in its way; matter in tons, if necessary, so long as such quantities are, in so mysterious and complicated a sphere, one of its conditions of activity. Above all, it takes kindly to that admirable philosophic view which makes of matter the mere encasement or sheath, thicker, thinner, coarser, finer, more transparent or more obstructive, of a spirit it has no more concern in producing than the baby-frame has in producing the intelligence of the baby—much as that intelligence may be so promoted.

I "like" to think, I may be held too artlessly to repeat, that this, that, and the other appearances are favorable to the idea of the independence, behind everything (*its* everything), of my individual soul; I "like" to think even at the risk of lumping myself with those shallow minds who are happily and foolishly able to believe what they would prefer. It isn't really a question of belief—which is a term I have made no use of in these remarks; it is on the other hand a question of desire, but of desire so confirmed, so thoroughly established and nourished, as to leave belief a comparatively irrelevant affair. There is one light, moreover, under which they come to the same thing—at least in presence of a question as insoluble as the one before us. If one acts from desire quite as one would from belief, it signifies little what name one gives to one's motive. By which term action I mean action of the mind, mean that I can encourage my consciousness to acquire that interest, to live in that elasticity and that affluence, which affect me as symptomatic and auspicious. I can't do less if I desire, but I shouldn't be able to do more if I believed. Just so I shouldn't be able to do more than cultivate belief; and it is exactly to cultivation that I subject my hopeful sense of the auspicious; with such success—or at least with such intensity—as to give me the splendid illusion of doing something myself for my prospect, or at all events for my own possibility, of immortality. There again, I recognize extremes "neatly meet"; one doesn't talk otherwise, doubtless, of one's working out one's salvation. But this coincidence too I am perfectly free to welcome—putting it, that is, that the theological provision happens to coincide with (or, for all I know, to have been, at bottom, insidiously built on) some such sense of appearances as my own. If I am talking, at all events, of what I "like" to think I may, in short, say all: I like to think it open to me to establish speculative and imaginative connections, to take up conceived presumptions and pledges, that have for me all the air of not being decently able to escape redeeming themselves. And when once such a mental relation to the question as that begins to hover and settle, who shall say over what fields of experience, past and current, and what immensities of perception and yearning, it shall *not* spread the protection of its wings? No, no, no—I reach beyond the laboratory-brain.

* * *

BOOK SEVEN

ON POLITICS AND SOCIETY

ALICE JAMES, wholly sympathetic with the Irish in their struggles against England, deplored that the family had come from "debased Ulster," and added: "What a humiliation for me. I suppose they didn't suspect what was to spring from them, or they would have managed better." One inextinguishable family trait was a keen sense for social injustice. Almost equally keen, except in HJ, was the love of a good fight.

Both the father and WJ were champions of the widest human freedom. Though a socialist, Henry Senior disowned all outward authority, and kept insisting on the superiority of man over any restricting institutions. He was far too committed to principle and far too heedless of the consequences of his ardent speech to be of any use in practical politics. Like John Jay Chapman in the next generation, he might have taken for his motto: "Never say in public what you won't regret." He was an intermittent writer of startling "letters to the editor," of which the most startling was his defense of Andrew Johnson for having been drunk on the day of his inauguration as Vice-President.

Johnson was not exactly one of the family's heroes. HJ, recalling their emotion at the time of Lincoln's death, contrasted him with his luckless successor: "It was vain to say that we had deliberately invoked the 'common' in authority and must drink the wine we had drawn. No countenance, no salience of aspect nor composed symbol, could superficially have referred itself less than Lincoln's mould-smashing mask to any mere matter-of-course type of propriety; but his admirable unrelated head had itself revealed a type—as if by the very fact that what had made in it for roughness of kind looked out only less than what had made in it for splendid final stamp, in other words for commanding Style." But if, as HJ anxiously examined the new President's picture in shop windows, it seemed to reveal anything but style, once Johnson's conduct had been attacked by the English papers, Henry Senior came warmly to his support.

The situation, grossly exaggerated and distorted by Johnson's enemies, was that the new Vice-President, who had not wholly recovered
from an attack of typhoid fever, felt weak on the morning of the
inauguration and asked Hannibal Hamlin to get him some whisky.
Once in the overheated Senate chamber, the alcohol overasserted itself, and he introduced into his speech some heartfelt expressions of
belief in the common man. He gloried in being "one who claims no
high descent, one who comes from the ranks of the people. . . . You,
Senators, and you who constitute the bench of the Supreme Court of
the United States, are but the creatures of the American people; your
exaltation is from them. . . . I, though a plebeian boy, am authorized
by the principles of the government under which I live to feel proudly
conscious that I am a man, and grave dignitaries are but men." According to reports, he also turned to where the foreign ministers were
sitting and added: "And you, gentlemen of the Diplomatic Corps,
with all your fine feathers and gewgaws."

What aroused Henry Senior's ardor were such editorials as the one
in the London *Saturday Review* which granted that Johnson's "vulgar
conceit" might be explained by intoxication, but went on to make its
case by adding: "It is difficult to say how much harm a reckless up-
start in supreme power might create. . . . Boasts of plebeian origin,
and an officious display of coarseness, probably indicate Jacobin tendencies." The *New York World*, to be sure, using the less delicate
language of American politics, had already termed Johnson "an insolent
drunken brute, in comparison with whom Caligula's horse was respectable." But by the time Henry Senior read the English reactions,
Lincoln had been assassinated, and Johnson was in the White House.
Furthermore, Henry Senior was true to his heritage in never brooking
an insult from an Englishman. Once his combative imagination was en-
kindled, he managed to find in Johnson's behavior another parable of
the greater worth of the heart over the head:

*　*　*　*　*

Tuesday, May 23, 1865

To the Editors of *The New York Evening Post*:

Have we really reached second childhood? or are we still men in
understanding? I ask these questions of you and your readers in view
of the astonishing amount of senility which the accident to Vice-President Johnson on inauguration day has provoked, first in some of our
own papers, and now at last in the more malignant echoes of the London
press. It is a well-understood thing among all those who desire to know
the truth upon the subject that the Vice-President, being disqualified
by illness and consequent nervous depression for taking part in the
inauguration ceremonies, and yet being persuaded against his own better
judgment to make the effort, sought a temporary access of strength

and exhilaration for that purpose in the use of stimulants; and that the effect of these remedial agents was to give him a somewhat larger liberty of speech than comported with conventional usage.

I have the same sincere aversion and disgust to vicious habits and indulgences in other people that my neighbors have; and if I thought any of our public men inclined to intemperance, for example, I should deem it a great misfortune, demanding extra vigilance on our part to obviate its possible disastrous consequences. Even then, however, I hope I should be incapable of any brutal denunciation of the peccant individual himself; incapable of any expression of feeling towards him which might wantonly enfeeble his self-respect and so harden him in vice. But if any private friend—much more any official person, clothed with a public responsibility—should upon any occasion be accidentally wrenched from his habitual ways to obey for a moment the siren voice of pleasure, I should consider myself dishonored in my own esteem if I did not overlook the occurrence and do my best to conceal it from the notice of others. It appears to me that I should shrink from exposing any similar delinquency on my own part, or in one of my own kindred. At all events, I am sure of this: that if through any latent Phariseeism of soul in me, either inherited or acquired, I should be surprised into a contrary course of action—should be led to parade the occurrence to public gaze and denounce it with well-simulated words of regard for public virtue—my flagrant inhumanity would ere long chase me out of my most specious concealments and scourge me into a premature grave.

With what loathing, then, does one read the insulting, insincere comments of the London *Times* and *Saturday Review* in application to the incident in question! Who that has a fibre of regard for Divine truth or goodness in his soul; who that has a fibre of self-respect or respect for human worth in his bosom, untainted by a persistent servility to aristocratic pretension, is not outraged by the odious epithets which these foulmouthed partisans and apologists of respectable iniquity bestow upon President Johnson? A zeal for virtue, indeed! How did this zeal manifest itself but in every form of abject adulation and hushed reverence, when George the Fourth turned his palaces into so many styes of drunkenness and lewd debauchery! How does it demean itself now, when the highest officer of the crown—the very head and front of English respectability now for long years—has been for all these long years living not only in open, but in what a distinguished Englishman who well weighs all his words, did not hesitate recently to pronounce "*ostentatious* adultery"? Not a breath of reprehension! Every honeyed word instead of graceful sycophancy and cunning admiration! Tell me, indeed, that the infamous tongue of these writers is animated by any regard for things human or things divine! No; rely upon it, the only intelligible motive of the scurrility is to be found in the fact that Mr. Johnson represents, as it was never before represented, the distinctively popular instinct in the working of our institutions.

I mentioned just now the *Saturday Review*, which is undoubtedly the best average expression to which English literary culture has yet attained. This *Review* as to its general conduct is a spirited though ungraceful imitation of the French literary scepticism; bearing the same relation to its original that a cask of creditable home-brewed ale bears to a generous natural vintage. It exhibits a more than ordinary University veneering and polish; but it betrays also, much more than the *Times*, the awkward self-consciousness impressed upon English manners by that other subtle tyranny which, next to the Universities, makes itself felt in English training—I mean the tyranny of the serv-ants' hall—and gives it a defiant, insolent air, fatal to all grace and innocence. To be sure the whole unconscious soul of the *Review* runs to preaching bluffly once a week what the *Times* insinuates more prudently every day, namely: that English manhood is substantially the only manhood, and that other people are men, therefore, just in the ratio of their approximation to Englishmen. But then I maintain that the *Saturday Review*, notwithstanding its comparative infrequency of appearance, is much more offensive to public decency for the lack of this same prudence that notoriously regulates the *Times*. It is seven times more afflictive to good taste than the *Times*, not only because the same amount of egotism and vulgar truculence makes a shriller squeal through a narrow vent than through a broad one, but chiefly because the *Review* writers exhibit a sort of feminine malignity, which is always the most depraved and hopeless. They represent the cultivated consciousness of the country, while the *Times* is more true to the common mind. The *Times* expresses the common instincts of the people so far as that course can be made pecuniarily profitable; and hence it enjoys a comparatively masculine inspiration. The *Saturday Review* represents the select or collegiate mind of the country, the class of per-sons in whom the national self-consciousness is intensified to the highest pitch, amounting, in fact to a *cultus;* and hence it has a certain emascu-late air, an air of acrid perverted virginity, which gives it the semblance of being written by a set of mettlesome, high-handed, unscrupulous, and yet frivolous spinsters. It is a ghastly chastity which is enshrined in eastern harems and guarantied only by eunuchs. Yet in looking at spiritual England, its highest interests, those of morality and religion, seem betrayed into the same unhandsome keeping; that is, are most loudly avouched by men whose whole temper of mind palpably dis-qualifies them for any living sympathy with God or man. I never take up any of their more characteristic periodicals, such as the *Saturday Review*, for example, without being reminded, by every explosion of its flippant insincere conservatism, of this spiteful hideous rage of the eunuch against incontinence.

But to return to my proper subject. Mr. Johnson said nothing on the occasion in question which *in substance* he ought not to have said. The only possible objection to what he did say lay in the unaccustomed frankness with which he referred to his own personal career, and sought to illustrate by it the striking practical impartiality of our institutions. His origin was more humble in a conventional regard than that of any previous incumbent of his office, and yet the popular will had exalted him to preside over its most august legislative body, and in certain contingencies over the nation itself. In these facts he beheld an unquestionable argument of the excellence of our form of government, and his manly heart was melted with devout gratitude that such things should really be—that such hope for man's advancing destiny on earth was to be providentially ratified by the ceremonial then and there to ensue. What wonder, then, if the profound emotion of the upright spontaneous heart, accidentally, or rather providentially, released for the moment from the custody of the wily conventional head, bubbled up in words of childlike religious joy and amazement! In words of such exquisite truth and profound religious pathos indeed to my ear, as to sound the knell of an old world of mere false pretension, and announce a new world of unblemished faith and honesty! It is very doubtful to me whether President Johnson would have given the frank utterance he did to the divine emotion which glowed in his soul, if he had been left to his ordinary carnal prudence. I doubt especially whether, under that base inspiration, he would have found courage pointedly to summon the attention of the representatives of foreign governments to the exquisitely humane lesson of the facts there transpiring. But I have no shadow of doubt that it was most becoming in him to do these things; that it was high time these most righteous inculcations of providential justice manifest in our extraordinary history should be commended to the world's reverent attention, and that therefore if Mr. Johnson was incapacitated by his normal self-control for the worthy performance of these offices, it is a thing not to groan over, but simply to be glad of, that he was freed for a moment from his own providence, and rendered frankly obedient to inspirations deeper than his own virtue. That the case was so reflects no individual discredit in my opinion upon Mr. Johnson. It is only a new argument of the adorable Wisdom, that when it is estopped from affecting its own ends by our conceited virtue, it makes our abject weakness the honored ministers of its pleasure. Thus, while I would not recommend inebriation as an improved editorial qualification for the conductors of the London *Times* or the Boston *Courier*, I am yet quite sure that if in some accidental experience of that condition which may befall those gentlemen—for we are all mortal—they shall utter anything half so grand and timely, half so encouraging to human hope, half so fragrant with an inward fire of worship, as the words that fell from the lips of the outraged and noble soul who now, equally with his lamented predecessor, honors the Presidential chair so long fouled by evil occupancy, all the world, white and black, will not only forgive their temporary obscuration, but never cease to remember them as far more virtuous in their own despite than they have ever yet been by their own concurrence.

H. J.

* * *

WJ had written to HJ from Brazil saying how much he wanted to see this letter, but during all the early part of his own career, he was far less concerned with politics than his father had been. The instinctive response of his thought, to be sure, was always for the new against the old, for heresy against orthodoxy, as when faith-healers wanted the right to practice in Massachusetts and he defended them, to the scandal of the reputable medical profession, on the ground that truth might often result from seemingly disreputable experiments. But when he alluded to "the labor question," in "What Makes a Life Significant?" [1] it was only to illustrate his contention that different groups failed to see the value in one another's point of view. He gave no indication of an awareness of the grim conditions that Henry George had documented some years before in *Progress and Poverty* (1879). When he wrote HJ about the Haymarket riot, he showed no such discernment of the real issue as enlisted Howells' courageous defense of the accused anarchists. He exulted in the free play of forces, and said: "Don't be alarmed by the labor troubles here. I am quite sure they are a most healthy phase of evolution, a little costly, but normal, and sure to do lots of good to all hands in the end. I don't speak of the senseless 'anarchist' riot in Chicago, which has nothing to do with 'Knights of Labor,' but is the work of a lot of pathological Germans and Poles."

Following his father in his distrust of fixed institutions, whether in church or state, WJ was much less abreast than Henry Senior had been with the new social thought of his own time. In celebrating WJ's centenary Max Otto remarked: "If he ever chanced upon the aphorism of Karl Marx, 'Philosophers merely give the world different interpretations, but the real job is to change it,' his response must have been enthusiastic, for this is exactly the criticism he himself made in philosophic terms." WJ's pragmatism insists that a thinker does not discover already existing truth, but makes truth dynamically for himself. But it is also undeniable, as Professor Otto went on to say, that WJ was singu-

---

[1] Pp. 417–19 above.

larly blind to the role played by economic forces in society, and in determining an individual's character and destiny.

For a long time WJ hardly thought in terms of a social context at all. Favored child of liberalism and *laissez faire*, he did not really begin, until his last dozen years, to reckon with the consequences of the "unlimited competition" that Henry Senior, half a century before, had pronounced "a system of rapacity and robbery."[1] During the 1870's and '80's WJ's political independence did not go beyond a dissatisfaction with both existing parties and a hope for civil service reform. His social sympathies, sure to be aroused on behalf of an underdog, broadened and deepened greatly during the period of the Spanish-American War and of the Dreyfus case. When our incipient imperialism caused him to see politics with fresh eyes, he spared no energy in denouncing what he called "the cold pot-grease" of McKinley's cant. When, in the face of their policy against Spain and the Philippines, McKinley and Roosevelt were nominated by the Republicans in 1900, he branded them as "a combination of slime and grit, soap and sand, that ought to scour anything away, even the moral sense of the country." Still, to his eyes, the election of Bryan would have meant no more than "a premature victory of a very mongrel kind of reform."

What he was most deeply disturbed by was our treatment of the Filipinos, and our departure from our previous foreign policy into reckless conquest based on a doctrine of racial superiority. Two of his letters on the subject deserve to be rescued from the files of the *Boston Transcript*, particularly since his description of a people's movement being mercilessly destroyed by our business civilization has as much bearing upon our present conduct in the Orient as it had fifty years ago:

* * * * *

THE PHILIPPINE TANGLE

March 1, 1899

To the Editor of the *Transcript*:

An observer who should judge solely by the sort of evidence which the newspapers present might easily suppose that the American people felt little concern about the performances of our Government in the Philippine Islands, and were practically indifferent to their moral aspects. The cannon of our gunboats at Manila and the ratification of the treaty have sent even the most vehement anti-imperialist journals temporarily to cover, and the bugbear of copperheadism has reduced the freest tongues for a while to silence. The excitement of battle, this time

---

[1] P. 12 above.

as always, has produced its cowing and disorganizing effect upon the opposition.

But it would be dangerous for the Administration to trust to these impressions. I will not say that I have been amazed, for I fully expected it; but I have been cheered and encouraged at the almost unanimous dismay and horror which I find individuals express in private conversation over the turn which things are taking. "A national infamy" is the comment on the case which I hear most commonly uttered. The fires of indignation are momentarily "banked," but they are anything but "out." They seem merely to be awaiting the properly concerted and organized signal to burst forth with far more vehemence than ever, as imperialism and the idol of a national destiny, based on martial excitement and mere "bigness," keep revealing their corrupting inwardness more and more unmistakably. The process of education has been too short for the older American nature not to feel the shock. We gave the fighting instinct and the passion of mastery their outing; we let them have the day to themselves, and temporarily committed our fortunes to their leading last spring, because we thought that, being harnessed in a cause which promised to be that of freedom, the results were fairly safe, and we could resume our permanent ideals and character when the fighting fit was done. We now see how we reckoned without our host. We see by the vividest of examples what an absolute savage and pirate the passion of military conquest always is, and how the only safeguard against the crimes to which it will infallibly drag the nation that gives way to it is to keep it chained for ever; is never to let it get its start. In the European nations it is kept chained by a greater mutual fear than they have ever before felt for one another. Here it should have been kept chained by a native wisdom nourished assiduously for a century on opposite ideals. And we can appreciate now that wisdom in those of us who, with our national Executive at their head, worked so desperately to keep it chained last spring.

But since then, Executive and all, we have been swept away by the overmastering flood. And now what it has swept us into is an adventure that in sober seriousness and definite English speech must be described as literally piratical. Our treatment of the Aguinaldo movement at Manila and at Iloilo is piracy positive and absolute, and the American people appear as pirates pure and simple, as day by day the real facts of the situation are coming to the light.

What was only vaguely apprehended is now clear with a definiteness that is startling indeed. Here was a people towards whom we felt no ill-will, against whom we had not even a slanderous rumor to bring; a people for whose tenacious struggle against their Spanish oppressors we have for years past spoken (so far as we spoke of them at all) with nothing but admiration and sympathy. Here was a leader who, as the Spanish lies about him, on which we were fed so long, drop off, and as the truth gets more and more known, appears as an exceptionally fine specimen of the patriot and national hero; not only daring, but honest; not only a fighter, but a governor and organizer of extraordinary power. Here were the precious beginnings of an indigenous national life, with which, if we had any responsibilities to these islands at all, it was our first duty to have squared ourselves. Aguinaldo's movement was, and evidently deserved to be, an ideal popular movement, which as far as it had had time to exist was showing itself "fit" to survive and likely to become a healthy piece of national self-development. It was all we had to build on, at any rate, so far—if we had any desire not to succeed to the Spaniards' inheritance of native execration.

And what did our Administration do? So far as the facts have leaked out, it issued instructions to the commanders on the ground simply to freeze Aguinaldo out, as a dangerous rival, with whom all compromising entanglement was sedulously to be avoided by the great Yankee business concern. We were not to "recognize" him, we were to deny him all account of our intentions; and in general to refuse any account of our intentions to anybody, except to declare in abstract terms their "benevolence," until the inhabitants, without a pledge of any sort from us, should turn over their country into our hands. Our President's bouffe-proclamation was the only thing vouchsafed: "We are here for your own good; therefore unconditionally surrender to our tender mercies, or we'll blow you into kingdom come."

Our own people meanwhile were vaguely uneasy, for the inhuman callousness and insult shown at Paris and Washington to the officially delegated mouthpieces of the wants and claims of the Filipinos seemed simply abominable from any moral point of view. But there must be reasons of state, we assumed, and good ones. Aguinaldo is evidently a pure adventurer "on the make," a blackmailer, sure in the end to betray our confidence, or our Government wouldn't treat him so, for our President is essentially methodistical and moral. Mr. McKinley must be in an intolerably perplexing situation, and we must not criticise him too soon. We assumed this, I say, though all the while there was a horribly suspicious look about the performance. On its face it reeked of the infernal adroitness of the great department store, which has reached perfect expertness in the art of killing silently and with no public squealing or commotion the neighboring small concern.

But that small concern, Aguinaldo, apparently not having the proper American business education, and being uninstructed on the irresistible character of our Republican party combine, neither offered to sell out nor to give up. So the Administration had to show its hand without disguise. It did so at last. We are now openly engaged in crushing out the sacredest thing in this great human world—the attempt of a people long enslaved to attain to the possession of itself, to organize its laws and government, to be free to follow its internal destinies according to its own ideals. War, said Moltke, aims at destruction, and at nothing else. And splendidly are we carrying out war's ideal. We are destroying the lives of these islanders by the thousand, their villages and their cities; for surely it is we who are solely responsible for all the incidental burnings that our operations entail. But these destructions are the smallest part of our sins. We are destroying down to the root every germ of a healthy national life in these unfortunate people, and we are surely helping to destroy for one generation at least their faith in God and man. No life shall you have, we say, except as a gift from our philanthropy after your unconditional submission to our will. So as they seem to be "slow pay" in the matter of submission, our yellow journals have abundant time in which to raise new monuments of capitals to the victories of Old Glory, and in which to extol the unrestrainable eagerness of our brave soldiers to rush into battles that remind them so much of rabbit hunts on Western plains.

It is horrible, simply horrible. Surely there cannot be many born and bred Americans who, when they look at the bare fact of what we are doing, the fact taken all by itself, do not feel this, and do not blush with burning shame at the unspeakable meanness and ignominy of the trick?

Why, then, do we go on? First, the war fever; and then the pride which always refuses to back down when under fire. But these are passions that interfere with the reasonable settlement of any affair; and in this affair we have to deal with a factor altogether peculiar with our belief, namely, in a national destiny which must be "big" at any cost, and which for some inscrutable reason it has become infamous for us to disbelieve in or refuse. We are to be missionaries of civilization, and to bear the white man's burden, painful as it often is. We must sow our ideals, plant our order, impose our God. The individual lives are nothing. Our duty and our destiny call, and civilization must go on.

Could there be a more damning indictment of that whole bloated idol termed "modern civilization" than this amounts to? Civilization is, then, the big, hollow, resounding, corrupting, sophisticating, confusing torrent of mere brutal momentum and irrationality that brings forth fruits like this! It is safe to say that one Christian missionary, whether primitive, Protestant or Catholic, of the original missionary type, one Buddhist or Mohammedan of a genuine saintly sort, one ethical reformer or philanthropist, or one disciple of Tolstoï would do more real good in these islands than our whole army and navy can possibly effect with our whole civilization at their back. He could build up realities, in however small a degree; we can only destroy the inner realities; and indeed destroy in a year more of them than a generation can make good.

It is by their moral fruits exclusively that these benighted brown people, "half-devil and half-child" [1] as they are, are condemned to judge a civilization. Ours is already execrated by them forever for its hideous fruits.

Shall it not in so far forth be execrated by ourselves? Shall the unsophisticated verdict upon its hideousness which the plain moral sense pronounces avail nothing to stem the torrent of mere empty "bigness" in our destiny, before which it is said we must all knock under, swallowing our higher sentiments with a gulp? The issue is perfectly plain at last. We are cold-bloodedly, wantonly and abominably destroying the soul of a people who never did us an atom of harm in their lives. It is bald, brutal piracy, impossible to dish up any longer in the cold potgrease of President McKinley's cant at the recent Boston banquet— surely as shamefully evasive a speech, considering the right of the public to know definite facts, as can often have fallen even from a professional politician's lips. The worst of our imperialists is that they do not themselves know where sincerity ends and insincerity begins. Their state of consciousness is so new, so mixed of primitively human passions and, in political circles, of calculations that are anything but primitively human; so at variance, moreover, with their former mental habits; and so empty of definite data and contents; that they face various ways at once, and their portraits should be taken with a squint. One reads the President's speech with a strange feeling—as if the very words were squinting on the page.

The impotence of the private individual, with imperialism under full headway as it is, is deplorable indeed. But every American has a voice or a pen, and may use it. So, impelled by my own sense of duty, I write these present words. One by one we shall creep from cover, and the opposition will organize itself. If the Filipinos hold out long enough, there is a good chance (the canting game being already pretty well played out, and the piracy having to show itself henceforward naked) of the older American beliefs and sentiments coming to their rights again, and of the Administration being terrified into a conciliatory policy towards the native government.

The programme for the opposition should, it seems to me, be radical. The infamy and iniquity of a war of conquest must stop. A "protectorate," of course, if they will have it, though after this they would probably rather welcome any European Power; and as regards the inner state of the island, freedom, "fit" or "unfit," that is, home rule without humbugging phrases, and whatever anarchy may go with it until the Filipinos learn from each other, not from us, how to govern themselves. . . . Until the opposition newspapers seriously begin, and the mass meetings are held, let every American who still wishes his country

---

[1] For WJ's own more penetrating ob-   p. 520 above.
jection to this phrase of Kipling's, see

to possess its ancient soul—soul a thousand times more dear than ever, now that it seems in danger of perdition—do what little he can in the way of open speech and writing, and above all let him give his representatives and senators in Washington a positive piece of his mind.

WILLIAM JAMES

GOVERNOR ROOSEVELT'S ORATION

April 15, 1899

To the Editor of the *Transcript*:

Shall Governor Roosevelt be allowed to crow all over our national barnyard and hear no equally shrill voice lifted in reply? Even the "prattlers who sit at home in peace with their silly mock humanitarianism" must feel their "ignoble" and "cowardly" blood stirred by such a challenge, and I, for one, feel that it would be ignominious to leave him in uncontradicted possession of the field.

In the Hegelian philosophy the worst vice that an oration or any other expression of human nature can have is abstractness. Abstractness means empty simplicity, non-reference to features essential in the case. Of all the carnivals of emptiness and abstractness that the world has seen, our national discussions over the Philippine policy probably bear away the palm. The arch abstractionists have been the promoters of expansion; and, of them all, Governor Roosevelt now writes himself down as the very chief. We miss in him, thank Heaven, the sanctimonious abstractions. Not a word about "elevating" the Filipinos. Not a word about giving them pure homes, free schools, American school books and ready-made pants to hide their indecent nudity. Not a word about "sending them Christ"—and for all that let us thank him. But of all the naked abstractions that were ever applied to human affairs, the outpourings of Governor Roosevelt's soul in this speech would seem the very nakedest. Although in middle life, as the years age, and in a situation of responsibility concrete enough, he still mentally in the Sturm and Drang period of early adolescence, treats human affairs, when he makes speeches about them, from the sole point of view of the organic excitement and difficulty they may bring, gushes over war as the ideal condition of human society, for the manly strenuousness which it involves, and treats peace as a condition of blubberlike and swollen ignobility, fit only for huckstering weaklings, dwelling in gray twilight and heedless of the higher life. Not a word of the cause—one foe is as good as another, for aught he tells us; not a word of the conditions of success. Just as revolution, per se, seems the ideal status to strata of the Parisian populace, bred in a certain condition, so war in the abstract and per se seems the ideal status to Governor Roosevelt: and peace in the abstract and per se is his notion of the ignominious human life.

In pure esthetic abstractness every human heart responds after a fashion. But when it comes to turn itself concretely into Shafter's policy of "Kill half the natives and govern the rest justly," one feels that abstract esthetic and organic emotionalities may need a policeman to keep them in check.

Governor Roosevelt's abstract war-worship carries no test of what is better or worse in the way of wars. He scathes and scores the "party of peace" in the war of secession—a party whom lately we have heard little about. But, strangely enough, he fails to praise explicitly the party of Jeff Davis. Yet civil war is war, and partakes of all its virility. The secessionists were certainly leading the strenuous life when they chose battle rather than Lincoln as president. And certainly in his heart of hearts Governor Roosevelt does bless them for what they did. They gave us four years of martial excitement, and a lot of heroes and matter for war historians; and therein for him lies the essence of all national "greatness."

But why then were the Bryanites not recreants to all true national greatness when they failed two years ago to march on Washington to prevent McKinley's inauguration? That was surely the more "adventurous" path. And why are not England's parties, with their edges all worn flabby by their mutual good nature, inferior to those of Guatemala and Peru, where every election is a revolution? Why is not the history of France, with its revolutions during all the century, the ideal for all other nations to imitate? Why did not the trained and disciplined restraint of the British government and press, when President Cleveland's threat of war was published, and when a single shrill word from Lord Salisbury would have thrown that nation into a war-fever like our own, trace the low-water mark of national infamy? They failed to go to war, when our whole coast lay at their mercy!

It is impossible to say what principles of discrimination Governor Roosevelt could use in these cases, for in his oration he swamps everything together in one flood of abstract bellicose emotion.

Roosevelt and the McKinley party make one understand the French revolution, so long an enigma to our English imaginative powers. How could such bald abstractions as Reason and the Rights of Man, spelt with capitals, and ignoring all the concrete facts of human nature, ever have let loose such a torrent of slaughter? The Philippine islanders well know how—that naked abstraction, "good government" firing the American soul, has done the like. We see how, by reading Governor Roosevelt's oration, "No parleying, no faltering in dealing with our foe," is keeping the ground red.

The crime of which we accuse Governor Roosevelt's party is that of treating an intensely living and concrete situation by a set of bald and hollow abstractions.

The abstractions are five in number:
1. "Responsibility" for the islands.
2. "Unfitness" of the natives.
3. "Good government" our duty.
4. "The supremacy of the flag" needful thereto; wherefore—
5. "No entanglement with Aguinaldo's crew." . . .

It grows tiresome to repeat the indictment, but "good government" in the concrete means a government that seeks to make some connection with the actual mental condition of the governed. It does not mean callous insult to all their representatives, and perfidy under the name of avoidance of entanglement.

Similarly "unfitness for self-control" means in the concrete a visible set of facts, and not a paper label pinned to a population beforehand by an assumption made thousands of miles away. Visibly the Filipinos were showing fitness for government by actually carrying it on; and the only anarchy the islands now show is that ensuing upon our president's proclamation, a declaration of war in fullest technical form, to which no known concrete race of human beings ever could be expected to submit tamely. This monstrous proclamation came before the Spaniards gave up their legal title; it came like a thunderbolt out of a clear sky; it came without any preliminary attempt to get into any kind of working partnership with the national leaders or to gain their good will by even entertaining the possibility of conciliating some of their ideals. The empty abstractions had unrestricted right of way—unfitness, anarchy, clean sweep, no entanglement, no parley, unconditional surrender, supremacy of the flag; then, indeed, good government, Christian civilization, freedom, brotherly protection, kind offices, all that the head of man or people can desire.

The one result that is obvious is that no more ignominious political blunder was ever made—no greater failure to profit by a magnificent opportunity. Or will Governor Roosevelt pretend that there is some law of nature which, if a man of different mental mold from President McKinley had been dictator for the past nine months, would have precluded him also from even trying a friendship-winning policy? Was there some iron decree of fate that doomed our name anyhow to become "from the word go" an object of execration to the Luzon population? That predestined every superior personality among them to become militant against us?

Hardly! It is safe to say that the governor perceives as much as any one the personal blundering and incapacity, and knows as much as any one that President McKinley is the sole culprit officially responsible.

Yet like any Hun or Tartar, like President McKinley himself, his only notion of a remedy, now that we have committed the crime, is to kill, kill, kill our way through all its witnesses and victims. It is strenuous war, divine and glorious, and accursed be the mock philanthropists and weaklings who presume to call a halt!

I submit to Governor Roosevelt that here is a matter for a perfectly definite political issue in these states. Shall the mere killing policy continue, or shall it stop? Is a brown man's government, that has for nine months carried on a war against the finest white army of its size in the world, being beaten in every special engagement and retreating, yet holding together and never losing heart, and foiling us completely when the campaign, as a whole, is taken—is such a government as completely "unfit" to even be allowed to try the task of domestic administration as we have abstractedly assumed it to be? No government ever proved its fitness for trial in any other way. For God's sake, we say, then, let up on the fine fellows; give them a fighting chance with their government and see what they will do. It will be time enough to fall to and massacre them again when they shall have begotten an anarchy remotely resembling that which the McKinley policy has wrought. Therefore speak, write, agitate, in season and out of season, until that policy is reversed, or its sole proprietors and inventors are driven out of power.

And I submit that Mr. Roosevelt's attempt to turn this concrete political issue into an abstract emotional comparison between two types of personal character, one strong and manly, the other weak and cowardly, is an evasion unworthy the student of history which he is. He knows that courage is equally distributed among persons of divergent opinions and that taking one human being with another, all are abstractly equally willing to fight. He knows that the only difference between them that betrays itself in politics is as to the sufficient cause for fighting. To enslave a weak but heroic people, or to brazen out a blunder, is a good enough cause, it appears, for Colonel Roosevelt. To us Massachusetts anti-imperialists, who have fought in better causes, it is not quite good enough. . .

William James

* * *

WJ continued to support the New England Anti-Imperialist League until, in an address before its membership in 1903, he had to confess that he and they had been beaten in their immediate objective, that " 'Duty and Destiny' have rolled over us like a Juggernaut car." But he then took the longer view that liberalism as an international force must prevail in the end:

"Angelic impulses and predatory lusts divide our heart exactly as they divide the hearts of other countries. . . . Political virtue does not follow geographical divisions. It follows the eternal division inside of each country between the more animal and the more intellectual kind of men, between the tory and the liberal tendencies, the jingoism and animal instinct that would run things by main force and brute possession, and the critical conscience that believes in educational methods and in rational rules of right. . . . The great international and cosmopolitan liberal party, the party of conscience and intelligence the world over, has, in short, absorbed us; and we are only its American section, carrying on the war against the powers of darkness here, playing our part in the long, long campaign for truth and fair dealing which must go on in all the countries of the world until the end of time. Let us cheerfully settle to our interminable task. Everywhere it is the same struggle under various names,—light against darkness, right against might, love against hate. The Lord of life is with us, and we cannot permanently fail."

He could nevertheless perceive some of the inherent weaknesses of liberalism. He commented upon its "chronic fault" of "lack of speed." After listening to two hours of five-minute speeches at a banquet, he came away "saddened by the sight of what I knew already, that when you get a lot of pure idealists together they don't show up as strong as an equal lot of practical men." Despite his opposition to Roosevelt's jingoism, he felt himself attracted by his contagious energy. WJ also revered the strenuous life in his own way, and after observing Roosevelt as President, he decided that his heart was "in the right place," since he was "an enemy of red tape and quibbling and everything that in general the word 'politician' stands for." WJ even hoped for a while, in one of those volatile bursts of enthusiasm that characterized him to the end, that Roosevelt might at the close of his national term become the next president of Harvard. But when T. R. made a speech in Cambridge and derided scholarship before the students, WJ quickly veered away again. He admired a fighter, but only for causes that he could respect.

The one constant political position that he adhered to was the nonexpendable value of the individual. He sometimes supported underdogs just because they were underdogs; if they had been top dogs, he would certainly have been against them. More often, however, he was moved by human vividness wherever he encountered it. After renewing his fondness for the *Waverley* novels in middle life, he wrote to a Baltimore friend: "The Scotch are the finest race in the world—except the Baltimoreans and Jews." When the Dreyfus case made racial prejudice a fighting issue, he commented on a hitherto favorite hotel: "The circular appears this year with the precious addition: 'Applications from Hebrews cannot be considered.' I propose to return the boycott." At the time of Dreyfus' conviction in the summer of 1899, WJ had not yet been defeated in his stand against American imperialism, and wrote to his brother-in-law from Europe:

"We must thank God for America; and hold fast to every advantage of our position. Talk about our corruption! It is a mere fly-speck of superficiality compared with the rooted and permanent forces of corruption that exist in the European states. The only serious permanent force of corruption in America is party spirit. All the other forces are shifting like the clouds, and have no partnerships with any permanently organized ideal. Millionaires and syndicates have their immediate cash to pay, but they have no intrenched prestige to work with, like the church sentiment, the army sentiment, the aristocracy and royalty sentiment, which here can be brought to bear in favor of every kind of individual and collective crime—appealing not only to the immediate pocket of the persons to be corrupted, but to the ideals of their imagination as well. . . . We 'intellectuals' in America must all work to keep our precious birthright of individualism, and freedom from these institutions. *Every* great institution is perforce a means of corruption —whatever good it may also do. Only in the free personal relation is full ideality to be found.—I have vomited all this out upon you in the hope that it may wake a responsive echo. One must do *something* to work off the effect of the Dreyfus sentence."

His opposition to all big institutions as such left WJ with no adequate fulcrum from which to operate upon modern society. He seemed to realize at times that he was living at a point of divide between conflicting attitudes. He wrote in that same summer of 1899:

"As for me, my bed is made: I am against all bigness and greatness in all their forms, and with the invisible molecular forces that work from individual to individual, stealing in through the crannies of the world like so many soft rootlets, or like the capillary oozing of water, and yet rending the hardest monuments of man's pride, if you give them time. The bigger the unit you deal with, the hollower, the more brutal, the more mendacious is the life displayed. So I am against all big organizations as such, national ones first and foremost; against all big successes and big results; and in favor of the eternal forces of truth which always work in the individual and immediately unsuccessful way, underdogs always, till history comes, after they are long dead, and puts them on the top."

Half a dozen years later he pursued this train of thought in commemorating his friend the free-lance philosopher Thomas Davidson:

"The memory of Davidson will always strengthen my faith in personal freedom and its spontaneities, and make me less unqualifiedly respectful than ever of 'Civilization,' with its herding and branding, licensing and degree-giving, authorizing and appointing, and in general regulating and administering by system the lives of human beings. Surely the individual, the person in the singular number, is the more fundamental phenomenon, and the social institution, of whatever grade, is but secondary and ministerial. Many as are the interests which social systems satisfy, always unsatisfied interests remain over, and among them are interests to which system, as such, does violence whenever it lays its hand upon us. The best Commonwealth will always be the one that most cherishes the men who represent the residual interests, the one that leaves the largest scope to their peculiarities."

The one potential leaven that he found in the social lump was the guiding example of educated men. He may have taken too hopeful a view of his own profession, and have spoken too often as a eupeptic moralist. But he was by no means unaware of the dangers confronting the future of American education. "We of the colleges," he remarked in a local speech on "The Social Value of the College-Bred," "must eradicate a curious notion which numbers of good people have about such ancient seats of learning as Harvard. To many ignorant outsiders, that name suggests little more than a sterilized conceit and incapacity for being pleased. . . . Real culture lives by sympathies and admirations, not by dislikes and disdains; under all misleading wrappings it pounces unerringly upon the human core. If a college, through the inferior human influences that have grown regnant there, fails to catch the robuster tone, its failure is colossal, for its social function stops: democracy gives it a wide berth, turns toward it a deaf ear."

As far as Harvard itself was concerned, he was often of a divided mind. He recognized that at its best, in its assemblage of scholars from all over the world, it was "perhaps a more cosmopolitan post of observation than is elsewhere to be found." But he sometimes felt, as Henry Adams had felt during his brief stay there as a professor of history, that the University failed in its opportunity to create anything like a living community. At the time he was finishing his *Psychology*, he gave voice to sentiments that many subsequent Harvard teachers must have shared: "The Eliots have just returned from a year of absence abroad. I have not seen 'em yet. Whether it be his cold figure at the helm, or what not; whether it be perhaps the fact that I myself never graduated here, I know not; one thing is certain, that although I *serve* Harvard College to the best of my ability, I have no *affection* at all for the institution, and would gladly desert it for anything that offered better pay." He never did desert it, though he was tempted once by an offer from Johns Hopkins. What held him to his post was largely his satisfaction in his contacts with the students and the companionship of a few colleagues.

He remained greatly impressed by the way the intellectuals of France had rallied to the cause of Dreyfus, and envisaged—and did his best to encourage—an equivalent group in America:

"In this very simple way does the value of our educated class define itself: we more than others should be able to divine the worthier and better leaders. The terms here are monstrously simplified, of course, but such a bird's-eye view lets us immediately take our bearings. In our democracy, where everything else is so shifting, we alumni and alumnæ of the colleges are the only permanent presence that corresponds to the aristocracy in older countries. We have continuous traditions, as they have; our motto, too, is *noblesse oblige;* and, unlike them, we stand for ideal interests solely, for we have no corporate selfishness and wield no powers of corruption. We ought to have our own class-consciousness. '*Les Intellectuels!*' What prouder club-name could there be than this one, used ironically by the party of 'redblood,' the party of every stupid prejudice and passion, during the anti-Dreyfus craze, to satirize the men in France who still retained some critical sense and judgment! Critical sense, it has to be confessed, is not an exciting term, hardly a banner to carry in processions. Affections for old habit, currents of self-interest, and gales of passion are the forces that keep the human ship moving; and the pressure of the judicious pilot's hand upon the tiller is a relatively insignificant energy. But the affections, passions, and interests are shifting, successive and distraught; they blow in alternation while the pilot's hand is steadfast. He knows the compass, and, with all the leeways he is obliged to tack toward, he always makes some headway. A small force, if it never lets up, will accumulate effects more considerable than those of much greater forces if these work inconsistently. The ceaseless whisper of the more permanent ideals, the steady tug of truth and justice, give them but time, *must* warp the world in their direction."

By the end of his life he had begun to recognize that the newest ideals wanted to warp the world in directions different from his liberal hopes. He wrote to HJ in 1908, after reading Lowes Dickinson's *Justice and Liberty:* "Stroke upon stroke, from pens of genius, the competitive regime so idolized seventy-five years ago, seems to be getting wounded to death. What will follow will be something better, but I never saw so clearly the slow effect of [the] accumulation of the influence of successive individuals in changing prevalent ideals. Wells and Dickinson will undoubtedly make the biggest steps of change." The effect upon him of Wells' Fabianism is to be seen in an essay that appeared in the month of his death, particularly in the remark: "I devoutly believe in the reign of peace and in the gradual advent of some sort of a socialistic equilibrium."

That essay was "The Moral Equivalent of War." In one of his earliest

pieces of writing, *What Constitutes the State*, Henry Senior had declared that "War is becoming an increasing abomination to all humane
hearts." Now WJ gave expression to similar feelings. In combining his
anti-militarism with a plea for the necessity of giving effective social
scope to men's energies in peacetime, he wrote his most far-reaching
political essay:

*   *   *   *

THE MORAL EQUIVALENT OF WAR

THE war against war is going to be no holiday excursion or camping
party. The military feelings are too deeply grounded to abdicate their
place among our ideals until better substitutes are offered than the glory
and shame that come to nations as well as to individuals from the ups
and downs of politics and the vicissitudes of trade. There is something
highly paradoxical in the modern man's relation to war. Ask all our
millions, north and south, whether they would vote now (were such a
thing possible) to have our war for the Union expunged from history,
and the record of a peaceful transition to the present time substituted
for that of its marches and battles, and probably hardly a handful of
eccentrics would say yes. Those ancestors, those efforts, those memories
and legends, are the most ideal part of what we now own together, a
sacred spiritual possession worth more than all the blood poured out.
Yet ask those same people whether they would be willing in cold blood
to start another civil war now to gain another similar possession, and
not one man or woman would vote for the proposition. In modern eyes,
precious though wars may be, they must not be waged solely for the
sake of the ideal harvest. Only when forced upon one, only when an
enemy's injustice leaves us no alternative, is a war now thought permissible.

It was not thus in ancient times. The earlier men were hunting men,
and to hunt a neighboring tribe, kill the males, loot the village and
possess the females, was the most profitable, as well as the most exciting,
way of living. Thus were the more martial tribes selected, and in chiefs
and people a pure pugnacity and love of glory came to mingle with the
more fundamental appetite for plunder.

Modern war is so expensive that we feel trade to be a better avenue to
plunder; but modern man inherits all the innate pugnacity and all the
love of glory of his ancestors. Showing war's irrationality and horror is
of no effect upon him. The horrors make the fascination. War is the
strong life; it is life *in extremis;* war-taxes are the only ones men never
hesitate to pay, as the budgets of all nations show us.

History is a bath of blood. The Iliad is one long recital of how Dio-
medes and Ajax, Sarpedon and Hector *killed*. No detail of the wounds

they made is spared us, and the Greek mind fed upon the story. Greek history is a panorama of jingoism and imperialism—war for war's sake, all the citizens being warriors. It is horrible reading, because of the irrationality of it all—save for the purpose of making "history"—and the history is that of the utter ruin of a civilization in intellectual respects perhaps the highest the earth has ever seen.

Those wars were purely piratical. Pride, gold, women, slaves, excitement, were their only motives. In the Peloponnesian war for example, the Athenians ask the inhabitants of Melos (the island where the "Venus of Milo" was found), hitherto neutral, to own their lordship. The envoys meet, and hold a debate which Thucydides gives in full, and which, for sweet reasonableness of form, would have satisfied Matthew Arnold. "The powerful exact what they can," said the Athenians, "and the weak grant what they must." When the Meleans say that sooner than be slaves they will appeal to the gods, the Athenians reply: "Of the gods we believe and of men we know that, by a law of their nature, wherever they can rule they will. This law was not made by us, and we are not the first to have acted upon it; we did but inherit it, and we know that you and all mankind, if you were as strong as we are, would do as we do. So much for the gods; we have told you why we expect to stand as high in their good opinion as you." Well, the Meleans still refused, and their town was taken. "The Athenians," Thucydides quietly says, "thereupon put to death all who were of military age and made slaves of the women and children. They then colonized the island, sending thither five hundred settlers of their own."

Alexander's career was piracy pure and simple, nothing but an orgy of power and plunder, made romantic by the character of the hero. There was no rational principle in it, and the moment he died his generals and governors attacked one another. The cruelty of those times is incredible. When Rome finally conquered Greece, Paulus Æmilius was told by the Roman Senate to reward his soldiers for their toil by "giving" them the old kingdom of Epirus. They sacked seventy cities and carried off a hundred and fifty thousand inhabitants as slaves. How many they killed I know not; but in Etolia they killed all the senators, five hundred and fifty in number. Brutus was "the noblest Roman of them all," but to reanimate his soldiers on the eve of Philippi he similarly promises to give them the cities of Sparta and Thessalonica to ravage, if they win the fight.

Such was the gory nurse that trained societies to cohesiveness. We inherit the warlike type; and for most of the capacities of heroism that the human race is full of we have to thank this cruel history. Dead men tell no tales, and if there were any tribes of other type than this they have left no survivors. Our ancestors have bred pugnacity into our bone and marrow, and thousands of years of peace won't breed it out of us.

The popular imagination fairly fattens on the thought of wars. Let public opinion once reach a certain fighting pitch, and no ruler can withstand it. In the Boer war both governments began with bluff but couldn't stay there, the military tension was too much for them. In 1898 our people had read the word "war" in letters three inches high for three months in every newspaper. The pliant politician McKinley was swept away by their eagerness, and our squalid war with Spain became a necessity.

At the present day, civilized opinion is a curious mental mixture. The military instincts and ideals are as strong as ever, but are confronted by reflective criticisms which sorely curb their ancient freedom. Innumerable writers are showing up the bestial side of military service. Pure loot and mastery seem no longer morally avowable motives, and pretexts must be found for attributing them solely to the enemy. England and we, our army and navy authorities repeat without ceasing, arm solely for "peace," Germany and Japan it is who are bent on loot and glory. "Peace" in military mouths today is a synonym for "war expected." The word has become a pure provocative, and no government wishing peace sincerely should allow it ever to be printed in a newspaper. Every up-to-date dictionary should say that "peace" and "war" mean the same thing, now *in posse*, now *in actu*. It may even reasonably be said that the intensely sharp competitive *preparation* for war by the nations *is the real war*, permanent, unceasing; and that the battles are only a sort of public verification of the mastery gained during the "peace"-interval.

It is plain that on this subject civilized man has developed a sort of double personality. If we take European nations, no legitimate interest of any one of them would seem to justify the tremendous destructions which a war to compass it would necessarily entail. It would seem as though common sense and reason ought to find a way to reach agreement in every conflict of honest interests. I myself think it our bounden duty to believe in such international rationality as possible. But, as things stand, I see how desperately hard it is to bring the peace-party and the war-party together, and I believe that the difficulty is due to to certain deficiencies in the program of pacificism which set the militarist imagination strongly, and to a certain extent justifiably, against it. In the whole discussion both sides are on imaginative and sentimental ground. It is but one utopia against another, and everything one says must be abstract and hypothetical. Subject to this criticism and caution, I will try to characterize in abstract strokes the opposite imaginative forces, and point out what to my own very fallible mind seems the best utopian hypothesis, the most promising line of conciliation.

In my remarks, pacificist though I am, I will refuse to speak of the bestial side of the war-*régime* (already done justice to by many writers) and consider only the higher aspects of militaristic sentiment. Patriotism no one thinks discreditable; nor does any one deny that war is the romance of history. But inordinate ambitions are the soul of every patriotism, and the possibility of violent death the soul of all romance. The militarily patriotic and romantic-minded everywhere, and especially the professional military class, refuse to admit for a moment that war may be a transitory phenomenon in social evolution. The notion of a sheep's paradise like that revolts, they say, our higher imagination. Where then would be the steeps of life? If war had ever stopped, we should have to re-invent it, on this view, to redeem life from flat degeneration.

Reflective apologists for war at the present day all take it religiously. It is a sort of sacrament. Its profits are to the vanquished as well as to the victor; and quite apart from any question of profit, it is an absolute good, we are told, for it is human nature at its highest dynamic. Its "horrors" are a cheap price to pay for rescue from the only alternative supposed, of a world of clerks and teachers, of co-education and zoophily, of "consumer's leagues" and "associated charities," of industrialism unlimited and femininism unabashed. No scorn, no hardness, no valor any more! Fie upon such a cattleyard of a planet!

So far as the central essence of this feeling goes, no healthy minded person, it seems to me, can help to some degree partaking of it. Militarism is the great preserver of our ideals of hardihood, and human life with no use for hardihood would be contemptible. Without risks or prizes for the darer, history would be insipid indeed; and there is a type of military character which every one feels that the race should never cease to breed, for every one is sensitive to its superiority. The duty is incumbent on mankind, of keeping military characters in stock—of keeping them, if not for use, then as ends in themselves and as pure pieces of perfection,—so that Roosevelt's weaklings and mollycoddles may not end by making everything else disappear from the face of nature.

This natural sort of feeling forms, I think, the innermost soul of army-writings. Without any exception known to me, militarist authors take a highly mystical view of their subject, and regard war as a biological or sociological necessity, uncontrolled by ordinary psychological checks and motives. When the time of development is ripe the war must come, reason or no reason, for the justifications pleaded are invariably fictitious. War is, in short, a permanent human *obligation*. General Homer Lea, in his recent book "The Valor of Ignorance," plants himself squarely on this ground. Readiness for war is for him the essence of nationality, and ability in it the supreme measure of the health of nations.

Nations, General Lea says, are never stationary—they must necessarily expand or shrink, according to their vitality or decrepitude. Japan now is culminating; and by the fatal law in question it is impossible that her statesmen should not long since have entered, with extraordinary foresight, upon a vast policy of conquest—the game in which the first moves were her wars with China and Russia and her treaty with England, and of which the final objective is the capture of the Philippines, the Hawaiian Islands, Alaska, and the whole of our Coast west of the Sierra Passes. This will give Japan what her ineluctable vocation as a state absolute forces her to claim, the possession of the entire Pacific Ocean; and to oppose these deep designs we Americans have, according to our author, nothing but our conceit, our ignorance, our commercialism, our corruption, and our feminism. General Lea makes a minute technical comparison of the military strength which we at present could oppose to the strength of Japan, and concludes that the islands, Alaska, Oregon, and Southern California, would fall almost without resistance, that San Francisco must surrender in a fortnight to a Japanese investment, that in three or four months the war would be over, and our republic, unable to regain what it had heedlessly neglected to protect sufficiently, would then "disintegrate," until perhaps some Cæsar should arise to weld us again into a nation.

A dismal forecast indeed! Yet not unplausible, if the mentality of Japan's statesmen be of the Cæsarian type of which history shows so many examples, and which is all that General Lea seems able to imagine. But there is no reason to think that women can no longer be the mothers of Napoleonic or Alexandrian characters; and if these come in Japan and find their opportunity, just such surprises as "The Valor of Ignorance" paints may lurk in ambush for us. Ignorant as we still are of the innermost recesses of Japanese mentality, we may be foolhardy to disregard such possibilities.

Other militarists are more complex and more moral in their considerations. The "Philosophie des Krieges," by S. R. Steinmetz is a good example. War, according to this author, is an ordeal instituted by God, who weighs the nations in its balance. It is the essential form of the State, and the only function in which peoples can employ all their powers at once and convergently. No victory is possible save as the resultant of a totality of virtues, no defeat for which some vice or weakness is not responsible. Fidelity, cohesiveness, tenacity, heroism, conscience, education, inventiveness, economy, wealth, physical health and vigor— there isn't a moral or intellectual point of superiority that doesn't tell, when God holds his assizes and hurls the peoples upon one another. *Die Weltgeschichte ist das Weltgericht;* and Dr. Steinmetz does not believe that in the long run chance and luck play any part in apportioning the issues.

The virtues that prevail, it must be noted, are virtues anyhow, superiorities that count in peaceful as well as in military competition; but the strain on them, being infinitely intenser in the latter case, makes war infinitely more searching as a trial. No ordeal is comparable to its winnowings. Its dread hammer is the welder of men into cohesive states, and nowhere but in such states can human nature adequately develop its capacity. The only alternative is "degeneration."

Dr. Steinmetz is a conscientious thinker, and his book, short as it is, takes much into account. Its upshot can, it seems to me, be summed up in Simon Patten's word, that mankind was nursed in pain and fear, and that the transition to a "pleasure-economy" may be fatal to a being wielding no powers of defence against its disintegrative influences. If we speak of the *fear of emancipation from the fear-régime*, we put the whole situation into a single phrase; fear regarding ourselves now taking the place of the ancient fear of the enemy.

Turn the fear over as I will in my mind, it all seems to lead back to two unwillingnesses of the imagination, one æsthetic, and the other moral; unwillingness, first to envisage a future in which army-life, with its many elements of charm, shall be forever impossible, and in which the destinies of peoples shall nevermore be decided quickly, thrillingly, and tragically, by force, but only gradually and insipidly by "evolution"; and, secondly, unwillingness to see the supreme theatre of human strenuousness closed, and the splendid military aptitudes of men doomed to keep always in a state of latency and never show themselves in action. These insistent unwillingnesses, no less than other æsthetic and ethical insistencies, have, it seems to me, to be listened to and respected. One cannot meet them effectively by mere counter-insistency on war's expensiveness and horror. The horror makes the thrill; and when the question is of getting the extremest and supremest out of human nature, talk of expense sounds ignominious. The weakness of so much merely negative criticism is evident—pacificism makes no converts from the military party. The military party denies neither the bestiality nor the horror, nor the expense; it only says that these things tell but half the story. It only says that war is *worth* them; that, taking human nature as a whole, its wars are its best protection against its weaker and more cowardly self, and that mankind cannot *afford* to adopt a peace-economy.

Pacificists ought to enter more deeply into the æsthetical and ethical point of view of their opponents. Do that first in any controversy, says J. J. Chapman, *then move the point*, and your opponent will follow. So long as anti-militarists propose no substitute for war's disciplinary function, no *moral equivalent* of war, analogous, as one might say, to the mechanical equivalent of heat, so long they fail to realize the full inwardness of the situation. And as a rule they do fail. The duties, penalties, and sanctions pictured in the utopias they paint are all too weak and tame to touch the military-minded. Tolstoï's pacificism is the only exception to this rule, for it is profoundly pessimistic as regards all this world's values, and makes the fear of the Lord furnish the moral spur provided elsewhere by the fear of the enemy. But our socialistic peace-advocates all believe absolutely in this world's values; and instead of the fear of the Lord and the fear of the enemy, the only fear they reckon with is the fear of poverty if one be lazy. This weakness pervades all the socialistic literature with which I am acquainted. Even in Lowes Dickinson's exquisite dialogue,[1] high wages and short hours are the only forces invoked for overcoming man's distaste for repulsive kinds of labor. Meanwhile men at large still live as they always have lived, under a pain-and-fear economy—for those of us who live in an ease-economy are but an island in the stormy ocean—and the whole atmosphere of present-day utopian literature tastes mawkish and dishwatery to people who still keep a sense for life's more bitter flavors. It suggests, in truth, ubiquitous inferiority.

Inferiority is always with us, and merciless scorn of it is the keynote of the military temper. "Dogs, would you live forever?" shouted Frederick the Great. "Yes," say our utopians, "let us live forever, and raise our level gradually." The best thing about our "inferiors" today is that they are as tough as nails, and physically and morally almost as insensitive. Utopianism would see them soft and squeamish, while militarism would keep their callousness, but transfigure it into a meritorious characteristic, needed by "the service," and redeemed by that from the suspicion of inferiority. All the qualities of a man acquire dignity when he knows that the service of the collectivity that owns him needs them. If proud of the collectivity, his own pride rises in proportion. No collectivity is like an army for nourishing such pride; but it has to be confessed that the only sentiment which the image of pacific cosmopolitan industrialism is capable of arousing in countless worthy breasts is shame at the idea of belonging to *such* a collectivity. It is obvious that the United States of America as they exist today impress a mind like General Lea's as so much human blubber. Where is the sharpness and precipitousness, the contempt for life, whether one's own, or another's? Where is the savage "yes" and "no," the unconditional duty? Where is the conscription? Where is the blood-tax? Where is anything that one feels honored by belonging to?

Having said thus much in preparation, I will now confess my own utopia. I devoutly believe in the reign of peace and in the gradual advent of some sort of a socialistic equilibrium. The fatalistic view of the war-function is to me nonsense, for I know that war-making is due to definite motives and subject to prudential checks and reasonable criti-

---

[1] "Justice and Liberty," N. Y., 1909.

cisms, just like any other form of enterprise. And when whole nations are the armies, and the science of destruction vies in intellectual refinement with the sciences of production, I see that war becomes absurd and impossible from its own monstrosity. Extravagant ambitions will have to be replaced by reasonable claims, and nations must make common cause against them. I see no reason why all this should not apply to yellow as well as to white countries, and I look forward to a future when acts of war shall be formally outlawed as between civilized peoples.

All these beliefs of mine put me squarely into the anti-militarist party. But I do not believe that peace either ought to be or will be permanent on this globe, unless the states pacifically organized preserve some of the old elements of army-discipline. A permanently successful peace-economy cannot be a simple pleasure-economy. In the more or less socialistic future towards which mankind seems drifting we must still subject ourselves collectively to those severities which answer to our real position upon this only partly hospitable globe. We must make new energies and hardihoods continue the manliness to which the military mind so faithfully clings. Martial virtues must be the enduring cement; intrepidity, contempt of softness, surrender of private interest, obedience to command, must still remain the rock upon which states are built—unless, indeed, we wish for dangerous reactions against commonwealths fit only for contempt, and liable to invite attack whenever a centre of crystallization for military-minded enterprise gets formed anywhere in their neighborhood.

The war-party is assuredly right in affirming and reaffirming that the martial virtues, although originally gained by the race through war, are absolute and permanent human goods. Patriotic pride and ambition in their military form are, after all, only specifications of a more general competitive passion. They are its first form, but that is no reason for supposing them to be its last form. Men now are proud of belonging to a conquering nation, and without a murmur they lay down their persons and their wealth, if by so doing they may fend off subjection. But who can be sure that *other aspects of one's country* may not, with time and education and suggestion enough, come to be regarded with similarly effective feelings of pride and shame? Why should men not some day feel that it is worth a blood-tax to belong to a collectivity superior in *any* ideal respect? Why should they not blush with indignant shame if the community that owns them is vile in any way whatsoever? Individuals, daily more numerous, now feel this civic passion. It is only a question of blowing on the spark till the whole population gets incandescent, and on the ruins of the old morals of military honor, a stable system of morals of civic honor builds itself up. What the whole community comes to believe in grasps the individual as in a vise. The war-function has grasped us so far; but constructive interests may some day seem no less imperative, and impose on the individual a hardly lighter burden.

Let me illustrate my idea more concretely. There is nothing to make one indignant in the mere fact that life is hard, that men should toil and suffer pain. The planetary conditions once for all are such, and we can stand it. But that so many men, by mere accidents of birth and opportunity, should have a life of *nothing else* but toil and pain and hardness and inferiority imposed upon them, should have *no* vacation, while others natively no more deserving never get any taste of this campaigning life at all,—*this* is capable of arousing indignation in reflective minds. It may end by seeming shameful to all of us that some of us have nothing but campaigning, and others nothing but unmanly ease. If now—and this is my idea—there were, instead of military conscription a conscription of the whole youthful population to form for a certain number of years a part of the army enlisted against *Nature*, the injustice would tend to be evened out, and numerous other goods to the commonwealth would follow. The military ideals of hardihood and discipline would be wrought into the growing fibre of the people; no one would remain blind as the luxurious classes now are blind, to man's relations to the globe he lives on, and to the permanently sour and hard foundations of his higher life. To coal and iron mines, to freight trains, to fishing fleets in December, to dishwashing, clothes-washing, and window-washing, to road-building and tunnel-making, to foundries and stoke-holes, and to the frames of skyscrapers, would our gilded youths be drafted off, according to their choice, to get the childishness knocked out of them, and to come back into society with healthier sympathies and soberer ideas. They would have paid their blood-tax, done their own part in the immemorial human warfare against nature; they would tread the earth more proudly, the women would value them more highly, they would be better fathers and teachers of the following generation.

Such a conscription, with the state of public opinion that would have required it, and the many moral fruits it would bear, would preserve in the midst of a pacific civilization the manly virtues which the military party is so afraid of seeing disappear in peace. We should get toughness without callousness, authority with as little criminal cruelty as possible, and painful work done cheerily because the duty is temporary, and threatens not, as now, to degrade the whole remainder of one's life. I spoke of the "moral equivalent" of war. So far, war has been the only force that can discipline a whole community, and until an equivalent discipline is organized, I believe that war must have its way. But I have no serious doubt that the ordinary prides and shames of social man, once developed to a certain intensity, are capable of organizing such a moral equivalent as I have sketched, or some other just as effective for preserving manliness of type. It is but a question of time, of skilful propagandism, and of opinion-making men seizing historic opportunities.

The martial type of character can be bred without war. Strenuous honor and disinterestedness abound elsewhere. Priests and medical men are in a fashion educated to it, and we should all feel some degree of it imperative if we were conscious of our work as an obligatory service to the state. We should be *owned*, as soldiers are by the army, and our pride would rise accordingly. We could be poor, then, without humiliation, as army officers now are. The only thing needed henceforward is to inflame the civic temper as past history has inflamed the military temper. H. G. Wells, as usual, sees the centre of the situation. "In many ways," he says, "military organization is the most peaceful of activities. When the contemporary man steps from the street, of clamorous insincere advertisement, push, adulteration, underselling and intermittent employment into the barrack-yard, he steps on to a higher social plane, into an atmosphere of service and coöperation and of infinitely more honorable emulations. Here at least men are not flung out of employment to degenerate because there is no immediate work for them to do. They are fed and drilled and trained for better services. Here at least a man is supposed to win promotion by self-forgetfulness and not by self-seeking. And beside the feeble and irregular endowment of research by commercialism, its little short-sighted snatches at profit by innovation and scientific economy, see how remarkable is the steady and rapid development of method and appliances in naval and military affairs! Nothing is more striking than to compare the progress of civil conveniences which has been left almost entirely to the trader, to the progress in military apparatus during the last few decades. The house-appliances of today, for example, are little better than they were fifty years ago. A house of today is still almost as ill-ventilated, badly heated by wasteful fires, clumsily arranged and furnished as the house of 1858. Houses a couple of hundred years old are still satisfactory places of residence, so little have our standards risen. But the rifle or battleship of fifty years ago was beyond all comparison inferior to those we possess; in power, in speed, in convenience alike. No one has a use now for such superannuated things." [1]

Wells adds [2] that he thinks that the conceptions of order and discipline, the tradition of service and devotion, of physical fitness, unstinted exertion, and universal responsibility, which universal military duty is now teaching European nations, will remain a permanent acquisition, when the last ammunition has been used in the fireworks that celebrate the final peace. I believe as he does. It would be simply pre-

---

[1] "First and Last Things," 1908, p. 215.   [2] Ibid., p. 226.

posterous if the only force that could work ideals of honor and standards of efficiency into English or American natures should be the fear
of being killed by the Germans or Japanese. Great indeed is Fear, but
it is not, as our military enthusiasts believe and try to make us believe,
the only stimulus known for awakening the higher ranges of men's spiritual energy. The amount of alteration in public opinion which my
utopia postulates is vastly less than the difference between the mentality of those black warriors who pursued Stanley's party on the
Congo with their cannibal war-cry of "Meat! Meat!" and that of the
"general staff" of any civilized nation. History has seen the latter interval bridged over: the former one can be bridged over much more
easily.

* * *

HJ was often at his flimsiest on the subject of politics. In contrast to
the equalitarianism of both his father and his brother, he grew to take
it for granted that democracy must inevitably level down; and on his
late return to America he worried about the new aliens in a way that
brought him dangerously near to a doctrine of Anglo-Saxon racial
superiority. He was consistent within his own terms in that he carried
his primary standard, his æsthetic perception of fitness, into all his
judgments. His typical process may be observed in his reaction to Edmund Gosse's essay on Björnson:

"Many thanks for the study of the roaring Norseman. . . . Björnson
has always been, I frankly confess, an untended prejudice—a hostile one
—of mine. . . . I don't think you justify him, *rank* him enough—
hardly quite enough for the attention you give him. At any rate he
sounds in your picture—to say nothing of looking, in his own!—like
the sort of literary fountain from which I am ever least eager to drink:
the big, splashing, blundering genius of the hit-or-miss, the *à peu près*,
family—without perfection, or the effort toward it, without the exquisite, the love of selection: a big superabundant and promiscuous
democrat."

In his later years he frequently declared that public events had become for him "a spectacle merely—a drama of great interest, but as to
which judgment and prophecy are withered in me, or at all events
absolutely checked." But like the trapped spectators in his fiction, he
continued to use his eyes with immense alertness.[1] In the face of his
seeming indifference to formal politics, it may seem odd to find him
asking WJ to send him a good photograph of President Hayes, and,

[1] The unforgettable impression that,
towards the end of HJ's life, this alertness left on younger men, was recorded
in Pound's seventh *Canto*:
    And the great domed head, *con gli
      occhi onesti e tardi*

Moves before me, phantom with
    weighted motion,
Grave incessu, drinking the tone of
    things,
And the old voice lifts itself
    weaving an endless sentence.

later, one of Cleveland. But he always wanted to scrutinize appearances for himself. And it is remarkable how much he could often see in what passed before him. By the mid-1880's he had watched the English upper class long enough to be able to liken them to the corrupt Roman world upon which the barbarians descended.[1] Out of such perceptions he wrote *The Princess Casamassima,* but no more than his sensitive hero, Hyacinth Robinson, could he ever take an effective stand against such corruption. To his distant view, revolution was something wholly destructive, a vindictive force from the impoverished underworld that might be goaded by its suffering to annihilate the treasures of an older civilization. He seems never to have speculated on the creative potentialities in social movements. His father had dwelt always on the promise of a new society that was about to come to birth. But HJ's thought was never dynamic. He liked to quote Tennyson's line: "The tender grace of a day that is dead," and though he did not look far back into time, he was the recorder of a society that he knew to be waning.

He did respond to WJ's late increase of interest in political topics. On hearing the results of the 1896 election, he wrote: "I don't feel that McKinley is the *end* of anything—least of all of big provincial iniquities and abuses and bloody billionaires. However he's more decent than the alternative." HJ was more consistent than WJ on the subject of Roosevelt, whom he pronounced, on his succession to the Presidency, "a dangerous and ominous Jingo," and, a dozen years later, "the mere monstrous embodiment of unprecedented resounding Noise."

Just before the outbreak of the Spanish-American War he declared to WJ: "I confess that the blaze about to come leaves me woefully cold, thrilling with no glorious thrill or holy blood-thirst whatever. I see nothing but the madness, the passion, the hideous clumsiness of rage, of mechanical reverberation; and I echo with all my heart your denouncement of the foul criminality of the screeching newspapers. They have long since become, for me, the danger that overtops all others." On the increasing menace of a vulgarized press the brothers continued to see eye to eye. A few years later WJ added: "The sensational press is the organ and promulgator of [a] state of mind which means . . . a new 'dark' ages that may last more centuries than the first one. Then illiteracy was brutal and dumb, and power was rapacious without disguise. Now illiteracy has an enormous literary organization, and power is sophistical; and the result is necessarily a new phenomenon in history—involving every kind of diseased sensationalism and insincerity in the collective mind."

But on the question of imperialism and on the Dreyfus case HJ took refuge once again in the spectator's role:

---

[1] P. 297 above.

"To live in England is, inevitably, to feel the 'imperial' question in a different way and take it at a different angle from what one might, with the same mind even, do in America. Expansion has so made the English what they are—for good or for ill, but on the whole for good—that one doesn't quite feel one's way to say for one's country 'No—I'll have *none* of it!' It has educated the English. Will it only demoralize *us*? I suppose the answer to that is that we can get at home a bigger education than they—in short as big a one as we require. Thank God, however, I've no *opinions*—not even on the Dreyfus case. I'm more and more only aware of things as a more or less mad panorama, phantasmagoria and dime museum."

Only after he had read WJ's communications to the *Transcript* did he come near to having a positive opinion, and then it was only an echo of WJ's reaction against "bigness":

"Your last letter on Roosevelt and the Philippines . . . commands all my admiration and sympathy. I agree with you no end—we have ceased to be, among the big nations, the one great thing that made up for our so many crudities, and made us above all superior and unique— the only one with clean hands and no record of across-the-sea murder and theft. *Terminato—terminato!* One would like to be a Swiss or a Montenegrin now. I applaud with all my heart the courage and 'scathing'-ness with which you drive it home."

Several years before, Alice James, contemplating the world from her sanatorium, had come to a more incisive understanding of some of the forces in modern society than either of her brothers. She might take her lead from something one of them had said, but she then pursued her own reflections further. She often discussed English society with HJ. They agreed on many of the symptoms, but she pushed on to a diagnosis quite beyond his scope in its thoroughness:

"I find myself, as the months pass, more and more oppressed by the all-pervasive sense of pharisaism in the British constitution of things. You don't feel it at first, and you can't put your finger upon it in your friends; but as the days go by you unfold it with your *Standard* in the morning, and it rises dense from the *Pall Mall Gazette* in the evening; it creeps through the cracks in the window frames like the fog, and envelopes you through the day. I asked H. once how it struck him from his wider and varied field, not wanting my view to become cramped upon conclusions drawn from my centimetre of observation; he said that he didn't think it could be exaggerated. It's woven of a multiplicity of minute details and incidents which elude you in the telling, but which seem to exist in the texture of things, and leave a dent in the mind as they file past. A monarchy to which they bow down in its tinsel capacity only, denying to it a manly movement of any sort! A boneless church, broadening itself out, up to date; the hysterical legislation over a dog with a broken leg, whilst society is engaged in making bags of four thousand pheasants, or gloating over foxes torn to pieces by a pack of hounds; the docility with which the classes enslave themselves to respectability or non-respectability, as the 'good-form' of the present may be; the 'sense of their betters' in the masses; the passivity with which the workingman allows himself to be patted and legislated out of all independence; then the profound irreconcilable in the bone and sinew conviction that outlying regions are their preserves, for they alone of the human races massacre savages out of pure virtue. It would ill become Americans to reflect upon the treatment of aboriginal races; but I never heard it suggested that our hideous dealing with the Indians was brotherly love masquerading under the disguise of pure 'cussedness.' "

On her most heartfelt subject, the question of Ireland, she was glad to find that WJ, having gone to pay his compliments there to the family of his Cambridge maid, had come away with the right general views:

"William was most amusing about Ireland. He seems sound enough on Home Rule; but how could a child of father's be anything else? He went to see the family of a little maid-servant they have, and such a welcome as he had! The refrain 'The Lord be praised that Kerry should have seen this day!' was repeated every five minutes during the two hours that he was with them. He says that they are an absolutely foreign people, much more excessive than they are with us, just like the stage Irishman. He was very funny about evictions, and says the horror of them entirely vanishes when you see the nature of the cabins,—existence without being so much preferable to existence within. He says that it is the most extraordinary thing to see coming out from the midst of all this filth, misery and squalor, this jovial, sociable, witty, intelligent race, supported and living entirely upon an idea. Oh, the tragedy of it!—when you think of the dauntless creatures flinging themselves and their ideal, for seven centuries, against the dead wall of British brutality, as incapable of an ideal inspiration or an imaginative movement as the beasts of the field."

WJ had probably not engaged in anything like that final reflection; or at least it would have been more in character for him to have celebrated the heroic rather than the tragic aspects, the value of the strife in itself. As AJ continued to meditate, she sounded far more like their father:

"The behaviour of the Unionist and Tory is simply the *bête* carried to its supreme expression. It is truly a great misfortune for a people to be so destitute of inspiration, and so completely without honour, as to be left absolutely naked to itself. If you could read, too, the chorus going up to heaven on all sides over the love of manliness and fairness

in the Briton's bosom!—those qualities of which they are always assuring the rest of the world they hold the monopoly. The Englishman,
however, should not be held accountable for being mentally so abject
before the Irishman; he is helpless, for there is absolutely nothing in his
organization wherewith he can conceive of him, and his self-respect
naturally has no other refuge save in loathing and despising him. He has
no wings to his mind to bear him whither his leaden feet are inapt for
carrying him; so that it is only now, at the end of seven centuries, that
he is beginning faintly to divine that in Ireland, above all other lands,
there are impalpable spiritualities which rise triumphant and imperishable before brutalities."

But the subject on which she most outdistanced her brothers was the
economic make-up of society, and the role of "the disinherited":

"The *Standard* this morning devotes the first paragraph of its summary of news to the thrilling fact that the infant daughter of the Duke
of Portland was christened in Windsor Chapel in presence of the
Queen; toward the end of the column comes the mention of the 'impressive' gathering in Hyde Park of the workingmen on the eight-
hours question—the first shall be last, and the last shall be first! How I
wish I could have seen a few of the faces of these masters of the world
in whose hands our material future lies, who can say how immediately?
Should the governments of Europe show the cowering, abject attitude
which they took on the first of May, what an impetus it will give;
it will almost seem as if one might live to see the remodelling. I shall
always be a bloated capitalist, I suppose,—an ignominy which, considering all things, I may as well submit to gracefully, for I shouldn't
bring much *body* to the proletariat; but I can't help having an illogical
feminine satisfaction that all my seven per cents and six per cents with
which I left home have melted into fours; I don't feel as if four per
cent is quite so base!

"Could anything exhibit more beautifully the solidarity of the race
than that by combining to walk through the streets on the same day,
these starvelings should make emperors, kings, presidents, and millionaires tremble the world over? Those who have every opportunity for
acquiring wisdom, and of inheriting noble, human, and generous instincts, have found no more inspired means of allaying their mutual
rapacities than shooting down vast hordes of innocent men, as helpless
as sheep; whilst these creatures, the disinherited, with savage instincts
all unsubdued, have divined that brotherly help is the path to victory.
What one of us, with his sentimental, emotional sympathy, ever stood
by his fellow starving, and watching his dwindling wife and children
for weeks? And yet at every strike thousands of the unfed, the un-
clothed, and the unread stand or fall together and make no boast."

In comparison with this comprehension of the meaning of a May

Day parade, HJ's notion of the revolutionary "underworld" is romantic melodrama; and WJ's moralizing over the mutual benefit that might result to both parties from the struggle, while full of good will, is academic. It was such passages in AJ's journal that, to do him justice, HJ must have had in mind when he wrote to WJ that her nature had been potentially that of the leader of a people's movement.[1]

HJ's own most matured views about society were expressed in *The American Scene*. We have noted WJ's brilliant description of the effect that book made upon him, as though it was composed "wholly out of impalpable materials, air, and the prismatic interferences of light, ingeniously focused by mirrors upon empty space." It is unquestionably one of the curiosities of our literature, far more difficult to read than its author's latest fiction, since HJ's stories generally build around a few central images, effectively heightened by repetition; whereas in *The American Scene* it is as though he were a gigantic camera-eye moving restlessly over the whole surface of the continent from New Hampshire to Florida. He deliberately restricted his narrative to reflections upon what he had seen for himself, and as a result several points are out of focus, since they are not weighted by their social background. For instance, he was inordinately impressed by the new development of the Country Club. In contrast with European exclusiveness, it struck him that such an institution was "one of the great garden-lamps in which the flame of Democracy burns whitest and steadiest." This observation wholly misses the social ladder of which the Country Club is the top, as any social realist like Dreiser could have told him.

But the most salient fact about *The American Scene* was that, despite WJ's ingenious metaphor, it was not made out of air. It was the product of one of the most trained pairs of eyes in our history, and when they were concentrated on what HJ could understand, they yielded some very solid criticism. He was unerring when he looked at the students passing in the Harvard Yard and reflected on "the business-face" and its implications regarding the relation between the sexes in forming our culture:

"This vision, for the moment, of a great dim, clustered but restlessly expansive Harvard, hushed to vacation stillness as to a deep ambitious dream, was, for the impressible story-seeker, practically the germ of the most engaging of the generalized images of reassurance, the furniture, so to speak, of the *other* scale, that the extension of his view was to cause him to cultivate. Reassurance is required, before the spectacle of American manners at large, whenever one most acutely perceives how little honor they tend to heap on the art of discrimination, and it is at such hours that, turning in his frequent stupefaction, the restless

---

[1] P. 285 above.

analyst reaches out for support to the nearest faint ghost of a constituted Faculty. It takes no exceptional exposure to the promiscuous life
to show almost any institution pretending to university form as stamped
here with the character and function of the life-saving monasteries of
the dark ages. They glow, the humblest of them, to the imagination—
the imagination that fixes the surrounding scene as a huge Rappacini-
garden, rank with each variety of the poison-plant of the money-
passion—they glow with all the vividness of the defined alternative,
the possible antidote, and seem to call on us to blow upon the flame
till it is made inextinguishable. So little time had it taken, at any rate,
to suggest to me that a new and higher price, in American conditions,
is attaching to the cloister, literally—the place inaccessible (to put it
most pertinently) to the shout of the newspaper, the place to perambu-
late, the place to think, apart from the crowd. Doubtless indeed I was
not all aware of it at the time, but the image I touch upon in connection with those first moments was to remain with me, the figure of
the rich old Harvard organism brooding, exactly, through the long
vacation, brooding through the summer night, on discriminations, on
insistences, on sublime and exquisite heresies to come.

". . . There could be no unrest of analysis worthy of the name that
failed to perceive how, after term had opened, the type of the young
men coming and going in the Yard gained, for vivacity of appeal,
through this more marked constitution of a *milieu* for it. Here, verily,
questions could swarm; for there was scarce an impression of the local
life at large that didn't play into them. One thing I had not yet done—
I had not been, under the best guidance, out to Ellis Island, the seat of
the Commissioner of Immigration, in the bay of New York, to catch in
the fact, as I was to catch later on, a couple of hours of the ceaseless
process of the recruiting of our race, of the plenishing of our huge national *pot au feu*, of the introduction of fresh—of perpetually fresh so
far it isn't perpetually stale—foreign matter into our heterogeneous system. But even without that a haunting wonder as to what might be becoming to us all, 'typically,' ethnically, and thereby physiognomically,
linguistically, *personally*, was always in order. The young men in their
degree, as they flocked candidly up to college, struck me as having
much to say about it, and there was always the sense of light on the
subject, for comparison and reference, that a long experience of other
types and other manners could supply. Swarming ingenuous youths,
whom did they look like the sons of?—that inquiry, as to any group,
any couple, any case, represented a game that it was positively thrilling
to play out. There was plenty to make it so, for there was, to begin
with, both the forecast of the thing that might easily settle the issue
and the forecast of the thing that might easily complicate it.

"No impression so promptly assaults the arriving visitor of the

United States as that of the overwhelming preponderance, wherever he turns and twists, of the unmitigated 'business-man' face, ranging through its various possibilities, its extraordinary actualities, of intensity. And I speak here of facial cast and expression alone, leaving out of account the questions of voice, tone, utterance and attitude, the chorus of which would vastly swell the testimony and in which I seem to discern, for these remarks at large, a treasure of illustration to come. Nothing, meanwhile, is more concomitantly striking than the fact that the women, over the land—allowing for every element of exception— appear to be of a markedly finer texture than the men, and that one of the liveliest signs of this difference is precisely in their less narrowly specialized, their less commercialized, distinctly more generalized, phys- iognomic character. The superiority thus noted, and which is quite another matter from the universal fact of the mere usual female fem- ininity, is far from constituting absolute distinction, but it constitutes relative, and it is a circumstance at which interested observation snatches, from the first, with an immense sense of its *portée*. There are, with all the qualifications it is yet open to, fifty reflections to be made upon the truth it seems to represent, the appearance of a queer deep split or chasm between the two stages of personal polish, the two levels of the conversible state, at which the sexes have arrived. It is at all events no exaggeration to say that the imagination at once embraces it as *the* feature of the social scene, recognizing it as a subject fruitful beyond the common, and wondering even if for pure drama, the drama of manners, anything anywhere else touches it. If it be a 'sub- ject,' verily—with the big vision of the intersexual relation as, at such an increasing rate, a prey to it—the right measure for it would seem to be offered in the art of the painter of life by the concrete example, the art of the dramatist or the novelist, rather than in that of the talker, the reporter at large. The only thing is that, from the moment the painter begins to look at American life brush in hand, he is in danger of seeing, in comparison, almost nothing else in it—nothing, that is, so characteristic as this apparent privation, for the man, of his right kind of woman, and this apparent privation, for the woman, of her right kind of man.

". . . It in any case remains vivid that American life may, as regards much of its manifestation, fall upon the earnest view as a society of women 'located' in a world of men, which is so different a matter from a collection of men of the world; the men supplying, as it were, all the canvas, and the women all the embroidery. Just this vividness it was that held up the torch, through the Cambridge autumn, to that question of the affiliation of the encountered Harvard undergraduate which I may not abandon. In what proportion of instances would it stick out that the canvas, rather than the embroidery, was what he had to show?

In what proportion would he wear the stamp of the unredeemed commercialism that should betray his paternity? In what proportion, in his appearance, would the different social 'value' imputable to his mother have succeeded in interposing?"

HJ gave far more of his space to New York than to Boston. From his first impression as he came up the harbor, he felt that the city, with its earliest skyscrapers, was too big for him to take in, too big, perhaps, like the continent stretching behind it, "for any human convenience," and with hardly "any deviation . . . into the liberal or charming." He sensed that someone with the crude power of a Zola would be needed even to suggest its vast "human aggregation." He had doubtless never heard the name of Dreiser, whose first novel, *Sister Carrie*, had been suppressed by its timid publisher only four years before. But HJ could recognize for himself that the key to the maze in front of him lay in understanding that it was the product of "an interested passion . . . restless beyond all passions," a passion whose sole command was: "Make so much money that you won't . . . mind anything."

He wanted to expose himself to whatever experience he could. He may have missed the worst poverty in the ghetto by his sense of how splendid some of its neighboring department stores were in contrast with the shops in similar quarters in Europe. But the crowded streets led him into an oblique realization of the merciless power of the trusts. When he used his ears as well as his eyes, he forecast also the increasing difference between the American speech of the future and the conservative English to which he clung:

"What struck me in the flaring streets (over and beyond the everywhere insistent, defiant, unhumorous, exotic face) was the blaze of the shops addressed to the New Jerusalem wants and the splendor with which these were taken for granted. . . . The wants, the gratifications, the aspirations of the 'poor,' as expressed in the shops (which were the shops of the 'poor'), denoted a new style of poverty; and this new style of poverty, from street to street, stuck out of the possible purchasers, one's jostling fellow-pedestrians, and made them, to every man and woman, individual throbs in the larger harmony. One can speak only of what one has seen, and there were grosser elements of the sordid and the squalid that I doubtless never saw. That, with a good deal of observation and of curiosity, I should have failed of this, the country over, affected me as by itself something of an indication. To miss that part of the spectacle, or to know it only by its having so unfamiliar a pitch, was an indication that made up for a great many others. It is when this one in particular is forced home to you—this immense, vivid *general* lift of poverty and general appreciation of the living unit's paying property in himself—that the picture seems most to clear and the way to jubilation most to open. For it meets you there,

HJ, by Alice Boughton, at the time he was gathering material for THE AMERICAN SCENE

at every turn, as the result most definitely attested. You are as constantly reminded, no doubt, that these rises in enjoyed value shrink and dwindle under the icy breath of Trusts and the weight of the new remorseless monopolies that operate as no madnesses of ancient personal power thrilling us on the historic page ever operated; the living unit's property in himself becoming more and more merely such a property as may consist with a relation to properties overwhelmingly greater and that allow the asking of no questions and the making, for coexistence with them, of no conditions. But that, in the fortunate phrase, is another story, and will be altogether, evidently, a new and different drama. There is such a thing, in the United States, it is hence to be inferred, as freedom to grow up to be blighted, and it may be the only freedom in store for the smaller fry of future generations. If it is accordingly of the smaller fry I speak, and of how large they massed on that evening of endless admonitions, this will be because I caught them thus in their comparative humility and at an early stage of their American growth. The life-thread has, I suppose, to be of a certain thickness for the great shears of Fate to feel for it. Put it, at the worst, that the Ogres were to devour them, they were but the more certainly to fatten into food for the Ogres.

"Their dream, at all events, as I noted it, was meanwhile sweet and undisguised—nowhere sweeter than in the half-dozen picked beer-houses and cafés in which our ingenuous *enquête*, that of my fellow-pilgrims and I, wound up. These establishments had each been selected for its playing off some facet of the jewel, and they wondrously testified, by their range and their individual color, to the spread of that lustre. It was a pious rosary of which I should like to tell each bead, but I must let the general sense of the adventure serve. Our successive stations were in no case of the 'seamy' order, an inquiry into seaminess having been unanimously pronounced futile, but each had its separate social connotation, and it was for the number and variety of these connotations, and their individual plentitude and prosperity, to set one thinking. Truly the Yiddish world was a vast world, with its own deeps and complexities, and what struck one above all was that it sat there at its cups (and in no instance vulgarly the worse for them) with a sublimity of good conscience that took away the breath, a protrusion of elbow never aggressive, but absolutely proof against jostling. It was the incurable man of letters under the skin of one of the party who gasped, I confess; for it was in the light of letters, that is in the light of our language as literature has hitherto known it, that one stared at this all-unconscious impudence of the agency of future ravage. The man of letters, in the United States, has his own difficulties to face and his own current to stem—for dealing with which his liveliest inspiration may be, I think, that they are still very much his own, even in an Amer-

icanized world, and that more than elsewhere they press him to intimate communion with his honor. For that honor, the honor that sits
astride of the consecrated English tradition, to his mind, quite as old
knighthood astride of its caparisoned charger, the dragon most rousing,
over the land, the proper spirit of St. George, is just this immensity of
the alien presence climbing higher and higher, climbing itself into the
very light of publicity.

"I scarce know why, but I saw it that evening as in some dim dawn
of that promise to its own consciousness, and perhaps this was precisely
what made it a little exasperating. Under the impression of the mere
mob the question doesn't come up, but in these haunts of comparative
civility we saw the mob sifted and strained, and the exasperation was
the sharper, no doubt, because what the process had left most visible
was just the various possibilities of the waiting spring of intelligence.
Such elements constituted the germ of a 'public,' and it was impossible
(possessed of a sensibility worth speaking of) to be exposed to them
without feeling how new a thing under the sun the resulting public
would be. That was where one's 'lettered' anguish came in—in the turn
of one's eye from face to face for some betrayal of a prehensile hook
for the linguistic tradition as one had known it. Each warm lighted and
supplied circle, each group of served tables and smoked pipes and fostered decencies and unprecedented accents, beneath the extravagant
lamps, took on thus, for the brooding critic, a likeness to that terrible
modernized and civilized room in the Tower of London, haunted by
the shade of Guy Fawkes, which had more than once formed part of
the scene of the critic's taking tea there. In this chamber of the present
urbanities the wretched man had been stretched on the rack, and the
critic's ear (how else should it have been a critic's?) could still always
catch, in pauses of talk, the faint groan of his ghost. Just so the East-
side cafés—and increasingly as their place in the scale was higher—
showed to my inner sense, beneath their bedizenment, as torture-rooms
of the living idiom; the piteous gasp of which at the portent of lacera-
tions to come could reach me in any drop of the surrounding Accent
of the Future. The accent of the very ultimate future, in the States,
may be destined to become the most beautiful on the globe and the
very music of humanity (here the 'ethnic' synthesis shrouds itself
thicker than ever); but whatever we shall know it for, certainly, we
shall not know it for English—in any sense for which there is an existing literary measure."

From there his camera-eye passed at once to the city's architecture.
Whatever building or monument it paused on was a cultural image
HJ could thoroughly apprehend. Seeking in the forms of art the index
to social coherence, he could read only social disorder in the jumble
of New York's styles. A sense of the need of some city planning, pos-

sessed in this country then by only a few pioneers, brought him hesitantly to perceive the limitations of uncontrolled individualism. He read once again his father's lesson of waste. Confronted with a work of art that he admired, with Saint-Gaudens' Sherman imposing its dignity upon the surrounding square, he made the kind of devious social criticism for which he was best fitted:

"The huge jagged city, it must be nevertheless said, has always at the worst, for propitiation, the resource of its easy reference to its almost incomparable river. New York may indeed be jagged, in her long leanness, where she lies looking at the sky in the manner of some colossal hair-comb turned upward and so deprived of half its teeth that the others, at their uneven intervals, count doubly as sharp spikes; but, unmistakably, you can bear with some of her aspects and her airs better when you have really taken in that reference—which I speak of as easy because she has in this latter time begun to make it with an appearance of some intention. She has come at last, far up on the West side, into possession of her birthright, into the roused consciousness that some possibility of a river-front may still remain to her; though, obviously, a justified pride in this property has yet to await the birth of a more responsible sense of style in her dealings with it, the dawn of some adequate plan or controlling idea. Splendid the elements of position, on the part of the new Riverside Drive (over the small suburbanizing name of which, as at the effect of a second-rate shop-worn article, we sigh as we pass); yet not less irresistible the pang of our seeing it settle itself on meagre, bourgeois, happy-go-lucky lines. The pity of this is sharp in proportion as the "chance" has been magnificent, and the soreness of perception of what merely might have been is as constant as the flippancy of the little vulgar "private houses" or the big vulgar "apartment hotels" that are having their own way, so unchallenged, with the whole question of composition and picture. The fatal "tall" pecuniary enterprise rises where it will, in the candid glee of new worlds to conquer; the intervals between take whatever foolish little form they like; the sky-line, eternal victim of the artless jumble, submits again to the type of the broken hair-comb turned up; the streets that abut from the East condescend at their corners to any crudity or poverty that may suit their convenience. And all this in presence of an occasion for noble congruity such as one scarce knows where to seek in the case of another great city.

"A sense of the waste of criticism, however, a sense that is almost in itself consoling, descends upon the fond critic after his vision has fixed the scene awhile in this light of its lost accessibility to some informed and benevolent despot, some power working in one great way and so that the interest of beauty should have been better saved. Is not criticism wasted, in other words, just by the reason of the constant remembrance, on New York soil, that one is almost impudently cheated by any part of the show that pretends to prolong its actuality or to rest on its present basis? Since every part, however blazingly new, fails to affect us as doing more than hold the ground for something else, some conceit of the bigger dividend, that is still to come, so we may bind up the æsthetic wound, I think, quite as promptly as we feel it open. The particular ugliness, or combination of uglinesses, is no more final than the particular felicity (since there are several even of these up and down the town to be noted), and whatever crudely-extemporized look the Riverside heights may wear to-day, the spectator of fifty years hence will find his sorrow, if not his joy, in a different extemporization. The whole thing is the vividest of lectures on the subject of individualism, and on the strange truth, no doubt, that this principle may in the field of art—at least if the art be architecture—often conjure away just that mystery of distinction which it sometimes so markedly promotes in the field of life. It is also quite as suggestive perhaps on the ever-interesting question, for the artist, of the entirely relative nature and value of 'treatment.' A manner so right in one relation may be so wrong in another, and a house-front so 'amusing' for its personal note, or its perversity, in a short perspective, may amid larger elements merely dishonor the harmony. And yet why *should* the charm ever fall out of the 'personal,' which is so often the very condition of the exquisite? Why should conformity and subordination, that acceptance of control and assent to collectivism in the name of which our age has seen such dreary things done, become on a given occasion the one *not* vulgar way of meeting a problem? . . .

"Were I not afraid of appearing to strike to excess the so-called pessimistic note, I should really make much of the interesting, appealing, touching vision of waste—I know not how else to name it—that flung its odd, melancholy mantle even over one's walks through the parts of the town supposedly noblest and fairest. For it proceeded, the vision, I think, from a source or two still deeper than the most obvious, the constant shocked sense of houses and rows, of recent expensive construction (that had cost thought as well as money, that had taken birth presumably as a *serious* demonstration, and that were thereby just beginning to live into history) marked for removal, for extinction, in their prime, and awaiting it with their handsome faces so fresh and yet so wan and so anxious. . . . I have had occasion to speak—and one can only speak with sympathy—of the really human, the communicative, side of that vivid show of a society trying to build itself, with every elaboration, into some coherent sense *of* itself, and literally putting forth interrogative feelers, as it goes, into the ambient air; literally reaching out (to the charmed beholder, say) for some measure and some test of its success. This effect of certain of the manifestations of wealth in New York is, so far as I know, unique; nowhere else does pecuniary power so beat its wings in the void, and so look round it for the charity of some hint as to the possible awkwardness or possible grace of its motion, some sign of whether it be flying, for good taste, too high or too low. In the other American cities, on the one hand, the flights are as yet less numerous—though already promising no small diversion; and amid the older congregations of men, in the proportion- ately rich cities of Europe, on the other hand, good taste is present, for reference and comparison, in a hundred embodied and consecrated forms. Which is why, to repeat, I found myself recognizing in the New York predicament a particular character and a particular pathos. The whole costly up-town demonstration was a record, in the last analysis, of individual loneliness; whence came, precisely, its insistent testimony to waste—waste of the still wider sort than the mere game of rebuild- ing. . . .

"It appeared at all events, on the late days of spring, just a response to the facility of things, and to much of their juvenile pleasantry, to find one's self 'liking,' without more ado, and very much even at the risk of one's life, the heterogeneous, miscellaneous apology for a Square marking the spot at which the main entrance, as I suppose it may be called, to the Park opens towards Fifth Avenue; opens towards the glittering monument to Sherman, towards the most death-dealing, per- haps, of all the climaxes of electric car cross-currents, towards the loosest of all the loose distributions of the overtopping 'apartment' and other hotel, towards the most jovial of all the sacrifices of precon- sidered composition, towards the finest of all the reckless revelations, in short, of the brave New York humor. The best thing in the picture, obviously, is Saint-Gaudens's great group, splendid in its golden ele- gance and doing more for the scene (by thus giving the beholder a point of such dignity for his orientation) than all its other elements together. Strange and seductive for any lover of the reasons of things this inordinate value, on the spot, of the dauntless refinement of the Sherman image; the comparative vulgarity of the environment drinking it up, on one side, like an insatiable sponge, and yet failing at the same time sensibly to impair its virtue. The refinement prevails and, as it were, succeeds; holds its own in the medley of accidents, where noth- ing else is refined unless it be the amplitude of the 'quiet' note in the front of the Metropolitan Club; amuses itself in short with being as extravagantly 'intellectual' as it likes. Why, therefore, given the sur- rounding medium, does it so triumphantly impose itself, and impose it- self not insidiously and gradually, but immediately and with force? Why does it not pay the penalty of expressing an idea and being founded on one?—such scant impunity seeming usually to be enjoyed among us, at this hour, by any artistic intention of the finer strain? But

I put these questions only to give them up—for what I feel beyond anything else is that Mr. Saint-Gaudens somehow takes care of himself.

"To what measureless extent he does this on occasion one was to learn, in due course, from his magnificent Lincoln at Chicago—the lesson there being simply that of a mystery exquisite, the absolute inscrutable; one of the happiest cases known to our time, known doubtless to any time, of the combination of intensity of effect with dissimulation, with deep disavowal, of process. After seeing the Lincoln one consents, for its author, to the drop of questions—that is the lame truth; a truth in the absence of which I should have risked another word or two, have addressed perhaps even a brief challenge to a certain ambiguity in the Sherman. Its idea, to which I have alluded, strikes me as equivocal, or more exactly as double; the image being, on the one side, and splendidly rendered, that of an overwhelming military advance, an irresistible march into an enemy's country—the strain forward, the very inflation of drapery with the rush, symbolizing the very breath of the Destroyer. But the idea is at the same time—which part of it is also admirably expressed—that the Destroyer is a messenger of peace, with the olive-branch too waved in the blast and with embodied grace, in the form of a beautiful American girl, attending his business. And I confess to a lapse of satisfaction in the presence of this interweaving—the result doubtless of a sharp suspicion of all attempts, however glittering and golden, to confound destroyers with benefactors. The military monument in the City Square responds evidently, wherever a pretext can be found for it, to a desire of men's hearts; but I would have it always as military as possible, and I would have the Destroyer, in intention at least, not docked of one of his bristles. I would have him deadly and terrible, and, if he be wanted beautiful, beautiful only as a war-god and crested not with peace, but with snakes. Peace is a long way round from him, and blood and ashes in between. So, with a less intimate perversity, I think, than that of Mr. Saint-Gaudens's brilliant scheme, I would have had a Sherman of the terrible march (the 'immortal' march, in all abundance, if that be the needed note), not irradiating benevolence, but signifying, by every ingenious device, the misery, the ruin and the vengeance of his track. It is not one's affair to attempt to teach an artist how such horrors may be monumentally signified; it is enough that their having been perpetrated is the very ground of the monument. And monuments should always have a clean, clear meaning."

HJ's lament for the destruction of the old city of his youth reached out also to embrace Newport. The image with which he symbolized its transformation, that of a little white open hand suddenly crammed with gold, was to remain in his mind until it yielded the setting for *The Ivory Tower*. As he contrasted the recent senseless luxury with the old Newport's "ivory idol" of leisure, he adumbrated the central symbol of that novel:

"The palaces, on the sites but the other day beyond price, stare silently seaward, monuments to the *blasé* state of their absent proprietors. Purer . . . I remind myself, was that stretch of years which I have reasons for thinking sacred, when the custom of seeking hibernation on the spot partly prevailed, when the local winter inherited something of the best social grace (as it liked at least to think) of the splendid summer, and when the strange sight might be seen of a considerable company of Americans, not gathered at a mere rest-cure, who confessed brazenly to not being in business. Do I grossly exaggerate in saying that this company, candidly, quite excitedly self-conscious, as all companies not commercial, in America, may be pleasantly noted as being, formed, for the time of its persistence, an almost unprecedented small body—unprecedented in American conditions; a collection of the detached, the slightly disenchanted and casually disqualified, and yet of the resigned and contented, of the socially orthodox: a handful of mild, oh delightfully mild, cosmopolites, united by three common circumstances, that of their having for the most part more or less lived in Europe, that of their sacrificing openly to the ivory idol whose name is leisure, and that, not least, of a formed critical habit. These things had been felt as making them excrescences on the American surface, where nobody ever criticised, especially after the grand tour, and where the great black ebony god of business was the only one recognized. So I see them, at all events, in fond memory, lasting as long as they could and finding no successors; and they are most embalmed for me, I confess, in that scented, somewhat tattered, but faintly spiced, wrapper of their various 'European' antecedents. I see them move about in the light of these, and I understand how it was this that made them ask what would have become of them, and where in the world, the hard American world, they *could* have hibernated, how they could even, in the Season, have bowed their ecónomic heads and lurked, if it hadn't been for Newport. I think of that question as, in their reduced establishments, over their winter whist, under their private theatricals, and pending, constantly, their loan and their return of the *Revue des Deux-Mondes*, their main conversational note. I find myself in fact tenderly evoking them as special instances of the great—or perhaps I have a right only to say of the small—American complication; the state of one's having been so pierced, betimes, by the sharp outland dart as to be able ever afterwards but to move about, vaguely and helplessly, with the shaft still in one's side.

"Their nostalgia, however exquisite, was, I none the less gather, sterile, for they appear to have left no seed. They must have died, some of them, in order to 'go back'—to go back, that is, to Paris. If I make, at all events, too much of them, it is for their propriety as a delicate subjective value matching with the intrinsic Newport delicacy. They must have felt that they, obviously, notably, notoriously, did match— the proof of which was in the fact that to them alone, of the customary thousands, was the beauty of the good walk, over the lovely little land, revealed. The customary thousands here, as throughout the United States, never set foot to earth—yet this had happened so, of old, to be the particular corner of *their* earth that made that adventure most possible. . . . So it was not only not our friends who had overloaded and overcrowded, but it was they at last, I infer, who gave way before that grossness. How should they have wished to leave seed only to be trampled by the white elephants?

"The white elephants, as one may best call them, all cry and no wool, all house and no garden, make now, for three or four miles, a barely interrupted chain, and I dare say I think of them best, and of the dis- tressful, inevitable waste they represent, as I recall the impression of a divine little drive, roundabout them. . . . What an idea, originally, to have seen this miniature spot of earth, where the sea-nymphs on the curved sands, at the worst, might have chanted back to the shepherds, as a mere breeding-ground for white elephants! They look queer and conscious and lumpish—some of them, as with an air of the brandished proboscis, really grotesque—while their averted owners, roused from a witless dream, wonder what in the world is to be done with them. The answer to which, I think, can only be that there is absolutely noth- ing to be done; nothing but to let them stand there always, vast and blank, for reminder to those concerned of the prohibited degrees of witlessness, and of the peculiarly awkward vengeances of affronted proportion and discretion."

If HJ was everywhere conscious, in the parts of America which he revisited, of relentless loss, when he turned to an America he had never known before and contemplated the traveling salesmen on the train taking him south, he could produce the trenchant passage that most delighted WJ.[1] Noting the desperate limitations of a business civiliza- tion, HJ foreshadowed some of the criticisms in *Main Street* and *Babbitt*. In the face of such an unilluminated mass, he realized the pathetic frailty of the one delicate counterpoise to it he had ever known, and delivered his swan song for the American girl:

"I was to find the obvious 'bagman,' the lusty 'drummer' of the Southern trains and inns (if there be not, as yet unrevealed to me, some later fond diminutive of designation for the ubiquitous commercial traveller)—I was to find, I say, this personage promptly insist on a

---

[1] See p. 342 above.

category of his own, a category which, at the moments I here recall, loomed so large as to threaten to block out of view almost every other object.

"Was I the victim of grave mischance, was my infelicity exceptional? —or was the type with which the scene so abounded, were the specimens I was thus to treasure, all of the common class and the usual frequency? I was to treasure them as specimens of something I had surely never yet so *undisputedly* encountered. They went, all by themselves, as it were, so far—were, as to facial character, vocal tone, primal rawness of speech, general accent and attitude, extraordinarily base and vulgar; and it was interesting to make out why this fact took on, for my edification, so unwonted an intensity. The fact of the influence, on the whole man, of a sordid and ravenous habit, was naturally no new thing; one had met him enough about the world, the brawny peddler more or less gorged with the fruits of misrepresentation and blatant and brazen in the key of his 'special line of goods' and the measure of his need. But if the figure was immemorial, why did it now usurp a value out of proportion to other values? What, for instance, were its remorseless reasons for treating the restless analyst, at the breakfast-hour perhaps above all, to so lurid a vision of its triumph? He had positively come to associate the breakfast-hour, from hotel to dining-car and from dining-car to hotel, with the perfect security of this exhibition, the sight of the type in completely unchallenged possession. I scarce know why my sensibility, at the juncture in question, so utterly gave way to it; why I appealed in vain from one of these so solemnly-feeding presences to another. They refused to the wondering mind any form of relief; they insisted, as I say, with the strange crudity of their air of commercial truculence, on being exactly as 'low' as they liked. And the affirmation was made, in the setting of the great greasy inelegant room, as quietly as possible, and without the least intention of offence: there were ladies and children all about—though indeed there may have been sometimes *but* the lone breakfasting child to reckon with; the little pale, carnivorous, coffee-drinking ogre or ogress, who prowls down in advance of its elders, engages a table—dread vision!—and has the 'run' of the bill of fare.

"The great blank decency, at all events, was no more broken than, on the general American scene, it ever is; yet the apprehension of marks and signs, the trick of speculation, declined none the less to drop. Whom were they constructed, such specimens, to talk with, to talk over, or to talk under, and what form of address or of intercourse, what uttered, what intelligible terms of introduction, of persuasion, of menace, what developed, what specific human process of any sort, was it possible to impute to them? What reciprocities did they imply, what presumptions did they, could they, create? what happened, inconceivably, when such Greeks met such Greeks, such faces looked into such faces, and such sounds, in especial, were exchanged with such sounds? What women did they live with, what women, living with them, could yet leave them as they were? What wives, daughters, sisters, did they in fine make credible; and what, in especial, was the speech, what the manners, what the general dietary, what most the monstrous morning meal, of ladies receiving at such hands the law or the license of life? Questions, these latter, some of which, all the while, were not imperceptibly answered—save that the vainest, no doubt, was that baffled inquiry as to the thinkable ground, amid such relations, of preliminary confidence. What *was* preliminary confidence, where it had to reckon so with the minimum of any finished appearance? How, when people were like that, did any one trust any one enough to begin, or understand any one enough to go on, or keep the peace with any one enough to survive? Wasn't it, however, at last, none the less, the sign of a fallacy somewhere in my impression that the peace *was* kept, precisely, while I so luxuriously wondered?—the consciousness of which presently led me round to something that was at the least a temporary, a working answer. My friends the drummers bore me company thus, in the smoking-car, through the deepening, sweetening South (where the rain soon gave way to a refinement of mildness) all the way to Savannah; at the end of which time, under the enchantment of the spreading scene, I had more or less issued from my maze.

"It was not, probably, that, inflated though they might be, after early refreshment, with the inward conflict of a greater number of strange sacrifices to appetite than I had ever before seen perpetrated at once, they were really more grewsome examples of a class at best disquieting than might elsewhere have been discovered; it was only that, by so sad a law of their situation, they were at once more exposed and less susceptible of bearing exposure. They so became, to my imagination, and by a mere turn of the hand of that precious faculty, something like victims and martyrs, creatures touchingly, tragically doomed. For they hadn't *asked*, when one reflected, to be almost the only figures in the social landscape—hadn't wanted the fierce light to beat *all* on themselves. They hadn't actively usurped the appearance of carrying on life without aid of any sort from other kinds of persons, other types, presences, classes. If these others were absent it wasn't *their* fault; and though they devoured, at a matutinal sitting, thirty little saucers of insane, of delirious food, this was yet a law which, over much of the land, appeared to recognize no difference of application for age, sex, condition or constitution, and it had not in short been their pretension to take over the whole social case. It would have been so different, this case, and the general effect, for the human scene, would have been so different, with a due proportion of other presences, other figures and characters, members of other professions, representatives of other interests, exemplars of other possibilities in man than the mere possibility of getting the better of his fellow-man over a 'trade.' Wondrous always to note is this sterility of aspect and this blight of vulgarity, humanly speaking, where a single type has had the game, as one may say, all in its hands. Character is developed to visible fineness only by friction and discipline on a large scale, only by its having to reckon with a complexity of forces—a process which results, at the worst, in a certain amount of social training.

"No kind of person—that was the admonition—is a very good kind, and still less a very pleasing kind, when its education has not been made to some extent by contact with other kinds, by a sense of the existence of other kinds, and, to that degree, by a certain relation with them. This education may easily, at a hundred points, transcend the teaching of the big brick schoolhouse, for all the latter's claim to universality. The last dose ever administered by the great wooden spoon so actively plied *there* is the precious bitter-sweet of a sense of proportion; yet to miss that taste, ever, at the table of civilization is to feel ourselves seated surely too much below the salt. We miss it when the social effect of it fails—when, all so dismally or so monstrously, every one strikes us as 'after' but one thing, and as thus not only unaware of the absent importances and values, but condemned and restricted, as a direct consequence of it, to the mere raw stage of their own particular connection. I so worked out, in a word, that what was the matter with my friends was not at all that they were viciously full-blown, as one might say, were the ultimate sort of monstrosity they had at first appeared; but that they were, on the contrary, just unformed, undeveloped, unrelated above all—unrelated to any merciful modifying terms of the great social proposition. They were not in their place—not relegated, shaded, embowered, protected; and, dreadful through this might be to a stray observer of the fact, it was much more dreadful for themselves. They had the helpless weakness and, I think even, somewhere in dim depths, deeper down still than the awful breakfast-habit, the vaguely troubled sense of it. They would fall into their place at a touch, were the social proposition, as I have called it, completed; they would then help, quite subordinately assist, the long sentence to read—relieved of their ridiculous charge of supplying all its clauses. I positively at last thought of them as appealing from this embarrassment; in which sublime patience I was floated, as I say, to Savannah.

"After that it was plain sailing; in the sense, I mean, of the respite—temporary at least—of speculation; of feeling impressions file in and seat themselves as quietly as decorous worshippers (say mild old ladies with neat prayer-books) taking possession of some long-drawn family pew. It was absurd what I made of Savannah—which consisted for me

but of a quarter of an hour's pause of the train under the wide arch
of the station, where, in the now quite confirmed blandness of the
Sunday noon, a bright, brief morning party appeared of a sudden to
have organized itself. Where was the charm?—if it wasn't already,
supremely, in the air, the latitude, the season, as well as in the imagination of the pilgrim capable not only of squeezing a sense from the important city on these easy terms and with that desperate economy, but
of reading heaven knows what instalment of romance into a mere railroad matter. It is a mere railroad matter, in the States, that a station
should appear at a given moment to yield to the invasion of a dozen or
so of bareheaded and vociferous young women in the company of
young men to match, and that they should all treat the place, in the
public eye, that of the crowded contemplative cars, quite as familiar,
domestic, intimate ground, set apart, it might be, for the discussion and
regulation of their little interests and affairs, and for that so oddly, so
innocently immodest ventilation of their puerile privacies at which the
moralizing visitor so frequently gasps. I recall my fleeting instants of
Savannah as the taste of a cup charged to the brim; I recall the swarming, the hatless, pretty girls, with their big-bowed cues, their romping
swains, their inveterate suggestion of their having more to say about
American manners than any other single class; I recall the thrill produced by the hawkers of scented Southern things, sprigs and specimens
of flower and fruit that mightn't as yet be of the last exoticism, but that
were native and fresh and over-priced, and so all that traveller could ask.

"But most of all, I think, I recall the quite lively resolve not to give
way, under the assault of the be-ribboned and 'shirt-waisted' fair, to the
provocation of *their* suggestiveness—even as I had fallen, reflectively
speaking, straight into the trap set for me by the Charleston bagmen;
a resolve taken, I blush to say, as a base economic precaution only, and
not because the spectacle before me failed to make reflections swarm.
They fairly hummed, my suppressed reflections, in the manner of bees
about a flower-bed, and burying their noses as deep in the *corollæ* of the
subject. Had I allowed myself time before the train resumed its direction, I should have thus found myself regarding the youths and the
maidens—but especially, for many reasons, the maidens—quite in the
light of my so earnestly-considered drummers, quite as creatures extraordinarily disconcerting, at first, as to the whole matter of their public
behavior, but covered a little by the mantle of charity as soon as it
became clear that what, like the poor drummers, they suffer from, is
the tragedy of their social, their cruel exposure, that treachery of fate
which has kept them so out of their place. It was a case, I more than
ever saw, like the case of the bagmen; the case of the bagmen lighted
it here, in the most interesting way, by propinquity and coincidence.
If the bagmen had seemed monstrous, in their occupancy of the scene,

by their disporportioned possession of it, so was not the hint sufficient that this also explains much of the effect of the American girl as encountered in the great glare of her publicity, her uncorrected, unrelated state? There had been moments, as I moved about the country, when she had seemed to me, for affirmation of presence, for immunity from competition, fairly to share the field but with the bagman, and fairly to speak as my inward ear had at last heard him speak.

" 'Ah, once *place* me and you'll see—I shall be different, I shall be better; for since I am, with my preposterous "position," falsely beguiled, pitilessly forsaken, thrust forth in my ignorance and folly, what do I know, helpless chit as I can but be, about manners or tone, about proportion or perspective, about modesty or mystery, about a condition of things that involves, for the interest and the grace of life, other forms of existence than this poor little mine—pathetically broken reed as it is, just to find itself waving all alone in the wind? How can I do *all* the grace, all the interest, as I'm expected to?—yes, literally all the interest that isn't the mere interest on the money. I'm expected to supply it all—while I wander and stray in the desert. Was there ever such a conspiracy, on the part of a whole social order, towards the exposure of incompetence? Were ever crude youth and crude presumption left so unadmonished as to their danger of giving themselves away? Who, at any turn, for an hour, ever pityingly overshadows or dispossesses me? By what combination of other presences ever am I disburdened, ever relegated and reduced, ever restored, in a word, to my right relation to the whole? All I want—that is all I need, for there is perhaps a difference—is, to put it simply, that my parents and my brothers and my male cousins should consent to exist otherwise than occultly, undiscoverably, or, as I suppose you'd call it, irresponsibly. That's a trouble, yes—but *we* take it, so why shouldn't they? The rest—don't you make it out for me?—would come of itself. Haven't I, however, as it is, been too long abandoned and too *much* betrayed? Isn't it too late, and am I not, don't you think, practically lost?' "

HJ, in outliving all his immediate family, had to face alone the first great crisis of the modern world. At the end of July 1914, on the eve of the outbreak of the war, he wrote:

"What one first feels one's self uttering, no doubt, is but the intense unthinkability of anything so blank and so infamous in an age that we have been living in and taking for our own as if it were of a high refinement of civilisation—in spite of all conscious incongruities; finding it after all carrying this abomination in its blood, finding this to have been what it *meant* all the while, is like suddenly having to recognise in one's family circle or group of best friends a band of murderers, swindlers and villains—it's just a similar shock. It makes us wonder whom in the world we are now to live with then—and even if with everything publicly and internationally so given away we can live, or want to live, at all. . . . Infamous seem to me in such a light all the *active* great ones of the earth, active for evil, in our time (to speak only of that,) from the monstrous Bismarck down! But il s'agit bien to protest in face of such a world—one can only possess one's soul in such dignity as may be precariously achievable. . . . With it all too is indeed the terrible sense that the people of this country may well—by some awful brutal justice—be going to get something bad for the exhibition that has gone on so long of their huge materialized stupidity and vulgarity. I mean the enormous national sacrifice to insensate amusement, without a redeeming idea or a generous passion, that has kept making one ask one's self, from so far back, how such grossness and folly and blatancy could possibly *not* be in the long run to be paid for. The rate at which we may witness the paying may be prodigious— and then no doubt one will pityingly and wretchedly feel that the *intention*, after all, was never so bad—only the stupidity constitutional and fatal. That is truly the dismal reflection . . . that if anything very bad does happen to the country, there isn't anything like the French intelligence to react—with the flannelled fool at the wicket, the muddied oaf and *tutti quanti*, representing so much of our *preferred* intelligence. However, let me pull up with the thought that when I am reduced to—or have come to—quoting Kipling for argument, there may be something the matter with my conclusion. One can but so distressfully wait and so wonderingly watch."

But as events rushed rapidly forward, he was pulled away from his habitual detachment. He felt as though he was strangely reliving his emotions of the Civil War, and he visited the hospitals with a shy approximation to Whitman's devotion to the soldiers. He became a wholehearted adherent to the English cause, and was soon referring to "the *louche* and sinister figure of Mr. Woodrow Wilson, who seems to be *aware* of nothing." When America did not enter the war after the sinking of the *Lusitania*, he felt that the only way he could witness his gratitude for almost forty years of residence in England was by changing his citizenship.

He lived less than a year thereafter. He wrote letters to the papers on behalf of the Belgian refugees and to stimulate interest in the American ambulance corps, and an introduction to Rupert Brooke's letters. But his mind could no longer concentrate on his own work, and *The Ivory Tower* and *The Sense of the Past*, as well as *The Middle Years*, were left unfinished at his death. What he wrote in August 1914 remained almost literally true: "Black and hideous to me is the tragedy that gathers, and I'm sick beyond cure to have lived on to see it."

He sounded his last full affirmation of life in the spring before. He had recently extended an encouraging hand to his nephew William, who, as a portrait-painter, was carrying HJ's devotion to art into the next generation. "Your fond old Uncle H" always entered sympathetically into any problems of craft:

"What you tell me of your own late work on Alice [1] and of your more assured view of your best manner of getting on fills me with confidence, curiosity and sympathy. Right indeed you must be as to facing and tackling the 'wrongnesses' of each case as it comes, and dealing with them in that case rather than sinking and postponing the question—*if you do deal with them to the finish and not to the chucking up of the particular piece.* This last is all important, and only if you observe that rule will such a process bear its best fruit in the way of teaching you Nerve. Treat your picture not as an experiment now any longer, but only and ever as a Production and Performance that you absolutely are committed to, and *then* work out or over the given wrongnesses as much as you like. But to no given wrongnesses should you ever sacrifice any saving rightnesses, *that time.* Treat every time now as the right time—for finish!"

Now he was writing to Henry Adams, to whose pessimistic theory of history WJ had previously taken exception.[2] Adams' reaction to *Notes of a Son and Brother* was to dwell on the futility of their old age. To this HJ responded with his belief in the endlessly renewed possibilities of creation. Challenged by Adams' gloom, he gave this answer, which, coming from a man of seventy-one, rings like a heroic trumpet call:

"I have your melancholy outpouring . . . and I know not how better to acknowledge it than by the full recognition of its unmitigated blackness. *Of course* we are lone survivors, of course the past that was our lives is at the bottom of an abyss—if the abyss *has* any bottom; of course, too, there's no use talking unless one particularly *wants* to. But the purpose, almost, of my printed divagations was to show you that one *can,* strange to say, still want to—or at least can behave as if one did. Behold me therefore so behaving—and apparently capable of continuing to do so. I still find my consciousness interesting—under *cultivation* of the interest. . . . You see I still, in presence of life (or of what you deny to be such,) have reactions—as many as possible—and the book I sent you is a proof of them. It's, I suppose, because I am that queer monster, the artist, an obstinate finality, an inexhaustible sensibility. Hence the reactions—appearances, memories, many things, go on playing upon it with consequences that I note and 'enjoy' (grim word!) noting. It all takes doing—and I *do.* I believe I shall do yet again—it is still an act of life."

---

[1] Alice Runnells James, wife of William James, Jr.

[2] See *The Letters of William James,* II, 344–7.

EPILOGUE

WILLIAM JAMES AND HENRY JAMES

"THERE IS very little difference between one man and another," said WJ, "but what little there is, *is very important*." After contemplating all the divergences between the brothers' minds, the reader might well conclude that, on the contrary, the differences between these two men, born hardly more than a year apart, and exposed to the same environment and to the same educational theory, were astonishingly great. All their other discrepancies in thought and expression would seem to stem back to their contrasting conceptions of knowledge, since the knower as actor and the knower as spectator are bound to behold different worlds, and to shape them to different ends.

It will not do, however, to array WJ and HJ on opposite sides of their father's antithesis between *doing* and *being*, since Henry Senior's *being*, unlike Henry Junior's, was dynamic rather than static. The pattern of relationship is further complicated by HJ's kind of detachment and WJ's kind of immersion. The one led to æsthetic contemplation as the primary mode of experience, the other to a view of life as an ethical proving ground for the will, where æsthetic standards were always subordinate. Here in particular the father would have found himself divided between his sons. His subordination of "moral" to "spiritual" put him on the side of contemplation, but his was the contemplation of the religious seer, not that of the artist. And when his attention was engaged with this world, Henry Senior had none of Henry Junior's aristocratic preferences; he was a more convinced equalitarian democrat even than WJ. Once again the basic differences are between modes of truth. For Henry Senior, truth was revelation, not something absorbed through the eyes and intelligence as it was for HJ, nor something made out of struggle as it was for WJ.

On such differences the changes could be rung indefinitely, and, as with other change-ringing, shortly to the point of stultification. But one other definition of the fundamental contrast between WJ and HJ is worth advancing, since it was first advanced by Santayana in his epoch-making formulation of "The Genteel Tradition in American Philosophy." Writing the year after WJ's death, his main point was the wide separation, from the time of Calvinism through that of transcendentalism, between the American mind and American experience, between the abstract intellect, pure and rarified, and the actual operative sphere of the pioneering will, aggressive and often brutal. Santayana cited Whitman as the one American writer who had "left the genteel tradition entirely behind." He instanced the James brothers as being "as tightly swaddled in the genteel tradition as any infant geniuses could be, for they were born before 1850, and in a Swedenborgian household. Yet they burst those bands almost entirely. The ways in which the two brothers freed themselves, however, are interestingly different. Mr. Henry James has done it by adopting the point of view of the outer world, and by turning the genteel American tradition, as he turns everything else, into a subject-matter for analysis. For him it is a curious habit of mind, intimately comprehended, to be compared with other habits of mind, also well known to him. Thus he has overcome the genteel tradition in the classic way, by understanding it. With William James too this infusion of worldly insight and European sympathies was a potent influence, especially in his earlier days; but the chief source of his liberty was another. It was his personal spontaneity, similar to that of Emerson, and his personal vitality, similar to that of nobody else. Convictions and ideas came to him, so to speak, from the subsoil. He had a prophetic sympathy with the dawning sentiments of the age, with the moods of the dumb majority. His scattered words caught fire in many parts of the world. His way of thinking and feeling represented the true America, and represented in a measure the whole ultra-modern, radical world. Thus he eluded the genteel tradition in the romantic way, by continuing it into its opposite."

There are many senses in which HJ is not a classicist and WJ is not a romantic, and these catch-all terms, almost exhausted of meaning by a century of hair-splitting conflict, are usually best excluded now from any critical discourse. But as Santayana employed them, they serve to distinguish the characteristic attitudes and productions of the brothers. WJ, to be sure, attacked the German romantic philosophers, and his radical empiricism held that experience was neither exclusively subjective, nor exclusively objective. But, as he announced in one introduction to his uncompleted metaphysics, "I prefer to start upon this work romantically"—that is to say, without formal justification, and in the mood of taking the open road to see where it would lead him. That had been the prevailing mood of his career, kindled by the animation and gusto of the intense individualist who was confident that what he found on the road would be worth finding. His delight in believing that Bergson had killed intellectualism was symptomatic of how he "continued the genteel tradition into its opposite." WJ escaped from abstract thought by embedding thought in life, but, to the eyes of a more deliberate philosopher like Santayana, he also escaped from any exact processes of thought into the more exciting but confused realm of the fervent pragmatic will.

HJ too was romantic in his nostalgia for distant joys, in his attribution of so much glamour to the "otherness" of Europe. If he was classic in his desire for comprehension, in his belief that literature is "our sum of intelligent life," any strict classicist might take exception to his analysis of the inner life as disproportionate, and to the length of his forms as excessive. Yet HJ might seem to be giving his own version of Aristotle's dictum that form "is all of the boat that is not the wood" by saying that form "is substance to that degree that there is absolutely no substance without it." And as an artist he was on the side of the classic craftsman, the trainer of talent, against the romantic genius of prophetic inspiration. He was the objective practitioner, finding his subjects outside himself and regarding them as technical problems to be solved. When we hear him saying, in relation to *The Ambassadors*, that "One's work should have composition because composition alone is positive beauty," we have reached the ground on which his work stands farthest from WJ's. For WJ's taste was for the unfinished and unformed as sources of further potentiality.

Santayana's view of WJ as a romantic might be substantiated by his great influence in our anything but classic age. But since much of that influence is not strictly relevant to the point Santayana was making, his terms had better be dropped at this juncture. WJ's clearest mark has been made on psychology rather than on philosophy. "The behaviorist, the gestaltist, and the psycho-analyst," as H. M. Kallen observed, "as well as the functionalist and the actionist, have drawn upon his insights." He remains as one of the founders of scientific method in this field, and yet he was eager, particularly at the close of his life, to curb the claims of a too arrogant science and to point out its limitations. The current exaltation of science into a faith seemed to him "a fanatic cult of the abstract."

The tendency of WJ to turn up on all sides of almost any question illustrates the futility of trying to pin him down by any one label. Like his father, he was an inexhaustible fountain. Like his master, Emerson, his greatest function was to awake and challenge others to find their own directions. It is significant of his quality as a philosopher, though not as a psychologist, that he has always spoken most directly to the amateur, even if many academic professionals have found him "unintelligible." He continued to trouble his colleagues from the time

that Chauncey Wright pronounced one of his first articles "boyish."
The rationalist Howison phrased the orthodox judgment of him: "Emerson and James were both great men of letters, great writers, yes, great thinkers, if you will, but they do not belong in the strict list of philosophers. Mastery in logic is the cardinal test of the true philosopher, and neither James nor Emerson possessed it. Both, on the contrary, did their best to discredit it." Leslie Stephen, who looked back to the solid standards of the eighteenth century, declared, after reading "The Dilemma of Determinism": "I have just read a denunciation of the wicked determinists from William James, who is a clever fellow, but, I think, rather flighty. I stick to Spinoza and Jonathan Edwards and Hume and all really clear-headed people."

The estimates of WJ that seem likely to carry most enduring weight are those held by his greatest immediate predecessor and follower in American philosophy, Peirce and Dewey. WJ's senior by only three years, Peirce was forever deploring his friend's "almost unexampled incapacity for mathematical thought." Into the tangled question of WJ's debt to Peirce we do not have to enter here—fortunately, since even WJ's devoted disciple Perry has had to declare that perhaps the most just answer is that "the modern movement known as pragmatism is largely the result of James' misunderstanding of Peirce."

They corresponded throughout their lives, and WJ tried unsuccessfully to secure a Harvard appointment for this unconventional and intransigent genius, whom, with his usual generosity, he recognized as having a more powerful mind that his own. WJ's friendliness was not dimmed at all by Peirce's efforts to make him over, by his exhortations to "try to learn to think with more exactitude," or by his deploring "your very exaggerated utterance." WJ was easily recognizable in Peirce's essay on "Minute Logic" (1902) as a "man of strength" who "proceeds slap-dash," and "has but the vaguest notion of how he has come by his principles." Yet, in the very same year that he wrote that, Peirce also showed where he believed WJ's strength to lie: he pronounced him to be "the first psychologist living or that ever lived." Their philosophies emphasized opposite aspects: Peirce was far more preoccupied with social than with individual values, and with order and coalescence and unity rather than with variety. But he did not fail to estimate WJ's pre-eminence in realms into which his own rigorous methodology did not carry. He thought of him as essentially an artist who could picture men's souls. He believed *The Varieties of Religious Experience* to be the best of WJ's books because of its "penetration into the hearts of people."

WJ tended to take for granted the kinship between his pragmatism and Dewey's, whereas Dewey regarded some of their differences as fundamental. More systematic, more concerned with the techniques of thought, Dewey also commented on WJ's lack of rigor. Though he was seventeen years younger than WJ, Dewey's first book, his *Psychology*, appeared four years before WJ's long-delayed volumes. WJ was not greatly impressed by this work: it struck him that Dewey had fallen short of grasping the living individual in his concrete wholeness. Dewey, on the other hand, hailed WJ's *Psychology* as "the spiritual progenitor" of the entire Chicago school. He dedicated his *Studies in Logical Theory* (1903) to WJ, who responded: "I feel so the inchoateness of all my publications that it surprises me to hear of anything definite accruing to others from them." Thereafter, as he embarked on his final battle for his philosophy, he considered Dewey a constant ally.

Although he took issue with several of WJ's formulations of pragmatism, in retrospect Dewey declared: "During the thirty years which have elapsed since his death, we have been able only to enlarge the openings which James has made." Dewey has returned to him many times. In the month after WJ died, Dewey saw that "his lasting achievement is to have laid upon this firm basis of scientific method a superstructure of unrivaled introspective refinement, accuracy and breadth. . . . With William James introspection meant genuine observation of genuine events, events that most persons are too conventional or too literal to note at all." Sounder than Peirce in his judgments, Dewey has continued to hold the *Psychology* the greatest of WJ's books. But just as Dewey cut through the usual academic objections to Emerson's "inconsistencies" and proclaimed him "the philosopher of democracy," so, too, in dealing with WJ, he has insisted that it is only a caricature to represent him as giving an endorsement to wishful thinking or to state that his philosophy is "a glorification of non-rational activity." On the contrary, Dewey has affirmed, WJ was a pioneer in his perception that experience is "an intimate union of emotion and knowledge."

Others have hailed WJ for abandoning the restrictions of mere reason. Unlike both Peirce and Dewey, Bergson agreed with him in holding that thought was essentially alien to the flow of experience, and that concepts were pale restrictions upon reality. Since WJ celebrated not only novelty but change, that aspect of his philosophy has been seized upon by various social movements. Wells called him his "second master," the first having been Huxley; but Mussolini also cited him, along with Nietzsche and Sorel, as one of his chief teachers. He claimed to have learned from James that "an action should be judged rather by its results than by its doctrinary basis," and also to have been quickened in "that ardent will to live and fight, to which Fascism owes a great part of its success." It seems probable that Mussolini knew James largely through the intermediary of Sorel's intensified version, *De l'utilité du pragmatisme*. Nevertheless, WJ could be regarded as an ally for having challenged the authority of the intellect. Nietzsche had found in Emerson the core of his conception of the *Übermensch*, in a way that would have startled that innocent celebrator of power. WJ would have been shocked at how different some of his doctrines could sound when the road was no longer the easy open one of the American nineteenth century, and when anti-intellectualism had become one of the sinister tools of violence.

From any such wide sweep of conflicting influence HJ's work has been almost entirely removed. Few readers have combined an equal taste for WJ and HJ; and at the time of their deaths the readers of WJ must have outnumbered those of HJ at least ten to one. What a hearty admirer of WJ like Wells could make of HJ is grimly on the record. The brothers had shared their enthusiasm for Wells' abundant vitality, and HJ, in particular, corresponded with him for several years. He believed that *Kipps* proved Wells to be "the most interesting 'literary man' of your generation"; and he relished *Tono-Bungay* and *Ann Veronica* as "very swagger" performances, the "vividness and colour" of which could have been the envy of Dickens. HJ was, to be sure, always taking exception to Wells' scorn of composition, and he pronounced him "perverse" for neglecting so many of the other demands of lasting craftsmanship. But these criticisms assumed a mutual respect, and he was bewildered when, in 1915, Wells published the heavy-handed satire that epitomized HJ as "the culmination of the Superficial type," whose characters were all "eviscerated," whose books were of "an elaborate, copious emptiness." "The thing his novel is *about* is always there. It is like a church lit but without a congregation to distract you, with every light and line focused on the high altar. And on the altar, very reverently placed, intensely there, is a dead kitten, an egg shell, a bit of string."

HJ's long and dignified answer and Wells' rejoinders [1] constitute a debate extremely symptomatic of the cleavage HJ had often noted between the small audience for serious art and the greater public. Wells declared flatly: "I had rather be called a journalist than an artist, that is the essence of it," and remained unconvinced by HJ's final declaration: "It is art that *makes* life, makes interest, makes importance, for our consideration and application of these things, and I know of no substitute whatever for the force and beauty of its process."

He had nothing to say to the generation of Wells and Arnold Bennett, to the "slice-of-life" novelists. His one immediate disciple was Edith Wharton, who understood the meaning of his insistence upon composition: "For him every great novel must first of all be based on a profound sense of moral values and then constructed with a classical unity and economy of means." He had perceptive English readers in

---

[1] *The Letters of Henry James*, II, 485–90.

Conrad and Rebecca West and Virginia Woolf, but the novel of "the stream of consciousness," the novel of Proust and Joyce, was to find its conceptions of time and memory and its psychological method through Bergson and Freud rather than through either James.

HJ's devotion to art was to bring him more explicit adherence from poets than from prose-writers. In the Georgian period of relaxed standards, HJ and Conrad, as Ezra Pound said, taught both Eliot and himself "that poetry ought to be as well written as prose." Eliot has also insisted on the importance of dramatic character in terms very similar to HJ's discussion in "The Art of Fiction," and he emulated HJ's development of a central reflecting intelligence like Strether in the Tiresias of *The Waste Land*. He penetrated to the deepest spiritual level in HJ —to the existence of which Wells was entirely oblivious—in emphasizing his "profound sensitiveness to good and evil." He observed thereby that HJ's "real progenitor" was Hawthorne, as WJ's was Emerson.

The next group of poets, the generation of Spender and Auden, have continued to regard HJ as one of the great masters of modern literature. His reputation in America, limited for many years to a handful of fellow craftsmen, seemed to renew itself during the period of the second World War, and to amplify its range. He had been dead sufficiently long for novelists of all schools to begin to profit by him. One did not have to accept his point of view to respond to his challenge to every mature writer of fiction to develop a point of view of his own; and on the basic matter of the exact presentation of material, naturalists no less than symbolists might learn from his discipline. Another cause for his access of readers in our time of intense outwardness has been that his inner dramas have provided a refuge—though hardly an escape. In the face of a breakdown of standards far more ruthless than anything he witnessed, he takes his readers away from sensationalism and violence to a realm where they must contemplate ethical issues, and he revives an awareness of the value of a far-distant kind of humane freedom.

The chief reason why HJ is capable of compelling our attention, despite the remoteness of his world from our own, is elucidated in his parable of the relation between the subject, the form, and the artist. "The house of fiction," he wrote in his preface to *The Portrait of a Lady*, "has not one window but a million." He then proceeded to expand this image and to drive its meaning home. At each of these windows hanging over the human scene "stands a figure with a pair of eyes. . . . He and his neighbours are watching the same show, but one seeing more where the other sees less, one seeing black where the other sees white, one seeing big where the other sees small, one seeing coarse where the other sees fine. And so on, and so on; there is fortunately no saying on what, for the particular pair of eyes, the window may *not* open; 'fortunately' by reason, precisely, of this incalculability of range. The spreading field, the human scene, is the 'choice of subject'; the pierced aperture, either broad or balconied or slit-like and low-browed, is the 'literary form'; but they are, singly or together, as nothing without the posted presence of the watcher—without, in other words, the consciousness of the artist. Tell me what the artist is, and I will tell you of what he has *been* conscious. Thereby I shall express to you at once his boundless freedom and his 'moral' reference."

That is the kind of talk, we are quickly reminded, to which WJ always kindled. Many of his sentences would fit directly into HJ's parable: for instance, the one about its being "the amount of life which a man feels that makes you value his mind"; or "a thing is important if anyone *think* it important"; or the one affirming that every philosopher worthy of the name must proceed from "a bias and a logic of his own." Only that last phrase happens to come from the preface to "The Figure in the Carpet" and to refer not to a philosopher but to an artist.

We are aware again, therefore, that no matter how wide the divergence between the directions taken by these brothers' minds, or between the curves of their reputations, they are held together by a solid core of values. Their kinship becomes even more striking when we recall the reasons HJ gave for using the symbol of the complex design in a Persian rug to reinforce his plea for analytic appreciation. He was bent on making the point that you could not understand an artist's work if you approached it merely from outside. You had to enter imaginatively into its pattern as a whole, into the "special beauty" that "pervades and controls and animates it." This is not "the 'esoteric meaning,' as the newspapers say; it's the *only* meaning, it's the very soul . . . of the work."

Isn't this exactly the same plea that WJ made in *A Pluralistic Universe?* "Place yourself . . . at the center of a man's philosophic vision and you understand at once all the different things it makes him write or say. But keep outside, use your post-mortem method, try to build the philosophy up out of the single phrases, taking first one and then another and seeking to make them fit, and of course you fail. You crawl over the thing like a myopic ant over a building, tumbling into every microscopic crack or fissure, finding nothing but inconsistencies, and never suspecting that a centre exists."

Both brothers thus insist not only upon the necessity of having a point of view, but also upon the willingness to stand sympathetically inside other points of view. It was most natural for both of them to speak in terms of seeing, since, as we have noted again and again, both lived by their eyes. Both therefore took delight in introducing into their writing their fullest resources of visual imagery. The art of fiction allowed HJ to develop his pictorial gifts to greater lengths, but WJ, in the most extended image he permitted himself, writes as though for once he might be vying with HJ's breath-taking elaborations. WJ wanted, in the exposition of his "Radical Empiricism," to instance the essential plurality of experience, how reality "is neither absolutely one nor absolutely many, but a stream whose parts coalesce where they touch," and then inevitably diverge. He made this conception as concrete as possible:

"*Prima facie*, if you should liken the universe of absolute idealism to an aquarium, a crystal globe in which goldfish are swimming, you would have to compare the empiricist universe to something more like one of those dried human heads with which the Dyaks of Borneo deck their lodges. The skull forms a solid nucleus; but innumerable feathers, leaves, strings, beads, and loose appendices of every description float and dangle from it, and, save that they terminate in it, seem to have nothing to do with one another. Even so my experiences and yours float and dangle, terminating, it is true, in a nucleus of common perception, but for the most part out of sight and irrelevant and unimaginable to one another."

The suspicion that WJ may have had HJ in mind is caused by the fact that, in all three of his late major novels, HJ had likened his social group to fishes held together "in a fathomless medium." Merton Densher had reflected, at the moment of Milly Theale's appearance in the Venetian palace, on how she seemed to "diffuse in wide warm waves the spell of a general, a beatific mildness. There was a deeper depth of it, doubtless, for some than for others; what he in particular knew of it was that he seemed to stand in it up to his neck. He moved about in it and it made no plash; he floated, he noiselessly swam in it, and they were all together, for that matter, like fishes in a crystal pool." Such a comparison is ambivalent, since Densher also feels that he is "immersed in an element more strangely than agreeably warm." He feels himself caught up, as does Strether somewhat less and Maggie Verver even more, in a densely involved and slowly circulating situation, all inescapably exposed to the observing eye.

To WJ such a world was far too static, far too attenuated in its æsthetic essences, for him to enter into it with much sympathy or even understanding. Though it is not likely that WJ was consciously directing his whole argument here against HJ, whom he would not have identified with "absolute idealism" or, indeed, with any strict philosophical position, nevertheless his image illustrates the essential relationship between them. For if many of HJ's phases were "unimaginable" to WJ, their minds came together in "a nucleus of common perception."

A passage in WJ's *Psychology* may elucidate this relationship a little further. WJ, as we might suspect from his mercurial temperament, belonged to the type that he described, following Galton and Binet, as making use "in memory, reasoning, and all their intellectual operations, of images derived from movement." When he represented this type in the man "of explosive will," he provided another comparison that is relevant to himself and HJ:

"He will be the king of his company, sing all the songs, and make all the speeches, lead the parties, carry out the practical jokes, kiss all the girls, fight the men, and, if need be, lead the forlorn hopes and enterprises, so that an onlooker would think he has more life in his little finger than can exist in the whole body of a correct judicious fellow. But the judicious fellow all the while may have all these possibilities . . . ready to break out . . . if only the brakes were taken off. It is the absence of scruples, of consequences, of considerations, the extraordinary simplification of each moment's mental outlook, that gives to the explosive individual such motor energy and ease; it need not be the greater intensity of any of his passions, motives, or thoughts."

Again one must not apply the comparison too literally, though it is fascinating how closely "the king of the company" approximates the "William" of HJ's autobiography. Furthermore, the peculiar intensity of HJ's most complex passages is bound up with the multiplication of "scruples" and "considerations." One of the most distinguishing features of his imagery, in contrast with that of "the motor type," is its suppression of sudden movement. More strictly a "visual" than WJ, he did not ignore violent action, but treated it in a way deliberately calculated to suggest its terrifying force.

A single example can suffice. One of the greatest scenes in all his fiction comes towards the end of *The Golden Bowl*, when Maggie Verver, fully aware now of the relation between her husband and Charlotte Stant, walks up and down the terrace, knowing that with one sudden gesture of denunciation she could stride in and break the situation to bits. But she wants more than anything to regain her husband's love, and this can be accomplished only by keeping up appearances. Therefore HJ's leading image is one of violence rejected: "the straight vindictive view," "the protests of passion" figured to Maggie "nothing nearer to experience than a wild eastern caravan, looming into view with crude colours in the sun, fierce pipes in the air, high spears against the sky, all a thrill, a natural joy to mingle with, but turning off short before it reached her and plunging into other defiles." Though the primitive release is denied her, though she does nothing to disturb the surface decorum, HJ manages—and this is the supremely important point—to intensify rather than to weaken thereby Maggie's dilemma: "the horror of finding evil seated all at its ease where she had only dreamed of good; the horror of the thing hideously *behind*, behind so much trusted, so much pretended, nobleness, cleverness, tenderness." Such passages render, in their brooding density, the mixed and tragic elements of life in a fashion quite beyond the scope of WJ's quicker and more buoyant simplicity.

But their central kinship, transcending all contrasts, lies in their belief in nothing less than the sacredness of the individual. For this they were indebted, as we have seen, to both their religious and their political background, to their father's Christian ethics as well as to the roots of Jeffersonian democracy. They affirmed this belief under widely different guises, and once again a passage from one of them, this time from HJ's preface to *The Spoils of Poynton*, may serve as an unintended basis for comparison. HJ, like WJ, was most interested in human behavior under pressure, even though the pressures that absorbed him were those of inner and not of outer conflict. He recognized that his choice of Fleda Vetch for a heroine was an instance of his "well-nigh extravagant insistence on the free spirit." Her freedom consists in the fact that she "both sees and feels," whereas Mona Brigstock "is *all* will, without the smallest leak into taste or tenderness or vision." Therefore, inevitably, Fleda goes down to defeat, she loses Owen Gereth to Mona. But HJ's conviction is that "the free spirit, always much tormented, and by no means always triumphant, is heroic, ironic, pathetic, or whatever, and, as exemplified in the record of Fleda Vetch, for instance, 'successful,' only through having remained free."

HJ unquestionably had no thought there of giving a warning to WJ, though some of the distorters of WJ's philosophy have seized upon its danger point in its too unguarded exaltation of the will. Fleda, though WJ may not have so recognized her, was essentially one of his underdogs; and WJ also tried to reverse the ruthless march of his age by decrying "the bitch-goddess Success" and by expressing his admiration for those "who do not close their hand on their possessions." He could, in turn, have indicated the psychological weaknesses in HJ's free spirits, in so far, at least, as they were represented by the extreme case of Fleda, who was fastidious to the point of being neurotic, and almost embraced renunciation as a goal, instead of as an end to be accepted only if absolutely necessary.

The free spirits of WJ and HJ themselves, throughout the long range of their careers, are among the most magnificent productions of our American nineteenth century. It does not lessen their value to recall that, in the fuller perspective of history, their father's greater emphasis on society stands closer to the norm. WJ and HJ, through the special circumstances of their expansive era, conceived of freedom largely in terms of separate individuals. Henry Senior's insight was more profound. He knew, as we are rediscovering now in our own more tragic times, that the ripest freedom comes through participation in society and not apart from it, that such freedom can be based only on the minimization of economic inequality, that such freedom is not lonely but finds its completion through fraternity, in solidarity.

CHRONOLOGY, NOTES,
and INDEX

CHRONOLOGY

1811 *Henry James, Senior, is born in Albany.*

1840 *Marries Mary Robertson Walsh.*

1842 *William James, born January 11.*

1843 *Henry James, Junior, born April 15.*

1845 *Birth of Garth Wilkinson James.*

1846 *Birth of Robertson James. Henry Senior*: WHAT CONSTITUTES THE STATE.

1847 *Henry Senior*: LETTER TO A SWEDENBORGIAN.

1848 *Birth of Alice James.*

1850 *Henry Senior*: MORALISM AND CHRISTIANITY.

1852 *Henry Senior*: LECTURES AND MISCELLANIES.

1854 *Henry Senior*: THE CHURCH OF CHRIST NOT AN ECCLESIAS-TICISM.

1855 *Henry Senior*: THE NATURE OF EVIL.

1857 *Henry Senior*: CHRISTIANITY THE LOGIC OF CREATION.

1861 *Henry Senior*: THE SOCIAL SIGNIFICANCE OF OUR INSTITUTIONS.

1866 *Henry Senior*: SUBSTANCE AND SHADOW.

1869 *Henry Senior*: THE SECRET OF SWEDENBORG.

1875 *HJ*: A PASSIONATE PILGRIM AND OTHER TALES *and* TRANSATLAN-TIC SKETCHES.

1876 *HJ*: RODERICK HUDSON.

1877 *HJ*: THE AMERICAN.

1878 *HJ*: FRENCH POETS AND NOVELISTS *and* THE EUROPEANS.

1879 *Henry Senior*: SOCIETY THE REDEEMED FORM OF MAN. *HJ*: THE MADONNA OF THE FUTURE AND OTHER TALES, DAISY MILLER, *and* HAWTHORNE.

1880 *HJ*: CONFIDENCE.

1881 *HJ*: WASHINGTON SQUARE *and* THE PORTRAIT OF A LADY.

1882 *Death of Mary Walsh James and of Henry James, Senior.*

1883   *Death of Garth Wilkinson James.* HJ: The Siege of London
        and Portraits of Places. Collection of Novels and Tales, *14
        volumes.*

1884   The Literary Remains of the late Henry James, *edited with
        an Introduction by William James.* HJ: Tales of Three Cities.

1885   HJ: A Little Tour in France *and* Stories Revived.

1886   HJ: The Bostonians *and* The Princess Casamassima.

1888   HJ: The Reverberator, The Aspern Papers, *and* Partial Por-
        traits.

1889   HJ: A London Life.

1890   WJ: The Principles of Psychology. HJ: The Tragic Muse.

1892   *Death of Alice James.* HJ: The Lesson of the Master.

1893   HJ: The Real Thing and Other Tales, Picture and Text,
        and Essays in London and Elsewhere.

1894   *Alice James' Journal, printed in four copies for the family.*
        HJ: Theatricals.

1895   HJ: Theatricals: Second Series *and* Terminations.

1896   HJ: The Figure in the Carpet *and* The Other House.

1897   WJ: The Will to Believe and Other Essays in Popular
        Philosophy. HJ: The Spoils of Poynton *and* What Maisie
        Knew.

1898   WJ: Human Immortality. HJ: The Turn of the Screw *and*
        Covering End.

1899   WJ: Talks to Teachers on Psychology and to Students on
        Some of Life's Ideals. HJ: The Awkward Age.

1900   HJ: The Soft Side.

1901   HJ: The Sacred Fount.

1902   WJ: The Varieties of Religious Experience. HJ: The Wings
        of the Dove.

1903   HJ: The Ambassadors, The Better Sort, *and* William Wet-
        more Story and His Friends.

1904   HJ: The Golden Bowl.

1905   HJ: English Hours.

1907   WJ: Pragmatism. HJ: The American Scene.

1907–9 HJ: Novels and Tales, *the New York Edition, 24 volumes.*

1909   WJ: A Pluralistic Universe *and* The Meaning of Truth.
        HJ: Italian Hours.

1910   *Death of Robertson James and William James.* HJ: The Finer
        Grain.

1911   WJ: Some Problems of Philosophy *and* Memories and
        Studies. HJ: The Outcry.

1912   WJ: Essays in Radical Empiricism.

1913   HJ: A Small Boy and Others.

1914   HJ: Notes of a Son and Brother *and* Notes on Novelists.

1916 *Death of Henry James.*

1917 HJ: THE IVORY TOWER, THE SENSE OF THE PAST, *and* THE MIDDLE YEARS.

1920 WJ: COLLECTED ESSAYS AND REVIEWS, *edited by Ralph Barton Perry.*

THE LETTERS OF WILLIAM JAMES, *edited by his son, Henry James.*

THE LETTERS OF HENRY JAMES, *edited by Percy Lubbock.*

1921–3 THE NOVELS AND STORIES OF HENRY JAMES, *35 volumes.*

1934 THE JOURNAL OF ALICE JAMES, *edited by Anna Robeson Burr.*

NOTES

Book I

Henry James, Senior

Page

3 "allowing them to absorb," *P*, I:59
"a danger, after all escaped," *NSB*, 117

4 "a very small sum," *LWJ*, I:2
"When old Billy James came," ibid., I:4
"of medium height," ibid., I:3
"a good wife and mother," *LRHJ*, 147, 148

5 "The rupture with my grandfather's tradition," *SBO*, 190
"the numerous dawnings," ibid., 14
"extravagant unregulated cluster," Henry James: *The Wings of the Dove* (Macmillan, 1923), I:100
"the bent of my nature," C. Hartley Grattan: *The Three Jameses* (1932), 89

6 "Some consider you," Austin Warren: *The Elder Henry James* (1934), 17
"The flesh said," *Journals of Ralph Waldo Emerson*, edited by Edward Waldo Emerson and Waldo Emerson Forbes (1909–14), IX:190
"the nothingness of selfhood," ibid., IX:90

7 "essential malignity," Henry James, Sr.: *Substance and Shadow* (1863), 165

Page

"as so much mere rubbish," Austin Warren: *The Elder Henry James*, 79

8 "the curse of mankind," Henry James, Sr.: *Society the Redeemed Form of Man* (1879), 47
"the gradual access of self-love," Henry James, Sr.: *The Nature of Evil* (1855), 129, 192
"His intellect appears to me," Henry James, Sr.: *Substance and Shadow*, 322
"our glorified natural humanity," Henry James, Sr.: *Society the Redeemed Form of Man*, 264
"the inmost and inseparable life," Henry James, Sr.: *Lectures and Miscellanies* (1852), 147
"That style of deity," Henry James, Sr.: *Society the Redeemed Form of Man*, 333–4
"true worship is always spontaneous," Henry James, Sr.: "William Blake's Poems," *The Spirit of the Age* (1850), I:113

9 "One animal preys upon another," Henry James, Sr.: *Christianity the Logic of Creation* (1857), 94–6
"A skeptical state," *NSB*, 235

10 "Henry James said to me," *P*, I:3

"Thanks for your cheering letter," Henry James, Sr., to Julia Kellogg: *Unpublished Letter*, 1869

"The other day," Henry James, Sr., to Julia Kellogg: *Unpublished Letter*, undated

11 "immense elation of freedom," William James: *The Varieties of Religious Experience* (1902), 272, 280

the "one great truth" in his ontology, cf. *P*, I:152

"it wholly ignores," Henry James, Sr.: *Letter to a Swedenborgian* (1847), 4

12 "the old conceptions," Henry James, Sr.: *Lectures and Miscellanies*, 3

"the democratic idea," ibid., 8–9

"our entire system of trade," Henry James, Sr.: *Moralism and Christianity* (1850), 33

"A true society," Henry James, Sr.: *Lectures and Miscellanies*, 87

"Life is simply the passage," *P*, I:71

"The measure of a man's goodness," Henry James, Sr.: *What Constitutes the State* (1846), 24

"the great unitary life," Henry James, Sr.: *Substance and Shadow*, 369, 145

13 "an astute and terrible searching," Stephen Pearl Andrews: *Love, Marriage and Divorce* (1889), 11

"tends powerfully toward metaphysical subtleties," ibid.

"of the class of purely ideal reformers," ibid., 10

"to a right-minded man," *Life and Letters of Edwin Laurence Godkin*, edited by Rollo Ogden (1907), II:117

"They talk so heartily," Austin Warren: *Henry James the Elder*, 184

"the school of seers and prophets," Stephen Pearl Andrews: *Love, Marriage and Divorce*, 11–12

14 "He was a writer," *Life and Letters of E. L. Godkin*, II:118

"substance or body from things," Henry James, Sr.: *The Secret of Swedenborg* (1869), 37

"make all my work sabbatical," *P*, I:23

"the stagnant slipslop," Stephen Pearl Andrews: *Love, Marriage and Divorce*, 26

"stale and mercenary circus tricks," Henry James, Sr.: *The Secret of Swedenborg*, 211

"Against this lurid power," C. H. Grattan: *The Three Jameses*, 69

"to burst asunder," ibid.

15 "elegant Billingsgate," *Journals of Ralph Waldo Emerson*, IX:520

"Please run your eye," C. H. Grattan: *The Three Jameses*, 78

"thoughts and dispositions," *P*, I:22

"Those who know the rich," ibid., II:110

"You need never go to them," Henry James, Sr.: *Society the Redeemed Form of Man*, 68

"true comfort—wise, gentle," *Journals of Ralph Waldo Emerson*, VIII:109

"a little fat, rosy Swedenborgian amateur," *Familiar Letters of Henry David Thoreau*, edited by F. B. Sanborn (1894), 145

16 "aninted with the Isle of Patmos," M. A. De Wolfe Howe: *Memories of a Hostess* (1922), 47

Autobiography

17 "He had often been urged," *LRHJ*, 7–8

"I will not attempt," *LRHJ*, 145–91

Letters to Emerson

39 "I listened to your address," *P*, I:39–41

40 "proudly and pressingly," *SBO*, 8

41 "To the Invisible Emerson," *P*, I:41–3

42 "Your letter was well-come," ibid., I:46–7

43 "Oh you man without a handle!" ibid., I:51

"makes humanity seem more erect," *Familiar Letters of H. D. Thoreau*, 95

"is a hearty man enough," ibid., 402

"was literally the most childlike," Austin Warren: *The Elder Henry James*, 182–3

44 "Mr. Alcott could not condone," ibid., 48

"most frank, cordial and friendly," ibid., 49

"beamed with delight," Edward Waldo Emerson: *The Early Years of the Saturday Club* (1918), 329
"I am horrified at the prospect," *P*, I:57–9
46 "Socialism is as good a topic," ibid., I:59
"before our migration," *NSB*, 198–200

"Your note finds me," *P*, I:71–2, who dates this letter in autumn of 1851.
47 "Father came back comfortable," ibid., I:105
"the busy, the tipsy, and Daniel Webster," *SBO*, 49
"I remember well," *NSB*, 68–70

Socialism and Civilization

49 "I propose to discuss," Henry James, Sr.: *Moralism and Christianity*, 39–42, 61–7, 80–94

The Social Significance of Our Institutions

59 "A friend observed to me," Henry James, Sr.: *The Social Significance* of Our Institutions (1861), 3–6, 7, 9–19

Book II
The Children's Education

69 "delighting ever in the truth," *SBO*, 220
"the literal played," ibid., 216
"He's really . . . a native," *P*, I:412
70 "I desire my child," Henry James, Sr.: *The Nature of Evil*, 99
"that almost eccentrically home-love habit," *SBO*, 72
71 "My dear Father,—We have had," *P*, I:188–9
"used to spoil our Christmasses," *AJ*, 125
"When I look back," ibid., 163
"felicities of destitution," *SBO*, 59
"the she-wolf of competition," ibid., 221
"all gentle and generous together," ibid., 177
"There could not be," *Life and Letters of E. L. Godkin*, II:118
"our excellent parents," *AJ*, 192
72 "the preoccupation (too strong, at least)," Henry James, Jr., to Mrs. William James: *Unpublished Letter*, April 26, 1900
"rag-bag of memory," *SBO*, 69, 92
"professed amazement," ibid., 68
"with anything but contempt," *LWJ*, I:20
73 "number and succession," *SBO*, 16
"We couldn't have changed oftener," ibid.
"It is beyond measure odd," ibid., 209
"entrancing interest," ibid., 30

"dawdling and gaping," ibid., 26
"I first 'realized' Fourteenth Street," ibid., 97
"quieter harmonies," ibid., 98
74 "the highest pleasure of sense," ibid., 228
"the oblong farinaceous compound," ibid.
"that of my brother's occupying," ibid., 8–10
"a 'motor,' and morally ill-adapted," *LWJ*, II:163
"the vivid image," *SBO*, 3
"constant comic star," ibid., 253
"the dreadful blight of arithmetic," ibid., 222
75 "my comparatively so indirect quality," ibid., 288
"One way of taking life," ibid., 290
"drawing, always drawing," ibid., 207
"I try at least to recover here," ibid., 259–64
77 "could suffer such elements," ibid., 214
"As I reconsider," ibid., 214–18
79 "'flagrant' morality," ibid., 68
"Mr. George Bradford had opened," *AJ*, 218–19
80 "No education avails," *SBO*, 26
"I see myself moreover," ibid., 24–6
81 "all our books," ibid., 81
"forever mounting on little platforms," ibid., 60
"succumbed to the spell," ibid., 65

"first experiment," ibid., 159

"The point exactly was," ibid., 162–4

82 "might have been," *NSB*, 180

"Our young liberty," *SBO*, 232–5

"Of course whenever we truly conceive," Henry James, Sr.: *Unpublished Letter on Incarnation*, January 4, 1874

84 "I wonder whether," *AJ*, 120

"I remember so distinctly," ibid., 166–7

85 "as a baby in long clothes," *SBO*, 53–4

"Looking back at it," ibid., 301–2

86 "only by a person incorrigible," ibid., 302

"I dare say," ibid., 304

"formative, fertilising . . . 'intellectual experience,'" ibid., 349

"that bridge over to Style," ibid., 346

"The beginning in short," ibid., 351–3

87 "Willy is very devoted," *P*, I:184

88 "felicity of idiom," *SBO*, 325

"a New England," *NSB*, 86

"The first time," *LHJ*, I:6–8

89 "incorrigible vagueness," *NSB*, 1

"a lost lamb," ibid., 6

"simply said to themselves," ibid., 4

90 "Whatever he might happen to be doing," ibid., 13–16

91 "a miserable, home-bred," *LWJ*, I:20

"Your hearts, I know," *P*, I:195

92 "I wish you would," ibid., I:196–8

93 "had always counted upon," ibid., I:191

"It is melancholy," Henry James, Sr.: *Moralism and Christianity*, 64

"the career of art," *SBO*, 51

"My brother challenges him," *NSB*, 50–2

94 "had gradually ceased," ibid., 61

"no brisk conductor," ibid., 62

95 "at the threshold," ibid., 82

"In a year or two," *P*, I:193

"I am myself a good draughtsman," William James: *Principles of Psychology* (1890), II:53

"I buried two of my children," *NSB*, 221–3

97 "a great revulsion of spirit," *NSB*, 112–16

99 "To me in my boyish fancy," *P*, I:202

"'The adipose and affectionate Wilky,'" E. W. Emerson: *The Early Years of the Saturday Club*, 328

"for his intimate experience," *NSB*, 444

100 "unconnected," ibid., 66

A Note on the Family Tongue

101 "the representations of Socrates," E. W. Emerson: *The Early Years of the Saturday Club*, 327

"The rich robustness," Alice James to Mrs. William James: *Unpublished Letter*, February 5, 1890

102 "Many times and bitterly today," William James to Mr. and Mrs. Henry James, Sr.: *Unpublished Letter*, Christmas 1861; and in a slightly revised form, *NSB*, 132–3

"Comment on the abundance," *NSB*, 134–5

103 "*Chérie de Jeune Balle*," William James to Alice James: *Unpublished Letter*, November 14, 1866; *LWJ*, I:80–1, in part

104 "*Süss Balchen!*" *LWJ*, I:115–18

105 "pleasantry of paradox," *NSB*, 134

"In this respect," *LWJ*, I:178

"You were good enough," ibid., I:15–16

106 "to say a thing," ibid., II:277

"the sudden word," ibid., II:89

107 "I don't care," ibid., I:341

"Isn't fertility better," ibid., II:86

"idiocyncrasies of diction," *P*, II:104–5

"who promised to read it," ibid., I:77

"I'm glad you like adverbs," *LHJ*, II:214–15

"laid hands upon the letters," Henry James, Jr., to his nephew Henry James: *Unpublished Letter*, November 15–18, 1913; *LHJ*, II:346–7, in part

109 "I may mention however," *LHJ*, II:347–8

110 "Très-cher et très-grand ami!" ibid., II:217–20

Father to Sons

113 "It is a delight," *P*, I:110

"Your long sickness," ibid., I:3–4

"a letter under date of May 1868," *NSB*, 52

114 "I had no sooner left," Henry
James, Sr., to James T. Fields: *Un-
published Letter*, May 2, 1868;
NSB, 52, in part
"Almost all my dear father," *NSB*, 53
"I think Father is the *wisest*," *P*,
I:142
"A skeptical state," *NSB*, 235
"as a means of delivering him," *Dictionary of American Biography*,
IX:594
"He is probably the greatest," *P*, I:
283
115 "I have been reading," ibid., I:151
"the first requisite," ibid., I:147
"I have read your article," ibid., II:
705-6, 706-7, 707-9
119 "I cannot understand," ibid., II:
709-11
"I acknowledged your metaphysical
letter," ibid., II:711
120 "You probably now see," ibid., II:
714-15
121 "Be very sure," Henry James, Jr.,

to Henry James, Sr.: *Unpublished
Letter*, January 14, 1870
"We had a sitting," Henry James,
Sr., to Henry James, Jr.: *Unpublished Letter*, January 14, 1873; *P*,
I:333-4, in part
123 "Dearest father—I have just received," Henry James, Jr., to
Henry James, Sr.: *Unpublished
Letter*, February 1, 1873
"I went to see Osgood," Henry James,
Sr., to Henry James, Jr.: *Unpublished Letter*, March 4, 1873; and
in a slightly revised form, *NSB*,
275-8
125 "As for the recital," *NSB*, 274
"I have rejoiced," Henry James, Jr.,
to Mrs. Henry James, Sr.: *Unpublished Letter*, March 24, 1873
126 "Beloved Brother— . . . I have
had," *P*, I:316-17
"nothing in the world," Henry James,
Jr., to Henry James, Sr.: *Unpublished Letter*, April 16, 1879

Death of the Mother and Father

127 "soundless and yet absolutely,"
NSB, 176-7
"Oh! my dear Boy," *LWJ*, I:9
"My dearest mother died," *P*, I:111
"My mother's death," *LHJ*, I:92
"On Sunday January 29th," Henry
James: *Unpublished Notebook*
129 "And now, my darling boy," *P*,
I:112-13
130 "The making of the book," Austin
Warren: *The Elder Henry James*,
186
"I stick by Almighty God," ibid., 188
"A week before Father died," *AJ*,
238-9
"Darling Father's weary longings,"
Alice James to Henry James, Jr.:
Unpublished Letter, December 20,
1882

131 "You will already have heard,"
Henry James, Jr., to William
James: *Unpublished Letter*, December 26, 1882; *LHJ*, I:97-8, in
part; *P*, I:114-15, in part
132 "Darling old Father . . . We have
been," *LWJ*, I:218-20
133 "Dear William . . . I went out,"
Henry James, Jr., to William
James: *Unpublished Letter*, January 1, 1883
"Your eagerly awaited letter," *P*, I:
165
"Father's boyhood," *LWJ*, I:221-2
134 "It is singular," ibid., I:222
"I fell upon Father's and Mother's,"
AJ, 130-2

The Tributes of the Sons to the Father

136 "public justice," *P*, I:165
"infinitely for granted," *NSB*, 155
"by designing a small cut," *LHJ*, I:9
"Now and then he'd break out," *Life
in Letters of William Dean Howells*, edited by Mildred Howells
(1928), I:164
"Father's book is out," *P*, I:306-7

138 "Father would find in me," *LWJ*,
I:310
"Religion is the great interest," ibid.,
II:58
"We have walked," Henry James,
Sr.: *Substance and Shadow*, 155
"it made experience possible," *LRHJ*,
224-5

"The true solution," *P*, II:426
"was too sensitive," ibid., I:324

139 "It has seemed to me," *LRHJ*, 7–119

187 "Three days ago," *LHJ*, I:111–12

188 "What a pity," *P*, I:148

"Your letter . . . was most welcome," *LWJ*, I:241–2

191 "We took his 'writing,' " *NSB*, 155–81

202 "A less vague or vain idealist," ibid., 224–30

Book III

Formulations: William James

209 "Much would I give," *P*, I:515
"in the 'queer' or the incalculable," *NSB*, 123
"Insomnia, digestive disorders," *LWJ*, I:84
"One year study chemistry," ibid., I:42

210 "The hours I spent," William James: *Memories and Studies* (1912), 14
"unspeakable disgust," *P*, II:271
"fugitive sequences," ibid., I:176
"earnest search for coherency," ibid., I:769
"a pathological repugnance," ibid., II:680
"the gaping contrast," William James: review of H. R. Marshall's *Pain, Pleasure, and Æsthetics* (1894), quoted by *P*, II:127
"to be born afresh every morning," *P*, II:686

211 "a thing is important," William James: *Principles of Psychology*, II:675
"realities are only," William James: *Pragmatism* (1907), 50
"the knower is not simply a mirror," William James: *Collected Essays and Reviews* (1920), 67
"If six years ago," *LWJ*, I:119–20

212 "It made me feel quite sad," ibid., I:127–33

216 "Today I about touched bottom," *P*, I:322
"It seems to me," *LWJ*, I:158
"the worst kind of melancholy," William James: *The Varieties of Religious Experience*, 159–60

217 "Whilst in this state," ibid., 160–1

218 "I think that yesterday," *LWJ*, I:147–8
"I originally studied medicine," *P*, I:228

219 "My eyes serve," ibid., I:328
"Willy goes on swimmingly," ibid., I:339–40

220 "I decide today to stick," ibid., I:335
"to fight it out," *LWJ*, I:170
"Yesterday I told Eliot," *P*, I:343
"I believe I told you," ibid., I:344

221 "This is the point," ibid., I:347
"My dear H.—The die is cast!" William James to Henry James, Jr.: *Unpublished Letter*, September 2, 1873
"The trouble with him," Mrs. Henry James, Sr., to Henry James, Jr.: *Unpublished Letters*, March 17, 1874 and July 6, 1874; *P*, II:673, in part
"If dear Harry," Mrs. Henry James, Sr., to Henry James, Jr.: *Unpublished Letter*, September 12, 1873

222 "The philosophical teaching," William James, "The Teaching of Philosophy in Our Colleges," the *Nation*, September 21, 1876; *LWJ*, I:189–91

223 "study of the mind," William James: *Principles of Psychology*, I:224, 225, 226, 229

224 "It is obvious and palpable," ibid., I:233–4, 237, 238–9

225 "I have often thought," *LWJ*, I:199–200
"I have been paying," ibid., I:261

226 "William expressed himself," *AJ*, 121
"In the relief of certain hysterias," *P*, II:123n
"I went there for one day," *LWJ*, II:327–8

227 "At most of our American colleges," William James: *The Will to Believe* (1898), vii–xii

230 "Divine truth has first," Henry James, Sr.: *Society the Redeemed Form of Man*, 35
"If this life be not," William James: *The Will to Believe*, 61–2

231 "What a curse," George Santayana:

Character and Opinion in the United States (1920), 92

"How you *have* misunderstood," *LWJ*, II:22–3

232 "A man's religion," *P*, II:328

"Remember that the whole point," ibid., II:331

"mere sanity is the most," ibid., II:333

"A perfect bog of reasonableness," ibid., II:697

"the supreme contemporary example," William James: *The Varieties of Religious Experience*, 84

"If we admit that evil," ibid., 131–4

234 "There is no need," ibid., 161–5

236 "My philosophy is what," *LWJ*, II:203–4

"I see now with absolute clearness," ibid., II:190

237 "I thank you for your congratulations," ibid., II:268

"the philosophy which is so impor-

tant," William James: *Pragmatism*, 4, 6–13

240 "a system that will combine," ibid., 20

"I am all aflame with it," *P*, II:452

"It is absolutely," ibid., II:457

"The name 'pragmatism,'" William James: *The Meaning of Truth* (1909), 184–6

241 "had enough of the squashy," *P*, II:338

"I am going, if I live," *LWJ*, II:179

"intellectual higgledy-piggledyism," *P*, I:774

"*technical* writing on *philosophical* subjects," ibid., II:387

"I believe that philosophy stands," ibid., II:662

242 "Say it is fragmentary," William James: *Some Problems of Philosophy* (1911), vii

"Let *my* last word," William James: *Memories and Studies*, 411

Formulations: Henry James

243 "I may remark," *SBO*, 175–6

244 "only form of riot or revel," ibid., 25

245 undistracted by "ideas," cf. T. S. Eliot: "On Henry James," the *Little Review*, August 1918; reprinted in F. W. Dupee: *The Question of Henry James* (1945), 110–11

"Henry James was not," T. S. Eliot: "The Education of Henry Adams," the *Athenæum*, May 23, 1919; quoted by F. O. Matthiessen: *The Achievement of T. S. Eliot* (1935), 12

"who preyed not upon ideas," Dupee: *The Question of Henry James*, 109–10

"so fine that no idea," ibid., 110

"It is the sensuous contributor," Matthiessen: *The Achievement of T. S. Eliot*, 12

"I had under stress," *NSB*, 243–6

247 "Scarce at all to be stated," ibid., 296–9

248 "through crazy juvenility," *LHJ*, I:317

249 "The feeling of that younger time," Henry James: *Unpublished Notebook*

"on the very vaguest grounds," *NSB*, 292

250 "quite prodigious," ibid., 344

"I have kept to this hour," ibid., 340–1

"playing with much thinner things," ibid., 265

251 "He is superficial," Henry James: "'Essays on Fiction' by Nassau W. Senior," *North American Review*, October 1864; reprinted in *Notes and Reviews* (1921), 2

"to what a use American matter," *NSB*, 411

"I found myself," Henry James: *The Middle Years* (1917), 3–6

253 "I have been debating," Henry James, Jr., to Mrs. Henry James, Sr.: *Unpublished Letter*, March 2, 1869

255 "I admire Raphael," Henry James, Jr., to William James: *Unpublished Letter*, May 13, 1869

"It is a great pity," *P*, I:309

"terrifically agitated," ibid., I:311

"Boulogne looked as if," Henry James, Jr., to Mrs. Henry James, Sr.: *Unpublished Letter*, May 17, 1869

256 "The smell of revolution," Henry James: *The Ambassadors* (Macmillan, 1923), II:246

"Paris continues to seem," Henry James, Jr., to William James: *Unpublished Letter*, September 22, 1872 "lively travel," Henry James, Jr., to Henry James, Sr.: *Unpublished Letter*, May 10, 1869

"There is another Atlantic Cable," Henry James, Jr., to his parents: *Unpublished Letter*, June 13, 1869

"I duly noted your injunction," Henry James, Jr., to Mrs. Henry James, Sr.: *Unpublished Letter*, June 28, 1869

257 "Indeed you are always," Henry James, Sr., to Henry James, Jr.: *Unpublished Letter*, August 8, 1873

258 "I have been cut off," Mrs. Henry James, Sr., to Henry James, Jr.: *Unpublished Letter*, July 24, 1869

259 "My mind is so full," Henry James, Jr., to William James: *Unpublished Letter*, March 29, 1870

264 "I have to forge every sentence," *LWJ*, I:225

Formulations: *Younger Sons*

265 "Poor Wilky cries aloud," *NSB*, 242

"My darling Father: My heart," Garth Wilkinson James to Henry James, Sr.: *Unpublished Letter*, April 27, 1865

266 "I have been rebaptized," *AJ*, 47–9

267 "God bless you forever," Robertson James to William Dean Howells: *Unpublished Letter*, December 8, 1889

268 "The act of reading," *NSB*, 33

"the wear and tear," Robertson James to Edward Henry Clement: *Unpublished Letter*, August 1, 1900

"After all my reading," Robertson James to William Dean Howells: *Unpublished Letter*, undated

"So at night," ibid.

269 "progressive nervous degeneracy," Alice James to Henry James, Jr.: *Unpublished Letter*, October 3, 1881

"an extraordinary instance," *AJ*, 103

"real beauty," Henry James, Jr., to Mrs. Henry James, Sr.: *Unpublished Letter*, January 31, 1877

"Although I lie so low and still," *NSB*, 377–8

270 "You speak of an autobiography," Robertson James to William James: *Unpublished Letter*, February 24, 1898

271 "How inestimable this," Alice James to Mrs. William James: *Unpublished Letter*, February 5, 1890

"of all the darkness and pain," *AJ*, 60

Formulations: *Alice*

272 "Oh woe, woe is me!" *AJ*, 175–6

"rheumatic gout," ibid., 231

273 "The fact is, I have been," ibid., 250

"She asked me if suicide," ibid., 76–7

"What a pity to hide it," ibid., 108

"Alice met all attempts," ibid., 79

"How I recall," ibid., 144–5

274 "I think that if I get," ibid., 87

"My circumstances allowing," ibid.

"How dreary to be somebody," ibid., 249

"Dr. Tuckey asked me," ibid.

275 "Sir: For several years past," ibid., 173–4

"You must continue," *P*, I:418

"Imagine my entertainment," *AJ*, 173

"If the aim of life," ibid., 211

"William says in his *Psychology*," ibid., 197

276 "William uses an excellent expression," ibid., 181–2

277 "I must 'abandon,'" ibid., 182

"I must try and pull," ibid., 106–7, 112, 150–1

280 "Her trouble is dreadful indigestion," Alice James to Mrs. William James: *Unpublished Letter*, August 2, 1890

"the formless vague," *AJ*, 231

"poor dear William," ibid., 232

"Dearest Alice,— . . . Of course," *LWJ*, I:309–11

282 "My dearest William,—A thousand thanks," Alice James to William James: *Unpublished Letter*, July 30, 1891

283 "Supposing that your being," Alice James to William James: *Unpublished Letter*, December 2, 1891

"*The American* died," *AJ*, 245

"It is reassuring to hear," ibid., 248

284 "Tenderest love to all," Alice James

to William James: *Unpublished Cablegram*, March 5, 1892
"Alice just passed away," Henry

James, Jr., to William James: *Unpublished Cablegram*, 1892
"As regards the life," *LHJ*, I:214–16

Europe and/or America

286 "I am somewhat disappointed," *P*, I:122–3

287 "I very much enjoy," ibid., I:251

288 "I somehow feel," ibid., I:283
"You must have been envying me," ibid.
"Within ten days," ibid., I:305–6

289 "My dearest William . . . Here I am," *LHJ*, I:24–5
"It is very good," *P*, I:134
"I'm sick unto death," ibid., I:313

290 "yield its secrets," *LHJ*, I:30
"Its a complex fate," ibid., I:13
"You have learned," Henry James, Jr., to William James: *Unpublished Letter*, September 24 and 28, 1872
"I am fast becoming," Henry James, Jr., to Henry James, Sr.: *Unpublished Letter*, November 1872
"But can't you find out," *P*, I:331
"Happy wretch!" ibid., I:330–1

291 "My dearest old Dad,—We left," ibid., I:162–3
"Italy is a very *delightful* place," ibid., II:258

292 "Willy, who at first hung fire," ibid., I:353–4
"Any gossip about Florence," ibid., I:355–6

293 "The great fact," *LHJ*, I:36–7
"Tell Willy I thank him," ibid., I:38–40

294 "Although I have not written," Mrs. Henry James, Sr., to Henry James, Jr.: *Unpublished Letter*, May 18, 1874
"I had long wished," Henry James, Jr., to William James: *Unpublished Letter*, May 29, 1878
"I am unlikely ever to marry," Henry James, Jr., to Grace Norton: *Unpublished Letter*, November 7, 1880

295 "a bright cold unremunerative winter," Henry James: *Unpublished Notebook*
"Harry James is gone abroad," *Life in Letters of William Dean Howells*, I:215
"the little American set," Henry James: *Unpublished Notebook*
"an eternal outsider," ibid.
"I take very kindly," Henry James,

Jr., to Mrs. Henry James, Sr.: *Unpublished Letter*, December 24, 1877
"Certain individuals read poetry," *P*, I:365
"I expect to spend many a year," *LHJ*, I:59–60

296 "I have said enough," ibid., I:64
"I have made my choice," Henry James: *Unpublished Notebook*

297 "The condition of that body," *LHJ*, I:124

298 "Dear William . . . You speak," *P*, I:387–9

299 "My dear Harry,—On my return," William James to Henry James, Jr.: *Unpublished Letter*, January 23, 1883; *P*, I:389–90, in part

300 "The complete absence," William James to Henry James, Jr.: *Unpublished Letter*, January 9, 1883; *P*, I:386–7, in part

301 "two or three pages," *P*, I:390
"You say you enjoyed," William James to Henry James, Jr.: *Unpublished Letter*, February 6, 1883; *P*, I:391

302 "I am getting to know," *LHJ*, I:87
"I enjoy the easier," ibid., I:141–2

303 "Your only drawback," ibid., II:285
"Harry is as nice," *LWJ*, I:288
"I have enjoyed being with Harry," *P*, I:412

304 "What enrichment of mind," Alice James to William James: *Unpublished Letter*, May 29, 1896
"I had an almost Gallic sense," *AJ*, 161–2
"One should not be a cosmopolitan," *P*, II:189
"I am up here," *LWJ*, I:346–7

305 "Strange how practically all," Henry James, Jr., to William James: *Unpublished Letter*, May 29, 1896
"The horrors of *not* living," *LWJ*, II:36

306 "Nothing you tell me," *LHJ*, I:316
"HJ has a real little *bijou*," *LWJ*, II:105

307 "When we return," ibid., II:158
"I should like to return," *P*, II:199–200
"The desire to go 'home,'" Henry James, Jr., to William James: *Unpublished Letter*, April 10, 1903; *LWJ*, II:188, in part
"Your . . . *inhaltsvoll* letter," *LWJ*, II:188–9
308 "There is—and there *was*," *LHJ*, I:416–21
311 "Your long and excitingly interesting," *LWJ*, II:195
"Poverty-stricken this New Hampshire country," ibid., II:192

"My brother Henry stayed," ibid., II:215
312 "Whenever one is with William," Henry James: *Unpublished Notebook*
"California, on these terms," *LHJ*, II:33
"You've seen this wonderful spot,' *LWJ*, II:241
"I found my native land," *LHJ*, II:48–9
313 "The first impression," *LWJ*, II:264
"We're a thousand years behindhand," *P*, II:254–5
"I like to think of your tranquil," *LHJ*, II:134–5

WJ and HJ: on Each Other's Work

315 "Harry has a story," *AJ*, 40
"I pine for Harry's," *P*, I:224
"Beloved 'Arry—I hope," *LWJ*, I:103–4
316 "I received about a fortnight ago," *P*, I:250–1
"I got a letter," ibid., I:252
"Both stories show," ibid., I:263–5
"Exactly what escaped me," ibid., I:270
318 "I have got your last," ibid., I:271
"the obvious criticism," Henry James: *Unpublished Notebook*
319 "On account of my back," *P*, I:293–4
"Dear Harry . . . Father has been," ibid., I:315–16
"Beloved Brother . . . I received," ibid., I:319
320 "I envy ye," ibid., I:327, 330
"Your letters to the *Nation*," ibid., I:327
"Your criticism of my *Nation* letters," Henry James, Jr., to William James: *Unpublished Letter*, September 22 and 28, 1872
321 "the first of William James' publications," *P*, I:329
"Your letters to the *Nation* have been," ibid.
"I send you today," ibid., I:330–1
"I take up my pen," ibid., I:340–1
322 "Dearest William . . . Looking over," ibid., I:345
323 "I read with great pleasure," Henry James, Jr., to William James: *Unpublished Letter*, September 15, 1873

"*Roderick Hudson* seems to be," *P*, I:363
"Keep watch and ward," ibid., I:370, 371
"Dear Wm. . . . I am much obliged," *LHJ*, I:51
324 "I was much depressed," *LHJ*, I:65–6
"I have just been reading," *P*, I:380
"Only a line to acknowledge," ibid., I:380
325 "Thank you for what you say," ibid., I:381
"It is very delightful," ibid.
"It is a better subject," Henry James, Jr., to William James: *Unpublished Letter*, October 5, 1884
326 "I am quite appalled," Henry James, Jr., to William James: *Unpublished Letter*, February 14, 1885; *LHJ*, I:115–17, in part
327 "I concur absolutely," Henry James, Jr., to William James: *Unpublished Letter*, October 9, 1885; *P*, I:392–3, in part
328 "Your letter from Paris," *P*, I:393
"He is simply to me," ibid., I:394
"I seize my pen," *LWJ*, I:250–2
329 "Thank you for your letter," Henry James, Jr., to William James: *Unpublished Letter*, June 13, 1886
330 "I have made a start," William James to Henry James, Jr.: *Unpublished Letter*, April 1, 1885
"I have been writing," William James to Henry James, Jr.: *Unpublished Letter*, March 10, 1887

"I hope indeed you may finish," *P*, I:400

"I have tried," ibid., I:398–9

"Your last letter," ibid., I:400

"I have followed your advice," ibid., I:406–7

331 "I must also thank," *LWJ*, I:280

"I hunger and thirst," *P*, I:408

"You are right in surmising," *LHJ*, I:142–3

332 "My dear Harry . . . The great event," *LWJ*, I:296

"At last you've done it," *P*, I:412–13

333 "I had from you," *LHJ*, I:170

"It gave me great pleasure," *P*, I:414–15

334 "College begins with many changes," William James to Henry James, Jr.: *Unpublished Letter*, September 28, 1890; *P*, II:112, in part

"Within the year," *AJ*, 234

"I blush to say," *LHJ*, I:180–1

"the most important," *P*, II:104–5

335 "A good letter," William James to Henry James, Jr.: *Unpublished Letter*, May 9, 1897

"Your *Theatricals* came," William James to Henry James, Jr.: *Unpublished Letter*, July 10, 1894

336 "My dear William,—I never cabled," *LHJ*, I:227–9

337 "been weaned," *LWJ*, II:62

"I got and have just read," William James to Henry James, Jr.: *Unpublished Letter*, September 6, 1896

"You have done the best thing," *LWJ*, I:342

"which I think," William James to Henry James, Jr.: *Unpublished Letter*, August 30, 1897

"You certainly excel," William James

to Henry James, Jr.: *Unpublished Letter*, April 7, 1903

338 "He and I are so utterly different," *LWJ*, II:169

"I am reading," Henry James, Jr., to Mr. and Mrs. William James: *Unpublished Letter*, July 4, 1902

"I have read *The Wings of the Dove*," William James to Henry James, Jr.: *Unpublished Letter*, October 25, 1902

"Your reflections on," Henry James, Jr., to William James, *Unpublished Letter*, November 11, 1902

"I have been pressing hard," Henry James, Jr., to William James: *Unpublished Letter*, April 13, 1904

"the most extravagant opinions," William James to Henry James, Jr.: *Unpublished Letter*, July 12, 1905

"I read your Balzac," William James to Henry James, Jr.: *Unpublished Letter*, August 20, 1905

339 "It put me," *P*, I:423–4

"I mean (in response . . .)," *LHJ*, II:43–4; *P*, I:424–5, in part

340 "Your last was your delightful reply," *LWJ*, II:240

341 "I have just read," ibid., II:252

"Dearest H. . . . I've been," ibid., II:277–80

343 "I enter immensely into," Henry James, Jr., to William James: *Unpublished Letter*, May 31, 1907

"I have just been reading," *LWJ*, II:299

"Why the devil," *LHJ*, II:83–4

344 "All this time," *P*, I:428

"I have beautiful communications," Henry James, Jr., to William James: *Unpublished Letter*, October 31, 1909; *LHJ*, II:140–2, in part

345 "I sit heavily stricken," *LHJ*, II:167

Book IV: Characteristic Maturity

349 "a sort of comprehensive manual," *LHJ*, II:99

"who of all novelists," Henry James: "Historical Novels," *Nation*, August 15, 1867

350 "a conscious moral purpose," Henry James: *Partial Portraits* (1888), 404

"It is the amount," *P*, I:234

"might be described," ibid., II:108

351 "with the actual," ibid., II:54

"appeal most urgently," William

James: *Principles of Psychology*, II:312

"Son of Man," ibid., II:315

"the willing department," William James: *The Will to Believe* (1896), 114

"it does not follow," *P*, II:241

"the only decent thing," *LWJ*, I:203

352 "the perception on which," *P*, II:265

353 "I should not have affixed," Henry James: *Partial Portraits*, 375–408

371 "No one could be," *LWJ*, I:294
"I came home very weary," ibid.,
I:295
"It seems to me," ibid., II:1
372 "I have kept close," William James:
Principles of Psychology, I:v–vii
373 "Were we to go through," ibid.,
II:447–54
379 "In the recently published Life,"

William James: *The Will to Believe*, 1–31
397 "I wish I were able," William
James: *Talks to Teachers* (1899),
v–vi
398 "Our judgments concerning the
worth," ibid., 229–34, 250–4, 257–9,
263–4
404 "In my previous talk," ibid., 265–
301

Book V: Partial Portraits
The Art of Criticism

423 "to give outward form," Henry
James, Sr.: *Lectures and Miscellanies*, 117
"Our highest mode of action," Henry
James, Sr.: *Moralism and Christianity*, 49
"Even the habit of excessive indulgence," William James: *Principles
of Psychology*, I:125–6
424 "Pragmatism is correct doctrine,"
P, II:424–5
"in estimating a work," Henry James,
Sr.: *Lectures and Miscellanies*, 113
"general principles," Henry James:
"A French Critic," review of Edmond Sherer's *Nouvelles Études
sur la littérature contemporaine*,
Nation, October 12, 1865; reprinted
in *Notes and Reviews*, 103, 102
"Criticism is appreciation," Henry
James: *Picture and Text* (1893), 13
425 "little of a moralist," Henry James:
"Saint-Beuve's Portraits," *Nation*,
June 4, 1868
"I have just read," Henry James, Jr.,
to Mr. and Mrs. Henry James, Sr.:
Unpublished Letter, October 13,
1869
"the measure," Henry James: "Mat-

thew Arnold," *English Illustrated
Magazine*, January 1884
"was not the narrow law-giver,"
Henry James: "Saint-Beuve," *North
American Review*, January 1880;
reprinted in *American Literary
Criticism*, edited by William Morton Payne (1904), 305–6
"The man has so much ability," *P*,
II:52
"there may be something," Henry
James: "Saint-Beuve," *American
Literary Criticism*, Payne, 301–2
"incurable preference for grace," M.
Roberts: *Henry James's Criticism*
(1929), 23
426 "a conservative taste," Henry
James: "Victor Hugo's 'Ninety-
Three,'" *Nation*, April 9, 1874
"are the noblest speculations," *LHJ*,
I:324
"He has a mighty fund," ibid., II:324
"undoubtedly the greatest novel,"
LWJ, II:40
"I don't like his fatalism," ibid., II:45
"Our sole inference," Henry James:
Notes on Novelists (1914), 336
"When you ask me," *LHJ*, II:237–8

Emerson

428 "Mr. Emerson has no spiritual insight," *LRHJ*, 267–8
429 "My father was a theologian,"
Henry James, Sr.: "Emerson," *Atlantic Monthly*, December 1904
430 "had somehow become," *NSB*, 352
"I 'visualise' . . . the winter," ibid.,
204–5
"We may smile," Henry James: *The
American Scene* (1907), 254–5

431 "The reading of the divine Emerson," *LWJ*, II:190
432 "modern transcendental idealism,"
William James: *The Varieties of
Religious Experience*, 31
"Platonic formulas," *P*, I:144
"Both are just man," ibid., I:442
"I am sure that an age," ibid., I:352
"Sow an action," ibid., I:90
"Heroism is always," ibid., II:272

433 "I wish you had been," *LWJ*, I:194
"I myself believe," ibid., II:196–7
434 "At all events," *LRHJ*, 293–302
438 "Mr. Elliot Cabot has made,"

Henry James: *Partial Portraits*, 1-11, 13–18, 19–25, 26–7, 27–33
453 "The pathos of death," William James: *Memories and Studies* (1912), 19–34

Carlyle

459 "Carlyle is the same," *P*, I:83
"Carlyle nowadays is," ibid., I:99–100
"aggressively *earnest* tone," Henry James: "Charles Kingsley's 'Hereward, the Last of the English,'" *Nation*, January 25, 1866; reprinted in *Notes and Reviews*, 144
"perhaps the very greatest," *LHJ*, I:123

460 "by his great pictorial energy," Henry James: "The Correspondence of Carlyle and Emerson," *Century Magazine*, June 1883
"gospel of work," William James: *The Will to Believe*, 87
"The only escape," ibid., 173–4
"Thomas Carlyle is incontestably dead," *LRHJ*, 421–33, 437–9, 439–46, 449–68

Hawthorne

479 "I am going to Concord," *P*, I:88–90
"must have been struck," Henry James: *Hawthorne* (1880), 78; noted by *P*, I:90

481 "is apt to spoil," Henry James: *Hawthorne*, 61–2
482 "must have lingered," ibid., 41
483 "I much regret," *Proceedings* of the Hawthorne Centenary Celebration at Salem (1904), 55–62

Whitman

488 "You ask me," *NSB*, 233
"human energy," *P*, I:512
"I've got much good," ibid., II:229
"Always things burst," *LWJ*, II:223
489 "Discriminations of the prosaic order," *NSB*, 310–11
"I had never before heard poetry," Edith Wharton: *A Backward Glance* (1934), 185–6
490 "It has been a melancholy task,"

Henry James: "Mr. Walt Whitman," *Nation*, November 16, 1865; reprinted in *Views and Reviews* (1908), 101–10
494 "What sense shall I speak of," Henry James: "American Letter," *Literature*, April 16, 1898
495 "The supreme contemporary example," William James: *The Varieties of Religious Experience*, 84–7

Howells

498 "Talking of talks," *Life in Letters of William Dean Howells*, I:116
"I must own to you," ibid., II:276–7
"He ignores the cause," ibid., II:395–6
499 "are the only English," *P*, I:399
"Howells edits, and observes," *LHJ*, I:30–1
"I rec'd some days ago," Henry James, Jr., to W. D. Howells: *Unpublished Letter*, May 3, 1874
500 "Yes, I see a good deal," Henry James, Jr., to W. D. Howells: *Unpublished Letter*, February 3, 1876
"I am supposed to be," Henry James,

Jr., to W. D. Howells: *Unpublished Letter*, March 30, 1877
501 "I am delighted to hear," Henry James, Jr., to W. D. Howells, *Unpublished Letter*, June 17, 1879
502 "Your review of my book," *LHJ*, I:71–4
503 "as little as possible," *P*, I:399
"I have been seeing," *LHJ*, I:104–5
504 "Mr. Howells has gone," Henry James: "William Dean Howells," *Harper's Weekly*, June 19, 1886
506 "I have been not writing," *LHJ*, I:163–6

508 "You've done it this time," *LWJ*,
I:298–9

"All the 'culture' on earth," Robertson James to W. D. Howells: *Unpublished Letter*, December 2, 1889

509 "So far as literary standing," *Life in Letters of William Dean Howells*, II:55

"I am indebted to you," *LHJ*, I:230

510 "Preoccupied with," ibid., I:357

511 "Ever since receiving," ibid., I:375–7

"I was struck last evening," Henry James: *Unpublished Notebook*

512 "Your most kind communication," Henry James, Jr., to W. D. Howells: *Unpublished Letter*, January 25, 1902

513 "Nothing more delightful," *LHJ*, I:407

514 "My actual attitude," ibid., II:99–102

515 "It is made known to me," ibid., II:221–6

A Family Miscellany

519 "was much the greater charlatan," Henry James: *French Poets and Novelists* (revised edition, 1893), 60

"among the men," *P*, I:305

520 "an Impression," Henry James: *Unpublished Notebook*

"Now that by his song-making power," *LWJ*, II:88

"His *Ballad* future," *LHJ*, I:270–1

521 "If literary criticism," Henry James: *Essays in London and Elsewhere* (1893), 259–66

525 "I was on the point," Henry James: *Picture and Text* (1893), 92–8, 100–1, 104–7, 114–15

529 "The one marvel," Henry James, Jr., to Henry James, Sr.: *Unpublished Letter*, May 10, 1869

530 "a cousin by marriage," Henry James, Jr., to Mr. and Mrs. Henry James, Sr.: *Unpublished Letter*, November 17, 1878

"Even on the way I quaked," Henry James: *The Middle Years*, 81–6

532 "Read the third volume," *AJ*, 97–9

533 "I was to breathe," Henry James: *The Middle Years*, 99–108

536 "The domestic muse," *AJ*, 249

537 "Harry came yesterday," ibid., 127–8

"It would be unnatural," William James: *Memories and Studies*, 3–16

542 "As for what you propose," *P*, I:723–4

"I am heartily glad," ibid., II:414

543 "You are still the centre," *LWJ*, II:136

544 "The great event in my life," ibid., II:122–3

"Palmer has just sent me," *P*, II:320–1

545 "Santayana's book is a great one," *LWJ*, II:234–5

546 "O my Bergson," ibid., II:290–1

The French Novelists

548 "I was much satisfied," *P*, I:309

"My dear Sir—It seems," ibid., I:137–9

549 "Nevertheless accept my heartfelt thanks," ibid., I:140

550 "I don't like their wares," *LHJ*, I:49

"I never heard you speak," *LWJ*, I:182, 185

"Her 'sapience,' " ibid., I:185

551 "than from anyone else," Henry James: *The Question of Our Speech* (1905), 70

"to wait an hour," *NSB*, 306

"Read . . . or rather skipped," *P*, I:215

"He is literally real," Henry James:

"Harriet Elizabeth Prescott's 'Azarian: An Episode,' " *North American Review*, January 1865; reprinted in *Notes and Reviews*, 24

"No one begins," Henry James: *The Question of Our Speech*, 110

"Balzac ought to come to life," *LWJ*, II:265

"you, Balzac, or Howells," ibid., I:318

552 "Money is the most general element," Henry James: *French Poets and Novelists*, 71

"the efficient combination," Henry James: *Essays in London*, 264

"I had also the other day," *LHJ*, I:46

"In poor old Flaubert," *P*, I:367

553 "I do not propose," Henry James:

The Question of Our Speech, 57
"We know of several," Henry James: *French Poets and Novelists,* 211–12, 216–17, 220–2, 249–51, 251–2
557 "When the mortal remains," Henry James: *Partial Portraits,* 291–9, 314–19, 322–3
565 "The greatest thing," Henry James: *French Poets and Novelists,* 116–18
566 "Stronger than ever," Henry James:

Notes on Novelists, 109, 109–10, 111–15, 117–18, 119, 120–1
570 "M. Flaubert's theory," Henry James: *French Poets and Novelists,* 201–3, 209–10
572 "His life was that," Henry James: *Essays in London,* 143–50
576 "There are many things," Henry James: *Notes on Novelists,* 77–9, 79–82, 82–3, 84–5, 89, 92, 93–4

Book VI: On Consciousness and Immortality

587 "Divine truth has first," Henry James, Sr.: *Society the Redeemed Form of Man,* 36
"the former is concerned," John Dewey: *Characters and Events* (1929), I:113
588 "perception and thinking," William James: *The Will to Believe,* 114
"I myself find," William James: *A Pluralistic Universe* (1909), 213
"every bit of us," ibid., 289
"so small a part," *Dictionary of American Biography,* IX:597
In lecturing on some "Supposed Objections" to immortality, cf. *P,* II: 132
"May not you and I," William James: *A Pluralistic Universe,* 290
"Out of my experience," William James: *Memories and Studies,* 204
589 "By the big part of me," *P,* II:356
"The demand for immortality," William James: *Principles of Psychology,* I:348
"Never keenly; but more strongly," *LWJ,* II:214
590 "I am as convinced," *P,* II:359
"The problem I have set," *LWJ,* II: 127
"as in a sense a study," *P,* II:325

"Here or nowhere," ibid., II:328–9
591 "At bottom it is the feud," ibid., II:332
"I can't possibly pray," *LWJ,* II:214
"a dissatisfaction with anything," *P,* II:259
"the terrible *fluidity,*" Henry James: Preface to *The Ambassadors* (Macmillan, 1923), I:xxi
"only extracts from his brain," André Gide: "Henry James," *Yale Review,* Spring 1930
592 "was in love with," A. R. Orage: *Readers and Writers* (1922), 10
593 "Before the sufferings of others," *LHJ,* I:100–1
594 "I am always praying," ibid., I:115
"desperately mundane," André Gide: "Henry James," *Yale Review,* Spring 1930
HJ was certainly as far removed, cf. Austin Warren: *The Elder Henry James,* 149
"As I have elsewhere written," William James: *The Varieties of Religious Experience,* 515–27
602 "I confess at the outset," *In After Days, Thoughts on the Future Life,* by Henry James, W. D. Howells and others (1910), 199–233

Book VII: On Politics and Society

617 "What a humiliation," *AJ,* 132
"It was vain to say," *NSB,* 431
618 "one who claims," George Fort Milton: *The Age of Hate* (1930), 146
"It is difficult to say," "American Officials," editorial in London *Saturday Review,* March 25, 1865
"an insolent drunken brute," editorial in *New York World,* March 7, 1865; cf. George Fort Milton: *The Age of Hate,* 149

"Have we really reached," Henry James, Sr.: "The English Journals and President Johnson," *New York Evening Post,* May 23, 1865
622 "Don't be alarmed," *LWJ,* I:252
"If he ever chanced upon," *William James the Man and Thinker* (1942), 22
623 "the cold pot-grease," *LWJ,* II:94
"An observer who should judge," William James: "The Philippine

Tangle," *Boston Evening Transcript*, March 1, 1899

628 "Shall Governor Roosevelt be allowed," William James: "Governor Roosevelt's Oration," ibid., April 15, 1899

631 " 'Duty and Destiny' have rolled," *P*, II:313

"Angelic impulses," ibid.

632 "chronic fault," ibid., II:299

"saddened by the sight," ibid., II:294

"in the right place," ibid., II:314

"The Scotch are the finest race," *LWJ*, I:309

"The circular appears," *P*, II:691–2

633 "We must thank God," *LWJ*, II:100–1

"As for me," ibid., II:90

"The memory of Davidson," William James: *Memories and Studies*, 102–3

634 "We of the colleges," ibid., 321–3

"perhaps a more cosmopolitan post," *P*, I:685

"The Eliots have just returned," ibid., II:679

635 "In this very simple way," William James: *Memories and Studies*, 319–20

"Stroke upon stroke," *LWJ*, II:318

"I devoutly believe," William James: *Memories and Studies*, 286

636 "War is becoming," Henry James: *What Constitutes the State* (1845), 5; cf. Austin Warren: *The Elder Henry James*, 91

"The war against war," William James: *Memories and Studies*, 267–96

646 "Many thanks for the study," *LHJ*, I:220–1

"A spectacle merely," ibid., I:295

647 "I don't feel that McKinley," ibid., I:249

"a dangerous and ominous Jingo," ibid., I:379

"the mere monstrous embodiment," ibid., II:273

"I confess that the blaze," ibid., I:280–1

"The sensational press," *P*, II:318

648 "To live in England," *LHJ*, I:310–11

"Your last letter on Roosevelt," Henry James, Jr., to William James: *Unpublished Letter*, June 3, 1899

"I find myself," *AJ*, 137–8

649 "William was most amusing," ibid., 109–10

"The behavior of the Unionist," ibid., 146–7

650 "The *Standard* this morning," ibid., 157–8

651 "one of the great garden-lamps," Henry James: *The American Scene*, 311

"This vision, for the moment," Henry James, ibid., 55–6, 61–3, 64

654 "for any human convenience," ibid., 119

"any deviation . . . into," ibid., 98

"human aggregation," ibid., 80

"an interested passion," ibid., 75

"Make so much money," ibid., 228

"What struck me," ibid., 131–5

657 "The huge jagged city," ibid., 135–8, 153, 153–4, 166–8

661 "The palaces, on the sites," ibid., 214–16, 217

662 "I was to find," ibid., 408–15

667 "What one first feels," *LHJ*, II:376–8

668 "the *louche* and sinister figure," ibid., II:442–3

"Black and hideous to me," ibid., II:389

669 "What you tell me," Henry James, Jr., to his nephew William James, Jr.: *Unpublished Letter*, spring 1914

"I have your melancholy outpouring," *LHJ*, II:360–1

Epilogue: William James and Henry James

673 "There is very little difference," William James: *The Will to Believe*, 256–7

674 "left the genteel tradition," George Santayana: *Winds of Doctrine* (1913), 202

"as tightly swaddled," ibid., 203–4

"I prefer to start," *P*, II:378

675 "our sum of intelligent life," *LHJ*, II:342

"is substance to that degree," ibid., II:237

"The behaviorist, the gestaltist," *In Commemoration of William James, 1842–1942* (1942), vi

"a fanatic cult of the abstract," ibid., 139

676 "boyish," *P*, I:530
"Emerson and James were both,"
G. W. Howison: "Josiah Royce:
The Significance of his work in
Philosophy," *Philosophical Review*
(1916), 241
"I have just read a denunciation," *P*,
I:607
"almost unexampled incapacity," ibid.,
I:540
"the modern movement known,"
ibid., I:409
"try to learn to think," ibid., I:437
"your very exaggerated utterance,"
ibid., I:438
"man of strength," ibid., II:422
"the first psychologist," ibid.
Peirce was far more preoccupied,
cf. *P*, II:411
"penetration into the hearts of people," ibid., II:286
WJ tended to take for granted, cf.
P, II:514
677 "the spiritual progenitor," *P*, II:521
"I feel so the inchoateness," ibid.,
II:523-4
"During the thirty years," *In Commemoration of William James,
1842-1942*, vi-vii
"his lasting achievement," John
Dewey: *Characters and Events*,
I:113-14
"a glorification of non-rational activity," *In Commemoration of William James, 1842-1942*, 56
"an intimate union," ibid., 57
"an action should be judged," Benito
Mussolini quoted in the London

Sunday Times, April 11, 1926; cf.
P, II:575
678 "the most interesting," *LHJ*, II:39
"very swagger," ibid., II:139
"vividness and colour," ibid., II:138
"the culmination of the Superficial
type," H. G. Wells: *Boon* (1915),
105, 108
"The thing his novel is about," ibid.,
109
"For him every great novel," R. M.
Lovett: *Edith Wharton* (1925), 55
679 "that poetry ought to be," quoted
in Matthiessen: *The Achievement
of T. S. Eliot*, 6
"profound sensitiveness to good and
evil," ibid., 7
680 "special beauty," Henry James: *Unpublished Notebook*
"Place yourself . . . at the center,"
William James: *A Pluralistic Universe* (1909), 263
681 "is neither absolutely one," *P*, II:684
"*Prima facie*, if you should," William
James: *Essays in Radical Empiricism* (1912), 46-7
"diffuse in wide warm waves," Henry
James: *Wings of the Dove* (Macmillan, 1923), 192
682 "in memory, reasoning," William
James: *Principles of Psychology*,
II:61
"He will be the king," ibid., II:538
"the straight vindictive view," Henry
James: *The Golden Bowl* (Macmillan, 1923), II:209
"the horror of finding evil," ibid.

INDEX

i

A Note ON THE TYPE IN WHICH

THIS BOOK IS SET

This book was set on the Linotype in Janson, a recutting made direct from the type cast from matrices made by Anton Janson some time between 1660 and 1687.

Of Janson's origin nothing is known. He may have been a relative of Justus Janson, a printer of Danish birth who practised in Leipzig from 1614 to 1635. Some time between 1657 and 1668 Anton Janson, a punch-cutter and type-founder, bought from the Leipzig printer Johann Erich Hahn the type-foundry which had formerly been a part of the printing house of M. Friedrich Lankisch. Janson's types were first shown in a specimen sheet issued at Leipzig about 1675.

The typography and the binding design are by
Warren Chappell

Composed, printed, and bound by Kingsport Press, Inc.
Kingsport, Tenn.